Wilhelm Roscher, Louis Wolowski, John Joseph Lalor

Principles of political Economy

Vol. II

Wilhelm Roscher, Louis Wolowski, John Joseph Lalor

Principles of political Economy
Vol. II

ISBN/EAN: 9783337077730

Printed in Europe, USA, Canada, Australia, Japan

Cover: Foto ©ninafisch / pixelio.de

More available books at **www.hansebooks.com**

PRINCIPLES

OF

POLITICAL ECONOMY

BY

WILLIAM ROSCHER,

PROFESSOR OF POLITICAL ECONOMY AT THE UNIVERSITY OF LEIPZIG, CORRESPONDING
MEMBER OF THE INSTITUTE OF FRANCE, PRIVY COUNSELOR TO HIS
MAJESTY, THE KING OF SAXONY.

FROM THE THIRTEENTH (1877) GERMAN EDITION.

WITH ADDITIONAL CHAPTERS FURNISHED BY THE AUTHOR, FOR THIS FIRST
ENGLISH AND AMERICAN EDITION, ON

PAPER MONEY, INTERNATIONAL TRADE, AND THE
PROTECTIVE SYSTEM;

AND A PRELIMINARY

ESSAY ON THE HISTORICAL METHOD IN POLITICAL ECONOMY.
(From the French)

By L. WOLOWSKI,

THE WHOLE TRANSLATED BY

JOHN J. LALOR, A. M.

VOL. II.

CHICAGO:
CALLAGHAN AND COMPANY.
1882.

TO

WILLIAM H. GAYLORD, Esq.,

COUNSELOR AT LAW,

OF CLEVELAND, OHIO,

TO WHOSE BROTHERLY CARE IT IS LARGELY DUE THAT I LIVED TO
TRANSLATE THEM,

THESE VOLUMES

ARE AFFECTIONATELY INSCRIBED.

BOOK III.

DISTRIBUTION OF GOODS.

CHAPTER I.

INCOME IN GENERAL.

SECTION CXLIV.

RECEIPTS. — INCOME. — PRODUCE.

The idea covered by the word receipts *(Einnahme)* embraces all the new additions successively made to one's resources within a given period of time.[1] Income, on the other hand, embraces only such receipts as are the results of economic activity. (See §§ 2, 11.) Produce *(Ertrag, produit)* is income, but not from the point of view of the person or *subject* engaged in a business of any kind, but from that of the business itself, or of the *object* with which the business is concerned, and on which it, so to speak, acts.

Income is made up of products, the results of labor and of the employment and use of resources. These products, the producer may either consume himself or exchange against other products, to satisfy a more urgent want.[2] Hence, spite

---

[1] Including of course, gifts, inheritances, lottery prizes etc.

[2] Thus the original income of the peasant consists in his corn, of the miller in his flour, of the baker in his bread, of the shoemaker in his shoes. The money which circulates among all these and the purchaser, is only the means of exchanging that part of their products which they cannot themselves use, for other goods. Money, on the other hand, was the original income of the producers of the gold or silver it contains. Compare *Mirabeau*, Philosophie rurale, 1763, ch. 3. *Adam Smith*, II, ch. 2. But especially,

Vol. II — 1

of the frequency with which we hear such expressions as these: "the laborer eats the bread of his employer;" "the capitalist lives by the sweat of the brow of labor;" or, again, a manufacturer or business man "lives from the income of his customers,"[3] they are entirely unwarranted. No man who manages his own affairs well, or those of a household, lives on the capital or income of another man; but every one lives on his own income, by the things he has himself produced; although with every further development of the division of labor, it becomes rarer that any one puts the finishing stroke to his own products, and can satisfy himself by their immediate consumption alone. Hence we should call nothing diverted or derived income except that which has been gratuitously obtained from another.[4]

SECTION CXLV.

INCOME — GROSS, FREE AND NET.

In all *income*, we may distinguish a *gross* amount, a *net* amount and a *free* amount.[1] The gross income of a year, for

---

see *J. B. Say*, Traité II, ch. 1, 5; and *Sismondi*, N. P., I, 90, 376, in which it is correctly said, that the quality which constitutes anything capital or income does not inhere in the thing itself, but depends on the person. Compare, however, I, 148; *Hermann*, Staatsw. Untersuch. 297 ff., 33 seq.

[3] A fundamental thought in *St. Chamans*, Du Système d'Impôt, 1820. Nouvel Essai sur la Richesse des Nations, 1824.

[4] Thus, for instance, the support given by the head of a family to the members thereof; also gifts, alms, thefts. Even *A. L. Schlözer*, St. A., II, 487, will allow that no one "eats the bread of another," but the person who has received it from the latter by way of favor and for nothing. In the case of a rented house, there is only an exchange of objects of income. The person to whom it is rented gives up a portion of his, and the renting party the use of his house. Similarly, in the case of personal services. Writers who maintain that only certain kinds of useful labor are productive, must of course extend the limits of diverted income much farther. See *Lotz*, Handbuch, III, § 133; *Rau*, Lehrbuch, I, §§ 248, 251. *Cantillon* thinks that if no landowner spent more than his income, it would be scarcely possible for any one else to grow rich. (Nature du Commerce, 75.) According to *Stein*, Lehrbuch, 347, every one gets his income from the income of other people!

[1] Similarly in *Sismondi*, N. P., II, 330, and *Rau*, Lehrbuch, I, § 71, a.

instance, consists of all the goods which have been newly produced within that time. The net[2] income is that portion of the former which remains after deducting the cost of production (§ 106), and which may therefore be consumed without diminishing the original resources. Only the new values incorporated in the new commodities make up the net income. Evidently, a great portion of what is considered in one business the cost of production is net income in a great many others; as for instance, what the person engaged in one enterprise in production has paid out in wages and interest on capital. By means of this outlay, a portion of his circulating capital is drawn by others as income, and, on the other hand, a portion of their original income is turned into a portion of his circulating capital.[3] *Free* income, I call that portion of net income which remains available to the producer after his indispensable wants have been satisfied.

An accurate kind of book-keeping which keeps these three elements of income separate is more generally praticable as civilization advances. We might call it the *economic balance*. Where commerce is very thriving it is even customary to provide by law that those classes who need it especially should have this species of book-keeping. People in a lower stage of cultivation, with their poetical nature, are unfriendly to such calculations.[4][5] And where natural-economy (*Natur-*

---

[2] Called by *Hermann*, loc. cit., simply income.

[3] This truth *J. B. Say* has exaggerated to the extent of claiming that gross and net income are one and the same so far as entire nations are concerned. (Traité, II, ch. 5; Cours pratique, III, 14; IV, 74.) But the gross profit of the entire production of any one year is much greater than the simultaneous net income of all the individuals engaged in it. This is accounted for by the fact that in such production an amount of circulating capital is invested which was saved from the net profit of previous economic times. Compare *Storch*, Nationaleinkommen, 90 ff. *Hermann*, loc. cit., 323 ff.

[4] In the East, a valuation by one's self of his property is considered a guilty kind of pride, usually punished by the loss of one's possessions. *(Burckhardt*, Travels in Arabia, I, 72 ff.) See *Samuel*, 24, on the census made by David. The Egyptians, however, as may be inferred from their monuments, must have very early and very extensively felt the want of some kind of

4 DISTRIBUTION OF GOODS. [B. III, Ch. I.

alwirthschaft) or barter prevails, a book-keeping of this kind of any accuracy is scarcely practicable. The ratio which net income bears to gross income is a very important element to enable us to judge of the advantageousness of any method of production. If every producer should succeed in consequence of keeping his books in this manner, in determining exactly the cost to him of each of his products, this would be an eco-

---

book-keeping such as we have mentioned. A very accurate sort of book-keeping among the more higly cultured Romans, with a daily memorandum and a monthly book with entries from the former *(adversaria-tabula expensi et accepti)*. Compare *Cicero*, pro Roscio, com. 2, 3; pro Cluent, 30; *Verr.*, II, 1, 23, 36. The Latin *putare*, from *putus*, pure, means: to make an account clear, and therefore corresponds to the American provincialism, "I reckon," i. e., I believe; and is a remarkable proof of a rigid method of keeping accounts. The Italian, or so-called double-entry method of book-keeping, which gives the most accurate information on the profit from every separate branch of business, became usual among the nations of modern Europe whose civilization was the first to ripen, about the end of the fifteenth century. Its invention is ascribed to the monk Luca Paciolo di Borgo S. Sepolcro.

In England, this kind of book-keeping is very gradually coming into use even among farmers, while *Simond*, Voyage en Angleterre, 2 ed., II, 64, *Dunoyer*, Liberté du Travail, VIII, 5, say, "it would in France be considered as ridiculous as the book-keeping of an apple vendor." In Germany, there have been for some time past, manufactories of commercial books. Besides, the remarkable difference brought out by the income tax in England between the exact statements made by large manufacturers etc., and by those engaged in industry on a medium or small scale, bears evidence of the better way in which the former keep their accounts, the cause and effect of their better business in general. Compare *Knies*, in the Tübing. Zeitschr., 1854, 513. On the best mode of determining income, see *Cazaux*, Eléments d' Économie publique et privée, Livre, II. It is especially necessary to keep an account of the increase or diminution, even when accidental, of the value of the fixed capital employed.

[5] The Code de Commerce, I, art. 8, requires that every merchant should keep a journal, paged and approved by the authorities, showing the receipts and disbursements of each day, on whatever account, and also the monthly expenditures of his family. Besides, he is required to make a yearly inventory of his, debits and credits, subscribe to it and preserve it. That such books were excellent judicial evidence may be shown by Italian statutes of the fourteenth century. *(Martens*, Ursprung des Wechselrechts, 23.) Those of Germany even in 1449. *(Hirsch*, Danziger Handelsgeschichte, 232.)

nomic progress similar to that of general spread of good chemical knowledge in the arts. On the amount of *free* income, on the other hand, depends all the higher enjoyment of life, all rational beneficence, and the progressive enrichment of mankind.[6]

SECTION CXLVI.

NATIONAL INCOME. — ITS STATISTICAL IMPORTANCE.

Among the most important[1] but also the most difficult objects of statistics, that book-keeping of nations, is national income. In estimating it, we may take our starting point from the goods which are elements of income, or from the persons who receive them as income.[2]

In the former case the gross national income consists:

A. Of the raw material newly obtained in the country.

B. Of imports from foreign countries, including that which is secured by piracy, as war-booty, contributions etc.

C. The increase of values which industry[3] and commerce

---

[6] Importance of the so-called "transferring to credit," where a business man considers his business as an independent entity and as distinct from himself.

[1] Not only to compare the happiness and power of different nations with one another, but also for purposes of taxation, the profitableness and innocousness of which suppose the most perfect adaptation to the income of the whole people.

[2] The former, in *Rau*, Lehrbuch, I, § 247; the latter in *Hermann*, 308 ff. The former mode of calculation gives us a means of judging of the comfort of the people, their control of natural forces etc.; the second, of the relation of classes among the people. (*v. Mangoldt*, Grundriss, 99. V. W. L., 316 ff.) Each member of the nation produces his income only in the whole of the nation's economy. Hence *Held*, Die Einkommensteuer, 1872, 70, 77, would, but indeed only under very abstract fictions, construct private income from the national, and not *vice versa*.

[3] On the average degree of this increase of values in different industries, see *Chaptal*, De l'Industrie française, II, passim. *Bolz*, Gewerbekalender für, 1833, 111. No such scale can be lastingly valid, because, for instance, almost all technic progress decreases the appreciation of values through industry, and every advance made by luxury raises the claims to refined quality etc. See *Hildebrand*, Jahrbücher für Nat-Œk., 1863, 248 ff.

add to the first two classes up to the time of their final consumption.

D. Services in the narrower sense and the produce *(Nutzungen)* of capital in use.

All these several elements, estimated at their average price in money, which supposes that all purchases, especially those under the head D, are made voluntarily⁴ and at their natural price.

To find the national net income, we must deduct the following items:

A. All the material employed in production which yields no immediate satisfaction to any personal want.⁵

B. The exports which pay for the imports.

C. The wear and tear of productive capital and capital in use.

In the second case the net national income is to be calculated from the following items:

A. From the net income of all independent private businesses etc.⁶

B. From the net income of the state, of municipalities,

---

⁴ Many items in Class D evade all calculation. Thus, for instance, the numberless cases of personal services which are enjoyed only by the doer himself; also the greater number of products *(Nutzungen=*usufruct) of capital in use for the consumption of the owner himself. (Latent income.) Only, it may be, in the case of dwelling houses, equipages etc., that the consumption by use can be estimated in accordance with the analogy of similarly rented goods.

⁵ The principal materials consumed in manufactures are of course not to be deducted here, because the increase in their value was taken into account above.

⁶ When an artist who earns $10,000 per annum appears in a country, the gross national income increases in a way similar to that in which it increases when a new commodity is found which would have a yearly increase of value equal to $10,000 over and above that of the raw material. Cost of production in the case of such a virtuoso is scarcely to be alluded to. Nearly his entire income, with the exception of his traveling expenses etc., is net, and the greater portion of it *free.* An income tax would affect his hearers after as it did before, and in his income, find a completely new object. *Per contra,* see Saggi economici, I, 176 f.

corporations and institutions, derived from their own resources.

C. Under the former heads must be taken into the account such parts of property as have been immediately consumed and enjoyed.[7]

D. Interest on debt must be added only on the side of the creditor, and deducted from the income of the debtor; otherwise, *error dupli*. This does not apply to taxes or church dues because the subjects of a good state and members of a good church purchase thereby things which are really new and of at least equal value to the outlay. Besides, in both instances, it is necessary to calculate the number of men who live from the national income, the average amount of their indispensable wants, and the average price in money of the same, in order to determine the *free* national income by deducting the sum total of these average wants, estimated at this average price.[8][9]

---

[7] For purposes of taxation, where a relative valuation is more the question than an absolute one, it would be sufficient to assume that every household consumed clothing, utensils etc., in proportion to the rest of their income. Hence, these items might, unhesitatingly, be omitted altogether.

[8] Mathematically demonstrated by *Fuoco*, Saggi economici, II, 102 ff.

[9] The gross income of British Europe is estimated by *Pebrer*, Histoire financière et statistique générale de l' Empire Br., 1834, II, 90, at £514,823,059, viz.: agriculture, £246,600,000; mining, 21,400,000; manufactures, after deduction made of the raw material, £148,050,000; internal and coast trade, £51,975,060; foreign commerce and navigation, £34,398,059; banking, £4,500,000; interest from foreign countries, £4,500,000. By *Moreau de Jonnès*, Statist de la Gr. Br., 1837, I, 312, it is estimated at 18,000,000,000 francs, from which, however, the raw material used in industry is not deducted. The net income of Great Britain was estimated by Pitt, in 1799, at £135,000,000, of which £25,000,000 were received by land-owners for rent, £25,000,000 by farmers, £5,000,000 were tithes, £3,000,000 from forests, canals, and mines, £6,000,000 from houses, £15,000,000 from state funds, £12,000,000 from foreign commerce, £28,000,000 from inland commerce and manufactures, £3,000,000 from fine arts, £80,000,000 from Scotland, £5,000,000 from foreign countries. (*Gentz*, Histor. Journ., 1799, I, 183 ff.) *Lowe*, England in its present Situation, 1822, p. 246, speaks of 255,000,000. About 1860, the incomes subject to taxation alone, that is, all above £100, amounted to 335,000,000. The remainder was certainly worth one-half of this. (Statist.

SECTION CXLVII.

NATIONAL INCOME.—ITS STATISTICAL IMPORTANCE.
[CONTINUED.]

The question frequently discussed, whether it is more advantageous to increase the gross income or the net income[1] of

Journ., 1864, 121.) *Baxter*, in 1867, assumed it to be £825,000,000. Compare *L. Levi*, on Taxation, 6.

In France, about forty years ago, according to Chaptal, Doudeauville, Balbi and others, about 6,500,000,000 francs gross national income could be counted on. *Schnitzler* speaks of 7,000,000,000 francs (Creation de la Richesse en France, 1842, I, 392), after deduction made of the raw material of manufacture. According to *Wolowski*, Statistique de la Fr., 1847, it was more than 12,000,000,000 francs. *M. Chevalier*, Revue des deux Mondes, March 15, 1848, has it 10,000,000,000 at most. In these four estimates, only material products are taken into account. *Ch. Dupin* thinks the income per capita was, in 1730, =108 francs; in 1780, =169; in 1830, =269. *Cazeaux*, Eléments, 163, estimated the net national income, in 1825, at 5,000,000,000 francs; *Cochut*, in 1861, at 16,000,000,000. (Revue des deux Mondes, XXXVII, 703.)

In Spain, *Borrego*, Nationalreichthum etc. Spaniens, 1834, 33, estimated the income from agriculture at 2,284,000,000 francs; from industry etc., 361,000,000; commerce, 124,000,000; from houses, 186,000,000; canals, streets etc., 8,500,000; personal services, 75,000,000; money in circulation (probably loaned capital), 85,000,000.

In the United States, in 1840, the national income was estimated at over $1,063,000,000; from agriculture, over $654,000,000; from manufactures, nearly $240,000,000; commerce, almost $80,000,000; mining, over $42,000,000; from lumber *(Wäldern,)*, almost $17,000,000; and from the fisheries, almost $12,000,000. The per capita amount of income was $62. It was largest in Rhode Island—$110; in Massachusetts it was $103; in Louisiana, $99; and in Iowa, smallest, $27; in Michigan, it was $33. Compare *Tucker*, Progress of the United States, 195 ff. The census of 1860 assumes the national wealth, slaves not included, at $14,183,000,000, that is $451 per capita, with a per capita annual income of $112. According to *Czörnig*, the gross income of Austria, from agriculture, the chase and fisheries, in 1861, was 2,119,000,000 florins; from mining, 41,000,000; from the industries, 1,200,000,000. In Prussia, the net national income, not including the revenue from state property, nor the income of the royal household, seems, from the returns of the income and *class* tax, to have been about 2,458,000,000 thalers, in 1874. *Engel*, Preuss. Statist. Ztschr., 1875, 133. The majority of the above estimates are obviously unreliable.

[1] The greater number of writers, at bottom, understand by this question

a people, may be readily answered with the assistance of our tripartite division. Since economic production has no other object than the satisfaction of human wants, the mere increase of the gross income of a people is a matter of indifference. An increase of the net income puts a people in a condition to increase either their numbers or their enjoyments. (See §§ 163 and 239.) The most desirable condition is where both these results are produced. It is fortunate for a people when the *free* income of the nation increases by reason of the absolute or relative decrease of the cost of production, which adds nothing to enjoyment. But it is politically and morally to be lamented when it increases at the expense of the satisfaction of man's necessary wants, especially if the majority of the people deny themselves in this respect to produce that end. Sir Thomas More called the sheep of his time, to make place for which so many farm houses were razed to the ground, ravenous beasts, which devoured men and laid waste city and country.[2]

---

only whether greater efforts should be made to increase the wages of the lower classes or the rent and rate of interest on capital paid to the higher. (*Schmoller*, in the Tüb. Zeitschrift, 1863, 22.)

[2] The difference between gross and net income was introduced into the science principally by the Physiocrates. *Vauban* (1707) had no conception of it, and thirty years later a French minister, in his instructions concerning the levy of the *vingtièmes*, dimly seeing that the aggregate amount of the harvest was not clear gain, ordered, to obtain the latter, that the cost of reaping and threshing should be deducted. (*Dupont*, Correspondence of *J. B. Say*, 404, éd. Daire.) By *produit net*, *Quesnay* means the excess of original production over its cost, considered from the personal point of view of the individual land-owner. This excess, it is claimed, can alone increase the national wealth and alone support the "steril" class.

The political and military bearing of this very clearly recognized. (102 ff., éd Daire.) Hence *Quesnay*, favors it in every way; by large farming instead of small, by stock raising on a large scale, supplanting home labor by cheaper foreign labor, by machinery and the employment of manual labor etc.; 91 ff., 200 ff., 274 ff. The elder *Mirabeau* teaches even that the goodness of a government or of a constitution, and even national morality may be inferred from the amount of the *produit net*. (Ph. rurale, ch. 5.) *Stewart*, Principles, I, ch. 20. *Adam Smith* gives greater prominence to the gross income,

SECTION CXLVIII.

THE TWO PHASES OF INCOME.

In every income which has anything to do with other incomes, it is necessary to distinguish its immediately productive side, and its profit or acquisition side. It is necessary, in the first place, that all the products made by private parties should, so to speak, be put into the common treasury of the national economy, and that each should thence draw his own private revenue. Justice requires that there should be a perfect correlation between the two; that each should enjoy precisely the quota of the national income to the production of

and grades the principal branches of national labor according as they increase the gross product of the nation's economy. (II, chs. 1, 5.) Similarly, *J. B. Say*, Traité, ch. 8, § 3; *Lauderdale*, Inquiry, 142.

Ricardo thoroughly reacts against this view, and considers it a matter of indifference whether a net product (interest on capital and rent) of a given amount be obtained by the labor of five or seven million other men, so long as only five million can live on it. (Principles, ch. 26.) Similarly *Ganilh*, Systèmes, I, 218 ff.; Théorie, II, 96. Controverted by *Malthus*, Principles, II, § 6. *Buquoy*, Theorie der Nat. Wirthsch., 1815, 310 ff. *Sismondi* has ridiculed this predilection for the net product which in *Ricardo* corresponds with what the Germans call free product (*freien Ertrage*), and which, contrary to Ricardo's own opinion, he calls Ricardo's ideal, saying that according to him, nothing more was to be desired but that "the king should remain alone on the island and, by turning a crank forever, do all the work of England through the instrumentality of automata." (N. P., II, 330 ff.) An entire people should value only gross product. (I, 183.) In his Etudes, Essai, II: Du Revenu Social, *Sismondi* distinguishes as elements of the gross national income: a, pure capital, the return of outlay; b, that which is at once both capital and income, and serves as family support (capital as a necessarily remaining supply, income as the product of the preceding year); c, net income, the excess of production over consumption.

The Socialists of our day would prefer to see the whole net income of a people employed in the satisfaction of the necessary wants of an ever increasing population. By this procedure, as a natural consequence, we should witness first the curtailing of the taxing power, of the funds for the satisfaction of the more refined wants and of the saving of capital, nor would it be long before even the existing generation would experience the bitterness

which his person or his property contributed. A just appreciation of the relative productive power of the divers branches of labor constitutes one of the chief bulwarks against the inroads of destructive socialistic theories. The person who calls a good doctor or a good judge unproductive should, to be consistent, call those who by their greater intelligence are fitted to superintend agricultural and industrial enterprises unproductive, also, as is done by the coarser socialists with their apotheosis of mere manual labor. Unfortunately, such a settlement as is above contemplated among the different factors of production, whose owners are desirous to divide the common product among them, is possible only where the factors of production are either of the same kind, or can be reduced to a common denominator.[1] But if justice pure and

---

of this "living from hand to mouth." After a time, even the possibility of progress and even of mere increase of population would cease.

Hermann, Staatsw. Untersuch., 297 ff., has better than almost any one else developed the theory of income, and he lays most stress on the satisfaction of wants as the chief aim of public economy. *Kröncke*, Das Steuerwesen, 1804, 381 ff.; Grundsätze einer gerechten Besteuerung, 1819, 93 f., may be considered the predecessor who prepared the way for him. Compare the profound work of *Bernhardi*, Versuch einer Kritik der Gründe die für grosses und kleines Grundeigenthum angeführt werden, St. Petersburg, 1848. Many controversies on this subject may be closed by a more accurate understanding as to terms. Thus, for instance, when *Rau*, Handbuch, embraces in the cost of production the necessary maintenance of material-workmen, and of those engaged in the labor of commerce; or when *Jacob*, Staatswissenschaft, § 496, and *Storch*, Einkommen, 116 ff., even the necessary support of every class useful to society, their valuation of the gross national income is in only apparent conflict with our doctrine on the subject.

[1] This is possible between labor and capital, at least in so far as a comparison can be instituted between the sacrifice of human rest there is in labor and the sacrifice of enjoyment in the building up of capital. But the person who introduces an entirely unimproved piece of land into the service of production, stands to the laborer as well as to the capitalist in a relation which is entirely incomparable with any other. (See § 156.) The doctrine of former agriculturists, that one-half of the harvest was to be ascribed to the soil and the other to the manure, would not suffice here, even if it were correct. Compare *Fraas*, Gesch. der Landbau- und Forstwissenschaft, 257. But in the production of a calf, the coöperation of a bull and cow are necessary.

simple were meted out, no man could subsist. Love or charity must supplement justice in order to assist those (and especially such as without any fault of theirs) who are not able to produce anything, or enough to supply those wants, for instance, children and the poor.

As the net national income, following the three great factors of all economic production, is divided into three great branches, rent, wages and interest on capital, the net income from any private business may be reduced to one or more of these branches.[2] The three great branches of income may be considered with advantage from a great many different points of view. We may inquire in the case of each of them: concerning its absolute magnitude, its relation to the aggregate national income, to the magnitude of the factor of production, of which it constitutes the remuneration; by what number of men it is shared, and what number of wants it satisfies.[3] Lastly, the difference between the amount stipulated for, and

---

Yet no one is in condition to determine what portion of the calf is to be accounted as belonging to either. If the bull and cow belong to different owners, the relation of supply and demand, and the deeper causes that determine them, decide in what proportion the value of the calf is to be divided among them.

[2] Among the greatest services rendered by *Adam Smith* is, his complete demonstration, that any income may be resolved into one or more of the three great branches of the national income. (I, ch. 6.)

[3] *Ricardo* has not unfrequently bewildered uncritical readers, by his habit — in which he is by no means always consistent — of using the expressions higher and lower wages, higher and lower profit of capital, to designate not the absolute greatness of these branches of income, either in money or in the wants of life, nor their greatness from a personal point of view, but only their relative greatness as compared with the aggregate income, the measure of the quota of the aggregate product which is divided among workmen, capitalists etc. And yet, in the case of most economic questions, this is without doubt the less interesting side. Compare the polemic of *R. Jones*, On the Distribution of Wealth, 1831, I, 288 ff.; *Senior*, Outlines, 142 seq.; *Carey*, On the Rate of Wages, 1834, 24. Thus, according to *Ricardo*, the increase of one branch is possible only at the expense of another, while in the case of flourishing nations, the three branches increase absolutely and together. *Ricardo*, himself, was by no means unacquainted with this, as may be seen from *Baumstark's* German translation of his work, pp. 37, 108 ff.

the original amount of both rent and wages, as well as the interest of capital, is of special importance. The former consists in the price paid by the borrower for the use of the factor of production to the owner; the latter in the immediate products which the employment of the same productive power brings on one's own account. Evidently, the original amount is, in the long run, the chief element in the determination of the stipulated amount. While the former depends more on the deeper and more durably effective elements of price, especially the cost of production, the value in use and the paying capacity of purchasers; the latter is conditioned more by the superficial variations of supply and demand, and even by custom. For our purposes, the former is by far the more important, but, at the same time, by far the more difficult to perceive.

CHAPTER II.

THE RENT OF LAND.

SECTION CXLIX.

THEORY OF RENT.

Rent is that portion of the regular net product of a piece of land which remains after deducting the wages of labor and the interest on the capital usual in the country, incorporated into it.[1] Hence it is the price paid for the using of the land itself, or for what Ricardo calls the original inexhaustible forces

---

[1] According to *von Thünen*, Der isolirte Staat. in Beziehung auf Landwirthschaft und Nat. Œk, 1850, I, 14: "what remains of the revenue of an estate after deducting the interest on all the objects of value which may be separated from the soil." According to *Whately*, it is surplus profit. The expression "regular product" supposes, among other things, an average skillfulness of the economic individual. Thus, for instance, the farm-rent of a piece of land generally includes besides the real rent of the land, interest on much capital which is more or less firmly fixed in the soil. The importance of the latter may be approximately determined from the fact that in the electorate of Hesse, for instance, the value of all meadow lands, woods, and agricultural lands is estimated at from 205 to 206 millions of thalers, and the value of all the houses at 100 millions. (*Hildebrand*, Statist. Mittheil. über die volkswirthschaftlichen Zustände Kurhessens, 1852, 37.) In the English income tax of 1843, the annual value of all lands in Great Britain was estimated at over 45 millions sterling, that of all houses at over 38 millions. However the farm-rent of a piece of land does not by any means always embrace the entire rent. A part of the rent is paid to the state in the form of taxes, and another portion to the payment of tithes. Short leasehold terms, frequent land sales, the comparatively great difficulty of disengaging capital invested in the cultivation of land, the union of landed proprietor, capitalist and laborer in one person easily obscure the law of rent.

of the soil which are capable of being appropriated.[2] This price also depends, of course, on the relation between demand and supply; the demand in turn, on the wants and means of payment of buyers, but the supply by no means on cost of production, which, from the definitions above given, is here unthinkable. However, land has this in common with other means of production, that its price is mainly determined by that of its products.

SECTION CL.

THEORY OF RENT.
(CONTINUED.)

Agricultural products of equal quantity and quality are produced on pieces of land of unequal fertility, even when the same amount of skill is displayed by the husbandman, with very different outlays of capital and labor.[1] And yet the price

---

[2] The stores of immediate plant-food in a piece of land, of minerals in a mine, of salt in a salt-mine etc., are subject to the law of rent only in so far as they may be considered inexhaustible; that is, they are not, strictly speaking, subject to it. Our definition applies all the more to the capacity for cultivation, and of support or bearing capacity mentioned in § 35; and hence it is easier to follow the law of rent in the case of land used for building purposes than for agriculture. When *v. Mangoldt* claims that the exhaustibility or inexhaustibility of the soil has nothing to do with rent so long as it flows evenly *(so lange sie eben fliesst)* he is in harmony with his own general conception of rarity-premiums *(Seltenheitsprämien).*

[1] *Flotow*, Anleitung zur Abschätzung der Grundstücke nach Klassen, 1820, 50 ff., estimates the cost of production of a *scheffel* of rye on land of the first class, at scarcely 1½ thalers; on land of the tenth class, at 3 thalers. In Hanover, it is estimated that about 60 per cent. of the land devoted to gardening and agricultural products produces only from 2 to 4 times the quantity of seed sown; over 35 per cent. from 5 to 8 times, and 4.5 per cent. from 9 to 12 times. *(Marcard,* Zur Beurtheilung des Nat. Wohlstandes im Königreich Hanover, Tab. 3.) In Prussia, the rates of net produce adopted by the central commission in 1862 vary from 3 to 420 silver groschens per *morgen*, in the case of agricultural land; from 6 to 420 in the case of meadow land; in the case of pasturage, from 1 to 360. *(v. Viebahn,* Statist. des Zollvereins, II, 966.) In England, parliamentary investigations (1821) have shown that the best land produces from 32 to 40, and the worst from 8 to 12 bushels per

of these products in the same market is uniformly the same. This price must, on the supposition of free and intelligent competition, be, in the long run, at least high enough to cover the cost of production on even the worst soil (the margin of cultivation according to Fawcett), which must be brought under cultivation in order to satisfy the aggregate want. (See § 110.) This worst land need yield no rent.[2] The better land which, with an equal outlay of labor and capital, produces a greater yield, furnishes an excess over the cost of production.[3] This excess is rent, which, as a rule, is obviously higher in proportion as the difference in fertility between the worst and the better land is greater. The person who cultivates the land of a stranger may unhesitatingly turn this rent over to the owner; since, notwithstanding his so doing, all that he has himself

acre of wheat. (Edinburgh Review, XL, 21.) As to the influence of the elevation of land, the royal Saxon commission for the assessment of the value of land, estimated that the net product of an acre of land at a height above the level of the sea,

In the case of 2d class land —	In the case of 11th class land —
Of 500 feet, 55 per cent.	42.9 per cent. of the gross yield.
Of 800 " 52½ "	39½ " " " "
Of 1600 " 48 "	34 " " " "
Of 2400 " 43.8 "	26 " " " "

[2] The English are very fond of assuming that the worst land for the time being under cultivation pays no rent. (*Ricardo*, Principles, II, 2.) This fact is frequently obscured by the aggregation into one economic whole of land that pays no rent and land that is able to pay rent. (*John Stuart Mill*, Principles, II, ch. 16, § 3.) True it is that there is a great deal of land which cannot be farmed out, but which can be used only by its owners. Compare *Salfeld*, in the Landwirthsch. Centralb., 1871, II, 182 ff. On land near Wetzlar which, notwithstanding the high price of land in the neighborhood, could not be farmed out at auction, because no one was desirous to lease it, and which was therefore turned over to the highest bidder for the preceding piece, see *Stöckhardt*, Zeitschr. für deutsche Landwirthe, 1861, 237. Where, however, all the land has its own proprietors, the competition of farmers may easily produce a rent for the worst land. It is a matter of complete indifference to the theory of rent, whether the worst land when possessed only by right of occupation or used as pasturage for cattle previous to its cultivation, had value or not. Compare *Nebenius*, Œff. Credit, I, 29; *Hermann*, Staatswirthsch. Unters., 170 seq.

[3] The analogous gradation in mining may make this clearer.

contributed to production in labor and capital of his own, returns to him entire in the product.[4]

According to § 34, a continual increase in the amount of labor and capital lavished on the fertilization of land, agricultural science remaining the same, leads, sooner or later to this, that every new addition of capital or labor becomes relatively less remunerative than the preceding.[5] The worse the land is,

---

[4] *Ricardo* illustrated this by the following example. An uncultivated tract of country is settled by a small colony. As long as there is here an excess of land of the best quality, and everyone may take possession of it without paying anything therefor, no rent of the land which is merely occupied is possible. But if all the first class land is under cultivation — land which perhaps with the employment of a small amount of capital yields 5 quarters an acre per annum; and the increasing population necessitates the cultivation of land of the second class, which with the same outlay of capital yields only 4 quarters an acre per annum, there arises a rent of 1 quarter an acre per annum for land of the first class. For the price, 4 quarters is now high enough to cover the cost of production per acre, and it must be a matter of complete indifference (complete indifference?) to a new comer whether he obtains 5 quarters from land of the first class as a farmer and pays out 1 quarter, or whether he harvests 4 quarters from second class land as proprietor. If there is a further increase of population, so that land of the third class also, which yields only 3 quarters per acre per annum, must be brought under cultivation, the price of corn rises again because the cost of production has now to be covered by three quarters. Land of the first class now pays a rent of 2 quarters and second class land of 1 quarter. (Ch. 2.)

[5] *v. Thünen*, der isolirte Staat, II, I, 179, estimates that a bed of manure $\frac{1}{3}$ of an inch thick on an acre of ground, increases the production by $\frac{1}{2}$; that a second $\frac{1}{2}$ inch of manure increases the yield only by a + of $\frac{5}{8}$ corn; the third of $\frac{1}{4}$ corn etc. *Geyer* is of opinion that, in Saxony, land of the average quality will yield a gross product of 60 thalers per acre, and 14 thalers net product per acre, in case it is managed with the greatest intelligence and the employment of a large amount of capital; when managed in a very ordinary way, it would yield 20 thalers gross, and 7$\frac{1}{2}$ thalers net product. *Thünen* gives the following formula determining when it is more advantageous to cultivate the old land with more *intensiveness* (higher farming) than to begin the cultivation of new: As long as p — aq is less than $\sqrt{ap}$, so long is an increase of the outlay of capital on the same land more profitable than the cultivation of new land, and *vice versa*. Here p = aggregate product obtained by a workman in a year from the amount of capital used by him; a = sum of his necessary yearly wants; a = the interest per annum of a capital = p; q = the amount of capital given to assist the individual workman.

the sooner is this point reached. Hence, it necessarily happens that, with an increase in the aggregate want of agricultural products, greater and greater amounts of labor and capital are employed in the further fertilization of land, and that there comes to be a greater difference between the fertility of the worst and better lands, in consequence of which the rent of the latter rises.*

SECTION CLI.

THEORY OF RENT.—LAND FAVORABLY SITUATED.

The favorable situation of a piece of land operates, in almost every politico-economical respect, in the same manner as its fertility.[1] If a market, to be fully supplied, needs to be fed from a circuit of ten miles, the price must be sufficient to make good not only the other cost of production but the freight over ten miles. Here, therefore, all producers living nearer to the market, who have to make a smaller outlay for transportation and yet obtain the same market price for their produce, make

---

* *Ricardo* had, in every case in which outlay of capital and labor of different degrees of productiveness had to be used on the same land, to suppose a price of the products = the cost of the least productive outlay. See the tables in *Ricardo's* work, On the Influence of a low Price of Corn on the Profits of Stock, 1815, 14 seq. *Schmoller*, on the other hand, rightly applies the principle of united costs of production in as far as the usual amount of profit of the producer is added to the cost of the commodity with the highest cost of production. Mittheilungen des Landwirthsch. Instituts zu Halle, 1865, 128. Compare *supra*, §§ 106, 110.

[1] *L'éloignement équivaut à la stérilité.* (*J. B. Say.*) If we imagine with *A. Walker* an entirely uncultivated country, equally fertile in every part, settled only on the coast, and divided into shares of equal breadth, equally accessible at all points, so that every settler has unlimited space to extend his possessions from the coast into the interior, the shares situated in the middle of the coast strip would be most eagerly sought after; since in its vicinity, prospectively, all the institutions of the country would come together. The colonist, therefore, who should obtain that share as his, would, unquestionably, be in a condition to pay a price for this preference, that is a rent. (Science of Wealth, 296.)

a profit exactly corresponding to the advantage of their situation.[2]

The situation of individual pieces of land relatively to farm buildings etc., operates in a similar way.[3]

SECTION CLII.

THE THEORY OF RENT.
[CONTINUED.]

From what we have said, it follows that the rent of the land of a country is equal at least to the sum of all the differences between the product of the least productive portions of capital which have been necessarily laid out in the cultivation of the soil and the product of the other portions more productively laid out by other husbandmen. It may rise higher than this on account of a coalition among land owners or immoderate competition among farmers, who may thereby be forced to surrrender a portion of their wages and interest on capital to the former; but it can never lastingly fall below this amount. If the land owners themselves were to surrender all claim to rent, the price of agricultural products would not sink if the market was kept fully supplied; and the excess obtained from the better land over and above the cost of production would go, but only in the nature of a gift, to the farmers, corn dealers and individual consumers.[1] Normal rent is not to

---

[2] It is a consequence both of their difference of situation and of their fertility that in the Himalaya the farmers low down on the sides pay 50 per cent. of the gross product as farm rent, and higher up, 20 per cent. less. *(Ritter, Erdkunde,* III, 878.) Both influences may be traced most accurately in East Friesland, and in similar places: marsh land, sandy land, heath land, and high moor land.

Its situation influences especially the money rent of land, and its quality the amount of produce. *(McCulloch,* Principles, III, 5.)

[3] We need only mention the hauling of the crops and of manure. According to the instructions of the royal Saxon commission, above mentioned, the cost is assumed to be 10 per cent. higher for a distance of 250 rods, and 20 per cent. higher for a distance of 500 rods.

[1] Compare *J. Anderson,* An Inquiry into the Nature of the Corn Laws,

be explained by any mysterious or peculiar productiveness [2] of the land that yields it, but on the contrary, by the fact that even material forces unexhaustible in themselves, but which can be productive only in combination with given parcels of land, uniformly oppose even successively greater difficulties to every successive and additional improvement.[3]

1777. Extracts from the same in the Edinburgh Review, LIV, 91 ff. On the other hand, *Buchanan*, on Adam Smith, IV, 134, thinks that rent arises exclusively from the monopoly of the owners, and that without it the price of corn would be lower. It is certain, however, that if the land of a country be considered as one great piece of property, and under one great system of husbandry, the products of the soil might be offered permanently at a price corresponding to the average cost of production, on the better and worse pieces of land. (*Umpfenbach*, N. Œk., 191.)

[2] *Malthus*, On the Policy of restricting the Importation of foreign Corn, 1815. Additions, 1817, to the Essay on the Principle of Population, III, ch. 8-12; Principles, 217 ff.

[3] *Ricardo* says that if air, water, elasticity and steam were of different qualities, and might be made objects of exclusive possession; and that if each kind could be had only in a moderate supply, they would, like land, produce a rent, according as they were brought into use, one kind after another. In the class of natural forces, also, the possession of a secret of production or of inimitable skill, or a legal right to its exclusive use, may produce something similar to rent. (*Senior*, Outlines, 91.) *Hermann*, Staatswirthsch. Unters., 163 ff., had already laid the foundation of this doctrine, and earlier yet, *Canard*, 17 seq., and *Hufeland*, I, 303 ff. See *supra*, § 120. Hence *v. Mangoldt* uses the word rent to designate all rarity-premiums. *John Stuart Mill*, III, ch. 5, 4. *Schäffle* speaks of the universal existence of a surplus; that is, of the factor of rent (Nat. Oek., I, Aufl., 140 ff.), and has recently developed this into a theory thoroughly systematic and detailed. (Nationalökonomische Theorie der ausschliessenden Absatzverhältnisse, 1867.)

According to him, rent is " the premium paid for the most economic course taken in the interest of society in general ;" and hence he finds rent as much in superior labor and in a very advantageous outlay of capital. Yet he grants, that " exclusive custom *(Kundschaft)* on the basis of natural advantages occurs only in the case of land-rent." (59.) And even granting that he is right, that no rent is by itself forever secure (74 seq.), and that much rent is a premium paid for a search after and the appropriation of the best land, divination of the best situations etc. (60 ff., 74 ff.), there still remains the great difference between rent and the extra income from labor and capital; that here the very transitory nature of the substratum, or basis, and the personal merit of the recipient, is the rule, while in the former case it is a rare exception. Willingly, therefore, as I recognize the possibility and fruit-

Moreover, the capital which becomes a part of the land to such an extent that it cannot be separated from it, and perhaps not even distinguished from it at sight, such for instance as has been laid out for purposes of drainage or in the purchase of material intended to modify the nature of the soil, partakes of the character of the land itself, and its yield obeys the laws of rent. How frequently it happens that such improvements made by the farmer without the least assistance from the owner of the land permanently contribute to an increase of the rent. (§ 181.)[4]

---

fulness of Schäffle's way of conceiving this subject (the latter, especially, for monographic purposes), I prefer, so far as the entire system is concerned, the keeping apart of the three branches of income corresponding to the three factors of production as has been usual since Adam Smith's time.

[4] *John Stuart Mill*, ch. 16, § 5. An example in *Fawcett*, Manual, 149 seq. This explains many objections to Ricardo's laws, which are the result of misconception. Thus, for instance, in *Schmalz*, Staatswirthschaftslehre, I, 81, Quarterly Review, XXXVI, 412 ff. *Bastiat*, Harmonies économiques, ch. 9, where rent is considered the interest on the capital laid out in bringing land under cultivation and improving it. If, however, we imagine an island to emerge suddenly from the waves in the vicinity of Naples, in consequence of an earthquake, no one can doubt that its land would sell at a very high rate and pay a very good rent. And yet no capital or labor has been laid out on it. A similar lesson is taught by the fact, that, in Scotland, rocks which are covered twice a day by the waves are leased for the sake of the sea-weed left on them. (*Adam Smith*, Wealth of Nations, I, ch. 11.) Also by the fact, that in Poulopinang, a cavity in which many edible swallows' nests are found, pays £500 a year rent. (Geogr. Ephemeriden, Oct., 1805, 134.) However, *Bastiat*, abstractly speaking, is right when he says, that every one by the importation of agricultural products from quarters which pay no rent, and still more by emigrating thither, may deprive the owners of land of the tribute imminent in rent.

But how would it be if the cost of transportation and emigration amounted to more than the rent? The case theoretically so important, in which all the land in the world is supposed to have been appropriated as private property, this writer, generally so lucid, treats in a surprisingly blind way (275 ff). It is remarkable that *A. Walker*, Science of Wealth, spite of his prejudices in favor of Bastiat's doctrines on the gratuitous nature of all natural forces, nevertheless follows, essentially, *Ricardo's* theory of rent, 294 ff.

A much more vulgar error yet is, that rent is the result of the capacity of the capital employed in the purchase of the land to produce some interest

SECTION CLIII.

THEORY OF RENT.
(CONTINUED.)

Ricardo says that rent can never, not even in the slightest degree, constitute an element in the price of corn. This is certainly not a very happy way of expressing the truth, that a high rent is not the cause, but the effect, of a relatively high price of corn.[1] Ricardo would have been nearer right had he said that rent was not a component part of the price of every portion of the supply of corn brought to market.

Is rent an addition to national income? Ricardo (ch. 31) answers this question in the negative, and says that it takes from the consumers what it gives to the owners of the land, and that it increases only the value in exchange of the national wealth.[2] It is evident that as thus stated, the question is not properly put. Neither interest on capital nor wages are any

---

Thus *Hamilton*, Reports to the Congress on the Manufactures of the United States, 1793, and *Canard*, Principes, sec. 5. Per *contra*, compare *Turgot's* view, *supra*, § 42, note 1. Even *Locke*, Considerations on the Lowering of Interest, Works, II, 17 ff., maintained the closest parallel between rent and interest to be possible, with this difference only, that money was all of a kind but pieces of land of different degrees of fertility. Similarly Sir D. North, Discourse upon Trade, 1791, with his parallel of landlord and stocklord.

[1] To be met with in this form even in *Adam Smith*, Wealth of Nations, I, ch. 11, pr. *John Stuart Mill*, Principles II, ch. 16, § 6, thus states the matter: "Whoever cultivates land, paying a rent for it, gets in return for his rent an instrument of superior power to other instruments of the same kind for which no rent is paid. The superiority of the instrument is in exact proportion to the rent paid for it." According to *v. Jacob*, Grundsätze der Nat.-Oek., I, 187, rent constitutes a much larger portion of the price of commodities than is generally supposed, in as much as wages depend so largely on the price of the means of subsistence. Per contra, *Baudrillart*, Manuel, 391 ff., who maintains that rent is practically insignificant.

[2] Similarly *Buchanan*, loc. cit., and *Sismondi*, Richesse commerciale, I, 49. Compare contra, *Malthus*, Inquiry into the Nature and Progress of Rent, 15. I would call attention *en passant* to the absurdity that there may be an increase in the value in exchange of a nation's entire resources without any increase in its value in use. *(Supra, § 8.)*

addition to a nation's income, but, like rent, only forms of trade, by means of which that income is distributed among the individuals constituting the nation. (§ 201.)

The special kind of product obtained from a piece of land influences its rent only in so far as the growth of that kind of product is exclusively confined either by nature, privilege or prejudice to certain land.[3] Adam Smith is of opinion that the rent of agricultural land is ordinarily (!) one-third of the gross product; that of coal mines, from one tenth to a maximum of one-fifth; of good lead and tin mines, one sixth (with the dues paid the state of twenty-one and two-thirds per cent.); of Peruvian silver mines, scarcely one-tenth; of gold mines, one-twentieth. And he thinks that rent grows less certain for every succeeding article.[4]

So far as this is based on facts, it may be explained as follows: The greater capacity an article has for transportation from one place to another, the less important is advantage of situation, which is generally one of the chief elements of rent. The more indispensable the commodity is, the more readily is the consumer induced to pay a price for it greater than the cost of production; that is, to pay a rent. This again is enhanced by the difficulty of the preservation of the commodity. Lastly, the more it is a mere product of nature,[5] the more difficult it is to simultaneously employ several portions of capital of different grades of productiveness in its production.

---

[3] Thus *Adam Smith* remarks that corn fields and rice fields pay very different rents, because it is not always possible to convert one into the other. (Wealth of Nat., I, ch. 11, 1.) Compare the tabular statistical view of the rent of land used for vineyards, gardens, meadows, pasturages, wood and farming purposes, in *Rau*, Lehrbuch, I, § 218. For a general theory of the rent of wooded land, see *Hermann*, Staatsw. Unters., 177 ff.; of vineyards, 181 seq.

[4] *Adam Smith*, Wealth of Nat., I, ch. 11, 3.

[5] It is hereby rendered akin to those low stages of civilization in which no rent is paid.

SECTION CLIV.

THEORY OF RENT.
(CONTINUED.)

As the purchase of a piece of land[1] is no more and no less than its exchange against a portion of capital in the shape of money,[2] its purchase-price depends generally on the amount it will rent for as compared with the interest on the capital to be given in exchange for it. The rate of interest remaining the same, it rises and falls with its rent. And *vice versa*, the rent remaining the same it rises and falls inversely as the rate of interest.[3] A rise in the price of land is not always a proof of the growing wealth of a people. It may proceed from a depreciation of the value of money, or from a decrease of the rate of interest caused by a decline in the number of loans which can be advantageously placed.

It is frequently said, that the price paid for land is greater than the money-capital which yields an equal revenue.[4] This, abstraction made of proletarian distress prices for small parcels of land and of the political and social privileges of land-owners, is accounted for by the assumed greater security of the latter,[5]

---

[1] In every day language, people say of a man who has purchased a piece of land, that he "put" as much capital as is equal to the purchase price "into his land;" or "laid out on it" as much. But this mode of expression is as inaccurate as is this other: "the sun is rising," or "the sun has gone down."

[2] *Macleod*, who is not fond of the natural mode of expression, maintains that the purchase price of a piece of land is equal to the discounted value of the sum of the values of all the future products to be obtained from the land. (Elements, 75.)

[3] C : i :: L : r in which C = the capital, i = its interest, L = the piece of land, and r = its rent.

[4] There are traces to be found of the fact among the ancient Greeks, that the farm rent of landed estates paid a smaller interest on the purchase money than was otherwise usual in the country. *Isaeus de Hagn.*, 42; *Salmasius*, De Modo Usur., 848.

[5] Thus even *North* and *Locke*, loc. cit.; *Cantillon*, Nature du Commerce,

which, however, fares ill enough in war times, and times of political disturbance. The fact itself is found to exist, I think, only in economically progressive times, when confidence prevails, and it is based on the pretty certain prospect that the rate of interest will decline, while rents will rise.[6]

It has been observed in Belgium, that the medium farm rent of land, in quarters remarkable for any economic peculiarity whatever, pays an interest lower, as compared with the purchase-money, in proportion as the country about is more thickly populated, and as its husbandry is carried on by farmers instead of by owners.[7] This phenomenon is doubtless correlated with these others, that the conditions just named are pretty regularly attendant on a high state of civilization, and that advanced civilization is attended uniformly by a decline in the rate of interest. (175).[8]

---

[6] Compare *List*, Werke II, 173. In Belgium, farm rent per *hectare* was, in 1830 = 57.25 francs, in 1835 = 62.78, in 1840 = 70.44, in 1846 = 74.50, on an average. This was at the rate of from 2.62 to 2.80, or an average of 2.67 per cent. on the purchase money. If to this we add the increase in the rise of land between 1830 and 1846, divided by 16, the yearly revenue rises from 2.67 to 3.91 per cent., that is pretty nearly the rate of interest on hypothecation, and is higher or lower in the different provinces, as the former is higher or lower. (*Heuschling*, Résumé du Récensement général de 1846, 89.) In France, land paid but from 2 to 3 per cent. on the purchase money; but both rents and the price of land have doubled between 1794 and 1844. (Journal des Econ., IX, 208.)

[7] Moreover, whole countries may, because of their great natural advantages, possess, so far as the commerce of the entire world is concerned, something analagous to rent. Thus, for instance, North America, although here, this world-rent finds expression in the national height of the wages of labor and of the rate of interest. (*v. Bernhardi*, Versuch einer Kritik der Gründe welche für grosses und kleines Grundeigenthum angeführt werden, 1848, 294.)

[8] Writers as old as *Culpeper*, A Tract against the high Rate of Usurie, 1623, and *Sir J. Child*, Discourse of Trade, p. 22 of the French translation, observed the connection existing between a low rate of interest, national wealth and a flourishing state of commerce on the one hand, and a high price of the necessaries of life and of land in the other. *Sir W. Petty* would estimate the rent of land as follows: If a calf pasturing in an open meadow gains as much flesh in a given time as is equal to the cost of the food of 50

SECTION CLV.

HISTORY OF RENT.

In poor nations, and in those in a low stage of civilization, men for a day, and a workman, on the same land, in the same time, produces food for 60 men, the rent of the land must be 50, and the rate of wages 10. (Political Anatomy of Ireland, 62 seq.; compare 54.) Besides, he accounts for the height of rents by the density of the population exclusively, and he would prefer to see both increase *ad infinitum*. (Several Essays on Political Arithmetic, 147 ff.)

The germs of the *Ricardo* law of rent, in *Boisguillebert:* the price of corn determines how far the cultivation may be extended; by manuring the land, as much corn as desired may be obtained, provided the cost of production is covered. (Traité des Grains, II, ch. 2 ff.) There is a foreshowing of the same law in the Physiocratic view that only in the production of raw material is there a real excess over and above the cost —*produit net*. Compare *Quesnay*, Probl., économique, 177 ff. Sur les travaux des artisans. (Daire.) *Auxiron*, Principes de tout Gouvernement, 1776, I, 126. *Adam Smith* came very near to the true principle in the case of coal mines, but was hindered reaching it in other cases by the false assumption that certain kinds of agricultural production always yield a rent, while others do so only under certain circumstances. Besides he always considered the interest of capital fixed in the soil; buildings, for instance, as part of the rent. (Wealth of Nat., I, ch. 11. Compare *Hume's* Letter to Adam Smith; *Burton's* Life and Correspondence of Hume, II, 486; *von Thünen*, Isolirter Staat., I, 15 ff.

The most immediate predecessors of *Ricardo*, Principles, 2, 3, 24, 31, are *Anderson* (§ 152); *West*, Essay on the Application of Capital to Land, 1815, and *Malthus*, Inquiry into the Nature and Progress of Rent, 1815. See § 152. It is wonderful how a theory which, in 1777, remained almost untouched, was in 1815 etc., attacked and defended with the greatest zeal, because it then affected the differences between the moneyed and landed interest. Yet *Ricardo* did not take into account at all the rent-creating influence of the situation of land in relation to the market, as well as to the "farm-office" *(dem Wirthschaftshofe)*. The influence of the system of husbandry on rent, first thoroughly treated by *v. Thünen*, loc. cit. What has recently been urged against *Ricardo* by, for instance, *J. B. Say*, Traité, II, ch. 9; *Sismondi*, N. P., III, ch. 12; *Jones*, Essay on the Distribution of Wealth, 1831 (see Edinburg Review, LIV), bears evidence either of a misunderstanding of the great thinker, or else contains only modifications of some individual abstract propositions of his, stated perhaps too strictly. In judging *Ricardo*, it must not be forgotten, that it was not his intention to write a text book on the science of Political Economy, but only to communicate to those versed in it the result of his

especially where the population is sparse, rent is wont to be low. In Turkistan, land is valued according to the capital

researches, in as brief a manner as possible. Hence he writes so frequently making certain assumptions; and his words are to be extended to other cases only after due consideration, or rather re-written to suit the changed case.

Baumstark very correctly says: " Rent rises, not because new capital has been invested, but when the circumstances of trade make a new addition to capital possible." (Volkswirthschaftliche Erläuterungen über Ricardo's System, 1838, 567.) *Fuoco's* Nuova Teoria della Rendita, Saggi economici, No. 1, is nothing but an Italian version of the doctrines of Malthus and Ricardo. The greater number of anti-Ricardo theories of rent have originated from the rapid and apparently unlimited growth of national husbandry in recent times. Thus it is a fundamental thought in *Rodbertus*, Sociale Briefe, 1851, No. 3, that an increase of the price of corn need not attend an increase of population, either uniformly or necessarily. According to *Carey*, The Past, the Present and the Future, ch. 1, 1848, the most fertile land is last brought under cultivation, because it is covered with swamps, forests etc.; and because it offers greater resistance to the work of the agriculturist, by reason of its luxurious vegetation. The more elevated lands are first cultivated which present fewer obstacles to cultivation on account of their dryness, their thinner crust etc. Carey generalizes this and thinks he has reversed the *Ricardo* law of rent! He overlooks entirely that *Ricardo* speaks only of the original powers of the soil. Now a swampy land which must be dried at the expense of a great deal of labor, possesses less of these original powers than a sandy soil which may be sown immediately. See *Carey*, Essay on the Rate of Wages, 232 ff., and the lengthy exposition of the same doctrine rank with inexact natural science and unhistorical history in the same author's Principles of Social Science, 1858, vol. I.

There is this much truth, however, in Carey's error that, with increasing economic progress, the superiority not only of situation, relatively to the market, but also of natural fertility, may of itself go over to other lands. Thus, for instance, the ancient Slaves used clay soil everywhere as pasturage, and cultivated the sandy soil, because their pick-axes could overcome the resistance only of the latter. *Langethal*, Geschicte der deutschen Landw., II, 66; *Waitz*, Schlesw. Holstein, Gesch., I, 17. Similarly in Australia: *Hearne*, Plutology, 1864. Compare, *Roscher*, Nationalökonomik des Ackerbaues, § 34. The word fertility should not be taken too exclusively in its present agricultural sense. In a lower stage of civilization, the facility of military defense or the *ut fons, ut nemus placuit — Tacit.*, Germ., 16 — may have more weight.

The chief difference in the theories of rent consists in this: whether rent is considered a result of production or only of distribution, and an equaliza-

invested in its irrigation.¹ In the interior of Buenos Ayres, at the beginning of the nineteenth century, landed estates were paid for in proportion to the magnitude of the live stock on them, so that it seemed, at least, as if the land was given for nothing, or simply thrown in with the purchase. And only a short time since, an English acre in the same country, fifteen *leguas* from the capital, was worth from three to four pence, and at a distance of fifty *leguas*, only two pence.² In Russia, also, not long since, the valuation of landed estates was made, not in proportion to the superficies, but according to the number of souls, that is, of male serfs, a *remnant* suggestive of the previous situation when no rent was paid.³ Where, in relatively uncivilized medieval times, instances of the farming out or leasing of land occur, farm-rents are so small that their payment can only be considered as a mere recognition of the owner's continuing right of property.

Under these circumstances, it is natural that great land owners, especially in the lower stages of civilization, should exert an especially great influence; and that their low tenants *(Hintersassen)* are more dependent in proportion to the want of capital and the absence of trade. Hence, these are wont to make up for the smallness of their rent by great honors paid

---

tion of gain. Compare *Behrens*, Krit. Dogmengeschichte der Grundrente, 1868, 48.

¹ *A. Burnes*, Reise nach Bukhara, II, 238.

² *W. Maccann*, Two Thousand Miles Ride through the Argentine Provinces, London, 1853, I, 20; II, 143. Ausland, 1843, No. 140. Frisian ancient documents in which parcels of land are described as *terræ 20 animalium, 48 animalium*, etc. *Lacomblet*, Urkundenbuch, I, 27. *Kindlinger*, Münster Beitr., I, Urkundenbuch, 24.

³ The custom began to be more usual in Russia also to say "so many *dessjatines* and the peasantry belonging thereto." This was especially so in the case of very fertile land, as for instance in Orel. See *v. Haxthausen*, Studien, II, 510. Formerly the bank loaned only 250 per soul, afterwards up to 300 R. Bco. (II, 81). Spite of this *v. Haxthausen* thinks that rent would be illusory, in Russia, in case agriculture was carried on with hired workmen. (I, Vorrede, XIII.) *Carey's* remark, "every one is familiar with the fact that farms sell for little more than the value of the improvements," may be true of the United States (The Past, Present and Future, 60.)

to their landlords, and great services, especially military service.[4] Besides, the lords of the manor, in almost every medieval period, have used their influence with the government to cut down the wages of labor by serfdom and other similar institutions, and the rate of interest on capital by prohibiting interest, by usury laws etc.; and thus, in both ways, to artificially increase their own share of the national income.

SECTION CLVI.

INFLUENCE OF ADVANCING CIVILIZATION ON RENT.

Advancing civilization contributes in three different ways to raise rents.[1] The growth of population necessitates either a more *intensive* agriculture (higher farming), or causes it to extend over less fertile parcels of land, or parcels less advantageously situated.[2] If the growth of population be attended by an increase of capital, this happens in a still higher degree. The people now consume, if not more, at least wheat of finer quality, more and better fed live stock; the consequence of which is, that the demands made on the land are increased. Lastly, if the population be gradually concentrated in large cities, this fact also must contribute to raise rents, because it requires a multitude of costly transportations of agricultural produce and so increases the cost of production (up

---

[4] This condition of things continued in the highlands of Scotland until the suppression of the revolt of 1745. The celebrated Cameron of Lochiel took the field with 800 tenants, although the rent of the land was scarcely £500. *(Senior,* Three Lectures on the Rate of Wages, 45.) "Poor 12,000 pound sterling per annum nearly subverted the constitution of these kingdoms!" *(Pennant.)*

[1] *Jung,* Lehrbuch der Cameralpraxis, 1790, 182, has so little idea of this that he is of opinion that farm-rent must grow ever smaller.

[2] According to *Schmoller,* in the Mittheilungen des landwirthschaftlich. Instituts zu Halle, 1865, 112 seq., the average farm-rent of the Prussian domains per *morgen,* and the population to the square mile, amounted:

to the time of consumption) on the less advantageously situated land.³ ⁴

District.	1849.	1864.	1849.	1858.
	Thalers.	Thalers.		
Königsberg, - - -	0.73	1.16	2076	2298
Gumbinnen, - - -	0.59	0.76	2059	2249
Danzig, - - - -	1.02	1.51	2656	2926
Marienwerder, - -	0.63	1.06	1944	2135
Posen, - - - -	0.69	1.07	2789	2857
Bromberg, - - -	0.69	1.10	2116	2322
Stettin, - - - -	1.07	1.73	2355	2614
Cöslin, - - -	0.83	1.30	1735	1940
Stralsund, - - -	0.95	1.50	2347	2549
Breslau, - - -	1.19	1.45	4733	5034
Liegnitz, - - -	1.17	1.75	3676	3763
Oppeln, - - -	0.86	1.20	3973	4433
Potsdam, - - - -	1.08	1.59	3317	3640
Frankfort, - - -	1.29	2.00	2446	2660
Magdeburg, - - -	2.31	2.98	3290	3508
Werseburg, - - -	2.35	3.03	3934	4270
Erfurt, - - - -	2.04	2.55	5621	5735
Münster, - - -	....	2.03	3192	3299
Minden, - - - -	2.48	2.62	4841	4808

Compare the review of rents in the states of the Zollverein, in *v. Viehbahn*, Statistik, II, 979. It is difcult to compare different countries with one another in this respect, because it is seldom certain whether the word rent means exactly the same thing in them. Besides, it should not be overlooked, how difficult it is to ascertain what rent, in the strict sense of the term, as used by *Ricardo*, is.

³ Moreover, the rise of rents, in so far as it depends on the greater cost of transportation to a growing market, becomes progressively slower. The concentric circles about that point increase in a greater ratio than the radii.

⁴ As to the history of rents in England, a comparison of the years from 1480 to 1484, with the most recent times, shows that the amount of rent estimated in money in agricultural districts, where no very great "improvements" have been made, have increased as 1 to 80–100, while the price of wheat has increased 12-fold and wages 10-fold. (*Rogers*, in the Statist. Journal, 1864, 77.) According to *Hume*, History of England, ch. 33, it seems that rents under Henry VIII. were only $\frac{1}{15}$ of those usually paid in his time, while the price of commodities was only ¼ of the modern. *Davenant*, Works, II, 217, 221, estimates the aggregate rent of land, houses and mines, at the beginning of the seventeenth century, at £6,000,000; about 1698, at £14,000,000; capitalized respectively at £72,000,000 and £252,000,000. About 1714, *J. Bellers*, Proposals for Employing the Poor, puts it at £15,000,000; about 1726, *Erasm. Phillips*, State of the Nation in Respect to Commerce

SEC. CLVI.   CIVILIZATION ON RENT.   31

As most of the symptoms of a higher civilization become apparent earliest, and in the most striking manner, in large cities, so also a rise in rents is first felt in them. The building of houses may be considered as the most *intensive* of all cultivation of land and that which is most firmly fixed to the soil.[5] Rent has nowhere an unsurpassable maximum any more than a necessary minimum.

---

etc., at £20,000,000; about 1771, *A. Young*, at £16,000,000; about 1800, *Beeke*, Observations on the Income-Tax, at £20,000,000; about 1804, *Wakefield*, Essay on Political Economy, at £28,000,000; about 1838, *McCulloch*, Statist., I, 535, at £29,500,000. The poor tax in England and Wales, in 1841, was on a valuation of £32,655,000. (*Porter*, Progress, VI, 2, 614); 1864-5, the annual value of lands, £46,403,853 (Stat. Journal, 1869.) Moreover, the income from houses, railroads etc. (real property other than lands), increased very much more than that received from pieces of farming land; between 1845 and 1864-5, the former by 392.8 per cent., and the latter by 27.9 per cent. (*Hildebrand's* Jahrbb., 1869, II, 383 seq.); and the income tax of 1857 on £47,109,000. There was a still more rapid growth of rent in Scotland. In 1770, it was only £1,000,000-1,200,000: in 1795, £2,000,000; in 1842, £5,586,000. (*McCulloch*, I, 576, ff.) In Ireland, about 1776, it was only $900,000, according to *Petty*. (Political Anatomy of Ireland, I, 113.) *A. Young* assumed it to be £6,000,000 in 1778; *Newenham*, View of Ireland, about 1808, £15,000,000. In many parts of the Rosendale Forest in Lancashire, the land is leased by the ell, at £121, and even at £131 per acre; i. e., more than the whole forest of 15,300 acres was rented for in the time of James I. In many of the moor-land portions of Lancashire, rent has risen in 150 years, 1,500 and even 3,000 per cent. (Edinburg Rev., 1843, Febr., 223.)

The amount of rents in Prussia, *Krug* assumed to be in 1804, 50,000,000 thalers, and *von Viebahn*, Zollverein Statistik, II, 974, in 1862, 116,500,000 thalers. *Lavergne* assumed the rents of France after 1850 to be 1,600,000,000 francs (Revue des deux Mondes, Mars, 1868); and *Dutot*, Journal des Economistes, Juin, 1870, in 1870, at 2,000,000,000. In Norway, the capitalized value of all the land was assessed at 13,000,000,000 thalers in specie, in 1665; in 1802, at 25,500,000; in 1839, at 64,000,000 thalers. *Blom*, Statistik von Norwegen, I, 145. The older such estimates are, the more unreliable they are.

[5] In Paris, in 1834, the square *toise* = 37 sq. feet, in the Rue Richelieu and Rue St. Honoré, cost 1,500 to 2,000 francs; in Rue neuve Vivienne, 2,500 to 3,500 francs; in 1857, from 200 to 500 francs per square meter, = 10 sq. feet, was very usual. (*Wolowski*.) Before the gates of Paris, the rent amounted to as high as 250 francs per *hectare;* at Fontainebleau, to only from 30 to 40. (Journal des Economistes, Mars, 1856, 337.) In Market Square, Philadelphia, land was worth from 3,000 to 4,000 francs per sq. *toise*, and in Wall

SECTION CLVII.

HISTORY OF RENT.—IMPROVEMENTS IN THE ART OF AGRICULTURE.

Improvements in the art of agriculture which are confined to individual husbandmen leave rent unaffected. They do not perceptibly lower the price of agricultural products, and only effect an increase of the reward of enterprise which is entirely personal to the more skillful producers and does not attach to the ground itself.

But how is it when these improvements become general throughout the country? If population and consumption remain unchanged, the supply of agricultural products will exceed the demand. This would compel farmers, if there be no avenue open to exports, to curtail their production. The least fertile and most disadvantageously situated parcels of land will be abandoned to a greater or less extent, and the least productive capital devoted to agriculture, withdrawn. In this way, rent goes down both relatively and absolutely, although the owners of land may be able to partially cover their loss by the gain which results to them as consumers and capitalists.[1] (§ 186). After a time, however, and as a conse-

Street, New York, about 4,000 francs. *(M. Chevalier*, Letters sur l'Amérique, 1836, I, 355.) In St. Petersburg, after 6 years, the house frequently falls to the owner of the area. *(Storch. by Rau*, I, 248 f.) In Manchester, the Custom House area cost from 10 to 12 pounds sterling per square yard; in the center of the city, as high of £40, that is, nearly £200,000 per acre. In Liverpool, in the neighborhood of the Exchange and of Town Hall, the cost is from 30 to 40 pounds sterling. (Athenæum, Dec. 4, 1852.) In London, a corner building on London street, erected for £70,000, with only three front windows, pays a rental of £22,000. (Allg. Zeitung, 1 Febr., 1866.) The villa at Misenum — a very beautiful location — which the mother of the Gracchi bought for about 5,000 thalers, came into the possession of L. Lucullus, consul in the year B. C. 74, for about 33 times as much. *Mommsen*, Römisch. Gesch., II, 382.

[1] Since it has seemed absurd to many writers to say that an improvement in the art of agriculture may cause rents to decline (compare *Malthus*, Principles, I, ch. 3, 8), *John Stuart Mill*, Principles, IV, ch. 3, § 4, prefers

quence of the diminished price of corn, population and consumption will increase, and entail an extension of agriculture and a consequent rise in rents.[2] If it, relatively speaking, reaches the same point as before, it still is absolutely much greater than before. Let us suppose that there are three classes

to put the question thus: whether the landowner is not injured by the improvement of the estates of other people, although his own is included in the improvement. Compare *Davenant*, Works, I, 361. And so the long agricultural crisis through which Germany passed at the beginning of the third decade of this century was produced mainly by the great impulse given to agriculture (*Thaer, Schwerz* etc.), while population did not keep pace with it. Similarly, at the same time, in England, *McCulloch*, Stat., I, 557 ff. Of course, the less fertile pieces of land declined even relatively most in price. From 1654 to 1663, Switzerland experienced a severe agricultural crisis, attended with oppressive cheapness of corn, a great decline in the price of land, innumerable cases of insolvency, revolts of the peasantry, emigration, etc. (*Meyer von Knonau*, Handbuch d. schweiz. Gesch., II, 43.) The Swiss had, precisely during the Thirty Years' War which spared them, so extensively developed their agricultural interests, that now that other countries began to compete with them, they could not find a market large enough for their products. For English instances of similar "agricultural distress" in the seventeenth and eighteenth centuries, see *Child*, Discourse on Trade, 73, 124 seq.; *Temple*, Observations upon the U. P., ch. 6; *Tooke*, History of Prices, I, 23 seq., 42. Even where there have been no technic improvements, a series of unusually good harvests may have the same results, of which there are many instances scattered through *Tooke's* first volume.

There is great importance attached in England to the difference between those agricultural reforms which save land and those which effect a saving in capital and labor. The latter, it is said, decrease the money rent of the land owner by depreciating the price of corn, but leave the corn-rent unaltered. The former, on the other hand, decrease the rent both in money and corn, but the money rent in a higher degree. (*Ricardo*, Principles, ch. 2; *J. S. Mill*, Principles, IV, ch. 3, 4.

[2] When the demand for products of the soil which minister to luxury, such as fat meat, milk, vegetables, is increasing, a greater cheapness of the necessary wheat may raise rent, for the reason that lands are now cultivated which were not formerly tillable. Thus, there is now land in Lancashire which could not formerly be planted with corn, because the laborers would have consumed more than the harvest yielded. Since the large imports of the means of subsistence from Ireland these lands have been transformed into artificial meadows, gardens etc. (*Torrens*, The Budget, 180 ff.) Compare *Adam Smith*, I, 257, ed. Bas. *Banfield* would misuse these facts to overturn the theory of Ricardo. (Organization of Industry, 1848, 49 ff.)

Vol. II — 3

of land of equal extent in a country, which for an equal outlay of capital produce 100,000, 80,000 and 70,000 bushels yearly. The rent of the land here would be equal to at least 40,000 bushels. If the yield of production now doubles, while the demand for agricultural products also doubles, the aggregate harvest will be 200,000 + 160,000 + 140,000 bushels; and consequently rent will have risen to at least 80,000 bushels. But this increase of rent has injured no one. If the population increases in a less degree than the productiveness of the land, the consumer may, to a certain extent, gain largely, and the land-owner better his condition. However, great agricultural improvements spread so gradually over a country, that, as a rule, the demand for agricultural products can keep pace with the increased supply. But even in this case, that transitory absolute decline of rent may be avoided; and it cannot be claimed universally, as it is by many who are satisfied with mumbling Ricardo's words after him, that an increase of rent is possible only by an enhancement of the price of the products of the soil. Where the development of a people's economy is a normal one, the rent of land is wont to increase gradually, but at the same time to constitute a diminishing quota of the entire national income.[3]

Improvements in milling,[4] and in the instruments of trans-

---

[3] The French testamentary tax was on an amount,
In 1835, of 552 mill. francs moveable property and 984 mill. immoveable.
In 1853, of 820 " " " " " 1,176 " "
In 1860, of 1,179 " " " " " 1,545 " "
So that the preponderance of immoveable property constituted a converging series of 78, 43, and 31 per cent. *(Parieu.)* In North America, with its great unoccupied territory, the reverse is the case. The census of 1850 gave a moveable property of 36 per cent.; that of 1860 of only 30 per cent. According to *Dubost*, the rent of land in Algeria was 80 per cent., a gross product of only 10–15 francs per *hectare;* in Corsica, 66 per cent., a gross yield of from 30–35 per cent.; in the Department du Nord, 17.5–24 per cent., a gross yield of from 500–740 francs. (Journal des Economistes, Juin, 1870, 336 ff.)

[4] The repeated sifting of the bran *(mouture économique)* had great influence in this respect. In France, in the sixteenth century, a *setier* of wheat gave

portation⁵ adapted to agricultural products, and the introduction of cheaper⁶ food, have the same effect as improvements of agricultural production. All such steps in advance render an increase in population, or in the nation's resources, possible without any corresponding increase in the amount paid to landowners as tribute money.⁷

---

only 144 pounds of bread. In 1767, according to *Malouin*, L'Art du Bonlanger, it gave 192 pounds. It now gives from 223 to 240 pounds. The gain in barley is still greater; the *setier* gives 115 pounds of flour, formerly only 58. (*Roquefort*, Histoire de la Vie Privée des Français, I, 72 ff. *Beckmann*, Beitr. zur Gesch. der Erfind., II, 54.)

⁵ In the beginning of the eighteenth century, the counties in the neighborhood of London addressed a petition to Parliament against the extension of the building of turnpike roads which caused their rents to decline, from the competition of distant districts. (*Adam Smith*, Wealth of Nat., I, ch. 11, 1.) Compare Sir *J. Stewart*, Principles, I, ch. 10. Improvements in transportation which affect the longest and shortest roads to a market in an absolutely equal degree, as, for instance, the bridging of a river very near the market, leave rent unaffected. (*von Mangoldt*, V. W. L., 480.)

⁶ *Malthus*, Principles, 231 ff. If the laboring class were to become satisfied with living on potatoes instead of meat and bread as hitherto, rents would immediately and greatly fall, since the necessities of the people might then be obtained from a much smaller superficies. But after a time, the consequent increase in population might lead to a much higher rent than before; since a great deal of land too unfertile for the cultivation of corn might be sown with potatoes, and thus the limits of cultivation be reached much later.

⁷ In France, between 1797 and 1847, the average price of wheat did not rise at all. *Hipp. Passy* mentions pieces of land which produced scarcely 12 hectolitres of wheat, but which now produce 20 — an increased yield of 170 francs, attended by an increase in the cost of only 75 francs. (Journal des Economistes, 15 Oct., 1848.) Moreover, it may be that a not unimportant part of modern rises in the price of corn may be accounted for by the better quality of the corn caused by higher farming. (*Inama Sternberg*, Gesch. der Preise, 10 seq.) Such facts, readily explainable by *Ricardo's* theory, remove the objection of *Carey, Banfield* and others, that the condition of the classes who own no land has, since the middle ages, unquestionably improved. Political Economy would be simply a theory of human degradation and impoverishment, if the law of rent was not counteracted by opposing causes. (*Ræsler*, Grundsätze, 210.) According to *Berens*, Krit. Dogmengeschichte, 213, the actual highness of rent is to be accounted for by the antagonism between the "soil-law *(Bodengesetz)* of the limited power of vegetation,"

The foregoing facts furnish us the data necessary to decide what influence permanent soil improvements have on the rent of land.[8] The improved parcels of land now grow more fertile. Their rentability also increases, while that of the others becomes not only relatively but absolutely less, if the demand remains unaltered. The whole is as if capital had been transformed into fertile land, and this added to the improved land.

SECTION CLVIII.

HISTORY OF RENT.—IN PERIODS OF DECLINE.

If a nation's economy be declining, in consequence of war for instance, the disastrous influence hereof on rent may be retarded by a still greater fall in wages or in the profit on capital. But it can be hardly retarded beyond a certain point.[1]

---

and the "progress of civilization" (but surely only to the extent that the latter improves the art of agriculture). Thus, too, *John Stuart Mill*, Principles, I, ch. 12; II, ch. 11, 15 seq.; III, ch. 4 seq.; IV, ch. 2 ff.

[8] Thus, for instance, drainage works which, where properly directed, have paid an interest of from 25 to 70 per cent. per annum in England and Belgium on the capital invested.

[1] "The falling of rents an infallible sign of the decay of wealth." *(Locke.)* In England, in 1450, land was bought at "14 years' purchase;" i. e., with a capital = 14 times the yearly rent paid; in 1470, at only "10 years' purchase." *(Eden, State of the Poor, III, App., I, XXXV.)* This was, doubtless, a consequence of the civil war raging in the meantime. The American war (1775–82) depressed the price of land in England to "23¼ years' purchase," whereas it had previously stood at 32. *(A. Young.)* The rent of land, in many places in France, declined from 10,000 to 2,000 livres, on account of the many wars during Louis XIV.'s reign. *(Madame de Sévigné's Lettres, 25 Dec., 1689.)* Even in 1677, it was only one-half of its former amount *(King, Life of Locke, I, 129.)* The whole Bekes county *(comitat)* in Hungary was sold for 150,000 florins under Charles VI.; after the unfortunate war with France. *(Mailath, Oesterreich, Gesch., IV, 523.)* Compare *Cantillon*, Nature du Commerce, 248. In Cologne, a new house was sold in the spring of 1848 for 1,000 thalers, the site of which alone had cost 3,000 thalers; and there are six building lots which formerly cost over 3,000 thalers, now valued at only 100 thalers. *(von Reden, Statist. Zeitschr., 1848, 366.)* On the other hand, Napoleon's war very much enhanced English rents *(Porter, Pro-*

As a rule, the decline of rents begins to be felt by the least fertile and least advantageously situated land.[2 3]

SECTION CLIX.

HISTORY OF RENT.—RENT AND THE GENERAL GOOD.

We so frequently hear rent called the result of the monopoly[1] of land, and an undeserved tribute paid by the whole people to land owners, that it is high time we should call attention to the common advantage it is to all. There is evidently danger that, with the rapid growth of population, the

---

gress of the Nation, II, 1, 150 ff.), because it affected England's national husbandry principally by hindering the importation of the means of subsistence. *(Passy,* Journal des Economistes, X, 354.)

[2] Thus the price of lands, in Mecklenburg, between 1817 and 1827, fell 30 to 40 per cent. in the least fertile quarters; in the better, from 15 to 20 per cent. *(von Thünen,* in *Jacob,* Tracts relating to the Corn Trade, 40, 187.) *Per contra,* see Hundeshagen Landwirthsch. Gewerbelehre, 1839, 64 seq., and *Carey,* Principles, I, 354.

[3] The average rent in England was, in 1815, 17s. 3d. In the counties, it was highest in Middlesex, 38s. 9d.; in Rutland, 38s. 2d.; Leicester, 27s. 3d.; lowest in Westmoreland, 9s. 1d. In Wales, the average was 7s. 10d.; highest in Anglesea, 19s.; lowest in Merioneth, 4s. 8d. In Scotland the average was 5s. 1½d.; highest, Midlothian, 24s. 6¼d.; lowest, Highland Caithness, Cromarthy, Inverness and Rosse, from 1s. 1d. to 1s. 5d.; Orkneys, 8½d.; Sutherland, 6d.; Shetlands, 3d. In Ireland, the average was 12s. 9d.; highest in Dublin, 20s. 1½d.; lowest, Donegal, 6s. *(McCulloch,* Stat., I, 544 ff.; Yearbook of general Information, 1843, 193.) In France, *Chaptal,* De l'Industrie Fr., 1819, I, 209 ff., estimates the average yield per *hectare* at 28 francs; in the Department of the Seine, 216; Nord, 69.56; Lower Seine, 67.85; in the upper Alps, 6.2; in the lower Alps, 5.99; in the Landes, 6.25. While in the Landes, only 20 francs a *hectare* are frequently paid, the purchase price in the neighboring Medoc is sometimes 25,000 francs. (Journal des Economistes, Jan. 15, 1851.) In Belgium, the average price of agricultural land is 52.46; in East Flanders, 53.19; in Namur, 29.24. *(Heuschling,* Statistique, 77.)

[1] "Rent is a tax levied by the land owners as monopolists." *(Hopkins,* Great Britain for the last forty Years, 1834.) For a very remarkable armed and successful resistance of farmers in the state of New York to the claims for rent of the Rensselaer family, represented by the government, see *Wappäus* Nord Amerika, 734.

mass of mankind should yield to the temptation of gradually confining themselves to the satisfaction of coarse, palpable wants; that all refined leisure, which makes life and the troubles that attend it worth enduring, and which is the indispensable foundation of all permanent progress and all higher activity, should be gradually surrendered. (See § 145.) Here rent constitutes a species of reserve-fund, which grows greater in proportion as these dangers impend by reason of the decline of wages and of the profit of capital, or interest.[2] Besides, precisely in times when rent is high, the sale and divisibility of landed estates act as a beneficent reaction against the monopoly of land, which is always akin to the condition of things created by rent.

But it is of immeasurably greater importance that high rents deter the people from abusing the soil in an anti-economic way; that they compel men to settle about the centers of commerce, to improve the means of transportation, and under certain circumstances to engage in the work of colonization; while, otherwise, idleness would soon reconcile itself to the heaping together of large swarms of men.[3] The anticipation of rent may render possible the construction of railroads, which enable the land to yield that very anticipated rent.

---

[2] *Malthus*, Additions to the Essay on Population, 1817, III, ch. 10; compare also *Verri*, Meditazioni, XXIV, 3. The Physiocrates call the land owners *classe disponible*, since, as they may live without labor, they are best adapted to military service, the civil service etc., either in person or by defraying the expenses of those engaged in them. (*Turgot*, Sur la Formation etc., § 15; Questions sur la Chine, 5.)

[3] Well discussed by *Schäffle*, Theorie, 65, 72, 83. *Malthus* considers the capital and labor expended in agriculture more productive than any other, because they produce not only the usual interest and wages, but also rent. If, therefore, the manufacturing and commercial profit of a country $= 12$ per cent., and the profit of capital employed in agriculture $= 10$ per cent., a corn-law which compelled the capital engaged in manufactures and commerce to be devoted to agriculture would be productive of advantage to the national husbandry in general, if the increase in rent should amount to about 3 per cent. (On the Effects of the Corn Laws and of a Rise or Fall in the Price of Corn on the Agriculture and the general Wealth of the Country, 1815. The Grounds of an Opinion on the Policy of Restricting the Impor-

CHAPTER III.

WAGES.

SECTION CLX.

THE PRICE OF COMMON LABOR.

Like the price of every commodity, the immediate wages of common labor is determined by the relation of the demand and supply of labor. Other circumstances being the same, every great plague[1] or emigration[2] is wont, by decreasing the supply, to increase the wages of labor; and a plague, the wages of the lowest kind of labor most.[3] And so, the in-

---

tation of Foreign Corn, 1815.) Compare *supra*, § 55, and the detailed rectification in *Roscher*, Nationalökonomik des Ackerbaues etc, § 159 ff.

[1] High rate of Italian wages after the plague in 1348, but also many complaints of the indolence and dissoluteness of workmen. (*M. Villani*, I, 2 ff., 57 seq. *Sismondi*, Gesch. der ital. Republiken in Mittelalter, VI, 39.) In England, the same plague increased the wages of threshers from an average of 1.7 d. in 1348, to 3.3 d. in 1349. Mowers received, during the 90 years previous, $\frac{1}{12}$ of a quarter of wheat per acre; in 1371—1390, from $\frac{1}{7}$ to $\frac{1}{4}$. The price of most of their wants was then from $\frac{1}{4}$ to $\frac{1}{12}$ as high as in *A. Young's* time, and wages $\frac{1}{2}$ as high. (*Rogers*, I, 306, 271, 691.) The great earthquake in Calabria, in 1783, produced similar effects. (*Galanti*, N. Beschreibung von Neapel, I, 450.) Compare *Jesaias*, 13, 12. On the other hand, depopulation caused by unfortunate wars is not very favorable to the rate of wages; instance, Prussia in 1453 ff, after the Polish struggle, and Germany, after the Thirty Years' War.

[2] How much it contributes to raise wages that workmen can, in a credible way, threaten to move to other places, is illustrated by the early high wages and personal freedom of sailors. Compare *Eden*, State of the Poor, I, 36. In consequence of the recent great emigration from Ireland, the weekly wages of farm hands in that country was 57.4 per cent. higher than in 1843-4. In Connaught, where the emigration was largest, it was 87 per cent. higher. (London Statist. Journ., 1862, 454.)

[3] Compare *Rogers*, I, 276, and *passim*.

creased demand, in harvest time, is wont to increase wages; and even day board during harvest time is wont to be better.[4][5] In winter the diminished demand lowers wages again.[6] Among the most effective tricks of socialistic sophistry is, unfortunately, to caricature the correct principle: "labor is a commodity," into this other: "the laborer is a commodity."

Moreover, common labor has this peculiarity, that those who have it to supply are generally much more numerous than those who want it; while the reverse is the case with most other commodities. Another important peculiarity of the "commodity" labor, is, that it can seldom be bought, without at the same time reducing the person of the seller to a species of dependence. Thus, for instance, the seller cannot

---

[4] And this in proportion as the uncertainty of the weather causes haste. In England, the harvest doubles wages. *(Eden.)* In East Friesland, it raises it from 8–10 ggr. to 2 thalers sometimes *(Steltzner);* in the steppes of southern Russia, from 12–15, to frequently 40–50 *kopeks*. This explains why the country people who come into the weekly market are anxious, during harvest time, to get rid of their stocks as fast as possible. According to the Statist. Journal, 1862, 434, 448, the average wages in harvest and other times, amounted to:

                                                In harvest time.   *Other times.*

In Scotland for	males,	18s. 7d.	12s. 11½d.
" "	females,	11s. 4d.	5s. 7d.
In Ireland "	males,	12s. 9d.	6s. 11½d.
" "	females,	8s. 3d.	3s. 9d.
" "	males,	15s. 4d.	7s. 1¼d.
" "	females,	7s. 1¾d.	3s. 11d.

The reason why the wages of females rises more in harvest time than the wages of males may be the same that in many places in Ireland has made emigration more largely increase the wages of women. (l. c., 454.) Every excess of workmen depresses, and every scarcity of workmen enhances the wages of the lowest strata relatively most.

[5] The wages of English sailors was usually 40–50 shillings a month. During the last naval war, it rose to from 100 to 120, on account of the great demand created by the English fleet. *(McCulloch,* On Taxation, 40.)

[6] The winter wages of German agricultural laborers varies between 6.1 and 20 silver groschens; summer wages between 7.9 and 27.5 silver groschens. *Emminghaus,* Allg. Gewerbelehre, 81, therefore, advises that in winter the meal time of workmen in the fields should be postponed to the end of the day, and winter wages then made less low than at present.

be in a place different from that in which his commodity is. Hence a change in the person etc. of the buyer very readily necessitates in the workman a radical change of life, and that the levelling adjustment of local excess and want is rendered so difficult in the case of this commodity.[7] Hence, it is that, if in the long run the exchange of labor against wages is to be an equitable one (§110), the master of labor must, so to speak, incorporate part of his own personality into it, have a heart for faithful workmen and thus attach them to himself.[8]

SECTION CLXI.

WAGES OF LABOR.—THE MINIMUM OF WAGES.

Human labor cannot, any more than any other commodity, be supplied, in the long run, at a price below the cost of production.[1][2] The cost of production here embraces not only the necessary or customary means of subsistence of the workman himself, but also of his family; that is, of the coming generation of workmen. The number of the latter depends essentially on the demand for labor. If this demand be such that it may be satisfied by an average of six children to a family, the rate of wages must be such as to support the workman himself and to cover the cost of bringing up six children.[3] Where it is

---

[7] *W. Thornton*, On Labour, its wrongful Claims and rightful Dues, its actual, Present and possible Future, 1869, II, ch. 1. *Harrison*, Fortnightly Review, III, 50.

[8] Just as the husband binds himself in marriage. While in concubinage there is apparent equality, it costs the woman a much greater sacrifice than the man.

[1] Compare *Engel's* beautiful lecture on the cost of labor to itself *(Selbstkosten=self-cost)*, Berlin, 1866.

[2] *Wolkoff* zealously and rightly argues, that the minimum wages is not the *taux naturel* of wages. (Lectures, 118 ff., 284.) *von Thünen* also divides wages into two component parts — that which the workman must lay out in his support in order to continue able to work, and that which he receives for his actual exertion. (Isolirter Staat., II, 1, 92 seq.)

[3] *Gasparin* distinguishes five periods in the career of a workman generally: a, he is supported by his parents; b, he supports himself and is in a

customary for the wife and child, as well as for the father, to work for wages, the father does not need to earn the entire support of the family, and hence individual wages may be smaller.[4] But if it were to fall below the cost mentioned above, it would not be long before increased mortality and emigration, and a diminution of marriages and births would produce a diminution of the supply; the result of which would be, if the demand remained the same, a renewed rise of wages. Conversely, it would be more difficult for the rate of wages to be maintained long much above that same cost, in proportion as the gratification of the sexual appetite was more generally considered the highest pleasure of sense, and the love of parents

---

condition to save something; c, he marries, and supports his children with trouble; d, the children are able to work, and the father lives more comfortably; e, his strength and resources decline. (*Villermé*, Tableau de l'Etat physique et moral des Ouvriers, 1840, II, 387.)

[4] *Cantillon*, Nature du Commerce etc., 1755, is of opinion that a day laborer, to bring up two children until they are grown, needs about as much as he does for his own support; and that his wife may, as a rule, support herself by her own work. (42 ff.) In Germany, it is estimated that, in the case of day laborers, a woman can earn only from $\frac{1}{3}$ to $\frac{1}{2}$ of what her husband does; mainly because she is so frequently incapacitated for work by pregnancy, nursing etc. (*Rau*, Lehrbuch, I, § 190.) In France, in 1832, a man working in the fields earned, on an average, 1$\frac{1}{4}$ francs a day, the wife $\frac{3}{4}$ of a franc (200 days to the year), the three children $\frac{38}{100}$ francs (250 days to the year), an aggregate of 650 francs per annum. (*Moreques.*) In England, the average amount earned in the country was for males, per annum, £27 17s.; munications relative to the Support and Maintenance of the Poor, 1834, p. LXXXVIII.) The wife of an English field hand, without children, earns $\frac{1}{3}$ more than one with children. In the case of mothers, a difference of fewer or more children is unnoticeable in the effects on wages. (London Statist. Journal, 1838, 182.) In the spinning factories in Manchester, in 1834, children between 9 and 10 years of age were paid, weekly, from 2s. 9d. to 2s. 10d.; between 10 and 12, from 3s. 6d. to 3s. 7d.; between 12 and 14, from 5s. 8d. to 5s. 9d.; between 14 and 16, from 7s. 5d. to 7s. 6d. (Report of the Poor Commissioners, 204.) Those manufactures which require great physical strength, like carpet and sail-cloth weaving, and those carried on in the open air and in all kinds of weather, allow of no such family competition and debasement of wages. (*Senior* in the Report of the parliamentary Committee on Hand Weavers, 1841.)

for their children as the most natural human duty. As Adam Smith says, where there is a great demand for men, there will always be a large supply of them.[5]

SECTION CXLII.

COST OF PRODUCTION OF LABOR.

The idea conveyed by the expression necessaries of life is, within certain limits, a relative one. In warm countries, a workman's family needs less clothing, shelter, fuel and even food[1] than in cold countries. This difference becomes still more striking when the warm countries possess absolutely cheaper food as, for instance, rice, Turkish wheat, bananas etc. Here, evidently, other circumstances being the same, the rate of wages may be lower.[2] The cultivation of the potato has operated in the same direction; since an acre of land planted with potatoes yields, on an average, twice as much food as the same acre planted with rye.[3] In France, two-

---

[5] Similarly, *J. Möser*, Patriot. Phant., I, 40. *Adam Smith* infers from the following symptoms in a country that wages are higher there than the indispensable minimum, viz.: if wages in summer are higher than in winter, since it is seldom that enough is saved in summer to satisfy the more numerous wants of winter; if wages vary less from year to year and more from place to place than the means of subsistence, if they are high even where the means of subsistence are cheapest. (Wealth of Nat., I, ch. 8.)

[1] Explained since *Liebig's* time by the fact that a part of food is consumed to preserve animal heat: means of respiration in contradistinction to means of nutrition. Recent research has shown that in cold weather more urea and also more carbonic acid are given off; hence the means of supplying this deficit should be greater in cold weather than in warm. This more rapid transformation is wont, when nutrition is sufficient, to be accompanied by more energetic activity. (*Moleschott*, Physiologie der Nahrungsmittel, 1850, 47, 50, 83.)

[2] This is opposed in part by the fact that a hot climate induces indolence, and that therefore he needs a greater incentive to overcome his disposition to idleness. Thus, in the cooler parts of Mexico, the rate of wages was 26 sous a day, in the warmer, 32 sous. (*Humboldt*, N. Espagne, III, 103.)

[3] According to *Engel*, Jahrbuch für Sachsen, I, 419, on acres similarly situated and under similar conditions, the lowest yielded:

thirds of the population lived almost without animal food, on chestnuts, Indian corn, and potatoes *(Dupin)*, while in England, malt, hops, sugar, brandy, tea, coffee, tobacco, soap, newspapers etc. are described as " articles chiefly used by the laboring classes." *(Carey.)*

The standard of decency of the working class also has great influence here. The use of blouses in Paris has nothing repulsive, nor that of wooden shoes in many of the provinces of France, nor the absence of shoes in lower Italy; while the English workman considers leather shoes indispensable, as he did only a short time ago a cloth coat. Compare *infra*, § 214.[4]

	Watery contents included.	Watery contents excluded.
Of wheat,	1,881 lbs.	1,680 lbs.
" rye,	1,549 "	1,404 "
" pease,	1,217 "	1,095 "
" potatoes,	21,029 "	5,257 "

The dry substance of these products yielded:

	Azotized Substance.	Fecula.	Mineral Matter.
Wheat,	282 lbs.	879 lbs.	49 lbs.
Rye,	243 "	661 "	34 lbs.
Pease,	309 "	431 "	33 lbs.
Potatoes,	525 "	3,785 "	178 lbs.

In Saxony, from 1838 to 1852, the average prices stood as follows.

	Of Rye.	Of Wheat.	Of Potatoes.
One lb. of dry substance,	1	1.28	.95
One lb. of protein substance,	1	1.11	1.78
One lb. of fecula,	1	1.14	0.72

(loc. cit.) The high price of protein in wheat depends probably on the more agreeable appearance and pleasanter taste of wheat flour; the still higher price of potato protein on the exceedingly easy mode of its preparation.

[4] As regards food alone, the cost of the support of a plowman on Count Podewil's estate, reduced by *Rau*, Lehrbuch, § 191, to the unit of rye, is annually 1,655 lbs. of rye. According to *Koppe*, it is 1,952 lbs.; to *Block*, 2,300 lbs.; to *Kleemann*, from 1,888 to 2,552 lbs.; to *Möllenger*, 2,171 lbs. The first three estimate the cost in meat at 78, 160 and 60 pounds. Compare *Block*, Beitr. Z. Landgüterschätzungskunde, 1840, 6. Exhaustive estimates for all Prussian governmental districts in *von Reden*, Preussische Erwerbs. und Verkehrsstatistik, 1853, I, 177 ff., according to which the requirement, per family, va-

SECTION CLXIII.

WAGES OF LABOR.—POWER OF THE WORKING CLASSES OVER THE RATE OF WAGES.

In this way, the working classes hold in their own hands one of the principal elements which determine the rate of wages; and it is wrong to speak of an "iron law" which, under

ries between 71 thalers in Gumbinnen and 204 thalers in Coblenz, the average being 105 thalers. According to more recent accounts, a laborer's family in East Prussia, gangmen not included, get along very well on 177 thalers per annum. *(von der Goltz,* Ländl. Arbeiterfrage, 1872, 9 ff.) In Mecklenburg, omitting *Hofgänger,* on 183 thalers. (Ann. des. patr. Vereins, 1865, No. 26.)

The necessary outlay of the family of an agricultural day laborer in England, in 1762, was estimated as follows: for bread and flour, £6 10s. per annum; for vegetables and fruit, £1 1⅔s.; for fuel, light and soap, 2-9⅞s.; for milk, butter and cheese, £1 1-6⅜s.; for meat, £1 6s.; for house rent, 1-6s.; for clothing, bedding etc., 2-16½s.; for salt, beer and colonial wares, 1-16⅜s.; for medicine, expenses attending confinement of wife, etc., 1-6¼ s. (*J. Wade,* History of the middle and working Classes, 1853, 545.) Concerning 1796, compare *Sir F. M. Eden,* State of the Poor, I, 660, 1823; *Lowe,* on the present Condition of England. Compare on the receipts and expenses of ten working families in and about Mühlhausen, the tables in the Journal des Economistes, October, 1861, 50; and further *Ducpétiaux,* Budgets économiques des Classes ouvrières en Belgique, 1855. According to *Playfair* in *Knop,* Agriculturchemie, I, 810, ff., different classes of grown men need daily food.

GRAMMES.	*1.*	*2.*	*3.*	*4.*	*5.*
Plastic material, -	56.70	70.87	119.07	155.92	184.27
Fat, - - -	14.70	28.35	51.03	70.87	70.87
Starch, - - -	340.20	340.20	530.15	567.00	567.00

Here 1 stands for a convalescent who can bear only enough to preserve life; 2, the condition of rest; 3, moderate motion of from 5 to 6 English miles' walk daily; 4, severe labor = a walk of 20 English miles daily; 5, very severe labor = to a day's walk of 14 English miles, with a load weighing 60 lbs. If the fat be given in terms of starch, the aggregate need of both substances in the case of 1 is 6.6 times as great as the need of plastic substance; in the case of 2, 3, 4, and 5, respectively 5.7, 5.2, 4.8 and 4.0 times as much.

the control of supply and demand, always reduces the average wages down to the means of subsistence.¹ For the moment, indeed, not only individual workmen, but the whole working class is master of the supply of its commodity only to a very small extent; since, as a rule, the care for existence compels it to carry, and that without interruption, its whole laborpower to market. But it is true that the future supply depends on its own will; since, with an increase or decrease in the size of the families of workingmen, that supply increases or diminishes. If, therefore, by a favorable combination of circumstances, wages have risen above the height of urgent necessity, there are two ways open to the working class to take advantage of that condition of things. The workman either raises his standard of living, which means not only that his necessary wants are better satisfied, his decencies increased and refined, but also and chiefly, that the intellectual want of a good prospect in the future, which so particularly distinguishes

---

A Dutch soldier doing garrison duty receives daily, in times of peace, 0.333 kilogrammes of wheat flour, 0.125 of meat, 0.850 of potatoes, 0.250 of vegetables, containing in the aggregate 60 grammes of albumen. In forts, where the service is more severe, he receives 0.50 kilogrammes of wheat flour, 0.06 of rice or groats, with an aggregate amount of 116 grammes of albumen. *(Mulder,* Die Ernährung in ihrem Zusammenhange mit dem Volksgeiste, übersetzt *von Moleschott,* 1847, 58 seq.) According to the researches of Dr. Smith, in order to avoid the diseases caused by hunger, a man needs, on an average, to take 4,300 grains of carbon and 200 grains of nitrogen in his daily food; a woman 3,900 grains of carbon and 180 grains of nitrogen. In 1862, the workmen in the famishing cotton industries of Lancashire were actually reduced to just about this minimum. *(Marx,* Kapital, I, 642.) Death from starvation occurs in all vertebrates when the loss of weight of the body, produced by a want of food, amounts to between two-fifths and one-half of what it was at the beginning of the experiment. *(Chossat,* Recherches expérimentales sur l' Inanition, 184, 3.)

¹ Compare *Lassalle,* Antwortschreiben an das Central Comite zur Berufung eines allg. deutschen Arbeitercongresses, 1863, 15; also *Turgot,* sur la Formation etc., § 6. When *Lassalle* says that when a varied standard of living has become a national habit it ceases to be felt as an improvement, he says what is in a certain sense true. But is the man to be pitied who, absolutely speaking, is getting on well enough; relatively speaking, better off than before; but who is only not better off than other men?

the honorable artisan from the proletarian is taken into consideration. And it is just here that a permanent workingmen's union, which should govern the whole class, might exert the greatest influence. Their improved economic state can be maintained only on condition that the laboring class shall create families no larger than they hope to be able to support consistently with their new wants.[2]

Or, the laboring class continues to live on as before, from hand to mouth, and employ their increased resources to gratify their sexual appetite earlier and longer than before, thus soon leading to an increase of population.

The English took the former course in the second quarter of the last century, when English national economy received a powerful impetus, and the large demand for labor rapidly enhanced the rate of wages. The Scotch did in like manner a generation later. The second alternative was taken by the Irish, when the simultaneous spread of the cultivation of the potato[3] and the union with England, at the beginning of the nineteenth century, gave an extraordinary extension to their resources of food. While the population of Great Britain, between 1720 and 1821, did little more than double, the population of Ireland increased from 2,000,000 to nearly 7,000,000 between 1731 and 1821. No wonder, therefore, that the average wages of labor was twenty to twenty-four pence per day in the former, and in the latter only five pence. (*McCulloch*.)[4]

Naturally enough, this difference of choice by the two peo-

---

[2] A case in Holstein, in which, in the first half of the eighteenth century, the serfs of a hard master conspired together not to marry, and thus soon forced him to sell his estate. (*Büsch*, Darstellung der Handlung, V, 3, 11.)

[3] On the otherwise remarkable economic advance in Ireland about 1750, see *Orrey*, Letters concerning the Life and Writings of Swift, 1751, 127; *Anderson*, Origin of Commerce, a., 1751.

[4] Compare especially *Malthus*, Principles, ch. 4, sec. 2. How little Adam Smith dreamt of this may be best seen in I, 115, Bas. Recently, the average wages per week amounted in England to 22½s., in Scotland to 20½s., in Ireland to 14⅓s. (*Levi*, Wages and Earnings of the working Classes, 1866.)

ples is to be explained by the difference in their previous circumstances. The Irish people, robbed by violence of their own higher classes, and, therefore, and on this account precisely, almost entirely destitute of a middle class, had lost the check on increase they possessed in the middle ages, without having as yet assimilated to themslves the checks which come with a higher stage of culture. Their political, ecclesiastical and social oppression allowed them no hope of rising by temporary sacrifices and energetic efforts permanently to a better condition as citizens or gentlemen. Only the free man cares for the future. Hence, the sexual thoughtlessness and blind good nature, the original tendencies of the Irish people, necessarily remained without anything to counterbalance them. It always supposes a high degree of intelligence and self-restraint among the lower classes, when an increase in the thing-value, or the real value of wages, does not produce an increase in the number of workmen, but in their well-being. The individual is too apt to think that it matters little to the whole community whether he brings children into the world or not, a species of egotism which has done most injury to the interests in common of mankind. As a rule, it requires a great and palpable enhancement of wages to make workmen, as a class, raise their standard of living.[5 6]

---

[5] Thus the unheard of long series of excellent harvests in England, between 1715 and 1765, contributed very largely to this favorable transformation. Day wages expressed in wheat, between 1660 and 1719, amounted on an average to only about ⅔ of a peck; between 1720 and 1750, to an entire peck. In the fifteenth century, a similar series of good harvests contributed very much to the flourishing condition of the "yeomanry." Under Henry VII., workmen earned from two to three times as much corn as they did a century later. And so in France, the greatRevolution at the end of the eighteenth century, by setting free a vast quantity of hitherto bound-up force, enhanced the productiveness of the entire economy of the nation, and made the division of the national income more nearly equal. There is an essential connection here between the rapidity of the transition and the facts, that the habits of consumption of the working class received a powerful impulse, and that population increased much less rapidly than the national income. Compare *John Stuart Mill*, Principles, II, ch. 11, 2. In our own days again,

SECTION CLXIV.

WAGES.—COST OF PRODUCTION OF LABOR.

As the cheapening of the means of subsistence, when the circle of wants of the laboring class has not correspondingly increased, leads to a decline of wages, so an enhancement of their price must, when wages are already so low as only to be able to satisfy indispensable wants, produce an increase in the rate of wages. The transition in the former case is as pleasing as in the latter it is replete with the saddest crises.[1] The

---

English workmen had a splendid opportunity to raise their standard of life. Emigration to Australia etc. preponderated over the natural increase of population to such an extent that, in 1852, for instance, only 217,000 more human beings were born in England and Wales than died, and 368,000 emigrated. At the same time, exports increased: in 1849, they were £63,000,000; in 1850 £71,000,000; about the end of 1853, something like £90,000,000.

This golden opportunity was used by the English laboring classes to both largely multiply marriages and to enhance the rate of wages. The number of marriages contracted in England yearly, from 1843 to 1847, was 136,200; from 1853 to 1857, 159,000. The number of births annually, from 1843 to 1847, was 544,800; from 1853 to 1857, 640,400. And wages, in a number of industries, rose, between 1839 and 1859, from about 18 to 24 per cent. (Quarterly Review, July, 1860, 86), while the prices of most of the necessaries of life declined. That, in the same time, the condition of English laborers was elevated, both intellectually and morally, is proved by many facts cited in *Jones' and Ludlow's* work on the social and political condition of the laboring classes in England. In Germany, the recent establishment of peace on a firm footing and the French war contributions have given the country an impulse which might be taken advantage of by the laboring class with the happiest results if they would accustom themselves to more worthy wants and at the same time preserve their accustomed industry.

⁶ The cheapening of the necessaries of life, experience shows, is more likely to lead to an increase of population; that of luxuries, to a raising of the standard of life or of comfort.

[1] According to *McCulloch*, Edition of *Adam Smith*, 472, the food of a day laborer's family constitutes between 40 and 60 per cent. of their entire support. In the case of Prussian field hands, it is generally 54 per cent. greatest in the province of Saxony, viz., 58 per cent., and lowest in Posen, 43 per cent. Compare *Rau*, Lehrbuch, I, § 191. This may serve as a point of departure, from which to measure the influence of a given enhancement of the

slower the rise in the price of the means of subsistence is, the more it is to be feared that the working classes will seek to meet it, not by emigration or by a diminished number of marriages, but by decreasing the measure of their wants, the introduction of a poorer quality of food etc.[2]

However, all this is true only of permanent changes in the average price of the means of subsistence, such as are produced, for instance, by the development of agriculture, by taxation etc. Transitory fluctuations, such as result, for instance, from a single good or bad harvest, cannot have this result.[3] It is, in poor countries at least, one of the worst effects of a bad harvest, that it tends to positively lower the rate of wages. A multitude of persons who would otherwise be able to purchase much labor are now deterred from doing so, by the enhancement of the price of food.[4] On the other hand, the supply in-

---

price of corn. In opposition to *Buchanan* (Edition of *Adam Smith*, 1817, 59), who had denied the influence of the price of the means of subsistence on the rate of wages, see *Ricardo*, Principles, ch. 16.

[2] How easily English farmers have accustomed themselves to the consequences of momentary calamities, may be seen from *John Stuart Mill*, Principles, II, ch. 11, 5 seq.; *Thornton*, Population and its Remedy, 1846, passim. *Malthus*, Principles, sec. 8, shows in opposition to *Ricardo*, Principles, ch. 8, that it is not all one to the laboring classes whether their wages rise while the price of the means of subsistence remains the same, or whether the rate of wages remaining nominally the same, the commodities to be purchased decline in price. If for instance, potato-food, physiologically considered, was just as good as flesh-food and wheat bread, yet an unmarried workman or a father with a number of children below the average would be able to save less from the former for the reason that it possesses less value in exchange. (Edinburg Rev., XII, 341.) Thus, e. g., in Ireland, between *A. Young* and *Newenham* (1778-1808), the rate of wages increased more than the price of potatoes, but all other means of subsistence in a still greater ratio. *(Newenham,* A view of Ireland, 1808.) Compare *Malthus*, On the Policy of Restricting the Importation of foreign Corn, 1815, 24 ff.; contru. *Torrens*, on the Corn trade, 1820, 374 ff.

[3] Compare *Garve* in *MacFarlan*, On Pauperism, 1785, 77. Thus, in the United States, the same quantities of coffee, leather, pork, rice, salt, sugar, cheese, tobacco, wool etc., could be earned in 1836 by 23.5 days' labor; in 1840, by 20.75; in 1843, by 14.8; in 1864, by 34.6. *(Walker,* Science of Wealth, 256.)

[4] The person who formerly consumed perhaps four suits of clothes in a

creases: many men who before would not work even for money, see themselves now compelled to do so. Those who have been workmen hitherto are compelled by want to make still greater exertions.[5]
In very cheap years, all this is naturally reversed.[6]

SECTION CLXV.

WAGES — THE DEMAND FOR LABOR.

The demand for labor, as for every other commodity, depends, on the one hand, on the value in use of it, and on the other, on the purchaser's capacity to pay for it (his solvability). These two elements determine the maximum limit of wages, as

---

year now limits himself to two, and forces the tailor to dismiss one journeyman. In Bavaria, the dear times, 1846-47, and probably also the disturbances of 1848-49, caused officials, pensioners, annuitants and professional men to discharge one-tenth of the female domestics they employed in 1840. (*Hermann*, Staatsw. Unters, II, Aufl., 467.)

[6] The labor of digging during the time of scarcity in England was paid one-third of the price usually paid in good years. (*Porter*, Progress of the Nation, III, 14, 454.) On the Sclavic portions of Silesia, see *Hildebrand's* Jahrb., 1872, I, 292. According to *Rogers*, I, 227 ff., 315 ff., and the table of prices in the appendix to *Eden*, State of the Poor, the price in England of a quarter of wheat and a day's wages was, in —

Year		Wheat		Wages
1287,	- - - -	2s. 10¼ d.	- -	3 d.
1315,	- - -	14s. 10⅞ d.	-	3 d
1316,	- - - -	15s. 11⅞ d.	- -	3⅞d.
1392,	- - -	3s. 2⅚ d.		5 d.
1407,	- - - -	3s. 4 d.	- -	3 d.
1439,	- - -	8s.–26s. 8 d.	-	4½d.
1466,	- - -	5s. 8 d.	- -	4–6 d.
1505,	- - -	6s. 8 d.	-	4 d.
1575,	- - - -	20s.		8 d.
1590,	- - -	21s.		3–6 d.
1600,	- - - -			10 d.

[6] *Petty*, Several Essays on Political Arithmetic, 133 ff. *Adam Smith*, Wealth of Nat., I, ch. 8. *Ricardo*, Principles, ch. 9. In Hesse, in consequence of a series of many rich harvests from 1240 to 1247, no servants could be had at all, so that the nobility and clergy were obliged to till their own lands. (*Anton*, Gesch. der deutschen Landwirthschaft, III, 209.)

the means of support considered indispensable by the workmen determine the minimum. There are circumstances conceivable under which the rise in wages might entirely eat up rents; but there must always be a portion of the national income reserved to reward capital (its profit). If wages were to absorb the latter also, the mere owner of capital would cease to have any interest in the progress of production. Capital would then be withdrawn from employment and consumed.[1] Obviously, no man engaged in any enterprise can give more as wages to his workmen than their work is worth to him.[2] Hence the additional product in any branch of industry, due to the labor of the workman last employed, has a controlling influence on the rate of the wages which can be paid to his fellow workmen. If the additional products of the workmen successively last employed constitute a diverging series,[3] the last term in the series is the natural expression of the unsurpassable maximum of wages; if they constitute a converging series, then the employer can pay the last workman higher wages than the additional product due to him; provided, however, that the reduction which is to be expected in the case of the workmen previously employed to the same level still leaves him a sufficiently high rate of profit.[4] Hence the growing skill of a workman, in

---

[1] *Storch*, Handbuch, I, 105 seq.

[2] Higher wages promised, for instance, as a reward for saving a human life or some other very precious thing in great danger of being destroyed. In the case of material production, labor is worth to the party engaged in the enterprise, at most, as much as the the price of the product after the remaining cost of reproducing it is deducted.

[3] Possibly in consequence of a better division of labor or of some other advance made in the technic arts.

[4] Thus, for instance, in harvesting potatoes, if, after they have been ploughed up, only those nearest the surface are collected, a laborer can gather over thirty Prussian *scheffels* in a day. But the fuller and completer the gathering of potatoes desired is, the smaller will be the product of one workman and of one day's labor. If, therefore, a man wants to gather even the last bushel in a potato field of 100 square rods, so much labor would be required to accomplish it that the workman would not gather enough to feed him during his work, to say nothing of supplying his other wants. Supposing that 100 *scheffels* of potatoes had grown on 100 square rods, and that of these were harvested —

and of itself, makes an increase of his wages possible;[5] while, conversely, if he can be replaced by capital, which always relatively decreases the value in use of his labor, there is a consequent pressure on his wages.

SECTION CLXVI.

WAGES.—PRICE OF COMMON LABOR.

In the case of a commodity as universally desired as human labor is, the idea of the purchasers' capacity to pay (solvability) must be nearly commensurate with the national income, or to speak more correctly, with the world's income.[1] In regard

When the number of men employed in gathering them was				Then the additional yield obtained by the last workman employed is	
4,	-	-	- 80 scheffels,	-	-
5,	-	-	- 86.6 "	-	6.6 scheffels.
6,	-	-	- 91 "	-	- 4.4 "
7,	-	-	- 94 "	-	3 "
8,	-	-	- 96 "	-	- 2 "

(*von Thünen*, Der isolirte Staat., II, 174 ff.)

[5] In Manchester, in 1828, the wages paid for spinning one pound of cotton yarn, No. 200, was 4s. 1d.; in 1831, only from 2s. 5d. to 2s. 8d. But, in the former year, the spinner worked with only 312 spools; in the latter, with 648; so that his wages increased in the ratio of 1274 to 1566. (*Senior*, Outlines.)

[1] *Senior* denies this. Let us suppose that agriculture in Ireland employs on every 200 acres ten working men's families, one-half of whom are used to satisfy the aggregate wants of the working people, and the other half in the production of wheat to be exported to England. If now the English market requires meat and wool instead of wheat, the Irish land owner will, perhaps, find it advantageous, of the ten laboring families, to employ one in stock raising, a second in obtaining food etc. to support the laborers, and to discharge all the others. If, then, the increased net product is employed in the purchase of other Irish labor, all goes on well enough; but if, instead of this, the land owners should import articles of English manufacture, the demand for labor in Ireland would doubtless decrease, notwithstanding the increase of its income. (Outlines, I, 154.) *Senior* here overlooks two things: first, that in the supposed case, if eight-ninths of Irish laborers are thrown out of employment, spite of the increased income of the owners of landed estates, Ireland's national income is on the whole probably diminished (§ 146), and secondly, that, possibly, the demand for labor in England experiences a greater

to the different kinds of labor, and especially to common labor, it is evident that the different kinds of consumption require very different quantities of them. Here, therefore, we depend on the direction which national consumption takes, and this in turn is most intimately related to the distribution of the national income.[2] If all workmen were employed in nothing but the production of articles consumed by workmen, the rate of wages would be determined almost exclusively by the ratio between the number of the working population and the amount of the national income. But, if this were the case, land-owners and capitalists would be obliged to live just as workmen do, and their highest luxury would have to consist in feeding idlers. (§ 226). The effect must be much the same, when the wealthy are exceedingly frugal and employ their savings as rapidly as possible in the employment of common home labor; while, on the other hand, the exportation of wheat, wood, and other articles, which the working classes consume, in exchange for diamonds, lace, champagne, diminishes the efficient demand for common labor in a country.[3]

The assumption frequently made, that the demand for labor depends on the size of the national capital, is far from exact.[4] Thus, for instance, every transformation of circulating into fixed capital, especially when the labor used in effecting this transformation is ended, diminishes the demand for other labor. That principle is not unconditionally true, even in the case of circulating capital. Thus, for instance, the rate of wages is wont to be raised by the transfer of capital from such

---

increase than the decrease in Ireland; since, with the addition to the world-income, there would be an increase in the world-demand for labor.

[2] Compare *Hermann*, Staatswirthsch. Untersuch., 280 ff. Earlier yet, *Malthus*, Principle of Population, II, ch. 13.

[3] Thus, *Thomas More*, Utopia, 96, 197, thinks that if every one was industrious and engaged in only really useful business, no one would need to fatigue himself very much; while, as it is now, the few real laborers there are wear themselves out in the service of the vanity of the rich, are poorly fed and worked exceedingly hard.

[4] *McCulloch*, Principles, 104, seq. 2d ed.

businesses as require little labor into such as require much.⁵ Only that part of circulating capital can have any weight here which is intended, directly or indirectly, for the purchase of labor and for the purchase of each kind of labor in particular.⁶ The capital of the employer is, by no means, the real source⁷ of the wages of even the workmen employed by him.

---

⁵ Thus, in France, during the continental blockade, distant ocean commerce declined, and manufactures flourished instead. (*Lotz*, Revision, III, 134.)

⁶ Thus, *Adam Smith* divides " the funds destined for the payment of wages" into two kinds: the excess of employers' income over their own maintenance, and the excess of their capital over the demands of their own use of it. (Wealth of Nat., I, ch. 8.) *Senior* considers it a self-evident principle, that the rate of wages depends on the size of the "fund for the maintenance of laborers compared with the number of laborers to be maintained." (Three Lectures on the Rate of Wages, 1830, Outlines, 153, ff.) But what determines the quota of the aggregate national wealth and national income that is to constitute this fund? *Carey*, Rate of Wages, 1835, has a very exhaustive commentary on *Senior*.

⁷ *Watts*, Statist. Journal, 1861, 500, asserts altogether too generally that an "increase of profit increases the future wages fund, and consequently the demand for laborers;" and that therefore every new machine useful in manufactures must also be of use to the laboring class. The employer engaged in any enterprise who has grown richer, *can* pay more wages, but whether he *will* do it depends on other causes, and even his ability to do it, in the long run, on his customers. When *John Stuart Mill*, Principles, I, ch. 5, 9, says that only the capital which comes into the hands of labor before the completion of their work contributes to their support, it is as if he were to explain the phenomena of prices by demand and supply, and nothing else, denying the influence of the cost of production, of value in use, and of the deeper determining causes upon them. *(Supra,* § 107, note 1.) Compare *Roesler*, Z. Kritik der Lehre vom Arbeitslohn, 1861, 104 ff. In England, the superstition which to a great extent attached to the idea "wages-fund," was first questioned by *F. Longe*, Refutation of the Wages-Fund Theory of modern Political Economy, 1866. See also *Thornton*, On Labour, II, ch. 1. Even *John Stuart Mill* dropped his earlier erroneous views on this subject. '(Fortnightly Review, May and June, 1869.) Not, however, without exaggeration, as is proved by his well-known saying, that laborers needed capital but no capitalists. Still, even here, he tenaciously holds that a rise in wages which increases the price of some classes of commodities, must decrease the aggregate demand for commodities. But better paid workmen may now increase their demand for commodities to the same extent that the purchasers of labor who do not gain as much as before, or the consumers of the goods

It is only the immediate reservoir through which wages are paid out, until the purchasers of the commodities produced by that labor make good the advance, and thereby encourage the undertaker to purchase additional labor. Correlated to this is the fact, that other circumstances being the same, those workmen usually receive the highest wages who have to do most immediately with the consumer.[8]

SECTION CLXVII.

DIFFERENCE OF WAGES IN DIFFERENT BRANCHES OF LABOR.

All the causes which make wages higher in some branches of labor, than in others, may be divided into three great categories.[1]

A. Rare personal acquirements. The supply of labor requiring rare personal ability will always be limited.[2] Such labor must, naturally, have great value in use, when a small supply of it is met by a great demand.[3] It sometimes

---

whose price has been enhanced diminish theirs. *(Brentano*, in Hildebrand's Jahrbb., 1871, 374.) Only, this increase need not affect the very commodities influenced by the decrease.

[8] Thus, the person who builds his own house is wont to pay his workmen better than a contractor or builder by profession; and the maker of the entire manufactured article, as a rule, suffers less frequently than the maker of only half of it. *(Hermann*, Staatsw. Unters., II, Aufl., 471.)

[1] Excellent germs thereof in *Adam Smith*, Wealth of Nat., I, ch. 10, 1. Earlier yet, in *Galiani*, Della Moneta, I, 2. *Cantillon*, Nature du Commerce, 24 ff.

[2] Even in the case of mere manual labor, for instance, a skillful packer of goods is paid higher wages than a mere day laborer; a sower better than a plowman or a digger; a vintner, in general, better than an agricultural laborer: in the Palatinate of the Rhine, in the ratio of 36:24. Thus, almost anyone can paint a door or a house, while an artist possesses a species of natural monopoly.

[3] Thus, the Greek juggler, who understood how to throw lintels from a certain distance through the eye of a needle, was very appropriately rewarded by his king with a bushel of lintels. On the other hand, the high fee

happens that a species of labor can be utilized only by a small circle of persons who demand it. But the wages for it is raised very high by the great solvability of those who do demand it. How frequently it happens, for instance, that a minister is paid a very high salary for the ability he possesses of making complicated and dry affairs of state attractive to the personal taste of his sovereign.[4] Here, particularly, the confidence which the workman inspires by his skill and fidelity enters as an element. Without this confidence, there are many kinds of business which would be crushed out entirely by the control it would be necessary to subject them to, and others would not be possible at all.[5] When, for instance, in a large manufacturing establishment, understrappers, workmen, foremen, subordinate superintendents, directors etc., draw different salaries, their pay, if equitably graduated, should be in harmony with the principles laid down in § 148. The head of a manufacturing establishment, for instance, who has organized a more perfect division and coöperation of labor, himself, and by means of which ten men are enabled to per-

---

paid for an operation for cataract depends both on the great importance of the eye which cannot be replaced in any way, and on the rarity of the courage among doctors to pierce the eye of a living man. Very remarkable achievements, which it requires great education to understand, are generally paid for at a very low rate. *(Stein*, Lehrbuch, 123.)

[4] I need only recall *Richelieu* and *Mazarin*, the last of whom left an estate worth 200,000,000 livres. *(Voltaire*, Siècle de Louis XIV, ch. 6.) In Parisian industries, few workmen are as well paid as those who are skilled in rapidly effecting changes of form. The so called *premières de modes* frequently received more than 1,800 francs a year, while the *apprêteuses* received only from 15 to 20 sous a day. (Revue des deux Mondes, Sept. 15, 1850.) There are women there paid very well for making pin-cushions, pen-wipers etc., each one of a different form; but as soon as any one form ceases to be a novelty, the wages paid for making it sinks to a minimum. *(M. Mohl*, Gewerbswissenschaftliche Reise durch Frankreich, 87.)

[5] Jewelers, lawyers, statesmen, generals. *Senior* says that of the income of £4,000 which a lawyer or a doctor draws, only £40 are wages for his labor; £3,000 are a rent paid for the possession of extraordinary talent, or for his good luck, and £960 as the interest on his intellectual capital, which is also the chief element of wealth. (Outline, 134.)

form the work before performed by twenty, may equitably retain, as the reward of his organizing power, a considerable amount of what was previously paid out in wages. Louis Blanc's proposition, that all should receive equal salaries is, as Bastiat remarks, equivalent to the assertion that a yard of cloth manufactured by a lazy or unskillful workman is worth as much as two yards manufactured by an industrious and skillful one.[6]

Such qualified labor, as is treated of here, may be most accurately estimated, the quality of which supposes a certain cost of acquisition. This cost may be considered as the outlay of so much capital, which, with interest,[7] should come back to the workman in his wages. Otherwise, others would be deterred from entering the same business by the example of his loss. Here, especially, it is necessary to take into account the long period of apprenticeship or tuition, and the large fees paid for the same; and this, whether they depend on the natural difficulties in the way of acquirement or on artificial obstacles opposed to freedom of competition.[8] The influence of these circumstances is particularly great in

---

[6] On the sad experience of the tailors' association founded by Louis Blanc himself, at Clichy, and in consequence of which they soon gave up paying equal wages and returned to piece wages, see Journal des Economistes, Mars, 1850, 349.

[7] As the interest on land improvements assumes the character of rent, so also does that of the education of labor the character of wages. The rate of interest usual in a country, and the average duration of the life of the workman affect the capital thus invested as a species of annuity.

[8] Wages in the country are generally lower than in the cities. In the electorate of Hesse, for instance, on the supposition of steady employment, males, in the country, received 69 thalers, 23 silver groschens a year; females, 55 thalers, 9 silver groschens; in the cities, on the other hand, males, 88 thalers, 23 silver groschens, and females 61 thalers, 28 silver groschens. (*Hildebrand*, statistische Mittheilungen, 101, 137.) And so, according to *Colquhoun*, Treatise on Indigence, 1806, the English agricultural laborers received, on an average, £31 per annum, and manufacturing workmen, £55. The reason of this is, besides the greater facility of learning how to perform agricultural labor, the greater dearness of living in cities, and in England also, because industry has developed much more rapidly than agriculture.

those kinds of labor which require a "liberal" education.[9] Among the costs of production proper, peculiar to this labor-force, must be included, also, the necessary support of the workman, during the interval between the completion of his studies and the beginning of his full reward.[10]

When a species of work requires special current expenses to be made in order to its proper performance, these also should of course be made good to the workman in his wages. Most intellectual labor, for instance, requires quiet surroundings. The brain-worker cannot share his study with his family, and, therefore should receive wages or remuneration large enough in amount to enable him to arrange his dwelling accordingly. A similar circumstance, only in a much higher degree, enhances the price paid for diplomatic service.

SECTION CLXVIII.

DIFFERENCE OF WAGES IN DIFFERENT BRANCHES OF LABOR.

(CONTINUED.)

B. The great economic risk of the work. When a branch of labor necessary to a country is, notwithstanding, attended

---

[9] The cost of bringing up a common laborer, in England, according to *Senior*, is £40; a gentleman, £2,040. (Outlines, 205.) The more expensive an education which one acquires for its own sake and without any special object beyond this in view, is, the less can the capital laid out in it affect wages. *(von Mangoldt,* V. W. L., 382.)

[10] If the salaries of clergymen are, on an average, lower than the income of a lawyer or a doctor, it is partly because theological candidates are provided for much earlier, and partly because of the lesser cost attending the study of theology. Thus, at the end of the eighteenth century, there were 350 students at the University of Tübingen who are maintained gratis, on foundation-money, and who had previously attended monastery schools, free of charge. *(Nicolai,* Reisebeschreibungen, XI, 73.) The remarkable contrast between the high wages of the Athenian sophists and the low wages of modern abbés, Adam Smith accounts for principally by the many scholarships of modern times. In Saxony, in 1850 etc., the outlay by the state and of foundation-funds for the education of a student amounted to an average of nearly 140 thalers. *(Engel.)*

by many chances of failure to the individual who devotes himself to it, a sufficient supply of the labor can be relied on only in case that the danger attending it is compensated for by a corresponding premium paid to success.[1] The choice of a profession or avocation, Adam Smith has compared to a lottery, in which the fortunate winners gain only what the unfortunate have lost. The greater the prizes, the greater also the number of blanks.[2] However, the surplus wages in risky kinds of labor are not sufficient to constitute a full insurance premium. This is connected with the vanity of men who, as a rule, over-estimate not only their talent but their good fortune,[3] and especially in youth, when they decide on the choice of a profession etc. According to this, wages must be specially low where even complete failure does not

---

[1] The greater the preparatory cost of labor is, the more difficult it is for workmen to go from one kind of labor to another; but, at the same time, the more certain it is that, without the inducement of a premium paid, there will be no after increase or recruiting of labor force.

[2] Thus, for instance, in the country, where doctors generally get along well enough, the most skillful never obtains any very distinguished position. But, in large cities, on the other hand, there is the greatest difference between first-class physicians and obscure practitioners. Great generals usually obtain a larger income and greater influence than great admirals; and so it is that prizes in the military lottery are greater, and there are therefore more blanks than in the naval lottery. The common soldier is almost everywhere worse paid than the common sailor. *(Adam Smith.)* To some extent, this depends on the prison-like life of the seaman in times of service, and in the absence of an attractive uniform. As to the extent that the lottery comparison is defective, see *Macleod*, Elements, 215.

[3] Who, otherwise, would have anything to do with a lottery in which the mass of players were certain to lose, and the keeper of it to gain? And this accounts for the fact well known to all financiers, that the amount of the budget remaining the same, a greater eagerness to enter the military service of the country is inspired by endowing the higher positions munificently — provided they are attainable by all — and paying the lower ones in a very niggardly way, than when the pay is made more uniform. Something similar is to be observed in the ecclesiastical service of the Roman and Protestant churches, inasmuch as the former, considered from an economic point of view, offers more magnificent prizes, but also more blanks, while the latter divides its emoluments more equally.

endanger the living or the social position of the workman. Partly on this account are the industries carried on by women so poorly remunerated;[4] as also such work as is done by a large class of people to fill up their leisure hours.[5] The prospect of frequent interruptions in any kind of labor must have the same effect on the wages paid for it as its economic or business risk.[6] Thus, for instance, a mason or roofer must earn at least enough, during the days he can work, to enable him to live during the time he is prevented working by bad weather. Hence, the highness of his wages

---

[4] As most seamstresses are, when the worst comes to the worst, supported by their parents, connections by marriage, brothers, etc., the condition of those who have to live by their needle must be a pretty hard one. Who is not familiar with the refrain to *Hood's* celebrated song of the shirt: "Oh God, that bread should be so dear, and flesh and blood so cheap!" There is a "distressed needlewoman's society" in London. They undoubtedly suffer from an overcrowding of their avocation, yet their chief desire is that the competition of all who do not live exclusively by the labor of their hands should be prohibited; for instance, that of seamstresses who are paid for their work outside of factories. (Edinb. Rev., 1851, 24.) In Paris, in 1845, the yearly earnings of women workers averaged 375 francs, their yearly wants 500 francs. (Journal des Economistes, X, 250.) This does not apply to female servants whose wages, especially in highly cultured localities as the vicinity of large cities (Holstein, Brandenburg), is very high. In England, the wages of female domestics is frequently higher than in the United States; and hence nearly two-thirds of all English girls between fifteen and twenty-five years of age serve as maids. *Browning*, Political and Domestic Condition of Great Britain, 413; *Carey*, Rate of Wages, 92. A remarkable indication that women thrive only in the family. (Compare § 250.)

[5] Thus, the darning of stockings in the sandy parts of North Germany, in the Highlands of Scotland, in the Faroe Islands, and formerly, even in the ante-rooms of the Russian nobility. *(Schlözer,* Anfangsgründe der Staatswirthsch, I, 126) Flax spinning and linen weaving in Westphalia and Ireland, and wool weaving in the East Indies. Manufacturing industries must be in a very highly developed condition, and machinery carried to a high degree of perfection to compete in price with these accessory industries. Cheapness of many products manufactured in convents and monasteries.

[6] Among these interruptions, may also be reckoned the prospect the laborer has of being early incapacitated for work, and thus of seeing himself cut off from every other source of support. This is is one of the principal reasons why opera singers are generally better paid than actors.

may, in some respects, be called an apparent one.[7] Wages paid by the week more generally tend to equality than wages paid by the day, and more so yet wages paid by the year, for then winter and summer compensate the one for the other. When the workman must be ever ready to perform his task, account must be taken not only of the number of hours he is engaged, but also of fractions of his waiting hours, which must be paid for likewise.[8] Two half days cost almost everywhere more than one whole one.

The number of holidays plays a very important part here. In Protestant countries, the workman must, in about three hundred work-days, earn enough to live on for about sixty holidays as well. In Catholic countries, before the time of Clement XIV., he had to earn enough in addition to support

---

[7] In Leipzig, in 1863, mason and carpenter journeymen earned during the summer, from twenty silver groschens to one thaler, ordinary garden workmen, 20 silver groschens, while shoemaker journeymen did not make much more than 3½ thalers a week, and manual laborers, only from 10 to 15 silver groschens a day. The masons of Paris have the reputation of being the best patrons of the savings banks, and, on that account, are more exposed to being attacked by thieves than any other class. *(Frégier*, Des Classes dangereuses, II, 3, 1.) High wages paid for threshing in East Prussia, because, the workman during the winter can be employed in very few different kinds of labor, and therefore must earn his entire support by threshing. In Paris, of 101,000 persons engaged in industry in 1860, 6,400 had to calculate on no interruption of their work, the remaining number, however, lost with a certain degree of regularity, from 2 to 4 months a year. (Revue des deux Mondes, 15 Fev., 1865.) If the interruption can be so accurately estimated in advance that the workman may engage in some business for himself during the interval, as for instance when the workmen in the Bavarian breweries work during the summer as masons, its influence on wages decreases. *(Storch,* Handbuch, I, 192.) As to how, in Switzerland, since 1850, the guaranty of full employment to masons in winter is considered as an addition to the wages of summer, see *Böhmert*, Arbeiterverhältnisse, I, 141.

[8] *Commissionaires*, hack-drivers, *Extraposthalter* in Germany, porters, nurses, guides, servants in watering places and countries visited by tourists. A London porter gets at least a shilling an hour. If employed by the day, he of course gets smaller wages. Image venders, who travel from house to house, sell their wares much lower at their own houses. The person who calls them in from the street is obliged to pay them not only for this one journey, but for several others which yielded them no profit.

himself for about one hundred and fifty holidays, on ninety of which he performed no work whatever.[9] So large a number of holidays produces a higher rate of wages or necessitates a low standard of life among the working classes.[10] Something similar is true of evening leisure and rest;[11] *i. e.*, of the time when labor ceases.

SECTION CLXIX.

THE DISAGREEABLENESS OF CERTAIN CLASSES OF LABOR.—ITS EFFECT ON WAGES.

C. Lastly, the personal disagreeableness of the work, which must be compensated for by higher wages. The uncleanness of a coal-worker's task, that of the chimney-sweep, and the repulsive labor of the butcher, demand high compensation, while other branches of business, themselves productive of pleasure, and therefore engaged in by many for pleasure's sake only, yield relatively little to those who engage in them as a regular industry.[1]

To this category belong the kinds of labor which require extraordinary effort,[2] or which put life or health in unusual

---

[9] If we call the minimum daily need or the absolute requirement of the workman $= m$, the rate of daily wages in the former case must amount to at least $m + \frac{m}{6}$; in the latter, on the other hand, to $m + \frac{m}{4}$. A Bavarian holiday estimated at a *minus* of much more than 1,000,000 florins. (*Hermann*, II, Anfl., 192.)

[10] *Von Sonnenfels*, Polit. Abhandlungen, 1777, 332 ff.

[11] In a part of Lower Bavaria, in which there were 204 holidays in a year, among them the anniversaries of the consecration of 40 churches in the country about, and a feast day following each such anniversary, as well as target-shooting festivals, the celebration begins at 4 o'clock P. M. of the preceding day. (*Rau*, Lehrbuch, I, § 193.)

[1] Thus the chase, fishing in rivers (compare *Theocrit.*, Idyll., 21), gardening, fine female manual labor, and literature.

[2] The high wages paid to mowers and threshers may be accounted for on this ground (§ 160). In countries that have a strong heavy soil, wages are frequently 20 per cent. higher than under circumstances otherwise similar

jeopardy.[3] But, indeed, when the danger attending any kind of work is made glorious by the romantic light of honor, or by still higher motives, it ceases to have any influence on wages.[4] On the other hand, the disreputableness of a business in itself raises wages;[5] whereas, scholars, poets etc., leaving the charm inherent in their occupations out of account, are for the most part remunerated only by the honor paid them, and, not

where it is sandy or light. In Mexico, a digger gets about twice the wages of an agricultural laborer. (*Senior*, On the Value of Money, 56.)

[3] Almost every trade predisposes to some special disease. Compare *Halfort*, Enstehung, Verlauf und Behandlung der Krankheiten der Künstler und Gewerbetreibenden, 1845. *Livy*, Traité d'Hygiène publique et privée, 1850, II, 755. It has been noticed, in Sheffield, that thoughtless steel polishers look unfavorably on certain new inventions intended to protect workmen against inhaling small particles of stone and iron dust. They dread that if these inventions come into general use, their wages would be lowered in consequence; and prefer a short and merry life to one longer and more quiet.

In places in which nearly all kinds of work are dangerous, the danger cannot of course relatively raise the wages of anyone. Thus, in the Thuringian forest, the wages of the haulers of wood are very low. (*Lotz*, Revision, III, 151.)

[4] Missionaries! Besides the extremely small wages paid to common soldiers (in the German infantry only 36.5 thalers cash per annum, to which in Leipzig, for instance, rations, etc., add about 34 thalers more) is an outlay made by the government principally to effect a levy of the tax of the compulsory labor that lies in conscription. (*Knies.*) In the volunteer system, the difference between officers and men is wont to be much smaller. Thus, *Gustav Wasa* paid his German mercenaries as follows: 6 marks a month to captains, five to lieutenants and 4 to common soldiers. (*Geijer*, Schwed. Gesch., II, 125 seq.) Similarly in the case of the Greek hired troops. (*Böckh*, Staatshaushalt der Athener, I, 165 ff.) As to how little at the outbreak of a war, soldier earnest money is increased, and positions as officers most sought after, see *Hermann*, II, Aufl., 479.

[5] Thus, for instance, the skinning or flaying of dead animals is comparatively well paid, to which the rarity of the application of the work of executioners contributes. (*J. Moser*, Patr. Ph., I, No. 34.) The high wages of actors, singers, dancers, and especially of the female members of the stage, depends principally on the contempt with which they were formerly looked upon; excommunicated by the Catholic church, and a scarcely milder sentence passed upon them by the Protestant, until about the middle of the eighteenth century. (*Schleiermacher*, Christliche Sitte, 681.) Compare even *J. J. Rousseau*, Lettre sur les Spectacles à Mr. d'Alembert sur son Article Genève.

unfrequently, only by fame after they have gone hence.[6] And yet their talents are so rare, the preparation so laborious, the economic risk so great! Nor is there for the really creative workman any such thing as evening rest. *(Riehl.)* Common intellectual labor is worse paid in our days than it was, comparatively speaking, a generation ago; because the increased average education makes it less burthensome to most people, and even seem positively agreeable to many. It would, indeed, be a dangerous retrogressive step towards barbarism, if it should come to such a pass, that labor preponderantly intellectual should be permanently more poorly remunerated than mere muscular labor.[7][8]

---

[6] *Schiller's* " Theilung der Erde." *Blanqui* says of the learned: " They are most frequently satisfied with a citizen-crown, and think themselves remunerated when justice has been done to their genius. Their magnanimity impels them, to their own injury, to diffuse their knowledge as rapidly as possible. Thus they are like the light of day which no one pays for, but which all enjoy, without thanking the giver as they ought." The reward of intellectual labor is called an *honorarium*. *(Riehl,* Die Deutsche Arbeit, 1861, 232.) According to *J. B. Say,* Traité, II, ch. 7, the poor wages of savants depends on the fact that they take to market, and all at once, a great quantity of what they produce, which cannot even be used up.

[7] In Switzerland, journeymen are often better paid than the clerks kept by the greater tradesmen. *(Böhmert,* Arbeiterverhältnisse, II, 168.) In England, also, since 1850, the wages for "unskilled labor" has risen, relatively, most. *(Tooke,* Hist. of Prices, VI, 177.) It would be a frightful peril to our whole civilization if school teachers and subordinate officials should be turned into enemies of the entire existing state of things by want.

[8] The high wages paid to engineers on railroads is accounted for by the wear, physical and mental, their employment entails, and also by their unavoidable expenses away from home; further, by the importance of the interests confided to their trust. On the Leipzig-Dresden Railway, locomotive engineers, for the most part previously journeymen blacksmiths, earned 900 thalers a year. Similarly, in the case of pilots. The high wages paid on board ships engaged in the slave-trade arose from the unhealthiness of the African coast, where formerly one-sixteenth of the crew died yearly (Edinburg Rev., 480), from the moral turpitude of the business, and from the severe penalties under which it was afterwards prohibited. On the other hand, the low wages paid to European mining laborers is largely the consequence of the certainty of being cared for in old age, of those so employed. Weavers' wages are low because the facility of learning the trade makes it possible for

SECTION CLXX.

RATE OF WAGES.—INFLUENCE OF CUSTOM.

Custom always exerts a great influence where there is question of choosing an avocation with the intention of devot-

the business to be carried on at home; and hence there is a comparatively great pressure to engage in it. (*Baines*, History of the Cotton Manufacture, 485 ff.)

According to the first annual report of the poor-law commissioners (202), the weekly wages in Manchester of hod-carriers was 12s.; of hand-weavers, 7–15s.; of diggers, 10–15s.; of pack-carriers, 14–15s.; of shoemakers, 15–16s.; of machine-weavers, 13–16⅜s.; of white-washers, 18s.; of tailors, 18s.; of dyers, 15–20s.; of plasterers, 19–21s.; of masons, 18–22s.; of tinsmiths, 22–24s.; of carpenters, 24s.; of spinners, 20–25s.; of machinists, 26–30s.; of iron founders and power-loom tenders, 28–30s. In Belgium, the average daily wages for male labor was 1.18 francs for agricultural laborers; for those engaged in industry, 1.48 francs; in the manufacture of linen, 80 francs; of cotton, 1.55; of woolens, 1.62; of silk, 1.25; of stockings, 1.14; of glass, 2.58; of coal, 1.33. All according to the Statistique générale de la B. In Athens, in the time of Aristophanes, a pack-carrier earned 4 oboli a day; a street sweeper, 3; a stone cutter on the public works, 6; a carpenter, 5; for roofing houses and taking down scaffoldings, each man, 6. The architects who superintended the building of the temple of Polias, on the other hand, got only 6 oboli per day, and the contractor 5. (*Böckh*, I, 165 ff.)

The Edictum Diocletiani of the year 301 after Christ contains the following provisions in relation to wages, besides "board:" shepherds, camel-drivers and muleteers, 20 denarii; agricultural laborers, water-carriers, scavengers, 25; bakers, masons, roofers, house-finishers and repairers of the inside, lime burners, wheelwrights and common clay moulders, 50; boatsmen, sailors, makers of marble or mosaic floors, 60; wall painters, 70; clay moulders for statues, 75; artistic painters, 150. (ed. *Mommsen*, cap. 7.) In slave countries, the price of different slaves is to be judged, mainly, by the above rules. Concerning the Greeks, see *Böckh*, I, 95 ff. *St. John*, The Hellenes, III, 23 ff. It is a characteristic fact that the Romans, after the Syrian war, began to pay high prices for the hitherto much despised kitchen slaves. (*Livy*, XXXIX, 6.) Remarkable fixed prices for slaves by *Justinian:* Cod. VI, 43, 3; VII, 7, 1, 5. Thus, in the Lex Burgundionum, tit. 10, the compensation for the murder of a common laborer is fixed at 30 solidi; of a carpenter, at 40; of a smith, at 50; of a silversmith, at 100; of a goldsmith, at 150. Advanced civilization is wont to raise the price of slaves who perform work of a higher quality, just as it raises the wages of labor of a higher quality.

ing one's self to it entirely and exclusively. There is a public opinion which fixes the gradation of the different classes of labor and their appropriate reward, which is slow to change, and which both determines, and is determined by the relation of supply and demand. There is an equilibrium between the pleasantness of work and the rate of wages only in the case of such kinds of labor as are on the same social footing. It frequently happens, however, that the most repulsive work has to be performed by those who are forced to accept any pay and to be satisfied with it.[1] There are many branches of labor those engaged in which still form a kind of exclusive caste; and the pay of the higher branches is maintained at a high rate, especially by the fact that the members of the castes to which they belong are provident in their marriages. The lower classes are not in a condition to meet the preparation necessary to engage in such professions, even if they were certain of being afterwards reimbursed with interest for the outlay.[2] One of the chief causes of the lowness of wages paid to women is, that so few branches of labor are traditionally open to them, that the few that are, are intended to supply luxuries, and are, besides, for the most part, over-crowded. The distribution of the aggregate wages earned by any industry, among the higher and lower classes of workmen who coöperate in it, depends very largely on their social position relatively to one another.[3,4] Here political forms and changes may exert the greatest influence.[5]

---

[1] At least where the supply of labor in general surpasses the demand. Compare *J. S. Mill*, Principles, II, ch. 14, 3d ed. The dangerous industries in which lead, quicksilver, arsenic etc. are manipulated or employed, should be and can be better paid than they actually are. In the Bavarian Palatinate, stone-cutters rarely reach their 45th year; and yet their wages are very low, because of the comparative over-population of the country. (*Rau*, *Haussen's* Archiv., N. T. X., 228.) But the lowness of wages here is certainly and mainly caused by the little thought the workmen themselves give to considerations of health.

[2] The lower the rate of wages of any class sinks, the more difficult it becomes for parents to devote their children to another career.

[3] In Paris, 24,463 workmen with less than 3 francs daily; 157,216, with from

Thus, the artificial increase of the wages of masters effected by the former guild-system was produced, to say the least, as much at the cost of the journeymen and apprentices as of the public. And if, on the other hand, it cannot be said that the most recent marked rise in wages, in so many countries, is merely the consequence of the extension of the parliamentary right of suffrage, certain it is that the two phenomena are very closely related, and that both are at once the effect and the cause of the intensified feeling of individuality and of the consciousness of constituting a class in the community of the lower strata of society.

---

3 to 5; 10,393, with from 5 to 20 and even 3 to 5 francs. It is remarkable, however, how uniform the average wages in the different trades is: *vêtements*, 3.33 francs; *fils et tissus*, 3.42; *boisellerie, vannerie*, 3.44; *garçons boulangers, bouchers* 3.50; *arts chimiques et céramiques* 3.71; *bâtiments*, 3.81; *carosserie*, 3.86; *peaux et cuirs*, 3.87; *ameublement*, 3.90; *articles de Paris*, 3.94; *métaux communs*, 3.98; *métaux précieux*, 4.17; *imprimerie*, 4.18. (Journal des Economistes, Janv. 1853, III.)

[4] How the Roman advocates were given to all sorts of ostentation, and even borrowed costly rings in order to raise their *honoraria*, see *Juvenal*, VII, 105, ff.

[5] The salaries paid to the employees in the office of the minister of finance in France and the United States were as follows: to the porter, 1,500 and 3,734 francs; the lowest clerk, 1,000 to 1,800, and 5,420 francs; to the head clerk, 3,200 to 3,600, and 8,672 francs; the secretary general, 20,000 and 10,840 francs; to the minister, 80,000 and 32,520 francs. (*Tocqueville*, Démocratie aux Etats-Unis, II, 74.) In the treasury department, at Washington, of 158 employees, only 6 received less than $1,000 salary, but only 2 over $2,000. (*M. Chevalier*, Lettres sur l'Amérique du Nord, II, 151, 456.) Compare *Büsch*, Geldumlauf, IV, 34. In Russia, the wages of the higher classes of laborers as compared with those paid the commoner class is much higher than in Germany. (*Kosegarten*, in *Haxthausen*, Studien, III, 583.) On the other hand, in England, since 1850, the rate of wages for unskilled labor has risen relatively more than any other. (*Tooke*, Hist. of Prices, VI, 177.)

SECTION CLXXI.

HISTORY OF THE WAGES OF COMMON LABOR — IN THE LOWER STAGES OF CIVILIZATION.

In very low stages of civilization, where there is scarcely any such thing as rent, and where capital is extremely rare, the wages of labor, notwithstanding its small amount absolutely speaking, must eat up the greatest part of the product.[1] With every further advance, the condition of the laboring class is modified, according as the natural decline in this relative amount of their wages is outweighed or counterbalanced, or neither outweighed nor counterbalanced, by the increase in the aggregate product; in other words, in the national income in general as compared with the number of workmen.

SECTION CLXXII.

HISTORY OF THE WAGES OF COMMON LABOR — IN FLOURISHING TIMES.

When, where a nation's economy[1] is growing and flourishing, capital increases more rapidly than population, there is a search for employment by capital still greater than the search

---

[1] *Adam Smith*, Wealth of Nat., I, ch. 8. Thus in the case of nations of hunters. The wages of free laborers in Russia, at the beginning of this century, were so high that mowers, in the vicinity of Moscow, received a good half of the corn mowed by them. (*von Schlözer*, Aufangsgründe, I, 65.) As a rule, the natural relation of the three branches of income is here postponed by the intervention of slavery. (§ 76, 155.) But, for instance, since the negroes have been emancipated, in the southern states of the American Union, it has become necessary to promise them one-half of the cotton crop as wages, and for the employer to run all the risk of a bad harvest. (*R. Somers*, The Southern States since the War, 1871.) On the wretched pay of domestic servants in the middle ages, see *Grimm*, D. Rechtsalterth., 357.

[1] Compare *Hermann*, Staatswirths. Unters., 241 ff.; *J. S. Mill*, Principles, ch. 3. As to how *Carey* confounds the rise and fall of the productiveness of labor with the rise and fall of wages, see *J. S. Mill's* views in *Lange*, 1866, 218 ff.

for employment by labor. The consequence is, of course, a decline in the rate of interest, and a rise in the rate of the wages of labor, although the latter may be compelled to surrender a part of its increase to rent, which also rises. If simultaneously with these phenomena, there have been great advances made in national productive skill, especially in the cultivation of land; if, therefore, labor and the capital consumed have become more prolific, the condition of the laboring class is improved in a two-fold manner; the condition of capitalists needs, to say the least, grow no worse, and the increase of rent paid to landowners may be avoided.[2]

---

[2] In England, wages from 1400 to 1420, estimated in produce, were much higher than from 1500 to 1533. (Statist. Journal, 1861, 544 ff.) Later, a quarter of wheat was earned by day labor as follows: under Elizabeth, in about 48 days; during the seventeenth century, in 43 days; between 1700 and 1766, in 32 days; between 1815 and 1848, in from 19 to at most 28¾ days. (*Hildebrand*, Nat. Œk. der Gegenwart und Zukunft.) Since 1860, it has been earned in about 14 days. About 1668, the wages paid to English laborers and servants was one-third higher than twenty years before. (*Sir J. Child*, Discourse on Trade, p. 43 of the French translation.) *D. Defoe*, Giving Alms no Charity, 1704, draws a much more favorable picture of the time next succeeding. *Adam Smith*, Wealth of Nat., I, ch. 8, shows how money-wages, in the eighteenth century, were higher and the price of corn lower than in the seventeenth century. Between 1737 and 1797, wages in most parts of England, except in the immediate neighborhood of the great cities, doubled. (*Eden*, I, 385.) In Scotland, about the year 1817, the wages of married farm servants, expressed in corn, were about 60 per cent. higher than in 1792. (*Sinclair*, Grundgesetze des Ackerbaues, 105.)

Boisguillebert, Traité des Grains, I, 2, estimates the wages in France, for agricultural laborers, at least from 7 to 8 sous, of present money, and at twice that amount in harvest time. In 1697, laborers in Paris received from 40 to 50 sous. (Détail de la France, I, ch. I, ch. 7.) *Vauban* estimates wages in large cities at 22½–45 sous; for country manual laborers, at 18 sous; for agricultural laborers, 12–13¼ sous. (Project d'une Dime royale, 89 Daire.) On the other hand, *Chaptal*, De l' Industrie, Fr. I, 245, 1819, speaks of an average wage — 25 sous. *Dureau de la Malle*, Economie polit. des Romains, I, 151, allows agricultural laborers, in 80 departments of France, only 20–25 sous. According to *Moreau de Joannés*, Journal des Econ., Oct. 1850, the average wages of a French agricultural family amounted per annum, in 1700, to 135 francs; in 1760, to 126; in 1788, to 161; in 1813, to 400; in 1840, to 500 francs. While *A. Young*, Travels in France, 1787–89, speaks of wages

SEC. CLXXII.]   WAGES OF COMMON LABOR.   71

This favorable development is most striking in the colonies of rich and highly civilized parent countries, where the labor, capital and social customs of an old and ripe civilization are found together with the overflowing natural forces inherent in a virgin soil, engaged in the work of economic production. Here the growth of national wealth is most rapid; and the rate of wages is here wont to be highest.³ With the high rate

---

of 20 sous a day; *Peuchet*, Statist. élémentaire, 1805, 361, assumes it to be 30 sous, although the price of corn was not much higher. Compare *Birkbeck*, Agricultural Tour of France, 13, who is of opinion even, that French laborers are better situated than the English (?). From 1830 to 1848, wages decreased about 30 per cent. (*L. Faucher*, Revue des deux Mondes, Avril, 1848.) *Levasseur*, Histoire des Classes ouvrières en France, II, 1858.

General data for whole countries are obviously very doubtful. In Germany, for instance, economically active places have witnessed an undoubted elevation of the condition of the laboring classes. Thus, in Hamburg and Lower Saxony, about the end of the eighteenth century (*Büsch*, Geldumlauf, II, 56 ff.); while in Thuringia, in 1556, a *sümmer* of rye was earned by 7 summer days' labor, and in 1830 ff. by 8. (*Lotz*, Handbuch, I, 404.) In Hessen, also, there has been but a very small increase in wages. (*Hildebrand*, Nat. Œk., I, 190.) According to *von der Goltz*, Ländliche Arbeiterfrage, 1872, 84 seq., wages in the country during the last twenty or thirty years have increased on an average, 50 per cent. at least; in Bavaria about 100 per cent.; in the Rhine province, male wages, about 100; female wages, from about 75 to 100 per cent. The masterly investigations of the wages of typesetters in Jena and Halle by *Strasburger* in *Hildebrand's* Jahrb., 1872, I ff., show that from 1717 to 1848, there was scarcely any change in them. A million m's was paid for in 1717-40 with 26.93 Prussian *sheffels* of rye; 1804-47 with from 24.80 to 28.80. Since then, a remarkable rise; so that in 1871, up to November, 76.26 was reached. The prices of food, dwellings, fuel, clothing, such as is in demand by such laborers, rose between 1850 and 1860, 16.7 per cent., and the wages for 1,000 m's in the same period of time rose about 14.3 and 43.7 per cent. In the industrious manufacturing vicinity of Moscow, wages in 1815 were four times as high as in 1670, while the means of subsistence rose relatively much less. (*Storch*, I, 203.)

³ In the United States, the wages of carpenters and masons, about the end of the last century, were $0.62 and $0.75; in 1835, of the former from $1.12 to $1.25, and for the latter from $1.37 to $1.50. In 1848, the general wage was $0.75. The price of corn, in the meantime, did not rise, and the price of manufactured articles was much smaller. (*Carey*, Rate of Wages, 26 seq.; Past, Present and Future, 154.) In New York, as far back as 1790, wages were much higher (*Ebeling*, Geschichte und Erdbeschreibung von Nord-

of interest that obtains where capital is rapidly saved, and with the low price of land, it is not a matter of difficulty for good workmen to enter into the ranks of land-owners and capitalists. In North America, and especially in the western part,[4] it is very frequently in the normal course of economic

amerika, II, 917); and between 40 and 50 years ago, a journeyman mason might earn over 700 thalers per annum. Agricultural laborers, in 1835, got $9 a month and their board, valued at $65 for the whole year. In the vicinity of large cities, both were higher. *(Carey,* 91.) The condition of the factory hands, in Lowell, is a very good one. In 1839, more than 100 of them had over $1,000 each in the savings banks, and pianos at their mess places. *(Boz,* Notes on America, 1842.) Most of them could save $1.50 a week. *Colton,* in his Public Economy (1849), says that a workman would consider himself in a bad way if he could not save half of his wages. Compare *Chevalier,* Lettres sur l'Amérique, II, 174, 122, 19; I, 221 ff.

Apprentices in the United States, in almost every instance, begin to be paid wages as soon as their work begins to prove useful. The work of half-grown children, who had not yet left the parental roof, was so well paid that it was estimated that a child earned for his parents, on the whole, £100 more than he cost them. What an incentive to marriage! *(Adam Smith,* Wealth of Nat., I, ch. 8.) In Canada, agricultural laborers earn between £24 and £30 per annum and their board. In and around Melbourne, agricultural laborers got from 15 to 20 shillings a week and lodging; herdsmen, £35 to £40 a year; girls, from £20 to £45 (Statist. Journal, 1872, 387 ff.); female cooks, from £35 to £40; male cooks, from £52 to £156. In hotels, girls, from £30 to £35; female cooks, from £50 to £100; domestic servants, £39 to £52; carpenters, masons etc., 10 shillings a day; the best tailors, from 60 to 75 shillings a week; shoemakers, from 40 to 55 shillings; bakers, from 40 to 66 shillings a week. (Statist. Journal, 1871, 396 seq.) In San Francisco, a short time since, servant girls got $25 a month; Chinese, $1 a day; common laborers, $2; skilled artisans, from $3 to $5. *(Whymper,* Alaska, 299, 326.) The wages of a European tradesman, in Rio Janeiro, was from 1 to 2 Spanish piasters a day. *(Martius,* Reise, I, 131.) In the English West Indies, a new-born negro was formerly worth £5. *(B. Edwards,* History of the West Indies, II, 128.) The high wages paid in young colonies are frequently made temporarily still higher, by a large influx of capital in the shape of money, brought by emigrants, and by government outlays. Thus, in Van Diemen's land, for instance, in 1824, carpenters, masons etc. got 12 shillings a day; in 1830, 10; in 1838, only from 6 to 7, although between 1830 and 1838, the export trade of the island trebled while the population scarcely doubled. *(Merivale,* On Colonies, II, 225.)

[4] As to how many workmen in the eastern part of North America buy land in the west, and so threaten their employers with immediate emigra-

development for young people to begin to work on wages, then to work on their own account, and finally to become themselves employers of labor.

SECTION CLXXIII.

HISTORY OF THE WAGES OF COMMON LABOR.—IN FLOURISHING NATIONS.

A permanently[1] high rate of wages[2] is, both as cause and effect, very intimately connected with a flourishing condition of national life. It proves on the one hand, great productiveness of the public economy of the people generally: prudence, self-respect and self-control, even of the lowest classes, virtues, which, however, are found, on the whole, only where political liberty exists, and where the lowest classes are rightly valued by the higher.[3] On the other hand, it produces a con-

---

tion, see *Brentano*, Arbeitergilden, II, 131. However, in Massachusetts, women's wages are in many instances so low that, considering the dearness of the means of subsistence, it is almost impossible to understand how they exist. (Statist. Journal, 1872, 236 ff.)

[1] A merely momentary rise in wages might be the result of a great calamity, destructive of human life, and might seduce workmen not intellectually prepared for it into idleness. Compare *von Taube*, Beschreib. von Slavonien etc., II, § 4.

[2] On the necessity of *free* wages, that is of an excess over and above the costs of support and of maintaining one's position, see *Roesler*, Grandsätze, 394.

[3] *Dans aucune histoire on ne rencontre un seul trait, qui prouve que l'aisance du peuple par le travail a nui à son obéissance, (Forbonnais.)* This is true only of well governed countries. When, in England, about the middle of the eighteenth century, a great improvement took place in the condition of the laboring classes, *Postlethwayt* (Great Britain's commercial Interests, 1759) was one of the first to recognize its general beneficial character; also *Th. Mortimer*. (Elements of Commerce, Politics and Finance, 1774, 82 ff.) *Benjamin Franklin*, before the American revolution, was of opinion that high wages made people lazy. (On the Price of Corn, 1776. On the laboring Poor, 1768.) He afterwards, however, acknowledged its generally good effect, and that even the products of labor might be cheapened thereby. (On the Augmentation of Wages, which will be occasioned in Europe by the

dition of the great majority of that portion of the population who have to support themselves on the wages they receive, worthy of human beings, a condition in which they can educate their children, enjoy the present and provide for the future. Equality before the law and participation in the affairs of government are empty phrases, and even tend to inflame the passions, where the rate of wages is not high. When the lower classes are dissatisfied, in highly civilized countries, with the sensitiveness and mobility of the whole national life, there can be no certainty of the freedom of the middle classes or of the rule of the upper. Here, in other respects, also, the philanthropy of employers harmonizes remarkably well with their reasonable self-interest. According to § 40, only the well-paid workman can accomplish anything really good, just as, conversely, only the good workman is on the whole, and in the long run, well paid. This suggests the physiological law, that where muscular activity is great, nutrition must be great, likewise; and the rapid waste and repair of tissues strengthens the muscles and gives tone to the whole physical life. With a correct insight into the relations of things, antiquity described its greatest worker, Herakles, as a great eater also. A well-paid workman, who costs and accomplishes as much in a day as two bad ones, is cheaper than they. He works much more cheerfully and faithfully, is, hence, more easily superintended, is less frequently sick, and later decrepid.[4] His childhood costs less, and his burial is not so expensive. In cases of need, he can more easily bear the

---

American Revolution. Works II, 435 ff.) See further, *Paoletti*, Veri Mezzi di render felici le Società, ch. 15; *Ricardo*, Principles, ch. 5. *Th. Brassey*, on Work and Wages, 1872. *Umpfenbach*, Nat.-Oek, 181, calls the costliness of labor to the purchaser of labor, "givers' wages," their purchasing power to the laborer himself, "receivers' wages," and is of opinion, that as civilization advances, the former declines and the latter rises.

[4] When in the department of the Tarn flesh food was introduced among journeymen smiths instead of mere vegetable diet, the sanitary improvement that followed was so great that the number of days lost by sickness in a year decreased from 15 to 3. (*Moleschott,.*)

SEC. CLXXIII. WAGES OF COMMON LABOR. 75

weight of taxation or a temporary lowering of wages.⁵ We might say of the granting of holidays and of evening leisure something similar to what we have said of the rate of wages. They are indispensable requisites to the development of a desirable individuality in the working classes; and when used for that purpose are certainly no detriment to the product of labor or to employers.⁶⁷

---

⁵ In high stages of civilization, it is always more profitable, the result being the same, to keep a few well fed cattle than many poorly fed. (*Roscher*, Nationalök. d. Ackerbaues, § 179.) *Infra*, § 231. When the drainage of Oxford street in London was made while wages were rising, it happened that the cubic foot of masonry work at 10 shillings per day was cheaper than it was formerly at 6 shillings per day. (*Brassey*, 68 ff.) *Senior* calls it an absurdity to consider the high wages paid in England as an obstacle in the way of its successful competition with other countries. Rather would he consider it as the necessary result of the excellence of English labor. Thus, in his Lectures on the mercantile Theory of Wealth, p. 76, he says that if the English employ a part of their labor injudiciously, they must pay it not in proportion to what it really accomplishes, but to what it might do if well employed. If a man calls in a doctor to cut his hair, he must pay him as a doctor. If he puts a man to throwing silk who might earn 3 ounces of silver a week spinning cotton, he must pay him weekly 3 ounces of silver, although he may deliver no more silk within that time than an Italian who gets only 1½ ounces.

⁶ Norfolk country workmen never worked more than 10 hours a day except in harvest and seed time. But a plowman there accomplished as much in 5 days as another in 8. (*Marshall*, Rural Economy of N., 138.) In southwestern Germany, the country working day is from 2 to 4 hours shorter than in the northeast, and yet just as much is accomplished in the former quarter. (*von der Goltz*, Ländl. Arbeiterfrage, 88, 131.) Thus the coal diggers of South Wales work 12 hours a day, those of Northumberland, 7; and yet the same achievement is 25 per cent. dearer in case of the former. In the construction of the Paris-Rouen Railroad, the English achieved more than the French, although the former worked from 6 A. M. to 5:30 P. M., and the latter from 5 A. M. to 7 P. M. (*Brassey*, 144 ff.) Examples from English manufactories in *Marx*, Kapital, I, 401 seq. In an English factory the hours worked were 12, and afterwards, 11. This caused the number of attendants of the evening school to grow from 27 to 98. (*Horner*.) Dollfuss, in Mühlhausen, reduced the number of hours worked from 12 to 11, and let the wages remain the same as before. The result was besides a great saving made in fuel and light, a surplus product of at least 1⅔ per cent. Something similar observed by *M. Chevalier*, Cours, I, 151.

In consideration of all the blessings attending a high rate of wages, we may well be induced to put up with a certain and frequently inconvenient external defiance of the lower classes which is wont to accompany it.[8] It teaches the upper classes many a moral lesson, and is surely a lesser sin in the lower, than the cowardly, malicious crimes of the oppressed. When wages are so low that they have to be supplemented by begging or public charity, the effect on morality is the same as when government officials, who cannot live on their salaries, resort to bribery or embezzlement.[9][10]

Hence *J. Möser*, Patr. Ph., III, 40, desired, on this account, that work in the evening should be prohibited by law. In England, not only the moral necessity, but also the economic general utility of leisure time of workmen has been defended, among others by *Postlethwayt*, Dictionary of Trade and Commerce, I, prelim. Discourse, 1751. A beautiful law, V Moses 24, 15. Only, care must be taken not to go to the other extreme, which is still more detrimental to personality. The North American ideal of 8 hours a day for work, 8 for eating, sleeping etc., and 8 for leisure, would be injurious except to workmen intellectually very active. But the provision to be met with in many states of the Union and in the arsenal employ of the government, that in case of doubt, the work day is to be tacitly assumed as of 8 hours, has, it is said, correspondingly lowered wages. See *supra*, § 168.

[7] In India, where the institution of caste is found, nearly half the year is made up of feast days, while in rationalistic China there is no Sunday and very few general holidays. (*Klemm*, A. Kulturgeschicht. VI, 405. *Wray*, The practical Sugar Planter, 1849.) The Judaic-Christian sanctification of the seventh day is a happy medium between these two extremes. Recuperation and collectedness get their due without its costing too much in action. *Ora et labora!* Compare *Sismondi*, N. P. II, ch. 5. Which is best, traveling on foot, to drag along all the time, or to walk decently and rest properly between times? The rest of Sunday, even leaving the work of recuperation and edification out of account, is necessary in the interests of the family and of cleanliness. The French *decadis* accomplished materially even too little: *ils ont à faire à deux ennemis, qui ne céderont pas, la barbe et la chemise blanche.* (*B. Constant.*) Hence, an English prize essay on the material advantages of Sunday found 1,045 competitors among English working men. (Tübinger Zeitschr., 1851, 363.)

[8] Thus *Parkinson*, A Tour in America, complains that with four servants in the house, he was obliged to polish his own shoes, and with his wife and children to milk the cows, while his people were still asleep. Strange servants bringing a message, come in with their hats on. All domestics are

SECTION CLXXIV.

HISTORY OF THE WAGES OF COMMON LABOR — IN DECLINING COUNTRIES AND TIMES.

When, circumstances being otherwise unaltered, the aggregate income of a nation decreases, the wages of labor are wont to be lower in proportion as the points above mentioned, and

called mister or misses. Servant maids are called "helps," and their masters, "employers." If a person at a hotel asks for a laundress, he is answered: "Yes, man, I will get a lady to wash your clothes." Similarly in *Fowler*, Lights and Shadows, ... three Years' Experience in Australia. But, at the same time, it is remarkable how seldom a native born white American accepts a fee. On the other hand, Russia is the classic land of fees. There is a popular story in that country to the effect that when God divided the earth among the different nations, they were all satisfied except the Russians, who begged a little drink-money or fee in addition. *(von Haxthausen,* Studien, I, 70.) Similarly in Egypt. *(Ebers,* Durch Gosen zum Sinai, 1873, 31 seq.) The system of feeing servants holds a middle place between the modern system of paying for everything lawfully and the medieval system in which people either rob, donate or beg.

⁹ Compare *Garve* in *Macfarlan*, 90. The wages of English wool workers in 1831 amounted to:

				Tax per capita of the population for support of the poor.
In				
Leeds,	-	-	-	22—22½s.	5s. 7d.
Gloucester,	-	-	-	13—15¼s.	8s. 8d.
Somerset,	-	-	-	16¾—19¾s.	8s. 9d.
Wilts,	-	-	-	13$\frac{7}{12}$—15$\frac{5}{12}$s.	16s. 6d.

Ure, Philosophy of Manufactures, 476. After an enthusiastic eulogy of high wages, *McCulloch* remarks especially that the English poor rates cost more than if the laborers were obliged to provide for themselves by getting higher wages. (Principles, III, 7.) Sad results of the system which came into vogue in the South of England in 1795, to supplement wages according to the price of corn and the number of children. Previously the laboring classes married only after the age of 25 and even at 35, and not until they had saved from £40 to £50. After the above mentioned system was adopted, even minors married. (Edinburg Review, LIII, 4, 7.)

¹⁰ *Von Thünen*, Isolirte Staat., II ,1, 154, gives the following formula as the expression of ideal wages: $\sqrt{ap}$, in which a = the necessary requirement for maintenance of the workmen, and p = the aggregate product of his labor. *von Thünen* attached so much importance to this formula that he had

which are unfavorable to the laborer in his competition, appear.[1] The worse distribution, also, of the national resources, when, instead of a numerous middle class, a few over-rich people monopolize all that is to be possessed, diminishes the wages of common labor and thus again produces a worse distribution than before.[2] In a similar way, wages must decline when the mode of life of the laboring class, or the quality of their work, has deteriorated. Some of these causes may exist transitorily

it engraved on his tomb-stone. But even if it were possible to reduce capital-generating labor and wage-labor to a common denominator, it would not be possible nor equitable to maintain the same dividing measure when capital and labor contributed in very different amounts to the production of the common product. An artist, for instance, who could make costly vessels out of very cheap clay and with cheap fuel would get too little by *von Thünen's* law; a mechanic who used a very efficient and costly machine, too much. The fundamental defect in his theory, *von Thünen* himself seems to have obscurely felt. Compare the letter in his Lebensbeschreibung, 1868, 239 and *Roscher*, Geschichte der Nat. Oek., in Deutschland, 895 ff.

[1] Hence *Adam Smith* says that it is not the richest countries in which wages are highest, but those which are becoming rich most rapidly.

[2] The classic lands of low wages and pauperism are especially the East Indies and China. A minister of Kienlong was punished after he had extorted about 20,000,000 thalers. (*Barrow*, II, 149.) In the confiscation of the well known *Keschen*, the authorities, according to their own accounts, found 683 pounds of gold and more than 6,000,000 pounds in silver. Considering the colossal banquets of the rich, embracing several hundred courses, of which *Meyen*, Reise um die Erde, II, 390, describes an example, the wretched food of the poor is doubly striking. Count *Görtz* relates that in Canton, rats and serpents are regularly exposed for sale. (Reise, 445.) The lowness of wages appears from the fact — one of many — that servants frequently get nothing but their board. (*Haussmann*, Voyage en Chine, etc.) In the cities, tradesmen with their tools run hither and thither about the streets begging for employment in the most imploring manner. Thousands live all their lives on rafts. Numberless instances of infanticide from want of food. (§ 251.) The influence of these circumstances on the morality of the people is best illustrated by the fact that *Keschen*, when he was ambassador to Thibet, preferred to confide his newly collected treasures to the escort of the French missionaries he persecuted rather than to the mandarins named by himself, so much more highly did he estimate European than Chinese honesty. (Edinburg Rev., 1851, 425 ff.) In the Chinese picture-writing, the word happiness was designated by a mouth well corked with rice. Chinese statisticians speak of mouths *(Maul)* where ours treat of the number of heads or souls. *Ritter*,

even among otherwise flourishing nations; as, for instance, in war times,[3] or when population for a while grows more rapidly than national wealth. But among nations universally declining, they are all wont to meet, and one strengthens the other.[4] One of the saddest symptoms of such a condition is the low value here put upon the life and strength of workmen. The cheapness of labor has indeed a charm for enterprising spirits,

---

Erdkunde, II, 1060. More favorable accounts in *Plath*, Münch. Akad., 1873, 784, 788 seq.

In the East Indies, a great many of the rejected castes live on carrion, dead fish, noxious insects, and even the middle class find wheat flour too dear, and therefore mix it with peas etc. *(Ritter*, VI, 1143.) It is said that Bengal, in the famine of 1770, lost more than one-third of its inhabitants. *(Mill*, History of British India, III, 432.) Eloquent description of misery in *Rickard*, India, or Facts submitted to illustrate the Character and Condition of the native Inhabitants, II, London, 1832. An immense number of badly paid servants of whom it may however be said that each one accomplishes very little. The Pindaries may pass for an extreme of Indian pauperism, corresponding to the pirate-calamity during the later Roman Republic. (Quarterly Review, XVIII, 466 ff.; *Ritter*, VI, 394 ff.)

[3] Thus, in England, during the last great war, wages rose less than the price of corn, and sank less after it. About 1810, wages were nearly 100 per cent. higher than in 1767; but, on the other hand, the price of wheat, 115; of meat, 146; of butter, 130, and of cheese, 153 per cent. (Edinburg Rev., XL., 28.) If it has some times been observed that crime, communistic machinations and revolutionary movements grow less frequent in times of war, the fact is not to be ascribed necessarily to a better condition of the laboring class. It might possibly be the consequence of the strongest and wildest elements of the laboring class finding some other career.

[4] *Adam Smith*, loc. cit., on this point describes China as a stationary country (according to *R. Fortune*, Wanderings in China, 1847, 9, a decided decline has been noticeable there for a long time), and Bengal as a declining one. On the condition of wages among the Romans, *Juvenal*, III, 21 ff., is one of the principal sources. Hence the desire to emigrate because honest labor had no longer any foothold (23 ff.). Poor dwellings of the laboring class, dark, exposed to danger from fire (166, 190 ff., 225), and yet comparatively dear (223 seq.). Numerous crowds of robbers and beggars (302 ff.; IV, 116 ff.; V, 8; XIV, 134). On beggary, see *Seneca*, Controv., V, 33. De Element., II, 6. De Vita beata, 25 ff. *Martial*, V, 81, XIV, 1, complains of the absence of outlook among the poorer classes. *Horace*, too, is rich in passages which might be appropriately cited in this connection. Characteristic question of the nabobs, in *Petron.*, 48, 5: What on earth is that thing called a pauper?

which induces them to employ human labor even where machinery, beasts etc., would economically be better adapted to the performance of the work.[5] Day-laborers are, on this account, more profitable to persons of enterprise *(Unternehmer = undertaker)* because they can more easily rid themselves of them. But such egotistic calculation should have no place even in the case of actual slaves.[6]

Besides, it not unfrequently happens, that the laboring class seek to oppose the decline of wages by increasing their industry, shortening their holidays and leisure, and by drawing their wives and children into their work. This may, under certain circumstances, result in an increase of the national income, and thus constitute a transition to the restoration of high wages, especially if beforehand there was reason to complain of the idleness of the working class. But if the other circumstances of competition are unfavorable to the working class, if especially they used their personally increased income to add to the population, it would not be long before they fell back to their previous state. In such case, the consequence is, that the same quantity of labor has become cheaper; that all permanent profit falls to the capitalists and land-owners, and

---

[5] Thus, in China, the East Indies etc., people travel in palanquins borne by men; in a multitude of cases, Chinese commodities are carried in wheelbarrows; and a great many roads are constructed, in reference not to wagons, properly so-called, but to this species of vehicle. How heartless the Chinese, who, before they save a drowning man, first higgle about the reward, and take pleasure in pestilence, famine etc., because those who survive profit by them. See *Finlaison,* Journey of the Mission to Siam, 1826, 62 ff.

[6] Hence *Menander* (342–290 before Christ) says it is better to be the slave of a good master than to live wretched in freedom. *(Stobæus,* Flor., 62, § 7. *Meinecke,* Fr. com. Gr., IV, 274.) *Libanios,* too, (Tom., 483, Reiske), in his " Blame of Poverty," represents slavery as better cared for, and freer from worry. Horrible contracts made even in Cæsar's time, from want, by freemen, to become gladiator-slaves. *Cicero,* pro Roscio, Am. 6; *Horat.,* Serm., II, 7, 58 ff.; *Petron.,* 117; *Seneca,* Epist., 37. And so by Justinian, cases of declined freedom are supposed. (L. 15, *Justin.,* Cod., VII, 2.) *" Dans une armée on estime bien moins un pionnier, qu'un cheval de caisson, parceque le cheval est fort cher, et qu'on a le pionier pour rien. La suppression de l'esclavage a fait passer ce calcul de la guerre dans la vie commune."* *(Linguet.)*

all that remains to the laboring class is only greater toil, a sadder home-life, and sadder children. The danger of such an issue is all the greater, because few things so much contribute to reckless marriages and the thoughtless procreation of children, as the industrial coöperation of wife and child.[7][8]

---

[7] *Sismondi* is guilty, however, of a philanthropic exaggeration when he says that the labor of children is always fruitless to the laboring classes. (R. P. I., 235.)

[8] The bringing into juxtaposition of the rates of wages in different countries is doubtless one of the most important objects of comparative statistics. Only it is necessary not to confine it to the money amount of wages, but to make it embrace the prices of the principal means of subsistence. Thus, in France, before the outbreak of the French Revolution, a French workman earned a cwt. of bread on an average of 10.5 days; one of meat in 36.8; an English workman, in 10.4 and 25.3 days. *(A. Young.)* In the interior of Russia, a female weaver earns, in a day, almost one Prussian *scheffel* of rye, in Bielefeld, only about one-tenth of a *scheffel;* a table-cloth weaver, in the former place, 18 silver groschens, while the *scheffel* costs from 12 to 15 silver groschens. *(von Haxthausen,* Studien, I, 119, 170.) According to *Humboldt*, the money-wages paid in Mexico were twice as high, and the price of corn two-thirds as dear, as in France. (N. Espagne, IV, 9.) According to *Rau*, Lehrbuch, I, § 180, the procuration of the following means of subsistence required in day labor in:

	Manchester. 1810–20	Hanover. 1700	Hanover. 1827	Upper Canada. 1830	Brandenburg. 1820–33	Gratz. 1826–45
Cwt. beef,	26	33	35	6.6	34	36
" potatoes,	1.85				1	2.68
" wheat,	5.5			2	7.6	11
" rye,		6.5	8.7	1.5	5.4	8.6
" butter,	42.3	87	64	22	83	84
" sugar,	96	181	128			

Estimated in silver, the East Indian laborer earns from £1 to £2 a year; the English, £9 to £15; the North American, £12 to £20. *(Senior.)* Hildebrand, Nat.-Œk., I, 195 ff., assures us that the average rate of wages in Germany, in 1848, amounted to 400 thalers a year; in England, to 300 thalers; and that the prices of the means of subsistence in the latter country were 1½ times higher than in the former. *Engel,* Ueber die arbeitenden Klassen in England, 1845, shows only the dark side of a real picture, and is silent on the other, and is well corrected by *Hildebrand,* I, 170 ff. Excellent statistics in

SECTION CLXXV.

WAGE POLICY — SET PRICE OF LABOR.

Among the artificial means employed to alter the existing rate of wages, we may mention first, a rate of wages fixed by governmental authority. These have, in many places, constituted an intermediate step between serfdom and the free wage-system. In most cases, this measure was intended in the interest of the upper classes to prevent the lower obtaining the full advantage of their freedom under the favoring circumstances of competition.[1] In later times, another cause has

Sir F. M. Eden, State of the Poor, I, 491–589. On the more recent times, compare the Edinburgh Review, April, 1851, April, 1862; Quarterly Rev., Oct., 1859, July, 1860. *Ludlow* and *Jones*, loc. cit. On the situation in France, see *Blanqui's* report in the Mémoires de l'Académie des Sciences morales et politiques, II, 7. *Leplay*, Les Ouvriers des deux Mondes, II, 1858. Very important are the "Reports from Her Majesty's diplomatic and consular Agents abroad respecting the Condition of the industrial Classes, and the Purchase-power of money in foreign Countries." (1871.)

[1] The plague known as the black death of 1348, which devastated the greater part of Europe, was followed by many complaints on the part of the buyers of labor, of the cupidity and malicious conspiracies of the working classes. See *supra* § 160.) Fixed rates of wages under Peter the Cruel of Castile, 1351; contemporaneously in France, Ordonnances, II, 350, and in England, 25 Edw. III, c. 2; 37 Edw. III, c. 3. In France, the wages of a thresher were fixed at the one-twentieth or the one-thirtieth of a *scheffel*, while in present Saxony it is from one-fourteenth to one-twelfth. In England, under the same ruler, who had seen his castle at Windsor built, not by day laborers for wages, but by vassal masons, vassal carpenters, etc., whom he got together from all parts of the kingdom. That the rates might not be evaded, the succeeding king forbade both the leaving of agriculture for industry and change of domicil without the consent of a justice of the peace. (12 Richard II., c. 3.) All such provisions were little heeded in the 16th century. *Rogers*, the Statist. Journal, 1861, 544 ff.)

Fixed rates of wages under Henry VII. and Henry VIII., in the interest of workmen. *(Gneist*, Verwaltungsrecht, II, Aufl., 461 ff.) The fact that in 5 Elizabeth, c. 4, another attempt was made to fix the rate of wages by governmental provisions, in which the person paying more than the sum fixed was threatened with 10 days' imprisonment, and the person receiving less with 12, was in part akin to the English poor laws. If a poor man had the

frequently been added to this, viz.: by diminishing the cost of production to increase foreign sales. (See § 106.) In the higher stages of civilization, nations will scarcely look with favor on the diminution of the rightful, for the most part, individually small gains of the most numerous, the poorest and most care-worn class of the community.[2] The purchasers of labor would, in consequence, be badly served, since they would have lost the possibility of obtaining better workmen by paying higher wages. Hence, there would, probably, be none but mediocre labor to be found.[3] On the other hand, fixed rates which keep within the limits described in § 114

---

right to be eventually employed and supported by the community, it was, of course, necessary that the justice of the peace should be able to determine at what wages anybody should be prepared to work before he could say: I can find no work. Extended by 2 James I., c. 6, to all kinds of work for which wages were paid. *(Eden,* State of the Poor, V, 123 ff., 140.) The buyers of labor in the eighteenth century frequently complained that these fixed wages were more to the advantage of workmen than of their masters. *(Brentano,* English Guilds., ed. by *Toulmin Smith,* 1870, Prelim. CXCI.)

In Germany, the depopulation caused by the Thirty Years' War explains why, before and after the peace of Westphalia. so many diets were concerned with fixing the rate of wages of servants. Compare *Spittler,* Gesch., Hanovers, II. 175. Among the most recent instances of English fixed rates of wages, is 8 George III., for London tailors, and the Spitalfields Act of 1773, for silk weavers who had, a short time before, revolted. Also in New South Wales, about the end of the last century, on account of the high rate of colonial wages. *(Collins,* Account of the English Colonies of New South Wales, 1798.) Later, *Mortimer,* Elements of Politics, Commerce and Finance, 1174, 72, maintains fixed rates of wages to be necessary. In Germany the imperial decree of 1830, tit., 24, and again the ordinance of Sept. 4, 1871, provide that each magistrate shall fix the rate of wages in his own district. *Chr. Wolf,* Vernunftige Gedanken vom gesellsch. Leben der Menschen, 1721, § 487, would have the rates so fixed that the laborers might live decently and work with pleasure.

[1] Proposal for a fixed sale of wages in the protocols of the Chamber of Lords of Nassau, 1821, 12.

[2] The Spitalfields Act was repealed in 1824, for the reason that the manufacturers themselves attributed the stationary condition of their industries for a hundred years to the fact that they were hampered by that act. *Ricardo's* and *Huskisson's* prophecies, on this occasion, fulfilled by the great impulse which the English silk industries soon afterwards received.

are, under certain circumstances, desirable. This is especially the case where the purchasers of labor on the one hand, and the buyers of labor on the other, have formed themselves into united groups, and where the rate fixed is only in the nature a treaty of peace under governmental sanction, when a war over prices had either broken out actually or there was danger to fear that one would break out. It must not be forgotten, that thus far common labor has scarcely had any thing similar to an "exchange."[4]

SECTION CLXXVI.

WAGES-POLICY — STRIKES.

Where the wages-receiving class feel themselves to be a special class, *vis-a-vis* of the purchasers of their labor, they have frequently endeavored, by the preconcerted suspension of labor upon a large scale, to force their masters to pay them higher wages, or grant them some other advantage.[1] It is

---

[4] Compare *Brentano*, Arbeitergilden der Gegenwart, II, 288. However, fixed rates of wages equitably arranged, in the establishment of which neither party has been given an advantage over the other, have continued to exist much longer than our distrustful and novelty-loving age would think possible. Thus compositors' wages in London, from 1785 to 1800, from 1800 to 1810, from 1810 to 1816, and from 1816 to 1866, remained unaltered; those of London ship builders, from 1824 to 1867; of London builders, from 1834 to 1853, and from 1853 to 1865. (*Brentano* II, 213. Compare II, 250, 267 ff.)

[1] Even *Boisguillebert*, Traité des Grains, was acquainted with instances of this kind in which from 600 to 800 workmen simultaneously left their masters. There are much earlier instances in Italy. Thus, in Sienna, in 1381 and 1384, in which the nobility sided with the workmen. (Rerum Ital. Sciiptores, XV, 224, 294.) Strikes of journeymen began to be much more frequent in Germany in the guilds, from the time of the prospect of their becoming masters themselves, and of their living in the family of the masters had decreased. On similar strikes at Spiers, in 1351, at Hagenau in 1409, and Mainz in 1423, see *Mone's*, Zeitschrift, XVII, 56; XIII, 155, and *Hegel*, Strassb. Chr., II, 1025. A remarkable strike of the Parisian book printers under Francis I. (*Hildebrand's* Jahrb., 1873, II, 375 ff.) In so-called " home manufactures," where the " manufacturer " is both orderer, preparer and sel

hard to say whether such strikes have more frequently failed or succeeded.[2] As a rule, a war over prices, carried on by such means, and without force on either side, must generally issue in the victory of the richer purchasers of labor.[3] The latter require the

---

ler, but strikes are scarcely possible without much fixed capital. The strike of the factory spinners in Lancashire in 1810 caused 30,000 workmen to stop work for four months.

Among the next following coalitions of labor, those of the Glasgow weavers in 1812 and 1822 were very important. In the latter, two workmen who would not participate with the strikers were blinded with sulphuric acid. In 1818, great strike by the Scotch miners. The Preston strike of 1853 lasted 36 weeks. It is said that 6,200 male and 11,800 female working people took part in it. *(Athenæum*, 30 Sept., 1854.) Compare *Morrison*, Essay on the Relations between Labor and Capital, 1854. For a history of Swiss strikes, especially of the Zürich compositors' strike in 1873, see *Böhmert*, Arbeiterverhältnisse, II, 287 ff. Comic type of a strike of married women in *Aristophanes*, Lysistrata. A practical one in Rome at the departure of the plebeians for the holy mountains, 492 before Christ. *(Livy*, II, 32,) then, on a small scale, on the removal of the pipers after Tiberius, 311 before Christ. *(Liv.*, IX, 30.)

[2] Instances of successful strikes: Fortnightly Review, Nov. 1865. Similarly in Germany, in 1865; but there, in truth, many strikes were only defensive and intended to restore the former thing-value of the declined money (Werke, XIII, 151). The English strikes, in 1866 and 1867, failed nearly all, so that wages again declined to their level in 1859, and in many places, to what they had been in the crisis-year 1857. (Ausland, 16 April, 1868.) As to how even in Victoria, strikes which opposed a decline of wages from 16 to from 8 to 10 shillings a day failed, after doing great injury, see Statist. Journ., 1861, 129 ff.

[3] The Preston strikers of 1853 got even from their non-striking colleagues, £30,000. Had their masters prevented this, the affair would have been terminated much sooner. (Quart. Rev., Oct. 1859.) But employers are much more frequently divided by rivalries than workmen, especially in strikes against new machines or when a manufacturer, who has too large a supply of goods on hand, desires a strike himself. On account of their smaller number, too, they are less in a condition to declare a recusant colleague in disgrace. *Adam Smith's* remark that coalitions of capitalists are much more frequent than those of workmen, only that much less is said of them, is hardly applicable to our time. (Wealth of Nat., I, ch. 8, p. 100, ed. Bas.) But, since the strike of the London builders in 1859, capitalists have begun to form more general opposing unions. On a very energetic one among the

uninterrupted continuation of labor for their convenience and profit; but the workmen need it to live. It is but seldom that the workmen will be in a condition to stop work for more than a few months, without feeling the sting of hunger. The purchaser of labor can live longer on his capital; and the victory here belongs to the party who, in the struggle, holds out longest. Hence, a strike that lasts more than six weeks may, for that reason alone, be considered a failure. The employers of labor, on account of their smaller number and greater education, make their counter-coalition much more secret and effective. How many instances there are in which labor-saving machines have come into use more rapidly than they otherwise would have come but for the influence of these coalitions![4]

On the other hand, it cannot be ignored that a host of workmen, by means of an organization which provides them with a unity of will, such as the heads of great enterprises naturally possess, must become much better skilled in carrying on a struggle for higher wages. Where wages in general tend to rise, but by force of custom, which is specially powerful here (§ 170), are kept below their natural level, a strike may very soon attain its end. And workmen are all the more to be wished God-speed here in proportion as employers are slow to decide of their own motion upon raising wages, and where, under

---

ship builders on the Clyde, see *Count de Paris*, Les Associations ouvrières en Angleterre, 1869, ch. 7. Examples on a smaller scale, Edinburg Review, LXXXIX, 327 ff. On the other hand, a "lock-out" on the part of capitalists is very difficult, from the fact that it is impossible to prevent idle workmen from being supported from the poor fund. Moreover, there can be no greater folly than for the workmen to add insult to their masters to their demand for higher wages, because then the limits within which the latter are willing to continue the business at all, are made much narrower, than they would be on a merely economic estimate.

[4] Thus the "iron man," by which a single person can put from 1,500 to 3,000 spindles in motion; also an improved plane-machine, by means of which several colors can be printed at once. (*Ure*, Philosophy of Manufactures, 366 ff.) Machines for riveting cauldrons. (*Dingler*, Polytechnisches Journal, LXXV, 413.)

certain circumstances,[5] a single cold-hearted master might force all his competitors to keep wages down. If even the entire working class should follow the example of the strikers, so that all commodities, in so far as they are products of labor, should grow dearer to an extent corresponding to the rise in wages, there would still remain an improvement of the condition of the working class at the cost of the interest paid on capital and the profits of enterprise. It is, of course, otherwise with the struggle of workmen against the natural conditions which determine the rate of their wages (§§ 161-166) in which they might, in turbulent times, possibly succeed[6] temporarily, but would, in the long run, have to fail.[7]

The working class will be best fortified in such a struggle for higher wages when their organization is a permanent one, and when they have taken care, during good times, to collect a certain amount of capital to protect their members, during their cessation from work, against acute want. This is the object of the trades-unions as they have grown up in England, especially since the total decline of the guild system and of governmental provisions relating to apprentices, fixed rates of wages[8] etc. But it cannot be denied that these unions, al-

---

[5] Compare the statements in the Statist. Journal, 1867, 7.

[6] Thus in several places in 1848, and in Paris in 1789, where even the lackeys and apothecary clerks formed such unions. (*Wachsmuth*, Gesch. Frankreichs im Revolutionszeitalter, I, 178.) Similarly, frequently in isolated factories.

[7] *Thornton* mentions six instances in which strikes and strike-unions may permanently raise wages: a, when those engaged in an enterprise have a virtual monopoly in their own neighborhood; b, when the country has, for the industry in question, great advantage over other lands; c, when the demand for the product of the industry is necessary on account of an increasing number and increasing capacity to pay of customers; d, when the progress of the arts, especially of machinery, makes the industry more productive; e, when the rise in the rate of wages affects all branches of industry to the same extent, and at the same time; f, when the industry is carried on on so large a scale that it yields greater profit, even while paying a smaller percentage than other industries. (On Labour, III, ch. 4.) It is easy to see that many of these conditions meet in the building industries in large cities.

[8] Compare *Brentano* in the Preliminary Essay to *T. Smith's* English Guilds,

though democratic in form, often exercise a very despotic sway over their members;[9] that they have, so far as the employers of labor are concerned, and the non-union laborers, gone back to a number of measures, outgrowths of the guild and embargo systems, which it was fondly hoped had been forever banished by the freedom of industry.[10] What many

---

ch. LXXII ff. The same author's Die Arbeitergilden der Gegenwart Bd., I, 1871.

[9] The greater number of strikes begin with a small minority, generally of the best paid workmen, whom the others follow unwillingly but blindly. (Edinb. Rev., 149, 422.) The despotic power of the Unions over their members depends principally on the fact that their treasury serves not only to maintain strikes but at the same time as an insurance fund for old age and sickness, and that every case of disobedience of a member is punished by expulsion, i. e., with the loss of everything he has contributed. Hence the Quart. Rev., Oct., 1867, advises that these two purposes which are so hard, technically speaking, to reconcile with each other, should be required to be kept separate, especially as most of the unions, considered as benevolent associations, are really insolvent. (Edinb. Review, Oct., 1867, 421 ff.) On the other hand, both the *Count of Paris*, ch. 3, and *Thornton* are favorable to the admixture of humane and offensive objects in the trades-unions, because the former contribute to make the latter milder. *Brentano*, I, 153, has no great objection to the insolvency shown by the books of the unions *vis-a-vis* of their duties as insurers, since, hitherto, the subscription of an extraordinary sum has never failed to make up the deficit. A strike is detrimental in proportion as the striking workmen represent more of the previous preliminary operations that go to finish a product; as when, for instance, the 50 or 60 spinners in a factory strike, and in consequence, from 700 to 800 other workmen are thrown out of employment and forced into idleness against their will. What might not have been the consequence of the great union of the coal miners of Durham and Northumberland, the members of which numbered 40,000 men, and stopped work from April to the beginning of September, 1864, so that at last it became necessary to carry Scotch coal to Newcastle! Compare *Engels*, Lage der arbeitenden Klassen in England, 314 ff.

[10] The English unions even forbid their members to exceed the established time of work, or the established task. Thus, for instance, a penalty of one shilling for carrying at any time more than eight bricks in the case of masons, and a similar penalty inflicted on the person's companions who witness the violation of the rule and do not report the guilty party. Equality of wages for all members; piece-wages allowed only when the surplus earned is divided among one's companions. Hence the complete discouragement of

of the friends of this system hope it may accomplish in the
future, viz.: regulate the whole relation between capital and
labor, and thus, on the whole, control the entire public economy
of a people,[11] is, fortunately, all the more certainly a chimera,
as any national or universal approximation to this end would
be the most efficacious way to compel employers of labor to
the formation of corresponding and probably far superior opposing unions. Notwithstanding this, however, I do not doubt
that the recent development of trades-unions in England is
both a cause and an effect of the rise in wages in the branches
of industry in question, as well as of the moral elevation of the
condition of the working class which has simultaneously taken

---

all skill or industry above the average. If an employer exceeds the prescribed number of apprentices; if he engages workmen not belonging to the
union; if he introduces new machines, a strike is ordered. With all this the
severest exclusion respectively of one class of tradesmen by the other. If a
carpenter lays a few stones, a strike immediately! (Quart. Rev., October,
1867, 363, 373.) Rigid shutting out of the products of one district from
another. (Edinburg Rev., October, 1867, 431.) The poor hand-weavers
were thus prevented going from their over-crowded trade into another. *(J.
Stuart Mill*, Principles, II, ch. 14, 6.) However, many trades-unions still
seem to be free from these degenerations, and the most influential unions the
most moderate in their proceedings. *(Count de Paris*, ch. 8, 9; *Thornton*,
III, ch. 2.) *Brentano* expressly assured us that such degeneration of the
unions in England is confined to the building trades-unions. (I, 68, 188.)

[11] "They have no notion of contenting themselves with an equal voice in
the settlement of labor questions; they tell us plainly that what they aspire
to is to control the destinies of labor, ... to dictate, to be able to arrange
the conditions of employment at their own discretion." *(Thornton*, III, ch.
1.) The membership of the English trades-unions was estimated, at the
Manchester Congress, June, 1868, at 500,000 by some, and at 800,000 by
others. *Brentano*, II, 310, speaks of 960,000. Since 1830, there have been
frequent endeavors to effect a great combination, with special organizations
of the different trades. During recent years, there have been even beginnings of an international organization, although in Germany, for instance,
at the end of 1874, there were 345 trades-unions, with a membership of over
21,000. *(M. Hirsch.)* A formal theory of workmen's unions to culminate
in popular representation, in *Dühring*, Arbeit und Kapital, 1866, especially, p.
233; while the American *Walker* accuses all such combinations, which used
compulsion on any one, of moral high treason against republican institutions.
(Science of Wealth, 272.)

place.[12] The mere possibility of a strike is of itself calculated, in the determination of the rate of wages, to procure for the equitable purchaser of labor the desirable preponderance over the inequitable.[13]

SECTION CLXXVII.

WAGES-POLICY—STRIKES AND THE STATE.

Should the state tolerate the existence of strikes or strike-unions? Legislation in the past most frequently gave a negative answer to the question, as well from a repugnance for high wages as for the self-help of the masses.[1] But even leaving

---

[12] The former view, for instance, of *Harriet Martineau*, "The tendence of strikes and sticks to produce low wages" (1834) is now unconditionally shared only by few. When *Sterling* says that the momentary success of a strike is followed by a two-fold reaction which restores the natural equilibrium, viz.: increase of the number of workmen and decrease of capital (Journal des Econ., 1870, 192), he overlooks not only the length of the transition time which would certainly be possible here, but also that an altered standard of life of the workmen prevents the former, and one of the capitalists the latter. The *Count of Paris* and *Thornton* do not doubt that the elevation of the condition of the English working classes, as proved by *Ludlow* and *Jones*, is to be ascribed, in part, to the effect of the trades-unions. Many of the unions work against the intemperance and quarrelsomeness of their members. The people's charter of 1835, came from the London "workingmen's association."

[13] On the great utility of the arbitration courts between masters and workingmen, by which the struggle for wages is terminated in a peaceable manner and without any interruption of work, see *Schäffle*, Kapitalismus und Socialismus, 659. More minutely in *Thornton*, III., ch. 5. *Faucher*, Vierteljahrsschr., 1869, III, 302, calls attention to the fact that such "boards" may be abused to oppress small manufacturers.

[1] Thus even 34 Edw. III., c. 9. Journeymen builders were forbidden by 3 Henry VI., c. 1, to form conspiracies to enhance the rate of wages, under pain of felony. Finally, 39 and 40 George III., c. 106, threatened any one who, by mere persuasion, should induce a workman to leave his master's service etc., with 2 months in the work-house, or 3 months' imprisonment. In France, as late as June and September, 1791, all conspiracies to raise wages were prohibited under penalty, the incentive to such prohibition being the opposition to all *intérêts intermédiaires* between the *intérêts particulier;* and the *intérêt général* which is characteristic of the entire revolution. Com-

the above reasons out of consideration, every strike is a severe injury to the national resources in general,[2] one which causes that part especially to suffer from which those engaged in the various enterprises and the working class draw their income. And, even for the latter, the damage endured is so great that it can be compensated for only by very permanently high wages.[3] How many a weak man has been misled by a long cessation from work during a strike, which ate up his savings, into lasting idleness and a devil-may-care kind of life. When employers, through fear of strikes, keep all

---

pare the law of 22 Germinal, 11. The German Empire on the 16th of August, 1731, threatened journeymen strikers even with death, "when accompanied by great refractoriness and productive of real damage." (Art. 15.)

[2] The strike of the spinners of Preston, to compel equal wages with those of Bolton, lasted from October to the end of December, 1836. The spinners got from their treasury 5 shillings a week (previously 22½ shillings wages); twisters, 2 to 3 shillings; carders and weavers lived on alms. In the middle of December, the funds of the union were exhausted. Altogether, the workmen lost 400,000 thalers; the manufacturers, over 250,000; and many merchants failed. (*H. Ashworth*, Inquiry into the Origin and Results of the Cotton Spinners' Strike.) The Preston strike of 1853 cost the employers £165,000, the workmen, £357,000. (Edinburgh Rev., July, 1854, 166.) The North-Stafford puddlers' strike, in 1865, cost the workmen in wages alone £320,000. Concerning 8 strikes that failed, mostly between 1859 and 1861, which cost in the aggregate £1,570,000, of which £1,353,000 were wages lost, see Statist. Journ., 1861, 503. A great mortality of the children of workingmen observed during strikes!

[3] *Watts* assumes that the strikers seek to attain, on an average, an advance in their wages of five per cent. Now, a week is about equivalent to two per cent. of the year. If, therefore, a strike lasted one month, the increase of wages it operates must last one and three-fifths years to compensate the workmen for their loss. A strike that lasts 12½ months would require 20 years to effect the same, and this does not include interest on lost wages. (Statist. Journal, 1861, 501 ff.) However, it is possible that the striking workingmen themselves should lose more than they gained, but that, for the whole working class, the gain should exceed the loss; since those who had not participated in the strike would participate in the increased wages. *Thornton* is of opinion that employers have won in most strikes, but surrendered in the intervals between strikes, so that now English workmen receive certainly £5,000,000 more in wages than they would be getting were it not for the trades-unions. (III, ch. 3-4.)

large orders etc. secret, the workmen are not in a condition to forecast their prospects and condition even for the near future. And in the end a dread of the frequent return of such disturbances may cause capital to emigrate.[4]

However, where there exists a very high degree of civilization, there is a balance of reasons in favor of the non-intervention of governments,[5] but only so long as the striking workmen are guilty of no breach of contract and of no crime. Where every one may legally throw up his employment, there is certainly no plausible legal objection to all of them doing so at once, and then forming new engagements. Coalitions of purchasers of labor for the purpose of lowering wages, which are most frequent though noiselessly formed, the police power of the state cannot prevent. If now it were attempted to keep the working class alone from endeavoring to correspondingly raise their wages, the impression would become general, and be entertained with right, that the authorities were given to measuring with different standards. Where the working classes so sensitively feel the influence of the government on the state of their wages, they would be only too much inclined to charge every chance pressure made by the circumstances of the times to the account of the state, and thus burthen it with a totally unbearable responsibility. Since 1824, freedom of competition has prevailed in this matter on both sides in England.[6] The

---

[4] By the Norwich strike, about the beginning of the fourth decade of this century, what remained of the industrial life of that city disappeared. (*Kohl*, Reise, II, 363 ff.) Similarly in Dublin. (Quart. Rev., October, 1859, 485 ff.) In Cork, the workingmen's union, in 1827, allowed no strange workmen to join them, and, it is said, committed twenty murders with a view to that end. The builders demanded 4s. 1d. a day wages. This discouraged the erection of new buildings, and it frequently happened that they found employment only one day in two weeks. (Eninb. Rev., XLVII, 212.) When workingmen struggle against a natural decline of the rate of wages, they, of course, add to their misfortune.

[5] The grounds on which *Brentano*, following *Ludlow* and *Harrison*, justifies the intervention of the state, have a very dangerous bearing, inasmuch as they do not suppose, as a condition precedent, a perfectly wise and impartial governmental authority.

[6] 5 George IV., c. 95: "provided no violence is used." Further, 6 George

dark side of the picture would be most easily brightened by a longer duration of contracts of labor.[7] Whether the trades-unions, when they shall have happily withstood the fermentative process now going on, shall be able to fill up the void created by the downfall of the economically active corporations of the latter part of the middle ages, we shall discuss in our future work, Die Nationalökonomik des Gewerbfleisses. One of the chief conditions precedent thereto is the strict justice of the state, which should protect members of the unions from all tyranny by their leaders, and from violations of the legal rights of non-members.[8]

IV., c. 129, and 122 Vict., c. 34. The law of 1871 declares the trades-unions lawful, allows them the right of registration, and thus empowers them to hold property. In France, the law of May 25, 1864, alters articles 414 to 416 of the *Code pénal* to the effect that only such strikes shall be punished as happen *à l' aide de violences, voies de fait, manoeuvres frauduleuses;* also coalitions against the *libre exercise du travail à l' aide d' amendes, défenses, proscriptions, interdictions.* But these amendments were rendered rather inoperative by the fact that meetings of more than 20 persons could be held only by permission of the police.

[7] As, for instance, the coal workers in the north of England required a half year's service. So long as the trades-unions consider themselves, by way of preference, as instruments of war, it is conceivable how they oppose all binding contracts for labor. So now among the German journeymen book-printers, and so, also, for the most part, in England. *(Brentano,* II, 108.) In quieter times, when the trades-unions shall have become peace institutions, this will be otherwise. We cannot even enjoy the bright side of the freedom of birds without enduring its dark side! In Switzerland, breaches of contract by railroad officers are guarded against by their giving security beforehand; in manufactures, by the holding back of from 3 to 14 days' wages. *(Böhmert,* Arbeiterverhältnisse, II, 91, 388 ff.)

[8] In Switzerland, the trades-unions have shown themselves very powerful against the employers of tradesmen, but rather powerless against manufacturing employers, and thus materially increased the already existing inferiority of the former. *(Böhmert,* II, 401.) They may, however, by further successful development, constitute the basis of a new smaller middle class, similar to the tradesmens' guilds at the end of the middle ages; and indeed by a new exclusiveness, in a downward direction. This would be a bulwark against the destructive inroads of socialism similar to that which the freed peasantry in France were and still are. While this is also *Brentano's* view, *R. Meyer,* Emancipationskampf des vierten Standes, 1874, I, 254 ff., calls the

SECTION CLXXVIII.

WAGES-POLICY — MINIMUM OF WAGES.

The demand[1] so frequently heard recently, that the state should guaranty an "equitable" minimum of wages, could be granted where the natural rate of wages has fallen below that minimum, only on condition that some of the working class in the distribution of the wages capital (no longer sufficient in all the less profitable branches of business) should go away entirely empty handed. Hence, as a rule, in addition to that wages-guaranty, the guaranty of the right to labor is also required. But as useful labor always finds purchasers (the word "useful" being here employed in the sense of the entire economy of a people, and understood in the light of the proper gradation of wants and the means of satisfying them), such a right to labor means no more and no less than that the state should force labor which no one can use, upon others.[2] Some-

---

trades-unions a practical preparation for socialism to which the English "morally went over" in 1869 (I, 751); which indeed loses much of the appearance of truth from the fact that *Marx (Brentano,* Arbeitergilden, II, 332) and the disciples of *Lassalle (Meyer,* I, 312) hold the trades-unions in contempt. *John Stuart Mill* approves of all trades-unions that seek to effect the better remuneration of labor, and opposes all which would bring the wages paid for good work and bad work to the same level. (Principles, II, ch. 14, 6; V, ch. 10, 5.) Compare *Tooke,* History of Prices, VI, 176. Reports of the Commissioners appointed to inquire into the Organization and Rules of Trades-Unions, 1857.

[1] Compare, besides, the Prussian A. L. R,. II, 19, 2. In *Turgot, droit du travail,* and *droit au travail* are still confounded one with the other. Oeuvres éd. *Daire,* II, 302 ff; especially 306. In such questions, people generally think only of factory hands. But have not writers just as good a *droit au travail* to readers whom the state should provide them with, lawyers to clients and doctors to patients?

[2] *L. Faucher* calls the *droit au travail* worse than the equal and compulsory distribution of all goods, because it lays hands on not only present products but even on the productive forces. It supposes that unlimited production is possible; that the state may regulate the market at pleasure to serve its pur-

thing similar is true of Louis Blanc's proposition that the rate of wages of the workmen should be determined and regulated by their own votes and among themselves.[3]

All such measures are injurious in proportion as they, by extending aid and the amount of the minimum, go beyond the limits of benevolence, and approach those of a community of goods. (§ 81 ff.) However, if they would be lasting and not pull workmen rapidly down to the very depths of universal and irremediable misery, these measures should be accompanied by the bestowal of power on the guarantor to hold the further increase of the human family within bounds.[4]

The condition of workmen can be continued good or materially improved only on condition that their numbers increase less rapidly than the capital destined for wages. The latter increases usually and most surely by savings. But only the middle classes are really saving. In England, for instance, the national capital increases every year by at least £50,000,000, while the working classes spend at least £60,000,000 in tobacco and spirituous liquors, *i. e.*, in numberless instances, only for a momentary injurious enjoyment by the adult males of the class, one in which their families have almost no share. According to this, every compulsory rise in wages would be a taking away from the saving class and a giving to a class that

---

poses; that, in fact, the state can give without having first taken what it gave. (Mélanges d' Economie politique, II, 148 ff.) The French national assembly rejected the "right to labor" on the 15th of September, 1848, by 596 ayes to 187 nays, after the provisional government had proclaimed it, February 25. Le Droit au Travail à l' Assemblée nationale avec des Observations de *Faucher, Wolowski, Bastiat* etc., by *J. Garnier*, Paris, 1848.

[3] *L. Blanc*, De L'Organization du Travail, 1849.

[4] "Every one has a right to live. We will suppose this granted. But no one has a right to bring creatures into life to be supported by other people. Whoever means to stand upon the first of these rights must renounce all pretension to the last. - - - Posterity will one day ask with astonishmet what sort of people it could be among whom such preachers could find proselytes." (*J. S. Mill*, Principles, II, ch. 12.)

effect no savings. Is not this to act after the manner of the savages who cut down a fruit tree in order more conveniently to relish its fruit?[5]

Benjamin Franklin calls out to workmen and says: If any one tells you that you can become rich in any other way than through industry and frugality, do not listen to him; he is a poisoner! And, in fact, only those changes permanently improve the condition of the working classes which are useful to the whole people: enhanced productiveness of every branch of business in the country, increased capital, the growth (also relative) of the industrial middle classes, the greater education, strength of character, skill and fidelity in labor of workmen themselves. Much especially depends upon their foresight and self-control as regards bringing children into the world. Without this latter virtue even the favorable circumstances would be soon trifled away.[6]

---

[5] Compare *Morrison*, loc. cit. Quarterly Rev., Jan. 1872, 260. The English savings in the savings banks, between 1839 and 1846, increased yearly in amount only £1,408,630, and scarcely half of this came from wages-workmen in the narrower sense of the term. What the latter contribute to the fund for the old and sick is not really productive capital but only individually deferred consumption. Let us suppose that a man had an income of $3,000 a year, of which he laid out yearly $2,000 ($1,000 for wages, $1,000 for rent and anterest on capital), and that he capitalizes $1,000. It now this man were, either through philanthropy or in furtherance of socialism, to double the wages he paid, the result would not be detrimental to the economic interests of the whole country only on the supposition that working classes who received the increased wages should either save what he is no longer able to save, or that by inventions or greater personal skill etc., they should increase the national income.

[6] According to *Hildebrand's* Jahrbb., 1870, I, 435, 193, North American workmen, the quality of work being supposed the same, now accomplish from 20 to 30 per cent. less than before 1860. Thus, in 1858, in New York, a steam engine was manufactured for $23,000, in 2,323 work days. In 1869, a similar one was built for $40,000 in 3,538 days. In the former case, the manufacturer made a profit. In the latter, he lost $5,000.

John Stuart Mill, II, ch. 13. Against the "philanthropists" who find it hard to preach to the poor, the only efficacious means of improving their condition, *Dunoyer*, L. du T., IV, ch. 10, says: The rich *do* employ it, although they have much less need of it! Even *Marlo* admits that a guar-

CHAPTER IV.

INTEREST ON CAPITAL.

SECTION CLXXIX.

THE RATE OF INTEREST IN GENERAL.

Interest on capital,[1] or the price paid for the use of capital, should not be confounded with the price of money (§42); although in common life people so frequently complain of want of money where there is only a want of capital, and sometimes even when there is a superabundance of money.[2] This error is connected with the fact, that for the sake of convenience, loans of capital are so often effected in the form of

---

anty of the right to labor, without any measures to limit population, would, in a short time, and irredeemably lead the country to destruction. (Welt-ökonomie, I, 2, 357.) *von Thünen*, der isolirte Staat., II, 1, 81 ff., would take a leap out of the vicious circle that those who live by the labor of their hands can produce no rise in their wages, because they are too little educated to hold their increase properly in check; and that, on the other hand, they cannot give their children a decent education, because their wages are too low; by suggesting that educational institutions should be established by the state, and that these should elevate the subsequent generation of workmen intellectually.

[1] In the case of fixed capital, we generally speak of rent; in the case of circulating capital, of interest. If interest be conceived as a fractional part of the capital itself, the relation between the two is called "the rate of interest," most generally expressed as a percentage, and for one year.

[2] In Russia, great depreciation of the assignats, and yet the people com-

money and that they are always at least estimated in money; but neither of these things is essential.

In reality, however, we as seldom meet with interest[3] pure and simple, as we do with rent pure and simple. A person who works with his own capital can, at best, by a comparison with others, determine where, in the returns of his business, wages stop and interest begins.[4] And even in the loaning of capital, it depends largely on supply and demand, whether the creditor shall suffer a deduction in consequence of the absence of care and labor attending his gain, and whether the debtor, in order to get some capital at all, shall sacrifice a a part of the wages of his labor.[5] When Adam Smith assumes it to be the rule that the "profit of stock" is about twice as great as the "interest of money,"[6] it is evident that a considerable amount of what is properly wages or profit of

---

plained of a "want of money." (*Storch*, Handbuch, II, 15.) According to the San Francisco correspondent of the Times, Jan. 31, 1850, one per cent. a day discount was paid there! Compare *North*, Discourse on Trade, 11 seq.

[3] Gross interest and net interest corresponding to the difference between gross product and net product.

[4] This is the natural rent of capital in contradistinction to the stipulated rent. (*Rau*, Lehrbuch, I, § 223.)

[5] Thus, for instance, a so-called beginner who is conscious of possessing great working capacity, but who possesses for the time being little credit. *Tooke*, Considerations on the State of the Currency, 1826, distinguishes three kinds of capitalists: a, those who are averse to running any risk whatever or incurring any trouble, or are not able to incur any risk or trouble, for whom every great increase of the sinking fund lowers the rate of interest, and every war loan raises it; b, those who will run no risk, but who are not averse to the trouble of looking after their investments and of endeavoring to obtain a higher rate of interest; c, such as, to obtain a higher rate of interest, unhesitatingly risk something. Borrowers he divides thus: a, those who employ the borrowed capital and their own in such a way as to enable them to meet their obligations and besides to earn a reasonable profit; b, those who need others' capital to make up for the momentary failure of the productiveness of their own; lastly c, unproductive consumers.

[6] Wealth of Nat., I, ch. 9. The gross product of English cotton industry was, in 1832, estimated at £32,000,000, viz: £8,000,000 worth of material, £20,000,000 wages, £2,000,000 interest, £2,000,000 undertaker's profits. (*Schön*, Nat. Oek, 104.)

the employer (*Unternehmer*=undertaker) is included in the former.

Many businesses have the reputation of paying a very large interest on the capital employed in them, when in reality they only pay the undertaker of them wages unusually high as compared with the amount of capital employed in them. Apothecaries, for instance, are called in some places " ninety-niners," because it is said that they earn 99 per cent. To discover the error, it would be sufficient to inquire the rate of interest on the capital borrowed by the apothecary on hypothecation, for instance, to enlarge his industry. But on the other hand, such a man who has more than any other manufacturer to do with the most delicate materials and with them in greater variety, requires proportionately greater caution and knowledge. Besides, as the guardian of the health and life of so many, and even as the comptroller of physicians, he should be a man who inspired universal and unqualified confidence.[7]
By the rate of interest customary in a country, we mean the average rate of the interest on money-capital employed safely and without trouble.

SECTION CLXXX.

RATE OF INTEREST IN GENERAL.— ITS LEVEL.

Within the limits of the same national-economic territory, the different employments of capital tend uniformly to pay the

---

[7] *Adam Smith*, I, ch. 10, 1: where the reasons why a shop-keeper in a small town apparently gets a larger interest than one in a large city, and yet gets rich less frequently, are developed. The high profit made from industrial secrets, Adam Smith very correctly considers wages (I, ch. 7). Why not also that made by inn-keepers? (I, ch. 10, 1.) When the returns of a business differ according to circumstances which depend on the person of the conductor of the business himself, and may by him be transferred into another business, etc.; when the competition in it is determined by personal agreeableness or disagreeableness, it is evident that the larger returns are to be ascribed rather to the highness of wages than of the rate of interest. The

same rate of interest.[1] If one branch of business were much more profitable than another, it would be to the interest of the owners of capital to allow it to flow into the former and out of the latter, until a level was reached.[2]

The most noticeable exception to this rule is only an apparent one. The revenue *(Nutzung)* derived from the use of capital must not be confounded with its partial restoration.[3] Thus, for instance, the rent of a house, if the entire capital is not to be sooner or later consumed entirely, must embrace, besides a payment for the use of the house, a sum sufficient to defray the expenses of repairing it, and even to effect a gradual accumulation of capital for the purpose of rebuilding. The risk attending the investment of capital plays a very large part and must be taken into special consideration. If the risk in a business be so great that ten who engage in it succeed and ten fail, the returns of the former, which are more than double those usual in the country, in reality pay, when the ten who failed are taken into the account, only the rate of interest customary in the country. The risk may depend on the uncertainty of the person to whom the capital is confided;[4] on the uncertainty of the branch of business in which it is intended to employ it,[5] or on the uncertainty of the commercial

---

profit also which a second-hand hirer makes is wages. *(Riedel, Nat. Oek., 376.)*

[1] Compare *Harris*, Essay on Money and Coins, 13. *Per contra, Ganilh,* Dictionnaire analyt., 107. According to *Hermann*, Staatsw. Untersuchungen, 147, a product which withdraws an amount of capital $=a$ from the immediate use of its owner for n months must bring in in its price a surplus, over and above the outlay of capital, which would bear the same ratio to the profit from another product which employed an amount of capital $=b$, m months, that an bears to bm.

[2] The class of bankers etc. which precisely in the higher stages of civilization is one so highly developed, is called upon to adjust these differences.

[3] Life annuities and annual revenues, *à fonds perdu.*

[4] Hence, for instance, good men engaged in industrial pursuits who employ borrowed capital productively pay lower interest than idlers who are suspected of desiring only to spend it in dissipation. High house-rent usually paid by proletarians.

[5] Thus even in *Anderson's* time, it was necessary that the profit of one

situation in general; but especially may it depend on the uncertainty of the laws.[6] The temporary lying idle of capital, for instance, in dwelling houses at bathing places during the winter season, increases the rate of interest much more than it does the rate of wages in the corresponding case of the lying idle of labor; for the reason that there is something pleasurable in the repose of the latter. *(Senior.)* On the whole, the vanity of mankind has an effect upon the rate of interest similar to that which it has on the rate of wages. (See § 168.) It causes the small chances of loss to be estimated below their real value, and the extraordinary chances of gain above it.[7]

---

good year in the whale fishery should compensate for the damage caused by six bad ones. (Origin of Commerce, III, 184.) Slave-traders made their calculations to lose from three to four out of five expeditions. (Athenæum, May 6, 1848.) Similarly in smuggling and contraband. High rate of interest in gross adventure trade and bottomry contracts, frequently 30 and even 50 per cent.; in ancient Athens, for a simple voyage to the Black Sea, 36 per cent., while the rate of interest customary in the country was only from 12 to 18 per cent.; the interest paid by rented houses only 8⅓, and by land leases only 8 per cent. *(Böckh,* Staatshaushalt der Athener, I, 175 ff.; *Issaeus de Hagn.,* Hered., 293.) In Rome, before Justinian's time, maritime interest was unlimited. *(Hudtwalker,* De Foenore nautico Romano, 1810.) And so in the manufacture of powder, the frequent explosion of the mills has to be taken into account: in France and Austria, 16 per cent. per annum. *(Hermann,* Principien, 119.) Here belong those new enterprises which, when they succeed, pay a high profit. *Thaer,* in reference to this insurance-premium, says: if the capital employed to purchase a landed estate yields 4 per cent., the inventory *(Inventar)* should bring in at least 6, and the working capital 12 per cent. (Ration. Landwirthschaft.)

[6] Compare *supra,* § 91; *infra,* §§ 184, 188.

[7] Thus *Friedr. Perthes,* in *Pölitz,* Jarhbüchern, Jan., 1829, 42, thinks that the publication of scientific books in Germany, since 1800, caused, on the whole, a loss of capital. In the Canadian lumber trade, also, speculators, in the aggregate, lost more than was gained. Yet the business goes on because of its lottery character. *(John Stuart Mill,* II, ch. 15, 4.) In lotteries, it is certain that the aggregate of players lose. So too in speculation in English stocks, on account of the costs to be paid the state. In the case of frightful losses, which may afford food for the imagination, the reverse is found. Thus, for instance, in England, fire insurance, stamp duties included, was paid for at a rate five times as high as mathematical calculation showed it to be worth.

SECTION CLXXXI.

RULE OF INTEREST IN GENERAL.—CAUSES OF DIFFERENT RATES.

The real exceptions to the above rules are caused by a prevention of the leveling influx and outflow of capital. Among nations in a low stage of civilization, there is wont to be a multitude of legal impediments in this respect. The existence of a difference of classes, of privileged corporations etc., not only restrains the transition of workmen, but also of capital from one branch of industry to another. But even the mere routine of capitalists, that blind distrust of everything new so frequently characteristic of easily contented men, may produce the same result.[1] In the higher stages of civilization, patents for inventions and bank privileges, are causes of a lastingly higher rate of interest than is usual in the country.[2] Finally, since in many enterprises only a large amount of capital can be used at all, or at least with most advantage, the aggregation of which from many small sources is ordinarily much more difficult than the division of a large one into small fractional parts; the rate of interest for very small amounts of capital, and especially in the higher stages of civilization, is usually lower than that of large amounts of capital. We need only mention interest paid by savings-bank investments.[3]

If circulating capital has been changed into fixed capital, its yield will depend upon the price of the particular goods in the production of which it has been made to serve. Com-

---

(*Senior*, Outlines, 212 ff.) Much here depends naturally on national character, which, in England for instance, or in the United States, is much more adventurous than in many quiet regions of continental Europe.

[1] Thus the rate of interest in the Schappach valley remained for a long time much lower than in the vicinity, for the reason that the peasantry who had grown rich through the lumber trade possessed notwithstanding little of the spirit of enterprise. (*Rau*, Lehrbuch, I, § 233.)

[2] Here the law produces a species of artificial fixation.

[3] *Von Mangoldt*, Unternehmergewinn, 150.

SEC. CLXXXI.] INTEREST — DIFFFRENT RATES. 103

pared with the cost of restoration of fixed capital, this yield may, in a favorable case, constitute an extraordinarily high rate of interest, in an unfavorable a very low one; and the former of these two extremes has a greater chance of being realized, in proportion as it is difficult to multiply fixed capital of the same kind; the latter, the more exclusively it can be employed in only one kind of production, and the longer time it takes to be used up by wear.[4] When fixed and circulating capital coöperate in production, the latter, because it can be more easily withdrawn, but also more easily replaced, first takes out its own profit, that is the profit usual in the country and leaves all the rest to the former. When fixed capital is sold, practically no attention is paid to what it originally cost. The purchaser pays only for the prospective revenue it will yield, which he capitalizes at the rate of interest usual in the country. The seller henceforth looks

---

[4] In other words, the more fixed they are Thus, for instance, dwelling houses in declining cities, canals etc. which have been supplanted by better commercial routes; or again, the shafts and stulms of a mine which has been abandoned. When Versailles ceased to be a royal residence, the value of inhabited houses sank to one-fourth of what it had been. *(Zinkeisen* in *Raumer's* histor. Taschenbuch, 1837, 426.) A rate of interest greater than that usual in a country is seldom found where freedom of competition prevails, since it is necessary there to distinguish between rent and interest on capital. When in an open city, the capital employed in the construction of dwelling houses *detractis detrahendis* pays 8 per cent., while the rate of interest customary in the country is only 4 per cent., the supply of houses will grow continually greater. Only the difficulties in the way of transferring capital from one business to another could here retard the leveling process, which where the political prospect for instance was bad, might last a long time — one of the principal reasons why, in 1848, the rent of houses declined much less than their purchase prices. The conjuncture was not serious enough to prevent the increase of population; but it entirely stopped the building of new houses. On the other hand, a bridge or railroad company may maintain a high rate of profit because competition cannot exist in the face of the great expense such enterprises require; but especially because the party who has here the advantage of priority may lower the price of transportation to such a point as to entirely discourage his rival. Compare *Hermann*, Staatsw. Untersuchungen, 145 ff. Interesting example of the London gas and water companies in *Senior*, Outlines, 101.

upon his gain as an accretion to capital, his loss as a diminution of capital, and no longer as high or low interest.[5] That accretion might be considered the wages, paid once for all, for the intelligent labor which governed the original investment of the capital, and *vice versa*.

SECTION CLXXXII.

VARIATIONS OF THE RATE OF DISCOUNT.

The fact that in commerce etc., the rate of interest on capital loaned for short periods of time (discount) is subject to great fluctuations, while the mortgage rate of interest, for instance, remains the same throughout, depends on similar causes.[1] Yet there are contingencies in trade which, when taken immediate advantage of, promise enormous profits, but

---

[5] Thus, for instance, Leipzig-Dresden railroad stock cost originally 100 thalers per share, and was taken at that rate. The yearly dividends amounted in 1856 to 13 thalers; that is, 13 per cent. for the original stockholders. But a person who on the 30th September, 1856, paid 285 thalers for a share, received but an interest of 4½ per cent. on his capital. It is characteristic, how *Serra*, Sulle Cause etc., 1613, I, 9, calls the high and the low rate of interest *prezzo basso e alto delle entrate*.

[1] *Nebenius*, Oeff. Credit, I, 74 ff. Thus, Hamburg discount towards the end of the last century fluctuated between 2½ and 12 per cent., while the capital invested in agriculture brought an interest almost invariably of 4 per cent. (*Büsch*, Geldumlauf, VI, 4, 19.) At the same time, in Pennsylvania, the usual rate of interest was 6 per cent. per annum, and the rate of discount not unfrequently from 2 to 3 per cent a month. (*Ebeling* Geschichte und Erdbeschreib. von Amerika, IV, 442.) During the crisis of 1837, it happened that ¼ per cent. a day was paid. (*Rau*, Archiv. N. F. IV, 382.) In the Prussian ports, during the crisis of 1810, it is said that in July the rate of discount was 2½ per cent. a month. (*Tooke*, Thoughts and Details, I, 111.) In Hamburg and Frankfort the rate of discount rose in the spring of 1848, but declined in June to 2; until December it was 1¼, until the summer of 1849, ¾ per cent. (Tüb. Zeitschr., 1856, 95.) Rate of discount in France, about 1798, at least 2 per cent. a month. (*Büsch*, loc. cit., IV, 52.) Half a year previous, capital employed in the purchase of land paid an interest of from 3 to 4 per cent. Legal interest was 5 per cent.; discount, at most, 6 per cent.; in very prosperous times 8–9 per cent. (*Forbonnais*, Recherches et Considérations, I, 372.)

which may disappear within a month; risks of the most dangerous kind which can be conjured only by the immediate aid of capital. These are both sufficient grounds of a high rate of interest. Again, there are times of the profoundest calm in the commercial world, during which capitalists are perfectly willing to make loans at a low rate of interest, provided they are sure to be able to get back their capital with the first favorable breeze that blows. Agriculture is too immovable to come opportunely to the assistance of capitalists, here as a receiver and there as a loaner of capital. As the cycle of its operations is gone through usually only in a series of years, sudden influxes or outflows of capital would cause it the greatest injury.[2]

SECTION CLXXXIII.

EFFECT OF INCREASED DEMAND FOR LOANS.

The price paid for the use of capital naturally depends on the relation between the supply and demand, and especially of circulating capital. The increase of the supply need no more unconditionally lower the rate of interest than the price of any other commodity. If 50 hunters kill 1,000 deer yearly, and give 100 deer per annum as interest to the capitalists who provided them with ammunition and rifles, a second capitalist with an equal number of rifles and an equal amount of ammunition may appear on the scene. If now 2,000 deer a year are killed, the rate of profit of the capitalists will probably remain the same. But if the woods are not rich enough in game for this, or the hunters not numerous enough, too indolent, or too easily satisfied, the rate of interest falls.[1]

---

[2] Remarkable case in *Cicero's* time in which bribery, carried on on a large scale, raised the rate of discount from 4 to 8 per cent. *Cicero* ad. Quint. M, 15; ad.Att. IV, 15.

[1] It is one of *Ricardo's* (Principles, ch. 21) chief merits, that he demonstrated the groundlessness of the opinion that the mere increase of capital must, on account of the competition of capitalists, lower the rate of interest,

The difficulties in the way of the desired increase of capital are here of great importance. The smaller the surplus over and above their absolutely necessary wants, which the people produce, the less their tendency to make savings, the less the inclination to capitalization; and the less the security afforded by the law is, the higher must the rate of interest be to induce people to face these difficulties. We may very well transfer the idea of cost of production to this condition.[2]

The demand for capital depends, on the one hand, on the number and the solvability of borrowers, especially of non-capitalists like land-owners and workmen; and, on the other hand, on the value in use of the capital itself. Hence the growth of population is, other circumstances being the same, a means to raise the rate of interest; because it infallibly increases the competition of borrowers of capital, even if the increased rate must take place at the expense of wages. The solvability or paying capacity of the land-owning class as contrasted with the capitalists can, in the last analysis, depend only on the extent and fertility of their lands and on the quality of their agricultural husbandry; the solvability or paying capacity of the working class, only on their skill and industry. Where these have grown, an increase of the rate of interest may be found in connection with an absolute growth of the rate of wages and of rent, because the aggregate income of the nation has become greater.

The value in use of capital, which is more homogeneous in proportion as it has the character of circulating capital *(res fungibiles)* is, in most instances, synonymous with the skill of the working class, and the richness of the natural forces connected with it. The deciding element, therefore, is the yield of the least productive investment of capital which must be made to employ all the capital seeking employment. This least productive employment of capital must

---

as is assumed by *Adam Smith*, I, ch. 9, *J. B. Say*, Traité, II, 8, and others. Compare also, *John Stuart Mill*, Principles, IV, ch. IV, 1.

[2] *Storch*, Handbuch, II, 20.

determine the rate of interest customary in a country precisely as cost of production on the most unfavorable land determines the price of corn (§§ 110, 150), and as the result of the work of the laborer last employed does the rate of wages. (§ 165.)

What portion of the total national income, after deduction is made of rent, shall go to the capitalists and what portion to the working class, will depend mainly on whether the capitalists compete more greedily for labor or the laboring classes for capital.[3] If, for instance, capital should increase more rapidly than population, there must be a relative increase in wages, and *vice versa*.[4] This is true especially of that peculiar

---

[3] Frequent withdrawals of capital must, other circumstances being the same, temporarily raise the rate of interest. In the long run, however, the question is decided by this: whether public opinion considers labor a greater sacrifice than the saving of capital. Compare *Roesler*, loc. cit., 8.

[4] Compare *Hermann*, Staatsw. Unters., 240 ff. Very much depends on whether the *new* increased consumption (of workmen when wages are rising, of capitalists when wages are declining) is of goods which are mainly the product of large capital, large factories etc., or chiefly of common labor. *(von Mangoldt*, Grundriss, 155 seq.) When *Adam Smith* suggests that the relation between wages and the profit of capital is determined by this: whether there is a market demand for more work or more commodities, for more "work to be done" or "work done" (I, ch. 7), he is, spite of appearances, very unsatisfactory. *Malthus* distinguishes a restrictive principle of the rate of interest, viz.: the return made to the least productive agricultural capital, and a regulative one, viz.: the reciprocal relation between demand and supply of capital and labor. (Principles, ch. 5, sec. 4.) *Ricardo*, ch. 6, makes the profit of capital at all times and in every country depend on the quantity of labor which it is necessary to expend on the land which pays no rent, in order to satisfy the wants of workmen — a very correct theory.

Only *Ricardo* himself (ch. 21) and his school postulate altogether too unconditionally that their wants would always coincide with the minimum of maintenance or support. Thus, for instance, *J. S. Mill*, Principles, IV, ch. 3, 4. However, *Mill* instead of *Ricardo's* "wages" employs the better expression, "cost of labor." *Senior* teaches that the distribution of the aggregate result between laborers and capitalists depends on the anterior course of both classes: on the value of the capital previously employed by capitalists to produce the means of satisfying working men's wants, and on the number of workmen which the previous laboring population have brought into existence. (Outlines, 188 ff.) Concerning *von Thünen's* vain attempt at

kind of higher wages which we shall (§ 145, ff.) designate as the "undertaker's profit." The smaller the number of persons engaged in enterprises is, in comparison with the number of retired persons who live on their rents, incomes etc., the smaller is the portion of the so-called net profit of enterprise the latter must be satisfied with in the shape of interest.[5]

SECTION CLXXXIV.

HISTORY OF THE RATE OF INTEREST.

Among barbarous nations, the loaning of capital is wont to happen so seldom, and to be limited so strictly to near relations, that it does not yet occur to any one to stipulate for a regular compensation therefor.[1] But, however, when they pass from this state to interest proper, the rate must be, of course, very high.[2] The premium for insurance is here very

---

a general formula, see *supra*, § 173. *Fourier's* idea that $\frac{1}{12}$ of the product should be distributed among labor, $\frac{4}{12}$ among talent, and $\frac{7}{12}$ among capital, is entirely baseless. (N. Monde, 309 ff.) *Considérant*, Destinée sociale, 192 ff. As early a writer as *H. Boden*, Fürstliche Machtkunst, 1700 and 1740, 42, came strikingly near the truth. According to him, a low rate of interest is produced by four circumstances: surplus capital, a dearth of landed estates, a want of credit and exact justice, and lastly, the heavy taxation of capital.

[5] Thus, in the last century, Spanish capitalists loaned capital readily to sure commercial companies, at from 2 to 3 per cent. per annum. (*Bourgoing*, Tableau de l'Espagne, I, 248.) The contemporary low rates of interest in Hannover, *Büsch*, Geldumlauf, VI, 4, 12, endeavors to explain by the absence of opportunities for investment, as no one dared to loan to any extent on fiefs or on the land of the peasantry, and because there was no law governing bills of exchange etc.

[1] *Tacit.*, Germ., 26; *Marculf*, Form., 18, 25 ff., 35; *Savigny*, Ueber das altrömische Schuldrecht, in the transactions of the Berlin Academy, 1833, 78 seq.

[2] According to the Lex Visig., V, 5, § 8, the maximum rate of interest allowed on loans of money was 12½ per cent., and on other *res fungibiles*, 50 per cent. From the 12th to the 14th century, the Lombards and the Jews in France and England took generally (?) 20 per cent. a year. (*Anderson*, Origin of Commerce, a., 1300.) Philip V. of France, in 1311, fixed the rate of interest at the fairs in Champagne at 15 per cent. (a species of discount) at **most, and** at a maximum everywhere of 20 per cent. (Ordonnances de la

great, the possibility and inclination to accumulate capital exceedingly small. Even of the existing supply of capital, a

---

France, I, 484, 494, 508.) The legal rate of interest in Verona, in 1288, was fixed at a maximum of 12½ per cent.; in Modena, 1270, at 20 per cent. (*Muratori*, Antiquitt. Ital., I, 894); in Bresica, 1268, at 10 per cent. (*v. Raumer*, Geschichte der Hohenstaufen, V, 395 ff.) Frederick II. wished to reduce it to 10 per cent. for Naples, but failed. (*Bianchini*, Storia delle Finanze di Nap., I, 299.) The tables of *Cibrario*, Economia polit. del medio Evo., III, 380, for 1306–1399, show for upper Italy interest to have been at 20, 15, 14, 10, and also 5½ per cent. About 1430 the Florentines, in order to moderate the enormously high rate of interest, called Jews to their city, and the latter promised not to charge over 20 per cent. (*Cibrario*, III, 318.) In the Rhine country, the Kowerzens, during the 14th century, took from 60 to 70 per cent., for which they had, however, to pay a heavy tax to the archbishop. (*Bodmann*, Rh. Alterthümer, 716.) Of Jewish maximum rates of interest, in the 14th and 15th centuries, see *Stobbe*, Juden in Deutschland während des M. Alters, 103, 110, 234 seq.; *Hegel*, Strassb. Chr., II, 977, 984.

The rate of interest usual in these countries must not however be calculated from the data furnished by these usurious rates and fixed rates of interest, simply. In Germany, the rate of interest promised by princes in the 13th and 14th centuries was usually 10 per cent. The Frankfort municipal loans made by Jews in the 14th century bore interest at the rate of 9, 11⅔, 13, 18, 26, and even 45 per cent. (*Kriegk*, F.'s Bürgerzwiste, 343, 539.) The rate of interest in the purchase of annuities continually declined between 1300 and 1500, especially in the time of the emancipation of manual laborers. Old Base documents give, between 1284 and 1580, as the highest rate, 11¾, and as the least, 5 per cent. The latter became more and more usual later, especially in the sale of house-rents (*Hauszins*), so that in 1841 all annuities (*Renten*) might be canceled by a payment of their amounts multiplied by 20. Until the beginning of the 15th century, in the city, the rule was 6 to 7 per cent.; outside of it, 8 to 10 per cent. (*Arnold*, Geschichte des Eigenthums in den deutschen Städten, 222 seq., 227 seq.) According to the Bremen Jahrb. of 1784, 164 seq., the rate of interest in the case of *Handfesten*, in 1295, =10 per cent., gradually sank: in the 15th century it was never over 6⅔; after 1450, generally 5; in 1511 only 4 per cent. In 1441 ff., in Augsburg, people were satisfied with a business profit of 7⅔ per cent., while the usual rate of interest paid by house-rent etc. was 5 per cent. (*Hegel*, Augsb. Chr., II, 134 seq., 157.) Handsome tables in the rate of interest in the purchase of annuities for all Germany, from 1215 to 1620, give as the rule, 7 to 10, scarcely ever over 15 per cent., in *M. Neumann*, Geschichte des Wuchers, 266 ff. For the upper Rhine, compare *Mone's* Zeitschr., 26 ff. Among the Fathers of the councils of Constance and Basil 5 per cent. was considered equitable. Compare *F. Hammerlin*, 1389–1457, De Emtione et

great part remains idle, because the faculty and the institutions necessary to concentrate it and permit it to flow are wanting. (§ 43.) The unskillfulness of labor is more than overcome by the excess of fertile and naturally productive land, of rich sites still unoccupied, the cream of which, as it were, needs only to be culled. Population is indeed sparse, but the usually prevailing absence of freedom of the lower classes prevents wages claiming the full benefit of competition.[3] This last circumstance is especially important.[4] For a given amount of the national income and of rent, every depression of wages must obviously raise the rate of interest, and every enhancement of wages lower it.[5]

Venditione unius pro viginti. Russian interest at 40 per cent., according to the laws of Jaroslaw (ob. 1054 after Christ). *Karamsin*, Russ. Gesch., II, 47.

[3] The high rate of interest in many countries at present may be thus accounted for. In the United States, during the last century, less than 8 per cent. was seldom paid. (*Ebeling*, III, 152.) According to *M. Chevalier*, Lettres sur l'Amérique du Nord, 1836, I, 59, the rate of interest in Pennsylvania was 6, in New York, 7, in most of the slave states, 8–9; in Louisiana, 10 per cent. In South Australia (1850) it was, with full security, 15–20 per cent. (*Reimer*, Südaustralien, 39.) In the West Indies, about the end of the last century, a strong negro might produce a revenue equal to one-fourth of his capital value. (*B. Edwards*, History of the British West Indies, II, 129.) In Brazil, the lowest rate of interest was at 9 per cent., and 12–18 per cent. was nothing unusual. (*Wappäus*, M. and S. Amerika, 1871, 1413.) In Cuba, for the government 10, for private parties, 12 to 16 per cent. (*Humboldt*, Cuba, I, 231.) In Potosi, in 1826, Temple got 30 per cent. interest on chattel mortgage, and from 2 to 4 per cent a month was offered, while the rate of interest in Buenos Ayres amounted to 15 per cent per annum. (*Temple*, Travels, II, 217.) In Russia, *Storch*, Haudbuch, I, 262, speaks of 8-10 per cent. According to *v. Haxthausen*, it was, in the interior, never less than from 8 to 12 per cent per annum; at Kiew and Odessa, 1¼, 1½ and 2 per cent. per month. (Studien, I, 58, 467; II, 495.) In Greece, the rate of interest on first mortgages is at least 10, on a second, 15–18 per cent. (Ausland, 1843, No. 82.)

[4] *Nebenius*, Oeff. Credit, I, 55.

[5] Only in this particular instance is what *Ricardo* so frequently insists on true, viz: that the rate of wages can be increased only at the expense of the profit of capital, and *vice versa*.

SECTION CLXXXV.

HISTORY OF THE RATE OF INTEREST.—INFLUENCE OF AN ADVANCE IN CIVILIZATION.

With an advance in civilization, the rate of interest is wont to decline.[1][2] One of the chief causes of this phenomenon is

---

[1] *Proudhon's* idea, that this decline might at last bring about a total abolition of interest, is based on the same error as this other: that since a man may keep diminishing his per diem quantum of food, he might finally dispense with food altogether. *Proudhon's* Banque du Peuple — People's Bank — which, by gradually diminishing the interest on its loans to the minimum cost of its administration, should compel other capitalists to follow its example.

[2] Thus, in England, by virtue of 37 Henry III., c. 9, the legal interest was = 10 per cent.; by 21 James I, c. 17 = 8; about 1651 = 6 per cent. (confirmed in 1660); by 12 Anne, ch. 16 = 5 per cent. In the time of George II., where the security was good, only 3 per cent. was, as a rule, paid. In France, the legal rate of interest, at the beginning of the 16th century, was $\frac{1}{10}$ of the capital; after 1657, $\frac{1}{14}$; 1601 *(Sully)*, $\frac{1}{16}$; 1634 *(Richelieu)*, $\frac{1}{18}$; 1665 *(Colbert)*, $\frac{1}{20}$. Compare *Forbonnais* Recherches et Considérations, I, 48, 225, 385 ff. It continued at this rate of 5 per cent. with short interruptions until the revolution. (*Warnkönig*, Franz. Staats. und Rechtsgeschichte, II, 588 seq.)

The rates of interest in Russia, in the 16th century, had already declined to 20 per cent. *(Herberstein,* Reise, 41 ff.; *Karamsin,* Russ. Geschichte, VII, 169.) In Holland, in 1623, it was estimated that land purchases paid 3 per cent.; hypothecations, 4 to 6; deposits, 5 to 6; a flourishing business, 10 per cent. Compare *Usselinx* in *Laspeyres,* Geschichte der volkswirthschaftl. Anschauungen der Niederländer, 76. About 1660, the rate of interest usual in Italy and Holland was at most 3 per cent. (in war times, 4); in France, 7; in Scotland, 10; in Ireland, 12; in Spain, 10 to 12; in Turkey, 20 per cent. *(Sir J. Child,* Discourse on Trade, French translation, 75 ff.) Side by side with 6 per cent. as the rate of interest in England, it was (a little later) 10 in Ireland. *Petty,* Political Anatomy of Ireland, 74.

The same course of things is to be observed in ancient times. In *Solon's* time, and again in that of *Lysias,* it was 18 per cent. *(Böckh,* Staatshaushalt der Athener, I, 143 ff.) I am of opinion that the rate of interest declined during this long interval, but rose again in consequence of the Peloponnesian war. Among friends, in the time of *Demosthenes,* 10 per cent. (adv. Onetor., I, 386.) *Aristotle,* Rhet., III, 10, mentions 12 per cent., which *Aeschines,* adv. Ctes., 104, and *Demosthenes,* adv. Aph., I, 820, 824, call low. The rate of commercial interest in Egypt (146 before Christ) seems to have been 12 per cent.

the necessity, as population and consumption increase, to employ capital in the fertilization of less productive land, and in less profitable investments.³ An increase in the stock of money does not necessarily depreciate the rate of interest. If this increase comes in connection with a corresponding depreciation of the individual pieces of metal, it cannot be said that the nation has thereby become richer in capital. All that would be required in such case is only a greater number of pounds of gold or silver, or more paper bills to represent the same capital.⁴ Only during the transition-period, during which the depreciation of money is still incomplete, is the rate of interest wont to be lowered; and all the more, since loaned capital is generally offered and sought after in the form of money.⁵ ⁶

---

per annum. (*Letronne*, Recompense promise à celui etc., 1833, 7.) Contemporaneously in Rome, a similar rate of interest must have been considered usurious. (*Cicero*, ad. Att., I, 12.) Under the emperor *Claudius*, 6 per cent. (*Columella*, De Re rust., III, 3.) *Justinian* allowed to *personae illustres* 4 per cent. per annum. (L. 26 Cod., IV, 32.)

³ A Huron with his bow and arrow kills 12 pieces of game; the European, with a much better capital, his rifle, only 5. Compare *v. Schözer*, Anfangsgründe, I, 28. *Malthus*, Principles, ch. 5. According to *Ricardo*, ch. 6, the decline of the rate of interest because of the necessity of carrying on agriculture under harder conditions, must make all capital of which raw material forms a part more valuable; while the possessors of money-capital particularly find no indemnification. *Wakefield*, England and America, 1853, accounts for it by saying that production, besides the coöperation of capital and labor, needs "a field of employment;" and *Bastiat*, Harmonies, ch, 5, 13, by saying that with the advance of civilization, the results of former services lose in value as compared with later ones, because performed under less favorable circumstances.

⁴ *D. Hume*, Discourses No. 4 On Interest.. Per contra, see *Locke*, Considerations of the Consequences of the Lowering of Interest; *Law*, sur l'Usage des Monaies, 1697 (Daire); and *Montesquieu*, Esprit des Lois XXII, 6. *Cantillon* draws a very nice distinction: If the increased amount of money in a state comes into the hands of loaners, it will decrease the current rate by increasing the number of loaners; but if it comes into the hands of consumers, the rate rises, because now the demand for commodities is so much greater. (Nature du Commerce, 284.)

⁵ The reviews in the Göttingen G. Anz., 1777, and of *von Iselin*, in the Ephemeriden der Menschheit, II, 170 ff., 177, question *Adam Smith's* (Wealth

SEC. CLXXXV.] HISTORY OF RATE OF INTEREST. 113

The decline of the rate of interest generally shows itself earliest in the large cities, which are everywhere the national organ, in which the good and bad symptoms of later civilization may be soonest observed.[7]

Moreover, the condition of capitalists is not necessarily made worse by a decline of the rate of interest. It is possible that, for a long time, the increase of capital should continue more rapid than the decrease of interest for each individual. (If, indeed, the aggregate interest of capital should become absolutely smaller, there is always a pleasant remedy available, viz.: to consume a part of the capital!) But, however, a decline of the rate of interest is nearly always followed by increased activity on the part of capitalists; and they come to

---

of Nat., II, ch. 4) entirely too positive denial of the influence of the American production of gold and silver on the diminution of the rate of interest, a view which was shared also by *Turgot*, Form. et Distr., § 78. See a beautiful comparison between a declining of the prices of the currency which promotes production, with the phenomena attending the growth of a tree, in *Schäffle*, N. Œk., II, Aufl., 249.

[6] Thus the rate of interest in Rome fell from 12 to 4 per cent. when Octavian suddenly threw the treasures of conquered Egypt upon the market, and the price of commodities only doubled. When later commerce had divided this amount of money among the provinces, it rose again. (*Sueton.*, Oct., 41; *Dio C.*, LI, 17, 21; Oros, IV, 19.) *Law's* emissions of paper, in colossal amounts, depressed the rate of interest to 1¼ per cent. (*Dutot*, Réflexions, 990 — Daire.) But as soon as the paper money had lost its value, the former condition returned. Similar observations in Rio de Janeiro: *Spix* und *Martius*, Reise, I, 131.

[7] While in Paris the capital safely invested paid 2½ to 3 per cent., 57 out of 61 *conseils généraux* declared, in 1845, that the rate of interest on hypothecations, in their departments, was always over 5 per cent.; 17 estimated it at an average of from 6 to 7 per cent.; 12 at from 7 to 10; some said 12 and 15, and even 22 per cent. in the case of small sums loaned for a short time. (*Chegarny*, Rapport au Nom de la Commission de la Réforme hypoth., 29 Avril, 1851.) In Russia, at the beginning of this century, the rate of interest in the Baltic provinces was 6 per cent.: in Moscow, 10; in Taurien, 25; in Astracan, 30 per cent. (*v. Schlözer*, Anfangsgründe I, 102.) In 1750, in Naples, the rate of interest was from 3 to 5 per cent., in the provinces from 7 to 9 per cent. (*Galiani*, della Moneta, IV, 1.) In Trajan's time in Rome, 6; in Bithynia, 12 per cent. (*Plin.*, Epist. VII, 18; X, 62.)

the resolve to retire later to enjoy the results of their previous labors. In Holland, after the time of Louis XIV., no branch of business was wont to pay more than from two to three per cent. In the case of the purchase of land, no one calculated on more than two per cent. Hence it was scarcely possible for small capitalists there to live on their interest; and the good sense of the people so well adapted itself to this state of things that to live in leisure on one's rents was considered a not entirely honorable mode of existence.[8] The lower the rate of interest, the larger, in highly civilized countries, is the stock on hand of cash apt to become, for the reason that business men then hope to gain more by the advantages of cash payments than by the saving of interest.[9][10]

SECTION CLXXXVI.

HISTORY OF THE RATE OF INTEREST.—CAUSES OF A HIGH RATE IN THRIVING COMMERCIAL NATIONS.

There are, however, even where a people's economy is in a flourishing condition, many obstacles which cause the decline of the rate of interest to take a retrogressive course, or which at least may delay it for a time.

---

[8] *Delacourt* Aanwysing, 1669, I, 7. *Temple*, Observations on the U. Provinces, ch. 6, Works L. 1854. Even *Descartes* says of Holland's *ubi nemo non exercet mercaturam*. Compare per contra, *II. Grotius*, Jus Belli et Pacis, II, 12, 22. Very large capitalists, in *Smith's* time, certainly lived generally on the interest of their money: Richesse de Hollande, II, 172. In England, at the present day, likewise, a vast number of persons who live on the interest of their money, occasionally take part in the speculation in commodities; which explains why so-called commercial crises are incomparably more extensive there, and reach incomparably deeper, than in Germany. Similarly, according to *Conring*, De Commerciis, 1666, c. 36, in Venice and Genoa.

[9] Hence the larger cash balances in England at the present day, which, however, are not kept in the form of coin, but of bank notes and bankers' deposits.

[10] As to how every frugal capitalist works to the injury of capitalists as a class, but to his own advantage, by lowering the rate of interest and increasing the rate of wages, see *Senior*, Outlines, 188 ff.

To this category belong all the modifications of a nation's economy alluded to in § 183.[1] Among them, therefore, is every extension of the limits of productive land. Let us suppose a nation which, its capital and labor remaining the same in every respect, should suddenly double its territory. The less productive places where investments were made in the old province are now abandoned, and labor and capital emigrate to the new. The result is, of course, an increase of the aggregate national income, and, at the same time, a decrease of rent. (§ 157.) Hence, the interest on capital and the wages of labor, taken together, must greatly increase. Which of these two branches shall profit most and longest by the increase will depend upon whether capital or the number of workmen increases most rapidly.[2] A similar effect must be produced when, by changes or modifications in the commercial situation, in the tariff etc., a nation is enabled to obtain the means of subsistence at cheaper rates from more fertile and less settled countries.[3]

---

[1] *Wolkoff* very well shows that the economic progress of mankind is effected partly by the improvement of production, and partly by saving. The former increases the rate of interest, the latter lowers it. (Lectures, 182, 189. Compare *supra*, § 45.)

[2] Thus the rate of interest in Russia rose, after Catherine II. had conquered the provinces situated on the Black Sea. *(Storch*, Handbuch, II, 34.) The same is still more strikingly apparent in the judicious planting of agricultural colonies.

[3] Abolition of the English corn laws! Foreign commerce when very advantageous, always adds to the well-being of the people; to the rate of interest, however, only to the extent that articles which are calculated to satisfy the wants of the working class become cheaper in consequence; and this in turn lowers the rate of wages. Let us suppose that a country had hitherto purchased yearly 10,000 barrels of wine for $1,000,000. It might now happen that, in consequence of an advantageous commercial treaty, for instance, the 10,000 barrels might be obtained for $500,000. If, after this, wine-drinkers want to spend $1,000,000 for wine as they did before, they of course double their consumption of wine, but the rate of interest remains unchanged. If, on the other hand, they leave their consumption of wine where it was before and apply the saved half million to effect an increased demand for home products, the capital required for this production is set free at the same time.

The introduction of better methods of production has very different immediate consequences, according as these methods affect the commodities which minister to the wants peculiar to workmen as a class, or do not. Let us suppose, as a first case, that the cost of ordinary clothing is reduced one half by reason of newly discovered material, better machines etc. As in the case of the whole people, so also in that of the owners of capital as consumers, there is, in consequence, an addition to their enjoyment of life. Their interest as well as their capital, compared with clothing material, would have become more valuable. But the relation between capital and interest, that is, the rate of interest, could not be directly changed. (Compare *infra*, note 3.) Only when the working class employ their materially increased wages to increase population; when in consequence hereof, their wages, estimated in money, again decline beyond what it was before; when, therefore, the price of a given quantity of labor declines, does the rate of interest rise, although a portion of that which the workmen have lost may be added to rent on account of the increased population?[4][5] If the applicability of the new method of production is confined to articles of luxury used by the upper classes, for instance to fine lace, the rate of interest

---

Hence, the relation between the supply and demand for capital has not changed, abstraction made of certain difficulties in the transaction. Compare *Ricardo*, Principles, ch. 7, rectifying *Adam Smith*, Wealth of Nat., I, ch. 9.

[4] An increase in the rate of interest caused by a diminution in the rate of wages does not last long. Capital now increases more rapidly, and the increase is accompanied by an increased demand for labor. If, in the mean time, workmen have become accustomed to a lower standard of life, the increasing wages are followed by an increase of population: then the necessity of having recourse to the cultivation of land of a worse quality is an additional cause of a decreasing rate of interest. (Edinb. Rev., March, 1824, 26.)

[5] According to this, it is easy to tell what influence the increasing skill or activity of the working class (for instance by a decrease in the number of holidays, coöperation of wife and child) must have. Where there has been no accompanying and corresponding elevation of the standard of life, and of the want of the class, the gain soon falls to the lot of the capitalists or landowners.

usual in the country will be affected thereby only to the extent that through the medium of commerce such products are exchanged with foreign nations against commodities consumed by the working classes. But there are very few improvements in production which have not led to a greater cheapness of those things which satisfy the wants of the working class; and this is especially clear in the improvements in the means of transportation so usual in our day.

However, the increase of fixed capital, such as machines, railroads etc., once they are completed, may, at first, cause a depression of the rate of wages, as well as an enhancement of the rate of interest; the former from the fact that a number of workmen is thereby, at least temporarily, thrown out of employment; the latter because the conversion of so much circulating into fixed capital must diminish the supply of the former.[6]

A second class of obstacles consists in the diminution of the supply of capital. War, for instance, always causes such a destruction of capital, and at the same time for the most part renders the reproduction of capital more difficult to such a degree that the rate of interest is wont to rise greatly.[7] Something similar is true of other great catastrophes and of extravagance on a large scale.[8] Every state loan, whether in-

---

[6] See the very clear but not entirely complete discussion in *John Stuart Mill*, Principles, IV, ch. 3 ff. When new railways, machines etc., before they are complete, simultaneously increase the rate of interest and the rate of wages, and even sometimes rent, although they do not immediately increase the national income in any way, the phenomena are to be explained, not by a distribution of income, but as the result of an advance of capital made.

[7] Compare *supra*, § 184. The rise of the rate of interest in Basil, between 1370 and 1393, *Arnold* (loc. cit.) accounts for by the wars and defeats of the upper German cities. Similarly in Zürich, 1457. (*Joh. Müller*, Schweizer Geschichte, IV, 211.) During the time immediately following the Spanish war of succession, the *usuriers les plus modérés* in France got 12–15 per cent. a year. (*Dutot*, Réflexions, 1866.) In Russia the rate of interest, after the war of 1805–15, rose by 4–5 per cent. (*Storch*, Handbuch, 35 seq.) Per contra, *Nebenius*, Oeff. Credit., 70 seq.

[8] Thus the Hamburg conflagration, combined with the bad harvests of 1841,

tended for direct consumption or to procure capital for use (*Nutzkapitalien*), decreases the supply of circulating capital which most directly determines the market rate of interest.[9][10]

SECTION CLXXXVII.

HISTORY OF THE RATE OF INTEREST.—EMIGRATION OF CAPITAL.

Midway between these classes of obstacles lies the very usual proceeding of highly civilized nations whose rate of interest is low, to transfer their capital into countries with a higher rate of interest, where the production of raw material is predominant.[1] This is most thoroughly accomplished by the

---

raised the rate of interest in Mecklenburg for a long series of years. Similarly in Würtemburg, the many bad harvests from 1845 to 1853, which are said to have caused a deficiency of 50,000,000 florins. Tübinger Zeitschr., 1856, 568.)

[9] In bad times, state loans are usually effected at a disproportionally high rate of interest. This also operates momentarily on the general rate of interest, to the injury of persons engaged in business enterprises; who, by the very fact of the withdrawal of so much capital, become involved in an unfavorable competition. In the long run, indeed, the high or low rates of interest paid by national debts, in so far as the creditor cannot demand reimbursement, has no influence on the rate of interest usual in the country. Such debts as cannot be declared due assume the character of stationary capital, the value in exchange of which is determined by their yearly return, capitalized at the rate of interest usual in the country. (*Hermann*, Staatswirthschatliche Untersuch., 223.)

[10] The coöperation of most of the causes above mentioned raised the English rate of interest which had sunk to 3 per cent. to an average of 5, from about 1760 to 1816. Thus *Gauss*, in a manuscript work which I have used, relates that the fund for the support of professors' widows in Göttingen was, in 1794, expected to pay only 3 per cent. In 1799, the trustees observed that their capital could often be safely invested at 4 per cent.; somewhat later the rate of interest rose to 5 per cent., at which point it remained for years. About 1843 ff. the rate of interest in old Bavaria was only 4 per cent.; in more highly cultured Rhenish Bavaria, 5 per cent.

[1] *Nebenius*, Der öffentliche Credit, 83 ff. After the end of the Napoleonic war, English capital flowed, by way of preference, towards South America, afterwards towards Spain and Portugal; after 1830, to North America; after

emigration for good of the capitalists themselves; but also least frequently, because the natural attachment of man to his native country is usually too powerful, among the well-to-do classes, to be overcome by the attraction of a higher rate of interest. Temporary settlements in foreign countries are by far more frequent. Either the capitalist removes there himself, for a time, to return enriched, at farthest, in his old age; or he establishes a permanent branch of his business there, and superintends it through the agency of a trusted representative. The inhabitants of northern Italy, during the last centuries of the middle ages, maintained such establishments, not only for the purpose of carrying on commerce in merchandise along the shores of the Levant, but also the money trade in the principal countries of the west.[2] Similarly, the Hanseatic

---

1840, towards Germany and France, to be invested in the construction of railways in the latter countries.

[2] The inhabitants of Asti began in 1226 to carry on the trade in money in trans-Alpine counties. In 1256, *Louis IX.* ordered 150 Asti money changers to be thrown into prison, and he confiscated the money they had loaned in France, to the amount of over 800,000 livres. They were afterwards turned over to their enemy, the Count of Savoy, as usurers. (*Muratori*, Scr. Rerum Ital., XI, 142 seq.) About 1268, Louis IX. banished all moneychangers of Lombard or Cahors origin: they were allowed only three months in which to collect their debts. (*Sismondi*, Histoire des Fr., VIII, 112.) About 1277, again all Italian money dealers were imprisoned, and 120,000 gold guldens extorted from them. (*Giov. Villani*, VII, 52.) After the Lombards had lost their freedom, the business passed into the hands of the Florentines and of the inhabitants of Lucca. (*Sismondi*, Gesch. der ital. Republiken, IV, 602; *Dante*, Inferno, XXI, 38.) Great part played by the brothers Franzesi as dealers in articles of luxury, and loaners on pledge etc., at the court of Philip IV. They seem to have instigated the persecution of other Italian money dealers, in 1291, from jealousy. (*Sismondi*, Histoire des Fr., VIII, 429 seq.) Great losses of the Florentines by the English-French war in 1337: Edward III. remained in the debt of his bankers Peruzzi and Bardi to the amounts respectively of 135,000 and 184,000 marks sterling; so that they and many others failed. France imprisoned all the Italian money dealers, and compelled them to pay a large amount of ransom-money. (*G. Villani*, XI, 71.) In 1376, the Pope who was engaged in a struggle with Florence, called upon all princes to despoil all Florentine merchants within their jurisdiction of their wealth, and to sell them as slaves;

cities contemporaneously in the north and northeast of Europe; and, to-day, the English in almost all the important seaport cities in the world.[3] Such enterprises are always somewhat dangerous, especially in countries but little advanced in civilization.[4]

The best means to facilitate the migration of capital is credit. It is, indeed, true, that in international trade, ordinary private loans are seldom made. To make such loans would be to run too many risks; risks through a want of knowledge of persons or circumstances, on account of the difficulties in the way of continued supervision, and of being able to assert and defend one's rights away from home.[5] Loans are much more readily made to foreign states, to great corporations, or joint-

---

and France and England actually did so. (*Sismondi*, Geschichte der ital. Republiken, V, 257 seq., VII, 74.)

[3] Shortly before the French Revolution, Cadiz had over 50 wholesale merchants against 30 retail, 30 modistes and at least 100 tradesmen from France. (*Bourgoing*, Tableau, III, 130.) Commercial colonies!

[4] Thus even the emperor Paul of Russia caused the property of English factors to be confiscated. The galleons which Holland and England captured in the Spanish war of succession belonged mostly to Amsterdam houses. (*Ranke*, Franz. Gesch., IV, 226.) Even *Galiani*, Della Moneta, IV, 3, thinks that, on this account, such commerce is incompatible with the warlike spirit. It is certain, however, that a government like the English would do well not to permit a war with such countries as Russia or the United States to break out too suddenly, that their subjects might have time to collect all their outstanding dues. When, in 1855, it was reported in London that all Russian drafts were dishonored, people looked upon that fact as the surest sign of coming war. English merchants had called in their advances to Russia during the preceding economic period, and refused to make new ones.

[5] This of course disappears when the borrowing country is dependent on the loaning country. Thus, the Canton of Uri formerly prohibited the inhabitants of the Livinerthal to borrow capital except from them. It is said that, at the beginning of this century, the Uri capital then loaned amounted to one-half a million florins, that is, an average of 250 per householder. Now it is not over one-fifth of that amount. (*Franscini*, Canton Tessin, 126.) Think also of the plantation colonies! But even the East Indies may be looked upon as a species of colony for England. Hence *Fawcett*, Manual, 105, is rightly of the opinion that no other country has the possibility of being as useful to the East Indies as England. And in fact, the East Indian railways obtained of their capital of £82,500,000, only a very small part,

stock companies, whose condition is well-known; and which, by reason of their perpetuity, have a deep and obvious interest in maintaining an honorable reputation. The issuing of certificates of stock etc., has greatly facilitated international trade in capital.[6] But the mode of loaning in foreign parts preferred is to sell them commodities, and to require payment for them only after some time has elapsed, of course, with interest. Purchases, on the contrary, are paid for immediately, possibly even in advance.[7] The lower the rate of interest in a

---

£800,000, in India itself, a very small proportion of which latter sum was subscribed by the native population. (Ausland 24, Juli, 1869.)

[6] What England is to-day, the Italian commercial cities were in the 16th and 17th centuries, viz.: the chief market for foreign loans. (Compare *Mun*, England's Treasure, 1664, ch. 4.) The Genovese loaned money in foreign countries at 2 and 3 per cent. *(Montanari*, Della Moneta, 1867, cap. 2.) It is said that the Dutch, in 1778 invested 1,500 millions of livres in foreign national debts, especially those of France and England. (Richesse de Hollande, II, 178.) According to *J. G. Forster*, Schriften, III, 335, in 1781 alone, in Europe, 800 millions loaned capital. The Niederl. Jaerboek of 1789, p. 729, estimates the amount of interest coming from abroad, English and French not included, at from 50 to 60 millions of florins. About 1844, according to official estimates, 1,000 million florins in foreign loans, that is one-third of whole national income. (Allgemeine Zeitung, 1844, No. 35.) Now, Belgium, 300 million florins, in Austrian evidences of indebtedness. (Quarterly Review, October, 1862, 402.) According to *Baumstark*, Staatswissensch. Versuche über Staatscredit etc., 1833, 77, foreign nations, between 1818 and 1825, borrowed in England £49,000,000; and, about the same time, England participated in Russian, French and North American loans to the extent of £55,500,000. It is said that there were, in 1843, £25,000,000 English capital in the canals, railroads and banks of the United States. *(Porter*, Progress of the Nation, III, 4, 634.)

[7] It is evident, from many of Demosthenes' orations on private matters, that Athens was in the habit of advancing the commercial capital needed by a great part of the inhabitants of the Mediterranean coast. Many colonial cities, Phaselis, for instance, had the very worst reputation in this respect. They were virtually pirates as regards Athens. (Adv. Lacrit., 931.) Here also it seems that the goods taken for the loan had to be brought to Athens. (941.) On the regular advances of Prussian merchants to their Lithuanian and Polish vendors, in the 15th century, while the former were forbidden even to buy on credit, see *Hirsch*, Geschichte des Danziger Handels, 167, 177. In Colbert's time, the Dutch gave 12 months credit in Europe. *(J. De Wit,*

country is, the longer and more cheaply can it give credit to others; a new reason why the less civilized countries are particularly fond of trading with the most civilized.[8][9]

Mémoires, 184.) In England, *Child* perceives a great advance in this: that in 1650, in all business in the interior, there was a credit of 3 to 18 months given; and in 1669, everything was paid for in cash. (Discourse on Trade, 45.) Concerning previous times, see *W. Raleigh*, Observations touching Trade and Commerce with the Hollander and other nations, 1603. (Works, VIII, 951 ff.) In North America, merchants in the interior frequently purchase their goods of importers on 6 months credit. *(Tellkampf,* Beiträge, I, 52.) In the West Indies, about the end of the last century, the English gave a credit, generally, of from 12 to 16 months. *(B. Edwards,* History of the British West Indies, II, 383.) In Brazil, in the case of imports, 4, 8 and even 12 months credit; payment in monthly installments, and frequently even longer delay, without interest. In the case of exports, when cash payments are not made, 1 per cent. a month. *(v. Reden,* Garn und Leinenhandel, 332.) Recently only about 40 per cent. of foreign advances are made at 12 to 20 months, 60 per cent. at from 50 to 70 days. (Tübing. Zeitschr., 1864, 517.

In Buenos Ayres, the producer or collector of export articles required price to be paid usually a long time in advance *(habilitacion),* a very bold but necessary procedure, on account of his poverty. *(Robertson,* Letters on S. America, I, 174 ff.) In the corn trade in South Russia, at least one-half of the purchase money was required to be paid in advance, and even before shipment, the other half as soon as the corn arrived in the harbor, and, hence, sometimes, long before it was put on board. *(W. Jacob,* On the Corn Trade of the Black Sea, 23.) Compare *Tooke,* View of the Russian Empire, I, 339, Richesse de Hollande, II, 43, *Storch,* Handbuch, II, 61 seq. Russia was, about 1770, a credit-giving nation to the still poorer Persians. *(Gmelin,* Reise, III, 413.) The Spaniards also, in their American colonies, had always an expedition ready and waiting, the payment for which was made on the arrival of the second. *(Depons,* Voyage dans la Terre Firme, II, 368.) Moreover, active commerce simply, especially when circuitous, may be considered as in some way an international loan; and thus it is that the favorable " balance," by means of which claim-rights are obtained in foreign countries, is secured.

[8] Notwithstanding the gratitude of the United States towards France, and spite of all the French ambassador could do, the English immediately after the conclusion of peace, attracted the greatest part of American trade to themselves. *(Chaptal,* de l'Industrie Fr., I, 103.) Countries with a low rate of interest have an advantage in this respect, which grows after the manner of compound interest, when the duration of the advance of capital is prolonged. *(Senior,* Outlines, 195.)

[9] How capitalists may, by the giving of international credit, fall into an

SECTION CLXXXVIII.

HISTORY OF THE RATE OF INTEREST—EFFECT OF A LOW RATE ON STATIONARY NATIONS.

Beneficial as the spur of a low rate of interest is for countries capable of development, it is a heavy drag on a stationary people, and more so on those who have lost a portion of the field for the investment of their capital by the competition of too powerful rivals.[1] A real superabundance of capital is attended with cares and temptations for the middle classes very similar to those caused by a so-called over-population, especially to dishonesty and extravagance.[2] When capital, population and the skillfulness of labor remaining the same, continues to increase, the enlarged capital may very readily have every succeeding year only the same return to divide among its owners, that the smaller had in previous years.[3] Hence additional saving here would produce no real enrichment of the people; and it might even happen that the instinct to accumulate capital might in

---

injurious habit, is shown by the late and troublesome building up of the Dutch railway system, while so many foreign railway enterprises were provided with Dutch capital.

[1] *Temple*, Works I, 102, assures us that the Dutch in his time considered the payment of the principal of a public debt a real misfortune: "they receive it with tears, not knowing how to dispose of it to interest with such safety and ease." On Italy, see *Bandini* (ob. 1760), Sopra le Maremme Sienese, 154 seq.; earlier *Montanari*, Della Moneta, 57. In the England of the present time, small capitalists especially belong to the so-called "uneasy" classes.

[2] Numberless bankrupts and unbounded extravagance in Holland. (Richesse de Hollande, II, 168.) In England, the hazardous enterprises of 1825 were very much promoted by the action of the government which a short time before reduced the interest on its state debt. (*Tooke*, History of Prices, II, 148 ff.)

[3] *J. S. Mill*, IV, ch. 4, 4. When *Ricardo*, ch. 6, says that every increase of productive capital must enhance the value in use, and still more the value in exchange, of a nation's property, but under such circumstances only to the advantage of the working class, and still more of the land owning class, he at least apparently presupposes an improvement, or increase of labor.

suppose a nation of fishermen with no private ownership in land and no capital, living naked in caverns, on sea-fish which the ebb of the ocean has left in the puddles along the shore, and which are caught only with the hand.[2] All workmen here may be equal, and each catch and consume three fish a day. Let us again suppose that some clever savage reduces his consumption to two fish a day, for one hundred days, and uses the stock of one hundred fish collected in this way to enable him to devote all his strength and labor, during fifty days, to the construction of a boat and a net. With the aid of this capital he, from the first, catches thirty per day. What now will his fellow tribesmen, who are not capable of such intelligent and systematic self control to do as he has done, do? What will they offer him for the use of his capital? In discussing this question both parties will very certainly consider not only the fifty days' labor spent in the construction of the boat etc., but also the one hundred and fifty days during which its maker had to abstain from his full ration of food. If the borrower, of the thirty fish which may be caught daily with the aid of his capital, gives twenty-seven away, his condition is at least no worse than it was at first. On the other hand, the lender, if compensated only for the wear and tear of his capital, would reap no profit whatever from his loan. The interest to be paid will be fixed somewhere between these two extremes by the relation between demand and supply. A loan which pays no interest is a donated use

---

born. In the loaning of capital productively invested, the creditor, in the interest received, consumes the real produce of his property. If the debtor has consumed the property unproductively, the creditor indeed lives on the debtor's other returns or supplies; which, however, without his intervention would probably have been consumed by their owner.

[2] We here, for the time being, make abstraction of all entangling surrounding circumstances. However, *Diodor.*, III, 15 ff., and *Strabo*, XVI, 773, describe a very similar condition of things among the Ichthyographs; also *Hildebrand*, Reise, um die Erde, III, 2, in China. In the Sudan, whole generations fetch water every day from a distant town, instead of working for a few weeks to dig a deep well nearer home. (*Barth*, Afr. Reise, III, 297.)

of capital. *(Knies.)*³ Interest may be called the reward of abstinence *(Senior)*, in the same way as wages is called the reward of industry.⁴ With the abolition of interest, exchange would be limited to the mere present, without any mediation between the past and the future. A great number of services would bring no equivalent in return, and, therefore, as a

---

³ The most recent relapse into the old error of the unproductiveness of capital, viz.: that of *Karl Marx* (Das Kapital; Kritik der polit. Oekonomie, I, 167) is a turning round and round of the author in the vicious circle of his demonstration. If the value of every commodity depends simply on the labor necessary to bring it into existence, or on the time of labor required to produce it, it is self-evident that the value of the capital consumed for the purpose of its production, can at most be only preserved in the new product, and that all the additional value *(Mehrwerth)* of the latter should be ascribed to labor. (172, and passim.) Hence, strictly speaking, the capitalist who advances capital to workmen, is still bound in duty to be grateful to the latter when the value of his advance is preserved to him undiminished, (§ 173) and all interest levied by him should be considered as a payment towards the extinguishment of the capital [debt] itself. (556.) Relying on such theories, many socialists admit private property and even the right of inheritance to means of enjoyment and use capital *(Gebrauchskapitalien)* provided only that land and productive capital should pass over into the "collective property" of society, with compensation, however, to their former owners. Considering the short duration of most goods used in enjoyment or consumed, the evil consequences of a community of goods mentioned in § 81, could not be avoided to any extent by this means.

How entirely fallacious the above assumption is, is seen most strikingly in the case of such goods as cigars, wine, cheese etc., which, without the least addition of labor, by merely postponing the consumption of them, obtain a much larger value both in exchange and in use. Or, how would it be possible, for instance, to reduce the value of a hundred-year-old tree, over and above the cost of planting it, to labor alone? Similarly, the fact that on a Chilian *hacienda*, 25 per cent. of the cattle can be slaughtered and no diminution of the herd take place. (*Wappäus*, M. und S. Amerika, 784.) *Strassburger* rightly inquires: if all the profit of capital is based on a cheating of workmen by capitalists, who is cheated in the case in which a manufacturer without workmen earns more with an increased capital than before with a small capital? (*Hildebrand's* Jahrb., I, 103.)

⁴ In a time full of nabobism and pauperism, when some can, without the least abstinence, make immense savings, and others none at all even with the greatest abstinence, we may comprehend where the socialists find food for their derision of the expression, "reward of abstinence."

rule, never be performed. Most of the charges commonly made in our day against the "tyranny of capital" are, at bottom, only a complaint that capital is not inexhaustible; and even those workmen who are obliged to pay most to capital would be much worse off without it.

SECTION CXC.

INTEREST-POLICY.—AVERSION TO INTEREST.

At the same time, there is a strong aversion to the taking of interest prevalent among nations in a low stage of civilization. Industrial enterprises of any importance do not as yet exist here at all, and agriculture is most advantageously carried on by means of a great many parcels of land, but with little capital. The purchase of land is so rare, and hampered by legal restrictions to such a degree, that loans for that purpose are almost unheard of. And just as seldom does it happen, by reason of the superabundance of land, that the heir of a land-owner borrows capital to effect an adjustment with his co-heirs, and thus enter alone into the possession of the estate. Here, as a rule, only absolute want leads to loaning.[1] If, in addition to this, we consider the natural height of the rate of wages in such times, the small number and importance of the capitalist class (§ 201), the tardy insight of man into the course and nature of economic production,[2] it will not be hard to un-

---

[1] Distress-debts in contradistinction to acquisition-debts. *(Schmalz,* Staatswirthsch. Lehre in Briefen, I, 227.) Compare *Hesiod.,* Opp., 647; also *Herodot.,* I, 138.

[2] Thus *Aristotle,* calls the taking of interest a gain against nature, since money is only a medium of exchange, and cannot produce its like. (Polit., 3, 23, Schn.) Similarly, *Plato,* De Legg., V, 742, and *Seneca,* De Benef., VII, 10. Compare, however, *Tacit.,* Annal, XIII, 42 seq. As late a writer as *Forbonnais,* 1754, accounts for interest thus: Some people hoard their money instead of spending it; hence a scarcity or want of money, and those who need it are obliged, in order to draw it out, to promise to pay interest. (Eléments de Commerce, II, 92 ff.)

derstand the odium attached in the middle age of every nation to so-called interest-usury[3] (*Zinswucher*). Most religions, the Christian excepted (the universal religion!), have been founded in the earlier stages of the nations who profess them, and have there, at least outwardly, exercised their greatest influence. No wonder, therefore, that so many religions have prohibited the taking of interest. Thus, for instance, the Jewish which, indeed, allows interest to be taken from foreigners, but raises loaning without interest among Jews in their commerce with one another, to the dignity of a duty binding on the conscience of the beneficent rich.[4][5] Similarly in the Koran.[6] The Fathers of the Church,

---

[3] Numerous disturbances on account of debt, during the first centuries of the Roman Republic, until finally (compare *Livy*, VII, 42), the taking of interest was in the year 349(?) before Christ, entirely prohibited. (*Tacit.*, Annal. VI, 16.) The public opinion in such matters may be understood from the words of Cato: *majores ita in legibus posuerunt, furem dupli condemnari, foeneratorem quadrupli.* (De Re rust.) The *foenerari* compared with the *hominem occidere.* (*Cato*, in *Cicero*, De Off., II, 25.) In the higher stages of civilization little heed was paid to the law, in practice (compare *Livy*, XXXV, 7; *Plut.*, Cato, I, 21.), although the democratic party always held fast to the legal perpetuation of the prohibition of interest. (*Mommsen*, Römisch. Gesch., III, 493.)

[4] Exod., 22, 25; Levit., 25, 35 ff.; Deuteron., 15, 7 seq.; 23, 19 seq.; Psalms, 15, 5; 109, 11; 112, 5; Proverbs, 28, 8; Jerem., 15, 10; *Hes.*, 18, 8. After the return from exile, the prohibition was restored. (Net. 5, 1 ff.) Was there, in the long duration of such prescriptions, an educational measure having reference to the peculiar fault towards which the Jewish national character had a special tendency? In Josephus's time even, usury practiced on one's country people was universally despised (Antiq. Jud., IV, 8, 25.), and the Talmud continues it. Compare *Michaelis*, De Mente ac Ratione Legis M. Usuram prohibentis. In Russia, the orthodox Jews are wont to evade the legal rate of interest by exacting one-half the profit, and estimating it approximately in advance at a probable sum. If, afterwards, the debtor declares under oath that he made no profit, the creditor has no more to say; but then the borrower would lose all credit in the future. (*Bonav. Mayer*, Die Juden unserer Zeit, 1842, 13 seq.)

[5] The Mosaic passages, however, only prohibit the taking of interest from poor people of one's own country.

[6] The prohibition in the Koran, ch. 2, 30, is regularly evaded in Persia, by

also, on the whole, look with disfavor on the taking of interest, relying upon well-known passages in the Old Testament, and, in part, on misunderstood expressions in the New.[7] This is especially true of the Fathers of the Church from the beginning of the fourth century, when the Roman empire was frightfully impoverished by the devastations of the barbarians, and as a consequence the conditions as to interest which prevail in the lowest stages of civilization had returned. Mercy towards the poor usually occupies the foreground in the demonstrations of the Fathers.[8]

SECTION CXCI.

INTEREST-POLICY.—THE CANON LAW ETC.

The canon law, from the first, endeavored to prevent contracts for interest. We may even say that the prohibition of interest-usury is the key-stone of the whole system of the political economy of the *Corpus Juris Canonici*. The development of that law coincides, as to time, with the senility of the Roman Empire and the childhood of modern nations.[1] In the

---

deducting the proper amount at the moment the loan is made. *(Chardin,* IV, 157 ff.) Under the Mongolian rulers, it was done by way of preference, by a fictitious sale for cash, at prices out of all proportion. "Why cannot capitalists either buy land or carry on trade?" asked Sultan Gazan, on an occasion when the prohibition of interest was strongly insisted on. *(d'Ohsson,* Histoire des Mongols, IV, 397.)

[7] For instance, *Luke,* 6, 34 ff., where interest is no more prohibited than in *Luke,* 14, 12 ff., the mutual invitation of friends to a feast. Not less groundless is the supposed allegorical allusion *(Matthew,* 21, 12) to interest-creditors. Rather might an approval of interest be inferred from *Matthew,* 25, 27.

[8] *Origen,* for instance, would have the creditor take no interest; but exhorts the debtor to return double the amount unasked. (Homil., III, ad. Ps., § 37.) Hence there is here no condemnation of interest, but only an effort to transform all legal relations into relations of love. Quite the reverse in *Lactant.,* Instit., VI, 12; *Basil,* ad. Matth., 5 ff.; *Ambrose,* De Off., III, 3; *Chrysost.,* ad. Matth. Hom., 56; Tim., VII, 373 ff. (Paris, 1727); *Hieronym.,* ad. Ezech., V, 367 c. (Francof, 1684); *Augustin.,* Epist., 54. Even *Cyprian,* 183, 318 (Paris, 1726).

[1] The apostolic canons and several decrees of councils of the fourth cen-

golden age of papal power, every interest-creditor was refused the communion, the *testamenti factio* and the right of ecclesiastical burial. Proceedings at law could not be instituted for the recovery of the principal debt until the creditor had restored all the interest obtained. In the council of Vienna, in 1311, it was declared heresy to defend the taking of interest. The universal antipathy of the church towards the growing importance of the *bourgeoisie*,[2] and the desire to give the spiritual courts an extensive jurisdiction in litigated cases, may have contributed largely to the adoption of these measures. In later medieval times, the secular power offered its services to execute these laws;[3] and, to judge of what public

---

tury prohibit the taking of interest by the clergy. A Spanish provincial council dared, in 313, to extend the prohibition to the laity. Pope Leo I. condemned the taking of interest by the laity also, but only in the form of a moral law. (443.) The synod of Constantinople (814) punished the violation of the prohibition with excommunication. See *Thomas Aquin.* (ob. 1274.) De Usuris, in the Quæstiones disputatae et quod libetales. The canon law, however, always permitted delay-interest *(Verzugszinsen)*, and Gregory IX, allowed *justa et moderata expensa et congruam satisfactionem damnorum* to be taken into account. (c. 17, X.) De Fora Comp. II, 2. A tacit recognition of the productiveness of capital is to be found in c. 7, X. De Donatt. inter. Virum. cett. IV, 20; and the later schoolmen, *Antonin* and *Bernhardin*, (ob. 1459 and 144) are pretty clear on the point. But *Albertus Magnus* had already recognized the *damnum emergens* and *Thomas Aquinas* the *lucrum cessans* as causes of interest. (Tübinger Zeitschr., 1869, 151, 159, 161.) The essentially modern character of Roman law, which, in the form it has finally assumed, is in harmony with a high development of national economy, accounts for the fact that the glosse of *Accursius* relying on *Irnerius* and *Bulgarus* entirely ignores the prohibition of interest. For a similar reason, in the 16th century, *Donellus* and *Cujacius* stand entirely on Roman ground. In the interval, indeed, men like *Bartolus* and *Baldus* were not disquieted by the canon law. *(Endemann*, Studien in der Römisch-Canonischen Wirtchafts- und Rechtslehre, I, 18, 27 seq. 61.) Compare the rich historical material in *Salmasius*, De Usuris, 1638; De Modo Usurarum, 1639, and De Mutuo, 1640.

[2] *A. Thierry*, Lettres sur l'Histoire de France, éd. 2., 248 ff.

[3] Thus the emperor Basil, in the year 867, as *Justinian* had before him, forbade the further payment of interest, once the amount already paid equaled the principal. (L. 29 seq.; Cod. IV, 32, Nov., 121, 2.) Compare Sachsenspiegel, I, 54. *Edward the Confessor* is said to have issued the first prohibition of interest. *(Anderson*, Origin of Commerce, a. 1045.) *Edward III*

opinion in this matter was, we need only call to mind the decided disapproval of interest by Dante, Luther and Shakespeare.[4]

The *Weddeschat*, a species of pledge or loan on security, constituted the transition from this state of things to the modern economic system of interest. The *Weddeschat* was a sale with a reserved right of redemption, by which the debtor gave his creditor the use and enjoyment of a piece of land a sort of interest in kind), but which he could at any time recover back, by payment of the principal. This was not very oppressive on the debtor, as he was the only party who could recall the contract.[5] In a higher stage of civilization,

---

forbade all interest as the ruin of commerce. (Idem a., 1341.) About 1391, the lower House had its zeal aroused against the "shameful vice of usury;" and again, in 1488, all interest on money and all rent-purchases stipulated for on unlawful conditions, were threatened with a fine of £20, the pillory, and six months imprisonment. *(Anderson,* a., 1488.) In France, the edict of Philip IV. of 1312. Compare *Beaumanoir,* Coûtumes, ch. 67, des Usures, No. 2.

[4] *Dante,* Inferno, XI, 106 ff., suggests that interest-creditors had violated the command of *Moses,* I, 3. *Macchiavelli* seems to judge otherwise: Compare Istoria Fior., VII, a, 1464; VIII, a, 1478. Very interesting discussions on the legitimateness of the taking of interest in 1353 seq., in which the Dominicans, up to the time of *Savonarola,* defended the strictest opinion. *(M. Villan,* 111, 166.) *Luther,* Tract on Trade and Money, 1524, and Sermon on Usury, 1519. Later still, *Luther* became more moderate. Thus, in his letter to the Danzig counsel, 1525, in *Neumann,* Geschichte des Wuchers in Deutschland, 617 ff., in which, for instance, he blames the forcible carrying out of interest-prohibitions, draws a distinction between rich and poor etc. So, too, in his letter: An die Pfarrherren, wider den Wucher zu predigen, 1540. *Melanchthon,* Phil. moral., 137 ff., is also more moderate. *Calvin* was clearer in this matter, and no longer recognized the canonical prohibition of interest. (Epistolæ et Responsa, Hanov., 1597, epist. 383.) Similarly *Zwinglius,* who will not praise interest, but considers it a natural consequence of property (Opp. ed. Tugur., 1530, I, 319 ff.), and even *Erasmus,* ad. Evang. Luc., 6, 44. Adagia v. Usuræ nautt. In *Shakespeare,* compare Merchant of Venice. *Bodinus* also rejects on principle, even Roman interest, which he held to be 1½ per cent. a year: De Republ., 1584, V. 2. Even the practical Dutch excluded the so-called "table-keepers," from the communion up to 1657. Compare the contests hereon in *Laspeyres,* Gesch. d. volkswirthsch. Ansich. d. Niederl., 258 ff.

[5] The mutual right of cancellation *(Kündbarkeit)* in the case of these con-

indeed the continuance of this species of land-pledge would be exceedingly disadvantageous, since the momentary possessor of a piece of land which might be bought back by another person at any time at a price fixed in advance, would scarcely think of improving it.[6]

And so, the introduction of rent-purchase *(Rentekauf)* was an important step in advance: the incumbrancing of a piece of land which remained in the possession of the debtor with an interest in kind paid to the creditor. The latter could never claim anything further, while the debtor and his heirs might redeem the land from this interest-incumbrance by paying back the purchase money.[7] As the Pope, on the 19th of January, 1569, renewed, in express terms, the prohibition of all interest not based on rent-purchase, so did the police ordinances of the Empire, of the sixteenth century, declare it to be the only lawful form of loaning at interest; provided, always, that only the debtor could demand the cancellation of

---

tracts during periods poor in capital and credit, would easily have ruined the debtor. Compare *J. Möser*, Patr. Ph., II, No. 18. Hence municipal rights in the latter part of the middle ages, which in many other respects are so antagonistic to Rome, have seldom anything to object to its measures in this matter.

[6] A reason why, as *A. Strüver* remarks, the Church which was more a creditor than a debtor, never approved the Weddeschat above mentioned.

[7] The institution of rent-purchase *(Rentekauf)* was already developed in the Hanse cities at the beginning of the fourteenth century. *(Stobbe*, in the Zeitschr. f. deutsches Recht, XIX, 189 ff.) About 1420, the bishops of Silesia inquired of the Pope, whether such contracts which had been the practice in Silesia for a century were lawful. The answer was a favorable one, although he left the rate of interest free in this particular case (Extr. Com. III, 5, 1. 2); after *Alexander IV.*, however, as early as 1258, had instructed inquisitors not to take part in litigations concerning usurious contracts. Formerly all such contracts were prohibited in express terms. (Decret. Greg., V. 19, 1, 2), although, in France, the ordinances of Louis IX. and Louis X. (1254 and 1315) had established fixed rates of interest therefor. Between pledge and rent-purchase, the right of the (virtual) loaner to expel the (virtual) borrower, which after fell into disquietude, occupies, so to speak, a middle place. (Compare *Eichhorn*, D. St.- und R. Gesch., II, § 361, a III, § 450.) It was decreed, in France, in 1565, that all rent in kind should be converted into money rent. *(Warnkönig*, Franz., St.- und R- Gesch, II, 585 ff.)

the contract.[8] We find, however, that, on the whole, at least Protestant countries had, before 1654, adopted the modern Roman law relating to interest.[9] [10]

---

[8] Magnum Bullar. Roman., II, 295.
[9] A Prussian law allowing interest even without a contract of rent-purchase as far back as 1385. (*Voigt*, Geschich. von Preussen, V, 467.) In Marseilles, in 1406, a rate of interest of ten per cent. allowed. (*Anderson*, Origin of Commerce, s. a.) Likewise in England, 37 Henry VIII., c. 9. In Brandenburg, 1565, 6 per cent. (*Mylius*, C. C., March, II, 1, 11.) A retrograde step by 5 and 6 Edward VI., c. 20; by which all interest was again prohibited. These laws had, practically, the effect of increasing interest to 14 per cent., and were therefore repealed in 1571. How unnatural the prohibition was is apparent from the fact that by 4 and 5 Philip and Mary, c. 2, the possessor of 1,000 marks was estimated equal to a person with £200 annual income. In Denmark, the taking of interest at 5 per cent. was allowed in 1554, since "although it is contrary to God's command, yet [according to an opinion given by *Melanchthon*] this commerce cannot be entirely abolished." (*Kolderup-Rosenvinge's* Dänische R. G., in *Homeyer*, § 142.) Similar views of the elector Augustus, 1583. (Cod. August I, 139 ff.)

The German Empire, in 1600, allowed the debtor to contract that, in case of delay, the contract might be declared annulled. In France, on the other hand, even during the 18th century, nearly all loans were made in the form of *rent-purchase (Law,* Trade and Money, 127), and the creditor could declare the contract void only in case the debtor did not pay him the rent. (*Warnkönig*, Franz. R. G., II, 585 ff. For strictly Catholic countries, the prohibition relating to the taking of interest still really remains. However, *Leo X.'s* bull, Inter multiplices, exempts the so-called *monti di pietà*, and by this means great obstacles in the way of saving, and promoted real usury. Of this last, *Niebuhr*, Briefe, II, 399, adduces very striking instances from the Pope's own temporal dominion. In the case of pledge, even 12 per cent. per annum is required. (Rom im Jahr, 1833, 163.) Yet, in 1830, the Poenitentiaria Romana instructed the clergy, without, however, deciding the chief question, not to disquiet people any longer in the confessional who had taken interest. (*Guillaumin*, Dictionnaire de l'Economie politique, art. usure.) On the Russian Sect, *Staroverzen*, which still condemns the taking of interest, see *Storch*, Handbuch, II, 19. By the Russian government it was permitted very early. *Ewers*, Aeltestes Recht der R., 323 seq.

[10] The first scientific defense of interest is generally considered to be that of *Salmasius*, loc. cit. Yet *Bacon*, Sermones fideles, C. 39 (after 1539), and at bottom also *H. Grotius*, De Jure Belli et Pacis, 1626, taught that it was lawful to take interest in so far as it was not against the love due to one's neighbor (*Endemann*, loc. cit., I, 62 ff.), and *Besold*, Quaestiones aliquot de Usuris, 1598, was as near the truth as *Samalsius*. Compare *supra*, note 4. How

SEC. CXCI.] INTEREST — THE CANON LAW. 135

However, the long persistence of the prohibition of the canon law in relation to interest, even with the refuge afforded by the introduction of the rent-purchase system, and of dormant partnerships *(Commanditen)* etc., so common in the sixteenth century,[11] would be unintelligible, if, contemporaneously, the Jews did not carry on an important and somewhat free trade in capital,[12] precisely as the Armenians, Hindoos and Jews do in the Mohammedan world of to-day.

---

earnestly *North* and *Locke* labored against the lowering of interest by governmental interference, see *Roscher*, Z. Gesch. der engl. Volkswirths., 90, 102 ff. The best writers, in strictly Catholic countries, did violence to themselves in this matter for a long time after. Thus *Galiani*, Della Moneta, II, 1 seq.; and one cannot help being greatly surprised at witnessing the subtleties which *Turgot*, Mémoire sur le Prêt d' Argent, 1769, had to have recourse to, to prove the clearest matters. Thus: at the moment of the loan, a sum of money is exchanged against the mere promise of the other party, which is certainly less valuable. [If it were not, why should he borrow?] This difference must, therefore, be made up in interest etc. *Mirabeau* even was a decided opponent of interest. (Philos. rurale, ch. 6.) Compare, however, the theological defense by *Viaixnes*, 1728, in the Traité des Prêts de Commerce, Amsterdam, 1759, IV, 19 ff.

[11] Of course, evaded in a thousand ways in practical life. Thus, for instance, people gave wheat, other commodities, and even uncoined gold and silver as loans, and had what interest they pleased promised them. In alienating the capital, they might stipulate *à fonds perdu*, as they thought best. (Turgot, I, c. § 29.) When debtors had promised under oath to make no complaint, the church ordered that they should be helped officially. When the temporal power showed itself lax, Alexander III. decreed that such questions should be brought before the spiritual courts. (Decret. Greg. V., tit. 19; 13 *Innocent*, Epist., VIII, 16; X, 61.) In England, *Richard of Cornwall* obtained a monopoly of the whole loaning business. *(Matth. Paris*, ed. 1694, 639: compare, also, 20 Henry III., 5.), from which fact the existence of the custom of taking interest about 1235, is apparent. Cases in which English kings borrowed and promised payment back *cum damnis, expensis et interesse:* Anderson, Origin of Commerce, a. 1274, 1339.

[12] Compare *Gioja*, Nuovo Prospetto, III, 190. The canon law desired to put an interdict on their taking interest also: Decret. Greg., V, tit. 19, 12, 18. Frequently, also, a minimum of interest was provided for them: Ordonnances de la Fr., L. 53 seq. II, 575. Receuil des anciennes, Lois, I, 149, 152. John of France extended this to four *deniers* per *livre* per week, that is, annually 86⅔ per cent.! *(J. B. Say*, Traité II, ch. 8.) In Austria, in 1244, 174 per cent. allowed! *(Rizy*, Ueber Zinstaxen und Wuchergesetze, 1859, 72 ff.)

SECTION CXCII.

INTEREST-POLICY.— GOVERNMENT INTERFERENCE.— FIXED RATES.

Instead of the medieval prohibition of interest, most modern states have established fixed rates of interest, the exceeding or evasion of which, by contract or otherwise, is declared null and void, and is usually punishable as usury.[1] If the fixing of the rate is intended to depress the rate of interest customary in the country,[2][3] it uniformly fails of its object. If

---

[1] This is, historically, the second meaning of the word usury, while in the middle ages, for instance in England, under Elizabeth *(D. Hume)*, the taking of any interest whatever was called usury. Science should employ this word only in the sense used in § 113.

[2] In Switzerland, at the end of the 17th century, not only were those punished who took more interest than the law prescribed, but those who took less. (Compare Rechtsquellen von Basel, Stadt und Land, 1865, Bd. II.)

[3] Fixed rates of interest of this kind are to be accounted for in part by a still continuing aversion of the legislator for interest in general; in part, by the opinion which prevails that precisely the most useful and most productive classes might be elevated by an artificial lowness of the rate of interest. (But most especially the government itself, which borrows more than it lends.) When Louis XIV. about 1665, lowered the rate of interest to 5 per cent., he claimed in the preamble to his decree that it would have the effect of promoting the welfare of landowners and business men, and of preventing idleness. Similarly *Sully*, Economies royales, L, XII. And so *J. Child*, Discourse of Trade, 69 ff., says that every lowering of the rate of interest, by law, produced a completely corresponding increase of the national wealth. He says, since the first reduction (?) of interest in 1545, the national wealth increased six fold; since the last, in 1651, the number of coaches increased a hundred fold; chamber-maids wore now better clothes than ladies formerly; on 'Change there were more persons with a fortune of £10,000 than before with £1,000. Similarly *Culpeper:* compare *Roscher*, Z. Geschichte der eng. Volkswirthsch., 57 ff. Later, the French generally thought that a lowering of the rate of interest would prove injurious to the *noblesse de la robe;* hence even in 1634, parliament was opposed to it. *(Forbonnais*, Recherches et Considérations, I, 48, 226.) *Darjes* says that information of all loans of capital should be made to the police authorities, and that the authorities might compel payment and the loaning of the principal over again to parties in need of capital. (Erste Gründe, 426 seq.) Something analogous practically pro-

governmental control were great enough, vigilant and rigid enough, which is scarcely imaginable, to prevent all violations of the law, it is certain that less capital would be loaned than had been, for the reason that every owner of capital would be largely interested in employing his capital in production of his own. More capital, too, would go into foreign parts, and there would be less saved by those not engaged in any enterprise of their own. All of this would happen to the undoubted prejudice of the nation's entire economy.[4][5]

If, on the other hand, the control by the government be not great enough, the law would, in most cases, be evaded; especially as each party, creditor as well as debtor, would find it to his advantage to evade it. The latter, who other-

---

vided for by the Würtemberg *Landesordnungen* of the 16th century. (Compare also *von Schröder*, F. Schatz-und Rentkammer, XXV, 3.)

[4] Precisely a high rate of interest is a powerful incentive to saving, and to the importation of capital.

[5] *Usurae palliatae*, interest taken out of the capital, or stem-interest, called also money-usury in contradistinction to patent interest-usury. To this category belong the written acknowledgments of indebtedness to a larger amount than that actually received; acknowledging it in a higher kind of money than that in which the loan was made; the compulsory taking by the debtor of commodities at a disproportionately high price, in the place of money, or at a disproportionately low one, by the creditor. See the enumeration of such things in the police regulations of the empire, 1530, art. 26, and 1548, art. 17. Thus, in Paris, jewels are "sold" to students hard-pressed for money, which immediately find their way to the *monts de piété*, and have to be paid for some time after to the usurious "seller," at a most exorbitant price. The person who loans $100 at 6 per cent., and retains the interest for the next following year from the date of the loan, takes in reality nearly 6.4 per cent. Fraudulent accessory expenses of all kinds, *faux frais*, expenses of registration, for prolongation, and extinguishment etc. Here belong, also, the provisions introduced into contracts to make redemption more difficult, the fixing of terms of payment in such a manner that the debtor is almost forced to let them slip by — called "usury in the conditions" in Austria. Remarkable instances from the 16th century in *Vasco*, Usura libera, § 57 ff. Recently, *Braun* und *Wirth*, Die Zinswuchergesetze, 1856, 190 ff. In view of the manifold business transactions behind which the interest-usurer may take refuge, the complete prevention of the latter would break the legs of commerce (loc. cit., 145 ff.).

wise would not be able to borrow at all, is, as a rule, more in need of obtaining the loan, than the creditor is to invest his capital. How easily, therefore, might he be induced to bind himself by oath or by word of honor![6] He would, moreover, be compelled to pay the creditor not only the natural interest and the ordinary insurance-premium, but also for the special risk he runs when he violates the law threatening him with a severe penalty.[7] Hence the last result is either a material enhancement of the difficulty of obtaining loans or an enhancement of the rate of interest.[8]

---

[6] If the state, by annulling such promises, should incite the people to violate them, it would be a frightful step towards the demoralization of the nation: "thus rewarding men for obtaining the property of others by false promises, and then, not only refusing payment, but invoking legal penalties on those who have helped them in their need." (*J. S. Mill*, Principles, V, ch. 10, 2.) Besides, the Austrian usury law of 1803 punishes the borrower also as a spendthrift, and imprisons him for six months (§ 18), or else it designates where he shall make his domicile (*Ortsverweisung*). Modern loaning on drafts and bills of exchange, the acceptance of which is forged with the knowledge of the creditor, corresponds to what *Plutarch*, Quaest., Gr., 53, relates of the Cretans, who had, especially in later times, the worst possible reputation for avarice and dishonesty. (*Polyb.*, VI, 46. *Paul* to Titus, I, 12.)

[7] He must insure him against the usury laws. (*Adam Smith.*) According to *Krug*, Staatsökonomie, the usury laws should be called so because they promote usury, not because they prevent it. Compare to some extent, *Montesquieu*, Esprit des Lois, XXII, 18 ff.

[8] When Catherine II. reduced the rate of interest in Livonia, in 1785, from 6 to 5 per cent., it soon became impossible, even on the best security, to borrow at less than 7 per cent. (*Storch*, Handbuch, II, 26.) And so, when in New York, in 1717, the rate of interest was reduced to 6 per cent., it became necessary, the following year, to raise it again to 8 per cent. The merchants, themselves, petitioned that it might be so raised, because they found it impossible to get any loans whatever. (*Ebeling*, Geschichte und Erdbeschreib. von Nord Amerika, III, 152.) In Chili, the legal rate of interest is 6 per cent., the actual rate, however, never under 12 per cent., and frequently 18 to 24 per cent. In Peru, on the other hand, the repeal of the usury laws rapidly reduced the rate of interest from 50 to 24 per cent., and finally to 12. (*Pöppig*, I, 118.)

SECTION CXCIII.

INTEREST-POLICY — EFFORTS TO AVOID THE EVIL EFFECTS OF A FIXED RATE.

It has been thought possible to avoid the evil effects of a fixed legal rate of interest, by regulating it in such a way as to make it coincident with the rate customary in the country.[1] But there are numberless transactions in which an insurance-premium, or premium for risk or certain expenses of administration[2] on the part of the loaner is inseparable from the true interest. Here, even the law which entered most into detail could never properly provide for the infinite gradations or shades of risk and trouble; and the rate in a great many transactions would, therefore, be placed below the natural height. Turgot long since observed that the value of a promise of future payment is different not only for different persons, but at different times. Thus, for instance, it is really less after there have been numerous cases of bankruptcy than at other times.[3] If, now, it was desired to fix the maximum rate of interest in such a way that it should equal the rate customary in the country, where the security is good, the best real property security for instance, the consequence would be, that those persons who had no such guaranty to offer (leaving the loaning " among brothers " out of the question) would either be unable to borrow money at all, or, by evading the law, only at an artificially higher rate. Hence the legislator causes injury where he wished to favor. This has been observed in England in almost all past commercial crises.[4] The man who

---

[1] In Austria, in 1803, in loaning on pledge, 4 per cent.; in other loans and in the trade of merchants with one another, 6 per cent. In France, since 1807, with merchants, 6 per cent.; with others, 5. *Salmasius*, De Mono Usur., c. 1, advises that the maximum should be fixed as high as that usual in the most unfavorable cases. The reduction from such rate, where possible, would regulate itself.

[2] *Petty*, Quantulumcunque concerning money, 1682.

[3] Sur le Prêt d'Argent, § 36.

[4] How many merchants would have avoided bankruptcy here if they had

makes it his business to loan his capital, on short time and in
small sums, undertakes a trade which the examination, and the
surveillance of a large number of small debtors, and the necessity of reinvesting the many small sums paid him, render ex-
ceeedingly troublesome and disagreeable. Moreover, in loaning on short terms of payment, there is always danger that
his money may lie idle for some length of time. These are
reasons sufficient, why, in such cases, when the whole compensation is denominated interest, a rate of interest greater
than usual in the country is equitable and even necessary.
(§ 179.)[5]

It has been frequently suggested that spendthrifts and ad-
venturers should be hindered using, or to speak more correctly, abusing the nation's wealth by laws prohibiting the rate
of interest at which they might be expected to obtain credit;
and this in the interest alike of the creditors they might possibly find and in their own.[6] But almost every inventor of

---

been allowed to borrow at 8 per cent.! The established rate of 5 per cent.
was certainly too low, considering the great demand for capital and the want
of confidence at the moment, to permit capital to be loaned at that rate.
Many saw themselves compelled to sell their merchandise or evidences of
state indebtedness at a loss of 30 per cent., in order to meet their obligations.
But the person who, to anticipate the receipts due in 6 months, for instance,
consents to suffer a loss of 30 per cent., pays, in a certain sense, interest at
the rate of 60 per cent. a year. Compare *Tooke*, Considerations on the State
of the Currency, 60, and History of Prices, II, 163, on the Crisis of 1825-26.
Since the Bank, least of all, could exceed the legal rate of interest, numberless applications were made to it in times of war in order to obtain the difference between the legal rate and the rate usual in the country. (*Thornton*, Paper Credit of Great Britain, ch. 10.) Prussia, November 27, 1857, sus-
pended the usury laws for 3 months, on account of the commercial crisis,
except the provisions relating to pawn-broker and minors.

[5] *Turgot* tells of Parisian "usurers" who made weekly advances to the
market women of la Halle, and received for 3 livres, 2 sous interest; that is
173 per cent. a year. The premium for insurance may have been very high
here. When such loaners were brought before the courts, and they were
sentenced to the galleys, the usual punishment for usury, their debtors came
and testified their gratitude by begging for mercy to them! (Mémoire sur le
Prêt d'Argent, § 14, 31.) Compare *Cantillon*, Nature du Commerce, 276.

[6] Thus, *Adam Smith*, Wealth of Nations, II, ch. 4. Similarly, *Roesler*

genius, from Columbus to Stephenson, has been obliged to be considered "an adventurer" for a time by "solid men." The law limits him thus, and more especially during the critical period of outlay which precedes the undoubted triumph of his idea, to his own means or the gifts of others.[7] And how inadequate, as rule, are both. The rich are as seldom discoverers, as discoverers are skillful supplicants. And, as regards spendthrifts, they may ruin themselves in so many thousands of ways, especially by buying or selling, and unhindered by the state, that it is scarcely apparent why the one way of borrowing should be legally closed to them.[8] How is it, if the law itself drives them into the hands of a worse class of creditors, and compels them to pay yet a higher rate of interest? Are they not simply more rapidly ruined? States, themselves, have scarcely ever given any heed to their own usury laws in borrowing or loaning.[9]

SECTION CXCIV.

INTEREST-POLICY. — REPEAL OF THE USURY LAWS.

However, the complete repeal of the usury laws[1] has not

Grundsätze, 495 ff. Compare, *per contra*, *Jer. Bentham*, Defense of Usury: showing the Impolicy of the present legal Restraints on the Terms of pecuniary Bargains in Letters to a Friend. To which is added a Letter to Adam Smith on the Discouragement imposed by the above Restraints to the Progress of inventive Industry, 1787; 3 ed., 1816.

[7] The first steamboat in the United States was, for a long time, called the "Fulton-folly!"

[8] It is just as hard to see why only money-capital should have a fixed rate of interest, and not buildings etc. likewise.

[9] In Holland, the legal rate of interest was lowered, in 1640, to 5 per cent., and in 1655 to 4; but not since. (*Sir J. Child*, Discourse of Trade, 151.) Besides, *Locke*, Considerations on the Lowering of Interest, Works, III, 34, assures us that, in his time, a man in England could make contracts for unlimited interest.

[1] In 1787, Joseph II. abolished the penalties for usury, but allowed the provisions denying a legal remedy, in cases of usurious demand of over 4 per cent. for hypothecations, 6 per cent. for bills and 5 per cent. for other loans,

under all circumstances accomplished what it was supposed it would; and the state should take great care, lest by an incautious framing of its laws, it should put judges in such a position that they may be compelled to coöperate in the execution of immoral contracts.[2] In the lowest strata, so to speak, of the loaning business, the medieval condition continues to exist (§ 190) after it has disappeared in the upper. Here, the loan is effected scarcely ever for the purposes of production, but most generally because of the most urgent necessity; and the debtor is not in a condition, from want of education, and especially from his ignorance of arithmetic, to estimate the magnitude of the burthen he has undertaken. The business of loaning is, under such circumstances, considered dishonorable, to some

---

to remain. Compare the prize essay by *Günther*, Versuch einer vollständigen Untersuchung über Wucher und Wuchergesetze, 1790; *v. Kees*, über die Aufhebung der Wuchergesetze, 1791; *Vasco*, Usura libera, 1792. The opposite view represented by *Ortes*, E. N., II, 24, and *v. Sonnenfels*, Ueber Wucher und Wuchergesetze, 1789, and zu Herrn *von Kees*, Abhandlung etc., 1791. The debates on the repeal of the usury laws in the French Chamber of Deputies, after which *Lherbette's* motion in favor of their repeal was rejected. In France they were, during the assignat-period of bewilderment virtually, and in 1804-1807 expressly (C. C., Art. 1907), but only provisionally repealed. In Würtemberg, all those having the right to draw bills of exchange were exempted from them in 1839. Since the law of 1848, governing bills of exchange, gave all persons capable of contracting, the right to draw bills of exchange, the usury laws have ceased to have any existence; without much noise before and without much complaint after. (A. Allgem. Ztg., 24 März, 1857.) Recent complete or partial repeal of the usury laws: in England, in 1854; in Denmark, in 1855; in Spain, in 1856; Sardinia, Holland, Norway and Geneva, 1857; Oldenburg, 1858; Bremen, 1859; in the kingdoms of Saxony and Sweden, in 1864; Belgium, 1865; Prussia, the North German Confederation, and to some extent Austria, in 1867.

[2] Compare *F. X. Funck*, Zins und Wucher, 1868, a moral theological treatise which rightly demands a more rigid popular morality in relation to real usury, after the repeal of the usury laws. The recent cases in which courts have juridically acquitted usurers because they could not do otherwise, but have branded them morally, are of very questionable propriety, in view of the facility with which high and usurious rates of interest may be confounded. *R. Meyer*, Emancipationskampf, I, 78, advises that the capitalist be allowed to ask whatever interest he wishes, but that the state, as judge and executor of the laws, should enforce payment only at a certain rate determined by law.

extent, by the public. And when a business necessary in itself is held disreputable by public opinion, the usual result is that bad men alone engage in it.[3] Real competition which would but fix the natural price is wanting here in proportion as the debtor is anxious for secrecy.[4]

Abuses in this respect are best guarded against by the establishment of government loan-institutions, and by the publicity of the administration of justice to debtors.[5] Besides, every contract might be prohibited the terms of which were such that an inexperienced borrower could not from them obtain a

---

[3] Many laws seem to purposely permit this, inasmuch as they allow a rate of interest, higher in proportion as the position of the creditor is less respectable. Thus, formerly, in some places, the Jews might require higher interest than the Christians. Justinian allows *personis illustribus* only 4 per cent.; ordinary private persons, 6 per cent.; money-changers etc., 8 per cent. (L. 26, Cod. IV, 32.) On the other hand, according to the Indian legislation of Menu, the Brahman is obliged to confine himself to 2, the warrior to 3, the *vaysya* to 4, the *sudra* to 5 per cent. per month at most. (Cap. 8.)

[4] *Turgot* considered that only the *prêteurs à la petite semaine*, pawnbrokers who loaned to hard-pressed people on the confines of the middle class and artisans, and the infamous characters who advanced money to the sons of rich men to spend in dissipation, still passed for usurers. Only the latter are injurious; not, however, because of the high rate of interest they charge, but because they help in a bad cause. (Sur le Prêt d'Argent, § 32.) According to *Colquhoun*, Police of the Metropolis, 167, there are women in London from whom the hucksteresses borrow 5 shillings every day and return them every evening with ½ shilling interest. Something analogous happens much more frequently in the country, especially in the loaning in kind of productive capital to poor persons. Thus, in Tessin, there are many "iron cattle" which the borrower is obliged to return at their original value, plus an interest of about 36 per cent. (*Frauscini*, C. Tessin, 152.) On the Rhine, frequently as much as 200 per cent. a year, is stipulated for in such contracts. *Morstadt*, der N. Œkonom. Heft., IX, 727.

[5] Compare *J. J. Becher*, Polit. Discurs, 1668, 219; *v. Schröder*, F. Schatz- und Rentkammer, Bd. §§ 123, 133 ff. The first *montes pictatis* were expressly intended to check the usury of the Jews. Thus, in Florence, in 1495, after the expulsion of the Jews, voluntary contributions were made to found a municipal loaning establishment. Similarly, *Tiberius*, Tacit. Ann., VI, 16 seq. *Count Soden*, Nat-Oek., IV, 57; V, 319, advises that all contracts for interest should be recorded in a public registry, under pain of their being held not actionable.

clear conception of the burthen he accepts, or which hindered him from paying the debt at a proper time.⁶

Lastly, there should be a rate of legal interest fixed by the state to be charged in such cases as interest is found to be in justice due, but in which none is provided for by contract; and this rate should approximate as nearly as possible to the rate usual in the country.⁷ ⁸

---

⁶ *Günther*, loc. cit., thinks that, in every contract in which the rate of interest is masked, its real rate should be expressed under penalty of invalidity. In addition to this, he would have those who have attained their majority put in full control of their fortune only after they had undergone an examination.

It seems opportune that the old prohibition against interest on interest *(Cicero*, ad. Att., V, 21, and L, 26, Digest, XIV, 6) and the provision that the interest should not be permitted to be greater than the *alterum tantum* (Digest, l. c.) should be permitted to continue. (Digest, l. c.) Both of these measures were first decreed by Lucullus, for the protection of Asia Minor. Compare § 115. Florentine law, of 1693, that interest in arrears, or that interest on interest beyond 7 years, should not be added to the principal without an express contract to that effect. *(Vasco*, Usura libera, § 155.) In England, the usury laws were by 2 and 3 Victor., c. 37, repealed, but only to the extent of excepting from their provisions bills of not over 12 months, and money loans not over £10. Compare *Rau*, Lehrbuch II, § 323.

⁷ Compare *Locke*, Considerations: Works, 10, 32 ff. In Spain, the Council of State is required to regulate the rate of legal interest yearly (law of 1856, art. 8); a thing which, according to *Braun*, would be better done in each individual case by the judges themselves. *(Faucher's* Vierteljahrsschrift, 1868, II, 13)

⁸ In Athens, the rate of interest in general was voluntary from the time of Solon, who, however, did away with slavery for debt. (Lysias adv. Theomn., 360.) Yet there was a legal rate of interest of 18 per cent. for the case in which a divorced husband delayed the return of his wife's dowry. Compare *Böckh*, Staatshaushalt der Athener, I, 148.

CHAPTER V.

THE UNDERTAKER'S PROFIT.
(UNTERNEHMERLOHN.)

SECTION CXCV.
THE REWARD OF ENTERPRISE.

The essence of an enterprise or undertaking, in the politico-economical sense of the word, consists in this, that the undertaking party engages in production for the purpose of commerce, at his own risk. In the earlier stages of a nation's economy, the production of consumers is, naturally enough, limited chiefly by their own personal wants. Somewhat later, when the division of labor has been further developed, the workman produces at first, enough to meet occasional determinate "orders;" and still later to meet them regularly and as a business. Later yet, and in stages of civilization yet higher, especially when the freedom of labor constantly grows, as it is wont to, here, and the freedom of capital and trade becomes more extensive, enterprise plays a part which grows more important as time rolls on, and is usually carried on more at one's own risk.[1] This transition is a great advance, inasmuch as the advantages of the coöperation of labor and of use may be utilized in a much higher degree by undertakers (*Unternehmer*) than by producers who labor only to satisfy their own household wants, or to meet "orders" already made.

---

[1] At first, usually imperfect enterprises in which the shop-instruments etc., are kept ready for present orders; and then complete or perfect enterprises. (*v. Mangoldt*, Volkswirthschaftslehre, 255.)

The awakening of latent wants, a matter of the utmost importance to a people who would advance in civilization, is something which can enter into the mind only of a man endowed with the spirit of enterprise (an undertaker).[2]

While most English political economists have confounded the personal gain of the undertaker with the interest on the capital used by him,[3] many German writers have called the "undertaker's earnings" or profit a special, and fourth, branch of the national income, coördinate with rent, wages, and the interest on capital.[4] Yet, the net income of every undertaker

---

[2] *v. Mangoldt*, Lehre vom Unternehmergewinn, 1855, 49 ff. The same author shows, in his Volkswirthschaftslehre, that it is better for the general good that the risk should be borne by the producer than by the consumer. In the case of the taking of orders, there is danger only of a technic failure, but in enterprise proper, there is possible also an economic miscarriage of the work, even when successful from a technic point of view. But in the case of the undertaker (man of enterprise), responsibility is much more of an incentive, production much more steady, and therefore much better able to exhaust all means of help. Consumers are much more certain in their steps, as regards price, etc., since they find what they want ready made.

[3] Thus *John Stuart Mill*, Principles, II, ch. 15, 4, teaches with a certain amount of emphasis that the "gross profits of stock" are different not so much in the different branches in which capital is employed, as according to the personal capacity of the capitalist himself or of his agents. There are scarcely two producers who produce at precisely the same cost, even when their products are equal in quality, and equally cheap. Nor are there two who turn over their capital in precisely the same time. These "gross profits" uniformly fall into three classes: reward for abstinence, indemnity for risk, remuneration for the labor and skill required for superintendence. *Mill* complains that there is in English no expression corresponding to the French *profit de l'entrepreneur*. [The translator has taken the liberty to use the expression "undertaker's profit," for what the French call the *profit de l'entrepreneur*, and the Germans *Unternehmerlohn*, spite of its funereal associations, and because Mill himself employed it, although he recognized that it was not in good usage.—TR.] (II, ch. 15, 1.) *Adam Smith* had the true doctrine in germ (Wealth of Nat., I, ch. 6), but those who came after him did little to develop it. Compare *Ricardo*, Principles, ch. 6, 21. *Read*, Political Economy, 1829, 262 ff., and *Senior*, Outlines, 130 seq., were the first to divide profit into two parts: interest-rent *(Zinsrente)* and industrial gain. Similarly, *Sismondi*, N. P., IV, ch. 6. According to *A. Walker*, Science of Wealth, 1867, 253, 285, "profits are wages received by the employer."

[4] *Hufeland*, Grundlegung, I, 290 ff.; *Schön*, Nat.-Oek., 87, 112 ff.; *Riedel*,

is either the fruit of his own land used for purposes of production and of his capital, in which case it is subject to the usual laws of development of rent and interest; or, it must be considered as wages paid for his labor.[5] These wages he earns, as a rule, by organizing and inspecting the work, calculating the chances of the whole enterprise; frequently by, at the same time, keeping the books and acting as cashier; and, in the case of small undertakings, as a common fellow-workman. (Tradesman, peasant). In every case, however, even when he

---

Nat.-Oek., II, 7 ff.; *v. Thünen*, Der isolirte Staat, II, 1 80 ff.; *v. Mangoldt*, Unternehmergewinn, 34 ff. The latter divides the undertaker's profit *(profit de l' entrepreneur)* into the following parts:

A. Indemnity for risk. If this be only an indemnity exactly corresponding to the risk, it cannot be looked upon at all as net income, but only as an indemnification for capital. If individual undertakers, favored by-fortune, receive a much larger indemnification than is necessary to cover their losses, such indemnification is not income either, but an extraordinary profit not unlike a lottery-gain, unless it be called, perhaps, the reward of extraordinary courage *(Eiselen)*, i. e., wages. If, lastly, the indemnity is uniformly somewhat larger than the risk, in order to compensate for the continual feeling that one is running a risk, it must be remembered that all remuneration for present sacrifice, made directly for the sake of production, is wont to be embraced under the name of wages.

B. Wages and interest for the labor and capital utilized only in one's own production, and which cannot be let. *v. Mangoldt* himself admits, that, in the long run, only certain qualified labor belongs to this category.

C. Undertaker's rent *(Unternehmerrente)* depending on the rarity of undertakers (men of enterprise) compared with the demand. This, therefore, is not a third component part, but only one which adds to the other two. *Storch*, Handbuch, I, 180, and *Rau*, Lehrbuch, I, § 237 ff., consider the profit of the undertaker as an admixture of wages and interest. Professor *J. Misczewicz* has given expression to an interesting thought in opposition to myself: that credit is a fourth factor of production (natural forces, labor and capital being the other three) produced by the three older factors, as capital by the two oldest. The undertaker's profit he then considers the product of this fourth factor, corresponding to rent, interest and wages.

[5] Compare *Canard*, Principes, ch. 3; *J. B. Say*, Traité, II, ch. 7, Cours pratique, V, 1-2, 7-9, distinguishes three branches of income: rent, interest and the profits of industry; and he divides the latter again into the profits of the *savant*, the undertaker and workmen. *(v. Jacob*, Grundsätze der Nat.-Oek., § 292; *Lotz*, Handbuch, I, 471; *Schmalz*, Staatswirthschaftslehre, I, 116; *Nebenius*, Oeff. Credit, I, Aufl., 466.)

puts an agent paid by himself in his place, he earns these wages from the fact that his name keeps the whole enterprise together; and for the reason that, in the last instance,[6] he has to bear the care and responsibility attending it.[7] When a business goes wrong, the salaried director or foreman may permit himself to be called on to engage in another; but the weary, watchful nights belong to the undertaker or man of enterprise, alone; and "how productive such nights frequently are!"[8]

This profit of the undertaker is subject essentially to the same natural law as wages in general are; only it differs in this from all other branches of income, that it can never be stipulated for in advance. Rather does it consist of the surplus which the product of the undertaking affords over and above all the rent stipulated for in advance or estimated at the rate usual in the country, the interest on capital, and wages of common labor.[9]

---

[6] I need only call attention to the influence that the mere name of a general sometimes exerts over the achievements and sometimes even over the composition of his army (Wallenstein!); and how important it sometimes is to keep his death a secret. And so the mere name of a minister of finance may facilitate loans etc.

[7] It is sufficient to mention the different positions occupied by the shareholders and preferred creditors of a joint-stock company.

[8] Compare *v. Thünen's* Isolirter Statt, II, 80 ff, and his Life, 1868, 96. *Meister muss sich immer plagen!* *(Schiller.)* See a long catalogue of books on the position of the undertaker in the principal different branches of industry in *Steinlein*, Handbuch der Volkswirthschaftslehre, I, 445 ff.

[9] *Tantièmes* occupy a middle place between wages and the undertaker's profit; dividends a middle place between undertaker's profit and the interest of capital. On this is based *Rodbertus's* view, that an increase of joint stock companies raises *ceteris paribus* the rate of interest, and an increase of productive associations the rate of wages, for the reason that in each instance, there is some admixture of "undertaker's profit," or reward of enterprise.

SECTION CXCVI.

UNDERTAKER'S PROFIT.—CIRCUMSTANCES ON WHICH IT DEPENDS.

As the wages or reward of labor, in all instances, depends on the circumstances mentioned in § 167 ff., so, also does the reward of enterprise; in other words, the undertaker's profit or wages. It depends, therefore:

A. On the rarity of the personal qualities required in a business, which qualities may be divided into technical and ethical qualities. Among the latter are, especially, the capacity to inspire capitalists with confidence and workmen with love for their task; the administrative talent to systematize a great whole made up of men and to order it properly, to keep it together by sternness of discipline in which pedantry has no part, and by economy with no admixture of avarice; and frequently endurance and even presence of mind. These ethical, statesmanlike qualities are, take them all in all, a more indispensable condition of high undertaker's profit than the technical are.[1]

B. On the risk of the undertaking in which not only one's property, but one's reputation, may be lost.[2]

C. As to the disagreeableness of the undertaking or enterprise, we must take into especial consideration the disinclination of capitalists in general to assume the care and trouble of concerning themselves directly with the employment of their capital. (§ 183.) The undertaker's profit is, besides, lower in proportion as he needs to care less for the profitable appli-

---

[1] Thus *Arkwright*, by his talent for organization principally, attained to royal wealth, while *Hargreaves*, a greater inventive genius, from a technic point of view, had to bear all the hardships of extreme poverty.

[2] An experienced Frenchman, *Godard*, estimates that of 100 industrial enterprises attempted or begun, 20 fail altogether before they have so much as taken root; that from 50 to 60 vegetate for a time in continual danger of failing altogether, and that, at the furthest, 10 succeed well, but scarcely with an enduring success. (Enquête commerciale de 1834, II, 233.)

cation of the different sources of production, and for their preservation. Hence it is, in general, higher for the direction of circulating than of fixed capital; in speculative trade and in wholesale trade which extends to the whole world, than in retail trade and merely local business.[3]

It has, indeed, been remarked, that the undertaker's profit is, as a rule, proportioned to the capital employed.[4] This may be true in most cases, but only as the accidental compromise between opposing forces. It is evident that the greater the enterprise is, the greater may be the surplus over and above the compensation stipulated for in advance of all the coöperating productive forces, and not only absolutely but also relatively. We need only call to mind the successful results attending the greater division of labor (§ 66) and the greater division of use *(Gebrauchstheilung)* (§ 207); the greater facility of using remains in production on a large scale, and the fact that all purchases, and all obtaining of capital are made, when the items are large, at cheaper rates, because of the more convenient conducting of the business.

This is true up to the point where the magnitude of the whole becomes so great as to render the conducting of it difficult. Considered even subjectively, the great undertaker, whose name and responsibility keep a great many productive forces together, may demand a higher reward, because there are so few persons competent to do the same. On the other hand, it cannot be denied that a support in keeping with his position may be called the amount of the cost of production of the undertaker's labor. If this cost is once fixed by custom, it will, of course, be relatively high in those branches of business which permit only of the employment of a small capital.[5]

---

[3] Thus *Ganilh*, Théorie de l'Economie politique I, p. 145, was of the opinion that in France's foreign trade the profit was only 20, and in its internal trade, scarcely 10 per cent. of the value put in circulation.

[4] *Hermann* loc. cit. 208.

[5] According to *Sinclair*, Grundgesetze des Ackerbaues, 1821, the profit on capital of English farmers was wont to be from 10 to 18 per cent. Only in very remarkable cases, by persons in very favorable circi mstances, was from

In the higher stages of civilization, the undertaker's profit has, like the rate of interest, a tendency to decline. This decline is, indeed, in part, only an apparent one, caused by the decreased risk and the smaller indemnity-premium. But it is, in part, a real one, produced by the increased competition of undertakers.⁶ The more intelligent land-owners and work-

---

15 to 20 per cent. earned; that is, on the whole, less than in commerce and industry. In the case of farmers of meadow-land, 15 per cent. and even more was not unusual; because there is a need of less outlay here, but more mercantile speculation, especially in the fattening of live stock.

At the end of the last century English farmers expected 10 per cent. profit on their capital. (*A. Young*, View of the Agriculture of Suffolk, 1797, 25.) And so *Senior* is of opinion that, in the England of to-day, industrial enterprises of £100,000 yield a profit of less than 10 per cent. a year; those of £40,000, at least 12½ per cent.; those of from £10,000 to £20,000, 15 per cent.; smaller ones 20 per cent. and even more. He makes mention of fruit hucksters who earned over 20 per cent. a day; that is, over 7,000 per cent. a year! (Outlines, 203 seq.) In Manchester, manufacturers, according to the same authority, turned over their capital twice a year at 5 per cent.; retail dealers, three times a year at 3½ per cent. (Ibid, 143.) *Torrens*, The Budget (1844), 108, designates 7 per cent. as the minimum profit which would induce an English capitalist to engage in an enterprise of his own. According to *v. Viebahn*, Statistik des Regierungsbezirks Düsseldorf, 836, I, 180, the undertaker's profit, i. e., the surplus money of the value of the manufactured articles, after deduction made of the raw material and wages, in the Berg country, amounted to, in 81 iron factories, 146,400 thalers; in 6 cotton factories, to 21,200 thalers; in 15 cloth factories, to 14,725 thalers; in 4 worsted factories, to 1,700 thalers; in 4 brush factories, to 800 thalers; in 2 tobacco factories to 10,220 thalers; in 2 paper factories, to 7,400 thalers; on an average, 1,924 thalers; although many undertakers earned only from 200 to 400 thalers, and some few from 5,000 to 10,000 thalers.

⁶ This is, of course somewhat oppressive to many individuals, and hence we find that in those countries which are unquestionably making great advances in civilization, there are so many complaints of alleged growing impoverishment. Compare *Sam. Fortrey*, England's Interest and Improvement, 1663; *R. Coke*, A Treatise wherein is demonstrated that the Church and State of England are in equal danger with the Trade of it, 1671. Britania languens, showing the Grounds and Reasons of the Increase and Decay of Land, etc., 1680. And per contra, England's great Happiness, wherein is demonstrated that a great Part of our Complaints are causeless, 1677. Analogous claims might be shown to exist in Germany by a collection of almost any number of opinions advanced during the last thirty years.

men become, the more readily do they acquire the capacity and desire to use the productive forces peculiar to them in undertakings of their own; and the number of retired persons who live from their rents grows smaller with the decline of the rate of interest. The strong competition of undertakers now leads to degeneration, and undertakings or enterprises become usual in which the gains or losses are subjective, and are destitute of all politico-economical productiveness; for instance, the purchase of growing fruits, and businesses carried on in "margins," or differences. It is self-evident that the circumstances which retard the rate of interest, or turn it retrograde, would have a similar effect on the undertaker's profit. (§ 186.) On the whole, a rapidly growing people meet with great gains and losses, but the preponderance is in favor of the former. A stationary people are wont to become more and more careful and cautious. A declining people underestimate the chances of loss, although in their case they tend more and more to preponderate over the chances of gain. *(v. Mangoldt.)*

SECTION CXCVI *(a.)*.

UNDERTAKER'S PROFIT.— HAVING THE "LEAD."

The undertaker's profit is that branch of the national income in which the greater number of new fortunes are made. If a land-owner has a large income, he generally considers himself obliged to make a correspondingly large outlay, one in keeping with his position; and workmen who are not undertakers themselves seldom have the means to make large savings. Besides, undertakers stand between the purchasers of their products and the lessors of the productive forces used by them in the peculiarly favorable situation which I may describe by the expression: having, as they say in card-playing, "the lead."[1] When, in the struggle for prices, one party occu-

---

[1] The same principle is effective in intermediate commerce, and in the intervention of bankers between government and state creditors.

pies a position which enables him to observe every change of circumstance much sooner than his opponent, the latter may always suffer from the effects of erroneous prices. If, for instance, the productiveness of business increases, even without any personal merit of the individual undertakers themselves, it will always be some time before the decline in the price of commodities and the rise in the rate of interest take place, as a result of the increased competition of undertakers, consequent upon the extraordinary rate of the undertaker's profit. It is difficult, and even impossible in most instances for the proprietors of the productive forces which they have rented out, to immediately estimate accurately the profit made by undertakers. On the other hand, the least enhancement of the price of the forces of production is immediately felt by the undertakers, and causes them to raise their prices. They just as quickly observe a decline of the prices of the commodities, and know how to make others bear it by lowering wages and the rate of interest.[2] It should not be forgotten that the persons most expert, far-seeing, active and expeditious in things economic, belong to the undertaking class.[3][4]

[2] This is much less the case in rents, for the reason that contracts here are made for a much longer term. Hence, here the farmer has as much to fear as to hope from a change of circumstances. Hence, too, we meet with a farmer who has grown rich much more seldom than with a manufacturer or a merchant.

[3] If an undertaker can cede his higher reward to another and guaranty its continuance, the circumstances which enable him to do this assume the nature of fixed capital; for instance, the trade or *clientèle* secured by custom or privilege. If the undertaker has not the power to dispose of it in this way, the increased profit either disappears with his retirement from the business or falls to the owner of the capital employed, and still more to the land owner. Thus, for instance, how frequently it has happened that a store, which has been largely resorted to by the public, drawn thither by the business tact of the lessee, has afterwards been rented by the owner at a higher rent! (*Hermann*, loc. cit. 210.)

[4] *Lassalle's* socialistic attacks on Political Economy have been directed mainly against the undertaker's profit or reward. Compare the work " Bastiat-Schulze von Delitzsch, der ökonom. Julian oder Kapital und Arbeit," 1863. By means of state credit, he would have this branch of income turned

CHAPTER VI.

CONCLUDING REMARKS ON
THE THREE BRANCHES OF INCOME.

SECTION CXCVII.

INFLUENCE OF THE BRANCHES OF INCOME ON THE PRICE OF COMMODITIES.

We have seen, § 106, that the cost of production of a commodity, considered from the point of view of individual economy, may be reduced to the payment for the use of the requisite productive forces rented or loaned to the producer. Hence every great variation in the relation of the three branches of income to one another must produce a corre-

---

over to common labor. *Dühring* also, Kapital und Arbeit 90, declaims not so much against capital as against "the absolutism of undertakers." *Schäffle* D. Vierteljahrsschrift Nr. 106, II, 223, objects to this, that undertakers give value in exchange to unfinished products, a great service rendered even to the laboring class, who otherwise would have to resign the advantages of the division of labor.

The undertaker's profit is precisely the part of the great politico-economical tree from which further growth chiefly takes place. To artificially arrest it, therefore, would be to hasten the stationary state, and thus make general and greater the pressure on workmen and capitalists, which it is sought to remove locally. Hence *Roesler*, Grundsätze, 507 ff., very appropriately calls the undertaker's profit the premium paid by society to those who most effectually combat the "law of rent." The importance of a good undertaker may be clearly seen when a joint stock manufacturing company pays a dividend of from 20 to 30 per cent., while one close by, of the same kind, produces no profit whatever. But, at the same time, the socialistic hatred of this branch of income may be easily accounted for, in a time full of stock-jobbing, which last never produces except a pseudo-undertaker's profit.

sponding variation in the price of commodities.[1] When, for instance, the rate of wages increases because they absorb a larger part of the national income, those commodities in the production of which human labor, directly employed, is the chief factor, must become dearer as compared with others. Whether this difference shall be felt principally by the products of nature or of capital (compare § 46 seq.), depends on the causes which brought about the enhancement of the rate of wages. Thus, a large decrease of population, or emigration on a large scale, will usually lower rent as well as the rate of interest;[2] an extraordinary improvement made in the art of agriculture, only the former; and an extraordinary increase of capital, only the latter. The usual course of things, namely that the growth of population necessitates a heavier draft on the resources of the soil, and thus causes rents to go up, and makes labor dear, must have the effect of raising the price of the products of labor and of natural forces, as compared with the products of capital; and all the more as it causes the rate of interest to suffer a positive decline. The products of mechanical labor become relatively cheaper; and cheaper in proportion as the producing machinery is more durable; therefore in proportion as, in the price of the services it renders, mere interest preponderates over compensation for its wear and tear.[3]

---

[1] Compare *Adam Smith*, I, ch. 7, fin. This relative increase or decrease of one branch of income at the expense or to the advantage of another, should be distinguished from the absolute change of its amount which does not affect the cost of production. Thus, for instance, when the rent of land indeed increases, but in consequence of a simultaneous improvement in agriculture, a decline in the rate of interest, and an enhancement of the price of wheat is avoided (§ 157). So, too, when individual wages increase on account of the greater skill and energy of labor, but the same quantity and quality of labor do not become dearer (§ 172 seq.); and lastly, when the rate of interest remaining unaltered, the receipts of capitalists are increased by reason of an increase of their capital (§ 185).

[2] After the great plague in the 14th century in England, when all the products of labor became dearer, skins and wool fell largely in price: *Rogers*, I, § 400.

[3] Anyone who carefully reads all the five divisions of *Ricardo's* first chap-

Let us, for a moment, leave ground-rent out of the question entirely, and suppose a nation's economy whose production is conducted by eleven undertakers employed on different commodities. Let us suppose that undertaker No. 1 uses machinery exclusively and employs only as many workmen as are strictly necessary to look after it, that undertaker No. 2 has a somewhat larger number of workmen and a somewhat smaller amount of fixed capital etc.; and that this increase in the number of workmen and decrease in the amount of fixed capital continues until we reach undertaker No. 11, who employs all his capital in the payment of wages. If now, the rate of wages were to rise, and the interest on capital to fall in the same proportion, the commodities produced by undertaker No. 11 would rise most in price, and those of No. 1 decline most. In the case of undertaker No. 6, the opposing influences would probably balance each other, and if the producers of money belonged to this sixth class, it would be very easy to get a view of the whole change in the circumstances of production, in the money-price of the different commodities.[4]

---

ter will soon find that this great thinker rightly understood the foregoing, although the great abstractness and hypothetical nature of his conclusions might easily lead the reader astray. The proposition which closes the second part, and which has been so frequently misunderstood by his disciples, can be maintained only on the supposition that the prices of all commodities hitherto have been made up of equal proportions of rent, capital and wages. But think of Brussels lace and South American skins!

[4] Compare *J. Mill*, Anfangsgründe der polit. Oekonomie, Jacob's translation, § 13 ff.; *McCulloch*, Principles, III, 6. *Adam Smith* was of opinion, that higher wages enhanced the price of commodities in an arithmetical ratio, a higher rate of interest in a geometrical one (I, ch. 9). Similarly *Child*, Discourse of Trade, 38. This last *Kraus*, Staatswirthschaft, better expresses by saying that an increase in the rate of interest operates in the ratio of the compounded interests.

SECTION CXCVIII.

REMEDY IN CASE ONE FACTOR OF PRODUCTION HAS BECOME DEARER.

When one of the three branches of income has grown as compared with the others; in other words, when the factor of production which it represents has become relatively dearer, it is to the interest of the undertaker and of the public, that it should be replaced where possible by another and cheaper productive force. (§ 47.) On this depends the advantageousness of *intensive* agriculture (high farming) in every higher stage of civilization. There land is dear and labor cheap. Hence, efforts are made to get along with the least amount of land-surface, and this minimum of land is made more productive by a number of expedients in cultivation, by manuring it, by seed-corn etc., of course also by the employment of journeymen laborers, oxen etc. And since the price of land is intimately connected with the price of most raw material, remains are here saved as much as possible, often with a great deal of trouble.[1] In a lower stage of civilization, such savings would be considered extravagance. As land is here cheap, and capital dear, it is necessary to carry on the cultivation of land *extensively;* that is, save in capital and labor, and allow the factor nature to perform the most possible. The clearing up of untilled land, or the draining of swampy land etc., would be frequently injurious here; for it would require the use of a very large amount of capital to obtain land of comparatively little value.

In large cities, it is customary to build houses high in proportion to the dearness of the land.[2] Thus, in England, where

---

[1] The sickle instead of the scythe; careful threshing by hand, and, where the rate of interest is low, threshing by machinery instead of the treading out of the sheaf by oxen. Thus in Paris the scraps from restaurants and soap-factories are made into stearin; and the remnants in shawl-factories in Vienna are sent to Belgium to be used by cloth manufacturers.

[2] Remarked in ancient times of Tyre, which was situated on a small

the rate of interest is low and wages high, labor is readily supplanted by capital. In countries like the East Indies or China, the reverse is the case. I need only call attention to the palanquins used in Asia instead of carriages; to the men who in South America carried ore down eighteen hundred steps to the smelting furnaces,³ and, on the other hand, to the "elevators," so much in favor in England, which are used in factories to carry people from one story to another inside to save them the trouble of going up stairs.⁴

SECTION CXCIX.

INFLUENCE OF FOREIGN TRADE.

Foreign trade, that great means of coöperation of labor among different nations, affords such a remedy in a very special manner. It very frequently happens that the undertakers of one country, when a certain factor of production seems too dear at home, borrow it elsewhere. Thus, for instance, a country with a high rate of wages draws on another for labor, and one with a high rate of interest on another for capital.¹ We elsewhere consider such a course of things from the standpoint of the supplying country, which in this way is healed of a heavy plethora of some single factor of production which disturbs the harmony of the whole. (§§ 187, 259, ff.) But, at the same time, the supplied country, considered from a

---

island, and, therefore, without the possibility of horizontal extension. (*Strabo*, XVI, 757.)

³ *Humbol lt*, N. Espagne II, ch. 5, II, ch. 11.

⁴ Thus, in England, the safety of railroad trains is not secured as in Germany by a multitude of watchmen etc.; but by solid barriers, by bridges at every crossing, in other words, by capital.

¹ "The transportation of productive capital and industrial forces from one point where their services are worse paid for, to another where they find a rich reward, will not be apt to be made so long as the equilibrium may be obtained [most frequently much more easily] by the interchange of the products." (*Nebenius*, Oeff. Credit, I, 48.) The repeal of the corn laws in England certainly diminished the emigration of English capital.

purely economic point of view, reaps decided advantages therefrom. If, for instance, a Swiss confectioner returns from Saint Petersburgh to his home, after having made a fortune in an honest way, no one can say that Russia has grown poorer by the amount of that fortune. This man made his own capital; if he were to remain in Russia, its national economy would be richer than before his immigration thither. Now, it is, at least, no poorer, and has in the meantime had the advantage of the more skilled labor of the foreigner.[2] And, so, when a capitalist living in Germany purchases Hungarian land, the national income of Hungary is diminished by the amount of the annual rent which now goes to Germany; but it receives an equal amount in the interest on capital, provided the purchase was an honorable one and the capital given in exchange for the land honestly invested.[3] If Hungary, in general, had a superabundance of land but a lack of capital, the economic advantage is undoubted.[4]

These economic rules, indeed, are applicable only to the ex-

[2] For an official declaration of the Brazilian state in this direction, see Novara Reise.

[3] Basing himself hereon, *Petty*, Political Anatomy of Ireland, 82 ff., questions the usual opinion, that Ireland suffered so much from absenteeism. He says that a prohibition of absenteeism carried out to its logical conclusion would require every man to sit on the sod he had tilled himself. *Carey*, On the Rate of Wages, 1835, 477, calls English capitalists who draw interest from America, absentees.

[4] The older political economists have, as a rule, ignored this law, and were wont to consider every payment of money to a foreign country as injurious. Thus, for instance, *Culpeper*, Tract against the high Rate of Usury, 1623, 1640, disapproves all loans made from foreign countries, because they draw more money in interest, and in repayment of the principal out of the nation, than they brought into it at first; and all the more, as the loan is generally procured, not in the precious metals, but in foreign goods, of which there is a superabundance in the home country. Similarly *Child*, Discourse of Trade, 1690, 79, who claims that the creditor was always fattened at the expense of the debtor. Hence *v. Schröder*, Fürst. Schatz.-und Rentkammar, 141, advises that the capital borrowed in foreign countries should be confiscated. Compare, also, *v. Justi*, Staatswirthschaft, II, 461. And yet the very simplest calculation shows, that if a man borrows $1,000 at 5 per cent. and makes 10, he is doing a good business with the borrowed capital. This *Locke*, Consid

tent that higher and national considerations do not in the interest of all, create exceptions to them. "Is not the life more than meat, and the body than raiment?" No rational people will allow certain services to be performed for them preponderantly by foreigners, even when they can be performed cheaper by the latter — the services of religion, of the army, of the state etc. The same is true of land-ownership; and all the truer in proportion as political and legal rights of presentation and other forms of patronage are attached to it. Lastly, hypothecation-debts which go beyond certain limits, may entail the same consequences as the complete alienation of the land;[5] and Raynal may have been, under certain circumstances, right when he said, that to admit foreigners to subscribe to the national debt was equivalent to ceding a province to them.[6] It is obvious that a great power may do much in this relation that would be a risk to a small state.[7][8]

---

erations, 9, recognizes very clearly. Compare, also, *J. B. Say*, Traité, II, ch. 10, and *Hermann*, Staatsw. Unters., 365 seq.

[5] Think of the English creditors in Portugal and the Genoese in Corsica! (*Steuart*, Principles, II, ch. 29.) Considered simply from an economic standpoint, the Edinburg Review, XX, 358, very clearly demonstrates that England should recruit her army from Ireland, where wages are so much lower than in Great Britain. But how dangerous in a political sense! In 1832, one-fourth of the stock of the United States Bank was in the hands of foreigners, and hence its opponents nick-named it the "British Bank." By the rules of the principal bank in Philadelphia, in 1836, only American citizens were allowed a vote in its proceedings. Similarly in the case of the Bank of France. (*M. Chevalier*, Lettres sur l' Amerique du N. I, 364.) It may be remarked in general, that the older political economists have based correct political views on false economic principles, while the more modern ignore them entirely.

[6] Compare *Montesquieu*, E. des Lois L, XXII, 17; *Blackstone*, Commentaries, I, 320.

[7] Thus Austria conceded, in 1854–55, a number of railways to French capitalists, and always favored the purchase of landed estates by small foreign princes. In the latter case, Austrian influence abroad was much more promoted by the measure than was foreign influence in Austria.

[8] Every nationality is not worth the sacrificing of the highest economic advantage or profit to it. Or, would it be preferable to leave the Hottentots and Caffirs, poor, barbarous and heathenish?

SECTION CC.

INFLUENCE OF THE BRANCHES OF INCOME ON THE PRICE OF COMMODITIES.

In relation to foreign trade, in the narrowest sense of the term, fears were formerly very frequently expressed and are sometimes even now, which in the last analysis are based on the assumption that one country might be underbid by another in all branches of commodities.[1] This is evidently absurd. Whoever wants to pay for foreign commodities can do it only in goods of his own. When he pays for them with money, the money is either the immediate product of his own husbandry (mining countries!), or the mediate product obtained by the previous surrender of products of his own. To receive from foreign countries all the objects which one has need of, would be to receive them as a gift.

It is just as absurd to fear that the three branches of income in the same country's economy should be all relatively high at the same time, and competition with foreign countries be thus made more difficult. Rent and interest especially in this respect have to demean themselves in ways diametrically opposed to each other.[2] When trade is entirely free, every nation will engage at last in those branches of production which require chiefly the productive forces which are cheapest in that country; that is which the relatively low level of the corresponding branch of income recommends to individual economy and enterprise. The merely absolute and personal height of the three branches of income has, as we have

---

[1] Thus, *Forbonnais*, Elements du Commerce I, 73. *J. Möser*, Patr. Ph., I, No. 2.

[2] For a thorough refutation of the error that everything is dearer in England than in France, see Journ des Econ., Mai, 1854, 295 seq. A distinguished architect assured me in 1858, that a person in London could build about as much for £1 as for from 6 to 7 thalers in Berlin; only the aggregate expense in both countries is made up of elements very different in their relative proportions.

said, no direct influence on the price of commodities. In this respect, all these may be higher in one country than in another. Thus, for instance, English land owners, capitalists and workmen may be all at the same time in a better economic condition respectively than Polish land owners, capitalists and workmen, when the national income of England stands to its area and population in general, in a much more favorable ratio than the Polish.[3]

---

[3] We very frequently hear that countries with high wages must be outflanked in a neutral market by countries with a low rate of wages. *Ricardo's* disciples reject this, because a decrease in the profit would put the undertaker in a condition to bear the loss caused by the high wages paid. See Report of the Select Committee on Artisans and Machinery. *Senior* ridicules such reasoning very appropriately by inquiring: "Might not the loss enable him to bear the loss?" Outlines, 146. And so *J. B. Say* thinks that wages are always lowest when undertakers are earning nothing. The truth is rather this: a country with a relatively high rate of wages cannot, in a neutral market, offer those commodities the chief factors required for the production of which is labor; but the comparatively low rate of interest or low rents, or the lowness of both found in connection therewith, must fit it to produce other commodities very advantageously. If, therefore, the rate of wages rises, the result will be to divert production and exports into other channels than those in which they have hitherto flowed. The old complaint of Saxon agriculturists, that there is a lack of labor in the country, is certainly very surprising in a nation as thickly populated as Saxony. But the remedy proposed by the most experienced practitioners consists chiefly in a higher rate of wages to enable workmen to care for themselves in old age, the introduction of the piece-work system and an increase of agricultural machines. But it seems to me, that the whole situation there points to the advantage of in part limiting the large farming hitherto practiced to live-stock raising and other branches in which labor may be spared, and in part of replacing it, by small farming of plants which are objects of trade.

Many points belonging to this subject have been very well discussed by *J. Tucker*, in his refutation of *Hume's* theory on the final and inevitable superiority of poor countries over rich ones in industrial matters. (Four Tracts on political and commercial Subjects, 1774, No. 1; *L. Lauderdale*, Inquiry, 206.)

SECTION CCI.

HARMONY OF THE THREE BRANCHES OF INCOME.—INDIVIDUAL DIFFERENCE IN THEM.

As national-economical civilization advances, the personal difference of the three branches of income is wont to become more and more sharply defined.[1] The struggle between landowners, farmers and workmen, which Ricardo necessarily assumed, did not exist at all in the middle ages; since landowners and farmers were then usually one and the same person, and since workmen, either as slaves or peasants, were protected against competition properly so called. And so in the industry of that time, based on the trades or on domestic industry.[2][3]

When, later, the division of labor increases, all the differences of men's aptitudes are turned to more advantage, and are more fully developed. In the same proportion that a

---

[1] Among nations in their decline, rent and interest fall into one possession again, because capitalists here are wont to buy the land. (*Roscher*, National-ökonomik des Ackerbaues, § 140 ff.)

[2] Related to this peculiarity of the middle ages is the fact that the canon law looked with disfavor on the personal separation of the three factors of production. So also in the prohibition of the *Weddeschat* referred to § 161, instead of rent-purchase (*Rentekauf*), also by extending the idea of partnership to a number of transactions which are only forms of loan. (*Endemann* in *Hildebrand's* Jahrb., 1863, 176 ff.) Antiquity also, with the independence of its οἶκος, with its slavery, etc., had not developed the difference between the three branches of industry to any extent. *Rodbertus*, in *Hildebrand's* Jahrbb., 1865, I, 343.

[3] If older writers, like *Steuart*, etc., speak so little of capital, labor and rent, and so much of city and country, it is not on account of ignorance simply. The contrast between the latter was then much more important than to-day, and that between the former much less developed. When, indeed, *Colton*, Public Economy of the United States, 1848, 155 ff., claims that because in America the three branches of income do not exist in so separated a condition as in Europe, therefore European Political Economy and its theories are not applicable to America, he forgets that science should not be simply a description or impression made of the reality, but an analysis of it.

working class is developed, the members of which are nothing but workmen, and can scarcely hope to possess capital or land,[4] there grows up, side by side with it, a class of mere capitalists, who come to obtain an ever-increasing importance.

Considered from a purely economic point of view, this transition has its great advantages. How much must the existence of a special class of capitalists facilitate the concentration of capital and the consequent promotion of production, as well as its (capital's) price-leveling influx and outflow! Even "idle" capitalists have this of good, that, without them, no competent man, destitute of means could engage in any independent enterprise. When, indeed, the gulf between these two classes passes certain bounds, it may, politically and socially, become a great evil. (§ 63.)[5]

SECTION CCII.

HARMONY OF THE THREE BRANCHES OF INCOME.—NECESSITY OF THE FEELING OF A COMMON INTEREST.

Every class corresponding to a branch of the national income must live with the consciousness that its interests coincide with the economic interests of the whole nation. Whenever the entire national income increases, each branch of it may increase without any injury to the others, and, as a rule,

---

[4] It is a very characteristic fact that, in our days, when workmen are spoken of, it is generally day laborers and tradesmen that are understood. In Prussia, in 1804, 17.8 per cent. of the population earned their living by letting out their labor; in 1846, 22.8 per cent. as day-laborers, servants, journeymen, tradesmen and factory hands. *(Dieterici.)*

[5] *Ricardo*, Principles, ch. 4, recognizes the bright side as well as *Sismondi*, N. P., I, 268, or *Buret*, De la Misère des Classes laborieuses en Angleterre et en France, 1841, its dark side. *Sismondi* thinks that land and the capital employed in its cultivation are found to the greatest disadvantage in the hands of the same person. The existence of a thrifty peasant class (also of a class of tradesmen) is one of the best means to prevent the too wide separation of the three branches of income.

does really increase.¹ But it is possible that the land owning class may be specially dependent on the prosperity of the whole people. How easy it is for workmen to emigrate; and how much easier yet for capital! England, to-day, can scarcely carry on a great war, in which it would not, at least at the beginning, have to fight English capital.² Where the treasure is, the heart is also! The land alone is immovable. It alone cannot be withdrawn from the pressure of taxation or from the distress of war. It alone cannot flee into foreign parts.³ ⁴ At the same time, it cannot be denied that the pos-

---

¹ The contrast between *Adam Smith*, at the end of the first book, and *Ricardo*, ch. 24, in regard to this point, is very characteristic of the times of those two authors. According to *Smith*, the private interests of the land-owners and laborers run entirely parallel; only both classes are easily deceived as to their own interests. Capitalists understand their own interest very well, and represent it with great energy; but their interest is in opposition to the common good, in so far as their profit among a poor and declining people is higher than among a rich and flourishing one. *Ricardo*, on the other hand, thinks that the interest of the land-owners is opposed to that of all others for the reason that they desire that the cost of the production of wheat etc. should be as high as possible.

Related to this is the fact that, in *Adam Smith's* time, the new theory of rent remained almost unnoticed, but that after 1815, it became rapidly popular. In a similar way, the socialists of the present time are wont to charge the undertaking class with opposing their own interests to those of the whole people, meaning by the whole the majority. (§ 196 a.)

² Towards the end of the 14th century the great Flemish merchants always sided with the absolutism of France in opposition to their own. *Artevelde*.

³ Hence it is, that in so many constitutions, charters of cities etc., the exercise of the higher rights of citizenship is conditioned by the possession of a certain quantity of land, and that land-ownership is considered as a species of public function.

I read, a short time ago, the life of a North-German noblemen who, in 1813, had fought bravely against the French, "although he was a man of large estates, and the enemy might therefore very easily have laid hands on them." If this "although" of his eulogist expressed the actual feeling of large landed proprietors, a great many old political institutions would have lost all foundation.

Ad. Müller was of opinion that the rights of primogeniture etc., might be an obstacle in the way of the development of the net income of a nation's economy; but that they gave to the state and to the national life the warlike tone so necessary to them etc. (Elemente, II, 90.)

sibility of being able to carry one's fortune out of a country in one's pocketbook and to be able to procure there with one's money the same conveniences, customs etc., to which one was accustomed at home, is, under certain circumstances, an important element of political and religious freedom. Moreover, the bright side and the dark of every class of owners, especially the dread of all unnecessary and also of all necessary change, must be common to rent and interest. Hence, where there is a marked and well-defined separation of the branches of income, it will be always considered a difficult but unavoidable problem, how to enable mere labor to take an active part in the affairs of the state.[5]

In times when calm prevails (not, however, in transition-crises such as are referred to in § 24), there is a public opinion concerning merit and reward, we might say a public conscience, by which a definite relation of the three branches of income to one another is declared equitable. Every "fair-minded man" feels satisfied when this relation is realized, and this feeling of satisfaction is one of the principal conditions precedent to the prosperity of production; inasmuch as upon it depends the participation (*Theilnahme*) of all owners of funds and forces. Every deviation from this relation or proportion is, of course, a misfortune,[6] but never so great as

[4] "The Roman capitalists on whom Pompey counted, left him in the lurch at the moment of danger, because Cæsar destroyed only the constitution, but respected their business relations." (*K. W. Nitsch.*)

[5] *Kosegarten*, Nat. Œk., 186, thinks that, on account of the struggle between the labor interest and the interest of capitalists, in our times, the "fourth estate" is not as well represented by persons belonging to the propertied classes as the constitutionalist party thinks. And in fact, *Jarke*, Principienfragen, 1854, 197, would have it represented by the government, in order to prevent the struggle between rich and poor. See *Cherbuliez*, Riche ou Pauvre, p. 242 seq.

[6] *A. Walker* shows, in a very happy manner, how no misfortune, however great, whether it come from heaven or from earth, in the shape of pestilence, drought, flood or oppressive taxation, so rapidly and hopelessly ruins a nation's economy as when the harmony which should exist between capital and labor is disturbed by foul play or legal frauds between labor or capital and their reward." (Sc. of Wealth, 66.)

when it takes place at the expense of the wages of labor. It should never be forgotten that rent is an appropriation of the gifts of nature, and that interest is a further fruit obtained by frugality from older labor already remunerated. Besides, the rate of wages when high, generally adds to the efficiency of labor, which cannot be claimed for interest or rent.⁷ The best means to preserve the harmony of the three branches of income is, however, universal activity. "Rich or poor, strong or weak, the idler is a knave." *(J. J. Rousseau.)*

---

⁷ Compare *Lotz*, Revision, III, 322 ff., 327, 334 ff. Handbuch, I, 511 ff. *Lafitte*, Sur la Réduction de la Rente, 56. *Fuoco* exaggerates this into the principle: *che la distribuzione, e non la produzione, sia la prima e principal operazione in economia.* (Saggi economici, II, p. 44.)

CHAPTER VII.

DISTRIBUTION OF NATIONAL INCOME.

SECTION CCIII.

EFFECT OF AN EQUAL DIVISION OF THE NATIONAL INCOME.

The best distribution of the national income among a people is that which enables them to enjoy the greatest amount and variety of real goods, and permanently to produce real goods in an increasing quantity and variety.

If the income of a people were divided equally among all, each one would indeed, be, to a very great extent, independent of all others. But then, no one would care to devote himself to the coarser and less agreeable occupations, and these would be either entirely neglected, or people would have to take turns in engaging in them.[1] (§ 9.) And thus would disappear one of the chief advantages of the division of labor, viz: that the higher orders of talent are devoted to the higher orders of labor. Besides, it is very doubtful, whether, under such circumstances, there would still be any solvent *(zahlungsfähige)* demand for the achievements of art.

Nor would the saving of capital prosper, where such equality prevailed. Most men consider the average outlay of their equals as an unavoidable want, and save only to the ex-

---

[1] According to *Schäffle*, System, II, 379 ff., "the distribution of the social return of production which conduces to the attainment of the highest measure of civilization in the moral association of men and in all the grades of that association, and thereby to the satisfaction of all true human wants in the highest degree." Thus only can a satisfactory line of demarkation be drawn between the profit of capital and the wages of labor (384).

tent that they possess more than others of their class. If, therefore, every one had an equal income, no one would consider himself in a condition to save.[2] The same consideration would deter most men from every economic venture, and yet no great progress is possible where no venture is made.[3][4]

SECTION CCIV.

DISTRIBUTION OF NATIONAL INCOME. — MONEYED ARISTOCRACIES AND PAUPERISM.

The extreme opposite of this, when the middle class disappears and the whole nation falls into a few over-rich men and numberless proletarians, we call the oligarchy of money, with pauperism as the reverse of the medal. Such a social condition has all the hardship of an aristocracy without its palliatives. As it is, as a rule, the offspring of a degenerated democracy,[1] it cannot in form depart too widely from the princi-

---

[2] See *Aristoph.*, Plut., 508 ff. Not taken into consideration sufficiently by *Benjamin Franklin*, in his eulogy of the equality of property: The internal State of America, 1784.

[3] The essential characteristic of the desert is, according to *Ritter*, Erdkunde, I, 1019 seq., its uniformity. No break in the horizontal plain, and hence no condensation of atmospheric vapor into bodies of water of any considerable size. The composition of the soil is everywhere the same; nothing but masses of silex and salt, hard and sharp. Lastly, extreme mobility of the surface, which undulates with every wind, so that no plant can take root in it. Nearly every feature in this picture finds its analogon in the extreme political and economic equality of men.

[4] *Les supériorités, qui ne sont dues qu'à un usage plus intelligent et mieux réglé de nos facultés naturelles, loin d'être un mal, sont un véritable bien. C'est dans la plus grande prospérité, qui accompagne un plus grand et plus heureux effort, qu'est le principe de tout développement.* (*Dunoyer*, Liberté du Travail, IV, 9, 10.) But, indeed, the rich man should never forget that society "inasmuch as it permits the concentration of wealth in his hands, expects that he will employ it to better advantage than the mass of mankind would if that same wealth were equally divided among them." (*Brentano.*)

[1] The more the lower classes degenerate into the rabble, and the more the national sovereignty comes into the hands of this rabble, the easier will it become for the rich to buy up the State.

ple of equality. Only get rich, they cry to the famishing poor; the law puts no obstacle in your way, and you shall immediately share our position.[2] Here the uniformity and centralization of the state, which are an abomination in the eyes of genuine aristocracy, are carried to the extreme. Capital takes the place of men, and is valued more than men. All life is made to depend on the state, that its masters, the great moneymen, may control it as they will. The falling away of all restrictions on trade, and of all uncommercial considerations relating to persons and circumstances, gives full play to capital, and speculators seek to win all that can be won. And, indeed, all colossal fortunes are generally made at the expense of others, either with the assistance of the state-power or by speculation in the fluctuations of values.[3] The dependence of proletarians on others is here all the greater, because from a complete absence of capital and land, so far as they are concerned, they are compelled, uninterruptedly, to carry their entire labor-force to market; and also because the supply of labor is made in masses embracing a large number of individuals, while the demand for labor lies in the hands of very few, and may be very readily and systematically concentrated.[4] So great and one-sided a dependence is, for men too far removed from one another for real mutual love, doubtless one of the greatest of moral temptations. It is as easy a matter for the hopelessly poor to hate the law, as it is for the over-rich to despise it.[5] Under such circumstances, the contagious power

---

[2] In the middle stages of the nation's economy, such as are described in §§ 62, 66, 90, 207, in which even the relative advantages of industry on a large scale over industry on a small scale, are not much developed the making political rights dependent on the possession of a certain amount of property is certainly a means of promoting equality. Hence, therefore, a reconciliation between the differences of class created by birth, may be effected for a long time here.

[3] *Hermann*, Staatsw. Untersuchungen, II, Aufl. 136.

[4] *Necker*, Législation et Commerce des Grains, 1775, I. passim. Compare *Bacon*, Serm fideles, 15, 29, 34, 39.

[5] *Schiller's* terrible words:
" *Etwas muss er sein eigen nennen,*
Oder der Mensch wird morden und brennen."

of communism, the dangers of which to order and freedom we have treated of in § 80, is great. There is a dreadful lesson in the fact of history, that six individuals owned one-half of the province of Africa, *when Nero had them put to death!*[6] Externally, a moneyed oligarchy will always be a weak state. The great majority who have nothing to lose take little interest in the perpetuation of its political independence. They rather rejoice at the downfall of their oppressors hitherto, and are cheered by the hope of obtaining a part of the general plunder.[7] The rich, too, separated from the neglected and propertyless masses of the nation, and rightly distrustful of them, begin to forget their nationality, and to balance its advantages against the sacrifices necessary to preserve it. But, a merely materialistic calculation leads doubtless to the conclusion, that universal empire is the most rational form of the state. The world-sovereignty of Rome was, by no circumstance more promoted than by the struggles between the rich and the poor, which devastated the *orbis terrarum*, and in which the Romans generally sided with the property classes.[8,9,10,11]

— i. e., " Something must he call his own, or man will murder and burn." It is one of *J. G. Fichte's* fundamental thoughts that as all property is based on mutual disclaimer, the person who has nothing of his own, has disclaimed nothing, and therefore reserves his original right to everything. (Geschlossener Handelstaat., Werke, III, 400, 445.)

[6] *Plin.*, H. N., XVIII, 7.

[7] How frequently this circumstance turned to the advantage of the Germans during the migration of nations! Compare *Salvian*, De Gubern, Dei, VII. Very remarkable answer given by a Roman taken prisoner by Attila, why it must be more agreeable to live among the Huns than in the over-civilized Roman Empire: Prisci legatio, in *Niebuhr*, Corp. histor. Byzant., I, 191 ff. And thus the conquest of Constantinople by the crusaders, took place amid the jubilation of the populace and of the country people: *Nicetas*, Chron. Hist. Urbs capta, § 11, 340. This law of nature becomes most apparent when one compares the preponderating power of Rome against Carthage, with its weakness against the Cimbri and Mithradates. May not Hannibal have been to his own country a phenomenon like that which Cæsar was afterwards to Rome? A healthy and united Carthage he certainly could have held against Italy.

[8] On the tendencies of the later times of the Jewish monarchy toward an

However, the worst horrors of the contrast here described can

oligarchy of money, see *Amos*, 2, 6 seq.; 6 1 ff.; 8, 5 ff.; *Micha*, 2; 2 *Isaias*, 5, 8 seq. Compare *Nehem.* 5. While Exodus, 30 and 38, mentions over 663,000 taxable men, the ten tribes comprising the kingdom of Israel had only 60,000. XII Kings, 15, 19. *Ewald*, Geschichte des Volkes Israel, II, 2, 320.

* The spirit of the Grecian moneyed oligarchy is best revealed by *Plato*, De Republ., VIII, and *Aristotle*, Polit., III, VI, passim, the first of whom considers the contrast between rich and poor as in itself demoralizing (IV, 422). All that can be called by the name of tradition, the political faith of a people, and the national feeling of right, had, in the Grecian world, been transformed into mere reasoning and concerned itself, with frightful exclusiveness, to the contrast existing between rich and poor. Compare *Aristot.*, Pol., II, 4, 1, with *Droysen*, Gesch. des Hellenismus, II, 496 etc., and the citations from *Menander* in *Stob.*, Serm., LXXXIX, 503, in which gold and silver are proclaimed almighty. It is a remarkable proof of the *omne venalia esse* in Greece that *Thucydides* (II, 65) lauds even *Pericles*, especially for his incorruptibility. *Demosthenes* says of his contemporaries, that it excited envy when any one was bribed, laughter when he confessed it; that he who was convicted of it (bribery) was pardoned, and he who blamed it, hated. (Phil., II, 121.) Compare the list in *Demosth.*, Pro. Cor., 324; *Pausan*, III, 10. In Athens, on the occasion of the census-constitution imposed forcibly on the state by *Antipater*, that in a population of 21,000 citizens, only 9,000 had a property worth 2,000 drachmas or more, that is, enough for a man to live on in the most niggardly way, on the highest interest it would yield. If, in addition to this, account be taken of the large number of slaves, the small number of the property class is all the more surprising, inasmuch as Lycurgus' financial administration bears evidence that the people were in a flourishing and comfortable condition; that afterwards, peace for the most part prevailed, and that Alexander's victories enabled Grecian commerce to make large gains. Compare *Boeckh*, Staatsh. IV, 3, 9.

In Sparta, the governing class finally numbered only 700 families, 100 of which owned all the land, and 600 of which were, therefore, only noble proletarians. It is well known that the social attempts at reform by. Agis and Kleomenes only precipitated the downfall of the state. *(Plutarch*, Agis and Kleomenes.) *Aratos* owed a great part of the consideration in which he was held to the reputation which he obtained by protecting the property of the Sicyonian exiles *(Thirlwall*, History of Greece, VIII, 167), while on the other hand, men like *Agathocles and Nabis* supported their faction by persecution of the rich, new debtor-laws and new division of land. *(Polyb.*, XIII, 6, XVI, 13, XVII, 17, XXVI, 2; *Livy*, XXXII, 38, 40, XXXIV, 31, XXXVIII, 34; *Plutarch*, Cleom, 20.) *Livy* expressly says that all the *optimates* were in favor of the Romans, and that the multitude wanted *novare omnia* (XXXV, 34). On the frightful struggle between these opposite parties, on the revolutions and counter revolutions, see also *Polyb.*, XIII, 1, 2;

occur only in slave-countries. Compare *Roscher*, National-ökonomik des Ackerbaues, § 141.

XVIII, 36 ff., XXX, 14; XXII, 21; XXXVIII, 2, 3; *Diodor.*, XIX, 6, 9; *Exc.*, 587, 623; *Livy*, XLI, 25, XLII, 5; *Pausan*, VII, 14. In Bœotia, no one was for 25 years, chosen by the people for the higher offices, from whom they did not expect a suspension of the administration of justice in the matter of crimes and debts, as well as the spending of the national treasure. (*Polyb.*, XX, 14, 5, 6.) The events at Corinth, before its conquest by the Romans, forcibly remind one of the Paris Commune of 1871. This decline had, as usual, begun earliest in the colonies: thus, in Sicily, even in *Thucyd.*, V, 4. Milesian struggle off the $\pi\lambda o \upsilon \tau i \varsigma$ and $\chi \varepsilon \iota \rho o \mu \acute{a} \chi a$ in *Plutarch*, Qu. Gr., 32; *Athen.*, XII, 524.

[10] The disappearance of the middle class in Rome, between the second and third Punic war, was brought about chiefly by the great foreign conquests made by it. An idea of the wealth which the governors of the provinces might extort may be formed from this among other facts, that Cicero originally demanded against Verres a fine of 5,000,000 thalers. (*Cic.*, in Verrem Div., 5.) Verres is related to have said, that he would be satisfied if he could retain the first year's booty; that during the second, he collected for his defenders; and during the third, for his judges! (*Cic.*, in Verr., I, 14.) Even *Cicero* became richer within the space of one year, in Cilicia, where it was well known he was not oppressive, by 110,000 thalers, which sum does not include numerous presents, pictures etc. (*Drumann*, Gesch. Roms., VI, 384.) On the frightful oppression and extortion practised by Brutus (!) in Asia, see *Cicero*, ad. Att., V, 21; VI, 1. *Sallust*, in his Jugurtha, has shown how such men waged war, and to what extremes their well-deserved want might push them in his Catiline. *Patricium scelus!* Most of the senators were in debt to Crassus; and this, together with his great political insurance-activity and power in elections, criminal cases at law etc., it depended that he, for a time, figured beside Cæsar and Pompey.

The wealth of these important personages must, and that not only relatively, have made the poor poorer and their luxury excited the covetousness of the people; but especially the great number of slaves they kept, combined with their pasturage system of husbandry, which rapidly spread over all of Italy after the provinces had emptied their granaries to supply the wants of the sovereign people, must have made it less and less possible for the proletarians to live by the work of their hands. Previously, the lower classes of the free born had been exempted from the military service, while slaves were conscripted for the fleet. Now, all this was changed; and thus was taken away one of the chief causes which had made the labor of free day laborers more advantageous on the larger estates. (*Nitzsch*, Gracchen, 124 ff., 235 ff.) The spoils of war and conquest caused the higher middle class to prefer to engage in the usurious loaning of money rather than in industry which would much

SECTION CCV.

DISTRIBUTION OF THE NATIONAL INCOME.—HEALTHY DISTRIBUTION.

Hence a harmony of the large, medium and small incomes more rapidly have formed a small middle class. (*Mommsen*, R. G. I, 622 ff.)

Hence, the *misera ac jejuna plebecula, concionalis hirudo aerarii*, according to *Cicero*, ad Att., I, 16, 6. At a time, when the Roman census showed a population of over 1,500,000, Philippus, 104 before Christ, otherwise a "moderate" man, could claim that there were not 2,000 citizens who had any property. (*Cic.*, de Off., II, 21.) True, those few were in such a position, that Crassus would allow that those only were rich, who could feed an army at their own expense. (*Cicero*, Parad., VI, 61; *Plin.*, H. N., XXXIII, 47. Concerning the colossal private fortunes under some of the earlier imperators, see *Seneca*, De Benef., II, 27; *Tacit.*, Ann., XII, 53, XIII, 32; XIV, 35; Dial. de Causis, 8, *Dio C.*, LXIII, 2 seq.

The clients of the time, that is the numerous poorly paid idlers treated as things of little value, in the service of the great, correspond, on a small scale, to the position of the great crowd in relation to the emperor. Compare *Friedländer*, Sittengeschichte Roms., I, 296 ff. As late as the West-Gothic storm, there were many houses which drew 4,000 pounds in gold, and about ⅓ as much in kind, from their estates, per annum. (*Plut.*, Bibl. Cod., 80, 63, Bekk.) Goddess Pecunia Majestas divitiarum, in *Juvenal*, I, 113.

If we take the Roman proletariat in its wider extent, the most frightful picture it presents is its slave-wars. Such a war Sicily had shortly before the *tribunate* of the elder Gracchus, cost over a million (?) livres; and at the same time there was a great uprising of slaves desolating Greece. (*Athen.*, VI, 83, 87 ff., 104.) A second war broke out in the time of Cimbri. But the most frightful was that under Spartacus, who collected 100,000 men, and the course of this uprising will always remain a type of proletarian and slave revolts. It originated among the most dangerous class of slaves, most dangerous because best prepared for the struggle, the gladiators, and among the immense *ergastula*, where they were held together in large masses. It spread with frightful rapidity, because the combustible material on which it fed was everywhere to be found. It was conducted with the most revolting cruelty. What the slaves demanded before all else was vengeance, and what dread had a gladiator of a death unaccompanied by torture?

After the first successes of the slaves dissensions broke out among them. Such hordes can nowhere long preserve a higher object than the momentary gratification of their passions — a fact which shields human society

may be considered the indispensable condition of the economic

---

from their rage. Piracy, also, is another side of this proletarian system. It found its strongest aliment in the system of spoliation practiced by the Romans in Asia Minor. The oppressed along the whole coast, joined the pirates "preferring to do violence rather than to suffer." *(Appian*, B. Mithr., 92, *Dio C.*, XXXII, 3.) The temples and the wealthy Romans were in special danger. But the worst feature in the horrible picture was that many of the great shared in the spoils with the robbers. They bought slaves and other booty from them at mock prices, even close by the gates of Rome. *(Strabo*, XIV, 668 seq., *Dio C.*, XXXVI, 5.) Precisely as the slave-wars were looked upon with pleasure by the poorer free men. Incendiarism was one of the chief weapons of mutinous pauperism. *(Drumann*, IV, 282.) The celebrated bacchanalian trial and the questions of poisoning which followed it as a consequence (186 before Christ) may be looked upon, in Rome, as the first marked symptoms of the disruption between the oligarchy of money and the proletariat. This put the morality of the higher classes in a bad light, while, at the same time, a large slave conspiracy in Apulia, which was not suppressed until the year 185, exhibited the reverse of the picture. Cato, the censor, endeavored to oppose this tendency by high sumptuary taxes, and by establishing proletarian colonies. At the same time we see the various parties among the nobility uniting and the publicans joining them. *Nitzsch*, Gracchen, 124 ff.) The history of the last hundred years of the Republic turns chiefly on the three great attempts made by the proletariat to overthrow the citadel of the moneyed oligarchy, under the Gracchi, under Marius and under Cæsar. The last was permanently successful but entailed the loss of the freedom of both parties.

Among the pretty nearly useless remedies employed, besides those described in § 79, I may mention the following also: the great number of agrarian laws intended to lessen estates of too great extent owned by one person, and to restore a free peasant population, in the years 133, 123, 100, 91, 59 before Christ; the law in Hannibal's time *(Livy*, XXI, 63) that no senator should own a ship with a capacity of more than 300 amphora; the provision *(Sueton*, Caes., 42) that all great herd-owners should take at least one-third of their shepherds from the ranks of freemen; the many laws *de repetundis*, the first of which was promulgated 149 before Christ, intended to protect the provinces against spoliation by the governors; the L. Gabinia, 56 before Christ, which prohibited the loaning by the provinces in Rome; lastly, a rigid enforcement of police provisions against slaves, especially against their bearing arms, which were carried to such an extent, that slaves who had killed a boar with a spear were crucified. *(Cicero*, in Verr., II, 3.) The chief rule of every real oligarchy of money is, while they hold the lower classes in general under their yoke with great severity, to keep dangerous elements in good humor at the expense of the state. Among these are es-

prosperity of a people.[1] This prosperity is best secured when the medium-class income prevails, when no citizen is so rich that he can buy the others, and no one so poor that he might be compelled to sell himself. *(J. J. Rousseau.)*[2] Where there is not a numerous class of citizens who have time enough to serve the state even gratis, as jurymen, overseers of the poor, municipal officers, representatives of the people etc. (compare § 63), and property enough to be independent of the whims and caprices of others, and to maintain themselves and the state in times of need, even the most excellent of constitutions must remain a dead letter. Nor should there be an entire absence of large fortunes, and even of inherited large fortunes. The changes of ministry which accompany constitutional government are fully possible only when the choice of men who would not lose their social position by a cessation of their salaries as public functionaries is not alto-

---

pecially the rabble in large cities and the soldiery. Compare *Roscher*, Betrachtungen über Socialismus und Communismus, 436, 437.

[11] In medieval Italy, also, popular freedom was lost through a moneyed oligarchy and a proletariat. *Popolo grasso* and *minuto (bourgeoisie — peuple)* in Florence. The former were reproached especially with the breach of trust in the matter of the public moneys *(Sismondi*, Gesch. der Ital. Republiken, II, 323, seq.), which reminds one of the French cry, *corruption* in 1847. *Machiavelli* gives a masterly description of the class contrasts during the last quarter of the fourteenth century, in his Istoria Fiorent., III, a. 1378, 4. The poor, whose spokesmen recall the most desperate shibboleths of modern socialists, dwell principally on this, that there is only one important difference, that between rich and poor; that all men are by nature entirely equal; that people get rich only through deceit or violence; that the poor want revenge etc. It is significant how, in Florence, the largest banker finally became absolute despot, and that contemporaneously in Genoa, the Bank of St. George, in a measure, absorbed the state; the former supported by numerous loans made to influential persons like Crassus *(Machiavelli*, Ist. Fior., VII); the latter by the overstraining of the system of national debt.

[1] *Verri* Meditazioni, VI.

[2] *Aristotle's* view that, in a good state, the middle class should preponderate. (Polit. IV, 6, Sch.) *Sismondi* says: *la richesse se réalise en jouissances; mais la jouissance de l'homme riche ne s'accroît pas avec ses richesses.* (Etudes sur l'Economie politique, 1837, I, 15.)

gether too limited.³ Thus the transaction of the most important political business, especially that which relates to foreign affairs, requires a peculiar elasticity of mind, and a capacity for routine on the grandest scale, which with very rare exceptions, can be acquired only by habituation to them from childhood, and which are lost as soon as the care for food is felt. The bird's-eye-view of those who are born "great" does not, by any means, embrace the whole truth of human things, but it does a very important side of it. Among this class, as a rule, it is easiest to find great party leaders, while leaders who have to be paid by their party, generally become in the long run, mere party tools.⁴ It is true that it requires great intellectual and moral power to resist the temptations which a brilliant hereditary condition presents; temptations especially to idleness, to pride and debauchery. For ordinary men, it is a moral and, in the end, an economic blessing, that they have to eat their bread in the sweat of their brow,⁵ and that they can grow rich only by long-continued frugality.⁶ However, the distribution of the national income, and every change in that same distribution, constitute one of the most important but

---

³ If state offices were to be filled by doctors or lawyers who live by their practice, after a time, only those could be had who had no large practice to sacrifice, that is, beginners or obscuranti.

⁴ Per contra, see *Bazard*, Doctrine de Saint Simon, 323. But *Sismondi* is certainly right: *nous ne croyons point, que les hommes qui doivent servir à l'humanité de flambeau naissent le plus souvent au sein de la classe riche; mais elle seule les apprécie et a le loisir de jouir de leurs travaux.* (Etudes, I, 174.)

⁵ To appreciate the demoralizing effects of an income obtained without labor and without trouble on men of small culture, we need only witness the bourgeoisie at great watering places, pilgrimage places, seats of courts and university cities supported largely by students. Similarly at Mecca, Medina, Meschhed, Rome, etc. (*Ritter*, Erdkunde VIII, 295 seq. IX, 32), and even in Palestine, during the crusades, when the miserable Pullanes counted on the tribute of the pilgrims. (*Wilken*, VII, 369, according to *Jacob de Vitriaco*.)

⁶ A man with $100,000 a year has a much less incentive to make savings than 100 men with $1,000 each per annum, for the reason that his economic wants are already all richly satisfied, and he can have little hope of improving it by saving. (*von Mangoldt*, V. W. L., 141.)

at the same time one of the most obscure departments of statistics.[7] When inequality increases because the lower classes absolutely decline, there is no use in talking any longer about the prosperity of the nation.[8] "It is different, of course, when

---

[7] *Harrington*'s fundamental thought (1611–1677, Works, 1700) is, that the nature of the constitution of a state depends on the distribution of the ownership of its land. "Balance of property!" Where, for instance, one person owns all the land or the larger portion of it, we have a despotism; where the distribution is more equal, a democracy etc. All real revolutions are based upon a displacement of the centre of gravity of property, since in the long run, superstructure and foundation can not be out of harmony with each other. For this reason, agrarian laws are the principal means to prevent revolutions. (*Roscher*, Gesch. der English. Volkswirthschaftslehre, 53 ff.) *Montesquieu* also pays special attention to the political consequences of the distribution of wealth. Thus, for instance, in monarchies, the creation of large fortunes should be promoted by the right of primogeniture; in aristocracies, on the other hand, the great wealth of a few nobles is as detrimental as that of extreme poverty. (Esprit des Lois, V, 8, 9.)

[8] The common assertion of the socialists, that the inequality of property is frightfully on the increase, is as far from being proved as is the opposite one of *Hildebrand*, Nat. Œk. der Gegenwart und Zukunft, I, 245 ff. According to *Macaulay*, Hist. of England, ch. 3, there were, in England, in 1685, only about three (ducal) families with an annual income of about £20,000 a year. The average income of a lord amounted to £3,000; of a baronet, to £900; of a member of the house of commons, to scarcely £800; and a lawyer with £1,000 per annum was considered a very important personage. At the same time, there were 160,000 families of free peasants, that is more than ⅓ of the whole population, whose average income amounted to from £60 to £70. For the year 1821, *Marshall*, Digest of all Accounts etc., II, 1833, assumes, that there were 4,000 families with over £5,000 yearly income; 52,000 families with from £1,500 to £5,000; 386,000 families with from £200 to £1,000; 2,500,000 families with less than £200. Compare, *per contra*, the Edinburg Review, 1835. The income tax statistics of 1847 show that 22 persons had an income of at least £50,000 a year; 376 persons, from £10,000 to £50,000; 788, from £5,000 to £10,000; 400, from £4,000 to £5,000; 703, from £3,000 to £4,000; 1,483, from £2,000 to £3,000; 5,234, from £1,000 to £2,000; 13,287, from £500 to £1,000; 91,101, from £150 to £500.

If we compare these numbers with the corresponding ones of the income tax of 1812, the numbers of those who returned an income of £150 to £500 increased 196 per cent.; of those with an income of from £500 to £1,000, 148 per cent.; of from £1,000 to £2,000, 148 per cent.; of from £2,000 to £5,000, 118 per cent.; of from £5,000 and more, 189 per cent.; while the population in general had increased by about 60 per cent. Compare Athenæum, Au-

only the higher classes become, relatively speaking, higher yet. But even this latter kind of inequality may operate disas-

gust, 1850; Edinburgh Rev., April, 1857. Between 1848 and 1857, the development was less favorable, so that the incomes of from £150 to £500 subject to taxation, increased only 7 per cent.; those from £500 to £1,000 about 9.56 per cent.; those from £10,000 to £50,000, by 42.4, and those over £50,000, 142.1 per cent. Between 1858 and 1864, the incomes derived from industry and commerce, subject to taxation below £200, had increased about 19.4 per cent.; those over £10,000, 59 per cent.; while the aggregate amount of all taxed incomes in this category increased 19 per cent. (Stat. Journal, 1865, 546.) According to *Baxter*, The National Income of the United Kingdom, 1868, there are now 8,500 persons with a yearly income of £5,000 and more, who draw in the aggregate 15.6 per cent. of the national British income, and on the average nearly £15,000 each. There are, further, 48,800 persons with a yearly income of from £1,000 to £5,000; 178,300 with from £300 to £1,000; 1,026,400 with from £100 to £300; and 1,497,000 with less than £100 a year from their property. In addition to this, 10,961,000 workmen on wages, with an aggregate income of £324,600,000. Compare §§ 172, 230.

In France, the number of so-called *électeurs*, who paid direct taxes to at least the amount of 200 francs was, in 1831, 166,583, and increased uninterruptedly until 1845, when it was 238,251, while the population had increased only 8.5 per cent.

In Prussia, the revenue from class-taxation up to 1840, increased, unfortunately, in a smaller proportion than the population: hence the lowest classes must have increased relatively more than the others. (*Hoffmann*, Lehre von den Steuern, 176 ff.) Between 1852 and 1873, according to the statistical returns from class-taxation and of the classified income tax, the growth of large incomes in the provinces of old Prussia, seems to have been much more rapid than that of the smaller ones. Thus, for every 100 tax-payers, with an income of from 400 to 1,000 thalers, there was an increase to 175.5; of from 1,000 to 1,600 thalers, for every previous 100, 210.2; from 1,600 to 3,200 thalers, 232.3; of from 3,200 to 6,000, 253.9; of from 6,000 to 12,000 thalers, 324.8; of from 12,000 to 24,000, 470.6; of from 24,000 to 52,000 thalers, 576.3; of from 52,000 to 100,000 thalers, 568.4; of from 100,000 to 200,000 thalers, 533.3; of over 200,000, 2,200. Hence, probably, a greater growth towards the top, than the general increase in the population will account for.

This concentration of property took place most noticeably in Berlin, where for instance, between 1853 and 1875 the incomes of from 1,000 to 1,600 thalers increased 212.2 per cent.; those from 24,000 to 52,000, 994.1 per cent. There are now in the whole state 2.24 per cent. of the population (including those dependent on them) subject to the income tax; that is, estimated as having a yearly income of 1,000 thalers. Of the remaining 97.76 per cent., more than a quarter, and probably more than one-half, are as a class free from tax-

trously, inasmuch as it nourishes the most dangerous tendency of democracy, that of envy towards those who are better off.

---

ation, because their income is presumably less than 140 thalers (6,049,699 against 532,367, exempt for other reasons and 4,850,791 belonging to classes subject to taxation: these three numbers probably not including dependents.) Among the payers of an income tax, there are 79,464 with an average income of 1,237 thalers per annum; 41,366 with 2,171 thalers; 12,305 with 4,279 thalers; 4,030 with 8,383 thalers; 1,655 with 16,527 thalers; 513 with 32,428 thalers; 163 with 65,595 thalers; 39 with 137,692 thalers; 21 with 427,·142 thalers; and one with 1,700,000 thalers per annum. (Preuss. statist. Ztschr., 1875, 116, 132, 142, 145, 149.) As the reverse of this picture, we may take the fact that, in 1870, of 1,047,974 cases of guardianship, there were only 208,614 in which there was any property to be looked after. (Justiz-Minist.-Blatt, 1872, No. 6.)

The figures from Bremen are very favorable. The incomes subject to taxation amounted, in 1847, to 71.6 thalers per capita; in 1869, to 131.2. The incomes subject to taxation in class No. 1, that is from 250 to 399 thalers, increased 78 per cent.; in class No. 2, 400 to 499 thalers, 45 per cent.; in class No. 3, 500 thalers and more, by 57 per cent. The average income of the third class amounted, in 1847-50, to 1,952 thalers; 1866-69, to 2,439 thalers. In 1848, there were, of estates of over 3,000 thalers subject to taxation, only 38 to every 1,000 inhabitants; in 1866, 49. (Jahrb. f. amtl. Statistik Bremens, 1871, Heft 2, p. 185 seq.)

BOOK IV.

CONSUMPTION OF GOODS.

CHAPTER I.

CONSUMPTION OF GOODS IN GENERAL.

SECTION CCVI.

NATURE AND KINDS OF CONSUMPTION.

As it is as little in the power of man to destroy matter as it is to create it, we mean by the consumption of goods, in the broad sense of the word, the abolition of or the doing away with an utility without any regard to the question whether another higher utility takes its place; in its narrower sense (consumption proper), a decrease of resources of any kind. Consumption is the counterpart of production (§ 30), the top of the tree of which production is the roots, and the circulation and distribution of goods the trunk. *(A. Walker.)* There is, also, what Riedel calls immaterial consumption, as when a utility disappears, either because the want itself to which it ministers disappears or because views have changed as to the means to be employed towards its satisfaction.[1]

---

[1] Diminutions of value, such, for instance, as an almanac, a newspaper, etc., undergoes simply from the appearance of the next years' etc.; of a shield or a part of an officer's uniform with the initials of the reigning sovereign, only because of the fact of a new succession to the throne. A boot or a glove loses a great part of its value when its mate is destroyed. *(Rau,* Lehrbuch, § 319.)

SECTION CCVII.

NATURE AND KIND OF CONSUMPTION—THE MOST USUAL KIND.

The commonest kind of consumption is that caused by the use of a thing, or by the employing of it for the purpose of acquisition or of enjoyment.[1] From time immemorial, enjoyment-consumption has been, preponderantly, the affair of women, as acquisition-consumption has been the business of men.[2] Other circumstances being equal, the degree or extent of consumption by use (use-consumption) is determined by national character. Thus, for instance, the cleanliness and love of order characteristic of the Dutch have contributed greatly to the long preservation in good condition of their dwellings and household articles.[3]

In the higher stages of civilization, the use of goods is wont to be divided more and more into special branches, according to the different peculiarities of the goods themselves, and of the different wants of men; a course of things which is, both as cause and effect, intimately related to the division of labor. I here speak of a principle of *division of use* (differentiation and specialization). Thus, for instance, Lorenz Lange, in 1722, found only one kind of tea in the trade between Russia and China; Müller, in 1750, found seven; Pallas, in 1772, ten; and Erman, in 1829, about seven hundred.[4] As the number of

---

[1] We should also mention here destructive consumption, where the defenders of a country destroy buildings, supplies, etc., only that the enemy may not use them.

[2] Compare Die Lebensaufgabe der Hausfrau, Leipzig, 1853; *von Stein*, Die Frau auf dem Gebiete der National Œkonomie, 1875, and the beautiful remarks of *Schäffle*, N. Œk., 166; and *Lotz*, Mikrokosmos, II, 370 ff.

[3] In Germany horses are said to last, on an average, 18 years; in England 25; in France and Belgium, only 12 years. (See for the proofs of this *Rau*, Handbuch II, § 168.) The more civilized a people are, the less do they completely destroy values by use; and the more do they use their old linen etc. as rags; their remains of food as manure etc. (*Roesler*, Grunds., 552.)

[4] *Ritter*, Erdkunde, III, 209. Thus, the French in the 13th century were

gradations of different kinds of the same goods increases with civilization, there is, in times of war, a retrogression in this respect, to a lower economic stage.[5]

acquainted with only three kinds of cabbage; in the 16th, with six, about 1651, with 12; they are now acquainted with more than 50; in the 16th century they knew only 4 kinds of sorrel; in 1651, 7; about 1574, only 4 kinds of lettuce; to-day they know over 50; under Henry II., they were acquainted with 2 or 3 kinds of melons; in the 17th century, with 7; now they are acquainted with over 40. (*Roquefort*, Histoire de la Vie privée des Fr., I, 179 ff.) Instead of the four kinds of pears mentioned by de Serre (1600), there were, in 1651, about 400. (I, 272.) Liebaud, 1570, knew only 19 kinds of grapes; de Serre, 41. (*Roquefort*, III, 29 ff.) According to the "Briefen eines Verstorbenen," IV) 390, the first kitchen-gardener in London, had 435 kinds of salad, 240 of potatoes, and 261 of pease.

And so precisely in ancient times. While the earlier Greeks speak of but one οἶνος, even at the most sumptuous feasts (compare, however, *Homer*, Il. XI, 641;) and while even in the time of Demosthenes only very few kinds of wine were known (*Becker*, Charicles, I, 455), *Pliny*, H. N. XIV, 13, was acquainted with about 80. In this respect the moderns have never returned to ancient simplicity; at least the fabliau, La Bataille des Vins, introduces us to 47 kinds of French wine in the 13th century. (Compare also *Wackernagel* in *Haupt's* Zeitschrift für deutsches Alterth., VI. 261 ff., and *Henderson*, History of ancient and modern Wines, 1824.) The Lacedemonians, with their intentional persistence in a lower stage of civilization, used the same garment in winter and summer (*Xenoph.*, De Rep. Laced., II, 4); while the contemporaries of Athenæos (III, 78 ff.) were acquainted with 72 kinds of bread. With what a delicate sense for good living the Romans in Caesar's time had discovered the best supply places for chickens, peacocks, cranes, thunny-fish, muraena, oysters and other shell-fish, chestnuts, dates, etc., may be seen in *Gellius*, N. A., VII, 16. Compare *Athen.*, XII, 540.

In the middle age of Italy, the houses had almost always three rooms: *domus* (kitchen), *thalamus, solarium*. (*Cibrario*, E. P. del medio Evo, III, 45.) The manors or masters' houses built on the estates of Charlemagne had 3 and 2 rooms, sometimes only 1, and sometimes 2 rooms and 2 bedrooms. According to an old document of 895, a shed was worth 5 sols, a well-built manor 12. (*Anthon*, Geschichte der deutschen Landwirth., I, 249 ff., 311.) The Lex Alamanorum, tit. 92, provided that a child, in order to be considered capable of living, should have seen the roof and four walls of the house! See an able essay, capable of being still further developed, by *E. Herrmann*, in which he endeavors to explain the *division of use* and of labor on Darwin's hypothesis of the origin of species in the D. Vierteljahrsschrift, Januar, 1867.

[5] Thus, 1785-1795, the best Silesian wool cost 60, the worst 26, thalers per

Opposed to this, we have the principle of the combination of use. There are numberless kinds of goods which may serve a great many just as well as they can one exclusive user; and this either successively or simultaneously, inasmuch as there is no necessity why, with the increasing use of the object, the size of the object itself should increase in an equal proportion. (According to Marlo: wealth usable by one; wealth usable by many; wealth usable by all.) Thus, for instance, a public library may be incomparably more complete, and accessible in a still higher degree than ten private libraries which together cost as much as it did. And so, a restaurant-keeper may serve a hundred guests at the same time, with a much greater table-variety, more to their taste, and at a more convenient time, than if each person made the same outlay for his private kitchen.[6] While formerly, only the great could travel rapidly, combination of use has enabled even the lower classes to do so in our own days. There is, doubtless, a dark side to this picture, too. Combination of use requires frequently great sacrifices of personal independence, which should not be underestimated when they affect individuality of character, or threaten the intimacy and closeness of family life. It is, however, a bad symptom when the divis-

---

cwt.; in 1805, on account of the great demand for cloth to make military uniforms, the former cost 78, the latter 50 thalers. (*Hoffmann*, Nachlass, 114.)

[6] The one large kitchen naturally requires much less place, masonry, fuel, fewer utensils etc., than 100 small ones. Think of the relatively large savings effected by the use of one oven kept always heated! Even the Lacedemonians called their meal associations φειδίτια, i. e., save-meals. Dainties proper can be consumed only in very small portions, but cannot well be prepared in such quantities. A guest at a first class Parisian restaurant has, at a moderate price, his choice of 12 *potâges*, 24 *hors d'oeuvres*, 15–20 *entrées de boeuf*, 20 *entrées de mouton*, 30 *entrées de volaille et gibier*, 15–20 *entrées de veau*, 12 *de pâtisserie*, 24 *de poisson*, 15 *de rôts*, 50 *entremets*, 50 *desserts;* and, in addition, perhaps 60 kinds of French wine alone. What more can a princely table offer in this respect? Compare *Brillat-Savarin*, Physiologie du Goût, Médit., 28.

ion of use increases without any corresponding combination of use.[7][8]

SECTION CCVIII.

NATURE AND KINDS OF CONSUMPTION.— NOTIONAL CONSUMPTION.

By the notional consumption *(Meinungsconsumtion)*, as Storch calls it, operated by a change of fashion, many goods lose their value, without as much as suffering the least change of form or leaving the merchant's shop. This kind of consumption, too, is exceedingly different in different nations. Thus, in Germany, for. instance, fashions are much more persistent than in France.[1] In the most flourishing times of Holland, only noblemen and officers changed with the fashions, while the merchants and other people wore their clothes until they

---

[7] In Diocletian's time, there was purple silk worth from 2½ thalers to 250 thalers per pound. *(Marquardt*, Röm. Privatalterthümer, II, 122.)

[8] Concerning the application of the above principle in industry and in the care of the poor, see *infra*. The advantages afforded by consumption in common, or the combination of use, have been enthusiastically dwelt upon by *Fourier*, and the organization of his phalansteries is based essentially on that principle. In these colossal palaces, which, spite of all their magnificence, cost less than the hundred huts of which they take the place, a ball is given every evening, because it is cheaper to light one large hall, in which all may congregate. The division of use, or of consumption also, is here developed in a high degree. When 12 persons eat at the same table they have 12 different kinds of cheese, 12 different kinds of soup etc. Even little children are allowed to yield to the full to their gluttonous propensities, since on them depends the productive activity of the so called *séries passsionnées*. Compare Nouveau Monde, 272. The Saint-Simonists also characterize the *association universelle* as the highest goal of human development. *Bazard*, Exposition, 144 ff.) On the danger of this development to family life, see *Sismondi*, Etudes I, 43.

[1] The consequences of this are very important to the character of French and German industry. *(Junghanns*, Fortschritte des Zollvereins, I, 28, 51, 56.) Rapidly as the Parisian fashions in dress make their way into the provinces, their fashions in the matter of the table are very slow to do so. *(Roquefort*, Hist. de la Vie privée des Fr., I, SS seq.)

went to pieces.² In the East, fashions in clothing are very constant;³ but the expensive custom there prevails, for a son, instead of moving into the house occupied by his father, to let it go to ruin, and to build a new one as a matter of preference. The same is true even in the case of royal castles. Hence, in Persia, most of the cities are half full of ruins, and are in time moved from one place to another.⁴

The national income of a country is, on the whole, much less affected by a change of fashion than the separate incomes of its people. The same whim which lowers the value of one commodity increases the value of another; and what has ceased to be in fashion among the rich, becomes accessible, properly speaking, to the poorer classes of the community for the first time.⁵ The want of varying his enjoyments is so peculiar to man, and so intimately connected with his capacity for progress, that it cannot in itself be blamed. But if this want be immoderately yielded to, if the well-to-do should despise every article which has not the charm of complete nov-

---

² *Sir W Temple*. Observations on the U. Provinces, ch. 6.

³ As most persons adorn themselves for the sake of the opposite sex, this invariability is caused by the oriental separation of two sexes. Our manufacturers would largely increase their market, if they could succeed in civilizing the East in this respect. In Persia, shawls are frequently inherited through many generations, and even persons of distinction buy clothes which had been worn before. *(Polak, Persien, I, 153.)* In China, the Minister of Ceremonies rigidly provided what clothes should be worn by all classes and under severe penalties. *(Davis, The Chinese, I, 352 seq.)*

⁴ *Jaubert*, Voyage en Perse, 1821. While cities like Seleucia, Ctesiphon, Almadin, Kufa, and even Bagdad, were built from the ruins of Babylon.

⁵ In Moscow, merchants close their accounts at Easter. Then begins a new cycle of fashions, after which all that remains is sold at mock-prices. *(Kohl, Reise, 98.)* In Paris, there are houses which buy up everything as it begins to go out of fashion and then send it into the provinces and to foreign parts. Thus, there are immense amounts of old clothing shipped from France and England to Ireland. Hence, the latter country can have no national costume appropriate to the different classes; and the traveler sees with regret, crowds of Irish going to work in ragged frock-coats, short trowsers and old silk hats. In Prussia, many of the peasantry, in the time of Frederick the Great, wore the discarded uniforms of the soldiery.

elty, the advantages of the whole pattern-system, by means of which the preparation of a large number of articles from the same model at a relatively small cost, would be lost. Besides, fashion, which makes production in large quantities, for the satisfaction of wants that are variable and free, possible, frequently means even a large saving in the cost of production.[s]

SECTION CCIX.

CONSUMPTION WHICH IS THE WORK OF NATURE.

The least enjoyable of all consumption *(loss-consumption)* is that which is the work of nature; and nature is certainly most consuming in the tropics. During the rainy season, in the region of the upper Ganges, mushrooms shoot up in every corner of the houses; books on shelves swell to such an extent that three occupy the place previously occupied by four; those left on the table get covered over with a coat of moss one-eighth of an inch in thickness. The saltpetre that gathers on the walls has to be removed every week in baskets, to keep it from eating into the bricks. Numberless moths devour the clothing. Schomburgk found that, in Guiana, iron instruments which lay on the ground during the rainy season became entirely useless within a few days, that silver coins oxydized etc.; evidently a great obstacle in the way of the employment of machinery. In summer, the soil of this same region, so rich in roots, is so parched by the heat, that subterranean fires sometimes cause the most frightful destruction.

In Spanish America, there are so many termites and other destructive insects that paper more than sixty years old is very seldom to be found there.[1]

The warmer portions of the temperate zone are naturally

---

[s] *Schäffle*, N. Œk. *Hermann*, Staatsw. Untersuchungen, II, Aufl., 100.

[1] *Ritter*, Erdkunde VI, 180 ff.; *Schomburgk* in the Ausland, 1843, Nr. 274; *Humboldt*, Relation hist., I, 306; Neuspanein, IV, 379; *Pöppig*, Reise, II, 197 ff., 237 ff. The ant, even in Marcgrav's time, was called the *rey do Brazil*.

most favorable to the preservation of stone monuments. Thus, for instance, in Persepolis, where there has been no intentional destruction, the stones lie so accurately superimposed the one on the other that the lines of junction can frequently be not even seen. The amphitheatre of Pola has lost in two thousand years only two lines from the angles of the stones.[2] The Elgin marble statues would certainly have lasted longer in Greece than they will in England. On the other hand, warm and dry climates have a very peculiar and exceedingly frightful species of nature-consumption in the locust plagues. The principal countries affected by such consumption are Asiatic and African Arabistan, the land of the Jordan and Euphrates, Asia Minor, parts of Northern India. On Sinai, locust plagues occur, on an average, every four or five years; but from 1811 to 1816, for instance, they destroyed everything each year. Their course is in its effects like an advancing conflagration. It turns the green country, frequently in a single day, into a brown desert; and famine and pestilence follow in its path.[3]

The colder regions of the temperate zone are exposed to danger and damage from land-slides in their long series of mountains, and from avalanches, from quicksands in many of their plains, from floods and the total destruction of land along

---

[2] *Ritter*, Erdkunde VIII, 895; *Burger*, Reise in Oberitalien, I, 7. The monuments of Nubia have suffered much less from the hand of time than those of Upper Egypt, because the air of the plateau is drier. The effects of climate have been most severely felt in Lower Egypt, where the air is most moist. (*Ritter*, I, 336, 701.) In the case of wood, on the other hand, dryness may be a great agent of destruction. Thus, in Thibet, wooden pillars, balconies, etc., have to be protected with woolen coverings to keep them from splitting. (*Turner*, Gesandtsreise, German translation, 393 ff.)

[3] Compare *Ritter*, Erdkunde, VIII, 789-815, especially the beautiful collection of passages from the Bible bearing on the locust plague, 812 ff. *Pliny*, H. N., XI, 85. *Volney*, Voyages en Syrie, I, 305. For account of an invasion of locusts, which, in 1835, covered half a square mile, four inches in thickness, see *v. Wrede*, R. in Hadhrammaut, 202. It is estimated that, in England, the destruction caused by rats, mice, insects etc., amounts to ten shillings an acre per year; i. e., to £10,000,000 per annum. (*Dingler*, Polyt. Journal, XXX, 237.)

their coasts;[4] but, on the other hand, they are, relatively speaking, freest from hurricanes, earthquakes and volcanoes, the ravages of which no human art or foresight is competent to cope with. From the point of view of civilization and of politics there is here a great advantage. See § 36. The former maritime power of Venice and of Holland is closely allied to the dangers with which the sea continually threatened them, and which was a continual spur to both. But, on the other hand, the danger from earthquakes which always impends over South America and Farther India, must produce consequences similar to those of anarchy or of despotism, because of the uncertainty with which they surround all relations. See § 39.[5]

SECTION CCX.

NECESSITY OF CONSIDERING WHAT IS REALLY CONSUMED.

Whenever there is question of consumption, it is necessary to examine with rigid scrutiny, what it is that has been really consumed; that is, that has lost in utility. The person, for instance, who pays twenty dollars for a coat, has consumed that amount of capital only when the coat has been worn out.[1] What is called the consumption of one's income in advance is nothing but the consumption of a portion of capital which the

---

[4] Origin of the gulf of Dollart in Friesland, 2½ square miles in area between 1177 and 1287; and of Biesboch of 2 square miles in 1421. On the repeated destruction of lands in Schleswig by inundations, see *Thaarup*, Dänische Statistik, I, 180 seq. It is a remarkable fact that in relation to the Mediterranean, *Strabo*, VII, 293, considers all such accounts fables.

[5] As to how the grandeur and irresistibleness etc. of this nature-consumption in the tropics leads men to superstition and the indulgence of wild fancies, see *Buckle*, History of Civilization in England, 1859, I, 102 ff. Since the conquest of Chili, sixteen earthquakes, which have destroyed large cities totally or in part, have been recorded.

[1] Compare *Mirabeau*, Philosophie rurale, ch. 1; *Prittwitz*; Kunst reich zu werden, 474.

consuming party intends to make good from his future income.[2] Fixed capital, too, can certainly be directly consumed; for instance, when the owner of a house treats the entire rent he receives from it as net income, makes no repairs, and no savings to put up a new building at some future time. As a rule, however, the owner of fixed capital must, in order to consume it, first exchange it against circulating capital. Thus the prodigality and dissipation, especially of courts of absolute princes, have found numerous defenders who have claimed that they are uninjurious, provided only the money spent in extravagance remained in the country.[3] The prodigality itself, that is, the unnecessary destruction of wealth is not, on that account, any the less disastrous. If, for instance, there are fire-works to the amount of 10,000 dollars, manufactured exclusively by the workmen of the country, ordered for a gala day; the night before they are used for purposes of display, the national wealth embraces two separate amounts, aggregating 20,000 dollars; that is, 10,000 dollars in silver and 10,000 in rockets etc. The day after, the 10,000 in silver are indeed still in existence, but of the 10,000 in rockets etc., there is nothing left.[4] If the order had been made from a foreign country the reverse would have been the case, the silver stores

---

[2] A very important principle for the understanding of the real effects of the spending of a state loan!

[3] In this way *Voltaire*, Siècle de Louis XIV., ch. 30, excuses for instance the extravagant (?) buildings at Versailles; and in a very similar way Catharine II. expressed herself in speaking to the Prince de Ligne: Mémoires et Mélanges par le Prince de Ligne, 1827, II, 358. *v. Schröder* even thinks that the Prince might consume as much and even more than "the entire capital" of the country amounted to; only, he would have him "let it get quickly among the people again." He is also in favor of the utmost splendor in dress, provided the public see to it that nothing was worn in the country which was not made in the country. (Fürstl. Schatz- u. Rentkammer, 47, 172.) Similarly even *Botero*, Della Ragion di Stato VII, 85; VIII, 191; and recently *v. Struensee*, Abhandlungen I, 190. The principle of Polycrates in *Herodotus* is nearly to the same effect. Compare, per contra, *Ferguson*, Hist. of Civil Society, V, 5.

[4] With the exception of the profit made by the manufacturers.

of the people would have been diminished, but their supply of powder would remain intact.

In a similar way, there is occasion given for the greatest misunderstanding when people so frequently speak of producers and consumers as if they were two different classes of people. Every man is a consumer of many kinds of goods; but, at the same time, he is a producer, unless he be a child, an invalid, a robber, a pick-pocket etc.[5] At the same time, Bastiat is right in saying that in case of doubt when the interests of production and of consumption come in conflict, the state, as the representative of the aggregate interest, should range itself on the side of the latter. If we carry things on both sides to their extremest consequences, the self-seeking desire of consumers would lead to the utmost cheapness, that is, to universal superfluity, and the self-seeking wish of producers to the utmost dearness, that is, to universal want.[6]

SECTION CCXI.

NATURE AND KINDS OF CONSUMPTION.—PRODUCTIVE CONSUMPTION.

There is no production possible without consumption. The embodiment of a special utility into any substance is a limitation of its general utility. Thus, for instance, when corn is baked into bread, it can no longer be used for the manufacture of brandy or of starch.[1]

---

[5] Strikingly ignored by *Sismondi*, N. P., IV, ch. 11.

[6] *Bastiat*, Sophismes économiques, 1847, ch. IV. Everything which, in the long run, either promotes or injures production, " steps over the producer and turns in the end to the gain or loss of the consumer." Only for this principle, inequality and dissensions among men would keep growing perpetually. All that the systems of Saint Simonism and communism contain that is relatively true is thus realized.

[1] Even when air-dried bricks are made from water and clay which cost nothing; when purely occupatory work is done, and purely intellectual labor performed, some consumption of the means of subsistence by the workmen is always necessary.

When, therefore, consumption is a condition (outlay) to production it is called productive (reproductive).[2] Here, indeed, the form of the consumed goods is destroyed, but the value of the goods lives on in the new product.

There are different degrees of productiveness in consumption also. Thus, to a scholar, his outlay for books in his own branch is immediately productive; but nevertheless, books in departments of literature very remote from his own, pleasure trips, etc. may serve as nutrition and as a stimulus to his mind. According to § 52, we are compelled to consider all consumption productive which constitutes a necessary means towards the satisfaction of a real economic want. We may, indeed, distinguish between productive consumption in aid of material goods, of personal goods and useful relations; but in estimating the productiveness of these different sorts of consumption we are concerned not so much with the nature of the consumption as the results in relation to the nation's wants. The powder that explodes when a powder magazine burns is consumed unproductively; but the powder shot away in war may be productively consumed just as that used to explode a mine may be unproductively consumed; for instance, when the war is a just and victorious one and the mining enterprise has failed.[3]

The maintenance or support of those workmen whom they themselves acknowledge to be productive is presumably accounted productive consumption by all political economists. Why not, therefore, the cost of supporting and educating our children, who, it is to be hoped, will grow up later to be productive workmen. Man's labor-power is, doubtless, one of the greatest of all economic goods. But without the means of subsistence, it would die out in a few days. Hence we may, and even without an atomistic enumeration of the individual services and products of labor, consider the continued dura-

---

[2] Χρηματιστικαί in contradistinction to ἀναλωτικαί, according to *Plato*, De Rep., VIII, 559. Temporary consumption. (*Umpfenbach.*)

[3] *Storch*, Handbuch, II, 450.

tion of that labor-power itself as the continued duration of the value of the consumed means of subsistence.[4]

SECTION CCXII.

UNPRODUCTIVE CONSUMPTION.

Moreover, unproductive consumption embraces not only every economic loss, every outlay for injurious purposes,[1] but also every superfluous outlay for useful purposes.[2] Yet, not to err in our classification here, it is necessary to possess the impartiality and many-sidedness of the historian, which enable one to put himself in the place of others and feel after them as they felt. The man, for instance, who, in cities like Regensburg and especially Rome, sees numberless churches often, so to speak, elbowing one another, cannot fail to recognize the difference between the buildings of to-day for business, political, educational and recreative pnrposes, and the medieval, for the satisfaction of spiritual wants. The latter also may, in their own sphere, and in their own time, have, as a rule, operated productively, as the former operate, often enough, by way of exception unproductively; as in the case of railway and canal speculations which have ended in failure. It would be difficult to decide between the relative value of the two kinds of wants, because the parties to the controversy do not, for the most part, share the want *(Bedürfniss)* of their respective opponents, frequently do not even

---

[4] Against the difference formerly usually assumed between productive and unproductive consumption, see *Jacob*, Grundsätze der Nat. Œk., II, 530. It is because of a too narrow view that *Hermann* (II, Aufl., 311), instead of reproductive consumption, speaks of technic consumption.

[1] Thus, for instance, food which spoils unused, and food which is stolen and which puts a thief in a condition to preserve his strength to steal still more.

[2] So far *Senior*, Outlines, 66, is right: the richer a nation or a man becomes, the greater does the national or personal productive consumption become.

understand it, and therefore despise it. Thus, there are semi-barbarous nations, who can entertain that respect for the laws which is necessary even from an economic point of view only to the extent that they see the person whose duty it is to cause them to be observed seated on a throne and surrounded by impressive splendor. Hence, such splendor here could not be considered merely unproductive consumption.[3]

We must, moreover, remark in this place as we did above, § 54, that it is easiest to pass the boundary line between productive and unproductive consumption in personal services. In 1830, the expenses of the state, in Spain, amounted to 897,000,000 of reals per annum; the outlay of municipal corporations, to 410,000,000, and that for external purposes of religion, 1,680,000,000. *(Borrego.)* This is certainly no salutary proportion; but it is scarcely evidence of a worse economic condition than the fact that in Prussia it would require a basin one Prussian mile in length, thirty-three and eight-tenths feet broad, and ten feet deep to hold all the brandy drunk in the country *(Dieterici);* or this other, that the British people spend yearly £68,000,000 sterling for taxes and £100,000,000 yearly for spirituous liquors.[4] Berkeley rightly says that the course practiced in Ireland, with its famishing proletarian population, of exporting the means of subsistence and exchanging them against delicate wines etc., is as if a mother should sell her children's bread to buy dainties and finery for herself with the proceeds.[5][6]

---

[3] Such gigantic constructions as the palaces, pyramids etc. of Egypt, Mexico or Peru are a certain sign of the oppression of the people by rulers, priests or nobles. One of the Egyptian pyramids is said to have occupied 360,000 men for twenty years. *(Diodor.,* I, 63; *Herodot.,* II, 175; *Prescott,* History of Mexico, I, 153, History of Peru, I, 18.)

[4] Edinburg Rev., Apr., 1873, 399.

[5] *Berkeley,* Querist, 168, 175, says that the national wants should be the guiding rule of commerce, and that besides, the most pressing wants of the majority should be first considered.

[6] *Ricardo,* Principles, p. 475, was of opinion that an outlay of the national or of private income in the payment of personal services increased the demand for labor and the wages of labor in a higher degree than an equal out-

SECTION CCXIII.

EQUILIBRIUM BETWEEN PRODUCTION AND CONSUMPTION.

In all cases economic production is a means to some kind of consumption as its end.[1] The sharpest spur to productive

lay for material things. The error at the foundation of this is well refuted by *Senior*, Outlines, 160 ff.

The first to zealously advocate and treat the theory of productive consumption was *J. B. Say*, Traité, III, ch. 2, seq.; Cours pratique, II, 265. But the germs of the doctrine are to be found in *Dutot*, Réflexions politiques sur le Commerce et les Finances, 1738, 974, éd. Daire. His distinctions are in part drawn with great accuracy. Thus he says that, among others, a manufacturer of cloth, productively consumes the results of his workmen, but that the workmen themselves who exchange these results for bread, consume the latter unproductively. *Say* is guilty of the inconsistency of claiming that only that consumption is productive which contributes directly to the creation of material exchangeable goods, spite of the fact that he gave the productiveness of labor a much wider scope. *Rau*, Lehrbuch, I, § 102 ff., 323 seq., is more consistent in so far as he applies the same limitation in both cases. (Compare also § 333, 336.) *Hermann*, Staatsw. Untersuchungen, 270 seq., 231 ff., would prefer to see the idea of productive consumption banished from the science, for the reason that if the value of the thing alleged to be consumed continues, there can be no such thing as its consumption. But, I would rejoin: in a good national economy, there would be, according to this, scarcely any consumption whatever, because the aggregate value of that which I have called above productive consumption is unquestionably preserved, and continues in the aggregate value of the national products.

Productive consumption is ultimately a stage of production, just as production itself is ultimately a means to an end, consumption, and therefore a preparation for the latter. Both ideas may be rigorously kept apart from each other, just as the expenses and receipts of a private business man, who makes a great portion of his outlay simply with the intention of reaping receipts therefrom, may be. Every one desires his production to be as large as possible, and his productive consumption, so far it does not fail of its object, as small as possible. *Riedel* rightly says that the theory of reproductive consumption serves Political Economy as the bridge which closes the circle formed by the action of production, distribution and consumption. (Nat. Oek. III, 49.) One of the chief fore-runners of the view we advocate was *McCulloch*, Principles, IV, 3 ff. *Gr. Soden*, Nat. Oek., distinguishes economic consumption, un-economic and anti-economic consumption. (Nat. Oek., I, 147.)

[1] We should not, indeed, say, on this account, with *Adam Smith*, IV, ch. 8,

activity is the feeling of want.² "Want teaches art, want teaches prayer, blessed want!" Well too has it been said: "Necessity is the mother of invention!" Leaving mere animals out of consideration,³ those men who experience very few wants, with the exception of some rare and highly intellectual natures, prefer rest to labor. Therefore, when European merchants desire to engage in trade with a savage nation they have uniformly to begin by sending them their nails, axes, looking-glasses, brandy etc., as gifts. Not until the savage has experienced a new enjoyment does the want of continuing it make itself felt; or is he prepared to produce for purposes of commerce.⁴ In a state of normal development, the complete and continuing satisfaction of the coarser wants should constitute the foundation for the higher.⁵

SECTION CCXIV.

CAUSES OF AN INCREASE OF PRODUCTION.

Only when wants increase does production increase also.¹

---

that "consumption is the sole end and purpose of all production," for labor and saving, besides their economic object have a higher one, imperishable and personal. Compare *Knies*, Polit. Œk. 129, and *supra*, § 30.

² According to *Sir F. M. Eden*, State of the Poor, I, 254, it is one of the most unambiguous symptoms of advanced civilization when families eat regularly at the same table; so also sleeping in real beds. "Bed and board!" It is said that the regularity of meal times was introduced among the Greeks by Palamedes. *Athen.* I, 11, after *Æschylus*.

³ Hibernating animals have supplies and dwellings, that is something analagous to capital.

⁴ This advance is generally observed to be introduced by the *jus fortioris*. *Steuart*, Principles I, ch. 7. (Compare §§ 45-6-8.) In this way, the earliest oriental despotisms have unwittingly been of great service to mankind. What the sultan here accomplished with his few favorites was done in the lower stages of civilization of the west by the aristocracy of great vassals, in a manner more worthy of human beings, and in a much more stable form. (*J S Mill*, Principles I, 14 ff.)

⁵ *Banfield*, Organization of Industry, 1848, 11.

¹ There is obviously here supposed besides the want thus increased, a ca-

The old maxim: *Si quem volueris esse divitem, non est quod augeas divitias, sed minuas cupiditates (Seneca)*, would, if consistently carried out, have thwarted the advance of civilization and frustrated the improvement of man's condition. On the other hand, most political economists, without more ado, assume that individuals, and still more nations, are wont to extend the aggregate of their enjoyments just as far as there is a possibility of satisfying their wants. But they forget here how great a part is played in the world, as men are constituted, by the principle of inertia.[2] At the first blush, what seems more natural than that the less labor a people need employ to obtain the most indispensable means of subsistence, the more time and taste would remain to them to satisfy their more refined wants. According to this, we should expect to discover a more refined civilization, especially, in intellectual matters, in the earliest periods, when population is small, when land exists in excess and is not yet exhausted. But, in reality, precisely the reverse is the case. In the earliest stages of civlization accessible to our observation, we find materialism prevailing in its coarsest form, and life absorbed entirely by the lowest physical wants. (Tropical lands.) Where bread grows on the trees, and one needs only to reach out his hand and pluck it; where all one wants to cover his nakedness is a few palm leaves, ordinary souls find no incentive to an ant-like activity, or to a union among themselves for economic pur-

---

pacity for development. Thus, for instance, the inhabitants of New Zealand brought with them, in what concerns clothing, dwellings, etc., the customs of a tropical into a colder country, and did not understand how to oppose the rigor of the new climate, except by building immoderately large fires, until they became acquainted with European teachers. (Edinb. Review, April, 1850, 466.)

[2] Compare *R. S. Zachariä*, Vierzig Bücher vom Staate, VII, 37. Men in the lower stages of civilization cherish a greater contempt for those more advanced than they are themselves visited with by the latter. Thus it was customary for the Siberian hunting races to utter a malediction: May your enemy live like a Tartar, and have the folly to engage in the breeding of cattle. (*Abulghazi Bahadur*, Histoire généalogique des Tartares.) Nomadic races look upon the inhabitants of cities as for the most part prisoners.

poses.³ When a Mexican countryman earns enough to keep himself and his family from absolute want by two days' labor in a week, he idles away the other five. It never occurs to him that he might devote his leisure time to putting his hut or his household furniture etc., in better shape. The necessity of foresight even is almost unknown; and in the most luxuriantly fertile country in the world, a bad harvest immediately leads to the most frightful famine. Humboldt was assured that there was no hope of making the people more industrious except by the destruction of the banana plantations.⁴ But, indeed, there would be little gained by such compulsory industry. To work for any other end than satiation, it is necessary that man should feel wants beyond the want created by mere hunger.⁵ There are so many conditions precedent (and mutually limiting one another) to a general advance in civilization, that such an advance can, as a rule, take place only very gradually. Let us suppose, for instance, a single Indian in Mexico, perfectly willing to work six days in the week, and in this way to cultivate a piece of land three times as great as his fellow Indians. Where would he get the land? He would, for a time find no purchasers for his surplus, and

---

³ The "happy, contented negroes," as Lord John Russel called them, work in Jamaica, on an average, only one hour a day since their emancipation. (Colonial Magazine, Nov. 1849, 458.) Egypt, India etc., from time immemorial, the classic lands of monkish laziness. Compare *Hume*, Discourses, No. 1, on Commerce. On the other hand, the person who has six months before him for which he must labor and lay up a store, if he would not famish or freeze, must necessarily be active and frugal; and there are other virtues which go along with these. (*List*, System der polit. Oek., I, 304.) According to *Humboldt*, the change of seasons compels man to get accustomed to different kinds of food, and thus fits him to migrate. The inhabitants of tropical countries are, on the other hand, like caterpillars, which cannot emigrate nor be made to emigrate, on account of the uniform nature of their food.

⁴ *Humboldt*, N. Espagne, IV, ch. 9, II, ch. 5. Similarly among the coarser Malayan tribes, the facility with which fish is caught and the cheapness of sago are the principal causes of their inertia and of their unprogressive uncivilization. *(Crawfurd.)*

⁵ *Le travail de la faim est toujours borné comme elle.* *(Raynal.)*

therefore not be in a condition to pay the landlord as much as the latter hitherto received from the pasturage alone. Not until cities are built and offer the rural population the products of industry in exchange for theirs, can they be incited to, or become capable of effecting a better cultivation of the land. This incentive and this capacity, are inseparably connected with each other. Where the agricultural population produce no real surplus, but after the fashion of medieval times, produce everything they want themselves, and consume all their own products with the exception of the part paid to the state as a tax, there can scarcely be an industrial class, a commercial class, or a class devoted to science, art etc. And, conversely, it is only the higher civilization which finds expression in the development of these classes, that, by a more skillful guidance of the national labor, can call forth its productiveness to an extent sufficient to yield a considerable surplus of agricultural commodities over and above the most immediate wants of the cultivators of the soil themselves. Hence, we find that precisely in those countries which are most advanced in the economic sense, there is relatively the smallest number of men engaged in agriculture, and relatively the largest number in production of a finer kind.[6] It is here as in private housekeeping: the poorer a man is, the greater is the portion of his income which he is wont to lay out for indispensable necessities.[7 8]

---

[6] Compare *Adam Smith*, I, ch. 11, 2; *supra*, § 54. In Russia, nearly 80 per cent. of the population live immediately from agriculture; in Great Britain, in 1835, only 35; in 1821, only 33; in 1831, only 31½; in 1841, only 26 per cent. (*Porter.*) According to *Marshall*, there were, in 1831, in British Europe, 1,116,000 persons who lived from their rents etc. In Ireland, there were, in 1831, over 65 per cent. of the population engaged in agriculture (*Porter*); in 1841, even 66 per cent.

[7] In Paris, in 1834, the average income per capita was estimated to be 1,029.9 francs, of which 46 francs were paid out for service; 55.7 for education; 11.5 for physicians' services etc.; 7 on theatrical shows; 36 for washing; 13.6 for public purposes. (*Dingler*, Polyt. Journal, LIII, 464.) According to *Ducpétiaux*, Budgets économiques des Classes ouvrières en

SECTION CCXV.

NECESSITY OF THE PROPER SIMULTANEOUS DEVELOPMENT OF PRODUCTION AND CONSUMPTION.

Hence, one of the most essential conditions of a prosperous national economy is that the development of consumption

Belgique, 1855, and *Engel*, Sächs. Statist. Ztschr., 1857, 170, the proportional percentage of family expenses for the following articles of consumption is:

Consumption Purpose.	EXPENSES OF			
	a laborer's family in comfortable circumstances.	*family of the middle class.*	*a well-to-do family.*	
	In Belgium per cent.	In Saxony. per cent.	In Saxony. per cent.	In Saxony. per cent.
Food,	61 ⎫	62 ⎫	55 ⎫	50 ⎫
Clothing,	15 ⎪	16 ⎪	18 ⎪	18 ⎪
Shelter,	10 ⎬ 95	12 ⎬ 95	12 ⎬ 90	12 ⎬ 85
Heating and lighting,	5 ⎪	5 ⎪	5 ⎪	5 ⎪
Utensils and tools,	4 ⎭			
Education, instruction,	2 ⎫	2 ⎫	3.5 ⎫	5.5 ⎫
Public security,	1 ⎬ 5	1 ⎬ 5	2 ⎬ 10	3 ⎬ 15
Sanitary purposes,	1 ⎪	1 ⎪	2 ⎪	3 ⎪
Personal services,	1 ⎭	1 ⎭	2.5 ⎭	3.5 ⎭

Hence *Engel* thinks that when the articles of food, clothing, shelter, heating and lighting have become dearer by 50 per cent., and other wants have not, and it is desired to proportionately increase the salaries of officials, salaries of 300, 600 and 1,000 thalers should be raised to 427.5, 800 and 1,275 thalers respectively. (Preuss. Statist. Zeitschr., 1875.) *E. Herrmann*, Pricipien der Wirthsch., 106, estimates that in all Europe, 45.6 of all consumption is for food, 13.2 for clothing, 5.7 for shelter, 4.6 for furnishing, 5.3 for heating and lighting, 2.6 for tools and utensils, 13.3 for public security, 6.6 for purposes of recreation. Compare *Leplay*, Les Ouvriers Européens, 1855, and *v. Prittwitz*, Kunst reich zu werden, 487 ff. The expenses for shelter, service and sociability are specially apt to increase with an increase of income.

* The necessity of an equilibrium between production and consumption was pretty clear to many of the older political economists. Thus, for instance, *Petty* calls the coarse absence of the feeling of higher wants among the Irish the chief cause of their idleness and poverty. Similarly *Temple*,

should keep equal pace with that of production, and supply with demand.[1] The growth of a nation's economy naturally

---

Observations on the N. Provinces, ch. 6, in which Ireland and Holland are compared in this relation. *North*, Discourses upon Trade, 14 seq.; Potscr. *Roscher*, Zur Geschichte der english. Volswirthschaftslehre, 83, 91, 127 ff. *Becher*, polit. Discurs., 1668, 17 ff., was of opinion that the principal cause keeping the three great estates together, the very soul of their connection, was consumption. Hence the peasant lived from the tradesman, and the tradesman from the merchant. *(Boisguillebert,* Détail de la France, I, 4, II, 9, 21.) According to *Berkeley*, Querist, No. 20, 107, the awakening of wants is the most probable way to lead a people to industry. And so *Hume,* loc. cit., *Forbonnais*, Eléments du Commerce, I, 364. The Physiocrates were in favor of active consumption. Thus *Quesnay*, Maximes générales, 21 seq.; *Letrosne*, De l' Interêt social, I, 12. *La reproduction et la consommation sont réciprocquement la mesure l'une de l'autre.* Some of them considered consumption even as the chief thing *(Mirabeau,* Philosophie rurale, ch. 1), which could never be too great. Further, *Verri,* Meditazioni, I, 1-4. *Büsch,* Geldumlauf, III, 11 ff.

The moderns have frequently inequitably neglected the doctrine of consumption. Thus it appears to be a very characteristic fact that in *Adam Smith's* great book, there is no division bearing the title "consumption," and in the Basel edition of 1801, that word does not occur in the index. *Droz* says that in reading the works of certain of his followers, one might think that products were not made for the sake of man, but man for their sake. But, on the other hand, there came a strong reaction with *Lauderdale*, Inquiry, ch. 5; *Sismondi*, N. Principes, L., II, passim; *Ganilh,* Dictionnaire Analytique, 93 ff., 159 ff.; but especially, and with important scientific discoveries, *Malthus,* Principles, B. II. *St. Chamans*, Nouvel Essai sur la Richesse des Nations, 1824, is an exaggerated carricature of the theory of consumption. For instance, he resolves the income of individuals into foreign demand or the demand of strangers (29); considers the first condition of public credit to lie in the making of outlay (32); and even calls entirely idle consumers productive, for the reason that they elevate by their demand a *utilité possible*, to the dignity of a *utilité réelle* (286 ff.) The view advocated by Mirabeau and referred to above, again represented by *E. Solly*, Considerations on Political Economy, 1814, and by *Weishaupt*, Ueb. die Staatsausgaben und Auflagen, 1819. And so according to *Carey,* Principles, ch. 35, § 6, the real difficulty does not lie in production, but in finding a purchaser for the products. But he overlooks the fact here that only the possessor of other products can appear as a purchaser. From another side, most socialists think almost exclusively of the wants of men, and scarcely consider it worth their while to pay any attention to the means of satisfying them.

[1] *Boisguillebert* lays the greatest weight on the harmony of the different

depends on this: that production should always be, so to speak, one step in advance of consumption, just as the organism of the animal body grows from the fact that the secretions always amount to something less than the amount of additional nutrition. A preponderance of secretions would here be disease; but so would be a too great preponderance of nutrition. Now, the politico-economical disease which is produced by the lagging behind of consumption, and by the supply being much in advance of the demand, is called a commercial (market) crisis. Its immediate consequence is, that for a great many commodities produced, no purchasers can be found. The effect of this is naturally to lower prices. The profit of capital and wages diminish. A transition into another branch of production, not overcrowded, is either not possible at all or is attended with care, great difficulties and loss. It is very seldom that all these disadvantages are confined to the one branch in which the disease had its original seat. For, since the resources of the one class of producers have diminished, they cannot purchase as much from others as usual. The most distant members of the politico-economic body may be thereby affected.[2]

---

branches of commerce. *L'équilibre l'unique conservateur de l'opulence générale;* this depends on there being always as many sales as purchases. The moment one link in the great chain suffers, all the others sympathise. Hence he opposes all taxation of commodities which would destroy this harmony. (Nature des Richesses, ch. 4, 5, 6; Factum de la France, ch. 4; Tr. des Grains I, 1.) Canard Principes d'E. politique, ch. 6, compares the relation between production and consumption in national economy with that between arteries and veins in the animal body. On the other hand, *Sismondi*, N. Principes I, 381, describes the bewilderment and want which are wont to arise when one wheel of the great politico–economical machine turns round more rapidly than the others.

[2] Thus, for instance, an occasional stagnation of the cotton factories of Lancashire has frequently the effect of "making all England seem like a sick man twisting and turning on his bed of pain." *(L. Faucher.)*

SECTION CCXVI.

COMMERCIAL CRISES IN GENERAL.—A GENERAL GLUT.

The greater number of such crises are doubtless special; that is, it is only in some branches of trade that supply outweighs demand. Most theorists deny the possibility of a general glut, although many practitioners stubbornly maintain it.[1] J. B. Say relies upon the principle that in the sale of products, as contradistinguished from gifts, inheritances etc., payment can always be made only in other products. If, therefore, in one branch there be so much supplied that the price declines; as a matter of course, the commodity wanted in exchange will command all the more, and, therefore, have a better vent. In the years 1812 and 1813, for instance, it was almost impossible to find a market for dry goods and other similar products. Merchants everywhere complained that nothing could be sold. At the same time, however, corn, meat and colonial products were very dear, and, therefore, paid a large profit to those who supplied them.[2] Every producer who wants to sell anything brings a demand into the market exactly corresponding to his supply. *(J. Mill.)* Every seller is *ex vi termini* also a buyer; if, therefore production is doubled, purchasing power is also doubled. *(J. S. Mill.)* Supply and demand are in the last analysis, really, only two different sides of one

---

[1] When those engaged in industrial pursuits speak of a lasting and ever-growing over-production, they have generally no other reason for their complaints than the declining of the rate of interest and of the undertaker's profit which always accompany an advance in civilization. Compare *J. S. Mill*, Principles, III, ch. 14, 4. However, the same author, I, 403, admits the possibility of something similar to a general over-production.

[2] *Say's* celebrated Théorie des Débouchés, called by McCulloch his chief merit, Traité, I, ch. 15. At about the same time the same theory was developed by *J. Mill*, Commerce defended, 1808. *Ricardo's* express adhesion, Principles, ch. 21. Important germs of the theory may be traced much farther back: *Mélon*, Essai politique sur le Commerce, 1734, ch. 2; *Tucker*, On the Naturalization Bill, 17; Sketch of the Advance and Decline of Nations, 1795, 182.

and the same transaction. And as long as we see men badly fed, badly clothed etc., so long, strictly speaking, shall we be scarcely able to say that too much food or too much clothing has been produced.[3]

SECTION CCXVII.

COMMERCIAL CRISES IN GENERAL.

All these allegations are undoubtedly true, in so far as the whole world is considered one great economic system, and the aggregate of all goods, including the medium of circulation, is borne in mind. The consolation which might otherwise lie herein is made indeed to some extent unrealizable by these conditions. It must not be forgotten in practice that men are

---

[3] Precisely the same commercial crisis, that of 1817 seq., which more than anything else led *Sismondi* to the conclusion that too much had been produced in all branches of trade, may most readily be reduced to *Say's* theory.

There was then a complaint, not only in Europe but also in America, Hindoostan, South Africa and Australia, of the unsaleableness of goods, overfull stores etc.; but this, when more closely examined, was found to be true only of manufactured articles and raw material, of clothing and objects of luxury, while the coarser means of subsistence found an excellent market, and were sold even at the highest prices. Hence, in this case, there was by no means any such thing as over-production. The trouble was that in the cultivation of corn and other similar products, too little was produced. There was a bad harvest even in 1816.

The most important authorities in favor of the possibility of a general glut are *Sismondi*, N. Principes, IV, ch. 4, and in the Revue encyclopédique, Mai, 1824: Sur la Balance des Consommations avec les Productions. Opposed by *Say* in the same periodical (Juilliet, 1824); where the controversy was afterwards reopened in June and July, 1827, by *Sismondi* and *Dunoyer*. Compare Etudes, vol. 1; *Ganilh*, Théorie, II, 348 ff.; *Malthus*, Principles, II, ch. 1, S. Compare *Rau*, *Malthus* und *Say*, über die Ursachen der jetzigen Handelsstockung, 1821. *Malthus'* views were surpassed by *Chalmers*, On Political Economy in Connexion with the moral State of Society, 1832. But even *Malthus* himself in his Definitions, ch. 10, No. 55, later, so defined a "general glut" that there could be no longer question of his holding to its universality. For an impartial criticism, see especially *Hermann*, Staatsw. Untersuchungen, 251, and *M. Chevalier*, Cours, 1, Leçon, 3.

actuated by other motives than that of consuming as much as possible.¹ As men are constituted, the full consciousness of this possibility is not always found in connection with the mere power to do, to say nothing of the will to do.² There are, everywhere, certain consumption-customs corresponding with the distribution of the national income. Every great and sudden change in the latter is therefore wont to produce a great glut of the market.³ The party who in such case wins, is not wont to extend his consumption as rapidly as the loser has to curtail his; partly for the reason that the former

---

¹ As *Ferguson*, History of Civil Society, says, the person who thinks that all violent passions are produced by the influence of gain or loss, err as greatly as the spectators of Othello's wrath who should attribute it to the loss of the handkerchief.

² If all the rich were suddenly to become misers, live on bread and water, and go about in the coarsest clothing, etc., it would not be long before all commodities, the circulating medium excepted, would feel the want of a proper market — all, including even the most necessary means of subsistence, because a multitude of former consumers, having no employment, would be obliged to discontinue their demand. Over-production would be greater yet if a great and general improvement in the industrial arts or in the art of agriculture had gone before. Compare, *Lauderdale* Inquiry, 88. This author calls attention to the fact that a market in which the middle class prevails must put branches of production in operation very different from those put in operation where there are only a few over-rich people, and numberless utterly poor ones: England, the United States — the East Indies, and France before the Revolution. (Ch. 5, especially p. 358.)

³ If England, for instance, became bankrupt as a nation, the country would not therefore become richer or poorer. The national creditors would lose about £28,000,000 per annum, but the taxpayers would save that sum every year. Now, of the former, there are not 300,000 families; of the latter there are at least 5,000,000. Hence, the loss would there amount to £100 a family per annum, and the gain here to not £6 per family. We may therefore assume with certainty that the two items would not balance each other as to consumption. The creditors of the nation, a numerous, and hitherto a largely consuming class, now impoverished, would be obliged to curtail their demand for commodities of every kind to a frightful extent; while a great many taxpayers would not feel justified in basing an immediate increase of their demand on so small a saving. Other revolutions, more political in character, may operate in the same direction by despoiling a brilliant court, a luxurious nobility or numerous official classes of their former income.

cannot calculate his profit as accurately as the latter can his loss.⁴

Thus laws, the barriers interposed by tariffs etc., may hinder the too-much of one country to flow over into the too-little of another. England, for instance might be suffering from a flood of manufactured articles and the United States from an oppressive depreciation in the value of raw material; but the tariff-laws places a hermetic dike between want on one side and superfluity on the other. Strong national antipathies and great differences of taste stubbornly adhered to may produce similar effects; for instance between the Chinese and Europeans. Even separation in space, especially when added to by badness of the means of transportation may be a sufficient hinderance especially when transportation makes commodities so dear that parties do not care to exchange. In such cases, it is certainly imaginable that there should be at once a want of proper vent or demand for all commodities; provided, we look upon each individual class of commodities the world over as one whole, and admit the exception that in individual places, certain parts of the whole more readily find a market because of the general crisis.

Lastly, the mere introduction of trade by money destroys as it were the use of the whole abstract theory.⁵ So long as original barter prevailed, supply and demand met face to face. But by the intervention of money, the seller is placed in a condition to purchase only after a time, that is, to postpone the oth-

---

⁴ The above truth has been exaggerated by Malthus and his school into the principle that a numerous class of "unproductive consumers," who consume more than they produce, is indispensable to a flourishing national economy. From this point of view, the magnitude of England's debt especially has been made a subject of congratulation. Compare *Malthus*, Principles, II, ch. 1, 9. Similarly *Ortes*, E. N., III, 17, to whom even the *impostori mezzani* and *ladri* seem to be a kind of necessity. (III, 23.) *Chalmers*, Political Economy, III ff. If it was only question of consumption here, all that would be needed would be to throw away the commodities produced in excess. Those writers forget that a consumer, to be desirable, should be able to offer countervalues.

⁵ *Malthus*, Principles, II, ch. 1, 3.

er half of the exchange-transaction as he wishes. Hence it follows that supply does not necessarily produce a corresponding demand in the real market. And thus a general crisis may be produced, especially by a sudden diminution of the medium of circulation.[6] And so, many very abundant harvests, which have produced a great decline in the value of raw material, and no less so a too large fixation of capital which stops before its completion,[7] may lead to general overproduction. In a word, production does not always carry with itself the guaranty that it shall find a proper market, but only when it is developed in all directions, where it is progressive and in harmony with the whole national econo-

---

[6] Let us suppose a country which has been used to effecting all its exchanges by means of $100,000,000. All prices have been fixed, or have regulated themselves accordingly. Let us now suppose that there has been a sudden exportation of $10,000,000, and under such circumstances as to delay the rapid filling up of the gap thus created. In the long run, the demand of a country for a circulation may be satisfied just as well with $90,000,000 as with $100,000,000; only it is necessary in the first instance that the circulation should be accelerated or that the price of money should rise 10 per cent. But neither of these accommodations is possible immediately. In the beginning, sellers will refuse to part with their goods 10 per cent. cheaper than they have been wont to. But so long as those engaged in commercial transactions have not become completely conscious of the revolution which has taken place in prices, and do not act accordingly, there is evidently a certain ebb in the channels of trade, and simultaneously in all. Demand and supply are kept apart from each other by the intervention of a generally prevailing error concerning the real price of the medium of circulation, and there must be, although only temporarily, buyers wanted by every seller, except the seller of money. In a country with a paper circulation, every great depreciation of the value of the paper money not produced by a corresponding increase of the same, may produce such results. *Say* is wrong when he says that a want of instruments of exchange may be always remedied immediately and without difficulty.

[7] Suppose a people, the country population of which produce annually $100,000,000 in corn over and above their own requirements, and thus open a market for those engaged in industrial pursuits to the extent of $100,000,000. And suppose that in consequence of three plentiful harvests, and because of an inability to export, the market should grow to be over-full, to such an extent that the much greater stores of corn have now (§ 5, 103) a much smaller value in exchange than usual. The latter may have declined to $70,000,-

my. To use Michel Chevalier's expression, the saliant angles of the one-half must correspond to the re-entrant angles of the other, or confusion will reign everywhere. Even in individual industrial enterprises, the proper combination of the different kinds of labor employed in them is an indispensable condition of success. Let us suppose a factory in which there are separate workmen occupied with nothing but the manufacture of ramrods. If these now exceed the proper limits of their production and have manufactured perhaps ten times as many ramrods as can be used in a year, can their colleagues, employed in the making of the locks or but-ends of the gun, profit by their outlay? Scarcely. There will be a stagnation of the entire business, because part of its capital is paralyzed, and all the workmen will suffer damage.[89]

SECTION CCXVIII

PRODIGALITY AND FRUGALITY.

Prodigality is less odious than avarice, less irreconcilable with certain virtues, but incomparably more detrimental to a nation's economy. The miser's treasures, even when they have been buried, may be employed productively, at least,

---

000. Hence the country people now can buy from the cities only $70,000,-000 of city wares. The cities, therefore, suffer from over-production. That people dispensing with the use of money should establish an immediate trade between wheat and manufactured articles, in which case the latter would exchange against a large quantity of the former, is not practicable, because no one can extend his consumption of corn beyond the capacity of his stomach, and the storage of wheat with the intention of selling it when the price advances is attended with the greatest difficulties.

[8] If, for instance, there are too many railroads in process of construction, all other commodities may in consequence lose in demand, and when the further construction begins to be arrested on account of a superfluity of roads, the new rail factories etc. are involved in the crisis.

[9] On the special pathology and therapeutics of this economic disease, compare *Roscher*, Die Productionskrisen, mit besonderer Rücksicht auf die letzen Jahrzente in der Gegenwart, Brockhaus, 1849, Bd., III, 721 ff., and his Ansichten der Volkswirthschaft, 1861, 279 ff.

after his death; but prodigality *destroys* resources. So, too, avarice is a repulsive vice, extravagance a seductive one. The practice of frugality[1] in every day life is as far removed from one extreme as the other. It is the "daughter of wisdom, the sister of temperance and the mother of freedom." Only with its assistance can liberality be true, lasting and successful. It is, in short, reason and virtue in their application to consumption.[2,3]

SECTION CCXIX.

EFFECT OF PRODIGALITY.

Prodigality destroys goods which either were capital or might have become capital. But, at the same time, it either directly or indirectly increases the demand for commodities. Hence, for a time, it raises not only the interest of capital, but the prices of many commodities. Consumers naturally suffer in consequence; many producers make a profit greater than that usual in the country until such time as the equilibrium between supply and demand has been restored by an increase of the supply of the coveted products. But the capital of spendthrifts is wont to be suddenly exhausted; demand suddenly decreases, and producers suffer a crisis. As Benjamin Franklin says, he who buys superfluities will at last have to sell necessities. Thus the extravagance of a court may con-

---

[1] Negatively: the principle of sparing; positively: the principle of making the utmost use of things. (*Schäffle*, Kapitalismus und Socialismus, 27.)

[2] Admirable description of economy in *B. Franklin's* Pennsylvanian Almanac, How poor Rich. Saunders got rich; also in *J. B. Say*, Traité, III, ch. 5. *Adam Smith*, W. of N., II, ch. 3, endeavors to explain why it is that, on the whole and on a large scale, the principle of economy predominates over the seductions of extravagance. This, however, is true only of progressive nations.

[3] The Savior Himself in His miracles, the highest pattern of economy: *Matth.*, 14, 20; *Mark*, 6, 43; 8, 8; *Luke*, 9, 17; *John*, 6, 12. That He did not intend to prohibit thereby all noble luxury is shown by passages such as *Matth.*, 26, 6 ff.; *John*, 2, 10.

tribute to the rapid prosperity of a place of princely residence.[1] But it should not be forgotten that all the food-sap artificially carried there had to be previously withdrawn from the provinces. The clear loss caused by the destruction of wealth should also be borne in mind.[2][3]

SECTION CCXX.

WHEN SAVING IS INJURIOUS.

The act of saving, if the consumption omitted was a productive one, is detrimental to the common good; because now a real want of the national economy remains unsatisfied.[1] The effecting of savings by curtailing unproductive consumption may embarrass those who had calculated on its continuance. But its utility or damage to the whole national economy will

---

[1] A rapid change of hands by money, as it is called in every day life. See, *per contra*, *Tucker*, Sermons, 31, 1774.

[2] Only the superficial observer is apt to notice this apparent prosperity of the capital much more readily than the decline of the rest of the country, which covers so much more territory. In like manner, many wars have had the appearance of promoting industry, for the reason that some branches grew largely in consequence of the increased demand of the state; but they grew at the expense of all others which had to meet the increased taxes. Compare *Jacob* in *Lowe*, England nach seinem gegenwartigen Zustande, 1823, cap. 2, 3; *Nebenius*, Œffentlicher Credit, I, Aufl., 419 ff.; *Hermann*, partment of the Seine, amounted, in 1850, to 497,000,000 francs; in the department of the Bouches du Rhone, to 39,000,000 francs; in 1855, on the other hand, they were, on account of the war, 887,000,000 francs and 141,000,000. (Journal des Econ., Juil., 1857, 32 ff.)

[3] The Journal des Economistes for March, 1854, very clearly shows, in opposition to the state-sophists who recommended extravagant balls etc. as a means of advancing industry, and who even advocated the paying officials higher salaries on this account, and making greater outlays by them compulsory, that such luxury when it comes of itself may be a symptom of national wealth, but that it is a very bad means to produce prosperity artificially.

[1] What evil influences such saving can have may be seen from Prussian frugality in its military system before 1806.

depend on the application or employment of what is saved.
Here two different cases are possible.
A. It is stored up and remains idle. If this happens to a
sum of money, the number of instruments of exchange in commerce is diminished. Hence, in consequence, there may be
either a general fall in the price of commodities, or some
commodities may remain unsold; that is, according to §217, a
commercial crisis of greater or smaller extent.[2] If it be objects
of immediate consumption that are stored up and lie idle, articles of food or clothing, for instance, the price of such commodities is wont to be raised by the new and unusual demand

[2] The custom of burying treasure is produced by a want of security (compare *Montanari*, Della Moneta, 1683-87, 97 Cust.), and by an absence of the spirit which leads to production. As *Burke* says, where property is not sacred, gold and silver fly back into the bosom of the earth whence they came. Hence, in the middle ages, this custom was frequent, and is yet, in most oriental despotic countries. (*Montesquieu*, E. des L., XXII, 2.) And so in Arabia: d' *Arvieux*, *Rosenmüller's* translation, 61 seq. *Fontanier*, Voyage dans l' Inde et dans le Golfe persique, 1644, I, 279. A Persian governor on his death bed refused to give any information as to where he had buried his treasure. His father had always murdered the slave who helped him to bury his money or any part of it. (*Klemm*, Kulturgeschichte, VII, 220.) In lower stages of civilization, it is a very usual luxury to have one's treasures buried with the corpse. In relation to David's grave, see *Joseph.*, Ant. Jud., VII, 15, 3, XIII, 8, 4; XVI, 7, 1. Hence the orientals believe that every unknown ruin hides a treasure, that every unintelligible inscription is a talisman to discover it by, and that every scientific traveler is a treasure-digger. (*v. Wrede*, R. in Hadhramaut, 113, 182 and *passim.*) Similarly in Sicily. (*Rehfues*, Neuester Zustand von S., 1807, I, 99.) In the East Indies every circumstance that weakens confidence in the power of the government increases the frequency of treasure-burial, as was noticed, for instance, after the Afghan defeat. Treasure-burial by the Spanish peasantry (*Borrego*, translated by Rottenkamp, 81), in Ireland (*Wakefield*, Account of I. I, 593), in the interior of Russia (*Storch*, Handbuch, I, 142), and among the Laplanders. The custom was very much strengthened among the latter when, in 1813, they lost 80 per cent. by the bankruptcy of the state through its paper money. (*Brooke*, Winter in Lapland, 1829, 119; compare *Blom*, Statistik von Norwegen, II, 205. As during the Thirty Years' War, so also in 1848, it is said that large amounts of money were burned by the Silesian and Austrian peasantry. Much of it is lost forever, but, on the whole, much treasure is wont to be found where much is buried; governments there make it a regal right to search for it.

for them, precisely as it is lowered afterwards when the stores are suddenly opened and thrown upon the market.[3]

B. If the saving effected be used to create fixed capital, there is as much consumption of goods, the same support of employed workmen, the same sale for industrial articles as in the previous unproductive consumption; only, there the stream is usually conducted into other channels. If a rich man now employs in house-building what he formerly paid out to mistresses; masons, carpenters etc. earn what was formerly claimed by hair-dressers, milliners etc.: there is less spent for truffles and champagne and more for bread and meat. The last result is a house which adds permanently either to personal enjoyment, or permanently increases the material products of the nation's economy.[4] And it is just so when the wealth saved is used as circulating capital. Here, the wealth saved is consumed in a shorter or longer time; and to superficial observers, this saving might seem like destruction; but it is distinguished from the last by this, that it always reproduces its full equivalent and more. However, the whole quantity of goods brought into the market by such new capital cannot be called its product. Only the use *(Nützung)* of the new capital can be so called; that is the holding together or the development in some other way of other forces which were already in existence until their achievements are perfected and ready for sale.[5][6]

---

[3] If the hoarding takes place in a time of superfluity, and the restitution of the stores in a time of want, there is of course no detrimental disturbance, but on the contrary the consequence is a beneficent equilibrium of prices. This is the fundamental idea in the storage of wheat.

[4] In the construction of national buildings etc., we have the following course of things: compulsory contributions made by taxpayers, or an invitation to the national creditors to desist somewhat from their usual amount of consumption, and to employ what is saved in the building of canals, roads etc. In France, for instance, after 1835, 100,000,000 francs per annum. *(M. Chevalier,* Cours, I, 109.) The higher and middle classes of England saved, not without much trouble, however, between 1844 and 1858, £134,500,000 in behalf of railway construction. *Tooke-Newmarch.*

[5] Such savings have sometimes been prescribed by the state. In ancient

SECTION CCXXI.

LIMITS TO THE SAVING OF CAPITAL.

It may be seen from the foregoing, that the mere saving of capital, if the nation is to be really enriched thereby, has its limits. Every consumer likes to extend his consumption-supply and his capital in use *(Gebrauchskapitalien)*; but not beyond a certain point.[1] Besides, as trade becomes more flourishing, smaller stores answer the same purpose. And no intelligent man can desire his productive capital increased except up to the limit that he expects a larger market for his enlarged production. What merchant or manufacturer is there who would rejoice or consider himself enriched, if the number of his customers and their desire to purchase remaining the same, he saw his stores of unsaleable articles increase every year by several thousands?

This is another difference between national resources or world-resources and private resources. The resources of a private person, which are only a link in the whole chain of trade, and which are, therefore, estimated at the value in exchange of their component parts should, indeed, always be increased by savings made. (§8.) For even the most ex-

---

Athens many prohibitions of consumption in order to allow the productive capital to first attain a certain height. Thus it was forbidden to slaughter sheep until they had lambed, or before they were shorn. *(Athen.,* IX, 375, I, 9.) Similarlly the old prohibition of the exportation of figs. (Ibid., III, 74.) Compare Petit. Leges. Atticae, V, 3. *Boeckh,* Staatshaushaltung, I, 62 seq.

* The process of the transformation of savings from a money-income, in a money-economy *(Geldwirthschaft),* into other products, more closely analyzed in *v. Mangoldt,* V. W. L., 152 ff.

[1] Up to this point, indeed, wants increase with the means of their satisfaction. The man who has two shirts always strives to get a dozen, while the person who has none at all, very frequently does not care for even one. And so the person who has silver spoons generally desires also to possess silver candle-sticks and silver plates. On Lucullus' 5,000 chlamydes, see *Horat.,* Epist, I, 6, 40 ff

cessive increase of supply in general, which largely lowers the price of a whole class of commodities, will never reduce the price of individual quantities of that commodity below zero, and scarcely to zero. It is quite otherwise in the case of national or world resources which must be estimated according to the value in use of their component parts. Every utility supposes a want. Where, therefore, the want of a commodity has not increased, and notwithstanding there is a continuing increase in the supply, the only result must be a corresponding decrease in the utility of each individual part.[2]

If a people were to save all that remained to them over and above their most urgent necessities, they would soon be obliged to seek a wider market in foreign countries, or loan their capital there; but they would make no advance what-

---

[2] That consumption and saving are not two opposites which exclude each other is one of *Adam Smith's* most beautiful discoveries. See Wealth of Nat., II, ch. 3. But compare *Pinto*, Du Crédit et de la Circulation, 1771, 335. Before his time most writers who were convinced of the necessity of consumption were apologists of extravagance. Thus *v. Schröder*, F. Schatz- und Rentkammer, 23 seq. 47, 172. Louis XIV's saying: "A King gives alms when he makes great outlays." According to *Montesquieu*, Esprit des Lois VII, 4, the poor die of hunger when the rich curtail their expenses. This view, which must have found great favor among the imitators of Louis XIV and Louis XV was entertained to some extent by the Physiocrats; for instance, *Quesnay*, Maximes générales, 21 seq. Compare *Turgot*, Oeuvres, éd, *Dare*, 424 ff. On the other hand, *Adam Smith*, loc. cit. says that the spendthrift is a public enemy, and the person who saves a public benefactor. *Lauderdale*, Inquiry, 219, reacts so forcibly against the one-sidedness which this involves that he believes no circumstance possible "which could so far change the nature of things as to turn parsimony into a means of increasing wealth. In his polemic against Pitts' sinking fund as inopportune and excessive, he assumes that all sums saved in that way are completely withdrawn from the national demand. See per contra *Hufeland* n. Grundlegung I, 32, 238. *Sismondi*, N. P. II, ch. 6, with his distinction between *production* and *revenu*, is more moderate; the former is converted into the latter only in as much as it is "realized," that is, finds a consumer who desires it, and pays for it. Now only can the producer rely on anything; can he restore his productive capital, estimate his profit, and use it in consumption, and lastly begin the whole business over again..... A stationary country must remain stationary in everything. It cannot increase its capital and widen its market while its aggregate want remains unaltered. (IV, ch. 1.)

ever in higher culture nor add anything to the gladness of life.³ On the other hand, if they would not save at all, they would be able to extend their enjoyments only at the expense of their capital and of their future. Yet these two extremes find their correctives in themselves. In the former case, a glut of the market would soon produce an increased consumption and a diminished production; in the latter the reverse. The ideal of progress demands that the increased outlay with increased production should be made only for worthy objects, and chiefly by the rich, while the middle and lower classes should continue to make savings and thus contribute to wipe out differences of fortune.⁴

SECTION CCXXII.

SPENDTHRIFT NATIONS.

As there are extravagant and frugal individuals, so also are there extravagant and frugal nations. Thus, for instance, we must ascribe great national frugality to the Swiss. In many well-to-do families in that country, it is a principle acted upon to require the daughters to look to the results of their white sewing, instead of giving them pin-money; to gather up the crumbs after coffee parties in the presence of the guests, and to make soup of them afterwards etc. Sons are generally neither supported nor helped to any great extent by their

---

³ Thus *John Stuart Mill* thinks that the American people derive from all their progress and all their favorable circumstances only this advantage: "that the life of the whole of one sex is devoted to dollar-hunting, and of the other to breeding dollar-hunters." (IV, ch. 6, 2.) In the popular edition of 1865, after the experience of the American civil war, he materially modified this judgment.

⁴ *Storch*, Nationaleinkommen, 125 ff. That there is at least not too much to be feared from the making of too great savings is shown by *Hermann*, St. Untersuch., 371 seq. On the other hand, there is less wealth destroyed by spendthrifts than is generally supposed, for spendthrifts are most frequently cheated by men who make savings themselves. (*J. S. Mill*, Principles, I, ch. 5, 5.)

parents in their lifetime, and are required to found their own homes. They, therefore, grow rich from inheritance only late in years, when they are accustomed to a retired and modest mode of life, and have little desire, from mere convenience sake, to change it for another. And so Temple informs us that it never occurs to the Dutch that their outlay should equal their income; and when this is the case they consider that they have spent the year in vain. Such a mode of life would cost a man his reputation there as much as vicious excess does in other countries. The greatest order and the most accurate calculation of all outlay in advance is found in union with this; so that Temple assures us he never heard of a public or private building which was not finished at the time stipulated for in advance.[1]

On the other hand, the Englishman lives rather luxuriantly. He is so used to enjoying comparative abundance, that when English travelers see the peasantry of the continent living in great frugality, they generally attribute it to poverty and not to their disposition to make savings. If England has grown rich, it is because of the colossal magnitude of its production, which is still more luxuriant and abundant than its consumption.[2] This contrast may be the effect in part of nationality and cli-

[1] *Temple*, Observations on the U. Provinces, Works, I, 136, 138 seq., 179. *Roscher*, Geschichte der engl. Volkswirthschaftsl., 129. Thus, for instance, the Richesse de Hollande, I, 305, desribes a rich town near Amsterdam in which a man with an income of 120,000 florins a year expended probably only 1,000 florins per annum on himself.

[2] As early a writer as *D. Defoe*, Giving Alms no Charity! 1704, says: the English get estates; the Dutch save them. An Englishman at that time with weekly wages of 20 shillings just made ends meet; while a Dutchman with the same grew rich, and left his children behind him in very prosperous circumstances, etc. *L. Faucher* draws a similar contrast between his fellow countrymen and the English. *Goethe's* ingenuous observations (Werke, Bd., 23, 246, ed. of 1840) in his Italian journey, show that the Italians, too, know how to save. *Molti pochi fanno un assai!* And so in Bohemia, the Czechs have a good reputation for frugality, sobriety etc. as workmen. They are more frugal than the Germans, although all the larger businesses belong to Germans, because when the Czech has saved something, he prefers to return to his village to putting his savings in jeopardy by speculation.

mate;³ but it is certainly the effect in part also of a difference in the stage of civilization which these countries have respectively reached. The elder Cato had a maxim that a widow might, indeed, allow her fortune to diminish, but that it was a man's duty to leave more behind him than he had inherited.⁴ And how prodigally did not the lords of the universe live in later times!

SECTION CCXXIII.

THE MOST DETRIMENTAL KIND OF EXTRAVAGANCE.

The kind of extravagance which it is most natural we should desire to see put an end to, is that which procures enjoyment to no one. I need call attention only to the excessive durability and solidity of certain buildings. It is more economical to build a house that will last 60 years for $10,000, than one which will last 400 years for $20,000; for in 60 years the interest saved on the $10,000 would be enough to build three such houses.¹ This is, of course, not applicable to houses built as works of art, or only to produce an imposing effect. The object the ancient Egyptians had in view in building their

---

³ Drunkenness a common vice of northern people: thus in antiquity the Thracians (*Athen.*, X, 42; *Xenoph.*, Exp. Cyri, VII, 3, 32), the Macedonians, for instance, Philip's (*Demosth.*, Olynth., II, 23) and Alexander's (*Plutarch*, Alex., 70; De Adulat., 13). To drink like a Scythian, meant, among the Greeks, to drink like a beast. (*Athen.*, X, 427; *Herod.*, VI, 84.) On North German drunkenness in the 16th century, see *Seb. Münster*, Cosmogr., 326, 730. *Kantzow*, Pomerania, II, 128.

⁴ *Plutarch*, Cato, I, 21.

¹ Compare *Minard*, Notions élémentaires d'Economie politique appliquée aux Travaux publics, 1850, 71 ff. He calls to mind the many strong castles of the age of chivalry, the Roman aqueducts, theaters etc., which are still in a good state of preservation, but which can be used by no one; so many bridges too narrow for our purposes, and so many roads too steep. The sluices at Dunkirk, made 12.60 metres in width by Vauban, were made 16 meters wider in 1822, and still are too narrow for Atlantic steamships. In England, private individuals have well learned to take all this into account. Compare *J. B. Say*, Cours pratique, translated by Morstadt, 1, 454 ff.

obelisks and pyramids continues to be realized even in our day.

I might also call attention to the premature casting away of things used. Our national economy has saved incredible sums since rags have been manufactured into paper. In Paris 4,000 persons make a living from what they pick up in the streets.²

---

² *Fregier*, Die gefährlichen Klassen, translated 1840, I, 2, 38. In Yorkshire it is said that woolen rags to the amount of £52,000,000 a year are manufactured into useful articles. (*Tooke*, Wool-Production, 196.) Compare The Use of Refuse: Quart. Rev., April, 1868. On the ancient Greek ragpickers the so-called σπερμολόγοις, see *St. John*, The Hellenes, III, 91; on the Roman *Centonariis:* Cato, R. R., 135; *Columella*, R. R., I, 8, 9; *Marquardt*, II, 476, V, 2, 187.

CHAPTER II.

LUXURY.

SECTION CCXXIV.

LUXURY IN GENERAL.

The idea conveyed by the word luxury is an essentially relative one. Every individual calls all consumption with which he can dispense himself, and every class that which seems not indispensable to themselves, luxury. The same is true of every age and nation. Just as young people ridicule every old fashion as pedantry, every new fashion is censured by old people as luxury.[1]

But (§ 1) a higher civilization always finds expression in an increased number and an increased urgency of satisfied wants. Yet, there is a limit at which new or intensified wants cease to be an element of higher civilization, and become elements of demoralization. Every immoral and every unwise want

---

[1] *Stuart*, Principles, II, ch. 30, *Ferguson*, History of Civil Society, VI, 2. Thus *Dandolus*, Chron. Venet., 247, tells of the wife of a doge at Constantinople who was so given to luxury that she ate with a golden fork instead of her fingers. But she was punished for this outrage upon nature: her body began to stink even while she was alive. In the introduction to *Hollinshed's* Chronicon, 1557, there is a bitter complaint that, a short time previous, so many chimneys had been erected in England, that so many earthen and tin dishes had been introduced in the place of wooden ones. Another author finds fault that oak was then used in building instead of willow, and adds that formerly the men were of oak but now of willow. *Slaney*, On rural Expenditure, 41. Compare *Xenoph.*, Cyrop., VIII, 8, 17.

exceeds this limit.² Immoral wants are not only those the satisfaction of which wounds the conscience, but also those in which the necessities of the soul are postponed to the affording of superfluities to the body; and where the enjoyment of the few is purchased at the expense of the wretchedness of the many. And not only those are unwise or imprudent for which the voluntary outlay is greater than one's income, but those also where the indispensable is made to suffer for the dispensable.

Thus it was in Athens, in the time of Demosthenes, when the festivities of the year cost more than the maintenance of the fleet; when Euripides' tragedies came dearer to the people than the Persian war in former times. There was even a law passed (Ol. 107, 4) prohibiting the application of the dramatic fund to purposes of war under pain of death.³

In the history of any individual people, it may be shown with approximate certainty at what point luxury exceeded its salutary limits. But in the case of two different nations, it is quite possible that what was criminal prodigality with the one, may have been a salutary enjoyment of life with the other; in case their economic *(wirthschaftlichen)* powers are different. Precisely as in the case of individuals, where for instance, the daily drinking of table wine may be simplicity in the rich and immoral luxury in the case of a poor father of a family.⁴ Healthy reason has this peculiarity, that where people will not listen to it, it never hesitates to make itself felt. *(Benjamin Franklin.)*⁵

However, the luxury of a period always throws itself, by way of preference, on those branches of commodities which are cheapest.

---

² Biblically determined: *Romans*, 13, 14.
³ *Plutarch*, De Gloria Athen., 348. *Athen.*, XIV, 623. Petit. Legg. Att., 385.
⁴ *Livy*, XXXIV, 6 ff.
⁵ Most writers who have treated of luxury at all have generally confined themselves to inquiring whether it was salutary or reprehensible. Aristippus and Antisthenes, Diogenes etc.; Epicureans and Stoics. The latter were re-

SECTION CCXXV.

THE HISTORY OF LUXURY.—IN THE MIDDLE AGES.

During the middle ages, industry and commerce had made as yet but little progress. Hence it was as difficult then for luxury to be ministered to by fine furniture as by the products of foreign countries. Individual ornamental pieces, especially arms and drinking cups,[1] were wont to be the only articles of

---

proached with being bad citizens, because their moderation in all things was a hindrance to trade. *(Athen.,* IV, 163.) The Aristotelian *Herakleides* declared luxury to be the principal means to inspire men with noble-mindedness; inspired by luxury, the Athenians conquered at Marathon. *(Athen.,* XII, 512.) *Pliny* was one of the most violent opponents of luxury. See *Pliny*, N. N., XXXIII, 1, 4, 13, and other places. The controversy has been renewed by the moderns, especially since the beginning of the 18th century, after luxury of every kind had previously (for the most part on theological grounds, but also by Hutten, for instance) been one-sidedly condemned. Among its defenders were *Mandeville*, The Fable of the Bees, 1706, who, however, calls everything a luxury which exceeds the baldest necessities of life; *Voltaire* in Le Mondain, the Apologie du Luxe, and Sur L'Usage de la Vie; *Mélon*, Essai politique sur le Commerce, ch. 9; *Hume*, Discourses, No. 2, On Refinement in the Arts; *Dumont*, Théorie du Luxe, 1771; *Filangieri*, Delle Leggi politiche ed economiche, II, 37; and the majority of the Mercantile school and of the Physiocrates. Among the opponents of luxury, *J. J. Rousseau* towers over almost all others. Further, *Fénélon*, Télémaque, 1699, L. XXII; *Pinto*, Essai sur le Luxe, 1762.

The reasons and counter-reasons advanced by those writers apply not only to luxury but to the lights and shades of high civilization in general. When a political economist declares for or against luxury in general, he resembles a doctor who should declare for or against the nerves in general. There has been luxury in every country and in every age. Among a healthy people, luxury is also healthy, an essential element in the general health of the nation. Among an unhealthy people luxury is a disease, and disease-engendering.

For an impartial examination of the question, see *Ferguson*, History of Civil Society, towards the end; see also *Beckmann*, in *Justis'* Grundsätzen der Polizei, 1782, § 308; *Rau*, Ueber den Luxus, 1817; *Roscher*, Uber den Luxus, in the Archiv der Politischen Œkonomie, 1843, and in his Ansichten der Volkswirthschaft, 1861, 399 ff.

[1] Here, as a rule, the value of the metal was greater than the form-value;

luxury. We have inventories of the domains of Charlemagne from which we find that in one of them, the only articles of linen owned were two bed-sheets, a table-cloth and a pocket handkerchief.[2] Fashion is here very constant; because clothing was comparatively dearer than at present. And so now in the East. In the matter of dwellings, too, more regard was had to size and durability, than to elegance and convenience. The palaces of Alfred the Great were so frailly built that the walls had to be covered with curtains as a protection against the wind, and the lights to be inclosed in lanterns.[3]

Hence the disposition to use the products of the home soil as articles of luxury was all the greater, but more as to quantity than to quality.[4] Since the knight could personally neither eat nor drink a quantity beyond the capacity of his own stomach, he kept a numerous suite to consume his surplus. It is well known what a great part was played among the ancient Germans by their retinues of devoted servants (comitatus), which many modern writers have looked upon as constituting the real kernel of the migration of nations.

In England, it was a maxim of state policy with Henry VII., whose reign there terminated the middle age, to prohibit the

---

and hence the medieval monasteries frequently made loans of silver vessels, where of course, the form could not be taken into consideration. On the other hand, in the case of the table service, presented by the king of Portugal to Lord Wellington, the metal cost £85,000 and the workmanship £86,000. (*Jacob*, Gesch. der edlen Metalle, translated by Kleinschrod, II, 5.) Compare *Hume*, History of England, ch. 44, App. 3. Similarly under Louis XIV. (*Sismondi*, Hist. des Français, XXVII, 45.) When Rome was highly civilized, C. Gracchus paid for very good silver ware, 15 times the value of the metal, and L. Crassus, (consul 95 before Christ) 18 times its value. *Mommsen*, R. Gesch. II, 383.

[2] *Specimen breviarii fiscalium Caroli Magni;* compare *Anton*, Gesch. der deutschen Landwirthsch. 244 ff.

[3] *Turner*, History of the Anglo Saxons, VII, ch. 6.

[4] In *Homer*, the kings live on nothing but meat, bread and wine: compare *Athen.*, I, 8. In the saga-poetry of Iceland, *H. Leo* does not remember to have heard any other food mentioned except oat-pap, milk, butter and cheese, fish, the flesh of domestic animals, and beer. (*Raumer's* Taschenbuch, 1835, 191.)

great liveried suites of the nobility (19 Henry VII., ch. 14) as Richard II., Henry IV. and Edward IV. had already attempted to do. But even under James I., we find ambassadors accompanied by a suite of 500 persons or 300 noblemen.[5]

The rich man welcomed every opportunity which enabled him to make others share in a dazzling manner the magnitude of his superfluous wealth: hence the numberless guests at weddings who were frequently entertained for weeks.[6] These festivities are memorable not because of the delicacies or great variety of the dishes, but because of their colossal magnitude. Even William of Orange, 1561, entertained at his wedding guests who had brought with them 5,647 horses; and he appeared himself with a suite of 1,100 men on horseback. There were consumed on the occasion 4,000 bushels of wheat, 8,000 of rye, 11,300 of oats, 3,600 *eimers* of wine, 1,600 barrels of beer.[7] In the ordinance of Münden regulating

---

[5] *Hume*, History of England, ch. 49, Append. Similarly among all nations which have still preserved much of the medieval. Thus the duke of Alba, about the end of the last century, had not a single commodious hall in his immense palace, but 400 rooms for his servants, since at least all his old servants, and even their widows and families, continued to live with him. In Madrid alone, he paid £1,000 a month wages to his servants; and the son of the duke, Medina-Celi, £4,000 per annum. (*Townsend*, II, 155, 158.) In many palaces in Moscow, previous to 1812, there were 1,000 and more servants, unskillful, clad for the most part as peasants, badly fed, and with so little to do that perhaps one had no service to perform but to fetch drinking water at noon, and another in the evening. Even poor noblemen kept 20 and 30 servants. (*v. Haxthausen*, Studien, I, 59.) *Forster*, Werke, VII, 347, explains Polish luxury in servants, by the poorness of the servants there: a good German maid could do more than three Polish servants. Thus, in Jamaica, it was customary to exempt from the slave-tax persons who kept fewer than 7 negroes. (*B. Edwards*, History of the W. Indies, I, 229.) Compare *Livy*, XXXIX, 11. The luxury of using torch-bearers instead of candelabra lasted until Louis XIV.'s time. (*Rocquefort*, Hist. de la Vie privée des Français, III, 171.) Compare *W. Scott*, Legend of Montrose, ch. 4.

[6] A Hungarian magnate, under king Sigismund, celebrated his son's wedding for a whole year. (*Fessler*, Gesch. von Ungarn, IV, 1267.)

[7] *Müller*, Annal. Saxon, 68. Several examples in *Schweinichen's* Leben von Büsching, I, 320 seq. *Krünitz*, Enclycopædie, Bd. 82, 84 ff. The wedding of the niece of Ottakar II. in 1264, has long been considered a most

weddings, promulgated in the year 1610, it is provided, that, at a large wedding there should not be over 24 tables, nor at a small one over 14, with 10 persons at each table.[8]

The hospitality of the lower stages of civilization[9] must be ascribed as well to this peculiar kind of luxury as to mere good nature. Arabian chiefs have their noon-day table set in the street and welcome every passer-by to it.[10] *(Pococke.)* And so, distinguished Indians keep an open cauldron on the fire cooking all the time, from which every person who comes in may help himself. *(Catlin.)*

Compared with this luxury of the rich, the poverty found side by side with it appears less oppressive. There is no great gap between the modes of life of the different classes.[11] This is the golden age of aristocracy, when no one questions its legitimateness. When, later, the nobleman, instead of keeping so many servants, begins to buy costly garments for himself, he, indeed, supports indirectly just as many and even more men; but these owe him nothing. Besides, in this last kind of luxury, it is very easily possible for him to go beyond his means, which is scarcely ever the case in the former.[12]

---

brilliant event in the history of medieval luxury. (*Palacky*, Gesch. von Böhmen, II, 191 ff.) Even yet, in Abyssinia, on the occasion of royal feasts, only meat and bread are eaten and mead drunk; but not only the great, but even common soldiers are entertained one after the other. (Ausland, 1846, No. 79.) Magnificent as was the table of a West Indian planter, it was in some respects very simple. A large ox was slaughtered for the feast, and everything had to be prepared from that: roast beef, beef steaks, beef pies, stews etc. (*Pinckard*, Notes on the W. Indies, II. 100 ff.)

[8] *Spittler*, Geschichte Hanovers, I, 381.

[9] *Tacitus*, Germ., 21 Leg., says of the Germans: *Convictibus et hospitiis non alia gens effusius indulget. Quemcunque mortalium arcere tecto, nefas habetur. Diem noctemque continuare potando, nulli probrum.*

[10] Entirely the same among the ancient Romans: *Valer. Max.*, II, 5. Compare per *contra*, *Euripid.*, Herc. fur., 304 seq.

[11] Think of nomadic races especially, where the rich can employ their wealth only to increase the number of their partisans, for war purposes etc.

[12] *Ferguson*, Hist. of Civil Society, VI, 3; *Adam Smith*, Wealth of Nat., IV, ch. 4. Compare *Contzen*, Politicorum, 1629, 662. As to how in the lower stages of civilization, guests are used to supply the place of the post-office service, see *Humboldt*, Relation hist., II, 61.

SECTION CCXXVI.

LUXURY IN BARBAROUS TIMES.

The luxury of that uncivilized age shows itself for the most part on particular occasions, and then all the more ostentatious, while in the periods following it, it rather permeates the whole of life. Even J. Möser excuses our forefathers for their mad celebration of their *kirmesses* and carnivals: *dulce est desipere in loco*, as Horace says, and that they sometimes carried it to the extent of drowning reason.[1] Among ourselves, the common man drinks brandy every day; in Russia, seldom, but then, to the greatest excess.[2] The well known peculiarity of feudal castles, that, besides one enormous hall, they were wont to have very small and inconvenient rooms for every day life, is accounted for in part by the great importance to them of festal occasions, and in part by the cordiality of the life led in them, in which lord and servants constituted one family. Nothing can be more erroneous than to ascribe great temperance in general to people in a low stage of civilization. Their

---

[1] *Möser*, Patr. Ph. IV, 7. On the feast of fools and the feast of asses of the middle ages, compare *Dutillet*, Mémoire pour sevir à l'Histoire de la Fête des Fous; *D. Sacchi*, Delle Feste popolari del medio Evo. During the latter half of the 16th century, the first Hannoverian minister received only 200 thalers salary and pieces of clothing, while the wedding of a certain von Saldern cost 5,600 thalers. (*Spittler*, Gesch. Hannovers, I, 333.)

[2] *v. Haxthausen*, Studien, II, 450, 513. Thus, in 1631, of those who had died suddenly, there were 957 who died of drunkenness. (*Bernouilli*, Populationistik, 303.) According to *v. Lengefeldt*, Russland im 19. Jahrh., 42, the number is now 1,474 to 1,911 per annum. On Poland, see *Klebs*, Landeskulturgesetzgebung in Posen, 78. When the South American Indians begin to drink, they do not stop until they fall down senseless. (*Ulloa*, Noticias Americanas, ch. 17.) The old Romans considered all barbarians to be drunkards. (*Plato*, De Legg., I, 638.) In eating, also, uncivilized people are extremely irregular. A Jackute or Tunguse consumes 40 pounds of meat; three men devour a whole reindeer at a meal. (*Cochrane*, Fussreise, 156.) One ate in 24 hours the back quarter of a large ox, or ½ a *pud* of fat, and drank an equal quantity of melted butter. (*Klemm*, Kulturgeschichte, III, 18.) Similarly among hunting races. See *Klemm*, I, 243, 339; II, 13, 255. On the South Sea Islanders, see *Hawkesworth*, III, 505; *Forster*, I, 255.

simplicity is a consequence of their ignorance rather than of their self-control. When nomadic races have once tasted the cup of more delicate enjoyment, it is wont to hurry them to destruction.[3]

SECTION CCXXVII.

INFLUENCE OF THE CHURCH AND OF THE CITY.

The change in this situation takes place first of all in the churches and in the cities. The Church has passed through almost every stage of development in advance of the State; and civilization, both in the good and bad sense of the term, has become general, and gradually acclimated in the rural districts, through the influence of the cities. In the Church, the earliest art endeavored to reach the beautiful. There, we first find music, painting, sculpture, foreign perfumes, incense and variegated garments.[1] In the cities, growing industry introduces a more attractive style of clothing and a more ornamental style of household furniture. Commerce, beginning to thrive, raises foreign commodities into wants,[2] and thus the old luxury of feudal times is modified.[3] The large number of idle servants is diminished. All the more refined pleasures are extended downward to wider circles of the people. In-

---

[3] Rapid degeneration of almost all barbaric dynasties as soon as they have subjugated civilized countries.

[1] The use of window-glass in churches in England dates from 674, in private houses from 1180. *(Anderson*, Origin of Commerce, s. a.) Even in 1567, it was so rare that during the absence of the lords from their country seats, the panes were taken out and stored for safe keeping. *(Eden*, State of the Poor, I, 77.) As to how Scotland developed in this respect still later, see *Buckle*, History of Civilization in England, II, 172.

[2] In our day, at the breakfast of a German of the middle class, may be found East Indian coffee, Chinese tea, West Indian sugar, English cheese, Spanish wine, and Russian caviar, without any surprising degree of luxury. Compare *Gellius*, N. A., VII, 16.

[3] In England, the transition is noticeable, especially under Elizabeth: *Hume* History, ch. 44, app. 3. In France, under Louis XIV; *Voltaire*, Siècle de Louis, XIV, ch. 29.

stead of individual bards, rhapsodists, skalds and minnesingers, we have the beginnings of the theater, and instead of tournaments, the shooting matches. (*Freischiessen.*)

But it is remarkable how much earlier here pomp and splendor are considered than convenience. The Spanish *romanceros* of the 12th century display wonderful splendor in their descriptions of the Cid, and the trousseau of his daughters. But, on the other hand, the wife of Charles VII. seems to have been the only French woman in the 15th century who had more than two linen chemises. Even in the 16th century, it frequently happened that a princess made a present to a prince of a single shirt. At this time the German middle class were wont to sleep naked.[4]

Even now, half-civilized nations look more to the outward appearance of commodities than to their intrinsic value. Thus, for instance, in Russia, we find large numbers of porcelain services extravagantly painted and gilded, awkward, the material of which is full of blisters; damaskeened knives, gilt sad-irons and candle-snuffers with landscapes engraved on them: but nothing fits into anything else; the angles are vicious, the hinges lame, and the whole soon goes to pieces. And so, among export merchants in Bremen, for instance, it is a rule, on all their wares intended for America, to put a label made of very beautiful paper, with their coat-of-arms or firm-name in real silver, and to do the packing in as elegant a manner as possible.[5] Cloths intended for America are usually exceedingly light, destitute of solidity, but very well dressed. The

---

[4] Poesias Castellanas anteriores al Siglo XV; Tom. I, 347, 327. *Roscher*, loc. cit. *J. Voight*, in *Raumer's* historischem Taschenbuche, 1831, 290; 1835, 324, seq. Thus, one of Henry VIII's wives, in order to get salad, had first to send for a gardener from Flanders; while at the time, a single ship imported into England from 3,000 to 4,000 pieces of clothing in gold brocade, satin or silk. (*Anderson*, a. 1509, 1524, 4; Henry VIII, c. 6.)

[5] Irish linen, worth from 30 to 35 shillings, is often provided with a label which cost 5 shillings. (*Kotelmann*, Statistische Uebersicht der landwirthschaftl. und industriellen Verhältnisse von Oesterreich und dem Zollverein, 215.)

cotton-printers who work for the African market prefer to employ false but cheap and dazzling colors.[6]

SECTION CCXXVIII.

HISTORY OF LUXURY IN HIGHLY CIVILIZED TIMES.

The direction which luxury takes in times when civilization is advanced, is towards the real, healthy and tasteful enjoyment of life, rather than an inconvenient display. This tendency is exceedingly well expressed by the English word *comfort*, and it is in modern England that the luxury of the second period has found it happiest development. It is found side by side with frugality; and it frequently even looks like a return to the unaffected love of nature.[1]

Thus, since Rousseau's time,[2] the so-called English gardens have dropped the former Versailles-Harlem style. Thus, too, modern fashion despises the awkward long wig, powdering etc.[3] Instead of garments embroidered, or faced with fur or lace, and instead of the galloon hat worn under Louis XIV. and Louis XV., the French revolution has introduced the simple citizen frock-coat and the round silk hat. The "exquisite" may even with these outshine others by the form he selects, the material he wears, or by frequent change, but

---

[6] Compare *Kohl*, Reise in Deutschland, II, 18, 250. *Roscher*, in the Göttinger Studien, 1845, II, 403, ff. About 1777, *Büsch* described the difference of goods manufactured in England " for the continent and home consumption," as being just the same as the difference now between goods for Africa and goods for Europe. (Darstellung der Handlung, Zusatz, 89.)

[1] The reformation of the sixteenth century had a remarkable tendency towards natural and manful fashions, as contradistinguished from the immediately preceding and the immediately following periods. Compare *J. Falke*, Deutsche Trachten und Modenwelt, II, 1858.

[2] *J. J. Rousseau*, N. Héloise, II, L. 11. Compare *Keysler*, Reise, I, 695.

[3] That a similar transition marked an epoch in the history of Grecian morals was recognized even by *Thucydides*, I, 6; compare *Asios*, in *Athen.*, XII, 528.

much less strikingly than before.[4] Since every one, in the purchase of household furniture etc., looks more to its use than to the honor of being sole possessor of an article or having something in advance of everybody else, it becomes possible for industry to manufacture its products in much larger quantities, and after the same model. and thus to furnish a much better article for the same price.[5] Besides, more recent industry has produced a multitude of cheap substitutes for costly objects of luxury: plated silver-leafing, cotton-velvet goods etc;[6] besides the many steel engravings, lithographs etc., which have exerted so beneficent an influence on æsthetic education.

In the England of our days, the houses are comparatively small, but convenient and attractive, and the salutary luxury of spending the pleasant season in the country very general.[7] The country-roads are narrow but kept in excellent order and provided with good inns.[8] More value is here attached to fine linen cloth than to lace;[9] to a few but nourishing meat-dishes

[4] It will always remain a want to own clothes for every-day wear and festal occasions. The frock coat satisfies this want in the cheapest way. As soon as people cease to distinguish clothing for festal occasions by the cut, gold-embroidery, fur-facing etc. will appear again, which would necessarily prove a great hardship to the propertyless classes of the educated, and even to the higher classes.

[5] On the striking contrast presented in this respect by the English and French, and even Russian customs, see *Storch*, Handbuch, II, 179 ff. *J. B. Say*, Cours pratique, translated into German by *Morstadt*, I, 435 ff.; Deutsche Vierteljahrsschrift, 1853, I, 182.

[6] Paper-hangings, instead of costly gobelins and leather hangings, were not known in France until after 1760, nor in the rest of Europe until much later. Busts of plaster were (*Martial*, IX, 17, and *Juvenal*, II, 4) usual among those who were less well off.

[7] Similarly even in *Giov. Villani*, XI, 93, the villas of the highly cultured Florentines appear finer than their city houses, while in Germany, at that time, even the richest citizens lived only in the city.

[8] Sidewalks in the cities, recommended by *J. J. Rousseau*, as a popular convenience and as a safeguard against the carriage-aristocracy

[9] In France, the luxury of lace was conquered by Marie Antoinette, but still more effectually by the Revolution. Previous to that time, many Parisians wore four manchettes to each shirt. (*Palliser*, History of Lace, 1865.)

than to any number of sauces and confections of continental kitchens.[10] Especially is the luxury of cleanliness, with its morally and intellectually beneficial results found only in well-to-do and highly cultured nations. As formerly in Holland, so now in England, it is carried to the highest point of development. In the latter country, the tax on soap is considered a tax on an indispensable article.[11] The reverse is the case in North America, if we can believe the most unprejudiced and friendly observers.[12] The person who lives in a log-house must, to feel at ease within his four walls, first satisfy a number of necessary wants.[13]

---

[10] During the middle ages, strongly seasoned food, ragouts etc., were more in favor than in even France to-day; compare *Legrand d' Aussy et Roquefort*, Histoire de la Vie privée des Français, passim. The wine even, at that time, used to be mixed with roots: *vin de romarin, clairet, hippocras, (W. Wackernagel*, Kl. Schriften I, 86,7.) The French kitchen became simpler and more natural, only after the middle of the 18th century. (*Roquefort*, III, 343.)

[11] The taxed consumption of soap amounted in England in 1801 to 4.84 and in 1845, 9.65 pounds per capita. (*Porter*, Progress of the Nation, V, 5, 579.) Soap-boiling in London dates from 1520 only. Before that time, all white soap was obtained from the continent. (*Howell*, Londinopolis, 208.) *Erasmus* charged that England, in his time, was an exceedingly dirty country. The Italians, on the other hand, were at that time greatly distinguished above northern people, especially the Germans, by their cleanliness. (*Buckhardt*, Kultur der Renaissance, 295.) The Vienna river-baths after 1870, *Nicolai*, Reise, III, 17, mentions as something deserving special note. The Leipzig river-baths date from 1774.

[12] *Birkbeck*, Notes on America, 39. Even in New York, it is not very long since there were no common sewers. Just as characteristic is the uncleanliness of the South African *boers (Mauch*, in *Petermann's* Mittheilungen, Ergänz-Heft, XXVII, 23), when compared with the celebrated cleanliness of the old Dutch.

Americans will certainly not agree with the "friendly and unprejudiced" observers mentioned in the text; for no one acquainted with genuine American home-life can deny that cleanliness is an American characteristic. It is only justice to the author to say that the above note (12), so far as it relates to America, appeared in the second edition of his work, and probably in the first; and that he is not so much to be blamed for it as the unfriendly and prejudiced, if not ignorant observers. It may be said, however, that, from the use of the word "log-house," in the context, the author does not intend to apply this remark to the older settlements.— TRANSLATOR.

[13] The most frightful uncleanliness prevails among the inhabitants of polar

SECTION CCXXIX.

EXTENT OF LUXURY IN HIGHLY CIVILIZED TIMES.

The luxury of this second period fills the whole of life and permeates every class of people. Hence we may most easily determine the degree of development a people have attained by the quantity of commodities of a finer quality which are, indeed, not indispensable to life, but which it is desirable should be consumed on as extensive a scale as possible by the nation, for the sake of the fullness of life and the freshness[1] of life to which they minister.

countries, who never bathe, because of the climate, avoid all ventilation, and because of the leathern clothing which they smear with grease etc. The Tunguses consider the after-birth cooked or roasted as a great delicacy. "Fathers and mothers wipe their childrens' noses with their mouth, and gulp the secretion down." *(Georgi,* Beschreib. aller Nationen des russ. Reiches, I, 287.) Among the Koruks, the suitor rinses his mouth with his sweetheart's water. (loc. cit., I, 349, 353.) Compare *Klemm,* Kulturgeschichte, III, 24, 57. In warmer climates, even less civilized nations are clean, for instance in the East and South-Sea Islands, etc. All the more surprising is the uncleanliness of the Hottentots and Bushmen, where the natural color is observable only under the eyes, where the tears produced by too much smoke has washed away the crust of dirt which, with this exception, covers the whole body. *(Klemm,* Kulturgeschichte, 333.) How long it takes for cleanliness to become a national trait, may be inferred from the history of water-closets, when, for instance, their introduction into every house during the 16th and even the 17th century, had to be provided for by law in Paris. *(Beckmann,* Beiträge, II, 358 ff.) The Göttingen statutes of 1342 had to expressly prohibit persons to *merdare* in public wine-cellars where persons ate and drank together. *(Spittler,* Gesch. Hannovers, I, 57.) Similarly in the courts of the German princes. On the other hand, universality of water-closets in England to-day.

In ancient times, too, the uncleanliness of the Spartans in body and clothing was very surprising to the Athenians: *Xenoph.,* Resp. Laced., II, 4; *Plutarch,* Lycurg, 16. *Just.,* Lac., 5. Still more that of many barbarians, for instance of the Illyrians: *Stobaeus,* V, 51, 132; *Gaisf. Aelian.,* V, II. IV, 1. The ancient Romans bathed only once a week *(Seneca,* Epist., 86), while under the Empire, "the baths embraced and filled up the whole life of man and all his wishes." *(Gerlach.)* Compare *Becker,* Gallus, II, 10 ff.; *Lamprid,* V, Comm., 11.

[1] Thus, for instance, the modern enjoyments of coffee, tea, newspapers, to-

Thus, for instance, as civilization has advanced, there has been almost everywhere a transition to a finer quality of the material of which bread is made. The number of consumers of white bread in France in 1700, was 33 per cent. of the population; in 1760, 40; in 1764, 39; in 1791, 37; in 1811, 42; in 1818, 45; in 1839, 60 per cent.[2] About 1758, in England and Wales, 3,750,000 of people lived on wheat bread; on barley bread, 739,000; on rye bread, 888,000; on oat bread, 623,000. The cultured southeastern population had almost nothing but wheat bread, while in the north and northwest, oat bread continued to be used a long time; and in Wales only 10 per cent. of the population ate wheat bread. This condition of things in England has since been much improved. But, at the extremities of the Hebrides, nine-tenths of the population still live on barley bread; and in Ireland it was estimated, in 1838, that with 8,000,000 inhabitants, potatoes were the chief article of food of 5,000,000, and oat bread of 2,500,000.[3]

---

bacco etc., promote domesticity with which antiquity was so little acquainted. *Zaccharia*, Vierzig Bücher, VI, 60.

[2] The food of the French people has improved also in point of quantity. At the beginning of the eighteenth century, of cereals there were 472 liters per capita, at present there are 541 liters; and in addition, now, 240 liters of potatoes and vegetables more than then. Compare *Moreau de Joannès*, Statistique de l' Agriculture de la France, 1848, and the same writer's Statistique céréale de la France, in the Journal des Economistes, 1842, Janv. On the recent decrease or increase in the consumption of meat, see the very different estimates of *M. Chevalier*, Cours., I, 113 seq., and Journal des Economistes, Mars, 1856, 438 ff.

[3] *Ch. Smith*, Tracts on the Corn Trade, 1758, 182. *Eden*, State of the Poor, I, 563, seq. In *McCulloch*, Statist., I, 316, 466 ff,, 548. Moreover, *Rogers* says that English workmen in the middle ages, for the most part, consumed wheat bread. (Statist. Journal, 1864, 73.) About the middle of the 13th century, only from 11 to 12 *malters* of wheat were produced on the estates of the bishop of Osnabrück; about 470 of oats, 300 of rye, and 120 of barley. *(J. Möser*, Osnabrück, Gesch., Werke, VII, 2. 166.) Even beer was brewed from oats in the earlier part of the middle ages. *(Guérard*, Polyptiques, I, 710 ff.) The ancients, also, in their lower stages of civilization, lived on barley bread by way of preference, and went over to wheat only at a later period; compare *Plin.*, H. N. XVIII, 14. *Heracl.*, Pont., fr. 2. *Athen.*, IV., 137, 141. *Plutarch*, Alcib., 23. As to how, in Rome, the transition from *far* to the much

And so, the consumption of meat in cities is uniformly much larger than in the country. In the cities of the Prussian monarchy and subject to the slaughter-house tax, it amounted in 1846, per capita: in East Prussia, to 61 ℔s.; in Pommerania, to 66; in Posen, to 70; in West Prussia, to 71; in Saxony, to 75; in the Rhine Province, to 83; in Silesia, to 86; in Brandenburg, to nearly 104; in Berlin alone, to 114: an average in the whole country, however, of scarcely 40 ℔s. per capita. *(Dictrici.)* In the kingdom of Saxony, the average consumption of beef and pork was, shortly before 1866, about 50 ℔s.; in Dresden alone, 86.7; in Leipzig, 136.9 ℔s.[4] The consumption of meat in England is exceedingly great, so that, for instance, in several orphan asylums in London, the daily meat ration amounts to an average of from 0.23 to 0.438 ℔s. The meat-consumption of a well-to-do family, children and servants included, Porter estimates at 370 ℔s. per capita per annum. The meat ration of soldiers in the field amounts in England to 676 grammes a day; in France, to 350.[5]

---

more costly *triticum*, was connected with the extension of the hide of land from 2 to 7 *jugera*, see *M. Voigt* in the Rhein. Museum f. Philol., 1868.

[4] To this, in Saxony, must be added about from 6 to 7 pounds of veal and mutton. The recent increase in the consumption of meat in Saxony is very encouraging: 1840, about 30 lbs. of beef and pork per capita; 1851-57, 40 lbs. (Sächs. Statist. Ztschr., 1867, 143 seq.) On the other hand, *Schmoller* estimated the consumption of meat in general in Prussia, in 1802, at 33.8; in 1816, at 22.5; in 1840, at 34.6; in 1867, at 34.9 lbs. *(Fühling*, N. Landw. Zeitg., XIX; Jahrg. Heft., 9 seq.) Paris consumed, in 1850, 145 pounds of butcher's meat per capita; in 1869, 194 pounds. In the year of the revolution, 1848, the consumption declined 45 per cent.; the consumption of wine in barrels, 16 per cent.; in bottles, 44 per cent.; of sea-fish, 25 per cent.; of oysters, 24 per cent.; of beer, 20 per cent.; of eggs, 19 per cent.; of butter, 13 per cent.; of fowl, 6 per cent. *(Cl. Juglar*, in the Journal des Economistes, March, 1870.)

[5] *Porter*, Progress of the Nation, V, 5, 591 ff.; *Hildesheim*, Normaldiet, 52 ff. Well-known English popular song: "Oh, the roast beef of old England" etc. Even at the end of the 17th century one-half of the nation partook of fresh meat scarcely once or twice a week; most of that consumed was salted. *(Macaulay*, History of England, ch. 3.) But even *Boisguillebert*, Traité des Grains, II, 7, characterizes the English as great beer-drinkers and meat-eaters, from the highest class to the lowest, while the French consumed

The consumption of sugar in 1734, in England, was about 10 ℔s. per capita; in 1845, in the whole of the British Empire, 20⅓ ℔s.; in 1849, almost 25 ℔s.; in 1865, over 34 ℔s.; but it must not be overlooked here, that in Ireland the consumption of sugar per capita was scarcely over 8 ℔s.[6] In the German Zollverein, the consumption of sugar, in 1834, amounted to an average of 2½ ℔s. per capita; in 1865, to more than 9 ℔s. In France, the consumption of the same article rose from 1.33 kilogrammes, the average from 1817 to 1821, to 7.35 ℔s. in 1865.[7] The population of the Zollverein rose 25.8 per cent. between 1834 and 1847, while the importation of coffee increased 117.5 per cent.; of spices, 58.2; southern fruits, 34.5, and cocoa, 246.2 per cent.[8]

A great many of vegetables and fruits, which seem to us to be almost indispensable articles of subsistence, have been cul-

almost nothing but bread. Similarly *J. J. Becher*, Physiologie, 1678, 202, 248, on the great consumption of meat and sugar in England.

[6] *Anderson*, Origin of Commerce, a. 1743; *Porter*, Progress, V, 4, 350 ff.; Meidinger, 154 ff.; Memorandum respecting British Commerce etc., before and since the Adoption of Free Trade, 1866. On men-of-war each man gets 35–45 ℔s. a year; in the poor-house, old men 22¾. (*Porter.*)

[7] In Henry IV.'s time, in France, sugar was sold by the apothecaries by the ounce!

[8] *Deiterici*, Statist. Uebersicht des Verkehrs etc. im Zollvereine, 4; Fortsetzung, 168 ff., 208, 265, 599. Thus, in Great Britain, the population between 1816 and 1828 grew, from 13½ million to nearly 16 million. On the other hand, consumption, when the average from 1816 to 1819 is compared with that from 1824 to 1828, increased in a much greater proportion: soap, from 67¾ to 100 million pounds; coffee, from 7,850,000 to 12,540,000 pounds; starch, from 3⅕ to 6⅓ million pounds. (Quart. Rev., Nov., 1829, 518.) The consumption of tea per capita in 1801 was 1.5 lbs., in 1871, 3.93 lbs. (Statist. Journ., 1872, 243.) In the matter of illumination, a very beneficent luxury has been obtained, inasmuch as, spite of the fact that gas-light is so generally used in recent times, i. e., since 1804, the consumption of oil has very much increased, on account of the lamps now so much in favor; and that of candles also has increased, relatively speaking, more rapidly than the population. The illumination produced is much richer now than formerly, a fact which, besides its sanitary advantages, has had a good influence in diminishing street robberies. (*Julius*, Gefängnisskunde, XXII.) During the middle ages, candles were very dear; according to *Rogers* (I, 415) 1⅕ to 2 shillings per pound.

tivated only a short time. Thus the English have been acquainted with artichokes, asparagus, several kinds of beans, salad etc. only since 1660.[9] Even in France, the finer kinds of fruits have appeared on the tables of the middle class only since the beginning of the last century.

The per capita consumption of wool in England, about a generation ago, amounted to about 4 ℔s. a year; in Prussia to 1.67; of cloth, to 5.76 and 2.17 ells; of leather, to 3.03 and 2.22 ℔s. respectively.[10] Of silk goods, England consumes half as much as the rest of all Europe, and an Englishman from 5 to 6 times as much as a Frenchman, although England does not produce a single pound of raw silk.[11]

SECTION CCXXX.

EQUALIZING TENDENCY OF LATER LUXURY.

The whole social character of this luxury has something equalizing[1] in it; but it supposes particularly that there is not too marked a difference in the resources of the people.

A proper gradation of national wants is best guarantied by a good distribution of the national resources.[2] The more unequal the latter is, the more is there spent on vain wants instead of on real ones; and the more numerous are the instances of rapid and even immoral consumption. Where there are only a few over-rich men, more foreign products and products

---

[9] Present state of England, 1683, III, 529; compare *Storch*, Handbuch, II, 337 seq.

[10] *Dieterici*, Statist. Uebersicht, 321 ff., 363, 399.

[11] *Bernouilli*, Technologie, II, 223. It is a striking symptom of the wealth or ostentation of the later period of the Empire that, according to *Ammian. Marcell*, (XXIII, 258—ed. Paris, 1636) silk goods were a want even among the lower classes, notwithstanding the fact that they had to be imported from China.

[1] Formerly the dress of citizens was a weak imitation of the court costume: at present the reverse is the case, and the court costume is only a heightening of the citizen costume. Compare *Riehl*, Bürgerl. Gesellschaft, 191.

[2] *Helvetius*, De l' Homme, 1771. sec. VI, ch. 5.

of capital are wont to be called for than home products and productions of labor; and luxury especially despises all those commodities manufactured in large institutions.³ Every change in the consumption-customs of a people, in this respect, should be most carefully observed; thus, for instance, whether brandy is exchanged for beer, tobacco for meat, cotton for cloth, or the reverse.⁴

One of the characteristics of this period is the endeavor to possess the best quality of whatever is possessed at all, and to be satisfied with less of it rather than purchase more of an inferior quality. This is, essentially, to practice frugality, inasmuch as certain production-services remain the same whether the commodity is of the best or the worst quality, and that commodities of the best quality are more superior to the worst in intrinsic goodness than they are in price. But this course supposes a certain well-being already existing.

In this period, also, the luxury of the state is wont to take the direction of those enjoyments which are accessible to all.⁵

---

³ *J. B. Say*, Traité, II, 4; *Sismondi*, N. P., IV, ch. 4. As early a writer as *Lauderdale*, Inquiry, 358 ff., thought the social leveling of modern times would promote English industry. In the East Indies, on the other hand, only the most expensive watches, rifles, candalabras etc. were sold, because the nabobs were the only persons who created any demand for European commodities (312 ff.). *Adam Smith*, Wealth of Nat., II, ch. 3, draws a very correct distinction between the luxury of durable goods and that of those which perish rapidly; the former is less calculated to impoverish an individual or a whole nation; and hence it is much more closely allied to frugality. Similarly even *Isocrates*, ad Niccol., 19; *Livy*, XXIV, 7; *Plin.*, H. N., XIII, 4; *Mariana*, 1598, De Rege et Regis Institutione, III, 10; *Sir W. Temple*, Works, I, 140 seq., who found this better kind of luxury in Holland: *Berkeley*, Querist, No. 296 ff.

⁴ *Schmoller*, loc. cit., considers it no favorable symptom, that in Prussia, between 1802 and 1867, the per capita consumption of milk decreased and that of wool increased. According to *L. Levi*, the consumption of brandy in England decreased from 1854 and 1870, from 1.13 to 1.01 gallons per capita; but, on the other hand, the consumption of malt increased from 1.45 to 1.84 bushels, and the consumption of wine from 0.23 to 0.45 gallons. The number of licenses to retail spirituous liquors was, in 1830, 6.30 per thousand of the population; in 1860–69, only 5.57. (Statist. Journal, 1872, 32 ff.)

⁵ Compare *Cicero*, pro Murena, 36. The Athenians under Pericles, in

SECTION CCXXXI.

THE ADVANTAGES OF LUXURY.

The favorable results which many writers ascribe to luxury in general are true evidently only of this period. And thus luxury, inasmuch as it is a spur to emulation, promotes production in general; just as the awarding of prizes in a school, although they can be carried away only by a few, excites the activity of all its attendants. A nation which begins to consume sugar will, as a rule, unless it surrenders some previous enjoyment, increase its production.[1] In countries where there is little or no legal security, in which, therefore, people must keep shy of making public the good condition they are in, this praise-worthy side of luxury is for the most part wanting.[2] All rational luxury constitutes a species of reserve fund for

---

times of peace, spent more than one-third of their state-income on plastic and architectural works of art. The annual state-income amounted to 1,000 talents *(Xenoph.,* Exp. Cyri, VII, 1, 27), while the propylea alone cost, within 5 years, 2,012 talents. *(Böckh,* Staatsh., I, 283.) On the other hand, *Demosthenes* complains of the shabbiness of public buildings, and the magnificence of private ones in his time. (adv. Aristocr., 689, Syntax., 174 seq.)

Demetrius Phalereus blames even Pericles, on account of his extravagance on the propylea, although Lycurgus had been, not long before, addicted to luxury after the manner of Pericles. *(Cicero,* De Off., II, 17.)

[1] Compare *Benjamin Franklin's* charming story, Works I, 134 ff.; ed. Robinson. *Colbert* recommended luxury chiefly on account of its service to production.

[2] Turkish magnates who keep several magnificent equipages ride to the sultan's in a very bad one. Risa Pascha, when at the height of his power, had his house near a villa of the sultan painted in the plainest and most unsightly manner possible. The walls of a park in Constantinople painted half in red and half in blue, to give it the appearance of being two *gardens.* (Alg. Zeitung, 16 Juli, 1849.) In Saxony, between 1847 and 1850, the number of luxury horses diminished from 6.11 to 5.64 per cent. of the total number of horses in the kingdom. *(Engel,* Jahrbuch, I, 305.) In the same country there were coined in 1848 over 64,000 silver marks, derived from other sources than the mines. *(Engel,* Statis. Zeitschr. I, 85. In England, on the other hand, the number of four-wheeled carriages increased more than 60 per cent. between 1821 and 1841, while the population increased only 30 per cent. *(Porter,* Progress, V, 3, 540.)

a future day of need. This is especially true of these luxuries which take the form of capital in use *(Nutzkapitalien.)* Where it is customary for every peasant girl to wear a gold head-dress,[3] and every apprentice a medal, a penny for a rainy day is always laid by among the lower classes. The luxury which is rapidly consumed has a tendency in the same direction. Where the majority of the population live on potatoes, as in Ireland, where, therefore, they are reduced to the smallest allowance of the means of subsistence, there is no refuge in case of a bad harvest. A people on the other hand, who live on wheat bread may go over to rye bread, and a people who live on rye bread to potatoes. The corn that in good years is consumed in the making of brandy may, in bad years, be baked into bread.[4] And the oats consumed by horses kept as luxuries may serve as food for man. Pleasure-gardens *(Lustgärten)* may be considered as a kind of last resort for a whole people in case of want of land.[5][6]

---

[3] Such a head dress may very easily be worth 300 guldens in Friesland. Gold crosses worn by the peasant women about Paris. *(Turgot,* Lettre sur la Liberté du Commerce des Grains.)

[4] So far it is of some significance, that nearly all not uncivilized nations use their principal article of food to prepare drinks that are luxuries. Thus, the Indians use rice, the Mexicans mais, the Africans the ignam-root. It is said that in ancient Egypt, beer-brewing was introduced by Osiris. *(Diodor.,* I, 34.) Compare *Jeremy Bentham*, Traité de Législation, I, 160. *Malthus,* Principle of Population, I, ch. 12; IV, ch. 11.

[5] While in thinly populated North America, space permits the beautiful luxury in cemeteries of ornamenting surroundings of each grave separately ('Gr. *Görtz,* Reise, 24), the Chinese garden-style seeks to effect a saving in every respect. In keeping with this is the fact that animal food has there been almost abolished. Compare, besides, *Verri,* Meditazioni, XXVI, 3.

[6] *Garve* thinks that luxury, when it takes the direction of a great many trifles, little conveniences, etc., has the effect of distracting the people. Here there are few men of towering ambition or of inextinguishable revenge, but at the same time, few entirely unselfish and incorruptible patriots. *(Versuche,* I, 232.)

SECTION CCXXXII.

LUXURY IN DECLINING NATIONS.

In declining nations, luxury assumes an imprudent and immoral character. Enormous sums are expended for insignificant enjoyments. It may even be said that costly consumption is carried on there for its own sake. The beautiful and the true enjoyment of life makes place for the monstrous and the effeminate.

Rome, in the earlier part of the empire, affords us an example of such luxury on the most extensive scale.[1] Nero paid three hundred talents for a murrhine vase. The two acres *(Morgen)* of land which sufficed to the ancient citizens for a farm *(Acker)* were not now enough to make a fish-pond for imperial slaves. The sums carried by the exiles with them, to cover their traveling expenses and to live on for a time, were now greater than the fortunes of the most distinguished citizens had been in former times.[2] There was such a struggle among the people to surpass one another in procuring the freshest sea-fish that, at last, they would taste only such as they had seen alive on the table. We have the most exalted descriptions of the beautiful changes of color undergone by the dying fish; and a special infusion was invented to enable the epicure better to enjoy the spectacle.[3] Of the transparent garments of his time, Seneca says that they neither protected the body nor covered the nakedness of nature. People kept herds of sheep dyed in purple, although their natural white must have been much more agreeable to

---

[1] *Meierotto*, Sitten und Lebensart des Römer, II, 1776; *Boettiger*, Sabina, II, 1803; *Friedländer*, Darstellungen aus der Sittengeschichte Roms, Bd. III, 1868; which latter work has been written with the aid of all that modern science can afford.

[2] *Plin.*, H. N., XXXVII, 7; XVIII, 2; *Seneca*, Quaest. Natur., I, 17; Consol. ad. Helviam, 12.

[3] *Seneca*, Quaest. Natur., III, 18; *Plin.*, H. N., IX, 30.

any one with an eye for the tasteful.⁴ Not only on the roofs of houses were fish-ponds to be seen, but gardens even hanging on towers, and which must have been as small, ugly and inconvenient as they were costly. Especially characteristic of the time was the custom of dissolving pearls in wine, not to make it more palateable, but more expensive.⁶ The emperor Caligula, from simple caprice, caused mountains to be built up and cut away: *nihil tam efficere concupiscebat, quam, quod posse effici negaretur*.⁷ This is the real maxim of the third period of luxury! People changed their dress at table, inconvenient as it was to do so, occasionally as often as eleven times. Perfumes were mixed with the wine that was drunk, much as it spoiled its taste, only that the drinkers might emit sweet odors from every pore. There were many so used to being waited on by slaves that they required to be reminded by them at what times they should eat and when they should sleep. It is related of one who affected superiority over others in this respect, that he was carried from his bath and placed on a cushion, when he asked his attendant: "Am I sitting down now?"⁸ It is no wonder, indeed, that an Apicius should reach out for the poisoned cup when his fortune had dwindled to only *centies sestertium*, *i. e.*, to more than half a million thalers.⁹

In this last period, the coarse debauchery of the earlier periods is added to the refined. Swarms of servants, reti-

---

⁴ *Seneca*, De Benef., VII, 9; *Plin.*, N. N., VIII, 74.
⁵ *Valer. Max.*, IX, 1; *Seneca*, Epist., 122. Thus Hortensius sprinkled his trees with wine. *Macrob.*, Sat., III, 13.
⁶ Besides Cleopatra, Caligula especially did this frequently. Compare also *Horat.*, Serm., II, 3, 239 ff. Similarly, the luxury of the actor Aesopus, when he placed a dish worth 6,000 *louis d'or* before his guests, consisting entirely of birds which had been taught to sing or speak. *Pliny*, H. N., X, 72. Compare *Horat.*, loc. cit., 345.
⁷ *Sueton*, Caligula, 37. *Hoc est luxuriae propositum, gaudere perversis*. *Seneca.*, Epist., 122. According to the same letter of Seneca, the luxury of Nero's time had its source rather in vanity than in sensuality and gluttony.
⁸ *Martial*, V, 79; *Plin.*, H. N. XIII, 5. *Seneca*, De Brev. Vitæ. I, 12.
⁹ *Seneca*, Cons. ad Helviam 10, *Martial*, III, 22.

nues of gladiators who might be even politically dangerous,[10] monster banquets, at which Cæsar, for instance, entertained the whole Roman people, colossal palaces such as Nero's *aurea domus*, which constituted a real city; annoying ostentation in dress[11] again becomes the order of the day. The more despotic a state becomes, the more is the craving for momentary enjoyment wont to grow; and for the same reason that great plagues diminish frugality and morality.[12]

SECTION CCXXXIII.

LUXURY-POLICY.

Sumptuary laws *(die Luxusgesetzgebung)* have been aimed, at all times, principally at the outlay for clothing, for the table and for funerals.[1] In most nations the policy of luxury

---

[10] Hence, early limited by law. *Sueton.* Caes, 10. Augustus limited the exiles to taking 20 slaves with them: *Dio Cass.* VII, 27. Special value attached to dwarfs, buffoons, hermaphrodites, eunuchs, precisely as among the moderns in the times of the degenerated absolutist courts, the luxury of which is closely allied in many respects to that of declining nations.

[11] Caligula's wife wore, on ordinary occasions, 40,000,000 sesterces worth of ornaments. *Plin.* H. N. IX, 58.

[12] *Gibbon*, History of the Decline and Fall of the Roman Empire, ch. 27. What a parallel between this later Roman luxury and the literary taste represented for instance by Seneca!

Let any one who would embrace the three periods of luxury in one view, compare the funeral ceremonies of the Greek age of chivalry *(Homer, II.)*, with those in *Thucyd.* (II, 34, ff.), *Demosth.* (Lept., 499 seq.), and the interment of Alexander the Great and, of his friend Hephaestion *(Diodor., XVII, 115, XVIII, 26 ff.)* Sullas (Serv. ad *Virgil*, Æneid VI, 861. *Plutarch*, Sulla, 38), and that of the wife of the emperor Nero *(Plin., H. N. XII, 41). Roscher*, loc. cit. 66 ff.

[1] Which of these three kinds of luxury specially preponderated has always depended on the peculiarities of national character. Thus, among the ancient Romans, it was the second; among the French, the first. In Germany the prohibitions relating to "toasts," or drinking one another's health have played a great part. Thus the well-known Cologne reformation of 1837. Compare *Seb. Münster*, Cosmogr., 326.

has its beginning in the transition from the first to the second period of luxury above described.² The extravagant feasts, which remain of the first period, seem vulgar to the new public opinion which is created. On the other hand, the conveniences of life, the universality, the refinement and variety of enjoyments characteristic of the second period are not acceptable to the austerity of old men, and are put down as effeminacy. In this period the bourgeoisie generally begin to rise in importance, and the feudal aristocracy to decay. The higher classes see the lower approximate to them in display, with jealous eyes. And, hence, dress is wont to be graded in strict accordance with the differences of class.³ But these

---

² In Greece, *Lycurgus*' legislation seems to have contained the first prohibition relating to luxury. No one should own a house or household article which had been made with a finer implement than an ax or a saw; and no Spartan cook should use any other spice than salt and vinegar. *(Plut.*, De Sanitate, 12; *Lycurg.*, 13. On Periander, see *Ephorus*, ed. *Marx*, fr. 106. *Heracb.*, Pont. ed.; *Köhler*, fr. 5; *Diog. Laert.*, I, 96 ff. The luxury-prohibitions of Solon were aimed especially at the female passion for dress and the pomp of funerals. Those who had the surveillance of the sex watched also over the luxury of banquets. *Athen.*, VI, 245; *Demosth.* in *Macart.*, 1070. In Rome, there were laws regulating the pomp of and display at funerals, dating from the time of the Kings; but especially are such laws to be found in the twelve tables. Lex Oppia de Cultu Mulierum in the year 215 before Christ. A very interesting debate concerning the abolition of this law in *Livy*, XXXIV, 1 ff. About 189, prohibition of several foreign articles of luxury. *Plin.*, H. N., XIII, 5, XIV, 16. Measures of Cato the censor. *(Livy*, XXXIX, 44.) First law relating to the table, L. Orchia, in the year 187; afterwards L. Fannia, 161, L. Didia, 143 before Christ. *(Macrob.*, Sat. V, 13; *Gellius*, N. A., II, 24. *Plin.*, H. N., X, 7.) After a long pause, sumptuary laws relating to food, funerals and games of chance, constitute an important part of Sulla's legislation

³ *Latus clavus* of the Roman senators; *annulus* of the knights. In the latter middle age, the knights were wont to be allowed to wear gold, and esquires only silver; the former, damask; the latter, satin or taffeta; but when the esquires also used damask, velvet was reserved for the knights alone. *St. Palaye*, Das Ritterwesen, by *Klüber*, IV, 107; II, 153 seq. But towards the end of the middle ages many sumptuary laws were enacted in cities by plebeian jealousy of the rich. The Venetian sumptuary laws were passed on account of the anxiety of the state that some rich men might shine above the rest of the oligarchs.

laws must be regarded as emanating from the tendency, which prevails in these times, of the state to act as the guardian of its wards, its subjects. The authority of the state waxes strong in such periods; and with the first consciousness of its power, it seeks to draw many things into its sphere, which it afterwards surrenders.

SECTION CCXXXIV.

HISTORY OF SUMPTUARY LAWS.

As in Italy, Frederick II., in Aragon, Iago I., in 1234, in England, Edward III., by 37, Edward III., c. 8 ff., so in France Philip IV. was the first who busied himself seriously with sumptuary legislation;[1] that is the same king who had introduced in so many things the modern political life into France. (For instance, the ordinance of 1294, regulating apparel and the luxury of the table.) In the 14th century, we find sumptuary laws directed mainly against expense for furs, and in the 16th mainly against that for articles of gold and silver. From the descriptions left us in such laws of the prohibited luxuries, we may learn as much of the history of technology and of fashion, as we may of the history of classes from the gradation of the things permitted. The fines imposed for violations of these laws, under Philip IV. went for the most part to the territorial lord; and in the 16th and 17th centuries to the foundation of charitable institutions. The state, as a rule, took no share of them; doubtless to avoid the odium which might attach to this kind of revenue.

---

[1] Ordonnances de France, I, 324, 531. Worms law of 1220. (*Riehl*, Pfälzer, 246.) Braunschweig law of 1228, that at weddings there should not be over 12 plates nor more than three musicians. (*Rehtmeyer*, Chron., 466. Danish sumptuary law of 1269. First law regulating dress in Prussia in 1269. (*Voigt*, Gesch. von Preussen, V, 97. On Henry II., see *v. Raumer*, Hohenstaufen, VI, 585. Some of the earlier restrictions on luxury, such as that of 190 in England and France, against scarlet ermine etc., may have been related to the religious fervor of the crusades. *St. Louis*, during the whole period of his crusades wore no articles of luxury.

Beginning with the end of the 16th century, the sumptuary laws of France relating to the luxuries permitted to the several classes of the people disappear. The legislator ceases to be guided by moral considerations and begins to be influenced by reasons partaking of a commercial and police character; and here we may very clearly demonstrate the origin of the so-called mercantile or protective system. Thus, in the declaration of Louis XIV. dated December 12, 1644, we find a complaint, that not only does the importation of foreign articles of luxury threaten to rob France of all its gold and silver, but also that the home manufacture of gold cloth etc., which at Lyons alone ate up 10,000 livres a week, had the same effect. Under Colbert, in 1672, it was specially provided for, in the prohibition of coarser silver ware, that all such ware should be brought to the mint.[2] In the edict of 1660, the king even says that he has in view especially the higher classes, officers, courtiers etc., in whom it was his duty to be most deeply interested. To preserve the latter from impoverishment was the main object of the law.

Under Louis XV. all sumptuary laws were practically a dead letter.[3] Their enforcement is, indeed, exceedingly diffi-

---

[2] The English prohibition against the wearing of silk on hats, caps, stockings etc. (1 and 2 Phil. and Mary, ch. 2.) was promulgated with the intention of promoting the home manufacture of wool. And so *Sully*, Economies, L, XII, XVI, was in favor of laws regulating outlay mainly from "mercantilistic" reasons, that the country might not be impoverished by the purchase of foreign expensive articles. The police ordinance of the Empire of 1548, tit. 9, desired to guard against both the "excessive" exportation of money and the obliteration of class differences; that of 1530, tit. 9, and the Austrian police ordinance of Ferdinand I. had only the second object in view. (*Mailath*, Gesch., von Oesterreich, II, 169 ff.) How, in Denmark, prohibitions of luxury grew very soon into prohibitions of imports with a protective intention, see in *Thaarup*, Dänische Statistik, I, 521 seq. On the mercantilistic object of the greater number of prohibitions of coffee, in the 18th century, see *Dohm*, über Kaffeegesetzgebung, in the D. Museum, Bd., II, St. 8, No. 4.

[3] *Des Essart*, Dictionnaire universel de Police, VI, 146. In Great Britain, the Scotch luxury-law of 1621 is the last. (*Anderson*, Origin of Commerce, a. 1621.) In Germany, there were some such laws until the end of the 18th

cult, as it is always harder to superintend consumption than production. The latter is carried on in definite localities, not unfrequently even in the open air. The former is carried on in the secrecy of a thousand homes. Besides, sumptuary laws have very often the effect to make the forbidden fruit all the sweeter. Where they are based on a difference of class, not only the passion for pleasure, but the vanity of the lower classes is an incentive to their violation.[4] Spite of the severity of the penalties attached to the violation of these laws, of redoubled measures of control, which are dreadful burdens on the intercourse between man and man,[5] the French government has been compelled to admit, after almost every internal commotion, and almost every external war, that its sumptuary laws fell into disuse.

SECTION CCXXXV.

DIFFICULTY OF ENFORCING SUMPTUARY LAWS.

The impossibility of enforcing sumptuary laws has been most strikingly observed, where it has been attempted to suppress the consumption of popular delicacies in the first stages

---

century; and the laws regulating mourning have lasted longest. Compare that of Frederick the Great of 1777, the Bamberg and Wurzberg laws of 1784, in *Schlözer*, Staatsanzeigen, IX, 460; fol. 141 ff. There are many men who have no desire to go to any heavy expense in mourning, but do not dare to give expression thereto in certain cases, and therefore look with favor on a law to which they may appeal as as excuse.

[4] Compare *N. Montaigne*, 1580, Essais, I, 63. A striking instance in antiquity: *Macrob.*, II, 13; most recently in *Lotz*, Revision, I, 407.

[5] Compare especially the French sumptuary law of 1567. Zaleucos went so far in his severity as to punish with death the drinking of unmixed wine, without the prescription of a physician. (*Athen.*, IX, 429.) The effort has sometimes been made to enlist the feeling of honor of the people in the controlling of luxury. Thus old Zaleucos forbade the wearing of gold rings or Milesian cloth unless the wearer desired to commit adultery, or to be guilty of sins against nature *(Diodor.*, XII, 21); but such laws are scarcely attended with success.

of their spread among the people. Thus, an effort was made in this direction in the sixteenth century, as regards brandy; in the seventeenth, as regards tobacco; in the eighteenth, as regards coffee; all which three articles were first allowed to be used only as medicines.[1] When governments discovered after some time the fruitlessness of the efforts, they gave up the prohibition of these luxuries and substituted taxes on them instead.[2] Thus an effort was made to combine a moral and a fiscal end. But it should not be lost sight of that the lower these taxes are, the greater the revenue they bring in; that is, the less the moral end is attained, the more is the fiscal end. Even Cato took this course. His office of censor, which united the highest moral superintendence with the highest financial guidance, must of itself have led him in this direction.[3] In modern times the most important excises and financial duties of entry have been evolved out of sumptuary laws. Even the Turks, after having long tried to prohibit tobacco-smoking in vain, afterwards found in the duties they imposed on that plant a rich source of income. That such taxes are among the best imposed, where they do not lead to frauds on the government,

---

[1] Hessian law that only apothecaries should retail brandy, 1530. English tobacco laws of 1604; *Rymer*, Fœdera, XVI, 601. Papal excommunication fulminated in 1624, against all who took snuff in church, and repeated in 1690. A Turkish law of 1610 provided that all smokers should have the pipe broken against their nose. A Russian law of 1634, prohibiting smoking under penalty of death. In Switzerland, even in the f7th century, no one could smoke except in secret. Coffee had a hard struggle even in its native place. *(Ritter,* Erdkunde, XIII, 574 ff.) Prohibited in Turkey in 1633, under pain of death. *v. Hammer*, Osmanische Staatsverwaltung, I, 75. In 1769, coffee was still prohibited in Basel, and was allowed to be sold by apothecaries only, and as medicine. *(Burkhardt,* C. Basel, I, 68.) Hanoverian prohibition of the coffee trade in the rural districts in 1780: *Schlözer*, Briefwechsel, VIII, 123 ff.

[2] According to *v. Seckendorff*, Christenstaat, 1685, 435 seq., a decidedly unchristian change.

[3] *Livy*, XXXIX, 44. In Athens, too, the highest police board in the matter of luxury was the areopagus, which was at the same time a high financial court. Sully transformed the prohibition of luxury in regard to banquets into a tax on delicacies. Similarly, in regard to funeral-luxuries, at an earlier date. *(Cicero,* ad. Att., XII, 35.)

become excessive, or diminish consumption to too great an extent, is universally conceded.

Beyond this there is, on the whole, little left of the old police regulations relating to luxury. Thus, governmental consent is, in most countries, required for the establishment of places where liquors are sold at retail, for the maintenance of public places of amusement, for shooting festivals, fairs etc.; and this consent should not be too freely granted. The police power prescribes certain hours at which drinking places shall be closed. Games of chance are wont to be either entirely prohibited or restricted to certain places and times (bathing places), or are reserved as the exclusive right of certain institutions, especially state institutions. The object of this is, on the one hand, to facilitate their supervision, and on the other, to diminish the number of seductive occasions. Here, too, belongs the appointment of guardians to spendthrifts, which is generally done on the motion of the family by the courts; but which, indeed, occurs too seldom to have any great influence on the national resources, or on national morals.[4]

SECTION CCXXXVI.

EXPEDIENCY OF SUMPTUARY LAWS.

To judge of the salutariness of sumptuary laws, we must keep the above three social periods in view throughout. At the close of the first period, every law which restricts the excesses of the immediately succeeding age (the middle age) is useful because it promotes the noble luxury of the second

---

[4] Customary even in the early Roman republic, and adjudged *exemplo furioso*. (*Ulpian*, in L. 1 Digest, XXVII, 10.) The immediate knights of the empire were in this respect very severe towards those of their own order. See *Kerner*, Reichsritterśch. Staatsrecht, II, 381 ff. *Sully* ordered the parliaments to warn spendthrifts, to punish them and place them under guardianship. (Economies royales, L, XXVI.) According to *Montesquieu*, it is a genuine aristocratic maxim to hold the nobility to a punctual payment of their debts. (Esprit des Lois, V, 8.)

period.¹ And so, in the third period, legislation may at least operate to drive the most immoral and most odious forms of vice under cover, and thus to diminish their contagious seduction. It is a matter of significance that, in Rome, the most estimable of the emperors always endeavored to restrict luxury.² But too much should not be expected of such laws. *Intra animum medendum est; nos pudor in melius mutet.*³ It is at least necessary, that the example given in high places should lend its positive aid, as did that of Vespasian, for instance, who thus really opposed a certain barrier to the disastrous flood of Roman luxury.⁴

But a strong and flourishing nation has no need of such leading strings.⁵ Where an excrescence has to be extirpated, the people can use the knife themselves. I need call attention only to the temperance societies of modern times (Boston, 1803), which spite of all their exaggeration⁶ may have a very

---

[1] Commendable laws relating to luxury in Florence in the beginning of the 15th century. The outlay for dress, for the table, for servants and equipages was limited; but, on the other hand, it was entirely unrestricted for churches, palaces, libraries, and works of art. The consequences of this legislation are felt even in our day. *(Sismondi,* Gesch. der Ital. Freistaaten im M. A., VIII, 261. Compare *Machiavelli,* Istor. Fior., VII, a., 1472.)

[2] Thus Nerva *(Xiphilin.,* exc. Dionis, LXVIII, 2); Hadrian *(Spartian V. Hadrian,* 22); Antoninus Pius (Capitol, 12); Marcus Aurelius (Capitol, 27); Pertinax (Capitol, 9); Severus Alexander *(Lamprid,* 4); Aurelian *(Lamprid,* 49); Tacitus *(Vopisc.,* 10 seq).

[3] Extracted from the remarkable speech made by the personally frugal Tiberius *(Sueton.,* Tib., 34) against sumptuary laws: *Tacit.,* Aanal., III, 52 ff. Compare, however, IV, 63.

[4] *Tacit.,* Ann., III, 55: but the differences in fortune had, at the same time, become less glaring. Henry IV. also dressed very simply for example's sake, as did also Sully, and ridiculed those *qui portaient leurs moulins et leur bois de haute-futaie sur leurs dos. (Péréfixe,* Histoire du Roi Henry le grand, 208.)

[5] The gross luxuries of drunkenness and gluttony are a direct consequence of universal grossness, and disappear of themselves when higher wants and means of satisfying them are introduced. *(v. Buch,* Reise durch Norwegen und Lappland, 1810, I, 166; II, 112 ff.)

[6] While, formerly, they cared only to abstain from spirits, the so-called "total abstinence" has prevailed since 1832. Most teetotallers compare

beneficial effect on the morally weak by the solemn nature of the pledge, and the control their members mutually exercise over one another. It is estimated that, of all who enter them, in the British Empire, at least 50 per cent. remain true to the pledge. In Ireland the government had endeavored for a long time to preserve the country from the ravages of alcohol by the imposition of the highest taxes and the severest penalties for smuggling. Every workman in an illegal distillery was transported for seven years, and every town in which such a one was found was subjected to a heavy fine. But all in vain. Only numberless acts of violence were now added to beastly drunkenness. On the other hand, the temperance societies of the country decreased the consumption of brandy between 1838 and 1842, from 12,296,000 gallons to 5,290,000 gallons. The excise on brandy decreased £750,000; but many other taxable articles yielded so much larger a revenue, that the aggregate government income there increased about £91,000.[7 8]

---

moderate drinking to moderate lying or moderate stealing; they even declare the moderate drinker worse than the drunkard, because his example is more apt to lead others astray, and he is harder to convert. (But, Psalm, 104, 15!) The coat of arms of the English temperance societies is a hand holding a hammer in the act of breaking a bottle. (Temperance poetry!)

[7] *McCulloch*, On Taxation, 342 ff. Speech of *O'Connell* in the House of Commons, 27 May, 1842. The more serious crimes decreased 1840-44, as compared with the average number during the five previous years by 28, and the most grievous by 50 per cent. *(Rau,* Lehrbuch, II, § 331.) Recently, the first enthusiasm awakened by Father Matthew has somewhat declined, and the consumption of brandy therefore increased. Yet, in the whole United Kingdom in 1853, only 30,164,000 gallons were taxed; in 1835, 31,-400,000; although the population had in the meantime increased from 10 to 11 per cent. In 1834, there were in the United States 7,000 temperance societies with a membership of 1,250,000. The members of these societies are sometimes paid higher wages in factories; and ships which allow no alcohol on board are insured at a premium of five per cent. less. *(Baird,* History of the Temperance Societies in the United States, 1837.)

[8] In the princedom of Osnabrück, the number of distilleries was noticeably diminished under the influence of the temperance societies; but the consumption of beer was rapidly increased twenty-fold. (Hannoverisches Magazin, 1843, 51. *Böttcher*, Gesch. der M. V. in der Norddeutschen Bundestaaten, 1841.)

The Puritanical laws which some of the United States of North America have passed prohibiting all sales of spirituous liquors except for ecclesiastical, medical or chemical purposes, have been found impossible of enforcement.[9][10]

---

[9] Even in 1838, Massachusetts had begun to restrict the sale at retail. The agitation for the suppression of the liquor shops begins in 1841. According to the Maine law of 1851, a government officer alone had the right to sell liquor, and only for the purposes mentioned in the text. The manufacture or importation of liquor for private use was left free to all. A severe system of house-searching, imprisonment and inquisitorial proceedings in order to enforce the law. Similarly in Vermont, Rhode Island, Massachusetts and Michigan. (Edinburg Rev., July, 1854.) There are, however, numberless instances related in which the law has been violated unpunished since 1856, and still more since 1872. See *R. Russell*, North America, its Agriculture and Climate, and Edinburg Rev., April, 1873, 404.

[10] From the foregoing, it is intelligible why most modern writers, even those otherwise opposed to luxury, are not favorably inclined towards sumptuary laws. "It is the highest impertinence and presumption in kings and ministers, to pretend to watch over the economy of private people and to restrain their expense, either by sumptuary laws or by prohibiting the importation of foreign luxuries. They are themselves always, and without any exception (?) the greatest spendthrifts in the society. If their own extravagance does not ruin the state, that of their subjects never will." *(Adam Smith*, I, ch. 3.) Compare *Rau*, Lehrbuch II, § 358 ff. *R. Mohl*, Polizeiwissenschaft, II, 434 ff.

Montesquieu's opinion that in monarchies luxury is necessary to preserve the difference of class but that in republics it is a cause of decline, is very peculiar. In the latter, therefore, luxury should be restricted in every way: agrarian laws should modify the too great difference in property and sumptuary laws restrain the too glaring manifestations of extravagance. (Esprit des Lois, VII, 4.) As an auxiliary to the history of sumptuary laws, compare *Boxmann*, De Legibus Romanorum sumptuarias, 1816. *Sempere y Guarinos*, Historia del Luxo y de las Leyes sumtuarias de Espana, II, 1788; *Vertot*, Sur l' Establissement des Lois somptuaires parmi les Français, in the Mémoires de l' Academie des Inscr., VI, 737 seq, besides the sections on the subject in *Delamarre*, Traité de la Police, 1772 ff.; *Penning*, De Luxu et Legibus sumtuariis, 1826. *(Holland.)*

CHAPTER III.

INSURANCE IN GENERAL.

SECTION CCXXXVII.

INSURANCE IN GENERAL.

The idea of societies for mutual assistance intended to divide the loss caused by destructive accidents which one person would not be able to recover from among a great many is very ancient. The insurance of their members against causes of impoverishment was one of the principal elements[1] of the strength of the medieval communities *(Gemeinden und Körperschaften.)* If we compare these insurance institutions of the middle ages with those of the present, we discover the well-known difference between a *corporation* and an *association*. There the members stand to one another in the relation of *persons* who, therefore, seek to guaranty their entire life in the one combination; here, they appear only as the representatives of limited portions of capital confronted with a definite

---

[1] The Icelandic *repps* consisting as a rule of 20 citizens subject to taxation, who mutually insured one another against the death of cattle (to the extent of at least one-fourth the value), and against damage from fire. After every fire three chambers of each house were replaced; so also the loss of clothing and of the means of subsistence, but not other goods or articles of display. *(Dahlmann,* Dänisch Gesch., II, 281 ff.) Scandinavian parish-duty, *(Gemeindepflicht),* of assistance in case of damage by fire: *Wilda,* Gesch. des deutschen Strafrechts, I, 142. Similarly Capitul. a. 779 in *Pertz*, Leges, I, 37. This matter plays an important part in the guilds out of which a large portion of the ancient cities were evolved: compare *Wilda,* Gildenwesen in M. Alter. 123.

risk, the average of which may be accurately determined. Hence, the former are of small extent, mostly local; the latter may extend over whole continents, and even over the whole earth. The former have uniformly equal members; the latter embrace men of the most different classes. While the former, therefore, simply govern themselves, often only on the occasion of their festive gatherings, the latter need a precise charter, an artificial tariff and a board of officers.

As the absolute monarchical police-state constitutes, generally, the bridge between the middle ages and modern times, so too the transition from the medieval to the modern system of insurance has been frequently introduced by state insurance.[2][3] This was very natural at a time when the guilds of the middle ages had lost their importance, and private industry was not ripe enough to supply the void left by them. The government of a country, far in advance intellectually of the majority of its subjects, may, by force, induce them to participate in the beneficent effects of insurance, and immediately provide institutions extensive enough to guaranty real safety. While it may be called a rule that mature private in-

---

[2] Proposed national fire insurance *(Landesbrandversicherung)* in which for the time being several villages should form a company, the surplus of which was to go to the ærarium, and the deficit to be made up by the same: *Georg Obrecht*, Fünf unterschiedliche Secreta, Strasburg, 1617, No. 3. A similar proposition made on financial grounds in 1609, and rejected in Oldenburg. *(Beckmann*, Beitr. zur Gesch. der Erfind, I, 219 ff.) The idea sometimes suggested in our day, of making the system of insurance a government prerogative, arises as much from the passion for centralization as from socialistic tendencies. Compare the Belgian Bulletin de la Commission de Statist. IV, 210, and *Oberländer*, Die Feuerversicherungsanstalten vor der Ständeversammlung des k. Sachsen, 1857.

[3] Maritime insurance is much older than insurance against risks on land; the Dutch institutions of Charles V.'s time seem to have existed long before. (Richesse de Hollande, I, 81 ff.) On Flemish, Portuguese and Italian maritime insurance in the 14th century, see *Sartorius*, Gesch. der Hanse, I, 215; *Schäfer*, Portug. Gesch. II, 103 ff., and *F. Bald. Pegolotti*, Tratato della Mercatura in Della decima etc., della Moneta e della Mercatura dei Fiorentini, 1765. The class engaged in maritime commerce are indeed especially and early rich in capital, speculative and calculating.

dustry satisfies wants more rapidly, in greater variety, and more cheaply than state industry; in the case of insurance against accidents, especially of insurance against fire, there are many peculiarities found which would make the entire cessation of the immediate action of the state in this sphere, or its limitation simply to a legislative and police supervision of insurance, seem a misfortune. A dwelling is one of the most universal and urgent of wants, and indeed a governing one in all the rest of the arrangements of life. If it be destroyed, it is especially difficult to find a substitute for it, or to restore it. And to the poorest class of those who need insurance, private insurance will, perhaps, be never properly accessible.[4] If German fire insurance and the German system of fire prevention be so superior to the English and North American etc., one of the principal causes is that German governmental institutions so powerfully participate in it.[5]

---

[4] In Berlin, in 1871, the movable property of 30.4 per cent. of all dwellings was insured; but with this great difference, that of the smallest (without any heatable rooms) only 5.3 per cent. were insured; while of dwellings having 5–7 heatable rooms, 84 per cent. had taken this precaution. (*Schwabe*, Volkszählung von 1871, 169.) But it should not be forgotten that private insurance, especially when speculative, is not in favor of having much to do with persons of small means, while public institutions are, for the most part, obliged to reject no proposition for insurance in their own line, except when coming from a few manufacturing quarters especially exposed to fire.

[5] Outside of Germany, public fire insurance is to be still found only in German Austria, in Denmark, Switzerland and Scandinavia. The Germans had, in 1871, an insurance-sum of 5,908,760,000 thalers, while the mutual private insurance companies had about 1,435,000,000 (of which, at most, 200,000,000 to 300,000,000 were on immovable property), and joint-stock insurance companies, after deducting re-insurance *(Rückversicherung)*, about 7,000,000,000. (Mittheilungen der öff. F. V. Anstalten, 1874, 84 ff.) Between 1865 and 1870, it was estimated that the per capita insurance of the population was: in Saxony, 407 thalers; in Würtemberg, 410; in Baden, 365; in Prussia, 332; in Switzerland, 425. On the other hand, in the much wealthier British Empire, only 325 per capita; in North America, 215. (loc. cit., 92.) Even in the case of joint-stock insurance companies, the average receipts of premiums (1867-70) were, in Germany, 2 per 1,000 of the insurance-sums; in the United Kingdom, 4.06 per 1,000; in the United States, 10.77; and the damage respectively 1.25, 2.28, 5.92 per 1,000 of the insurance-sum. (loc. cit., 93.)

SECTION CCXXXVII (a).

INSURANCE IN GENERAL.—MUTUAL AND SPECULATIVE INSTITUTIONS.

All insurance institutions fall into two classes:

A. Mutual insurance companies, in which the insured are also as a society the insurers, and share the aggregate damage, of a year, for instance, among themselves.

B. Speculative institutions, in which a party, generally a joint-stock company, in consideration of a certain definite compensation (premium agreed upon and paid in advance), assumes the risk.[1]

So far as security is concerned, no absolute preference can be accorded to either of these classes. Mutual insurance companies require to extend their business very largely[2] to be able to meet great damage. And even where the liability of the members is unlimited, care must be taken to distinguish between the legally and the actually possible.[3] The joint capital of a well

---

[1] We might, however, improperly add another class, that of self-insurance, which lies in the proper distribution of a large capital over a great many points. When, for instance, a large state insures its buildings, this seems a superfluous outlay of public money for the benefit of private associations. Or does England insure its ships? On this account, in Prussia, the insurance of post-offices which Frederick William favored, has recently been done away with. (*Stephan*, Gesch. der Preuss. Post, 195, 803.)

[2] According to *Brüggemann* (D. Allg. Ztg., 1849, No., 75 ff.), 100 million thalers of an insurance sum. Actual American legislation prescribes in the case of mutual insurance a minimum number of members of from 200 to 400, a minimum amount of annual premiums of from $25,000 to $200,000, of cash payments on the annual premium of from 10 to 40 per cent. of cash-paid yearly premiums, $5,000 to $40,000; and a maximum amount of premium notes made by a member of $500. (Compare Mittheilungen, 26 ff.)

[3] Hence several mutual companies limit themselves to a maximum liability. Thus, for instance, the Gotha Fire Insurance Company requires from each member a bond that in case of necessity, four times the amount of the presumptive contribution paid in advance shall be paid after; in Altona, six times the yearly premium is the maximum.

organized[4] premium-association affords, in this respect sufficient security from the first, but the ratio between its security-fund and the amount of its assumed liabilities becomes less favorable as the business is extended, in case the fund itself is not enlarged.[5] Mutual insurance may accomplish something analogous to that accomplished by a joint-stock fund by collecting a reserve of yearly dues in advance, thus modifying the burdensome vacillation of the amount payable each year.[6] Experience, however, teaches, that the strongest form of mutual insurance, that supported either by municipalities or by the state, has been able to meet extraordinary damage from fire much better than premium-institutions, which are too quickly left in the lurch by the stockholders when the damage is greater than the amount of the stock subscribed. So also loss from fire caused by war or riots is for the most part and on principle, excluded by speculative insurance institutions.[7]

---

[4] In France, every premium-insurance-company has to be approved by the government (Cod. de Comm., art 37), and the approval is not given until ¼ of the joint-stock capital has been deposited. *(Block,* Dictionn. de l' administration, Fr. 153.) Many recent American laws require that the shares of insurance companies should be registered with the name of the owner.

[5] The Aix-Munich Fire Insurance Association raised its joint-stock capital after the Hamburg fire from 1 to 3 million thalers.

[6] Usually so that the regular yearly contribution is higher than the average damage and cost of administration; this excess is then returned in the form of a dividend, either immediately at the close of the yearly account, or which is still safer, after several years. In the Stuttgart private insurance company, the reserve must amount to one per cent. of the amount insured, before the premium-surplus is returned. The Gotha fire insurance company, between 1821 and 1842, paid back an average of 46 per cent.; and even in 1842, after the Hamburg conflagration, there was an after-payment of only 98 per cent. necessary. This collection in advance of a fund for extraordinary losses is more secure than borrowing in case of need, and paying back in good years. Thus, the Baden Landes-Brandkasse had a debt in 1837 of 800,000 florins. *(Rau,* in the Archiv., III, 320 ff.) In a mutual insurance company, where entrance and exit are free, this would be scarcely possible.

[7] Nearly three-fourths of the public insurance institutions insure also against fire caused by war (Mitth., 1874, 85), a matter of importance even as war is waged in our own days, since in 1870-71, the damage from fire by the

In point of cheapness to the insured, mutual insurance seems to have the advantage, since it contemplates no profit.[8] From a national-economical point of view, also, it is very much of a question, whether the active competition of premium institutions, in a sphere which affords little room for industry proper, is more of a spur to make them "puff up" their claims *(Reclamen)* or to the simplification of their administration.[9] However, premium-institutions are more easily capable of extending the circle of their business;[10] which of itself decreases the general expenses and strengthens their insuring power. Premium-insurance supposes a greater development of capitalistic speculation than does mutual insurance. But, even in the highest stages of civilization, the competition of some mutual insurance companies is desirable to protect the insured from a too high rate of profit to the insurers.[11][12] And since the principle of

---

Franco-Prussian war in France was estimated at 141,000,000 francs. (Mitth., 1873, 33.)

[8] In Prussia, the mutual fire insurance companies, in 1865 and 1866 had an administration outlay of 0.24 and 0.22 per 1,000 of the amount insured; the premium insurance companies of 0.80 and 0.96; the latter doubtless including large assessments for common purposes. (Preuss. Statist. Ztschr., 1868, 269.) In all Germany, the outlay for administration is, for public institutions, 4 per cent. of the contributions; for premium institutions, inclusive of their dividends, 37.1 per cent.; for the more important French private institutions, even 68.8 per cent. (Mitth., 1874, 89, 92.)

[9] German public fire insurance institutions generally have a territory of their own, in which that institution is the only one of the kind. On the other hand, the premium institutions in the whole empire keep about 80,000 agents, i. e., a number 50 times as large as the number of officers of the former. (loc. cit. 90.)

[10] Mutual insurance companies, as they have extended, have sometimes split up into several; for instance, the insurance companies against damage by hail at Lübeck, Güstrow, Sshwedt and Griefswald, daughters of that at New Brandenburg.

[11] The founder of the Mutual Fire Insurance Company of Gotha expressed the hope that in it, it would be possible to insure 60 per cent. cheaper than was customary in the joint stock companies of the time. In the system of agricultural *Einzelhöfe* in Germany, small mutual insurance companies are possible, and insurance then may be very cheap.

[12] On the premium associations, *Bernouilli*, Ueber die Vorzüge der gegen-

mutual insurance has so little attraction for capitalists in a time like that in which we live that it can be maintained perhaps only by the support of the state or of municipalities, we may consider the desirableness of the state's continuing to participate in some way in the matter of insurance as established.

SECTION CCXXXVII (b).

INSURANCE IN GENERAL.—ECONOMIC ADVANTAGES OF INSURANCE.

The national-economic advantage of insurance consists in this, that the damage which is divided among many, and which, therefore, is felt but lightly by each one, is probably made up for, not by an inroad upon the body of still existing original resources, but by savings made from income. This, indeed, is unconditionally true only of such damage as does not depend at all on the will of man, such as, for instance, the damage caused by hail. On the other hand, there is especially in maritime[1] and fire insurance,[2] a great temptation to culpable and even criminal destruction; to the latter, when the object insured is estimated at too high a value. (Speculation-fires!) And it is difficult to say whether this drawback or that advantage is the greater. But, on the other hand, every kind of insurance is attended by good conse-

---

seitige Brandassecuranzen vor Prämiengesellschaften, 1827. *Per contra*, *Masius*, Lehre der Versicherung und Statische Nachweisung aller V. Anstalten in Deutschland, 1846. In Prussia, premium associations are growing more rapidly than mutual: the per capita amount on the whole population insured in the former against damage from fire in 1861 was 116.6 thalers; in 1866, 154.2; in 1869, 176.6; in the latter in 1861, 103,5; 1866, 124,3; 1869, 154.3 thalers. (*Engel*, Statist. Zeitschr., 1868, 268 ff.; 1871, 284 ff.) In France, in the former, in 1857, almost 36 milliards of francs; in the latter, in 1864, 13 milliards. (Mitth., 1871, 51.)

[1] Even in Demosthenes' oration against Zenothemis, we may see how easily the analogy of maritime insurance may lead to criminal destruction of property. Similar cases mentioned by *Pegolotti* before the middle of the 14th century. (Della Decima dei Fiorentini, III, 132.)

[2] French experience teaches that during a commercial crisis there are

quences to the credit of a people. It is of advantage to personal credit, since it prevents sudden impoverishment; but it is by far more advantageous to real-credit *(Realcredit=material credit)* the pledges of which, while their forms may be destroyed, it preserves the value of; that is their economic essence. This last is most clearly manifest in the case of public insurance institutions, with compulsory participation; while in the case of entirely voluntary insurance, the creditor can

---

more fires in mercantile magazines than at other times; while in times when sugar is a drug in the market etc., many sugar factories are burned. (Dictionnaire de l'Econ. polit., I, 88.) The style of our house-building and fire-extinguishing institutions is wont to improve with economic culture. Hence, for instance, in Mecklenburg, 1651 to 1799, cities burned down, in whole or in greatest part, 72 times; 1800 to 1850, only once. *(Boll*, Gesch., von Mecklenb., II, 618 ff.) However, in many countries the damage caused by fire has largely increased: in Baden, for instance, by 100,000 florins a year. Insurance capital, 1809 to 1818, 65 fl.; 1819 to 1828, 128 fl.; 1829 to 1836, 152 fl. *(Rau*, Archiv, III, 322.) Similarly in Switzerland. In Bavaria, of every 10,000 buildings insured, in 1856–60, there were 4.6 fires per annum; 1861–65, 5.04; 1866–69, 8.67. (Preuss. Statist. Ztschr., 1871, 315.)

In Saxony, in 1849–53, there was one fire in every 290 buildings; 1854–58, in every 201; 1859–63, in every 180. Of these fires, 68 per cent. of the whole number were from known causes, i. e., 36.4 per cent. from incendiarism; 28.5 per cent. from negligence. (Sächs. Statist. Ztschr., 1866, 106, 115.) Even in antiquity, similar evil consequences attended the generosity which gratuitously compensated damage by fire. Compare *Juvenal*, III, 215 ff.; *Martial*, III, 52. In England, of every 128 cases of damage by fire of " farming stock," 49 were caused by incendiaries, for the most part actuated by revenge. Hence, there, a notice is posted on insured buildings by the insurance companies which runs: "this farm is insured; the fire office will be the only sufferer in the event of a fire." In London, of every seven fires among the small trading class, one is estimated to have been the work of an incendiary, and of all fires at least one-third (Athenæum, 2, Nov., 1867), if not one-half (Mitth., 1879, 100). One of the largest English fire insurance companies estimates that the introduction of the lucifer match has caused it a damage of £10,000 per annum. Of 9,345 fires, 932 were ascribed to gas, 89 to certain, and 76 to doubtful, incendiarism, 127 to lucifer matches, 8 to storms, 100 to negligence, 80 to drunkenness, 2,511 to the catching fire of curtains, 1,178 to candles, 1,555 to chimnies, 494 to stoves, 1,323 to unknown causes. (Quart. Rev., Dec., 1854, 14 ff.) Fires originate from criminal *(dolose)* causes most frequently when a new stage in the politico-economical development of a people is reached, which renders the buildings put up in a former and lower stage of development insufficient.

never be certain that his debtor has not neglected something necessary. The aggregate danger is less than the sum of individual dangers, for the reason that it is more certain, and that uncertainty of itself is an element of danger.[34]

SECTION CCXXXVII (c).

FIRE INSURANCE.

The present system of fire insurance has been introduced in many places by the establishment of so-called domanial fire-guilds *(Domanial-Brandgilden)*, by which the country population on crown-lands bound themselves to mutually assist one another by furnishing thatch, and horse and hand power in the rebuilding of burned houses. Whatever was wanting after this was made up by gratuitous supplies of wood from the public forests, by the granting of governmental fire-licenses to beg *(begging letters)*, by permission to have collections made in the churches[1] etc. The next step was generally the establish-

---

[3] A Prussian fire insurance regulation, as far back as 1720, expressly says: "everybody scruples to make the least loan on pledged houses in towns." "Every care shall be taken to make the least possible amount of loans in cities." *(Jacobi,* in *Engel's* Zeitschr., 1862, 122.) *Leib*, Dritte Periode etc., 1708, cites a proverb to the effect that, in Hamburg, "no house takes fire;" that is, at a time that its fire-fund-system *(Brandkassenwesen)* had as yet found few imitators. *v. Justi's* proposition to combine the insurance of houses against fire with a loaning-bank for houses. (Polizeiwissenschaft, 1756, I, § 7, 8 ff.) In Russia, in 1815, the loaning bank was the only fire insurance company, which however assumed risks only on stone houses at three-fourths of their value in consideration of 15 per 1,000 annual premium. *(Rau,* Lehrbuch, I, 229.)

[4] *Spittler*, Politik., 441, objects to insurance that it diminishes benevolence and approximates to communism, thus hitting the dark side of all very high civilization.

[1] Thus in Austria, even after the middle of the 18th century: *Schopf*, L. W. des öst. Kaiserstaates, I. p. 175. In the mandate of the electorate of Saxony of Dec. 7, 1715; but the fire-fund *(Feuerkasse)* of 1729 depended on voluntary but regular collections, besides which it obtained certain contributions from the state and the church. Those who gave nothing, however, were threatened with getting nothing, or very little, in case of fire. Parties

ment of public insurance *(Landes-Assecuranz)* only for houses,[2] but with compulsory membership. This compulsion was justified by the continuing interest of the state in the payment of the house-tax, as well as by the interest of the eventual owner of the estate, and of hypothecation-creditors.[3][4] The insurance

---

desiring to rebuild massively had especially much to expect. (Cod. August Forst., I, 538.) The charters of the oldest German *Landesbrandkassen* contain a provision that, in future, no further fire-collections shall be allowed.

[2] The English Hand-in-Hand Fire Office for houses, founded in 1696; the Union Fire O., for houses and movable property, in 1714: both mutual institutions. The premium-institution, the Sun Fire Office, 1710 *(Frankenberg,* Europ. Herold, 1705, II, 181), mentions fire insurance as a special characteristic of England. But we may trace fire insurance on buildings and harvest supplies in the low countries about the Vistula in Prussia, even as far back as 1623. *(Jacobi,* loc. cit., 131.) Brandenburg fire-fund, 1705, with voluntary admittance of all houses, and fixed relation between the yearly contribution and the insurance capital. If a fire happened, the fund repaired the damage caused to the fullest extent its means allowed. *(Mylius,* Corp. Const. March. V., I, 174 seq.) Even in 1706, it became necessary to prohibit speaking ill of the institution. It was, therefore, abolished later. The first Würtemberg private fire insurance company, 1754, founded on similar principles, and which was still existing in 1760, had a like fate *(Bergius,* Polizei und Cameralmagazin, III, 40 ff.), but it was exchanged in 1773 for a mutual public company. In Berlin a mutual insurance company in 1718 *(Bergius,* Cameralistenbibliothek, 151); in Denmark, 1830 *(Thaarup,* Dän. Statist., II, 173 seq.); in Silesea, 1742; Calenberg-Grubenhagen, 1750; in Baden, 1750, in Kurmark, 1765; in Hildesheim, 1765; in Hesse-Darmstadt, 1777. In France, the Parisian institution of 1745 is considered the oldest. *(Beckmann,* Beitr. z. Gesch. d. Erfindd., I, 218.)

[3] In Galenberg-Grubenhagen only the *Bauerhöfe* subject to the common burthens were obliged to enter, in Hildesheim, all houses subject to taxation; in Darmstadt all house-owners who were allowed only a *dominium utile.* In Kurmark, the subjects of the estate might be compelled to enter by their lords, but could not be kept out. Of Prussian companies in 1846, entrance was compulsory only in those of East Prussia and Posen. In Würtemberg compulsion since 1773; confirmed in 1853. Also in Zurich, Jan. 24, 1832; in Schaffhausen Nov. 27, 1835. In Berne, only for state, municipal and mortgaged houses; for the latter only so far as it was not expressly left to the creditor. Introduced into Baden in 1807, after most of the parishes *(Gemeinden)* had voluntarily accepted it; confirmed in 1840. The provision that at least no judicial hypothecation should be made on an un-insured house is found in the Darmstadt law of 1777, § 13, and in that of Mainz of 1780, art. I, § 15. *Rau,* Lehrbuch, II, § 25 a., finds compulsion in the case of

of moveable property is much more recent, both by reason of the nature of the property itself, which becomes of importance only at a later date, and also on account of the much greater difficulty of carrying on such insurance.[5] The thought of making this species of insurance compulsory, or of turning it over to the state, has seldom been suggested.

SECTION CCXXXVII (d).

REQUISITES OF A GOOD SYSTEM OF FIRE INSURANCE.

Among the chief requisites of a good fire insurance system are the following:

---

property in common and in that of property belonging to other persons very appropriate. It is a matter worthy of thought, that, in cities like Berlin, Breslau, Thorn and Stettin, compulsory fire insurance is still retained. In Upper Silesia, the abolition of compulsory provisions has had for effect to cause 52 per cent. of all buildings to be insured. (Press Zeitschr, 1867, 329).

[4] Question of introducing state insurance into Hungary. As a cultured land, and one rich in capital, is better adapted to insurance, it would be folly to "emancipate" ones self from Trieste etc. in this respect. But, on the other hand, only state-insurance can attract the Hungarians and make them feel universally the want of insurance. A reconciliation of these opposing views might be effected by compelling the peasantry to insure their farm-houses, and allowing complete liberty in the cities and with reference to movable property.

[5] Even *Bergins*, Polizei und Cameralmag., III, 80, 1768 ff., doubts the possibility of the insurance of movable property. Insurance of movable property of the Evangelical clergy in the electorate of Mark, in which, however, only movable property of the value of 400 thalers is considered. But by this provision the changeableness of the object, which so facilitates fraud, was done away with. Hamburg joint-stock company for the insurance of movable property, 1779. Electorate of Saxony fire-fund for movable property, 1784-1818, which, however, made good, as a rule, only 25 per cent. of the damage caused. In Prussia, in 1814, there were only 12 insurance companies in which movable property could be insured. In the aggregate even they were but of little extent, and had generally a partnership, guild, or communal basis. (*Jacobi*, loc. cit., 123.) On the other hand, in 1869, there were in all the mutual insurance companies, 530,600,000 thalers worth of movable property insured, besides 2,814,800,000 thalers worth of immovable property, and 366,100,000 thalers worth of property of a mixed nature, partly movable and partly immovable. (Preuss. Statist. Zeitschr., 1876, 298.)

A. The adoption in insuring of measures for the prevention of criminal abuse on the part of the insured. No one should be benefited by the burning of his insured goods.[1] Hence, the rates of insurance should be rigidly fixed according to the real value in exchange.[2] In the case of houses, the value of the incombustible elements of value should be deducted; also the value of the ground and the value it possesses from being advantageously situated etc. The simultaneous insurance of the same object in several companies without proper notice being given should be unconditionally prohibited.[3] The control

---

[1] The former almost unrestricted liberty of the American system of insurance has recently been curtailed, in most of the states, by a rigid governmental superintendence, by special insurance boards with power to permit companies to engage in the business of insurance, and endowed with the right of imposing proper penalties, but of declaring the privilege forfeited at the end of any year. Compare *Brämer* in III, Ergänzungshefte der Preuss. Statist. Ztschr. und Mitth., 1871, No. 1.

[2] The first fire insurance provisions or regulations paid little attention to the danger of over-valuation. Similarly *v. Justi*, Abh. von der Macht, Glückseligkeit, etc., eines Staats. 1860, 81. Also *Krünitz*, Oekonom. Encyclopædie, 1788, XIII, considers it improbable that any one would have his home insured at a higher than its real value. On the other hand, there were formerly bitter complaints made in the United States that the agents, on whom the determination of the rate of premium and the control of the insurance-sum depended chiefly, were led to make over-valuations in furtherance of their own interests. (Mitth., 1871, 3; 1874, 95.)

[3] If the valuation were made to depend on the purchase-price or on the cost of replacing or restoring the damaged property, even this would be some temptation to not entirely upright men. Hence the Baden law of 1840 expressly provides that instead of this, the selling price shall be the basis; the law of 1852, § 17, the medium cost of the combustible parts. after deduction made of the diminution in value caused by age. The fixing of premiums in the case of houses should be repeated from time to time on account of wear. According to the Calenb. Grubenh. law of 1823, § 21, every 10 years. According to the Baden law of 1852, § 28, 33, and the Württemberg law of 1853, § 12, the city council should examine annually in what cases a new valuation was necessary. The more certainly over-insurance is avoided, the less need is there of the superintendence policy adapted to a rather barbarous state of insurance, that only a part of the value shall be made good. The Phœnix fire insurance company in Baden for the insurance of movable property has reserved the right to investigate at any time and to satisfy

of all this may be greatly facilitated by requiring foreign insurance companies to obtain a special permit to carry on their business in the country, and to allow them to effect insurance only through responsible home agents.[4] Most insurance companies exclude from insurance personal property which may be easily secreted, such, for instance, as jewels, cash money, valuable documents etc.

B. There should be a just proportion between the insurance premium and the risk. This depends not only on the style of building of the houses themselves and of those in the neighborhood,[5] on the situation, the too great intricacy *(Complicirung)*

---

itself as to the value of the insured object, and to lower the amount insured in accordance with its own opinion. The provision that the valuation shall be made by the authorities of the place, or that it shall be approved by them is frequently found. In Saxony, for instance (law of Nov. 14, 1835), the Leipzig city council gives its approval when it finds the amount insured in keeping with the means of the insured, and entertains no suspicions as to his honesty. To what a bad state of things a less liberal course leads, see in *Masius*, loc. cit., 85. This indeed is only difficult in large cities. It is also to be considered that it is not so much the many small amounts, but the few large ones that are dangerous to insurance. The Prussian scheme wanted to give up the police superintendence of insurance, but to punish over-insurance of more than 5 per cent. of the common value, by imposing a fine equal to the amount of over-insurance on the insured, the agents, and on the conductors of the business. *(Jacobi*, in II. Ergänzhefte der Preuss. Statist. Ztschr., 1869.) The provision that the amount paid as damages for a burned house shall be immediately employed in rebuilding, is to be explained in part by requisite A; in part also by the same police-guardianship against presumed negligence which introduced compulsory insurance.

[4] Compare *Brügemann*, Die Mobiliar V. in Preussen nach dem G. von 1837.

[5] *Oberländer*, loc. cit. 108, calls insurance without classification of risks, a " mutual benevolent institution;" and one rigidly classified according to the probable period of burning, "an institution for the making of advances " *(Vorschuss-Anstalt.)* In Baden, even in 1737, there was no difference made between a massive building and a wooden hut with a straw roof in the Black forest. *(Rau*, Archiv., III, 324.) Here, there was in 1844 to 1849, an average damage by fire in houses with brick roofs of 1,302 florins, with thatch roofs of 1,786 florins, with shingle roofs of 2,292 florins, to say nothing of the greater frequency of such damage in each succeeding class. *(Rau*, Lehrbuch, II, 1, § 26, a.) In Württemberg, before 1843, the owners of insured personal prop-

of which extends the ravages of fire, as its too great isolation makes assistance difficult;[6] but also on the nature of the business carried on in them,[7] and on the condition of the local development of fire police. Highly cultured places, especially large cities, are really much less exposed to damage from fire. To not take this into account would be not only to compulsorily dole out charity to the poorer classes of the people, and to the less cultivated portions of the country,[8] but it would indi-

---

erty, in houses with thatch roofs, had, in the same time, received 22 per 1,000 compensation for damage; in houses with brick roofs, from 8 to 9 per 1,000. *(Rau,* loc. cit.) In 17 German insurance companies, between 1866 and 1869, massive buildings with hard roofs paid 1,003,000 thalers and received 612,000 thalers; the not massive with hard roofs paid 1,544,000 thalers and received 1,339,000; houses with soft roofs paid 2,420,000 and received 2,792,000. (Preuss, Statist. Zeitschr. 1861, 327.) Similar observations made in Berne during 23 years.

[6] While in most English insurance companies, there are only three classes: common, hazardous, and doubly hazardous, in Rheinish Prussian insurance companies, there are seven, according to the style of building, and in each class two subdivisions, according to the location.

[7] According to an English average of 15 years, there is some damage from fire yearly in the following classes of buildings and on the following percentages: *Of the whole number.*

Match factories,	30.00
Lodging houses,	16.5
Hat makers,	7.7
Cloth makers,	2.6
Candle makers,	3.8
Smiths,	2.4
Carpenters,	2.2
Oil and color dealers,	1.5
Book dealers,	1.1
Coffee houses,	1.2
Beer houses,	1.3
Bakeries,	0.75
Wine dealers,	0.61
Small dealers in spices,	0.34
Eating houses,	0.86

(Quart. Rev., 1854, 23.) There is indeed a difference in the intensity of these fires. For instance, in inns, there have been a great many; but the damage has been for the most part insignificant.

[8] In Paris the houses insured had a value of 2,370,000,000 francs, but the

rectly put an obstacle in the way of a transition to the massive construction of houses, and of good, that is, as a rule, of costly fire-extinguishing institutions.[9] On the other hand, administration must be rendered much more difficult by the taking of risks of many degrees of danger, especially as it is scarcely possible, for a long time, to even hope for a statistically unassailable basis of a tariff graded in exact accordance with the risk.[10] If those objects especially exposed to danger should be excluded altogether, the common utility of the institution would be largely diminished; and the insured least exposed to danger would nevertheless have to complain of a relatively too high contribution.[11] If every peculiar class of risks were

damage from fire amounted to only 0.016 per 1,000! (Dictionn. d'Econ. politique, I, 89.) On an average, the premiums in France amount to 0.85 per 1,000. In Prussia, 1867-69 on an average: in the province of Prussia, 9.46 per 1,000; Posen, 3.75; Brandenburg, Berlin not included, 2.82; Pomerania, 2.52; Westphalia, 2.15; Schleswig-Holstein, 2.09; Hanover, 1.99; Silesia, 1.68; Saxony, 1.47; Hesse-Nassau, 1.46; the Rhine country, 1.34; Sigmaringen, 0.56; city of Berlin, 0.28 per 1,000. (Preuss Statist. Zeitschr., 1871, 289.) How largely a higher civilization tends to arrest the spread of fire by the reason of the great facilities of rendering assistance is shown by the fact that for 100 buildings totally consumed in Posen, in 1837-40, there were 13.4 only injured: in 1866-69, 32 were injured for 100 totally consumed. In Prussian Saxony, 1839-44, 34; 1867-69, 57. (loc. cit., 329.) In Baden, the district called the *Seekreis* got from the fire-fund, in 1845-49, 80 per cent. more than it contributed to it; the middle Rhine district contributed 37 per cent. more than it received. The Bavarian Reza district, 1828-29, received only 11.4 per cent. for damages, and paid 19 per cent. of all premiums; the Lower Danube district, 10 and 8.8 per cent. (*Rau*, Lehrbuch, II, § 28, 26.) The city of Leipzig contributed from $\frac{1}{16}$ to $\frac{1}{17}$ of the insurance paid, 1864-68, to the insurance companies taking risks on real property in the kingdom of Saxony, and received back only from $\frac{1}{502}$ to $\frac{1}{717}$, although its fire extinguishing institutions cost, in 1870, 26,182 thalers. (Official.)

[9] Even premium-institutions have frequently very different rates for the same risk, according as they fear greater or less competition, or desire to recommend themselves in a new place etc. Hence the tricks of the trade with which most of them surround their tariff.

[10] In Würtemberg, theaters, powder mills, places where brick and lime are burned, porcelain factories, iron-works etc. cannot be insured at all. In Calenb-Grubenh. and Bremen-Verden, shingle-roofed houses can be insured only at ⅔ of their real value.

[11] Thus, for instance, in the electorate of Mark, each of the four classes of

to be treated as one whole, the insuring principle itself would suffer.[12] Where the nation or municipality engages in the business of compulsory insurance, its too rigid system of rate-fixing has something inequitable in it, inasmuch as it makes the most provident housekeeper suffer from the danger from fire of his neighbor's establishment, a gas-factory, for instance.

C. The certainty of compensation for damage suffered. The government should see to it that the institution does not promise more than it can perform with its joint-stock capital and by means of its premiums.[13] The good will of foreign institutions to keep their promises to the letter is best assured by requiring them as a condition precedent of carrying on their business in a country, to bind themselves to litigate only in the home courts. They protect themselves against the

---

houses bears its own loss alone. To the fourth class, for instance, belong smithies, brick factories, and buildings with steam engines etc.. The Baden law of 1852 puts the same burthen in the same place, upon houses exposed to danger in a greater or lesser degree; but provides for 4 classes *(Gemeindeclassen)* with different rates of contribution, and assigns each *Gemeinde* every year, according to the relative magnitude of the losses of the previous year, to one of those classes. How risky it is for large cities to confine their insurance, because of the ordinarily small amount of damage to them from fire, only to insurance institutions of their own, is shown by the case of Hamburg in the year 1842, where three joint stock insurance companies could pay only from 75 to 80 per cent., and the Bieber Mutual Insurance Company, only 20 per cent.

[12] In the case of buildings, the greater risk is generally calculated by correspondingly multiplying the insurance-value, but in case of damage by fire, it is simply made good.

[13] In the insurance companies specified by *Masius*, loc. cit., 176, the aggregate amount of their insurance, stood to the amount necessary to cover it, by means of receipts from premiums, reserve, and joint-stock capital:

In the Leipzig Fire Insurance Company, as - - 100:1.87
In the Trieste Fire Insurance Company, as - - 100:1.80
In the Elberfeld Fire Insurance Company, as - 100:1.19
In the Aix-Munich Fire Insurance Company, as - 100:1.15
In the Cologne Colonia Fire Insurance Company, as 100:2.44
In the Karlsruhe Phœnix Fire Insurance Company, as 100:3.7
In the Berlin Fire insurance Company, as - - 100:6.3
In the Gotha (including the four fold after payment
    note), about as - - - - - - 100:2.6

risk of very large insurances by the system of re-insurance, by transferring a portion of the premium as well as of the risk to one or more other insurance companies.[14]

D. In all highly cultured quarters, the almost entirely voluntary fire-extinguishing system, in which the people turned out in a body to battle with the flames, made way for the fire-militia system; and if the latter should make place for what we may designate as a standing fire-army which is most easily attained in connection with the fire-insurance system, we should reach the ideal of such a system, especially if the business of insurance was in the hands of the state or of the municipality. Such a system would be in accordance with the principle of the division of labor, and, also, with the fact that usually the most vital interest is the greatest spur to action.[15]

In the same companies the amount of damage and of expense for the last preceding year were, on every 100 thalers of insurance, 46 pfennigs ($\frac{1}{500}$ thalers), 44, 29, 48, 67, 55, 35, 42; an average of 45, that is 1½ per 1,000. Besides, much depends on the degree to which the joint-stock capital can be applied. Thus, for instance, in Berlin, on every 1,000 thalers 200 are paid in cash, and a note *(Solawechsel)* given for the rest, payable in two months after notice. Where the unpaid remaining stock is but a mere book-debt, and may even be evaded by disclaiming the stock itself, it of course affords very little security.

[14] Compare *Volz*. Tübinger Zeitschr. 1847, 349 ff.

[15] The preparatory steps towards this ideal were taken long ago. Thus, for instance, the personal-property insurance companies have offered premiums for special merit in extinguishing fires (Calenb.-Grubenh., 1814, § 35), saving things from a burning house is looked after by the agents of personal property insurance companies; compensation is almost universally made not only for the damage done by fire, but also that caused while the fire is being extinguished. The excellent fire-extinguishing institutions of England are maintained by the common action of the insurance companies. There have been complaints, however, that they have shown a preference for insured objects. (Mitth., 1874, 113.)

BOOK V.

ON POPULATION.

CHAPTER I.

THEORY OF POPULATION.

SECTION CCXXXVIII.

INCREASE OF POPULATION IN GENERAL.

That amid the thousand dangers which threaten the existence of the individual the species may endure, the Creator has endowed every class of organic beings with such reproductive power, and so much pleasure in propagating their kind, that if the action of these were entirely unrestricted, it would soon fill up the earth.[1] In the case of the human race, also, the physiological possibility of propagation has very wide limits.[2] It

---

[1] Thus, for instance, the sturgeon can, according to *Leuckart*, produce 3,000,000 eggs in a year. According to *Burdach*, the posterity of a pair of rabbits may be over 1,000,000 in four years; and that of a plant-louse, according to *Bonnet*, over a 1,000,000,000 in a few weeks. The prolificacy of a species of animals is wont to be greater in proportion as the structure-material *(Bildungsmaterial)* saved within a given time during the course of individual life, is greater, and as material wants during the embryonic period are limited; also (teleologically), in proportion as to the danger the individual is exposed to. Compare *Leuckart* in *R. Wagner's* physiolog. Wörterbuche, Art. Zeugung. Teleogically, *Bastiat* says: *cette surabondance paraît calculée partout en raison inverse de la sensibilité, de l'intelligence et de la force avec laquelle chaque espèce résiste à la déstruction.* (Harmonies, ch. 16.)

[2] The researches of modern physiology make it probable that an ovum is detached from the ovaries at each period of healthy menstruation. *(Bischoff, Beweis der von der Begattung unabhängigen periodischen Reifung und*

would be nothing extraordinary that a healthy pair, living in wedlock from the 20th to the 42nd year of the woman's life, that is, during the whole time of her full capacity to bear children, should rear six children to the age of puberty. This would, therefore, suffice to treble the population in a single generation; provided that all who had grown up should marry. According to Euler,[3] when the births were 5 per cent. and the deaths 2 per cent., the population doubled in not quite 24 years; when the increase was 2½ per annum, in 28 years; when 2, in 35 years, and when 1½ per cent. in 47 years.

The United States furnish us with a striking illustration of

Lösung der Eier bei den Säugethieren und Menschen, 1844.) It is hardly possible to ascertain how many of these ova are capable of fecundation. Among the animals, on which the greater number of accurate observations have been made, that is in the case of horses, it has been found that, in the two districts of Prussia most favorably conditioned, of 100 mares that had been lined, 63.3 became pregnant, and 53.5 gave birth to live foals; in the rest of the Prussian monarchy, the births were only 46 per cent. Compare *Schubert*, Staatskunde, VII, 1, 98. In the Belgian *haras* (places for breeding horses), between 1841 and 1850, about 30 per cent. of the "leaps" proved fruitful, from 2 to 3 per cent. aborted, the rest were either probably or certainly unfruitful. *(Horn.,* Statist. Gemälde, 171.) In the human species, also, the great number of first-born generated in the first weeks of marriage, bears witness to a high degree of procreative susceptibility.

On the other hand, the healthy male semen ejected during a single act of coition contains innumerable germs, a very few of which are sufficient to produce fecundation. *(Leuckart,* loc. cit., 907.) According to *Oesterlen*, Handbuch der medicischen Statistik, 1865, 196, from 10 to 20 per cent. of all marriages were childless. In the United Kingdom, *Farr*, report on the Census of 1851, estimated that in a population of 27,511,000, there were 1,000,000 childless families, when the term is allowed to embrace widows and widowers as well as married couples.

[3] See the exhaustive table in *Euler*, Mémoires de l' Académie de Berlin 1756, in *Süssmilch*, Göttl. Ordnung, I, § 160. Bridge has constructed the following formula:

Log. A = Log. P + n × Log. $(1 + \frac{m-b}{m\,b})$. Here P stands for the actually existing population, $\frac{1}{m}$ = the ratio between the annual mortality and the number of the living, $\frac{1}{b}$, the ratio of the number of annual births to the number of the living, n the number of years, A, the population at the end of three years, the quantity sought for.

this doctrine, and on the grandest scale. There the natural increase of the white population, from 1790 to 1840, was 400.4 per cent.; that is in the first decade 33.9 per cent. of the population in 1790; in the second 33.1, in the third 32.1, in the fourth 30.9, in the fifth 29.6 per cent.[4][5]

SECTION CCXXXIX.
LIMITS TO THE INCREASE OF POPULATION.

There is certainly one limit which the increase of no organic being can exceed: the limit of the necessary means of subsistence. But, so far as the human race is concerned, this notion is somewhat more extensive, inasmuch as it embraces besides food, also clothing, shelter, fuel, and a great many other goods which are not, indeed, necessary to life, but which are so considered.[1] We may illustrate the matter by a simple example

[4] *Tucker*, Progress of the United States, 89, ff. 98. Here deduction is already made of immigrants and their posterity, who after subtracting the loss by emigration back to the old country, amounted to over 1,000,000. It probably amounted to more yet. If, as *Wappäus* does (Bevölekerungsstatistik, 1859, I, 93, 122 ff.), we calculate the rate of increase per annum, we have an average during the first decade of 2.89, during the second of 2.83, the third of 2.74, the fourth of 2.52, the seventh of 2.39, the eighth (1860-70) of probably 2.25 per cent. On the still greater ratio of increase in earlier times, see *Price*, Observations on reversionary Payments, 1769, 4 ed. 1783, I, 282 seq., I, 260.

It was nothing unheard of to see an old man with a living posterity of 100. *Franklin*, Observations concerning the Increase of Mankind, and the Peopling of New Countries, 1751.) It is said that in the region about Contendas, in Brazil, there were on from 70 to 80 births a mortality of from 3 to 4 per annum (how long?), and an unfortunate birth *(unglücklichen)* was scarcely ever heard of. Mothers 20 years of age had from 8 to 10 children; and one woman in the fifties had a posterity of 204 living persons. *(Spix und Martius*, Reise III, 525).

[5] Immense increase of the Israelites in Egypt. (Genesis 46, 27; Numbers, 1.

[1] When it is known that, in the Hebrides, one-third of all the labor of the people has to be employed in procuring combustible material *(McCulloch*, Statist. Account, I, 319), it will no longer excite surprise that, according to Scotch statistics, some parishes increase in population after coal has been found in them, and others decrease when their turf-beds are exhausted.

in the rule of division. If we take the aggregate of the means of subsistence as a dividend, the number of mankind as divisor; then the average share of each is the quotient. Where two of these quantities are given, the third may be found. Only when the dividend has largely increased can the divisor and quotient increase at the same time (prosperous increase of population). If, however, the quotient remains unchanged, the increase of the divisor can take place only at the expense of the quotient (proletarian increase of population).[2] Hence it is to be expected that the quantity of the means of subsistence being given and also the requirement of each individual, the number of births and the number of deaths should condition each other. Where, for instance, the number of church livings has not been increased, only as many candidates can marry as clergymen who held such livings have died. The greater the average age of the latter is, the later do the former marry, in the average, and *vice versa*. And so, in the case of whole nations, when their economic consumption and production remain unaltered.[3] A basin entirely filled with

---

[2] Compare *Isaias*, 9: 3. According to *Courcelle-Seneuil*, Traité théorique et pratique d'Economie politique, I, 1858, the *chiffre nécessaire de la population égal à la somme des revenus de la société diminuée de la somme des inégalités de consommation et divisée par le minimum de consommation:* $P = \dfrac{R-J}{M}$

[3] Thus *Süssmilch*, Göttliche Ordnung in den Veränderungen des menschlichen Geschlechts, 1st ed., 1742, 4th ed., 1775, I, 126 ff., assumes that one marriage a year takes place, on from every 107 to every 113 persons living. On the other hand, 22 Dutch towns gave an average of 1 in every 64. This abnormal proportion is very correctly ascribed by *Malthus*, Principles of Population, II, ch. 4, to the great mortality of those towns: viz., a death for every 22 or 23 persons living, while the average is 1 : 36. The Swiss, *Müret*, (in the Mémoires de la Société économique de Berne, 1766, I, 15 ff.), could not help wondering that the villages with the largest average duration of life should be those in which there were fewest births. "So much life-power and yet so few procreative resources!" Here too, *Malthus*, II, ch. 5, solved the enigma. The question was concerned with Alpine villages with an almost stationary cow-herd business: no one married until one cow-herd cottage had become free; and precisely because the tenants lived so long, the new comers obtained their places so late. Compare *d' Ivernois*, Enquête sur les Causes patentes et occulte de la faible Proportion de Naissances à Mon

SEC. CCXXXIX.]   INCREASE OF POPULATION.   277

water can be made to contain more only in case it is either increased itself, or a means is found to compress its contents. Otherwise as much must flow out on the one side as is poured in on the other. And so, everything else remaining stationary, the fruitfulness of marriages must, at least in the long run, be in the inverse ratio of their frequency. (See § 247.)⁴ ⁵

treux: yearly 1:46, of the persons living, while the average in all Switzerland was 1:28.

In France according to *Quételet*, Sur l'Homme, 1835, I, 83 ff., there was:

In	One marriage a year for every	Children to a marriage	One death yearly for every
4 Departments	110–120 inhabitants	3.79	35.4 inhabitants.
15 "	120–130 "	3.79	39.2 "
23 "	130–140 "	4.17	39.0 "
18 "	140–150 "	4 36	40.6 "
10 "	150–160 "	4.43	40.3 "
9 "	160–170 "	4.48	42.7 "
6 "	170 and more "	4.48	46.4 "

The two departments of Orne and Finisterre present a very glaring contrast: in the former, one birth per annum on every 44.8 (1851 = 51.6), a marriage on every 147.5, a death on every 52.4 (1851 = 54.1) living persons; in the latter, on the contrary, on every 26 (1851 = 29.8), 113.9 and 30.4 (1851 = 34.2). In Namur, the proportions were 30.1, 141, 51.8; in Zeeland, 21.9, 113.2, 28.5. (*Quételet*, I, 142.) The Mexican province, Guanaxuato, presents the most frightful extreme: one birth per annum on every 16.08 of the population living, and one death in every 19.7. (*Quételet*, I, 110.)

⁴ Compare even *Steuart*, Principles, I, ch. 13. *Sadler*, Law of Population, 1830, II, 514:

	Marriages per annum on every 10,000 inhabitants	Children on every 100 Marriages
⁵ In the purely Flemish provinces of Belgium	128	481
In the purely Wallonic provinces of Belgium	139	448
In the mixed provinces of Belgium - -	152	425
In Holland - - - - - - -	148	476
In Lombardy - - - - - -	166	489
In Bohemia - - - - - -	173	413
In the kingdom of Saxony - - -	170	410

SECTION CCXL.

INFLUENCE OF AN INCREASE OF THE MEANS OF SUBSISTENCE.

The sexual instinct and the love for children are incentives of such universality and power, that an increase of the means of subsistence is uniformily followed by an increase in the numbers of mankind. *Partout, où deux personnes peuvent vivre commodément, il se fait un mariage.* (*Montesquieu.*) Thus after a good harvest, the number of marriages and births is wont to considerably increase; and conversely to diminish after bad harvests.[1 2 3] In the former case, it is rather hope than

---

Compare *Horn*, Bevölkerungswissenschaftliche Studien, I, 162 ff., 191, 252 ff. In most countries, there is a much larger number of children to a marriage in the rural districts than in the cities; but at the same time, marriages are much less frequent there. In Saxony, however, where the cities show a greater marital productiveness, the rural districts present a large number of marriages. Of the 10 countries compared by *Wappäus*, II, 481 ff., only Prussia and Schleswig are exceptions to the rule.

[1] That rich food directly increased prolificacy is proved from the fact that, for instance, our domestic animals are much more prolific than wild ones of the same species. Compare *Villermé*, in the Journ. des Economistes VI, 400 ff. The months richest in conceptions fall universally in the spring, and again in the pleasant season immediately following the harvest. On the other hand, during the seasons of fast in the Catholic church the number of cases of conception is below the average. (Jour. des Econ., 1857, 808).

[2] Thus the annual mean number of marriages amounted to:

	Between 1841 *and* 1850.	*In* 1847 *alone.*
In Saxony,	15,505	14,220
In Holland,	22,352	19,280
In Belgium,	28,968	24,145
In France,	280,330	249,797

Horn, loc. cit. I, 167. In the governmental district (*Regierungsbezirke*) of Düsseldorf, there was in the years of scarcity, 1817 and 1818, one marriage for every 134 and 137 souls; on the other hand, in 1834 nd 1835, in every 103 and 105. (*Viebahn*, I, 120 seq.) In England, the variations in the yearly

actual possession which constitutes the incentive to the founding of new families. Hence the greatest increase is not found in connection with the absolutely lowest price of corn, but

price of corn are reflected in the variations in the number of yearly marriages. Thus, in 1800, 114 shillings per quarter; 1801, 122 shillings; 1802 (Peace of Amiens), 70 shillings; 1803, 58 shillings. The number of marriages in the four years respectively was 69,851, 67,288, 90,396, 94,379. (*Porter*, Progress of the Nation, III, ch. 14, 453.)

Similarly in Germany, in 1851, the conclusion of peace increased the number of marriages, and the scarcity of 1817 diminished it. In Prussia, in 1816, there was one marriage for every 88.1 of the population; in 1828, for every 121.4; in 1834 (origin of the great Zollverein), for every 104; in 1855, for every 136.4; in 1858 (hope of a new era), in every 105.9. (*v. Viebahn.* Statistik des Zollvereins II, 206.)

In Austria, the price of rye was:

	Per Metze.	No. of Marriages.
In 1851,	2.47 florins	336,800
In 1852.	2.11 "	316,800
In 1853,	3.38 "	283,400
In 1854,	4.36 "	258,000
In 1855,	4.43 "	245,400 (*Czörnig.*)

On Sweden, see Wargentin in *Malthus*, II, ch. 2.

The decreased number of births in consequence of a bad harvest, and *vice versa*, appears of course only during the following calendar year. Thus, in 1847, as compared with the average of the years 1844 and 1845, there were fewer children born in England by 4 per 1,000, in Saxony by 7 per 1,000, in Lombardy by 59, in France by 63, in Prussia by 82, in Belgium by 122, in Holland by 159 per 1,000. (*Horn*, I, 239 ff.) In Germany, the conscription-years corresponding to the scarcity time, 1816-17, gave a *minus* of 25 per cent. in many places below the average. (*Bernouilli*, Populationistik, 219.) In the case of marriage, the relative increase or decrease is still more characteristic, so far as our purpose is concerned, than the absolute increase or decrease. Thus in Belgium, for instance, against 1,000 marriages dissolved by death, there were, in 1846, only 971 new ones contracted, and in 1847 only 747; while in 1850 there were 1,500. The falling off in Flanders alone was still greater. Thus, in 1847, there were only 447 marriages contracted for 1,000 dissolved. (*Horn*, I, 170 ff.) However, *Berg*, using Sweden as an illustration, rightly calls attention to the fact, that the variations in the number of marriages and births is determined in part by the number of adults, that is, of the number of births 20 and more years before. Compare *Engel's* Statist. Zeitschr., 1869, 7.

with those prices which present the most striking contrast to those of a previous bad year.⁴

The introduction of the potato has promoted the rapid increase of population in most countries. Thus, the population of Ireland in 1695, was only 1,034,000; in 1654, when the cultivation of the potato became somewhat more common it was 2,372,000; in 1805, 5,395,000; in 1823, 6,801,827; in 1841, 8,175,000. In 1851, after the fearful spread of the potato-rot it fell again to 6,515,000.⁵ In general, every new or increasing branch of industry, as soon as it yields a real net product is wont to invite an increase of population. Machines, however, have not this effect only when they operate to produce rather a more unequal division of the national income than an absolute increase of that income.⁶

---

³ Sometimes, a sudden increase in the frequency of marriages may have very accidental and transitory causes. Thus, for instance, in France in 1813, when the unmarried were so largely conscripted, the number of marriages rose to 387,000, whereas the average of the five previous years was 229,000. (*Bernouilli*, Populationistik, 103.)

⁴ Thus, for instance, in nearly all countries affected by the movement of 1848, there were, during the last months of that year, an unusually large number of conceptions. (*Horn.*, I, 241 seq.) According to *Dieterici*, Abh. der Berliner Akademie, 1855, 321 ff., there was one birth a year for the number of persons living.

	Ten years' average.	1849 alone.
In France, - - - - -	36.19	35.79
In Tuscany, - - - - -	24.42	22.82
In Saxony, - - - - -	24.51	23.08
In Prussia, - - - - -	25.5	23.62

The great majority of men at that time believed all they liked to believe.

⁵ *Marshall*, Digest of all Accounts, I, 15. *Porter*, I, ch. I, 9.

⁶ *Wallace*, in this respect, places industry far behind agriculture. (On the Numbers of mankind in ancient and modern Times.) The county of Lancashire had, in 1760, that is shortly before the introduction of the great machine industry, 297,000 inhabitants; in 1801, 672,000; in 1831, 1,336,000; in 1861, 2,490,000. Saxony has, in almost every place, a relatively large number of births in proportion as in any locality, commerce and industry prepond-

SECTION CCXLI.

EFFECT OF WARS ON POPULATION.

We may now understand why it is that only those wars which are accompanied by a diminution of the sources of the means of support decrease population. The loss in the numbers of mankind produced by wars, hardships etc., would, as a rule, be readily made up for by increased procreation.[1] Thus, for instance, in Holland, the long Spanish war permitted an increase of the population for the reason that the national wealth increased at the same time; while the short war with Cromwell, which curtailed commerce, caused 3,000 houses in Amsterdam alone to remain empty.[2] In England and Wales, the population increased during the most fright-

---

crate over agriculture, and *vice versa*. See *Engel*, Bewegung der Bevölkerung im K. Sachsen, 1854. But this should not be generalized into a universal law. For instance, Prussia and Posen have an average number of births greater than that of the Rhine country and Westphalia. (*v. Viebahn*, Statistik des L. V, II, 222.)

[1] The war of 1870–71 cost Germany 44,890 lives. (Preuss. Statist. Ztschr., 1872, 293.) This number is not quite 20 per cent. of the excess of births (794,206) over deaths (563,065) in Prussia in the year 1865. On the other hand, in from 1856 to 1861 there were 10,000 cases of murder and manslaughter in all Europe, Turkey excepted. (*Hausner*, Vergl. Statistik, I, 145.) About the end of the last century, it was estimated that about 1,000,000 children were born annually in France. (*Necker*, Administration des Finances, I, 256.) Of these, about 600,000 outlived their 18th year. (*Peuschel*, Essai de Statistique, 31.) There were, annually, about 220,000 marriages. Hence the number of the unmarried was increased annually by 80,000 young men, who, according to *Peuschel* (32), amounted to over 1,450,000. According to this, the number of recruits, per annum, might amount to hundreds of thousands without causing any appreciable diminution in the number of births and marriages. Compare *Malthus*, Principle of Population, II, ch. 6. On the other hand, long continued wars have the effect of keeping the men physically strongest from marriage, and so to deteriorate the race.

[2] Richesse de Hollande, I, 149. During the Amsterdam commercial crisis, from 1795 to 1814, there were for every 4 births an average of 7 deaths. So that the population, in 1795, was still 217,000, and in 1815, only 180,000. (*Bickes*, Bewegung der Bevölkerung Anhang, 28.)

ful war of modern times, from 8,540,000 in 1790, to over 12,000,000 in 1821; in France, from, probably, 26,000,000 or 27,000,000 in 1791, to 29,217,000 in 1817. England, indeed, was itself never the seat of war, and its commerce was increased by the war in some directions as much as it was diminished by it in others. France's own territory was devastated only in the first and in the last years of the war. But the Revolution had, on the whole, once the storms of the Reign of Terror were over, not only more equally divided the means of subsistence in France, but it had developed them in a higher degree.[3][4]

---

[3] On the other hand, the population of East Prussia, between 1807 and 1815 diminished 14 per cent. *(v. Haxthausen*, Ländl. Verfassung der Preuss. Monarchie, I, 93.) The battles of the Seven Years' War are said to have consumed 120,000 Russians, 140,000 Austrians, 200,000 Frenchmen, 160,000 Englishmen, Hanoverians etc., 25,000 Swedes, 28,000 of the troops of the empire, and 180,000 Prussians. Yet the population of Prussia fell off 1,500,000. *(Frédéric*, Oeuvres posthumes, IV, 414; Preuss. Gesch. Friedrich's M., II, 349.) During the Thirty Years' War, the population of Bohemia fell from 3,000,000 to 780,000. *(Mailath*, Gesch. von Oesterr, III, 455.) Württemberg, according to the military recruiting lists had a population, in 1622, of 300,000 inhabitants. *(Spittler*, Werke, XII, 34.) In 1641, the population was only 48,000; according to a promotion-speech of *J. B. Andreä*. But between 1628 and 1650, more than 58,000,000 florins were lost by war contributions, and about 60,000,000 florins by plunder; about 36,000 private houses were in ruins. *(Spittler*, Württ. Gesch., 254.) On Alsace, Freisingen and Göttingen, see *Loudorp*, Bellum sexenn., II, 563; *Zschocke*, Bayerische Geschichte, III, 302; *Spittler*, Hanov. Gesch., II, 37 ff., 114. On Germany generally, see *R. F. Hanser*, Deutschland nach dem dreissigjährigen Kriege, 1862. However, many estimates of the diminution of the population are exaggerated, because it has not been considered that a great part of the men who disappeared in one place fled to another, for the time being more secure. Compare *Kius* in *Hildebrand's* Jahrb., 1870, I ff.

The population of Massachusetts increased 8,310 yearly, before the War of Independence; during the war, only 1,161, although the enemy scarcely ever entered the country. *(Ebeling*, Gesch. und Erdbeschreib. der V. Staaten I, 236.) Russia had a mortality during the war years, 1853–55, of 2,272,000, 2,148,000, and 2,541,000; in the years of peace previous, 2,000,000 at most.

[4] Besides the mere loss of men, war operates destructively on production, since it affects especially the most productive classes as to age, while pestilence, famine, etc., carry off children, old people, and the feeble. Hence, a

It cannot even be unconditionally predicated of emigration, that it hinders the increase of population. As soon as people have begun to calculate upon emigration, as a resort for themselves in case of distress, or upon the emigration of others, by which they would be left a larger field for action at home, a number of marriages is contracted and a number of children born; which would otherwise not have been the case. Most men, especially when young and enamoured, hope for the realization of all their wishes. Favorable chances, open to a great number of men alike and which every one thinks himself competent to calculate, are commonly over-estimated by the majority.[5] (See § 259.)

SECTION CCXLII.

COUNTER TENDENCIES TO THE INCREASE OF POPULATION.

The extension of economic production is always a labor; the surrender of one's ordinary means of subsistence to new comers, a sacrifice; but, on the other hand, the procreation of children is a pleasure. Hence it seems to be incontestibly true that the powers of increase of population, considered from an entirely sensuous point of view, tend to go beyond the bounds of the field of food. Malthus gave expression to this fact by saying that population had a tendency to increase in a geometrical progression, but the means of subsistence, even under the most favorable conditions, only in an arithmetical progression.[1] If the word "tendency" be correctly understood in the

---

people's public economy recovers more readily from the last named misfortune than from war.

[5] Compare *Giov. Botero*, Della Cause della Grandezza della Città, L. II, and Ragion di Stato, VIII, 95; where colonization is compared to the swarming of bees. *W. Raleigh*, Discourse of War in general, Works VIII. 257 ff. Similarly *Child*, Discourse of Trade, 371 ff. *Ustariz*, Teoria y Practica del Commercio, 1724, ch. 4. *Franklin*, Observations on the Increase of Mankind, which reminds one of the continued growth of polyps.

[1] Principle of Population, I, ch. 1. Adam Smith also implicitly held the

sense in which Malthus employed it, so that the reality appears as the product of several and partly opposite tendencies,[2] the first half of his allegation can scarcely be contested.[3] If a father has three sons, and each of the three three in turn, the love of procreation and the power of procreation, all being in the normal condition of health, are precisely three times as great in the second generation as in the first, and nine times as great in the third etc. The second half of Malthus's principle is more open to doubt. If it be true, as has been asserted, that man's means of subsistence consist solely of animals and plants, and these, as well as man, increase in a geometrical ratio, and usually even with a much larger multiplier, yet it is here, surprisingly enough, overlooked that their natural increase is interrupted by the consumption of them by man. On the other hand, it is true that even raw material, by means of more skillful technic processes (§ 134, 157), and the values by which man ennobles them, may always increase in a greater ratio than a merely arithmetical one. (§ 33).[4] But, that, in the long run, the means of subsistence should keep pace with the extreme of sensuous desire and of physiological power, is utterly incredible. Hence, the latter tendency is limited by others.

A. And indeed, firstly, by repressive counter-tendencies. As soon as there is a larger population in existence than can be supported, the surplus population must yield to a mournful necessity; in a favorable case, to that of emigration, but usually to hunger, disease and misery generally.

"The earth," says Sismondi, "again swallows the children she cannot support." It is the weakest especially who are

---

view that the demand for the means of subsistence is always in advance of them. Wealth of Nat., I, ch. 11, pref. and P. I.

[2] This may be represented by what physicists call the "parallelogram of forces." Compare *Senior*, Outlines, 47. *Malthus'* own explanation of "tendency," in his letter at the end of *Senior*, Two Lectures on Population, 1829.

[3] On the inaccuracy of the expression, "geometrical progression," in the present case, see *Moser*, Gesetze des Lebensdauer, 1839, 132.

[4] *Weyland*, Principles of Population and Production, 1816, 25 ff.

elbowed off the bridge of life, over which we pass from birth to the normal death from old age, because there is not room enough on it for all. Hence the frightful mortality among the poorer classes and in childhood. Now it is the absence of a healthy habitation,[5] or of proper clothing, or, in the case of children, of rational superintendence[6] which sows the germs of a thousand diseases; and now the absence of proper care, rest etc., which intensifies these diseases. Every bad harvest is wont, when its consequences are not alleviated by a high and

[5] In Paris the mortality is greater in the *arrondissements* in proportion to their poverty, of which the relative numbers of untaxed dwellings afford a criterion. According to this, between 1822 and 1826,

The Arrondissement	Had a yearly mortality of 1 in every	Locations non imposées.
II,	71 of population.	0.07
III,	67 "	0.11
I,	66 "	0.11
IV,	62 "	0.15
XI,	61 "	0.19
VI,	58 "	0.21
V,	64 "	0.22
VII,	59 "	0.22
X,	49 "	0.23
IX,	50 "	0.31
VIII,	46 "	0.32
XII,	44 "	0.38

Villermé, in the Journal des Econ., Novbr. 1853. The average house-rent in *arrondissement* II, amounted to 605 francs per annum; in III, to 426; in I, to 498; in IX, to 172; in VIII, to 173; in XII, to 148 francs. Doctor Holland divided all the streets in Manchester into three classes, and each class, in turn, into three sub-classes, according to the qualities of the dwellings. The yearly mortality in I a was 1:51; in I b = 1:45; I c = 36; II a = 1:55; II b = 1:38; III c = 1:25. (Report of Inquiry into the State of large Towns and Populous Districts, 1843.)

[6] In Prussia, the Jewish population, between 1822 and 1840, increased 34½ per cent.; the Christians only 28½ per cent.; although among the Jews there was only one marriage a year in every 139, and one birth in every 28; among the Christians, in every 112 and 25. This is accounted for, mainly by the favorable circumstances that Jewish mothers leave their homes seldomer to work outside, and thereby devote more attention, even in the lower classes, to the care of their children.

healthy civilization, to increase mortality. (§ 246, 9). Thus, in Sweden, during the second half of the 18th century, the average yearly mortality was $=1:39$-40. On the other hand, in the bad year $1771 = 1:35.7$; $1772 = 1:26.7$, and in 1773, as an after consequence, $1:19.3$. In this last, although it was a fertile year, there were only 48 births to every 100 deaths.[7] Among nations low down in civilization, the repressive counter tendency may assume a very violent character. How many cases of murder, human sacrifice, and even war, have been occasioned by over-population and famine.

B. Secondly, by preventive counter tendencies.[8] The person who believes himself unable to support children refrains from begetting them. This, we may call one of the most natural of duties. We might even say that the person who begets a child which he knows he is not in a condition to support, is guilty of a grievous sin against civil society, and of a still more grievous one against his poor child. Strange! To beget a child with countless wants, with an immortal soul! That is certainly an act the most pregnant with consequences which any ordinary man can perform in his life; and yet how thoughtlessly it is performed by the majority!

---

[7] *Wappäus*, Allg. Bevölkerungsstatistik, I, 315. In Thurgau, in 1815, the mortality was $=2,143$, in $1817 = 3,440$; in Luzerne, in $1820 = 1,543$, in $1817 = 3,511$. (*Bernouilli*, Populationistik, 219.) And so in London between 1601 and 1800, when the five dearest and five cheapest years of each decade are taken together, the aggregate mortality in the dearest was 1,971,076, in the cheapest, 1,830,835. (*Farr*, in the Statist. Journal, 1846, 163 ff.) The rule did not apply to the time 1801–1820; but it did again to the time 1821–1840 (l. c., 174). Compare *Messance*, Recherches sur la Population, 311; *Roscher*, Kornhandel und Theuerungspolitik, 54 ff. When scarcity continues a longer time, the mortality sometimes decreases on account of the largely diminished number of small children. In Lancashire, the number of deaths during the commercial crisis, 1846–47, was 36 per cent. greater than the average of the three last preceding years; in 1857–8 it was 11.9 per cent. greater. (*Ausland*, 1862, No. 44.)

[8] *Malthus* uses the word "preventive check," while he calls the repressive counter-tendencies "positive." *R. Mohl*, Polizeiwissenschaft, I, 88, speaks of preventive and destructive causes. Anteriorly and subsequently operating causes. (*Knapp*).

This counter-tendency is to be found only in the case of man. Plants and animals yield to the sexual instinct regardless of everything.[9] Where there is no question whatever of having food enough to support children, as is the case with the better-to-do classes, the dread of losing the decencies of life, or of "losing caste," acts as a preventive [10][11] to the found-

---

[9] Hence the infinite productiveness of irrational organisms is limited only by their mutual struggle for the means of support. That which cannot live there dies. "In this case there can be no artificial increase of food, and no prudential restraint from marriage." *(Darwin,* Origin of species, 4 ed. 1866, 73.) Compare *B. Franklin,* Observations concerning the Increase of Mankind, § 21. *Lamennais,* indeed, asserts that no plant and no animal takes away food from any other; that the earth has room for all!

[10] The rule that population tends to extend everywhere as far as the means of subsistence will permit, *Sismondi,* N. Principes, VII, ch. 3, has taken occasion to ridicule, basing himself on the example of the Montmorency family. This family has, notoriously, always lived in superabundance, and is, notwithstanding, on the verge of extinction. *Sismondi* here forgets the relativity of the idea "means of subsistence." Persons occupying an exalted social position not only think that they want more in this respect, but they are wont in forming marriage contracts to use the greatest and frequently exaggerated caution. Hence it is that families of this rank become, relatively speaking, frequently extinct; and, moreover, such a fact is here most frequently taken notice of. *Sadler,* Law of Population, 1830, infers from the frequent extinction of English noble families, that wealth leads to sterility; and, on the other hand, poverty (but not famine!) to prolificacy; and *Doubleday's* (True Law of Population, 12 ff.) suggestion, in explanation hereof, that over-fed animals and over-manured plants are sterile, as ably refuted in the Edinburg Rev., LI. It is there shown that the marriages of the English peers are fruitful above the average; that their extinction is partly due to the fact that the younger sons seldom married, and that hence there is a lack of collateral relations. But, in great part, such extinction is only apparent; since such a family is said to be extinct when only the male stem is extinct. The French nobility, from the 9th to the 11th century, continually increased in number. After this, the succession of females and cases of extinction became more frequent, because the nobility, in order to keep their estates together, began to not desire many sons. *Sismondi,* Hist. des Français, V, 182. Compare *Benoiston de Châteauneuf,* De la Durée des Familes nobles en France, in the proceedings of the Académie des Sciences morales et politiques, II, 792 ff. Besides, between 1611 and 1819, 763 English baronet families became actually extinct, 653 continued to exist, and 139 had been raised to the peerage; an average of from 3 to 4 peer families became extinct yearly. (Statist. Journal, 1869, 224.) There were, about 1569

ing a family, or increasing the numbers of one. Unfortunately, abstinence from the procreation of children may be exercised not only in accordance with the moral law,[12] but also, in contravention of it.[13] There is a necessary connection between human reason and human freedom and the possibility of misusing them. And it is certainly the inevitable fate of man either to place a morally rational check on the sexual impulse, or to be forcibly held within the limits of the means of subsistence, since they cannot be over-stepped by him — through the agency of vice and misery.[14][15]

2,219 Venetian *nobili;* in 1581, 1,843 *(Daru,* VI, 240 ff.); in Addison's time (1705), only 1,500. On the decrease of the Roman patricians, see *Dionys.,* Hal., I, 85; *Tacit.,* Ann., XI, 25; on that of the Spartan knights: *Clinton,* Fasti Hellenici, II, 407 ff.; of the *chrbaren Geschlechter,* at Nürnberg: *Hegel,* N. Stadtchroniken, 1862, 214. Compare, also, Westminster Rev., Oct., 1849.

[11] How, in England, not only many distinguished persons, but also their servants, are kept from marriage in this way, because they are sure of not being able to satisfy the wants of their bachelorhood as fathers of families, see in *Malthus,* P. of P., II, ch. 8. A description of the general misery which would result if all men consumed only that which was physically indispensable, in *Senior,* Outlines, 39.

[12] See *Bastiat's* beautiful words, in which he characterizes the holy ignorance of children, the modesty of young maidens, the severity of public opinion etc., as a law of limitation: (Harmonies, 437 seq.)

[13] Compare *Proudhon,* Contradictions, ch. 13.

[14] That want of employment or of business has rather a preventive tendency, see *Malthus,* Principle of Population, VII, ch. 14.

[15] *Malthus,* P. of P., II, ch. 13. I formerly called this natural law by the name of the investigator who earned the largest share of scientific merit in connection therewith. It cannot, indeed, be said, that he was the first to observe it. Compare even *Machiavelli,* Discorsi (between 1515 and 1518), II, 5. And so *Giovanni Botero* taught that the number of the population depended not so much on the number of *congiungimenti* so much as on the rearing of children. (Ragion di Stato, 1592, VII, 93 ff.) The *virtù generativa degli uomini,* which is always the same, is found face to face with the *virtù nutritiva delle citta.* The former would continue to operate *ad infinitum,* if the latter did not limit it. The larger a city is, the more difficult it is to provide it with the means of subsistence. In the last instance, the slave-sales of Guinea, the cannibalism of the Indians, the robber-system of the Arabians and the Tartars, the migration of nations, crimes, litigation etc., are traced back to the narrowness of the means of subsistence. (Delle Cause della Grandezza delle Città, 1598, Libr. III.) Sir Walter Raleigh (ob. 1618),

SECTION CCXLIII.

OPPONENTS OF MALTHUS.

Of Malthus' opponents, John Stuart Mill has said, that a confused notion of the causes which, at most times and places,

was of opinion that the earth would not only be full but overflowing with human beings were it not that hunger, pestilence, crime, war, abstinence welcome sterility etc. did away with the surplus population. (History of the World, I, ch. 8, 4. Discourse of war: Works, VII, 257 ff.) According to *Child*, Discourse of Trade, 371 ff., 149, the population is always in proportion to the amount of employment.

If England could employ only 100 men while 150 were reared, 50 would have to emigrate or perish; and so, too, conversely, occasional vacancies would soon be filled. Similarly *Davenant*, Works II, 233, 185; who, however, in the practical application of this law of nature, adopts the error of his contemporary, G. King, the statistician, according to whom the population of England would increase to 11,000,000 (II, 176) only after 600 years. *Benjamin Franklin's* Observations Concerning the Increase of Mankind, Peopling of new Countries, etc., 1751, are very good. Franklin here shows that the same tables of mortality do not apply to town and country, nor to old nations and new ones. The nation increases more rapidly in proportion as it is easy to contract marriage. Hence the increase is smallest in luxurious cities and thickly populated countries. Other circumstances, being equal, hunting nations require the largest quantity of land for the purpose of subsistence, and industrial nations least. In Europe, there was a marriage in every 100 of the population per annum; in America, on every 50; 4 children to a marriage in the former, and 8 in the latter.

Population diminishes as a consequence of subjugation, bad government, the introduction of slavery, loss of territory, loss of trade and food. He who promotes the opposite advantages may well be called the "father of his country." Further, *D. Hume*, Of the Populousness of the Ancient Nations: Discourses No. 10. *Per contra*, *Wallace*, On the Numbers of Mankind in Ancient and Modern Times, in which the superior populousness of antiquity is maintained, 1753. *Wallace* relied chiefly on the more equable distribution of land, and the smaller luxury of the ancient nations. *Herbert*, Essai sur le Police des Grains (1755), 319 ff. Les Intérêts de la France mal entendus, par un Citoyen (Amsterd., 1757), I, 197.

Steuart threw light especially on the connection between mortality and the number of marriages (Principles, I, 13); and he claims, with the utmost confidence; that only the want of the means of subsistence, using the expression in its broadest sense (I, 15), can put a limit to the increase of population

keep the actual increase of mankind so far behind their capacity for increase, has every now and then given birth to some ephemeral theory, speedily forgotten; as if the law of the increase of population were a different one under different circumstances, and as if the fecundity of the human species,

---

(I, 14). He calls wrongful procreation *(falsche Zeugung)* the chief cause of pauperism (II, 1), and his views on public charity have a strong Malthusian complexion (I, 14). Compare further *A. Young*, Political Arithmetics (1774), I, ch. 7. *Townsend*, Dissertation on the Poor Laws (1786), makes a happy use of the example of the Island of Juan Fernandez, in which a colony of goats was developed, first alone, and afterwards in a struggle with a colony of dogs, to illustrate the laws of the development of population as limited by the supply of food. Compare the same author's Journey through Spain, II, 8 seq.; 358 ff., III, 107. *G. M. Ortes*, Reflessioni sulla Populazione, delle Nazione per rapporto all'Economia nazionale, 1790, ascribes geometrical progression to the increase of population (cap. 1) precisely as in the case of other animals; only, in the case of the latter, a limit is put to their increase by *forza*, and in the case of man, by *ragione*. When the population of a country has attained its proper development, celibacy is as necessary in order to keep it so as marriage. Otherwise the door would be opened to extreme pauperism, to the debauchery of the "venus vaga," to eunuchism and polygamy (4). Strangely enough, *Ortes* asserts that no people are richer per capita than any other. The distribution of wealth among the apparently richer, operates to make individuals heap wealth together in greater quantities (8).

Malthus himself wrote his classical work under the influence of a very intelligible reaction (1st ed., 1798; 2d ed., 1803). For a whole generation, the European public had had no other view broached but that the tree of human kind might keep on growing even until it reached the heavens, if care were only taken to manure the ground, to water the roots and prune the branches according to the latest world-improving recipes. *Malthus*, in opposition thereto, called attention to the limits placed by nature to the number of mankind. He demonstrated that it was not merely arbitrary laws which opposed the Utopian happiness of all, but in part the niggardliness of nature; and in greater part the passions and sins of men themselves. If he sometimes described the limits as narrower than they really are, and if an occasional coarse expression escaped him, we need not wonder. His polemic was well founded, and he was at the time still a young man (born 1766, ob. 1834). He modified much in the later editions of his work. For instance, he stopped the unsavory sentence in which he says that a man born into the world already occupied, whose family cannot support him, and whose labor society does not need, has not the smallest right to demand the smallest particle of food, and is really superfluous in the world; that there is no place for him at

by direct divine decree, was in keeping with the wants of society for the time being.[1]

The majority of such theories are based on the proof that Malthus' description of one stage of civilization is not true of another, although the great discoverer, who, with his admirable many-sidedness, had investigated the law of population in and throughout all the stages of civilization, had, as a rule, himself given due weight to all of this. The objection of unwarranted generalization applies to Malthus much less than to the majority of his opponents. Since, for instance, in young colonies, even the natural forces, which are in themselves limited or exhaustible, afford a wide field of operation for a long time; many American writers have supposed that labor alone was the source of wealth, and that, to say the least, wealth should increase in the same ratio as mankind; and even in a still greater ratio, since the division of labor grows easier as population increases in density.[2] But here it is for-

---

the great banquet of nature; that nature bids him go hence and does not hesitate herself to execute the command. *P. Leroux* in a small pamphlet in answer to *Malthus*, quotes this sentence at least forty times. Moreover, *Möser*, who certainly is not considered a misanthrope, was not only acquainted with the Malthusian law, but develops it in words, and with consequences which strongly recall the very words which raised such a storm against *Malthus*. Compare Patr. Phant. I, 42: II, 1; IV, 15 (against vaccination); V, 26.

The opinions of political economists in our own day are, as might be expected, divided on some of Malthus' expressions and on his practical counsels. He has indeed but few such one-sided followers as *Th. Chalmers*, On Political Economy in Connexion with the moral State and moral Prospects of Society, 1832. Malthus' fundamental views, however, are truly scientific. ($K\tau\tilde{\eta}\mu\alpha$ $\dot{\epsilon}\varsigma$ $\dot{\alpha}\epsilon\iota$!) Compare *Baudrillart*, Manuel, 424 seq., and *A Walker*, Science of Wealth, who strangely enough (452) opposes Malthus, and yet is (458) virtually of the same opinion. Even the better class of socialists base themselves on the same view, without, however, thanking Malthus for it. Thus for instance, *K. Marlo*, System der Weltökonomie (1848, 52), passim. For an excellent history of the theory of population, see *R. Mohl*, Gesch. und Literatur der Staatswissenschaften, III, 409 ff. (1858).

[1] *J. S. Mill*, Principles I, ch. 10.

[2] *Everett*, New ideas on population, with remarks on the theories of Malthus and Goodwin, 1823. Similarly *Carey*, Principles of Social Science, I,

gotten that in every instance of economic production, there are many factors engaged, each one of which can take the place of another only up to a certain point. There are others, especially Grahame and Carey,[3] who allude to the possibility of emigration, which is still so far from being exhausted. But Malthus had nothing to say of the impossibility of emigration. He spoke only of the great difficulties in its way. (III. ch. 4.) There are many writers who would wish simply to ship emigrants off, like a great many doctors who send their patients away to die! (§ 259 ff.) When Sadler says that human prolificacy, circumstances remaining the same, is inversely as the density of population, he uses, to say the least, a very inaccurate mode of expression.[4] The grain of truth

---

88 ff., who, with a "natural philosophical" generalization, shows that the more the matter existing on the earth takes the form of men, the greater becomes the power of the latter to give direction to natural forces with an ever accelerated movement. So also *Fontenay*, in the Journal des Economistes, Oct., 1850, says: *un nombre de travailleurs doublé produit plus du double et ne consomme pas le double de ce que produisaient et consommaient les travailleurs de l'époque précédente*. Even *Bastiat* inclines to the same over-estimation of one factor of production. He promises in the introduction to his Harmonies économiques to prove the proposition: *toutes choses égales d'ailleurs, la densité croissante de population équivaut à une facilité croissante de production*. (Absolutely it is true, but whether relatively, quaere.)

[3] *Grahame*, Inquiry into the Principle of Population, 1816; *Carey*, Rate of Wages, 236 ff.

[4] Varies inversely as their numbers: *M. Th. Sadler*, The Law of Population, a treatise in Disproof of the Superfecundity of human Beings, and developing the real Principles of their Increase, III, 1830. There were, for instance —

	Inhabitants per English sq. mile	Number of children to a marriage
The Cape	1	5.48
The United States	4	5.22
Russia in Europe	23	4.94
Denmark	73	4.89
Prussia	100	4.70
France	150	4.22
England	160	3.66

hidden in this assertion does certainly not come from Gray's theory, that in the higher stages of civilization, the better living usual is a hinderance to the increase of population, and that the prevailing influence of large cities increases mortality;[5] but from influences, or, to speak more correctly, from free human considerations, on which no one has thrown so much light as Malthus. And indeed, where is the man who has better understood or more warmly recommended the "aristocratic" impulse which should, in well ordered civil society, hold the sexual instinct in equilibrium?[6] Malthus himself pleasantly derides his opponents, who, to explain how the same rifle, charged with the same powder and provided with the same ball, produces an effect varying with the nature of the object at which it is fired, prefer, instead of calculating the force of resistance of the latter, to take refuge in a mysterious faculty by virtue of which the powder has a different explosive force, according to the greater or less resistance the ball meets when it strikes.[7] The peculiarity of Godwin's polemics may be inferred from the fact that he considered it very doubtful

---

Most of these figures are very uncertain; and even if they were true, they would afford a very bad proof of his assertion. Besides, *Sadler* was one of those extreme tories who resorted almost to Jacobin measures in opposition to the reforms advocated by Huskisson, Peel and Wellington. Like Sadler, *A. Guillard*, Elements de Statistique humaine ou Démographie comparée, 1855. But, for instance, in Saxony, population has for a long time increased most rapidly, in those places where it is already densest. Compare *Engel*, loc. cit. The five German kingdoms and Mecklenburg-Strelitz hold the same relative rank, on a ten-year average, in relation to the number of births that they do to density of population. *v. Vichbahn*, Statistik des Z. V., II, 321 seq.)

[5] *Gray*, The Happiness of States, or an Inquiry concerning Population, 1875. *Weyland*, Principles of Population and Production, 1816, had already ascribed to industry in itself a tendency to make the increase of Population less rapid!

[6] Compare *Rossi*, Cours d' Economie politique, I, 303 ff.

[7] *Malthus*, Principle of Population, V, ch. 3. Thus *J. B. Say* asks those population-mystics: if in thickly populated countries the power of procreation diminishes of itself, how comes it that even here the extraordinay voids made by pestilence etc. are so rapidly filled up?

whether the population of England had increased during the four preceding generations; and that he traces the increase of the population of the United States to the influence of emigration almost exclusively, and allows the desertion of whole English regiments in 1812 ff. to play a part in accounting for that increase.[8]

Malthus has been accused of rejoicing over the evils which are wont to decimate surplus population; but the same charge might be brought against those physicians who trace the diseases back to the causes that produce them. He has also been branded as the enemy of the lower classes, spite of the fact that he is the very first who took a scientific interest in their prosperity.[9] As John Stuart Mill has said, the idea that all human progress must at last end in misery was so far from Malthus' mind, that it can be thoroughly combated only by carrying Malthus' principles into practice.[10]

---

[8] *Godwin*, Inquiry concerning the Power of Increase in the Numbers of Mankind, III, 1821; III, ch. IV. Compare the same socialistic writer's essay: Inquiry concerning public Justice (II, 1793), which in part provoked Malthus' book. *David Booth* (in Godwin's first book) had the misfortune to ridicule Malthus by comparing his law with the law of gravitation, which he said did not freely operate in nature and was undemonstrable in space void of air! From a better point of view, Bastiat says of Malthus' traducers, that they might as well blame Newton when they were injured by a fall.

[9] Principle of Population, III, ch. 13. His moral severity in other respects is apparent especially in IV, ch. 13, towards the end.

[10] Every good family takes care of their children even before their birth. How far from practical is the view that the means of subsistence come as a matter of course, provided only that men are here before them!

CHAPTER II.

HISTORY OF POPULATION.

SECTION CCXLIV.

HISTORY OF POPULATION.—UNCIVILIZED TIMES.

In the case of those wild tribes which can only use the forces of nature by way of occupation, the small extent of the field of food is filled up by even a very sparse population. And the principal means by which population is there limited are the following: the overburthening and ill treatment of the women,[1] by which the simultaneous rearing of several small children is rendered impossible;[2] the inordinately long time

---

[1] In New Holland they are beaten by their husbands even on the day of their confinement. Their heads are sometimes covered with countless scars. *Collins* says that for mere pity one might wish a young woman there death rather than marriage. (Account of N. S. Wales, 560 ff.) South American Indian women actually kill their daughters, with a view of improving the condition of women. (*Azara*, Reisen in S. Amerika, II, 63.) How the women among the aboriginal inhabitants of North America were oppressed is best illustrated by the absence of ornaments among the women, while the men were very gaudily decked, and carried small hand-mirrors with them. (*Prinz Neuwied*, N. A. Reise, II, 108 seq.) The early decay of female beauty among all barbarous nations is related to the ill-treatment they receive.

[2] The custom of killing one of twins immediately after birth or of burying a child at the breast with its mother, prevails extensively among savage nations. On New Holland, see *Collins*, 362; on North America, Lettres édifi-. antes, IX, 140; on the Hottentots, *Kolb*, I, 144.

that children are kept at the breast;³ the wide-spread practice of abortion;⁴ numerous cases of murder, especially of the old and weak;⁵ everlasting war carried on by hunting nations to extend their hunting territory, found in conjunction with cannibalism in many tribes.⁶ Besides, nations of hunters are frequently decimated by famine and pestilence, the latter

³ In many Indian tribes, children are kept at the breast until their fifth year. *(Klemm,* Kulturgeschichte I, 236; II, 85.) Among the Greenlanders, until the third or fourth year *(Klemm,* I, 208); among the Laplanders and Tonguses, likewise *(Klemm,* III, 57); among the Mongols and Kalmucks, longer yet. *(Klemm,* III, 171.)

⁴ The New Hollanders have a special word to express the killing of the fœtus by pressure. *(Collins.)* Among certain of the Brazilian tribes, this is performed by every woman until her 30th year; and in many more the custom prevails for a woman when she becomes pregnant to fast, or to be frequently bled. *(Spix und Martius,* Reise, I, 261.) Compare *Azara.*, II, 79.

⁵ On the Bushmen, see *Barrow,* Journey in Africa, 379 ff.; on the Hottentots, among whom even the wealthy aged are killed by exposure, see *Kolb,* Caput bonæ Spei, 1719, I, 321; on the Scandinavian, old Germanans, Wendes, Prussians, *Grimm,* D. Rechtsalterthümer, 486 ff.; on the most ancient Romans, *Cicero,* pro Rosc. Amer, 35, and Festus v. Depontani, Sexagenarios: on Ceos, *Strabo,* X, 486; on the ancient Indians, *Herodot.*, III, 38, 99; on the Massagetes, *Herodot.*, I, 216; on the Caspians, *Strabo,* XI, 517, 520. Touching picture of an old man abandoned in the desert, unable to follow his tribe compelled to emigrate for want of food: *Catlin,* N. American Indians, I, 216 ff. We here see how the killing of helpless old people may be considered a blessing among many nations. Death is also sometimes desired by reason of superstition. For instance, the Figians think that after death they will continue to live of the same age as that at which they died. *(Williams,* Figi and the Figians, I, 183.) The Germans who died of disease did not get to Walhalla! *(W. Wackernagel,* Kl. Schriften, I, 16.)

⁶ On the frightful cannibalism practiced on the upper Nile, see *Schweinfurth* in *Petermann's* geogr. Mettheilungen, IV, 138, seq. Australian women seldom outlive their 30th year. *Lubbock,* Prehistoric Times, 449. Many are eaten by the men as soon as they begin to get old. (Transactions of the Ethnolog. Society, New Series, III, 248.) A chief of Figi-Islands who died recently had eaten 872 men in his life-time. *Lawry,* Visit to the Friendly and Fejee Islands, 1850. Even the more highly civtilzed Mexicans had preserved this abomination. According to *Gomara,* Cronica de la N. Espana, 229, there were here from 20,060 to 25,000 human sacrifices a year; according to *Torquemada,* Indiana, VII, 21, even 20,000 children a year. *B. Diaz,* on the other hand, puts the number down at 2,500 only. Compare *Klemm,* Kulturgeschichte, V, 103, 207, 216.

generally a consequence of never-ending alternation between gluttony and famine.[1]

Most negro nations live in such a state of legal insecurity that it is impossible for a higher civilization with its attendant increase of the means of subsistence to take root among them. At the same time, their sexual impulses are very strong.[8] Here the slave trade constituted the chief preventive of overpopulation. If this traffic were suppressed simply and no care taken through the instrumentality of commerce and of missions to improve the moral and economical condition of the negroes, the only probable but questionable gain would be that the prisoners made in the numberless wars generated by famine would be murdered instead of being sold.

Nomadic races, with their universal chivalry, are wont to treat their women well enough to enable them bear children without any great hardship.[9] But the mere use of natural pasturage can never be carried to great intensity. The transition to agriculture with its greater yield of food but with the diminished freedom by which it is accompanied is a thing to which these warlike men are so averse that it directs the surplus population by the way of emigration into neighboring civilized countries, where they either obtain victory, booty and supremacy, or are rapidly subjugated. Such mi-

---

[1] The usual coldness, so much spoken of, of the Indians, seems to have an economic rather than a physiological cause. At least, it has also been observed among the Hottentots. (*Levaillant*, Voyage, I, 12 seq.), and under favorable economic conditions the Indians have sometimes increased very rapidly. (Lettres édifiantes, VIII, 243.) Whether the practice in vogue among the Botocuds to carry the organ of generation continually in a rather narrow envelope, or that among the Patachos of lacing the foreskin with the tendrils of a plant, is not a "preventive check," quære. Compare *Prinz Neuwied*, Bras. Reise, II, 10; I, 226.

[8] On the gold coast, people become fathers in their 12th year even, and mothers at 10. (*Ritter*, Erdkunde, I, 313.) In the whole of the Soudan the climate is so exciting that the intercourse of the sexes is said to be a "physical necessity," and an unmarried man of eighteen is universally despised. But, indeed, the individual is little valued in Africa, on account of the great prolificacy of the African race. (*Ritter*, I, 385.)

[9] *Herodot.*, IV, 26.

grations are a standing chapter in the history of all Asiatic kingdoms; they for a long time disturb declining civilized states, finally conquering them, and begin the same cycle in the new kingdom.[10] Where nomadic races see themselves cut off from such migrations their marriages are wont to be unfruitful.[11]

SECTION CCXLV.

INFLUENCE OF A COMMUNITY OF WOMEN AND POLYGAMY.

Most barbarous nations live very unchaste;[1] so that, as Tacitus observes, the ancient Germans were a brilliant exception to the rule.[2] Vices of unchastity always limit the other-

---

[10] Compare *Machiavelli*, at the beginning of his Istoria Fiorentina. The migration of the Germani is accounted for simply by the family and marriage relations of the Germans, which necessarily favored prolificacy: *Severa matrimonia .... singulis uxoribus contenti sunt .... septae pudicitia .... paucissima adulteria .... publicatae pudicitiae nulla venia .... nemo vitia ridet .... numerum liberorum finire, flagitium habetur ... sua quemque mater uberibus alit .... sera juvenum Venus eoque inexhausta pubertas .... quanto plus propinquorum, tanto gratiosior senectus. Tacit.*, Germ., 14. Entirely similar in character were the migrations of the Normans, which lasted just as long as the resistance to the countries they would invade, seemed to them a matter of less difficulty than the transition to a higher civilization in their own country. *Malthus* has corrected the extravagant notions concerning the former density of population in the North — the *vagina nationum*, according to Jornandes! *(Malthus,* I, ch. 6.) Compare, however, *Friedrich M.*, in Antimachiavel, ch. 21, and the later view: Ouevres, IX, 196.

[11] Among the Bedouins even three children are considered a large family; and they even complain of that number. *(Burckhardt.)*

[1] Impurity of the Kamtschatdales, bordering on a community of women. *(Klemm,* Kulturgeschichte, I, 287 ff., 350 ff.; II, 206, 297 seq.) On Lapland, see *Klemm*, III, 55. In their purely nomadic period, even the Getes, afterwards remarkable for their noble character *(Horat.,* Carm., III, 24), have had very loose relations of the sexes. *(Menander,* in *Strabo,* VII, 297.)

[2] Very unlike the Celts: *Strabo,* IV, 199. But the Germans even at the time when the compensation-system alone prevailed, imposed a disgraceful death on the *corpore infames. (Tacit.,* Germ., 12.) In keeping with this purity of the Germans was the deep gravity and the genuine heartiness of their ancient nuptial ceremonies. *(Tacit.,* Germ., 18.) Similarly, in England

wise natural increase of population. Premature enjoyment exhausts the sources of fruitfulness in the case of many.[3] The life of the child conceived in sin is generally little valued by its parents. Hence the numerous instances of exposure and infanticide.[4] We have already seen how closely, psychologically speaking, a community of goods is allied to a community of women. (§ 85.) And, indeed, in the lower stages of civilization, we find as close an approximation to the latter as to the former; and it is difficult to believe that, among men living in a state of nudity, the marriage of one man to one woman could properly exist.[5] But it is as little possible to reconcile

---

throughout the middle ages. (*Lappenberg*, Engl., Gesch. I, 596.) Great moral severity of the Scandinavians (*Weinhold*, Altnord. Leben, 255), so that the gratification of the sexual appetite outside of marriage was punishable with death. (*Adam Brem.*, IV, 6, 21.)

[3] Abuse of young girls in New Holland (*Collins*, 563); among the American aborigines (*Charlevoix*, Histoire de la N. France, III, 304; Lettres édifiantes, VII, 20 ff.); among the negroes (*Buffon*, Histoire naturelle de l' Homme, VI, 255).

[4] Infanticide in Kamtschatka, *Klemm*, I, 349.

[5] In most mythical histories, the institutions of property and of marriage are ascribed to the same name (Menes Cecrops, the Athenian Thesmophories.) Among the Indian tribes of Terra Firma, the exchange of wives and the *jus primæ noctis* of the chiefs are very common. *Depons* Voyage, I, 304, ff.) In North America, the Indians are very eager to rent out their wives for a glass of brandy. (*Prinz Neuwied*, N. A. Reise, I, 572 seq.) Compare *Lewis* and *Clarke*, Travels to the Source of the Missouri and the Pacific Ocean, 1804-1806. Almost always on entering a higher age-class it is one the principal conditions to leave one's wife for a time to the more distinguished. On feast days, prayer days etc., the women give themselves publicly up to vice; and this can be commuted only by a gift. (*Prinz Nenwied*, I, 129 ff., 272.) Community of women in California. *Bagert*, Nachrichten von der Halbinsel C. 1772.) In many of the South Sea Islands, the youth of the higher classes were wont to form themselves into so-called *arreyo-societies*, the object of which was the most unlimited intercourse of the sexes (a pair being united generally only from 2 to 3 days), and the murder of the new born children. The girls principally were murdered, and hence the missionaries at Otaheite (New Cytheria) found only $\frac{1}{4}$ as many women as men. *Chaque femme semble être la femme de tous les hommes chaque homme le mari de toutes les femmes.* (*Marchand*, I, 122.) The many governing queens here are characteristic. Compare *Forster*, Reise II, 100, 128; *Kotzebue*, Reise,

a community of women with density of population as great national wealth with a community of goods. Any one acquainted with the condition and capacities of new born children knows that the weak little flame easily goes out when not nursed by family care.[6]
Polygamy also is a hinderance to the increase of population. Abstract physiology must, indeed, admit that a man may, even without any danger to his health, generate more children

III, 119; European Magazine, June, 1806; *Reybaud*, Voyages, et marines, 128, and the quotations in *Klemm*, Kulturgesch., IV, 307.

Similar customs are found among the nomads. The Bedouins dissolve their marriages so easily that a man forty-five years old had 50 wives; family secrets are a thing unknown there. *(Burckhardt*, Notes on the Bedouins, 64; Travels app. II, 448; *Ritter*, Erdkunde, XII, 205, 211, 983.) On the Libyans, see *Herodot.*, IV, 168, 172, 186, 180: on the Massagetes, *Herodot.*, I, 216; on the Taprobanes, *Diod.*, II, 58; on the Troglodytes, *Pomp, Mella.*, I, 8, *Agatharch*, 30. Community of women among the ancient Britons, *Caesar*, B. G. V, 14 seq.; also among the naked, tatooed Caledonians, *Dio Cass.*, LXXVI, 12; probably also among the cannibal Irish. *Strabo*, IV, 201. Great laxity of the marriage tie in Moelmud's laws of Wales, *(Palgrave*, Rise and Progress of the English Commonwealth, I, 458 ff.) in which country a species of tenure in common of land and servants was customary. (*Wachsmuth*, Europ. Sittengesch. II, 225.) In Russia, in very ancient times, only the Polanes had real marriages. *(Nestor v. Schlözer*, I, 125 seq.) Something very analogous even among the Spartans: same education for boys and girls, ad mittance for men to the female gymnasiums; marriage in the form of an abduction, and afterwards fornication. *(Xenoph.*, De rep. Laced. I, 6: *Plutarch*, Lycurg. 15.) Adultery tolerated by law in countless cases. *(Xenoph.*, II, 7 ff.; *St. John*, The Hellenes, I, 394.) History of the origin of the so-called Parthenix; *Strabo*, VI, 279. *(Supra*, § 83.) The custom which prevails among so many barbarous nations to designate one's progeny by the name of the mother, *Sanchoniathan* traces to the licentiousness of women. (p. 16, Orell.) Traces of this also in Egypt: *Schmidt*, Papyrusurkunden, 321 ff. Avunculus means little grand-father. Many proofs which *Peschel*, Völkerkunde, 243 seq. explains otherwise, but which seem to me to point to an original community of wives.

[6] The relation existing between the so-called organization of labor (§ 82) and a community of wealth is repeated in the relation of a community of wives to the situation in Dahomey, where every man has to purchase his wife from the king. *Gumprecht*, Afrika, 196. Similarly among the Incas: *Prescott*, Hist. of Peru, I, 159. Even the sale of wives is a step in advance as compared with a community of wives (§ 67 seq).

SEC. CCXLV.] POPULATION—UNCIVILIZED TIMES. 301

than a woman can bear.[7] But, in reality, the simultaneous enjoyment of several women leads to excess and early exhaustion;[8] and if one of them is married after the other, the older who might still bear children for a long time are neglected by the man.[9] Monogamy is, doubtless, the Creator's law, since only in monogamous countries can we expect to find the intimate union of family life, the beauties of social intercourse and free citizenship.[10] "God made them male and female."[11] And yet in all countries with which we are statistically acquainted, there is a somewhat larger number of boys than of girls born;[12] but this excess is removed by the time

---

[7] It is said that a German prince of the 18th century had 352 natural children. (*Dohm*, Denkwürdigkeiten, IV, 67.) Feth Ali, shah of Persia, had made 49 of his own sons provincial governors, and he had besides 140 daughters. (*Ker Porter*, II, 508.)

[8] Turkish married men are frequently impotent at the age of 30. (*Volney*, Voyage dans la Turquie, II, 445.) Similarly in Arabia. (*Niebuhr*, Beschreibung, 74.) The use of aphrodisiac means very wide spread in the East. According to *Niebuhr* (76), monogamous marriages produced absolutely more children than polygamous. Compare *G. Botero*, Ragion di Stato, VIII, 93 ff.; *Montesquieu*, Lettres Persannes, N., 114; *Süssmilch*, Göttl. Ordnung, I, Kap., 11. On the other hand, *Th. L. Lau*, Aufrichtiger Vorschlag von .... Einrichtung der Intraden (1719), 6, recommends the allowing of polygamy as a means of increasing population.

[9] Rehoboam had 18 wives and 60 concubines, and only 88 children (II Chron., 11, 21); that is not much more than one child by each.

[10] The high esteem for woman requisite to true love seems to be almost irreconcilable with polygamy. The wife stands to the husband in the relation of a mistress; and, in reference to the latter, fidelity has scarcely any meaning. The husband also has no confidence in his wife; and hence the seclusion of the harem. But the domestic tyrant is easily made the slave of a higher power. And what becomes of fraternal love with the half-brother feeling of children of different mothers?

[11] Genesis 1, 27; 5, 12; 7, 13.

[12] Compare *J. Graunt*, Natural and Political Observations on the Bills of Mortality (1662). During the course of the 19th century, according to averages made from long series of years, there were, for every 1,000 girls born alive in Lombardy, 1,070 boys; in Bohemia, 1,062; in France, 1,058; in Holland, 1,057; in Saxony, 1,056; in Belgium, 1,052; in England, 1,050; in Prussia, 1,048. On the whole, the ratio in 70,000,000 children born alive was as 100 : 105.83. The excess of males over females in bastards is smaller than

that puberty sets in, by reason of the greater mortality of boys. Only extraordinary conditions which thin the ranks of males, such as war and emigration, leave a preponderance of the number of women.[13] Hence, among barbarous nations, who live in everlasting strife (§§ 67, 70), polygamy is very generally established. Men are seldom deterred therefrom by a solicitude concerning what they shall eat, since the women are treated as slaves, and rather support the men than are supported by them.[14] But in the civilized countries of the east, the polygamy of the great may actually lead to the compulsory singleness of many of the lower classes, as a species of compensation.[15] The monstrous institution of eunuchism,

---

in the case of legitimate children, in towns than in the country. Everything considered, the number of boys born seems to be greater than the number of girls in proportion as the father is in advance of his wife in years. Compare *Sadler*, Law of Population, II, 343. *Hofacker*, Ueber die Eigenschaften die sich vererben, 51 ff. *Wappäus*, Allg. Bevölkerungstatistik, II, 151, 160 ff., 306 ff. *Per contra*, we have *Legoyt's* supposition that the number of boys born is greater in proportion as the parents are more nearly of an age: Statistique comparée, 500.

[13] According to the censuses between 1856 and 1861, there are for every 1,000 men in Belgium 994 women; in Austria, 1,004; in Prussia, 1,004; in France, 1,001; in England, 1,039; in Holland, 1,038. The majority of the latter seems to have diminished everywhere the greater the distance in time from the most recent great wars; and to belong only to those age-classes which were coeval with those wars. (Preuss. amtliche Tabellen für 1849, I, 292.) In the United States there were, 1800–1844, for every 1,000 women, 1,033–1,050 men; mainly accounted for by large immigration. Between 1819 and 1855 the immigration was 2,713,391 men and 1,720,305 women. (*W. Bromwell*, History of Immigration to the United States, New York, 1856. In Switzerland, among the population belonging to the cantons, there were for every 1,000 men, 1,038 women; among the foreign Swiss, 970; among foreigners, 650. (*Bernouilli*, Populationistik, 31.) Compare *Horn*, loc. cit., I, 105 ff., who supposes a natural principle of equilibrium: the greater the preponderance of the number of women, the more does it happen that only the younger women are married; the greater consequently the difference between the ages of the married couple, and the more probable the birth of boys, and *vice versa*. (115 ff.)

[14] Compare *Catlin*, N. American Indians, I, 118 ff. Even Strabo believed that among the Median mountaineers each man had five wives! (XI, 526.)

[15] Concerning Solomon's 700 wives and 300 concubines, see I Kings, 11,

which has existed time out of mind in the east, is a consequence of this condition of things as well as of the natural jealousy of the harem.[16]

SECTION CCXLVI.

HISTORY OF POPULATION—IN HIGHLY CIVILIZED TIMES.

The conditions of population among mature and flourishing nations is characterized by this, that the moral and rational preventive tendencies counter to over-population decidedly preponderate. Here so much value is attached to the life, and

---

3; according to the Canticle of Canticles, only 60 wives and 80 concubines. According to *Mirkhond* and *Khondemir*, there was in the place in which the Sassand shah resided, 3,000 women of the harem and 12,000 female slaves. Polygamy among the latter class is seldom possible or thought of. Of 2,800 Moslems in Bombay, only 100 lived in polygamy, and only 5 had three wives each. (*Ritter*, Erdkunde, 1088.) I lay no weight here on the assertion so frequently repeated of travelers in the east, that more girls than boys are born there; for the reason that there is there no real statistics, and that the infidel travelers can be permitted few glimpses into the secrecy of family life. *Lady Sheil* indeed assures us that in Persia itself the opinion prevails that there are a great many more women than men. Glimpses of Life and Manners in Persia, 1855. Similar pretense among the Mormons.

[16] We find, even on Egyptian temples, pictures representing the castration of prisoners. *Franck*, in the Mémoires sur l'Egypte, IV, 126. On Babylon, see *Hellanicus*, apud. Donat. ad Terent. Eunuch., I, 2, 87. This province, besides Assyria (the ancient seat of sultan glory), delivered 500 castrated boys per annum to the king of Persia. (*Herodot.*, III, 92.) Of the califs, Soliman is said to be the first (at the beginning of the 8th century) who had his harem superintended by eunuchs; a very sensual master who frequently changed his wives. (*Reiske Z. Abulfeda*, I, 109 ff.; *Weil*, Gesch. der Kalifen, I, 573.) At an audience which the calif Moktadir gave to a Byzantine ambassador, there appeared 4,000 white and 3,000 black eunuchs. (*Rehm*, Gesch. des Mittelalters, I, 2, 32.) In the harems of the present Persian persons of rank, there are usually from 6 to 8 eunuchs. *Rosenmüller*, Altes und Neues Morgenland, IV, 290. In Upper Egypt, the castration of handsome boys by monks (!) is a regular trade. About 2 per cent. die in consequence of the operation, the others rise in consequence in price from 200–300 to 1,000 piasters. (*Ritter*, Erdkunde, I, 548.) In the Frankish middle age, the merchants of Verdun castrated persons to sell them in Spain. Compare *Liutprand*, Hist., VI, 3, in *Muratori*, Script. Rerum Ital., II, 1, 470.

to the healthy and comfortable life of human beings already
in existence that even the majority of the lower classes take
care to bring no more children into the world than can be
properly supported, nor to bring them into being in advance of
food. Here, too, mortality is relatively small, which when
population is stationary is found in connection with a higher
average duration of human life.[1] While among savage and

---

[1] The so-called *Populationistikers* are wont to distinguish between the average and probable duration of life *(vie moyenne — vie probable);* and understand by the former the number of years which, on an average, have been accorded to one deceased; by the latter, the number of years after the expiration of which one-half of a given number of human beings have disappeared. If x deceased persons have lived an aggregate of s years, their average duration of life $= \frac{s}{x}$ In the case of a whole people, indeed, even the many-years' average of the duration of life of those deceased expresses the true average duration of life only when (a rare case) the aggregate population remains stationary. For, when the population is increasiug, the average age of the deceased is smaller than the average duration of life, and, when population is decreasing, larger. In the saddest case of all, when there are no births whatever, and the nation is gradually dying out, there would be an increase from year to year of the average age. In all such cases, strictly speaking, only the actual observation and following up of those born, until they die, can afford a safe result. This is *Hermann's* method, introduced in to Bavaria since 1835. Compare the XIII. and XVII. numbers of the official Bavarian statistics with *G. Mayer's* criticism in *Hildebrand's* Jahrbüchern, 1867, I. And indeed *Hopf*, Preuss. Statist. Zeitschr., says that a complete table of mortality can be made, according to the best method, only after centuries of observation.

Compare *Kopf*, in the 3d edition of *Kolb's* Handbuch der Statistik, and the solid works of *G. F. Knapp*, Ueber die Ermittelung der Sterblichkeit (1868) and Die Sterblichkeit in Sachsen (1869). *Price's* mode of calculation of which *Deparcieux* is the real author, which divides the number of the living by the arithmetical mean of the number of births and deaths is not only inaccurate *(Meyer,* loc. cit., 43 ff.) but erroneous in principle, since it allows two countries of equal population to be the same, the one of which has 120,000 births and a mortality of 80,000, and the other, on the contrary, 80,000 births and a mortality of 120,000. *Engel* recommends as the measure of real vitality the ratio between the "living years" and the "dead years," meaning by the former the sum of the years which those still living have lived through, and by the latter the sum of the years lived through by those who have died within a given period. (Preuss. Statist.Zeitschr., 1861, 348 ff.) But the inference which may be drawn from a high or a low average of life

SEC. CCXLVI.] POPULATION — CIVILIZED TIMES. 305

semi-savage nations, travelers are struck by no phenomenon as much as by the total absence of old men,[2] in most European nations the average duration of life has, during the last centuries, seemed to noticeably increase. In France, for instance, between 1771 and 1780, on a population of 29,000,000 at most, there were as many deaths as on 35,000,000 between 1844 and 1853.[3] In Sweden, the classic land of statistics relating to population, mortality from 1749 to 1855 had diminished 0.107 per cent. per annum.[4][5]

---

is altogether ambiguous. A high average may as well be produced by a great mortality among children as by a favorable mortality among those of mature age; and a low average as well by a relatively small number of births as by a relatively short duration of life. *(Meyer,* loc. cit., 23, 24.)

[2] On the aborigines of America, see Lettres édifiantes, VII, 317 ff. *Cook,* Third Voyage, III, ch. 2. *La Pérouse,* Voyage, ch. 9. *Robertson,* Hist. of America B., IV. *Raynal,* Histoire des Indes L., XV. On the African negroes: *M. Park,* ch. 1. They are said to manifest the symptoms of old age at 40, and very seldom to live to be over 55 or 60 years of age.

[3] *Necker,* De l'Administration des Finances de la France, 1784, I, 205 ff., gives for 1771–80 the average number of births, per annum, 940,935; of deaths, 818,391; the population at 24,229,000. *Legoyt,* Statist. Comp., estimates the last, in 1784, at at least 26,748,843, probably even at 28,718,000. During the period, 1844–53, 35,000,000 to 36,000,000 Frenchmen had only about as many births (956,317) and deaths (815,723) as a much smaller population before the Revolution — the latter numbers, according to official estimation, omitting the still-born — which *Necker* also scarcely took into consideration. *C'est la différence entre un peuple de prolétaires et une nation, dont les deux tiers jouissent des bienfaits de la propriété.* *(Moreau de Jonnès.)* In France, there was one death, in 1784, on every 30 living; in 1801, on every 35.8 living; in 1834–5, on every 38 living; in 1844, on every 39.9 living; in 1855–57 (average), on every 41.1 living; in 1860–65 (average), on every 43.7 living. It is also probable, that the average duration of life in France increased from the fact that, from 1800 to 1807, the number of persons subject to conscription was only 45 per cent. of the whole corresponding number of births; but that from 1822 to 1825 it was 61 per cent. *(Bernoulli,* Populationistik, 452.) On Paris alone, see *Villermé,* Mémoire lu à l'Académie des Sciences, 29 Nov., 1824. Compare *supra,* § 10.

[4] *Wappäus,* Allg. Bevölkerungsstatistik. In Prussia, in the less cultured provinces (the eastern), the mortality and number of births is greatest; but in the whole country the relative mortality seems to have remained stationary since 1748. *(Engel,* Preuss. Statist. Zeitschr., 1861, 336 seq.) And even the average age of the deceased decreased even between 1820 and 1860 (344 ff.) In

No reasonable man considers mere living the highest good; but, from an average prolongation of life, we may with great probability infer an improvement in the means of subsistence, in hygienic measures etc., even for the lower classes, who everywhere constitute the great majority of the population. *Aisance est vitalité!* — at least on the supposition that morality remains the same.[6] How great may not have been the effect,

---

Berlin alone, the arithmetical mean of the number of births and deaths shows no improvement, at least (loc. cit. 1862, 195).

[5] In Geneva, where there have been almost uninterrupted tables of mortality, giving the age at the time of death, the average duration of life during the 2d half of the 16th century is estimated at $21\frac{1}{5}$ years; during the 17th century, at $25\frac{3}{4}$ years; from 1701 to 1750, at $32\frac{7}{13}$ years; from 1750 to 1800, at $34\frac{1}{7}$ years; from 1814 to 1833, at $40\frac{2}{3}$ years. Compare *Mallet*, Recherches historiques et statistiques sur la Population de Genève, 1837, 98 ff., 104 ff., and *Bernouilli*, Schweiz, Archiv., II, 77; *per contra*, *d'Ivernois*, sur la Mortalité proportionelle des peuples considérée comme Mesure de leur Aisance et Civilization, 1833, 12 ff. But little can be inferred from this, on account of the large immigration, of adults for the most part. Geneva is said to have had, in the 16th century, never much more than 13,000 inhabitants; at the end of the 17th century it had 17,000; in 1789, 26,000; between 1695 and 1795 there was an increase of 6,000 at least from abroad. (*Bernouilli*, Populationistik, 369 seq.) Compare *Wappäus* in the Götting. Gesellsch. der Wissensch. Bd., VIII, 1860, who, however, as well as *Neison*, Contributions to Vital Statistics, VI ff., is too skeptical as regards modern progress in vitality.

[6] Higher civilization, indeed, instead of leading to higher vitality, may lead to immoderate toil and immoderate enjoyment. (*Schäffle*, in the D. Vierteljahrsschrift, April, 1862, 340.) *Engel* says that, in general, life is more intense in our day, and hence leads to a more rapid exhaustion of individual life-force. (Preuss. Statist. Ztschr., 1862, 53.) According to English experience of the well-fed classes, those have the greatest duration of life who otherwise live in modest circumstances. Thus, for instance, clergymen thirty years of age have still an average expectation of life of 39.49 years; members of the learned professions, 38.86; country gentlemen, 40.22; members of the aristocracy, 37.31; princes of the blood, only 34.04; sovereigns, only 27.16 (Statist. Journal, 1859, 356 ff.); while agricultural laborers, who have sufficient means and intelligence to participate in the so-called friendly societies, have an expectation of life of 40.6 years after their thirtieth year. (*Neison*, loc. cit.) On the whole, it seems to be in harmony with the democratic leveling tendencies of our own age, that the better care of children and of the sick has lengthened short lives, and that the unrest of the times has shortened the long lives, although the level of the general average

for instance, of the healthier mode of the building of modern
cities, of the disappearance of the greater number of fortifications etc., the more rational character of the healing art, the
extension of vaccination,[7] the hygienic measures adopted by
governments,[8] the better care of the poor and especially the

continually rises, notwithstanding. Thus, in Geneva, the proportion of those
who outlived their thirtieth year was: in the 16th century, after 1549, 29.87;
in the 17th century, 37.29; in the 18th century, 49.39; in the 19th century,
until 1833, 58.85 per cent. of the number of births. On the other hand, the
expectation of life of those who had attained their 80th year, was in these
four centuries respectively 6.22, 5.87, 4.40 and 3.84 years. *(Mallet,* l. c., and
Statist. Journal, 1851, 316 ff.) In keeping with this is, that according to *Guy's*
researches, the average duration of life of the English peerage and baronetage
was, in 1500–1550, 71.27 years; 1550–1600, 68.25 years; 1600–1650, 63.95 years;
1650–1700, 62.40 years; 1700–1745, 64.13 years. (Statist. Journal, 1845, 74.)
However, we may most directly infer a favorable condition of things from
the diminished mortality of children, for the reason that this, far more directly than the mortality of adults, is conditioned by the quality of food.
The younger a child is, the more exclusively is its life-force the product of
these two factors: the physical constitution of its parents and the care bestowed upon it. Compare *F. J. Neumann,* Die Gestaltung der mittleren Lebensdauer in Preussen, 1865, 26 ff. In Prussia, in 1751–60, only 312 in 1,000
outlived their tenth year; in 1861–70, 633 in 1,000. Yet, since 1856, the mortality of children has again begun to increase. *(Knapp,* Mittheilungen des
Statist. Bureaus, VIII, p. 8.)

[7] *Duvillard,* Analyse ou Tableau de l'Influence da la petite Vérole, 1806,
is of opinion that before vaccination only 4 per cent. of those over 30 years
of age were spared by the small-pox; that two-thirds of all new-born children were attacked by the disease sooner or later, and that from one-eighth
to one-seventh of those attacked died; and of small children even one-third.
Hence, in many countries, the average duration of life was increased 3½
years by reason of vaccination. In London, between 1770 and 1779, of 1,000
deaths, 102 were caused by the small-pox; in from 1830 to 1836, only 25 in
1,000. *(Porter,* Progress of the Nation, I, 1, 39.) In Berlin, between 1792
and 1801, 4,999 persons died of the small-pox; between 1812 and 1822, only
555. *(Casper.)* That this is really a consequence of vaccination is proved
by the facts of the Chemnitz small-pox epidemic of 1870–71, during which,
in four of the streets principally visited by it, 9 per cent. were taken ill. Of
4,375 persons who had been vaccinated, 2.12 per cent. were attacked; of 644
who were not vaccinated, 54.38 per cent. Of those attacked, 2.1 per cent. of
the former and 11.3 per cent. of the latter died. (Leipzig Tageblatt, 5 Mai,
1871.)

[8] Among the earliest institutions of medical police are the following: the

asylums for small children! The modern system of agriculture and of the corn trade make famines less destructive of life.[9] (§ 115). The modern quarantine-system has protected us entirely against a number of plagues; and the worst epidemics of our day cannot be compared with those of earlier periods or in less civilized countries. In the second half of the 17th century, it was estimated in London that a plague would occur once in every 20 years, each of which swept away one-fifth of the entire population.[10] And in that very city the an-

---

Swedish Collegium medicum under Charles XI; the Prussian, 1724; the Danish, 1740; the quarantine law of Louis XIV, of 1683; the Parisian bureau of nurses, 1715; lying-in establishments since 1728; French institutions for the saving of drowned persons, 1740; English institutions for the saving of persons in cases of apparent death, 1744; bathing largely promoted by government since the eighteenth century; prohibition by Maria Theresa of burial in churches and of locating cemeteries too near dwelling houses, in 1778. Even *Thomasius*, De Jure Principum circa Sepultur., § 8, had advised this; and, in Italy, *Fr. Patricius*, De Inst. Republ. V, 10. On ancient medical police, see *Pyls* Repertorium für öffentliche und gerichtliche Arzneiwissenschaft, II 167, ff. III, 1 ff.

[9] In France, the number of deaths in the cheap years, 1816 and 1819, amounted to an average of 755,877; of the dear years, 1817 and 1818, to an average of 750,065. (Ann. d'Economie politique, 1847, 333.) Thus, the same scarcity in Pomerania increased its otherwise smaller mortality relatively less than in Posen. *(Hildebrand's* Jahrbb. 1872, I, 292.) It is a good sign that in Altenburg, between 1835 and 1864, the variation in the price of corn had no influence on its mortality, although the number of marriages and of births was conditioned by it. *(v. Scheel* in *Hildebrand's* Jahrbb., 1866, I, 161 ff.)

[10] *Sir W. Petty*, Several Essays, 31 seq. Great regularity of epidemics in the tropical world: *Humboldt*, N. Espagne, II, 5. The great plague in the middle of the 14th century is said to have destroyed ⅔ of the population of Norway, of Upland, ⅛; in the mountain districts of Wermeland only 1 boy and 2 girls were left. *(Geijer*, Schwed. Gesch., I, 186.) According to *Sismondi*, Gesch. der Italien. Republiken, VI, 27, ⅔ of the whole population of Europe died at that time. How the cholera would have raged among our forefathers in the middle ages! Certainly, as it does now in the East Indies; since, when of those really attacked by the disease among ourselves so many die, we cannot attribute our small number of deaths from cholera to the smaller intensity of the disease or to the greater skill of our doctors, but chiefly to the better nourishment of our people, to their better dwellings and greater cleanliness. Compare *Heberden*, On the Increase and Decrease of Disease, 1801.

nual mortality between 1740 and 1750 varied three-fifths, during the second half of the 18th century only one-third, during the 19th century only one-fifth in the same decade; a clear proof of the diminished fatality of epidemics.[11][12]

SECTION CCXLVII.

HISTORY OF POPULATION.—NUMBER OF BIRTHS AND DEATHS.

There is found to be in most states, where a decrease in mortality has been observed, a diminished number of births likewise.[1] This, indeed, happens necessarily only in the case in which the means of subsistence either do not increase at all, or in a less degree than mortality has decreased. Thus, to-

---

[11] *Bernouilli*, Populationistik, 363, seq. Whether, on this account, we can infer the increased health of the people, is very much doubted by the aged *laudatores temporis acti*. They would have us believe that it is possible that the prolongation of the average of human life is to be explained by taking into account the case of numerous valetudinarians who formerly died early, but who are *now* preserved to drag out a miserable existence. The relative number of those who have died of old age did not noticeably increase between 1816 and 1860 either in Berlin or in the Prussian state. (*'Engel*, Zeitschr., 1862, 222.) Compare, per contra, *Marx*, Ueber die Abnahme der Krankheiten durch die Zunahme der Civilization: transactions of the Göttinger Gessellschaft der Wissenschaften, 1842-44, 43, ff. The extreme limit of the decrease of mortality, where there are no other causes of death but inevitable weakness of childhood and age, *J. G. Hoffmann* thinks would be one death per annum for every 52-53 living, and *Wappäus*, one in 57-58. (Allg. Bevölkerungsstatistik, I, 231, 340); (*Schäffle*, System, I, 571); according to Capeland observations, one for every fifty.

[12] This much, however, is clear, that the life insurance companies of the present day cannot rely on the calculations made in earlier stages of civilization; on *Süssmilch's*, for instance; and just as little on those of the old Romans in L. Digest. ad Leg. Falcidiam. Compare *Schmelzer*, De Probabilitate Vitae ejusque Usu forensi, 1788.

[1] In France there was one child born alive,

In 1801–1805,	on every	30.9 living.	In 1826–1830,	on every	33.0	living.
In 1806–1810	"	31.6 "	In 1831–1836,	"	34.0	"
In 1811–1815,	"	41.5 "	In 1846–1850,	"	37.8	"
In 1816–1820,	"	31.6 "	In 1851–1854,	"	37.88	"
In 1821–1825,	"	32.1 "	In 1860–1864,	"	37.56	"

wards the end of the 18th century, Norway was the country where the increase and decrease of the population were most remarkable for their smallness. There was only one death between 1775 and 1784 for every 48 living persons; but, at the same time, only one marriage for every 130 living.[2] The organization of labor was so little developed among the Norwegians, especially in the absence of important cities, the industries of which might have been able to absorb the surplus population, that almost every one of its inhabitants was in a condition to calculate in advance whether or not he would have enough to support a family. A person born in the country remained generally in his native village all his life. To found a family he had either to own a peasant's estate himself or wait until one of the day laborer's huts *(Kathe)*, of which there were several attached to each such estate, was vacant. A too large family would certainly have died of hunger in the winter time. The clear sober sense of the people recognized this fact, and all the farm houses of the peasants were without any appreciable injury to morality filled with unmarried servants of both sexes who were, indeed, supplied with clothes and food but who at the same time were indolent and incapable of advancement.[3] Where a nation's economy is rapidly advancing, there is no necessity why the most natural and when properly directed the most beneficent human impulse should be sacrificed to a higher average duration of life. But if this must be, when the distribution of the national resources is pretty nearly equal, it is

---

[2] *Malthus*, Principle of Population, II, ch. 1. In Denmark, at the same time, 1 in 37 and 114. (*Thaarup*, Dänische Statistik., II, 1, 4.)

[3] In modern times, the intellectual and legal conditions which existed in Norway have been loosened to a great extent, and population in that country has, in consequence, made rapid advances. In 1769 the population was only 723,000; in 1855, it was 1,490,000. But the above customs for the most part continue still. Between 1831 and 1835, there was one marriage a year for every 138 living persons. The relative number of marriages is smaller than before. In 1769, there were, in every 1,000, 376 married persons; in 1801, 347; in 1825, 345; in 1835, 322. In 1805, there were only 63 illegitimate births to every 1,000 births; in 1835, the proportion was 71.5 in every 1,000. (*Blom*, Statistik von N., II, 168, 173.)

not so much the number of marriages as the average fruitfulness of marriages that will diminish; that is as many persons as before may enter the married state but most of them are obliged either to postpone doing so until a later age, which places a greater interval between generation and generation, and causes the number of those living at any one time to decrease; or they cease to procreate children at an earlier period in their married life. The latter is found especially in France.[4][5]

---

[4] In England, there were, in 1838–47, of every 1,000 contracting marriage, 94 who had not yet completed their 21st year; in Belgium, 1840–50, only 54; but the famine year, 1846–47, noticeably lowered the relative number of minors in both countries. There were married —

	In Belgium, 1841–50.	*In the purely Flemish provinces.*	*In the purely Walloon provinces.*	Sweden, 1831–35.
	per 1,000	per 1,000	per 1,000	
Before their 21st year	56	32	74	359 per 1,000 males.
From 22 to 25 years..	219	181	259	463 per 1,000 females.
From 26 to 35 years..	503	511	490	458 males, 387 females, per 1,000.
From 36 to 45 years..	161	191	129	183 per 1,000 males.
After their 45th year	61	75	48	150 per 1,000 females.

But it must not be overlooked here, that the Flemish provinces of Belgium had been for a long time in a sad economic condition. (*Horn*, Studien, I, 75 ff.) No less characteristic of the well-being of a people and their providence in entering into the married state is the relative age at which they contract marriage. If we divide ages into four classes (up to the 30th year, between 31 and 45, between 46 and 60, and after 60), we find, for instance, that from 1841 to 1845, there were in West Flanders 585 per 1,000 marriages between persons of the same age-class, 305 in which the husband, and 110 in which the wife belonged to an older class; in Namur, on the other hand, 683, 234 and 83. In dear years, the relative number of marriages between persons belonging to different age-classes, and the relative difference in age of parties to the marriage contract increases.

And so, the frequency of second marriages of widows and widowers is no favorable symptom of the facility of founding a family. Naturally every woman prefers a man who was never married before to a widower; and every man a maiden to a widow; but where there is a want of room to establish a new household, the possession of such one by a widower may readily prepon

But, on the other hand, where the distribution of the national

derate over all counter considerations. Thus, for instance, in the Flemish provinces of Belgium, of 1,000 widowers, from 365 to 395 marry again; in the Wallonic, only from 293 to 308. Of 1,000 brides, 98 are widows in West Flanders, and in Namur, 41. A similar proportion in Bavaria between the Palatinate and the hither-districts. *(Hermann*, Bewegung der Bevölkerung in Bayern, p. 14.) The less the frequency of marriage in general, the greater is the relative probability of second marriage for widows and widowers; and hence, in years of scarcity, the latter relatively increase. *(Horn*, Studien, I, 201 ff.) Sometimes this increase is absolute: in Austria, during the cheap year 1852, there were 231,900 marriages between persons never before married, and 85,000 in which at least one of the contracting parties had been married before. On the other hand, during the dear year 1855, there were only 156,000 of the former and 89,000 of the latter. Something analogous observed in antiquity. *(Pausan.*, II, 21, 8; X, 38, 6; *Propert.*, II, 11, 36.) *Tacitus*, Germ., 19, describes the moral feelings of the ancient Germans as averse to the second marriage of widows, and he apparently approves it.

*In 19 European countries, with an aggregate population of 121,000,000, the number of the married amounted to an average of 34.88 per cent. of the whole population. France is at the head with 38.94 per cent. (1866), even 40.5. In these countries, of all adults, there is a percentage of 65.98 who marry. France is here, also, at the head, with a percentage of 73.58. And the number of the unmarried has continually decreased in post-revolutionary France. In 1806, there were only 35.84 per cent. of the population married. (*Wappäus*, A. Bevölk erungsstatistik, II, 219, 223, 229.) In relation also to the frequency of first marriages and of marriage at the proper age, France is the best situated country. (*Haushofer*, Lehr-und Handbuch der Statistik, 40 ff.) But at the same time, in what concerns the fruitfulness of marriage, it is the farthest behind.; and since 1780 prolificacy has continually decreased there. Thus, 1800–1815, 3.93 legitimate children to a marriage; 1856–60, only 3.03; 1861–6, again 3.08. (*Legoyt* in the Journal des Econ. Oct. 1870, 28.) How little this depends upon physiological causes may be inferred from the fact that *Strabo* commends the women of the Gallic race for their peculiar adaptability to bearing and rearing children. (IV, 178, 196.) The "prudential checks" must play a principal part in producing a low birth rate. (Statist. Journal, 1866, 262), as we find in France

In	Yearly per 100 inhabitants.		Women who marry before their 25th year.
	Marriages.	Births.	
Brittany,	7.0	29.8	42.7 per cent.
Adour,	6.9	25.0	47.3 "
Lower Garonne,	8.3	22.0	59.7 "
Upper Seine,	8.0	23.7	60.0 "

SEC. CCXLVII.] POPULATION.—BIRTHS AND DEATHS. 313

resources is very unequal, the rich may afterwards as well as before continue to follow out their inclination to marry at as early a day and age as they wish; but the less fortunate must remain unmarried through life. Here, therefore, the average number of children to a marriage does not diminish; but the aggregate number of marriages does.[6] If the relative frequency of marriages in most European countries has diminished during the last century, the cause has been in part directly the long duration of life of married couples. Hence, we are not always warranted in consequence, to infer a diminished number of existing marriages.[7]

In many countries, it has been recently observed that the average number of persons to a family is a decreasing one. Thus for, instance, in 1840, in Holland, there were to every

---

That, however, the shorter duration and smaller fruitfulness of marriage by no means necessarily accompany one another, France also proves, since it possesses the longer average duration of marriage: 26.4 years against 20.7 in Prussia. (*Wappäus*, II, 311, 315.)

[6] The proportion of the married to the whole population declined in Prussia from 35.09 in 1816, to 33.09 per cent. in 1852; in Sweden, from 36.41 in 1751 to 32.59 per cent. in 1855; in Norway, from 37.60 per cent. in 1769 to 32.21 per cent. in 1855; in Saxony, from 35.52 per cent. in 1834, to 34.98 per cent. in 1849. (*Wappäus*, II, 229.) If all who are at least 20 years of age be considered competent to marry, there are of every 1,000 thus competent in Belgium, 520 actually married; in the Flemish provinces alone, 489; in the most favorably situated Wallonie, 554. (*Horn*, Bevölk. Studien, I, 139 ff.) In Rome, under Augustus, the proportion was much less satisfactory. In the higher classes, a large majority did not marry at all. (*Dio. Cass.*, I, VI, 1.)

[7] In Halle, in 1700, there was one marriage for every 77 of the population; in 1715, for every 99; in 1735, for every 140; in 1755, for every 167. In Leipzig, in 1620, there was one for every 82; 1741-1756, for every 118; 1868, for every 92.8. In Augsburg, 1510, one in 86; in 1610, in 108; in 1660, in every 101; in 1750, in every 123. The provinces of Magdeburg, Halberstadt, Cleve, Mark, Munden, Brandenburg, Pommerania and Prussia had, about the end of the seventeenth century, one marriage per annum for every 76-95 of the population; the Prussian monarchy, 1822-1828, one marriage for every 109-121. Compare *Süssmilch* Göttl. Ordnung, I., 131, ff., *Schubert* Staatskunde des preuss. Staates I., 364. In France, 1801-1805, there was one marriage per annum in every 137 living; in 1821-5, for every 129; in 1831-35, for every 127; in 1842-51, for every 125.39; in 1860, for every 124.7

hundred families 497 persons, in 1850, only 481; in Saxony, in 1832, 460; in 1840, only 443; in Bavaria, in 1827, 480, in 1846, only 448. In cities also the average size of families is usually smaller than in the country.[8] This is intimately connected with this other fact that in the higher stages of civilization a larger number of independent households consists of single persons in contradistinction to married couples.[9][10]

SECTION CCXLVIII.

HISTORY OF POPULATION.—NUMBER OF BIRTHS AND DEATHS.

So far as the mere number of the population is concerned, it is obviously a matter of indifference whether there are annually 1,000 births and 800 deaths, or 2,000 births and 1,800 deaths. But we see in the former an element of higher civilization,[1] especially, on account of the conditions which determine it. It can occur only where even the most numerous, that is the lower class, feel other wants than those of the mere means of existence and of the satisfaction of the sexual instinct: wants, duties which probably could not be satisfied in a state of mar-

---

[8] In Prussia, in 1849, there were in every one hundred families in the cities, 492 individuals; in the country, 512. In Belgium, in 1846, 459 and 497 respectively. (*Horn*, Bevölk. Studien, I, 88, ff.) In France, in 1853, in the cities, 358; in Paris alone, 299. In the Zollverein, the number of individuals in a family increased in 1852–55, 5.81 per cent.; the population only 3.02 per cent.; the population of those over fourteen* years of age, by 4.41 per cent.; of minors by 1.02 per cent. Only in Saxony and the cities of Hanover was the reverse the case. (*v. Viebahn*, II, 278, seq.)

[9] Thus, for instance, in Belgium, for every 100 households, there are 74 marriages; in the cities of Belgium, 70; in the Belgian country parishes, 75; in Prussia in 1849, 84. (*Horn*, I, 93 seq.) It is estimated that in Prussia, only 3 per cent. of the adult population live outside of the family. (*Viebahn*., II, 273.)

[10] It is strange that *Süssmilch*, Göttl. Ordnung, I, § 13, considers mortality an unalterable law, while he fully recognizes the social grounds which caused the frequency and prolificacy of marriages to vary (I, § 56, 99).

[1] *J. Möser* did not even dream of this. Patr. Phant., I, 15.

riage thoughtlessly entered into; where the virtues both of foresight and self-control are very generally practiced.

And then let us consider the consequences. The efficacy of the repressive hinderances to over-population either consists in immoral acts or easily leads to immorality. Until a "surplus" child has died, what a series of troubles for good parents, and what a chain of evil deeds for bad ones, to say nothing of the poor child itself.

Further, every man, no matter how short or long his life, requires a large advance of capital and trouble which he has later to return to society through the activity of his riper years. If he dies before his maturity, this advance has been made in vain. The more, therefore, the population of a country, in order to maintain itself within the bounds of its field of food, has to calculate on the death of children, the greater is this loss.[1] Hence, from a national-economic point of view, it is to be considered a great advance, that in England in 1780, there was one death among its people under 20 years of age in every 76 of the population, in 1801, in every 96, in 1830, in every 124, in 1833, one only in every 137. *(Porter.)* Lastly, the longer the average duration of life of a child, the greater, other circumstances remaining the same, the number of grown people as compared with that of the children; but grown people are,

---

[1] *Rossi*, Cours d'Economie politique, I, 371, estimates the cost of bringing up a child to its 16th year at a minimum of 1,000 francs. Hence, a country with 1,000,000 births annually, in which only 50 per cent. reach that age, would lose 500,000,000 francs per annum. However, over one-third of the children in question die in the first years of childhood, and the rest do not reach on an average their 16th year, but die between the age of 7 and 8: *Bernouilli*, Populationistik, 259. *Engel* estimates Saxony's "man-capital" at 4 times the value of all the land in the country, and at 10 times the value of all movable property. (Sächs., Statist. Zeitschr., 1855, No. 9. Preuss. Statist. Zeitschr., 1861, 324.) One of the chief advocates of the view that there is an investment of capital in every child is *Chadwick* in the opening address delivered by him before an English learned society at Cambridge: Statist. Journal, Dec., 1862. Lancashire alone pays a penalty per annum for preventable deaths of £4,000,000, for the funeral and medical expenses; to say nothing of the capital lost (506).

as a rule, independent, capable of self-defense, economically productive, competent to discharge all the rights and duties of citizenship, while children are dependent, incapable of self-defense, unproductive, immature. Only he who knows the relative numbers of the different age-classes of a nation can draw fruitful conclusions from the data per capita relating to taxation, from the statistics of crime, suicides, illegitimate births, of school-children etc., or judge correctly of a locality's military contingent.[3][4] Here, indeed, it should not be overlooked that in the highest age-classes, human beings return in many respects to the helplessness of childhood. Yet, as a rule, to reach a good old age is generally considered a personal good fortune; and the existence of a great many aged persons in a country, if not in itself an advantageous element in its economy, may, nevertheless, be called a pleasing symptom.[5] On an average there is only one person over sixty to every twelve under fifteen years of age. (*J. G. Hoffmann.*) We may, hence, readily measure what an advantage France possesses in this, that in 1861, in every 1,000 inhabitants, only 273 were under fifteen years of age, 524 between sixteen and fifty, the most vigorous years of life, and 203 over fifty years old. The average age of the French population was 31.06 years against 27.22 in Sardinia and 25.32 in Ireland.

---

[3] *Bernouilli*, Populationistik, 51 ff. *Quetelet*, Recherches statist. sur le Royaume des Pays-Bas, 1827, 1, 9, and Du Système social, 1848, 176 ff., specially called attention to the important differences in this relation, between the productive and unproductive years of life. Thus it should not be forgotten, when reading of the greater mortality of the poor quarters of Paris, that strangers who are for the most part in the vigorous years of life, live there least of all.

[4] In Russia, it seems that only 36 per cent. of all those born outlive their 20th year; in England, 55 per cent. (*Porter*, Progress, ch. I, 29.) The Russian peasants are said to have from 10 to 12 children, only about one-third of whom grow to maturity. (*v. Haxthausen*, I, 128.) In the United States, the population was in 1820 divided into two nearly equal parts as to age, the 16th year of age forming the dividing point; in England the same was the case, only the dividing point was 20 years of age. (*Tucker*, Progress of the United States, 16, 63.)

However, a positively unfavorable conclusion from a relatively large number of children in a nation should not be drawn except in the case of a people the limits of whose field of food cannot be extended. (§ 239.) Where the nation's economy has a rapid growth, as for instance in young colonies, the comparatively easy rearing of children which there obtains, without any corresponding mortality, is not so much considered a burthen[6] as a symptom of their good fortune and

[5] There were in

	Years.	From 0 to 15 years of age.	From 16 to 50 years of age.	Over 50 years of age.
		Per 1,000 of the pop.	Per 1,000 of the pop.	Per 1,000 of the pop.
Belgium,	1846	323	509	168
Prussia,	1849	370	504	126
Great Britain,	1851	354	504	142
Holland,	1849	333	509	158
Saxony,	1840	339	505	156
Sweden,	1850	328	511	161

In Great Britain, the census of 1851 gave 596,030 persons over 70 years of age; 9,847, over 90; 2,038, over 95; 319, over 100 years of age. (Athen., 12 Aug., 1854.) In France, in 1851, there were 1,319,960 persons seventy years of age and over. In the United States the population of —

	Per English square mile.		Relative number of children under ten years.	
	1800	1840	1800	1840
			per cent.	per cent.
New England,	19.2	34.8	63.5	51.1
The Middle States,	15.3	43.6	70.7	55.7
The Southern States,	8.9	15.9	73.0	67.8
The Southwestern States,	1.3	13.7	77.6	75.5
The Northwestern States,	2.3	25.5	84.9	73.8

In the whole Union, in 1830, the age classes up to 20 years embraced 56.12 per cent. of the population; in 1840, 54.62 per cent.; in 1850, 51.85 per cent. Compare *Horn*, Bevölk. Studien, I, 126; *Wappäus*, A. Bevölk. Stat., II, 44, 125 ff., 88; *Tucker*, Progress of the United States, 105.

[6] As *Wappäus* says that in America an equal number of adults must work for at least a third larger number of children than in Europe: "a much more

even a positive good.⁷ On the other hand, of the Belgian provinces, for instance, suffering Flanders had relatively the smallest number of children, because it had the largest child-mortality.⁸

Almost all the signs which, according to the above paragraphs, distinguish a higher stage of civilization from a lower, may be shown within the limits of the same age and nation to characterize the upper classes as compared with the lower. We may even claim that the greater foresight and self-control of the former in the matter of marriage and in the procreation of children, since the abolition of the greater number of legal advantages of class, are by far the most important of the elements constituting their superiority over the latter. The word proletariat, from *proles*, means first of all, having many children *(Vielkinderei)!*

SECTION CCXLIX.

HISTORY OF POPULATION.—IN PERIODS OF DECLINE.

Nations involved in political and religious decline are wont to lose the moral foundation of the situation last described. Here, therefore, again, both the repressive (which are almost always immoral) tendencies counter to over-population, and the viciously preventive occupy the most prominent place.

---

unfavorable situation, so far as production-force is concerned." (A. Bevölk. St., II, 44.)

⁷ *Horn*, I, 127 ff. The Becoming is not only more pleasant than the Having become, but it may even stand higher in so far as the latter consists only in being resigned to further development.

⁸ *Les mendiants sont dans le cas des peuples naissants* etc. *Montesquieu*, E. der Lois, LXXIII, 11. In England and Wales in 1851–60, there died yearly before their sixth year, 7.24 per cent. of all male children born, but in the families of peers, only 2.22 per cent. (Stat. Journal, Sept., 1865.) If we grade the quarters of the city of Berlin according to the well-being of their inhabitants, we find that in the lower, the number of married men between 18 and 25 years is successively geater: 1.1, 1.4, 2.4 and 3.4 per cent. *(Schwabe,* Völkszählung von, 1871, 24.)

We may most completely observe this spectacle among the heathen nations of later antiquity. But, unfortunately, even among modern nations, we find some analogies to the ancient, to which the political economist may point with the finger of warning. "For unto every one that hath shall be given, and he shall have abundance; but from him that hath not shall be taken away even that which he hath." This universally applicable truth explains the fact that all successive acts of immorality, the more frequently they occur the less severely are they branded by public opinion.

A. We are not warranted, from the relative[1] number of illegitimate births, to draw too direct an inference in relation to the morality of a people. Where, for instance, as in the kingdom of Saxony, the annual frequency of marriage was 0.017 of the population, every illegitimate birth bears evidence of a greater absence of self control than in Bavaria, where, on every one thousand living, there were only thirteen marriages a year.[2] In many quarters, where the economic relations are very stable, and where peasant estates *(geschlossene Bauergüter)* are subject to a species of entailing, where consequently the son can engage in marriage only after the death of the father, illegitimate children are in great part legitimatized by subsequent marriage at a later time, and meanwhile brought up in the family of the mother like legitimate children.[3] Evi-

---

[1] The ratio between the number of illegitimate births and legitimate, so generally brought forward, leads to no correct conclusions whatever. The ratio between the number of illegitimate births, on the other hand, and marriageable men and women, especially of those who are yet unmarried, may afford a basis for valuable inferences. Compare *Hoffmann*, in the Preuss. Staatszeitung, 1837, No. 18. In Prussia, nearly 75 per cent. of all women between 17 and 75 are married. (*v. Viebahn*, II, 189.)

[2] In Bavaria, not only was the frequency of marriage surprisingly small (one marriage a year in every 151.59 inhabitants, while the average in 14 European countries was 1 in 123.9), but marriage was there contracted at a surprisingly advanced age. Of 10,000 of both sexes engaging in marriage, there were, in Bavaria, only 2,081 25 years of age and less, while in England, there were 5,528. Compare *Wappäus*, A. Bevölk. Statistik, II, 241, 270.

[3] In Oldenburg, it is estimated that 48 per cent. of its illegitimate children are legitimatized *per subsequens matrimonium* (*Rau-Hanssen* Archiv. N. F., I

dently the guilty inconstancy creative of ephemeral *liaisons*, and the neglect of the children born of them, do not here produce the sad effects which they are wont to in the large cities, where illegitimate relations are made and dissolved with shocking rapidity. However, births are seldom heard of in the case of ruined debauchees.

At the same time, the frequency of illegitimate births is always an evidence that the rightful founding of a home is made difficult[4] by the economic condition of the police provis-

---

7), in the agricultural districts of Nassau even 70 per cent. *Faucher's* Vierteljahrsschrift, 1864, II, 19), in the whole of Bavaria, 15 per cent.; in the Palatinate, 29.7 per cent. *(Hermann*, Bewegung der Bevolkerung, 20); in the Kingdom of Saxony, 1865, at least 21 per cent. (Statist. Zeitschr. 1868, 184.) In France 10 per cent. of the marriages contracted legitimatize children. *(Legoyt*, Stat. Comp., 501); in Saxony, 1865, 11.7; in Bavaria up to 1852, about ¼ of the marriages belonged to this category; 1858–61, ⅓; 1861–64, nearly ¼. Compare Heft XII, of the official statistics. In the manufacturing towns of France, especially the border ones, a large number of the children of female operatives and of males having their domicile in foreign parts, are legitamatized by marriage: thus in Mühlhausen, 23.7 per cent. Recherches statist. sur M., 1843, 62.

[4] In Mecklenburg-Schwerin there was one marriage

	1841.	*1850.*
On domanial lands, on every	137 of pop'la'n.	every 149 of population.
On manor "	" 145 "	" 269 "
On monastery "	" 163 "	" 175 "
In the cities "	" 115 "	" 104 "

The number of illegitimate births stood to the aggregate number of births in 1800, as 1:16; in 1851, as 1:4.5; in 1850–55, as 14.8; in 1856–59, as 1:5.04; in 1865, as 1:4.0; in 1866, as 1:4.8; in 1867, as 1:5.33; in 1868, as 1:6.0; in 1869, as 1:7.2; in 1870, as 1:7.08. In 260 localities, in 1851, ⅓ and more of the aggregate number of births were illegitimate; in 209, ½ and more, and in 79 the entire number! The small improvement afterwards made was probably due in great part to emigration, which from 1850 to 1859 must have amounted to 45,000. How relative the idea of over-population even in this respect is, is shown by the small number of illegitimate births in very densely populated parts of England — Lancashire, Middlesex, Warwick, Stafford, West York — while districts as thinly populated as North York, Salop, Cumberland, Westmoreland, have very many illegitimate births. The number increases in the best educated districts, where their "education" begins to cause them to make "prudent" and long delays in marrying. *(Lumley*, Statistics of Illegitimacy: Statist. Journal, 1862.)

ions of a country; and that the moral force of the people does not suffice to resist the temptation [5] which such condition and provisions suppose. In the latter respect, this phenomenon may be considered, not only as a symptom but also as a cause: since bastards are generally very badly brought up. A large parthenic population is always an element of great danger in a state.[6] The frequency of illegitimate children must, however, be designated as a tendency counter to over-population, for the reason that still-born births and early deaths occur much more frequently among them than among legitimate children.[7]

---

[5] Strikingly more favorable influence of the *ecclesia pressa*. In Prussia, in 1855, the Evangelicals had 12.3 legitimate births for one illegitimate; the Catholics 19.4, the Jews 36.7, the Mennonites 211.5. *(v. Viebahn,* II, 226.)

[6] The relative number of illegitimate births in many nations of to-day is unfortunately an increasing one. In France, in 1801, only 4.6 per cent. of all live births were illegitimate; in 1811, 6.09; in 1821, 7.07; in 1830, 7.2; in 1857, 7.5; 1861–65, 7.56 per cent. The German especially must confess with deep shame that the southern half of the fatherland presents a very unfavorable picture in this respect. Can a nation be free when its capital, Vienna (1853–56), counts on an average 10,330 illegitimate and 11,099 legitimate births? Compare *Stein-Wappäus,* Handbuch der Geogr., IV, 1, 193. According to observations made between 1850 and 1860, in England between 1845 and 1860, there were in Holland for every 1,000 legitimate births 44 illegitimate, in Spain 59, in England and Wales 71, in France 80, in Belgium 86, in Prussia 91, in Norway 96, in Sweden 96, in Austria 98, in Hanover 114, in Saxony 182, in Bavaria 279. (Statist. Journ., 1868, 153.) Compare *Wappäus,* A. Bevölk. Stat., II, 387. In Russia, according to *v. Lengefeld,* 36.9; in the electorate of Mark, 1724–31, 1 in 18. *(Süssmilch,* I, § 239. During the 17th century it is estimated that the ratio of illegitimate to legitimate births in Merseburg was as 1 : 22–30, in Quedlinburg as 1 : 23–24, in Erfurt as 1 : 13½. (From the Kirchenbücher in *Tholuck's* Kirchliches Leben etc., I, 315 seq.) In Berlin in 1640, only 1–2 per cent. of illegitimate births. *(König,* Berlin, I, 235.) In Leipzig, 1696–1700, 3 per cent.; 1861–65, 20 per cent. *Knapp,* Mitth. des. Leipz. Statist. Bureaus, VI, p. X.

[7] Thus, in 1811–20, the still-born births in Berlin, Breslau and Königsberg amounted to five per cent. of the legitimate, and to eight per cent of the illegitimate; in the country places in Prussia, to 2¾ and 4¾ per cent. Of 384 illegitimate children born in Stettin in 1864, 45 were still-born and 279 died in their first year. *(v. Oettingen,* Moralstatistik, 879.) In the whole monarchy, 1857–58, three to 4 per cent. of legitimate children died at birth, and

B. The trade of the women of the town is indeed an exceedingly old one.[8] But this evil assumes large dimensions only where a large class of men and women have no prospect to marry at all, or only late in life; especially when, at the same time, families have become unaccustomed to keeping together for life.[9] Prostitution may be considered a counterpoise to over population, not only because of the polyandry it involves, but also of the infecundity of its victims.[10] Even the

---

5 to 6 per cent. of the illegitimate; while during the first year of their age 18–19 per cent. of the former, and 34–36 per cent. of the latter, died *(v. Vicbahn,* II, 235). In France, in 1841-54, of the legitimate births, an average of 4 per cent., and of illegitimate 7 per cent., was still-born; and the probability of death during the first year of life was 2.12 times as great for an illegitimate child as for one born in lawful wedlock. *(Legoyt.)* After the first year the proportion changes.

[8] Genesis, 38; Joshua, 1, ff.; Judges, 16, 1, ff. It must not here be overlooked that the Canaanites possessed a much higher degree of economic culture than the contemporary Jews. In Athens, Solon seems to have established brothels to protect virtuous women. *(Athen.,* XIII, 59.) In France, as early a ruler as Charlemagne took severe measures against prostitution. *(Delamarre,*Traité de Police, I, 489.) Compare L. Visigoth., III, 4, 17, 5.

[9] Travelers are wont to be the first to make use of prostitution. I need only mention the extremely licentious worship of Aphrodite (Aschera) which the Phoenicians spread on every side: in Cypria, Cytherae, Eryx etc. Connected with this was the mercenary character of the Babylonian women *(Herodot.,* I, 199); similarly in Byblos *(Lucian,* De dea Syria, 6); Eryx *(Strabo,* VI, 272: *Diod.,* IV, 83), in Cypria; *(Herodot,* I, 105, 199); Cytherin *(Pausan.,* I, 14); Athenian prostitutes in Piräeus and very early Ionian in Naucratis. *(Herodot.,* II, 135.) In all the oases on the grand highways of the caravans, the women have a very bad reputation. Temporary marriages of merchants in Yarkand, Augila etc. *(Ritter,* Erdkunde, I, 999, 1011, 1013, II, 360; VII, 472; XIII, 414.) It is remarkable how the legislation of German cities at the very beginning of their rise was directed against male bawds and prostitutes; at times with great severity, the death penalty being provided for against the former and exile against the latter, while the earlier legislation of the people was directed only against rape. *(Spittler,* Gesch. Hannovers, I, 57 ff.)

[10] Conception in the case of women of the town is indeed not a thing unheard of, but abortion generally takes place or is produced; their confinement is extremely dangerous, and nearly all the children born of them die in the first year of their life. *(Parent Du Chatelet,* Prostitution de Paris, 1836, I, ch. 3.)

diseases which it propagates are not without importance in this regard. The love of change and impatience of restraint which it produces keeps many a man who, economically considered, might very well engage in marriage, in a state of criminal celibacy.[11] This moral poisoning of the nation's blood is more pernicious in proportion as vice is decked with the charms of intellect,[12] and reflected in literature and art.[13] When Phryne had wealth enough to project the rebuilding of Thebes, and boldness enough to ask to be allowed to put this inscription on its walls: " Alexander destroyed them, but Phryne, the hetæra, rebuilt them," not only the dignity but the nationality of Greece was gasping for the last time for breath.[14][15]

---

[11] In the time of Demosthenes, even the more rigid were wont to say that people kept hetæras for pleasure, concubines to take better care of them, wives for the procreation of children and as housekeepers. (adv. Neæram., 1386.)

[12] In Greece as well as in Rome, only slaves, freedmen and strangers sold their bodies for hire; but under the Emperors, prostitution ascended even into the higher classes. *(Tacit.*, Ann. II, 85; *Sueton.*, Tiber, 35; *Calig.*, 41; *Martial*, IV, 81.) Concerning the Empress Messalina, see *Juvenal*, VI, 117 ff. Address of Heliogabalus to the assembled courtesans of the capital, whom the Emperor harrangued as *commilitones.* *(Lamprid,* V.; Heliogabali, 26.) In Cicero's time, even a man of such exalted position as M. Coelius was paid for cohabitation with Clodia, and even moved into her house. *(Drumann*, Gesch. Roms., II., 377.) Even in Socrates' time, the hetæras at Athens were probably better educated than wives: Compare *Xenophon*, Memorabilia, III, 11.

[13] On the Pornographs of antiquity, see *Athen.*, XIII, 21. Even *Aristophanes* was acquainted with some of the species. (Ranæ, 13, 10 ff.) Compare *Aristot.*, Polit., III, 17. *Martial*, XII, 43, 96. Of modern nations, Italy seems to have been the first to produce such poison flowers: *Antonius Panormita* (ob. 1471); *Petrus Aretinus* (ob. 1556). Of the disastrous influence on morals, during his time, of obscene pictures, *Propert*, II, 5, complains. It is dreadfully characteristic that even a Parrhasios painted wanton deeds of shame. *(Sueton*, Tiber, 44), and that Praxiteles did not disdain to glorify the triumph of a *meretrix gaudens* over a *flens matrona.* *(Plin.*, II. N., XXXIV, 19.) But indeed also Giulio Romano!

[14] Compare *Jacobs'* Vermischte Schriften, IV, 311 ff.: *Murr*, Die Mediceinische Venus und Phryne, 1804.

[15] The number of registered prostitutes in Paris, in 1832, amounted to

C. I know no sadder picture in all history than the wide diffusion and even sovereignty which unnatural vice possessed among the declining nations of antiquity. Egypt and Syria seem to have been the original seat of this moral plague.[16] In Greece, there was a time noted for the brilliancy of its literature and art, when the poetic fancy, in its dreams of love, pictured to itself only the forms of beautiful boys; and that this love was generally an impure one, there is, unfortunately, no room to doubt.[17] In more ancient Rome, it was most severely punished;[18] but afterwards, again, it seemed reprehensible to a Tibullus only when it was bought with money.[19]

3,558; in 1854, to 4,620 (*Parent Duchatelet*, ch. 1, 2); in 1870, to 3,656. These figures are evidently much below the real ones. Compare the extracts from the abundant, but, in particulars, very unreliable literature on the great sin of great cities, in *v. Oettingen*, Moralstatistik, 452 ff. According to the Journal des Econ., Juin, 1870, 378 ff., there was an aggregate of 120,000 *femmes, qui ne vivent que de galauterie.*

[16] *Nequitias tellus scit dare nulla magis*, says *Martial*, of Egypt. Worship of Isis, in Rome: *Juvenal*, VI, 488 ff. See, further, *Herodot.*, II, 46, 89; *Strabo*, XVII, 802. On Syria, see Genesis, 19, 4 ff., 9 seq.; Leviticus, 18, 22 seq., 20, 13, 15. The *cunnilingere* of Phoenician origin. (*Heysch, v.* σκύλαξ.) Frightful frequency of the *fellare* and *irrumare* in Tarsis: *Dio Chrysost.*, Orat., 33. The Scythians also seem to have learned the νοῦσος θήλεια (pederasty?) in Syria: *Herodot.*, I, 105. Similarly during the crusades.

[17] Compare *Becker*, Charicles, I, 347 ff. *Æschines* condemns this vice only when one prostitutes himself for money (in Timarch., 137). *Lysias*, adv. Simon, unhesitatingly speaks to a court about a contract for hire for purposes of pederasty. Compare *Æschin.*, l. c., 159, 119, where such a contract is formally sued on. Industrial tax on pederastic brothels. (*Æschin.*, I, c. R.) *Aristophanes* alludes to obscenity still more shameful: Equitt., 280 ff.; Vespp., 1274 ff., 1347; Pax., 885; Ranæ, 1349.

[18] *Valer. Max.*, VI, 1, 7, 9 ff. The Lex Julia treats it only as *stuprum:* L. 34, § 1. Digest, 48, 5; Paulli Sentt. receptt., II, 26, 13. Permitted later until Philip's time, in consideration of a license-fee. *Aurel. Vict.*, Caes., 28. Earliest traces of this vice in the year 321 before Christ. (*Suidas*, v. Γάϊος Λαιτώριος. Later, it caused much scandal when the great Marcellus accused the ædile Scatinus of making shameful advances to his son. (*Plutarch*, Marcell., 2.)

[19] *Tibull*, I, 4. Even the "severe" *Juvenal* was not entirely disinclined to pederasty, and *Martial* does not hesitate to boast of his own pederasty and onanism. (II, 43, XI, 43, 58, 73, XII, 97.)

Even under Cæsar, a censor could threaten an ædile with a charge of sodomy; the latter reciprocate the threat, and think it witty to invite a man like Cicero to assist at the curious argument which such a case might call forth, before a pretor with a reputation of being guilty of the same vice.[20] When the horrible deeds of which Tiberius was guilty are known, we cannot consider them capable of exaggeration. But Tiberius, at least, sought secrecy, while Nero, Commodus and Heliogabalus felt a special delight in the publicity of their shame.[21][22][23]

SECTION CCL.

INFLUENCE OF THE PROFANATION OF MARRIAGE ON POPULATION.

D. In the preceding paragraphs, we treated of the wild shoots of the tree of population. But the roots of the tree are still more directly attacked by all those influences which diminish the sacredness of the marriage bond. It is obvious how heartless *marriages de convenance*,[1] inconsiderate divorces

---

[20] *Cicero*, ad. Div., VIII, 12, 14.

[21] *Sueton.*, Tiber, 43 ff.; Nero, 27 ff. *Tacit.*, Ann., VI, 1; Lamprid. Commod., 5, 10 seq.; Heliog. passim. On the *greges exoletorum*, see also *Dio Cass.*, LXII, 28; LXIII, 13; *Tacit.*, Ann., XV, 37. *Tatian*, ad Graecos, p. 100. Even Trajan, the best of the Roman emperors, held similar ones. (Ael. Spartian, V, Hadr., 2.) Trade in the prostitution of children at the breast. (*Martial*, IX, 9.) The collection of nearly all the obscene passages in the ancient classics elucidated with a shameful knowledge of the subject in the additions to *F. C. Forberg's* edition of the Hermaphroditus of *Antonius Panormita*, 1824.

[22] How long this moral corruption lasted may be inferred from the glaring contrast between the purity of the Vandals at the time of the migration of nations. Compare *Salvian*, De Gubern. Dei, VII, passim.

[23] In keeping with the vicious counter tendencies described in this section, is the increasing frequency of the rape of children in France. The average number of cases between 1826 and 1830 was 136; between 1841 and 1845, 346; between 1856 and 1859, 692. Infanticide also increased between 1826 and 1860, 119 per cent. (*Legoyt*, Stat. comparée, 394.)

[1] This expression is applicable only in times of higher civilization where

and frequent adulteries mutually promote one another. And the period of Roman decline also is the classic period of this evil. I need only cite the political speculation in which Caesar gave his only daughter to the much older Pompey, or the case of Octavia, who when pregnant was compelled to marry the libertine Antonius.[2] Instead of the Lucretias and Virginias of older and better times, we now find women of whom it was said: *non consulum numero, sed maritorum annos suos computant.*[3] In the numerous class of young people

individual disposition of self is considered the most essential want. During the middle ages, when the family tie is yet so strong, the contract of marriage was generally formed by the family; but this was not, as a rule, felt a restraint. In France, at the present time, of 1,000 men who marry before their 20th year, 30.8 marry women from 35 to 50 years of age, and 4.8 who marry women over 50 years of age. (*Wappäus*, A. Bevölkerung. Stat. II, 291.)

[2] *Propertius* bitterly complains of the corruption prevalent in love affairs in his time. (III, 12.). In the Hellenic world, also, among the successors of Alexander the Great, there was a revoltingly large number of *marriages de convenance*, so that even the old Seleucos took to wife the grand-daughter of his competitor Antegonos, Lysimachos the daughter of Ptolemy etc. *Dante's* lament over the anxiety of fathers to whom daughters are born concerning their future dowry: Paradiso, XV, 103. Florentine law of 1509, against large dowries: *Machiavelli*, Lett. fam., 60. In the United States, marriage dowries are of little importance. (*Graf Görtz*, Reise um die Welt, 116.)

[3] *Seneca*, de Benef., III, 16 — a frightful chapter. Also, I, 9. *Juvenal* speaks of ladies who in five years had married eight men (IV, 229, seq.), and *Jerome* saw a woman buried by her 23d husband, who himself had had 21 wives, one after another. (ad. Agcruch, I, 908.) The first instance of a formal divorce *diffareatio* is said to have occurred in the year 523, after the building of the city (*Gellius*, IV, 3), a clear proof that the Romulian description of marriage, as κοινωνία ἁπάντων ἱερῶν καὶ χρημάτων (Dionys., A. R. II., 25), was long a true one. The old manus-marriage certainly supposes great confidence of the wife and her parents in the fidelity of the husband, while the marriage law of the time of the emperors relating to estates never lost sight of the possibility of divorce. The facility of obtaining amicable divorces (the most dangerous of all) appears from the gifts allowed, *divorti causa*, in L., 11, 12, 13, 60, 61, 62; Dig., XXIV, 1. In Greece, we meet with the characteristic contrast, that, in earlier times, wives were bought, but that later, large dowries had to be insured to them or the risk of divorce at pleasure be assumed. (*Hermann*, Privatalterthümer, § 30.)

who live without the prospect of any married happiness of their own, we find a multitude of dangerous persons who ruin the married happiness of others, especially where marriage has been contracted between persons too widely separated by years. *Corrumpere et corrumpi sæculum vocatur. (Tacitus).*[4] It is easy to understand how all this must have diminished the the desire of men to marry. Even Metellus Macedonicus (131 before Christ) had declared marriage to be a necessary evil.[5][6]

How women themselves married again, even on the day of their divorce, see *Demosth.*, adv. Onet., 873; adv. Eubul., 1311. On Palestine, see Gospel of *John*, 4, 17 ff. Concerning present Egypt, where prostitution is carried on especially by cast-off wives, see *Wachenhusen*, vom ägypt, armen Mann, II, 139. During the great French revolution, divorces were so easily obtained that but little was wanted to make a community of wives. (Vierzig Bücher, IV, 205; Handbuch des französischen Civilrechts, § 450.) The more divorces there are in a Prussian province, the more illegitimate births also. Thus, for instance, Brandenburg, 1860–64, had 1,721 divorces, and one illegitimate birth for every 7.8 legitimate (max.). Rhenish Prussia, four divorces and one illegitimate birth for every 25.4 legitimate (min.). In the cities of Saxony, it is estimated there are, for every 10,000 inhabitants, 36 divorced persons; in the country, only 19 (*Haushofer*, Statistik, 487 seq.); in Württemberg, 20; Thuringia, 33; all Prussia, 19; Berlin, 83. (*Schwabe*, Volkszählung von, 1867 p. XLV.)

[4] *Cicero*, in his speech for Cluentius, gives us a picture of the depth to which families in his time had fallen through avarice, lust etc., which it makes one shudder to contemplate. Moreover, of the numerous families mentioned in *Drumann's* history, there are exceedingly few which, either actively or passively had not had some share in some odious scandal. Concerning even Cato, see *Plutatch*, Cato, II, 25. Messalina's systematic patronage of adultery: *Dio Cass.*, LX, 18.

[5] *Gellius*, I, 6. In Greece, the same symptoms appear clearly enough, even in *Aristophanes:* compare especially his Thesmophoriazasuses. The frequently cited woman-hatred of Euripides is part and parcel hereof; also the fact that since Socrates' time, the most celebrated Grecian scholars lived in celibacy. (*Athen.*, XIII, 6 seq.; *Plin.*, H. N., XXXV, 10.) Compare Theophrast in Hieronym. adv. Jovin, I, 47, and *Antipater*, in *Stobæus*, Serm., LXVII, 25.

[6] In modern Italy, the monstrosity known as cicisbeism had not assumed any great proportions before the 17th century, in consequence of the bad custom which permitted no woman to appear in public without such attendant, and ridiculed the husband for accompanying his own. In the time of the republics, the conventual seclusion of girls and the duenna system were

In such ages young girls are kept subject to a convent-like discipline, that their reputation may be protected and that they may be able to get husbands; but once married they are wont to be all the more lawless. In a pure moral atmosphere, precisely the opposite course obtains.[7]

And so it has been frequently observed, that among declining nations the social differences between the two sexes are first obliterated and afterwards even the intellectual differences. The more masculine the women become, the more effeminate become the men. It is no good symptom when there are almost as many female writers and female rulers as there are male. Such was the case, for instance, in the Hellenistic kingdoms, and in the age of the Cæsars.[8] What to-

---

not yet customary. *(Sismondi,* Gesch. der Italienischen Republiken, XVI, 251, ff., 498, ff.) Adultery punished with death in many cities of medieval Italy: for instance, the Jus Municipale Vicentinum, 135. Concerning the Spanish cicisbeos, who evince as much shamelessness as fidelity, see *Townsend,* Journey, II, 142, ff. *Bourgoing,* Tableau, II, 308, ff. The so-called *cortejos* are generally young clerics or young officers.

[7] A young American woman says to Mrs. Butler: "We enjoy ourselves before marriage, but in your country girls marry to obtain a greater degree of freedom, and indulge in the pleasures and dissipations of society." While the young girls are always to be met with in the streets, wives are to be found always in the kitchen. *(Mrs. Butler,* American Journal, II, 183.) Compare *Beaumont,* Marie ou l'Esclavage aux Etats-Unis, I, 25 ff. 349. The opposite extreme in Italy, where, therefore, too favorable an inference should not be drawn from the small number of illegitimate births. Morally considered, one act of adultery outweighs 10 *stupra!* Even in the age of the rennaissance, the free intercourse of young girls in England and the Netherlands made a favorable impression on Italian travelers; *Bandello,* Nov., II, 42; IV, 27.

Similar contrast in antiquity between Ionian and Dorian women. Wives were more rigidly excluded from entering gymnasia for males in Sparta than young girls. *(Pausan.,* V, 6, 5; VI, 20, 6; *Plato,* De Legg., VII, 805; *Xenoph.,* De Rep. Laced., 1. Compare *K. O. Müller,* Dorier, II, 276 ff.

[8] *Plato,* De Legg., VI, 774, and *Aristotle,* Polit., II, 6; V, 9, 6; VI, 2, 12, complain of the too great supremacy of women in their day. Colossal land ownership of Lacedemonian women. *(Aristot.,* Polit., II, 6, 11.) And yet even Plato advises that women be allowed to participate in the gymnasia, in the assemblies and to hold public office, etc. They were indeed different from men, but not as regards those qualities which fit for ruling. (De Rep.,

day is called by many the emancipation of woman would ultimately end in the dissolution of the family, and, if carried out, render poor service to the majority of women. If man and woman were placed entirely on the same level, and if in the competition between the two sexes nothing but an actual superiority should decide, it is to be feared that woman would soon be relegated to a condition as hard as that in which she is found among all barbarous nations. It is precisely family-life and higher civilization that have emancipated woman. Those theorizers who, led astray by the dark side of higher civilization, preach a community of goods, generally contemplate in their simultaneous recomrniendation of the emancipation of woman a more or less developed form of a community of wives. The grounds of the two institutions are very similar. The use of property and marriage is condemned because there is evidence of so much abuse of both. Men despair of making the advantages that accompany them accessible to all, and hence would refuse them to every one; they would improve the world without asking men to make a sacrifice of their evil desires. The result, also, would be about the same in both cases. (§ 81.) So far would prostitution and illegitimacy be from disappearing that every woman would be

---

V, 451 ff.; De Legg., VI, 780; VII, 806.) That the Roman courtesans wore the male toga and were therefore called togatæ. *Horat.*, Serm., I, 2, 63 ff., 80 ff.; *Martial*, VI, 64, recalls certain caricatures of very recent times; for instance, Bakunius' demand that both sexes should wear the same kind of dress. (*R. Meyer*, Emancipationskampf des 4 Standes, I, 43.) Later, concerning witish men, see *Apuleius*, Metam., VIII; *Salvian*, Gubern. Dei VII. We are led to a related subject in noticing that in England of persons charged with serious crimes there were 10 women to 30 men; in Russia only 10 women to 81 men. (*v. Oettingen*, 758.) As *Riehl* remarks, Famille 15, the undeniable *consensus gentium*, that the costume of men should differ from that of women, is an equally undeniable protest against this species of emancipation. I would add that, as among ourselves in the earliest years of childhood, so also among lowly civilized peoples, the difference in costumes of the sexes is least apparent. (*Tacit.*, Germ., 17; Plan. Carpin., Voyage en Tartarie; Add. éd. Bergeron, art. 2.) Even the physical difference is smaller there (*Waitz*, Anthropologie der Naturvölker, I, 76), especially in the size of the pelvis. (*Peschel*, Völkerkunde, 81, 86.)

a woman of the town and every child a bastard. There would, indeed, be a frightful hinderance under such circumstances to the increase of population. The whole world would be, so to speak, one vast foundling asylum.[9]

---

[9] Even *Plato* complains of the unnatural relations of the sexes to one another, and would instead have the unions of couples of short duration introduced, and complete community of children under the direction of the state. (De Rep., V.) The Stoic Chrysippos approves the procreation of children by parent and child, brother and sister. (*Diog. Laert.*, VII, 188.) In the time of Epictetus (Fr. 53, ed. Duebner), the Roman women liked to read Plato's republic, because in his community of wives they found an excuse for their own course. The Anabaptists appealed to Christ's saying that he who would not lose what he loved could not be his disciple. Thus the women should sacrifice their honor and suffer shame for Christ's sake. Publicans and prostitutes were fitter for heaven than honorable wives etc. (*Hagen*, Deutschlands Verhältnisse im Reformationszeitalter, III, 221.)

In our days, the theory inimical to the family is based rather on misconceived ideas of freedom and science. The Christian mortification of the flesh is, it is said, one-sidedness; and that the flesh no less than the spirit is of God. Hence it is that Saint Simonism would reconcile the two, and "emancipate" the flesh. (*Enfantin*, Economie politique, 2d ed., 1832.) *Fourier*, in his Harmonie, allows each woman to have one *époux* and two children by him; one *géniteur* and one child by him; one *favori* and as many *amants* with no legal rights as she wishes. His "harmonic" world he would protect against over-population by four organic measures: the *régime gastrosophique*, the object of which is by first-class food to oppose fecundity; *la vigeur des femmes*, because sickly women have most children; *l'exercise intégral*, since by the exercise of all the organs of the body the organs of generation are latest developed; lastly the *mœurs phanérogames*, the minuter description of which *Fourier's* disciples omitted in the later editions. (*N. Monde*, 377, ff.) *Fourier* was of opinion that only one-eighth of the mothers should be occupied with the bringing up of the children, and that a child's own parents were least adapted to bringing it up, as is proved by the natural aversion of the child to mind the advice or obey the injunctions of its own parents. (186 ff.) If all were left free to choose their employment, two-thirds of all men would devote themselves to the sciences, and one-third of all women; the fine arts would be cultivated by one-third of the men and two-thirds of the women. In agriculture, two-thirds of the men and one-third of the women would take to large farming, and to small farming one-third of the men and two-thirds of the women.

The Communistic Journal, L'Humanitaire, is in favor of a community of wives proper, while *Cabet* leaves the question an open one. Compare, besides, *Godwin* on Political Justice, 1793, VIII, ch. 8. In beautiful contrast

But there is another sense to the expression emancipation of woman. It should not be ignored that, in fully peopled countries, there is urgent need of a certain reform in the social condition of woman. The less the probability of marriage for a large part of the young women of a country becomes, the more uncertain the refuge which home with its slackened bonds offers them for old age, the more readily should the legal or traditional barriers which exclude women from so many callings to which they are naturally adapted be done away with.[10] This is only a continuation of the course of things which has led to the abolition of the old guardianship of the sex. It may be unavoidable not to go much farther sometimes; but such a necessity is a lamentable one.[11] The best division of labor is that which makes the woman the glory of her household, only it is unfortunately frequently impossible.

---

to this are *J. G. Fichte's* (compare, *supra*, § 2) views on marriage and the family in the appendix to his Naturrecht, although he, too, would largely facilitate divorce.

[10] *J. Bentham*, Traité de Legislation, II, 237, seq., says that it is scarcely decent for men to engage in the toy trade, the millinery business, in the making of ladies' dresses, shoes etc. Compare *M. Wolstoncraft*, Rettung der Rechte des Weibes, translated by Salzmann, 1793; *v. Hippel*, über die bürgerliche Verbesserung der Weiber, 1792. Rich in remarks on the woman question are *K. Marlo*, System der Weltőkonomie, and *Schäffle*, Kapitalismus und Socialismus, 444 ff., who, for the most part, supports him. Compare *Josephine Butler*, Woman's Work and Woman's Culture: a Series of Essays, 1792; *Leroy-Beaulieu*, Le Travail des Femmes au. 19, siècle, 1873. Between 1867 and 1871, the number of men dependent on their own action in Berlin, increased 22.9 per cent.; of women dependent on their own labor, 36.6 per cent. (*Schwabe*, Volkszählung, 1871, 84.)

[11] *J. S. Mill*, on the other hand, rejoices over the great economic independence of women, and expects from it especially a decrease in the number of thoughtless marriages. (Principles, IV, ch. 7, 3. Compare by the same author, The Subjection of Women, 1869.) I need only mention the dramatic art and the factory proletariat, where the independence in question obtains and indeed with very different results! It is very characteristic of the time, that *Homer* (Il., XII, 433) considered the spinning for wages as despicable, while *Socrates*, in the mournful period following the Peloponnesian war, earnestly counsels that free women without fortune should employ themselves with home industries. (*Xenoph.*, Memor., II, 7.) It is in keeping

SECTION CCLI.

POLYANDRY—EXPOSURE OF CHILDREN.

In some of the countries of farther Asia, the immoral tendencies counter to over-population which with us take the direction of illegitimate births and acts of adultery, assume the guise of formal institutions established by law. I need only cite the polyandry of East India, Thibet and other mountainous regions of Asia, which is indeed modified somewhat by the fact that, as a rule, only several brothers have one wife in common.[1]

That unnatural institution is, in many localities, based on this, that a great many of the newly born female children are killed or at least sold in foreign parts after they have grown.[2]

---

with this that during the time of scarcity after the Peloponnesian war even female citizens hired themselves out as nurses. (*Demosth.*, adv. Eubul., 1309, 1313.) The frequency of such engagements has, in many respects, causes related to these which produce a frequency of illegitimate births.

[1] *Turner*, Embassy to Thibet, II, 349, tells of five brothers who lived satisfied thus under one roof. (*Jacquemont*, Voyage en Inde, 402.) In Ladakh, all the children are ascribed to the eldest brother, to whom also the property belongs; all the younger brothers are his servants and may be expelled the house by him. (*Neumann*, Ausland, 1866, No. 16 seq.) In Bissahir, on the other hand, the eldest child belongs to the eldest brother, the second to the second etc. Here the wife is bought by all the brothers together and treated precisely as a slave. (*Ritter*, Erdkunde, III, 752.) In Bhutan, the men move into the house of the woman, who is frequently old, and who before marriage, and up to her 25th or 30th year, has generally lived very lawlessly. (*Ritter*, IV, 195.) Among the Garos, the wife may leave the man at pleasure and not lose her property or her children, while her husband by her rejection of him loses both. (*Ritter*, V, 403.) Even in Mahabarata, polyandry occurs among the Northern Indians. Similarly, among the Indo-Germanic tribes in Middle Asia (*Ritter*, VII, 608); according to Chinese sources in ancient Tokharestan (*Ritter*, VII, 699), and among the Sabæans (*Strabo*, XVI, 768). Even in ancient Sparta. (*Polyb.*, XII, 6.)

[2] In lower Nerbudda, the poisoning of new born female children was very common about the beginning of this century. In Kutch, people prefer to marry persons from foreign countries, and murder their own daughters. (*Ritter*, VI, 623, 1054.) Similarly, even in the Indian Arcadia, the land of

In addition to this, we have the very great encouragement given to celibacy in the Himalayas, so that only monks can attain to a higher education and to the higher honors.[3] In many parts of the East Indies, we find a legally recognized community of wives, which is but slightly modified[4] by the difference of caste; and almost everywhere, that looseness of general morality which usually characterizes declining nations.[5]

China is, as a rule, considered the classic land of child-exposure. And a writer of the country, who is considered one of the principal authorities against the exposure of children, actually claims that it is reprehensible only when one has property enough to support them. The murder of daughters he especially reprobates as "a struggle against the harmony of nature; the more a father performs this act, the more daughters are born to him; and no one has ever heard that the birth of sons was promoted in this way."[6] Moreover, the exposure of

---

the Nilgherrys (V, 1035 seq.). In Cashmir, all the beautiful girls are sold in the Punjab and in India from their eighth year upwards. (VII, 78.) Similarly in the Caucasus and in the mountainous region of Badakschan. (VII, 798 ff.) *v. Haxthausen*, transkaukasia, 1856, I, ch. 1, tells how the Russians captured a vessel carrying Circassian slaves into Turkey. They left them their choice, to go back home, marry in Russia, or to continue their journey to Constantinople. They all unhesitatingly chose the last! There is an echo of something analogous even in the Semiramis saga.

[3] In many parts of Thibet and Rhutan the fourth son, and in some places the half of the young men, become lamas. *(Ritter,* Erdkunde, IV, 149, 206.)

[4] Among the Garos and Nairs, as well as among the Cossyahs, in Northwestern Farther India, the children have no father, but consider their brothers on the mother's side their nearest male relatives. Inheritance also takes this direction. *(J. Mill*, History of British India, I, 395 seq. *Buchanan,* Journey through Mysore, II, 411 seq. *Ritter,* V, 390 seq., 753.) Similarly, among the Lycians: *Herodot.,* I, 173. Whether the peculiar custom of many old German people, of which *Tacitus,* Germ., 20, makes mention, does not point to an original community of wives, *quære.*

[5] Even the most debauched European is a pattern of modesty compared with the Indians themselves. (Edinb. Rev., XX, 484.) On the frightful development of unnatural as well as natural crimes against chastity among the Chinese, see *G. Schlegel*, in the memoirs of the Genoostchap van Kunsten en Wetenschappen in Batavia, Band. XXXII, and Ausland, Januar., 1868.

[6] According to *J. Bowring's* official report: Athenæum, 17 Nov., 1855.

children in the later periods of antiquity played an important part. In Athens, the right of a father to expose his child was recognized by law. Even a Socrates accounts it one of the occasional duties of midwives to expose children.[7] Considered from a moral point of view, Aristotle has nothing to say against abortion.[8] In Rome, a very ancient law, which was still in existence in 475 before Christ, made it the duty of every citizen to have and to bring up children.[9] It was very different in the time of the emperors,[10] and until Christianity, made the religion of the state, caused a legal prohibition against the exposure of children to be passed.[11] [12]

That the exposure of children is allowed by law in China, and that many poor couples marry with the intention of exposing them, is unquestionable. But the reports concerning the extent of the evil differ materially. The Jesuits estimated that in Pekin alone from 2,000 to 3,000 children were exposed in the streets. To this must be added the many thrown into the water or smothered in a bath-tub immediately after birth. Compare Lettres édif., XVI, 394 ff.; *Barrow*, 166 ff. The street-foundlings were picked up by the police and placed in wagons, living and dead together, and cast into one pit in a part of the city. Other accounts are much more favorable: thus that of *Ellis*, Voyage, ch. 7, who was there in 1816, and of *Timkowski*, Reise, II, 359. Compare the quotations in *Klemm*, Kulturgeschichte, VI, 212.

[7] *Petit*, Legg. Att., 144. Compare *Becker*, Charicles, I, 21 ff.; *Plato*, Theæt., 150 ff. In Plato's state, a system of exposure on a large scale is one of the most essential foundations of the whole. (De Re., V, 461.)

[8] Aristotle advised that males should not marry before their 37th year, and that at least after their 55th year they should bring no more children into the world. No family was allowed to have more than a definite number of children. (Polit., VII, 14.) There are even yet pictures of Venus trampling an embryo under foot. (*R. O. Müller*, Denkmäler der alten Kunst, II, No. 265.) Compare, *per contra*, Stobaeus, Serm., LXXIV, 91; LXXI, 15.

[9] *Dionys. Hal.*, Ant. Rom., IX, 22.

[10] *Plutarch*, De Amore Prol., 2, Minut. Felix Octav., 30. That it seemed entirely right, when persons had "enough" children, to put the others to death, is proved by the catastrophe in *Longus'* idyllic romance, IV, 24, 35. Even men like *Seneca* (Contr., IX, 26; X, 33) and *Tacitus* (Ann., III, 25 ff.) were actually in favor of the right of exposing children. On the frequency of artificial abortion, see *Juvenal*, VI, 594. Semi-castration of young slaves for libidinous women who did not want to bear children. (*Juvenal*, VI, 371 ff.; *Martial*, I, V67.)

[11] Under Constantine the Great, 315 after Christ. *Theod.*, Cod., XI, 27, 1

SECTION CCLII.

POSITIVE DECREASE OF POPULATION.

The way of vice is steep. Where the aversion to the sacrifices and to the limitations of liberty imposed by marriage, has permeated the great body of the people; where, indeed, the immoral tendencies counter to population described in § 249 ff. have been largely developed, they very readily cease to be mere checks, and population may positively decline. While in the case of fresh and vigorous nations, the mere loss of men caused by wars, pestilence etc., is very easily made up;[1]

[1*] It is an unfortunate fact that many modern nations approximate more closely to this abomination of the ancients than is generally supposed. The infrequency of illegitimate children in Romanic southern nations is offset by the enormous number of exposures almost after the manner of the Chinese. See the tables in *v. Oettingen*, Anhang, 95. In Milan, between 1780 and 1789, there were, in the aggregate, 9,954 children abandoned; between 1840 and 1849, 39,436. (*v. Oettingen*, 587.) On abortion in North America, and the numberless bold advertisements of doctors there that they are ready to remove all impediments to menstruation "from whatever cause," see *v. Oettingen*. 523, and Allg. Zeitung, 1867, No. 309. It would be a very mournful sign of the times if the work: Principles of Social Science, or physical, sexual and natural Religion; an Exposition of the real Cause and Cure of the three great Evils of Society, Pauperism, Prostitution and Celibacy, by a Doctor of Medicine (Berlin, 1871), were really a translation of an alleged English original. It is throughout atheistic, materialistic and immoral, concerned only with one fundamental idea: to instruct women how to prevent conception!

[1] It is said that the plague which, in 1709 and 1710, decimated Prussia and Litthuanian, carried away one-third of the inhabitants, and even one-half of those at Dantzig. While previously the number of marriages annually was, on an average, 6,082, it rose in 1711 to 12,028. In 1712 it was 6,267, and sank some years afterwards on account of the decrease in population, to 5,000. (*Süssmilch*, Göttl. Ordnung, I, Tab. 21. Similar effects of the plague at Marseilles, 1720. (*Messance*, Recherches sur la Population, 766.) In Russia, too, it was observed after the devastation produced by the black death in 1347 and the succeeding years, that the population again increased at an extraordinarily rapid rate; and that an unusual number of twins and triplets were born (?). (*Karamsin*, Russ. Gesch., IV, 230.) Compare *Dalin*

that reproductive power may here be too much enfeebled to fill up the gap again. It has happened more than once that the decline of a period has been frightfully promoted by great plagues, which have swept away in whole masses the remnants of a former and better generation.[2] The return of the relatively small population of its childhood to a nation in its senility cannot be ascribed exclusively to a decrease in its means of subsistence and to a less advantageous distribution of them.[3][4] The depopulation, however, of Greece and Rome in their decline might be hard to understand were it not for the slavery of the lower class.[5]

Schwed. Gesch., II, 384; *Montfaucon*, Monuments de la Monarchie Française, I, 282.

[2] I would mention the Athenian pestilence during the last years or Pericles; the Roman in the *orbis terrarum*, between 250 and 265 B. C., which is said to have destroyed one-half of the population of Alexandria. (*Gibbon*, Hist. of the Roman Empire, ch. 10.) It also made frightful ravages, intellectually, on the nationality of the Romans. (*Niebuhr.*) Thus, in England, the black death contributed very largely to cause the disappearance of the medieval spirit. (*Rogers.*) Of great political importance was the pestilence of Bagdad, which, in 1831, carried off ⅔ of the inhabitants. All national bonds seemed dissolved, robbers ruled the country; the army of the powerful Doud Pascha was carried off entirely, and his whole political system, constructed after the model of that of Mehemet-Ali, fell into ruin. Compare *Anth. Groves*, Missionary Journal of a Residence at Bagdad, 1832.

[3] Among the Maoris, the number of sterile women is 9 times as great as the average in Europe. Compare Reise der Novara, III, 129.

[4] The decreasing number of English Quakers, among whom, in 1680–89, there occurred 2,598 marriages, and in 1840–49 only 659, finds expression in the unfrequency of marriage, a comparatively small number of women and a small number of children, all in conjunction with a small mortality. (Statist. Journ., 1859, 208 ff.) There is no reason to have recourse here to vice as a cause, and scarcely to physiological reasons for an explanation, because these phenomena are accounted for in great part by the fact that adult males so frequently leave the sect.

[5] In this respect, however, there is a great difference between bondage and slavery. As early a writer as *Polybius* speaks of the depopulation of Greece. (*Polyb.*, II, 55; XXXVII, 4.) He looks for the cause in this, that in every family, for luxury's sake, either no children whatever were wanted, or at most from one to two, that the latter might be left rich. (Exc. Vat., 448.) Very remarkable, *Seneca*, Cons. ad. Marc., 19. Further, *Cicero*, ad. Div., II,

CHAPTER III.

POPULATION-POLICY.

SECTION CCLIII.

DENSE POPULATION.—OVER POPULATION.

The nation's economy attains its full development wherever the greatest number of human beings simultaneously find the fullest satisfaction of their wants.

A dense population is not only a symptom of the existence of great productive forces carried to a high point of utilization;[1]

[5.] *Strabo*, VII, 501; VIII, 595; IX, 617, 629. *Pausan.*, VII, 18; VIII, 7; X, 4; *Dio Chr.*, VII, 34, 121; XXXIII, 25. *Plutarch* claimed that Hellas could, in his time, number scarcely 3,000 hoplites, while in the time of Themistocles, Megaris alone had put as many in the field. (De Defectu Orac., 8.) Antium and Tarentum similarly declined under Nero. (*Tacit.*, Ann., XIV, 27.) The depopulation even of the capital, which began under Tiberius, is apparent from *Tacit.*, Ann., IV, 4, 27. National beauty also declined with the nation's populousness. *Æschines* saw a great many beautiful youths in Athens (adv. Timarch., 31); *Cotta*, only very few *(Cicero*, de Nat. Deorum, I, 28); *Dio Chrysostomus*, almost none at all (Orat., XXI). On the necessary lowering of the military standard of measure, see *Theod.*, Cod., VII, 13, 3. *Verget*, de Re milit., I, 5. The depopulation of the later *orbis terrarum* is confirmed by the easiness of the new division of land with the German conquerors. Compare *Gaupp*, Die Germanischen Niederlassungen und Landtheilungen (1845), passim.

[1] A map of Europe, which would show the density of population by the intensity of shade, would be darkest in the vicinity of the lines between Sicily and Scotland, between Paris and Saxony, and grow lighter in proportion to the distance from their point of intersection. Italy is the country with the earliest highly developed national economy of modern times, and England that which possesses the most highly cultivated national economy;

but is itself a productive force,[2] and of the utmost importance as a spur and as an auxiliary to the utilization of all other forces. The new is always attractive, by reason of its newness; but at the same time, we hold to the old too precisely because of its age: and the force of inertia would always turn the scales in favor of the latter. This inertia, both physical and mental is so general, that perhaps the majority of mankind would continue forever satisfied with their traditional field of occupation and with their traditional circle of food, were it not that an impulse as powerful and universal as the sexual and that of the love of children compelled them to extend the limits of both. That man might subdue the whole earth it was necessary that the Creator should make the tendency of man to multiply his kind more powerful than the original production-tendency of his earlist home. The unknown far-away deters as much as it attracts.[3] It is easy to see how the division and

as the Rhine is, from the standpoint of civilization, the most important river in Europe. It is remarkable, in this connection, how slowly population increased in all European countries during the 18th century, and how rapidly after the beginning of the 19th, and especially since 1825. According to *Dieterici* (Berliner Akademie. 16 Mai, 1850), the population increased annually per geographical square mile:

In	1700–1800.	1800–1825.	1824–1846.
	BY	BY	BY
France,	4	16	32
Naples,	15	18	49
Piedmont,	6	8	50
Lombardy,	19	40	80
England and Wales,	16	42	136
Scotland,	3	16	34
Ireland,	17	80	77
Holland,	13	14	95
Belgium,	15	44	136
Prussia,	7	17	68
Hanover,	6	12	32
Württemberg,	17	12	56
Bohemia,	16	27	73

[1] "The useful rearing of children the most productive of all outlay." (*Roesler.*)

[2] Compare *J. Harrington* (ob. 1677), Prerogative of a popular Government,

combination of labor become uniformly easier as population increases in density. Think only of large cities as compared with the country.[4] "Under-populated"[5] countries, which

---

I, ch. 11; *Sir J. Stewart*, Principles, I, ch. 18; *Malthus*, Principle of Population, IV, ch. 1; *McCulloch* very happily shows how seldom those who can live comfortably without it are extraordinarily active. The Malthusian law prevents this ever becoming the condition of the majority. Precisely during those years that man is most capable of labor, there is a prospect of a great increase of outlay, in case one does not remain single, which would inevitably degrade every one, a few over-rich excepted, who had not taken care to provide for a corresponding increase of income. Were it not for this, human progress would become slower and slower, for the reason that the *dura necessitas* would be felt less and less.

[4] According to *Purves*, Principles of Population, 1818, 456, there were, in England (London not included):

	In the seven most densely populated counties.	*In the seven counties of average population.*	*In the five most sparsely populated counties.*
Inhabitants per geographical sq. mile,	4,904	2,229	1,061
One man with £60 income in every -	34 inhab'ts	37	77
One man with £200 income in every -	193 "	199	472
Aggregate of all incomes over £200 per square mile, - - - - -	£25,118	£12,676	£2,441

Compare *Rau*, Lehrbuch, II, § 13. Something analogous has frequently been observed as to taxation capacity. Thus, for instance, the Hessian provinces paid in direct taxation and taxation on wines, liquors etc.; and the density of the population was in the ratio—
In Rhenish Hessen, - - - - - - - 100 100.
In Starkenburg, - - - - - - - 65 64.
In Upper Hessen, - - - - - - - 64 59.
(*Rau*, Lehrbuch, III, § 280.) In many European countries, the population has for a long period of time, and in a comfortable way, increased most rapidly where it has been densest. Thus, for instance, the kingdom of Saxony was, in 1837, the most densely populated of all the monarchical states of Germany (6,076 inhabitants per square mile), Hanover (2,416) and Mecklenburg-Schwerin (2,004) were among the most sparsely peopled. And yet the annual increase of population between 1837 and 1858 was greatest in Saxony (1.36 per cent.) while Hanover (0.44) and Mecklenburg-Schwerin (0.59) stood very low in this respect. In very thinly populated countries, nature permits even

might easily support a large number of human beings, and which, notwithstanding have for a long period of time had only few inhabitants, are on this account abodes of poverty, regions where education and progress are unknown. While, therefore, it cannot be questioned that a nation under otherwise equal circumstances is more powerful and flourishing in proportion as its population embraces a large number of vigorous, well-to-do, educated and happy human beings, the last mentioned attributes should not be left out of consideration.

The possibility of over-population is contested by a great many theorizers (§ 243); and, indeed, the complaints on this score are in most cases only a baseless pretext of the inertia which feels the pressure of the population without being helped and spurred thereby to an increase of the means of subsistence. This inertia itself, especially when it governs a whole nation, is a fact which cannot be ignored. Over-population, as I use the term, exists whenever the disproportion between the population and the means of subsistence operates in such a way that the average portion of the latter which falls to the share of each is oppressively small, whether the effect produced thereby manifest itself in a surprisingly large mortality, or in the limitation of marriages and of the procreation of children carried to the point of hardship. Over-population of this kind is, as a rule, curable by extending the limits of the field of food, either as a result of the advance of civilization at home, or by emigration.

---

the civilized man to deteriorate: thus the French in Canada, the Spaniard in the valley of the La Plata.

ᵇ This excellent expression seems to have been first used by *Gerstner*, Grundlehren der Staatsverwaltung, 1864, II, 1, 176 ff. It must indeed be distinguished from a rapidly growing, but for the time being, a sparsely settled country. A nation with an equal population on a larger surface is, frequently in the immediate present weaker than another in which the population is more dense; but it has the advantage of a greater possibility of growth in the future. Think of the electorates of Saxe and of Brandenburg in the sixteenth century. Just as *Thaer*, Landwirthschaftliche Gewerbelehre, § 149, advises that a mere annuitant should, values being the same, rather purchase a smaller fertile estate; a very able husbandman the reverse.

That the whole earth should be incurably over-peopled is an exceedingly remote contingency.[6] But where, within a smaller circle, by reason of the great stupidity or weakness of mankind, or by the too great power of circumstances, over-population cannot act as a spur to new activity, it is indeed one of the most serious and most dangerous political diseases.[7] The immoderate competition of workmen involves the majority of the nation in misery, not only materially but also morally; one of the most dangerous temptations, for the rich to a contempt for human kind, for the poor to envy, dishonesty and prostitution. In every suffocating crowd, the animal part of man is wont to obtain the victory over the intellectual. Precisely the simplest, most universal and most necessary relations are most radically and disastrously affected by the difficulty or impossibility of contracting marriage, and the sore solicitude for the future of one's children.[8]

---

[6] We need only call to mind such facts as for instance that the United States wealth of coal is 22 times as great as that of Great Britain. (*Rogers*, The Coal Formation and a Description of the Coal Fields of North America and Great Britain, 1858.) In addition to this, only about 16 per cent. of the combustible material is really used in the way furnaces are now generally filled, only 10 per cent. in foundry furnaces, and from 14 to 15 per cent. in the transportation of passengers on railways. The Falls of Niagara afford a water-power equal to ⅔ of all the steam engines which existed, a short time since, in the whole world. (*E. Hermann*, Principien der Wirthschaft, 1873, p. 49, 153, 243.) But that single families, houses, branches of business, etc. may be over-peopled, and the impoverishing disproportion between numbers and the means of subsistence not be susceptible of immediate removal by the unaided power of the crowded circle, cannot be questioned.

[7] *Aristotle* had recognized the possibility of over-population. (Polit., II, 4, 3, 7, 4; VII, 4, 5; VII, 14.) *Schmitthenner*, Staatswissenschaften, I, distinguishes between relative and absolute over-population: the former is remediable by intellectual and especially by political development, while the latter borders on the extreme physical and possible limits of the means of subsistence. *W. Thornton*, Over-population and its Remedy, 1849, 9, considers a country in English circumstances over-populated when a man between twenty and seventy years of age is not in a condition to support, by means of his wages, 1¼ persons in need of assistance (children under 10, women over 60, and men over 70 years of age).

[8] Thus, for instance, in war, one million of peasants are infinitely more

SECTION CCLIV.

THE IDEAL OF POPULATION.

Hence it was not an erroneous policy that most governments have sought to promote the increase of population in undeveloped nations. So far as the influence of the acts of government can reach, such a course must tend to the earliei maturity of a people's economy. Much more questionable are positive provisions by government intended to hinder the further increase of population in a country already supposed to be fully peopled; if for no other reason, because even the deepest, most varied and extensive knowledge can scarcely ever predict with certainty that no further extension of the field of food is possible under the spur of momentary overpopulation; and also because questions of population reach so far into the life and tenderest feelings of the individual that a government which has regard for the personal freedom of its subjects, instead of promoting or hindering marriage, emigration etc. by police regulations, cannot but limit itself to a statistical knowledge and legislative regulation of these relations.[1][2]

---

powerful, especially in case of a protracted defensive war, than two millions of proletarians. Alaric's saying: "thick-growing grass is most easily mowed."

[1] Compare *R. Mohl*, Polizeiwissenschaft, I, § 15.

[2] There may be observed a regular ebb and flow in the opinions of theorizers on this subject. During the latter, great enthusiasm is manifested over the increase of population, which is considered an unqualified benefit; later, over-population gives rise to uneasiness. Not many had as much insight as Henry IV.: *la force et la richesse des rois consistent dans le nombre et dans l'opulence des sujets*. (Edict., in *Wolowski* in the Mémoires de l'Acad. des Sciences morales et politiques, 1855.) Thus, for instance, *Luther*, in his sermons on the married state, advises all young men to marry at 20, and all young women at from 15 to 18 years of age. The person who fails to marry because he cannot support a family has no real confidence in God. God will not allow those who obey his command to want the necessaries of life. Werke by *Irmischer*, XX, 77 ff. In England, great dread of depopulation under the first two Tudors: 4 Henry VII., c. 19; 3 Henry VIII., c. 8. *J. Bodinus*, De Rep., VI, is charmed with the Lex Julia et Papia Poppæa. Its

Whether the population of a country increase in a well-to-do or proletarian manner; whether, therefore, the state should rejoice or lament over such increase, may generally be inferred

repeal was immediately followed by the greatest looseness of morals and by depopulation.

On the other hand, a great dread of over-population prevailed among English political economists at the end of the sixteenth and the beginning of the seventeenth century. They recommended their colonial projects by saying that they desired to avert this danger. Thus, for instance, *Raleigh*, History of the World, I, ch. 4; *Bacon*, Sermones fid., 15, 33, and his essay, De Colonies in Hiberniam deducendis. Compare *Roscher*, Zur Geschichte der englischen Volkswirthschaftslehre, 24, 26, 31, 34, 42. Similarly, at the end of the fifteenth century, in highly developed Italy, which had become stationary. According to *F. Patricius* (De Inst. Republ., VI, 4; VII, 12): *incolarum multitudo periculosa est in omni populo*. Since *Colbert's* time, the opposite opinion has become the prevailing one. The densest population had been observed in the wealthiest and relatively the most powerful countries, and people thought they had here sufficient data for a wide generalization. The thought of military conscription by degrees obtained weight in this connection. Thus, *Saavedra Faxardo*, Idea Principis christiano-politici (1649), Symb. 66; *De la Court*, Aanwysing (1699), I, 9. Sir *W. Temple*, says that the fundamental cause of all commerce and wealth lies in a dense population, which compels men to the practice of industry and frugality. (Works, I, 162 ff., 171, III, 2.) *Imperii potentia ex civium numero æstimanda est. (Spinoza*, Tract. politicus, VII, 18.)

Thus *Petty* says that 1,000 acres which can support 1,000 men are better than 10,000 which do the same thing. He would give Scotland and Ireland up entirely, and have the inhabitants settle in England. In this way all combination for common purposes would be facilitated. (Several Essays, 107 seq., 147 ff.) Peter the Great is said to have entertained a similar view: Oeuvres de Frédéric le Grand, II, 23. More moderate is *Child*, Discourse of Trade, 298, and still more so in 368 ff.; *Locke*, Works, I, 73 ff.; II, 3, 6, 191. In Germany, *v. Seckendorff* advises that great establishments for children should be erected, in which orphans and even the children of poor parents should be brought up at the expense of the state, simply with the object of increasing the number of healthy men. (Teutscher Fürstenstaat, ed. 1678, 203, Add. 179.) *Becher*, Polit. Discours, 21, would have murderers punished because they detract from population, although he elsewhere in his definition of a city, "a nourishing populous community," is no blind enthusiast over population. According to *v. Horneck*, Oesterreich über Alles, 1684, 29 ff., the third fundamental rule of public economy is the greatest possible increase and employment of men. *Vera regni potestas in hominem numero consistit; ubi enim sunt homines, ibi substantiæ et vires. (Leibnitz*, ed., Dutens,

with some certainty from the other conditions of the country's economy, especially from the height of the rate of wages and from the consumption of the nation (§ 230). Thus, for in-

---

IV, 2, 502.) According to *Vauban*, Dîme royale, 150, Daire, no child can be born of a subject by which the king is not a gainer. Compare 46, 145. Numbers of People the greatest riches. *(Law*, Trade and Money, 209.) Similarly, Law's disciple *Mélon*, Essai politique sur le Commerce, ch. 1, 3. The number of people is both means and motive to industry *(Berkeley*, Works, II, 187) and hence the public are interested in nothing so much as in the production of competent citizens. (Querist, Nr., 206.) *Süssmilch*, Göttl. Ordnung, I, Kap. 10; Oeuvres de Frédéric M. IV, 4; VI, 82.

About the middle of the 18th century, we find a whole school of political thinkers who decide every question from the standpoint of the influence of the solution on the increase of population. (Excellently refuted by *Schlözer*, Anfangsgründe, II, 15 ff.) Thus especially *Tucker*, Important Questions, IV, 11; V, 5; VII, 4; VIII, 5. Four Tracts, 70. *Forbonnais*, Finances de France, I, 351, who considered it one of the principal objects of a good industrial policy to employ the greatest possible number of men. *Necker*, Sur le Commerce et la Législation des Grains, 1776. *v. Sonnenfels*, Grundsätze der Polizei, Handlung und Finanz (1765), in which the principle of population is called the highest principle of all four sciences of the state (I, § 25 ff.). These writers understand the " balance of trade " in such a way, that a nation always operates most advantageously which gives employment to the largest number of men with its export articles. *(v. Sonnenfels*, II, § 210 ff., 354 ff.) *v. Justi*, Staatswissenschaft, I, 160 ff., says plainly that a country can never have too many men. According to *Darjes*, Erste Gründe, 370, "even the increase of beggars brings something into the treasury by means of the excise tax which they pay." Compare, also, *J. J. Rousseau*, Contrat Social, III, 9; *Galiani*, Della Moneta, II, 4; *Verri*, Opuscoli, 325; *Filangieri*, Leggi Politche ed Economiche, II, 2; *Paley*, Moral and Political Philosophy, III, ch. 11. On similar grounds, *A. Young* laments that the increase of proletarians is greatly hindered by the English poor laws. (In later writings it is somewhat different: compare Travels in France, I, ch. 12.) How deeply such ideas had penetrated public opinion is apparent from the opening words of the Vicar of Wakefield, as well as from the declaration of *Pitt* in parliament in 1796, that a man who had enriched his country with a number of children had a claim upon its assistance to educate them. Much more correctly, *Voltaire*, Dict. Philosophique, art. Population, sect. 2.

The reaction which attained its height in the Malthusians proper, set in with the Physiocrates and *Steuart: Quesnay*, Maximes générales, No. 26; *Mirabeau*, Phil. rurale. ch. 8, and Ami des Hommes (1762), VIII, 84. Similarly, *J. J. Reinhard*, who calls Baden over peopled "for its present system of agriculture." (Vermischte Schriften, 1760, I, 1 ff.; II, Varr.) *Möser*

stance, the population of England, between 1815 and 1847, increased 47 per cent.; but during the same period the value of its exports increased 63 per cent.; the tonnage of its merchant marine, 55 per cent.; the amount yielded by the tax on legacies, and therefore moveable property, by 93 per cent.; the value of immoveable property by 78 per cent. Wherever in agriculture the ancient system of triennial rotation *(Dreifelder-system=three-field system)* has been exchanged for the so-called English system, not only is a greater number of men supported, but, as a rule, each is more abundantly provided for.[3] The construction of new houses is an especially good symptom, because a habitation is a want which governs many others, and which, at the same time, may be much curtailed

---

Patr. Phant., I, 33, 42; II, 1; IV, 15; V, 26. Also Minister *v. Stein:* Leben von Pertz, V, 72; VI, 539, 887, 1184. Compare *supra*, § 242. Of certain modern economists, it may be said that they deplore and condemn the birth of every child for whose support there has not been established a life long annuity in advance. A remarkable but unsuccessful attempt is made by *Ch. Périn*, De la Richesse dans les Sociétés Chrétiennes, at the end of the first volume, to reconcile the opposing views. Périn reproaches the Malthusians, and especially *Dunoyer* and *J. S. Mill*, with the advocacy of *l'onanisme conjugal*, and thus desiring to restore the old heathen situation. Only the Church holds the proper mean between defect and excess, inasmuch as it permits complete continency or the procreation of children regardless of circumstances to its members; while, on the other hand, it, by celibacy and by the inculcation of industry, frugality etc., guards against over-population. (How well the Roman Church has succeeded in this is best proved by the Roman Compagna!)

In Greece, too, in its first economic periods, especially at the time that the first colonies were sent out, great fears were expressed of over-population. *Hesiod* weighs the advantages and disadvantages of the married state against one another with great thoroughness. (Theog., 600 ff. In the Cypria, even the Trojan war was explained by a divine decree, emitted with the intention of removing over-population.

[3] *A. Young*, Political Arithmetik, 160 ff. In the United States, in ten years, the increase of wealth to that of population, was as 61:33. *(Tucker*, Progress of the United States, 202 ff.) As a good measure for the well-being of the masses, *J. J. Neumann* recommends the relative number attending higher schools, also that of shoemakers, tailors, etc., because the magnitude of the consumption of wool, leather etc., can scarcely be directly ascertained. *(Hildebrand's* Jahrbb., 1872, I, 283, 294.)

in case of need. Only, there should be no thoughtless building speculations, the existence or absence of which may readily be inferred from the ratio between the rent of houses and the rate of interest usual in the country. In England and Wales there was, in 1801, one house to every 5.7 inhabitants; in 1821, to every 5.8; in 1841, to every 5.4; in 1861, to every 5.39; in 1871, to every 5.35.[4]

The taking of the census at regular intervals in accordance with the principles of modern science, and with the apparatus of modern art, is one of the chief means to enable us to form a correct judgment of the health of the national life and of the goodness of the state.[5]

---

[4] Statist. Journ., 1861, 251. In Liverpool, between 1831 and 1841, the population increased 40 per cent., and the number of houses 24 per cent., on account of the large immigration of Irish proletarians. (Edinb. Rev. LXXX, 80.) According to *Fregier*, les Classes dangereuses, the number of good buildings continually increased under Louis Phillippe, and that of the worst lodging houses continually diminished. In Prussia, between 1819 and 1858, the population increased 60.8 per cent., the number of houses, 30.1 per cent.; but the insurance-value of the houses seems to have increased in a still greater proportion. *(v. Viebahn,* Zollverein's Statist., II, 291, ff., 299.) According to *Horn*, Bevölk. Studien, I, 62, ff., there are to every 100 persons in France, 20 dwelling houses; in Belgium, 19; in Great Britain, 18; in Holland, 16; in Austria, 14; in Prussia, 12. Too much should not be inferred from this mere table, as, for instance, in English cities, a house is, on an average, smaller than in the Prussian. A French house has, on an average, only 5½ windows and doors; a Belgian house, on the other hand, 3½ rooms. And so, in villages, it is found that there are uniformly fewer persons to a house than in cities, especially large ones. In Belgium, for instance, the cities have to every 100 inhabitants, 66 rooms, the country only 62. In the largest parishes of France (over 5,000 inhabitants), the number of doors and windows is on the average almost six times as great as in the smallest (under 5,000 inhabitants); but only 4 times as many persons live in them. *(Horn,* loc. cit. I, 76 ff.)

[5] It was very well remarked, even of the Servian census: *ut omnia patrimonii, dignitatis, ætatis, artium officiorumque discrimina in tabulas referrentur, ac sic maxima civitas minimæ domus diligentia contineretur .... ut ipsa se nosset respublica.* *(Florus,* I, 6, 8.)

SECTION CCLV.

MEANS OF PROMOTING POPULATION.

The following are the principal means which have been used to artificially promote the increase of population:

A. Making marriage and the procreation of children obligatory by direct command. Among almost all medieval nations so strong is the family feeling, that it seems to men to be a sacred duty to keep their family from becoming extinct. Where a person is not in a condition physically to fulfill this duty, the law supplies a means of accomplishing it by juridical substitution[1] at least. Most national religions[2] operate in the same direction, as well as the influence of political law-givers, who fully share in the contempt for willful old bachelors and sterile women, which runs through the national feeling of all medieval times.[3] In addition to this, there are the positive

---

[1] In Sparta, impotent husbands were obliged to allow another man to have access to their young wives. *(Xenoph.,* De Rep. Laced., 1. *Plutarch,* Lycurg., 15.) Compare *J. Grimm,* Weisthümer, III, 42. Great importance of adoption in Roman law.

[2] Thus, the Indian laws of Menu, concerned principally with the necessity of sacrifices to assure parents an existence after death. Similarly, Zoroaster and Mohammed. In the Bible the periods should be accurately distinguished: I Moses, 2, 18; V Moses, 26, 5; Judges, 10, 4; 13, 14; Proverbs, 14, 28; 17, 6, and the Preacher, 4, 8 apparently agree; also I Corinth., 7, written under essentially different circumstances but precisely on this account not in contradiction with those passages of the Old Testament.

[3] Genesis, 30, 23. In Sparta, willful bachelorhood was almost infamous. *(Plutarch,* Lycurg., 15.) In Athens, a person might be charged with *agamy* as with a crime. *(Pollux,* VIII, 40.) Concerning the ancient censorial punishments inflicted on those who had no children and the rewards of prolificacy, see *Valer. Max.,* II, 9, 1; *Livy,* XLV, 15; *Gellius,* I, 6: V, 19. Festus v. Uxorium. Many German cities made marriage a qualification for the holding of certain public offices etc. In some places, the public treasury was made the heir of bachelors, a custom not abolished in Hanover until 1732. Compare *Ludewig,* on the Hagestolziatu (1727), but also *Selchow,* Elem. Juris Germ., § 290. On the fines imposed on old bachelors in Spain, during the middle ages, see *Gans,* Erbrecht, III, 401 seq. Recently recommended very strongly by *Hermes,* Sophiens Reise (3 aufl.), I, 660.

rewards offered for large families of children.⁴ Even Colbert, in 1666, decreed that whoever married before his 20th year should be exempt from taxation until his 25th; that anyone who had 10 legitimate children living, not priests, should be exempt from taxation for all time;⁵ that a nobleman having 10 children living should receive a pension of 1,000 livres, and one having 12, 2,000 livres. Persons not belonging to the nobility were to receive one-half of this, and to be released from all municipal burthens.⁶ Such premiums are, indeed, entirely superfluous. No nobleman would desire 12 children simply to obtain a pension of 2,000 livres! Colbert himself abandoned this system of premiums shortly before his death.⁷ ⁸

---

⁴ Yearly rewards for *polytekny* in Persia: *Herodot.*, I 136. In Sparta, a father with three children was relieved of guard duty; and one with four, of all public burthens. (*Aristot.*, Polit., II, 6, 13. *Aelian*, V. H., VI, 6.) Between 1816 and 1823, 250 fathers received the royal gift made to godchildren at their christening in the district of Oppeln, for the seventh son. (*v. Zedlitz*, Staatskräfte der preuss. Monarchie, I, 285.) The king of Hannover paid annually about 900 thalers in such gifts. *Lehzen*, Hannovers Staatshaushalt, II, 346.

⁵ Children who had fallen in the service of their country were considered as still living. Precisely similar laws had existed in Spain from 1623 (*de Laet*, Hispania Cap., 4); in Savoy from 1648 (*Keysslers*, Reise, I, 209).

⁶ Russian law which required the serf master to emancipate his male serfs who were not married by their 20th year, and female serfs not married by their 18th. He could not charge them with desertion in such case, even where combined with theft. (*Karamsin*, Russ. Gesch., XI, 59.) An ancient Prussian law provides that the country people shall marry at the age of 25. Corpus Const., March, V, 3, 148, 274.

⁷ Lettres etc. de Colbert, éd. Clément, II, 68, 120. *Voltaire*, Siècle de Louis XIV. ch. 29, bitterly complains of this; and also *Berkeley*, Works, II, 187, and *Forbonnais*, Finances de France, I, 391. On the other hand, *Ferguson*, Hist. of Civil Society, III, 4, asks: what fuel can the statesman add to the fires of youth? Similarly, *Franklin*, Observations etc. It should not be forgotten that the taxes necessary to supply the so-called marriage-fund, intended to enable poor couples to marry at the expense of the state, make marriage more difficult for other couples. (*Krug*, Staats-Œk., 31.)

⁸ Frederick the Great limited the mourning time of widowers to 3 months and of widows to 9. His abolition of ecclesiastical punishment for those who had fallen, and his prohibition of censuring them under penalty of fine, was based as much on his population policy as on philanthropic grounds. (Preuss.

In the case of morally degenerated nations, in which an aversion to the married state had gained ground, efforts have sometimes been made to work against it by means of new premiums. Thus, especially in Rome, since the times of Cæsar and Augustus, although with poor success. It little becomes one who is himself a great adulterer to preach the sixth commandment.[9]

SECTION CCLVI.

IMMIGRATION.

B. Calling for immigrants. This is a means all the more in favor, inasmuch as it provides the country not only with new-born children, but with mature men, who frequently, when they come from thickly peopled and highly civilized

---

Geschichte, Friedrich's M., II, 337.) Similarly in Sweden: *Schlözer*, V. W., V, 43. In Iceland, after a great plague, even in the last century, it was provided that it should be no disgrace to a young woman to have as many as six illegitimate children. *(Zacchariä,* Vierzig Bücher vom Staate, II, 112.) The marshal of Saxony wished, in the interest of the recruiting of the army, that marriages should be contracted only for a term of five years. (Rêveries de Maurice etc., 345.) The sterile women of Egypt visit the Tantah, a place of pilgrimage and fair-town, where, under the cloak of religion, they give themselves up to unbridled and promiscuous intercourse. *(Wachenhufen,* vom ägypt. armen Mann, II, 151 ff.)

[9] Even in the year 131 B. C., the censor Metellus demanded that citizens should, for political reasons be compelled to marry. *(Livy,* LIX, *Sueton,* Oct. 89.) *Aes uxorium* for bachelors. *(Valer. Max.,* II, 9, 1.) Cæsar distributed land by way of preference among those who had three or more children. *(Sueton.,* Cæs. 20.) Augustus' celebrated Lex Julia et Papia Poppæa sought to urge even widows to marry again in opposition to the moral public conscience. (Partly augendo ærario: *Tacit.,* Ann., III, 25.) *Dio Cass.,* LVI, 1 ff. Trajan did more yet, inasmuch as he gave great assistance to impoverished parents, even of the highest classes, to enable them to educate their children. *Sub te liberos tollere libet, expedit!* *(Plin.,* Paneg., 26.) Of what little assistance all this really was, *Tacitus,* Ann., III, 25, IV, 16, and *Plin.,* Epist. IV, 15, bear witness. If, under the Cæsars, the damage done to the childless in the case of inheritance was a frequent motive of divorce *(Friedländer,* Sittengeschichte I, 389), the L. Julia, in fact, operated in a direction contrary to that in which it was intended to work.

countries, promote the industries of the country of their adoption, and become the teachers of a higher civilization. I need only mention the inhabitants of the Low Countries, who in the twelfth century settled as agriculturists in Northern Germany,[1] and in the fourteenth and sixteenth centuries in England, as artisans; the German miners and inhabitants of cities, who, during the middle ages, colonized Hungary, Transylvania[2] and Poland,[3] and the French Huguenots, who fled to the Independent Protestant countries. Nearly all the remarkable Russian princes since Ivan III. have endeavored in this way to induce Germans to settle in Russia, and, for the same reason, Peter the Great refused to give up his Swedish prisoners of war.[4] The great Prussian rulers have cultivated the policy of immigration on an extensive scale, and thus maintained the original character of their parent provinces as the colonial land of the German people.[5,6]

---

[1] *v. Wersebe*, Ueber die Niederländischen Kolonien in Deutschland, II, 1826.

[2] The immigration of the so-called Saxons into Transylvania began between 1141 and 1161, in consequence of the great inundations in the Netherlands. Compare *Schlözer*, Kritische Sammlungen zur Gesch. der Deutschen in Siebenb., 1795.

[3] In Poland, a multitude of German colonists established themselves during the thirteenth century on the domains of the crown and of the church. As a rule, they obtained the land in consideration of moderate services and rents, which, however, did not begin to run until after eight years, nor until after thirty for uncleared land. In addition to this, they were governed by the German law, and their communal authorities were for the most part German. (*Roepell*, Gesch. von Polen, I, 572 ff.)

[4] Later, the ambassador of Peter the Great endeavored to attract into Russia the Swedes, whom the Russian invasion had prevented from continuing the operation of their mines, saw mills etc. (*Schlosser*, Gesch. des 18 Jahrhund, I, 205.) Catherine's colonization, especially on the Volga and in Southern Russia, 1765 and 1783. About 1830, the number of the colonists was estimated at 130,000, mostly Germans.

[5] It is estimated that Frederick William I. spent 5,000.000 thalers in establishing colonists. Up to 1728, 20,000 new families were received into Prussia alone. *Stenzel*, Preuss. Gesch. III, 412 ff. Frederick the Great endeavored above all to retain in the country the strangers who came there periodically. Thus, the harvesters of Vogtland, in the neighborhood of Magdeburg, and the Vogtland masons in the suburbs of the capital (1752). Com-

Such immigrants have been generally accorded a release from taxation and from military duty for a number of years; a proper measure since the state thereby only surrendered an advantage temporarily which it otherwise would not have possessed at all. Where the land of the state receiving the immigrants was still almost valueless, it has frequently been made over in parcels to well-to-do colonists without consideration.[7] Assistance exceeding these limits is a very questionable boon. It should not be forgotten that the influx of men who bring no capital whatever with them, and who are not good workmen, is of no advantage. Nor are they always the best elements of a people who emigrate. They are very frequently men who, through their own fault, did not prosper at home, and who come to the new country, with all their old faults.[8] This is, of course not true of those who emigrate

---

pare *v. Lamotte* Abhandlungen, 1793, 160 ff. He is said to have settled 42,600 families, mostly foreigners, in 539 villas and hamlets. Besides, the population of Prussia, between 1823 and 1840, increased by 751,749 immigrants, without any positive favors shown them *(Hoffmann*, Kleine Schriften, 5 ff.), and the greater part of these were not very poor.

[6] In antiquity, nothing so much contributed to the rise of Athens and Rome as their reception of noble refugees during its earlier periods.

[7] In Russia, the Emperor Alexander, in 1803, promised the colonists a full release from taxation during ten years, a reduction of taxation for ten more, and freedom from civil and military service for all time; besides 60 *dessatines* of land per family gratis, an advance of 300 rubles for housebuilding etc. and money to enable them to maintain themselves until their first harvest. The provision relating to Poland (1833) was much less favorable: importation of movable property free of duty, freedom from military duty and from taxation for six years, and perpetual quit rents *(Erbzinsgüter)* to agriculturists who owned a certain amount of capital. Brazil promised immigrants, in 1820, land and ten years' freedom from taxation. Compare *Jahn*, Beiträge, z. Einwanderung und Kolonisation in Br. (1874), 37 ff. Hungary, in 1723, accorded settlers freedom from taxation for six years and artisans for fifteen years. *(Mailath*, Oesterreichische Gesch., IV, 525.) The ordinance of 1858 affords too little security for non-Catholics and is not adapted to farmers, but only to purchasers.

[8] Many of Frederick the Great's colonists turned out very badly. They were attracted only by the premiums offered, and they became dissolute after they had consumed them. Many of them thought that they were to

from their attachment to some great principle; for instance, it is not true of those who emigrate in search of freedom of conscience. These may become, provided they are in harmony with their new environment, a support and ornament to their adopted country.[9] But there is always danger that they may not be able to adapt themselves to their new economic relations, and that thus they may in consequence succumb to the pressure of circumstances.[10]

Oriental despotisms have frequently endeavored to assure themselves the possession of newly conquered countries by

---

be of use only by giving children to the state *(Meissner,* Leben des Herrn v. Brenkenhof, 1782), and that the land donated them was to be cultivated by others at the expense of the state! *Dohm* mentions villages of colonists which had to a great extent changed hands four times in 20 years. Whether the king would not have better attained his object had he employed the younger sons of Prussian peasants as colonists, *quære.* (*Dohm,* Denkwürdigkeiten, IV, 390 ff.) Even *Süssmilch* says: "A native subject is, in most cases and for most purposes, better than two colonists." (Göttl. Ordnung, I, 14, 275.) Compare the work: Wie dem Bauernstande Freiheit und Eigenthum verschafft werden könne, 1769, 16. Every family of colonists in South and new East Prussia is said to have cost the state 1,500 thalers. (*Weber,* Lehrbuch der polit. Œconomie, 1806, II, 172); but according to *Büsching* (Beiträge z. Regierungsgeschichte Friedrichs, II, 239), only 400 thalers. *J. Möser* is strongly opposed to the encouragement of immigration by direct appeals to it. (P. Ph., I, 60.) According to *Bülau,* Staatswirthschaftslehre, 24, only those immigrants are welcome who are attracted to the country by the whole character of its national institutions and circumstances. It is a different matter when, for instance, the government in New South Wales permits the colonists, by the payment of very moderate contributions, to have their workmen, friends and relations come after them from England in ships owned by the government. Between 1832 and 1858, £1,700,000 were paid out for such transportation. (Novara-Reise, III, 53.)

[9] Dutch Remonstrants since 1619 in Schleswig; Huguenots established since 1685, in Prussia, to the number of about 11,000; Waldenses in Prussia since 1686; natives of Salsburg and of the Palatinate in Prussia. For a state which is the representative of a religious or political principle, it may be a matter of honor, and then certainly useful, to afford an asylum to persons, adherents of that principle.

[10] On the German colonists whom Olavides settled in Spain, in 1768 etc., see *Schlözer's* Briefwechsel, 1779, IV, 587 ff. See adv.: Ueber Sitten, Temperament etc, Spaniens von einem reisenden Beobachter in den J., 1777 end 1778, Leipzig, 1781, p. 260, ff.

transporting its most vigorous inhabitants in whole masses to a distant part of their old empire. Thus, the Jews were carried into Assyria and Babylon; the Eretrians into Persia; the inhabitants of Caffa by Mohammed II.; the Armenians by Abbas the Great. The Russians, too, undertook a similar transportation of people under the Ivans.[11]

C. The prohibition of emigration, which, in the case of serfs, vassals and state-villeins, it seems natural enough, was very usual in periods of absolute monarchical power. Thus, for instance, Frederick William I. forbade the emigration of Prussian peasants under penalty of death. Whoever captured an emigrant received a reward of two hundred thalers.[12] The public opinion of modern times is very decidedly opposed to this compulsion, which would make the state a prison.[13] "A really excessive population would still find an exit to

---

[11] Canale Crimea, III, 346 ff. *Karamsin*, Russ. Geschichte, VIII, 97, 424.

[12] Ordinance of 1721. Compare *Wolf's* Vernünftige Gedanken, § 483, who at that time highly disapproved of such compulsion. Quite the reverse, the Prussian Landrecht, II, Tit. 17, § 133 ff. On the other hand, in Spiers, in 1765 and 1784, persons of good conduct, good workmen and others of sufficient means, were forbidden to emigrate. Prohibition under pain of death, in Spanish Milan; Novæ Constitut., 29, 145. The work: Les Interests de la France malentendus (1752), 258, advocates the prohibition of emigration as a species of *les majesté*.

[13] *Beccaria*, Dei Delitti e delle Pene, 1765, cap. 52. Similarly, *Mirabeau*, in his congratulatory letter to Fred. Wil. II., and *Benjamin Franklin*, On a proposed Act for preventing Emigration: Works, IV, 458 ff. The Dutch were very early advocates of freedom of emigration. Compare *U. Huber*, De Jure Civit., 1672, II, 4: *Pufendorff*, Jus. Natur. (1672), VIII, 11. Theorizers otherwise the most opposite in their views are here agreed. *Jeremy Bentham* says that properly speaking a prohibition against emigration should begin with the words: We, who do not understand the art of making our subjects happy; in consideration that if we should allow them to take flight, they would all betake themselves to strange and better governed countries etc. Des Recompenses et des Peines, II, 310. But also *K. L. v. Haller*, Restauration der Staatswissenschaft, I, 429 ff., 508, demands most strenuously that there should be freedom of emigration, for the reason that every man, without prejudice to any one else, might seek the state constitution which he wanted. *J. Tucker* entirely approved the English law prohibiting the emigration of workmen. Compare also *J. Bodin*, De Republ., I, 6.

escape, namely, through the gates of death." *(J. B. Say.)* The statesman, on the other hand, who opposes the withdrawal of political or ecclesiastical malcontents should take care, lest he act like the physician who prevents the discharge of diseased matter from the sick body, and causes it to take its seat in some vital organ.[14] Hence, even where emigration is considered detrimental to the country, no governmental condition should be attached to it, except that the person desiring to emigrate should give timely notice of his intention, and receive his passport only after it has been shown that he has discharged all his military duties, paid his taxes and his debts.[15][16]

The severe penalties imposed in Athens on emigration, after the defeat at Chæronea, when general discouragement threatened the state with total dissolution, belong to an entirely different mode of thought.[17]

---

[14] English prohibition of emigration under Charles I., 1637. *Rymer*, Fœdera XX, 143. The story that Cromwell and Hampden were thus detained in the country may be false, however. (*Bancroft*, History of the United States, I, 445.) Earlier prohibition of emigration of the Norwegian king in relation to Iceland. (*Schlegel*, Grâgas, Comment Crit. p. XV. In ancient Greece, the restriction of emigration by foreign powers contributed very largely to the democratization of the mother country. Something similar is impending over Germany if the present emigration towards North America should be much weakened by a change of circumstances there.

[15] Many governments require proof that the person emigrating will be admitted into his contemplated new home, and that he has the means to cover the expenses of the journey. The threat of not receiving back returning emigrants has very little effect, for the reason that it is the most thoughtless who at the moment of emigration entertain the most rose-colored hopes.

[16] I shall treat of the so-called after-tax (*Nachsteuer*) in the fourth volume of my System.

[17] Compare *Lycurg.*, adv., Leocrat. *Cæsar* forbade all persons of senatorial rank to emigrate out of Italy; other persons between 20 and 40 years of age were not to remain absent over three consecutive years at most. For the same reason, the time of military service was shortened. (*Mommsen*, R. G., III, 491.)

SECTION CCLVII.

SANITARY POLICE.

D. Hygienic measures and the improvement of the sanitary police of a country are of the utmost importance, not only to increase the number of inhabitants, but also to produce the conditions of population described in § 246.[1]

E. It is the indispensable condition precedent of all the measures which we have examined, if they would attain their end, that the means of subsistence of the people should be increased or at least more equally divided among them. Where this has been done the increase of population will, as a rule, take care of itself; where it has not, the artificially increased procreation of children can only produce new victims for the angel of death. A merely more equable distribution can, however, improve the condition of the people only in exceedingly rare cases. (§ 204). As a rule, the diseases which it is attempted to thus cure grow worse, or they at least increase in extent. (§ 80, ff., 250.) It is quite different, of course, when the more equable distribution coincides with an absolute growth of the nation's economy. We shall see, later, that, for instance, the freedom of land alienation and of industrial pursuits, when not accompanied by an important advance in the corresponding branches of economy may do more harm than good; but that under favorable circumstances a multitude of dormant forces are thereby awakened, and that then the national-economical dividend may be increased much more than the divisor. (§ 239. *Roscher*, Nationalökonomik des Ackerbaues, § 99, 139 ff.)

---

[1] *Bacon* in his History of Life and Death, or of the Prolongation of Life, hopes the better physicians "will not employ their times wholly in the sordidness of cures, neither be honoured for necessities only; but that they will become coadjutors and instruments of the divine omnipotence and clemence in prolonging and renewing the life of man."

SECTION CCLVIII.

MEANS OF LIMITING THE INCREASE OF POPULATION.

A. The means which consists in rendering marriage less easy by legislation is surrounded with peculiar difficulties in densely populated countries, which are always highly civilized. The state would have here to swim against the stream, and it would be generally a much less difficult task to enlarge the field of food. If there remained from a former period any inducements held out to promote marriage, it is self evident that they should now be discontinued. A voluntary bachelor must now no longer be considered as a man who permits one more woman to become an old maid, but as one who facilitates marriage to another couple.[1] On the other hand, it should not be forgotten that for men, generally, marriage is not only an occasion of increased outlay, but also an incentive to increased activity and greater economy.[2] Many states have endeavored to condition the founding of a family by requiring evidence that the father has a prospect of being able to support one.[3]

---

[1] In Ireland, the unsalaried condition of the Catholic clergy who depended entirely on marriage fees (as high as £20 being paid by poor farmers. Quart. Rev. No. 289), baptismal fees, burial fees, etc., operated as an artificial stimulus to the increase of population under the most unfavorable conditions. See § 254.

[2] It is very noteworthy in this connection that married people commit relatively fewer crimes than single persons. Thus, for instance, in Prussia, in 1861, of every 1,000 unmarried men over 16 years of age, 1.18 were sent to the house of correction; of every 1,000 married men, only 0.59; of every 1,000 divorced, 13.71! (Preuss. Statist. Zeitschr., 1864, 318 seq. In Austria, 1858–59, there was one person under sentence in every 203 unmarried persons, in every 669 married, and in every 1,053 widows and widowers. Of the married, there was a larger proportion of criminals among the childless than among those with children (49.8 per cent. against 42.6 per cent.). Compare v. Oettingen, Moralstatistik, 759. This evidence is all the stronger since, circumstances being otherwise the same, fathers of families are harder pressed by cares for food than single persons.

[3] In Würtemberg, the authorities were for the first time enjoined in 1633, to dissuade people from untimely marriages; in 1712 the consent of the au-

Distinguished theorizers accede to this condition, inasmuch as they deny the right of over-population.[4] But, unfortunately, it is impossible, except in a few extreme cases, to assert or deny a prospect of being able to support a family.[5] How easily is the most remunerative power of labor destroyed by physical or mental disease. Scarcely less subject to change is the so-called certain opportunity of acquisition afforded by a profession or a trade, when it is not guarantied by the possession of considerable capital or of landed property, or by some legal privilege. The amount of property required by many laws is so small that it alone would suffice to support the family only for a few years.[6] And yet it has been gener-

---

thorities to a marriage was made dependent on the evidence of a religious education and the capacity to support a family. Between 1807 and 1828, all restrictions on marriage because of incapacity to support a family were removed. According to the Bavarian Penal Code of 1751 (I, 11, § 7), persons who had married without governmental authorization, and who could not afterwards support themselves except by begging, were sentenced to at least one year in the workhouse and to be whipped once a week. Only a short time ago scarcely any one in Bavaria had a real and unquestionable right to marry. *(Braun*, Zwangscölibat für Mittellose in *Faucher's* Vierteljahrsschrift, 1867, IV, 8.) Austrian law relating to the proof of the certainty of maintaining one's self by one's trade etc: 12 Jan., 1815; 4 Sept., 1825.

[4] *R. Mohl*, in the 3d edition of his Polizeiwissenschaft, I, 152 ff., requires proof of the possession of a sufficiency of food, at least of the means to begin house-keeping. According to *Marlo*, Weltökonomie, III, 84 ff., and *Schäffle*, Kapitalismus und Socialismus, 689 ff., the compulsory insurance of widow and children should precede marriage.

[5] Thus the Württemberg law of 1833 prohibits the marriage of those who are under prosecution on account of repeated thefts, fraud, or carrying on the trade of a beggar; also all such as have been criminally punished within the two next preceding years, and all who within the three next preceding years have received alms from the public treasury, except in cases of misfortune, of the causes of which they were innocent. The Bavarian law of April 16, 1868, gives the parish a right of veto. According to the royal Saxon ordinance of 1840, male recipients of alms are permitted to marry only when their marriage makes an important amelioration of their circumstances probable, and does away with the necessity of public assistance in the future.

[6] During Iceland's middle age, prohibition of marriage for all who did not possess at least from 100 ounces of silver or 600 ells *vadhmal*. (*K. Maurer*, Island, 443 seq.) In Bavaria (July 1, 1831), the right of domicile is made to

ally provided that the proof of such a property gave one an unconditional right to establish a domicile and to marry. It is only where this is wanting that special consent is required. But who shall exercise this right of consent? The parish, perhaps, because on it the impoverished family would fall as a burthen. But it is to be feared that the course of procedure here would be too severe. Local narrow-heartedness might refuse the right of domicile to skillful and industrious candidates, who are in the best situation to maintain a family, but whose competition the older members of the parish might dread.[7] Hence, in most countries, the parish is treated as a party, on whose protest against the marriage the state itself

---

depend on a land-ownership free of debt, and a *steuersimplum* of from 1 to 2 florins (in towns more) in country parishes; on the real (reales) right of carrying on a trade, or on a personal trade-concession sufficient for support. A tax of 1 florin in 1852 meant about 1,200 florins worth of property. In other cases it depended on whether the parish recognized the existence "complete and permanent of the means of livelihood." Here good repute and the possession of a considerable savings bank deposit were to be particularly considered. In cases of competition, discharged soldiers who had served out their term, and good servants of 15 years service were to be preferred. In Württemberg (1833) a sufficient guaranty that a person contemplating marriage possessed the means of support was: the personal capacity to exercise a liberal art or to follow a scientific career, to engage in commerce or agriculture, or some branch of industry, or follow a trade, with sufficient income therefrom to support a family; or the possession of a property, according to locality, of 1,000, 800 or 600 florins. The law of May 5, 1852, was more exacting, and required, besides personal competency, evidence that one's calling yielded a sufficient income, as well as of an amount of property free of debt, of the value of from 150 to 200 florins. In Baden (1831) a property considered sufficient to insure the means of livelihood amounted in the four largest cities to 1,000 florins, in 10 smaller ones to 600; in the remaining communities to 300 florins. In the electorate of Hesse, the amount (1834) was from 150 thalers (for small country communities) to 1,000 thalers. (Kassel.) An irreproachable character is required by many laws (in Württemburg, since 1832, the good reputation of both parties), and the community is empowered to dispense with the other material conditions. Long-continued savings-bank deposit speaks well for the parties' competency to support a family, because it bears testimony to an excellent economic disposition.

[7] Remarkable instance in *Rau*, Lehrbuch, II, § 15 a., note b.

decides.⁸ If the state authorities were to give the immediate decisions in such cases, we might expect, in ordinary times, a liberality which would frustrate the object of the law; but sometimes, also, considerable chicanery on grounds of so-called higher police.

Where there still exist classes and corporations with real independence, the members of which still attach a real value to the body, the matter takes care of itself. The journeyman, for instance, voluntarily retards his marriage until he has become a master workman, and once he has attained that degree, he "works the golden mine of his trade."⁹ But wherever a numerous proletariat exists, the individuals of which have no better future to expect, whatever their present sacrifices and self-denial, and who know nothing of class-wants or class-honor, prohibitions of marriage are severely felt, and are far from being well enforced.¹⁰ The rule which excites least opposition is the fixing of a normal age for marriage, under which males should not be allowed to undertake its engagements.¹¹ Of all privileges those attaching to age are viewed

---

⁸ In Bavaria, in 1808, the decision reserved to the royal boards of police.

⁹ Those callings in which a certain *esprit de corps* prevails such as that, for instance, of officials and officers, submit willingly to restrictions on marriage authoritatively imposed. The Catholic clergy submit even to a full prohibition of marriage. Such measures uniformly strengthen the isolation of the class from the nation as a whole. It is well known that, during the middle ages, theological views on the meritoriousness of all self-denial made voluntary celibacy very common. The Franciscan order counted at one time 150,000 monks and 28,000 nuns, the so-called members of the third order, or penitents, not included. (*Helyot*, Gesch. der Kloster und Ritterorden, V, 33.) The severity of the laws relating to fasting might also, according to *Villermé*, be regarded as a "preventive check." Compare *supra*, § 240, note I.

¹⁰ The Prussian law authorizing parents and guardians to put an interdict on marriages, because of a want of the necessary means, of vicious habits, disease etc., may constitute a check in very good families and families of the middle class, but scarcely so in proletarian circles.

¹¹ Besides Württemberg, Baden also prescribed 25 years; in Saxony and Hessen-Darmstadt, 21 sufficed; in Prussia even 18. *Schäffle* advocates a minimum age of 25 years for males and 22 years for women (loc. cit.). Similarly, *Mohl*, loc. cit.

with least aversion. Something similar is effected in most countries to-day by military conscription, which, on this account, in young countries, has a very restrictive effect on the increase of population.[12] The best means against thoughtless marriages certainly consists in increasing the measure of individual wants (§ 163); assuming, of course, that the added wants are proper and worthy.[13] There is always the consideration that all limitation of marriage, even voluntary self-. limitation, by decreasing or postponing marriage, may prove disastrous to morals. It should, however, not be forgotten that there are other sins besides impurity, and that complete poverty constitutes one of the worst of temptations. Especially is it not the angel guardian of chastity.[14]

In England[15] and France, all governmental hinderances to marriage have long since ceased, and in Prussia, at least all general police hinderances; and we can by no means say that the consequences have been evil. On the other hand, no favorable results as to their influence on pauperism can be shown statistically from the restrictive laws of Württemberg. Rather do statistics point here to the unfavorable probable

---

[12] Why, hitherto, in Sweden, by way of exception, military service promoted early marriage, see *Wappäus*, Bevölkerungsstatistik, 11, 357. In France, on the other hand, the increase of population since 1815 has been almost exactly in the inverse ratio of the strength of the military levy. Acad. des Sc. Morales et Polit., 1867, II, 159.

[13] *Malthus*, Principle of Population, 10, ch. 13.

[14] *Malthus*, Principle of Population, IV, ch. 4, 5. It is a great error to suppose that the number of immoral acts increases and decreases with the frequency of temptation. In Ireland, farmers very frequently keep their men servants and maid servants even after the latter have married. But the very facility with which a fall is legalized, increases very largely the number of reckless marriages. (*Meidinger*, Reise, II, 187 seq.) In the country about Göttingen also, where the people marry much earlier on an average than in that about Calenberg, illegitimate births are much more frequent.

[15] Even no other legal obstacle which could make marriage more difficult occurred to *Malthus*, except that which consists in the refusal of public assistance after the expiration of a fixed period of time. (Principle of Population, IV, ch. 8; V, ch. 2.)

result of an increase of illegitimate births.[16] According to the law of the North German Confederation of 1868, the contract of marriage, except in the case of soldiers, officials, clergymen and teachers, is so free, so far as police influence is concerned, that even actual poverty is no impediment.[17][18][19]

---

[16] See the tables in the Tübinger Zeitschrift, 1868, 624 ff. Thus, formerly, in Rhenish Bavaria, where there was complete liberty allowed in this matter, the poor rates compared with the population, were only 34.6 per cent. of the average in the rest of Bavaria; and the number of illegitimate births was not so unfavorable by one-half. (*Rivet*, in the Archiv der polit. Oekonomie, N. F., I, 39.) The Bavarian law of the 16th of April, 1868, which provides that the community or parish can object to a person's marriage only on account of unpaid parish taxes or poor rates (art. 36) largely increased the number of marriages and diminished the illegitimate births; In the first year to 22.2 per cent., in the second to 17, and in 1873 to 13.2 per cent. (Allg. luth Kirchenztg., 12 März, 1875.) According to official statement, this law did more to improve the condition of workmen in the towns than any other cause. Compare *Thudichum*, Ueber unzulässige Beschränkungen des Rechts der Verehelichung, 1868. Per contra, *E. Schübler*, Ueber Niederlassung und Verehelichung in den verschiedenen deutschen Staaten, 1855.

[17] *Reinhold* has recommended the direct limitation of the procreation of children by the process of *infibulation* practiced on boys fourteen years of age and continued until they arrive at a marriageable age or are able to support illegitimate children. Un der Uebervolkerung in Milleleuropa, 1827. Ueber die Population und Industrié, oder Beweis dass die Bevölkerung in hoch kultivirten Ländern stets den Gewerbfleiss übereile, 1828. Ueber das menschliche Elend, welches durch Missbrauch der Zeugung herbeigeführt wird, 1828. Das Gleichgewicht der Bevölkerung als Grundlage der Wohlfahrt, 1829. The ancients proceeded sometimes in a similar way in the case of slave actors: *Juvenal*, VI, 73. Compare *Winckelmann*, Antichi inediti, Tav. 188.

[18] The obstacles formerly placed in many countries in the way of the marriage of Jews of allowing only the first-born to marry, and this only when a vacancy occurred in the number of families by death (Austria), was not based on a solicitude about population, but on religio-national intolerance, in part also on commercial police grounds.

[19] *Fisher*, Gesch. des deutschen Handels (1785 ff.), still considers war as a remedy for over-population, but *M. Wirth*, Grundzüge der N. Oek., rightly remarks that war destroys not so much children, women and the infirm as the most productive of the male population, and immense amounts of capital.

SECTION CCLIX.

EFFECTS OF EMIGRATION.

B. It is sufficiently evident that emigration from an over-populated country[1] may be attended with good consequences, especially when it takes place in organized bodies.[2] There is little danger that one who knows how to work and pray will go to the bad in a young agricultural colony. In a wilderness which has not yet been cleared, the greater number of proletarian vices spontaneously disappear. There is here no opportunity for jealousy or theft; little for intemperance, the gaming table, licentiousness or quarrelsomeness. Here labor is a necessity, and the rewards of industry and saving soon take a palpable shape. As the emigrant, in such a situation, can scarcely help marrying, children far from being a burthen, soon become companions to their parents in their solitude and, later, helpmates in business. The colonist belonging to the lower middle class is most certain of improving his condition. It may, indeed, require many and toilsome years before he can feel comfortable himself; but his children who would probably have led a proletarian life in the mother country may calculate with certainty on future well-being. The father's small capital which the outlay for education alone would have exhausted at home, here becomes the seed of a number of prosperous households.[3] It is otherwise with the mass of the

---

[1] Compare *R. Mohl*, in the Tübinger Zeitschrift für Staatswissenschaft, 1847, 320 ff.; *Roscher*, Nationalökonomische Ansichten über die Deutsche Auswanderung in the Deutschen Viertejahrsschrift, 1848, No. 43, 96 ff., the same author's Kolonien, Kolonialpolitik und Auswanderung, 2 Aufl., 1856, 342 ff.; *J. Fröbel*, Die Deutsche Auswanderung und ihre Kulturhistorische Bedeutung, 1858.

[2] Unfortunately, emigration in groups has recently become very rare,

[3] Unfortunately, emigration in groups has recently become very rare, whereas, during the middle ages, it took place preponderantly, first in armies and then in communities.

[3] According to parliamentary investigations, the Irish laborer in Australia, Canada etc., improves in a few years to such an extent that he can scarcely be distinguished from the Anglo-Saxon. He becomes industrious, self-

people who remain at home. (Compare § 241.)⁴ It is a matter of much more difficulty than is generally supposed by those who have not made a study of the matter, that the yearly emigration from countries like Germany should counterbalance the excess of births over deaths.⁵ It is not to

---

reliant etc. (Edinb. Rev., 1950, 25.) In North America, however, the Irish seldom become really well off, or occupy a position of consequence in society. *(Görtz,* Reise, 88.)

⁴ *E. G. Wakefield,* in other respects so intelligent a writer on the theory of colonization, is of opinion that every nation might, by giving a proper direction to emigration, establish such a density of population as it desired. Thus, for instance, if there were 10,000 marriages contracted every year in a country, and it was provided that each of these 10,000 couples should be sent to some colony immediately after marriage, the whole mother country would become extinct in from 60 to 70 years. This extreme is of course not desired by any one; but the way to be followed in order to attain a desirable limit is hereby pointed out. That emigration has in so few instances checked the advance of population, Wakefield accounts for by the fact that the means furnished to emigration have to a certain extent been wasted, and that old men, children etc., who either had no influence on population as yet, or could have no more in future, constituted a large proportion of those who left the country. (England and America.)

Evidently an important consideration is here omitted, viz.: that there is no such a thing as a normal year of marriages etc. If, for instance, all males were to wait until their 30th year, and all females until their 20th, to enter the married state, and that the government were to send all competent persons as soon as they had reached this age to America, what would be the consequence ? Numberless situations affording the means of supporting a family would be vacant, and a number of young men of 29 and of young women of 19 would be induced to marry etc. The number of children to a marriage in England in 1838–44 was 4.13; 1845–49, 3.96; 1850–54, 3.26; 1855–59, 4.15. (Journal des. Econ., Oct., 1861.

⁵ *Benjamin Franklin,* in 1751, estimated the aggregate number of English inhabitants in the North American colonies at 1,000,000, of whom only 80,000 had immigrated into the country. Hence, from 1790 to 1840, the United States, the promised land of European emigrants, received only about 1,500,000 emigrants. From 1820 to 1859, the number (according to *Bromwell* and *Hübner)* was 4,509,612; according to a report of the New York Chamber of Commerce (1874), 9,054,132 since 1824. An annual immigration of 100,000 was reached for the first time in 1842. According to the census of 1870, there were in the United States 5,567,229 persons born in foreign countries, of which number 1,690,410 were born in Germany, 1,855,827 in Ireland, and 5,550,904 in England. The aggregate emigration from the British empire,

be supposed that men who are really useless at home should be of any service in the colonies. How violently have not

which unquestionably possesses most colonies and the largest marine, was, on an average, between 1825 and 1835, only about 55,000; 1836 to 1845, over 80,000; in 1845 alone, over 93,000, while the yearly excess of births over deaths between 1841 and 1848, according to *Porter*, was in England and Wales alone, on an average, 169,000. During the succeeding years emigration received an extraordinary stimulus (which changed the proportion) in the influence of the discovery of the Californian and Australian mines, and in the Irish famine. Hence the emigration was, at least, in

	Persons.			Persons.
1847,	258,000	1858–60,	(average)	96,000
1848,	248,000	1862,	"	121,000
1849,	299,000	1863,	"	223,000
1850,	280,000	1865,	"	181,000
1852, (maxim.)	368,000	1867,	"	105,161
1853,	329,000	1870,	"	202,511
1855,	176,000	1871,	"	174,930
1857,	212,000			

while the excess of births over deaths (in Great Britain alone) amounted, in 1856, to 309,000. Between 1815 and 1870, there emigrated from the United Kingdom to the United States, 4,472,672 persons; to the British North American Colonies, 1,391,771; to Australia, 988,423; to other points, 160,771; an aggregate of 7,013,637. (Statist. Journal, 1872, 115.) On the other hand, between 1861 and 1871, 543,015 persons either returned or immigrated to the United Kingdom. It is estimated, (according to *Hübner's* Jahrb. der Volkswirthschaft und Statistik, 263 ff.; VIII, 222, and the Rudolst. Auswandererzeitung) that in no year before 1844 were there more than 33,000 emigrants from Germany. On the other hand, in

	At least.		At least.
1844,	43,000	1856.	98,000
1845,	67,000	1857,	115,000
1846,	94,000	1858–61, (average)	4,620
1847,	109,000	1866,	137,000
1848,	81,000	1867,	151,000
1849,	89,000	By Hamburg and	
1850,	82,000	Bremen alone —	
1851,	112,000	1867–71, (average)	33,355 & 48,296
1852,	162,000	1872,	57,621 & 66,919
1853,	156,000	1873,	51,432 & 48,603
1854, (maxim.)	250,000	1874,	24,093 & 17,913
1855,	81,000		

English colonies opposed the advent of settlers from the poor-houses of the mother country. The classes which are readiest to emigrate: idlers, fickle characters, fathers of families with altogether too many children, artisans who by a revolution in industry have lost the means of making a livelihood, are precisely those who find it most difficult to obtain employment on the other side of the water.[6] Most colonies refuse to receive persons over forty years of age at their own expense. But a young man intellectually and physically able to work, can always make his way even in the old world; only the weaker

while the natural increase of population in Prussia alone (1843-55) amounted to almost 150,000 per annum; in the kingdom of Saxony (1834-49), to over 18,000; in Austro-Germany and the five German kingdoms together, 305,000. *(Wappäus,* Bevölkerungsstatistik, I, 133.) In New York alone, in 1852, 118,600 Germans arrived; in 1853, 119,500; in 1854, over 178,000. That, at present, emigration is, on the whole, so much more frequent than formerly, is accounted for by the largely improved means of communication. However, it was estimated a century ago, that Europe sent at least 100,000 persons per annum to the East and West Indies. Between 1700 and 1719, an aggregate of 105,972 persons emigrated to the Dutch East Indies; between 1747 and 1766, 162,598. *(Saalfeld,* Gesch. des Holländ. Ostindiens, II, 189.) It should not be ignored, however, that the readiness to forsake the fatherland, which only a short time ago was so usual in Germany (in England, it prevails chiefly among the Irish), justified the greatest solicitude for the roots of German national life. How little Germany really suffers from over-population, is shown especially by the circumstance that, for instance, in Prussia, it is precisely the most densely populated districts to which immigration is largest. Compare *v. Viebahn,* Zollverein. Statist., II, 242.

According to *C. Negri,* about 40,000 Italians emigrate every year at present; and it is said that there are, in Turkey, Egypt and Tunis, 70,000; in Peru, 14,000, and in Buenos Ayres, 84,000 Italians living. (I. Jahresbericht der Hamburg. geogr. Gesellsch., 1874.) In other Romanic and Sclavic countries emigration is as yet insignificant. On the other hand, there were, in 1870, 214,574 native Scandinavians in the United States.

[6] While the most active demand for labor, for instance, existed in Australia generally, three government ships carrying emigrants arrived: one with English agricultural laborers, the second with former factory hands, the third with Irish. The agricultural laborers found places very rapidly a few days after their arrival; the factory hands did only tolerably well, while of the poor Irish not one-half could find anything to do, and became a burthen on the benevolence of the public. *(Merivale,* Lectures on Colonization and Colonies, II, 30 ff.)

succumb under the pressure of over-population. Lastly, it should be considered what an amount of capital is required for purposes of emigration and settlement. If emigrants, on the average, take more capital with them than is estimated to be the *per capita* amount of capital possessed by those remaining at home,[7] the consequence would be that, as a result of this very successful emigration, the ratio of consumers to the amount of capital in the country would become more and more unfavorable. The emigrating portion of the country might experience the advantage of this, but the great mass of the population remaining at home would become poorer in capital and in vigorous men,[8] and richer in the comparatively

---

[7] It is estimated that the first 21,200 settlers of New England brought about $1,000,000 with them. (*Bancroft*, Hist. of the United States.) The 50,000 emigrants who came to Quebec in 1832 were estimated to be worth $3,000,-000. It is thought that German emigrants to America, bring with them, on an average, 280 thalers, to which must be added 40 thalers passage money. This seems very high, while German estimates are generally too low, because no emigrant has any interest to overestimate his property, but frequently to underestimate it. Thus, for instance, in 1848–49, 8,780 persons emigrated from Prussia with 1,713,370 thalers of property, i. e., 195 thalers each. (Amtl. Tabellen, f., 1849, I, 290.) It is said that between 1844 and 1851, 45,300 persons emigrated from Bavaria with governmental consent, and that they carried with them property to the amount of 19,233,000 florins; that is, 424 florins each. (Beiträge zur Statistik des Kgr. Bayern, III, 322 seq.) Here the average amount of means carried away by emigrants seems to decrease; a sign that the mass of those emigrating come from successively lower strata of the population. (*Hermann*, Bewegung der Bevölk., 26 seq.)

A still smaller amount of capital would suffice for the purpose of emigration itself. Persons who settled in Canada (1823) cost the English nation £22 per capita, which amount provided them with cows, seeds, agricultural implements, help in building, and food for twelve months. According to the Edinburg Rev., Dec., 1826, only £15, 4s. were necessary for the same purpose. If it be borne in mind that many of these settlers afterwards caused five times as many relatives to come over at their own expense, the necessary outlay per capita would seem very small indeed; frequently not more than one year's maintenance in the poorhouse would have cost. Almost £1,000,000 are sent every year from the United States through banks and emigration bureaus, by emigrants, to the United Kingdom, to bring over their relatives. (Statist. Journal, 1872, 386.)

[8] It is said that in Mecklenburg agricultural labor has much deteriorated

needy. The comfortless contrast between colossal wealth and beggarly want could only be thereby increased, since it is almost exclusively the lower middle class who emigrate to agricultural colonies. The over-rich, as a rule, will not, and proletarians can not, go thither.[9][10]

SECTION CCLX.

COLONIST EMIGRATION.

All these dangers disappear when the portion of the nation which has emigrated continues economically connected with the body of the nation remaining at home. (Colonizing emigration.) Here emigration not only provides "elbow room" in the mother country, but there arises at the same time an increased demand for manufactured articles, an increased supply of raw material, by means of which an absolute growth

---

because the strong men emigrate and because the old and children remain at home. *(Bassewitz-Schumacher*, Comm. Bericht über die Verhältnisse der ländl. Arbeiterklassen, 1873.

[9] *J. S. Mill*, indeed, thinks that even where there is a larger emigration of capital than of men, the combined pressure which both exert on the natural forces of the country emigrated from must become less. (Principles, IV, ch. 5, 1.) Compare *Hermann*, loc. cit. 28 ff. *Hermann* also shows very clearly how emigrants to America would frequently like to return; but the expense of returning deters them from the undertaking, and they manage to get along by great effort, which, however, would have afforded them a livelihood if they had remained at home. Staatsw. Unters. II, Aufl. 480.

[10] Against real over-population, the emigration of women would be much more effective than that of men; and yet the emigration of the latter occurs much less frequently in large numbers. Thus, between 1853 and 1858, 3,694 males emigrated from Saxony and only 2,609 females. Between 1866 and 1874, there were 1,754,231 male immigrants to the United States, and only 1,147,446 females. According to *Rümelin* (Allg. Ztg., December, 1865), the large emigration from Württemberg produced by the years of scarcity — 1850 ff. — left such a preponderance of women that ⅛ of all the young women who have reached a marriageable age at present, would remain unmarried, even if all the marriageable young men were to engage in matrimony. Thus negative emigration does very little to cure the social disease of involuntary celibacy.

of population is made possible.[1] England has hitherto enjoyed these advantages to the fullest extent, Germany scarcely at all. German emigrants to Russia, America, Australia, or Algiers, were, together with all they have and are, for the most part lost to their fatherland. They become the customers and suppliers of foreign countries, and frequently enough the competitors and even enemies of Germany.[2][3]

---

[1] As *Torrens* shows there is no kind of trade that so much promotes production, or which is so capable of growth as the exchange of the means of subsistence and raw materials against manufactured articles. The Budget: On Commercial and Colonial Policy, 1841 ff.

[2] Care should be taken not to allow one's self to be misled here by relative numbers. In the United States, the amount of imports was, from —

	The British Empire.	France.	Germany without Austria.
1840–41,	$51,000,000	$24,000,000	$2,450,000
1849–50,	85,000,000	27,600,000	8,780,000
1859–60,	138,600,000	43,200,000	18,500,000

Hence, absolutely, the German exports increased in 19 years only about $16,000,000; the French (without any emigration), over $19,000,000; the English, more than five times the German. Of the 30,633 emigrants who sailed from Bremen in 1874, only 72 did not go to the United States. (D. Ausw. Ztg., 5 Jul., 1875.) The total exports of the United Kingdom to its colonies amounted, 1840–44, to an average value of £7,833,000; 1865–69, to £27,146,000; while those to foreign countries amounted, during the same periods of time, to only from £28,871,000 to £93,558,000. English colonial trade amounted, in 1866, to £6 2s. per capita of the colonial population; the trade with the East Indies, to only 9s. 7d. per capita of the East Indian population. (Statist. Journal, 1872, 123 ff.)

[3] There has hitherto been little to rejoice over in the condition of German emigrants. The greater number of them had received so little education that they were by no means in a way to oppose the weapons of attack of Anglo-Americans. The glorious literature of their old home scarcely existed for them. Almost the only national peculiarity which they held to with any tenacity was the disposition to a want of union among themselves. Hence they were necessarily de-Germanized in a few generations, after a toilsome and quarrelsome period of transition. How seldom, even in Ohio, did German names occur in the list of public officials, while in New York the number of German names on the poor list is very considerable. The situation, however, seems to have improved in modern times, and the na-

It might be very different if the stream of German emigration was directed towards German colonies for instance, as happened in later medieval times, towards the fertile but thinly populated parts of Hungary, towards the provinces of Austria and Prussia; perhaps, as List wished, towards those parts of Turkey which, God willing, shall yet constitute the inheritance of the German people. Thus, through the instrumentality of emigration, might a new Germany arise, which would directly or indirectly and necessarily ally itself to the old, politically, and at the same time constitute the surest bulwark against the danger from Slavic power.

Politico-economically, this country might be utilized by Germany as the United States uses the Mississippi valley and the Far West, especially as concerns the exclusiveness of the use. It is true, that emigrants could be invited to these quarters in good conscience only when the soil had been prepared for them. They should find there, on their arrival, complete legal security, especially for the landed property to be acquired by them; likewise, at least, full personal, religious, and also commercial freedom.[4]

It may be asked, whether there are places in the other quarters of the world adapted to German colonization in the higher sense of the word. These should of course be countries adapted to agriculture as practiced by the Germans,[5] with an easily accessible coast and provided in the interior with navigable streams. Here the Germans should be able not only to live together in large numbers, but the rest of the population should be inferior to them in political training and in national feeling. Otherwise, there would in time be

---

tional coherency and political power of the mother country have gone hand in hand with the revival of attachment on the part of the emigrants to the land of their nativity. How beautifully was this attachment manifested during the Franco-Prussian war in 1870-71!

[4] Compare *Fr. List*, in the D. Vierteljahrsschrift, 1842, No. IV. *Dieterici*, über Aus- und Einwanderungen, 1847, 18.

[5] No Mosquito-coast!

danger of their losing the German character and feeling.[6] The difficulty of establishing German colonies in the southern temperate parts of Chili and Brazil would be aggravated by the very same causes which prevented the creation of a German navy for centuries; and they would almost certainly have to calculate on the jealousy of all other colonial powers and of the United States.[7] We should not forget that from Raleigh's time to the present, almost every speculation having for its object the founding of a colony, whether originating with individual capitalists or with joint-stock companies, has been, considered from a mercantile point of view, a failure. The fruits of new colonization are generally reaped in the succeeding generation; and such delay is scarcely in harmony with the ideas of our own times. Almost every settlement has had its critical period when the settlers almost despaired. This produced less harm in the 17th century; for they were for the most part compelled to persevere. In our day, they would probably disband and go in search of an easier life in colonies already existing. And yet, Germany must make haste if it would not soon see the last appropriate locality occupied by other and more resolute nations.[8][9]

---

[6] How tenaciously have the Germans held to their nationality in Transylvania and the Baltic provinces, and how rapidly they lost it in Pennsylvania!

[7] On emigration to Brazil, see *v. Tschudi's* report of Oct. 6 to the Swiss parliament, 1860.

[8] Think only of the project of the Belgian East Indian Company, which Austria could not carry out at the beginning of the preceding century. Proposition by *Fröbel* (loc. cit., 87 ff.) that England and Prussia should together found a German colony in the valley of the La Plata, to which *Wappäus* rightly objects, that there are few places there in which peasant emigrants would like to acquire land. (Mittel- und Südamerika, 1866, 1027.)

[9] Compare *Wappäus*, Deutsche Auswanderung und Kolonisation, 1846.

SECTION CCLXI.

STATE AID TO EMIGRANTS.

The inquiry, What can the state reasonably do for emigration, must, of course, receive a very different answer according as there is question of merely negative (§ 259) or colonizing emigration (§ 262). To give the latter a pröper impulse requires so great an outlay of capital and labor that it can be made only by the state; and in Germany, on a large scale, only by a union of several states. We must not here deceive ourselves. Emigrants will go uniformly where they have the nearest prospect of a comfortable future. Whether in emigrating they shall continue their connection with their old home, or whether their children shall be completely denationalized is a matter with which very few emigrants concern themselves; and considering the amount of education they generally possess, this need excite no surprise. Hence, if Germany would unite its departing children in a colony permanently German, and therefore new,[1] it would be necessary for it to offer them, at its own expense, at least the same advantages which they would find in older and fully established colonies. He who would reap should not endeavor to evade the sacrifice incident to the sowing.[2] Even great sacrifices in this direction would certainly be richly rewarded if properly made. Probably the outlay would never be directly returned to the national treasury; but there is all the more reason, on this account, that there should be an indirect return by the increase of duties and other indirect taxes.

---

[1] Much might be gained if German emigrants to the United States would concentrate themselves in one state, and thus soon make it a German state. For many reasons Wisconsin is best adapted to such a purpose.

[2] Provision made to put the colonists in possession of lands well explored and surveyed, to have the preliminary labor performed by persons already acclimated — labor which is the most injurious to health, the clearing of the land, the construction of buildings — purchasing the agricultural implements at wholesale etc.

On the other hand, the costly assistance of the state in the case of merely negative emigration would, as a rule, be folly. Who would compel the children of the great national family, who necessarily or voluntarily remain faithful to the paternal roof, to pay tribute to those who turn their backs on the old home for ever? The wealthy especially who remain in the country have to put up with the disadvantage of paying higher wages for labor.

Simple humanity requires that the state should not be blind to the movement of emigration, nor abandon it to all the risks of improvident liberty. Hence it should endeavor to remove the ignorance prevailing on questions of emigration. It should require personal and other guaranties that emigration agents are not simply dealers in men, and that the contracts made with ship-owners by emigrants are really performed. It should exercise a strict superintendence over the mode of transportation of emigrants, and see to it that its consuls accredited to America etc. assist them by word and deed.[3] The legislation of Bremen is a model in this respect, and has contributed largely to make that port a principal outlet for German emigration.[4] The provisions of the laws of October

---

[3] *v. Gessler* (Tübinger Zeitschr., 1862, 398 ff.), recommends the establishment of an "asylum" in the neighborhood of the locality where the emigrants are likely to settle. In this asylum they might, during the time immediately following their arrival, find shelter, food, medicines etc., and all the implements necessary to a settler, at cost. The institution might be established either by the home government, by a humanitarian emigration society, or by a land company in the colony itself.

[4] There passed

	In 1854.	In 1867.
Through Bremen,	76,875 emigrants.	73,971 emigrants.
Through Hamburg,	50,819 "	42,845 "
(Of these directly only	32,310) "	(38,170) "
Through Havre,	95,849 "	22,753 "
Through Antwerp,	25,843 "	12,086 "
Through other ports,	2,500 "	

1, 1832, of July 14, 1854, of July 9, 1866, etc., embrace among others the following: Only a citizen of Bremen, of good repute, and who has given security to the amount of five thousand thalers, shall be entitled to receive and contract with emigrants for passage; to each passenger shall be allotted a space of at least twelve square feet of surface and six feet high; provision shall be made for the longest possible time of passage; for instance, for thirteen weeks for a voyage northerly from the equator. At the same time, the ship-owner is required to give security that in case of accident to the vessel, disabling it in such a way as to unfit it to continue the journey, he shall return the fare of all passengers saved, and pay them an additional sum of from twenty to forty thalers, according to the length of the passage, to cover the cost of salvage, to support themselves for the time being, and enable them to continue their journey. The entire matter is controlled by a rigid system of ship-investigation, and is under the superintendence of a board of officers, made up of senators and members of the chamber of commerce.⁵ Among English provisions⁶ particu-

---

The trade of Bremen has, as the result of this transportation of emigrants, grown just as that of the Italian sea coast cities by the transportation of the crusaders in the Middle Ages. Here, as in so many other cases, genuine philanthropy, in the long run, moves nearly parallel with real economic advantage. And in fact, the Statuta civitatis Messiliæ of 1228 (IV, 24 seq., 28, 30) contain provisions in relation to the crusaders which forcibly remind one of the modern Bremen laws. Similarly in Venice: Compare *Depping*, Histoire du Commerce entre le Levant et l'Europe, 284; II, 313 seq.

⁵ Similar provisions in Hamburg, June 3, 1850, revised February 26, 1855; in France, January 15, 1855; in the United States of America, March 2, 1855. Compare *Hübner*, Statistisches Jahrbuch, 1856, 289 ff. However, there were serious complaints, a short time since, concerning German emigrant transportation, especially of the treatment of women: Novara-Reise, III, 49 ff. Ausland, 1863, No. 8. One of the principal wants is that emigration agents should be held responsible for detaining their clients a long time and at a heavy expense, in places of embarkation.

⁶ Compare *McCulloch*, Commercial Dictionary, v. Colonies, 9 George, IV., ch. 21. The law of June 30, 1852, carries solicitude for the lot of emigrants very far. It embraces 91 articles and 11 additions. Everything is most minutely provided for, even the form of the passage ticket. The old law of

larly worthy of imitation is that which requires the government agents in Canada etc. to furnish information gratis to emigrants. But to keep their clients from the practice of idling about, so ruinous to themselves, the agents refuse aid to all emigrants who, without sufficient reason, remain over eight days in the harbor.

SECTION CCLXII.

EMIGRATION AND PAUPERISM.

As a very rare exception, an emigration suddenly undertaken, well directed and on a very large scale, may be made to constitute the efficient means preparatory to the abolition of pauperism. Where, for instance, by reason of the subdivision of the land into extremely small parcels, farming on a diminutive scale has come to preponderate; where the popular home-industries have been reduced to a miserable condition by the immoderate competition of great foreign manufacturers and machinery, the hopelessness of the situation consists principally in this: that every improvement made must be preceded by a concentration of the forces of labor, and their combination with the powers of capital; which for the moment renders a great number of those who have been laborers hitherto entirely superfluous. That is, to raise the level of the whole public economy and provide a decent livelihood for 10,000 men, it would be necessary to condemn another 10,000 to death from starvation! Most political doctors recoil at the thought of this transition-crisis. They content themselves

---

1803, drawn up in accordance with the advice of the Scotch Highland Society, was apparently devised in the interest of the emigrants; but it contained a multitude of minute requirements suggested by a desire on the part of the advisers to restrict emigration. Hence it was, in practice, by consent of both parties, always evaded. Compare *Lord Selkirk*, Observations on the present State of the Highlands of Scotland, with a View of the Causes and probable Consequences of Emigration (1805). Edinburgh R., December, 1826, 61; January, 1828.

with palliatives which, in the end, cost much and afford no help. The simplest remedy here would evidently be to cause those workmen who have become superfluous to emigrate at the expense of the state. Next, the necessary economic reforms should be carried out at home and the return of the evil prevented by rigid legislation. The more sudden this emigration is, the nearer it comes to taking place, so to speak, all at once, the less possible it is that the increase of population should keep even pace with it. The condition of the proletarians who remained at home could not fail to have a favorable influence in this respect; for nothing leads men so much into contracting reckless marriages as the total absence of any prospect of amelioration of their condition in the future.[1] [2]

SECTION CCLXII (a).

TEMPORARY EMIGRATION.

Besides definitive emigration, temporary emigration deserves special consideration. If the wages of labor are much lower

---

[1] Many of the most competent thinkers have designated such emigration as the only remedy for the overpopulation of Ireland. Compare *Torrens*, The Budget, passim; *J. S. Mill*, Principles, II, ch. 10; Edinburg Rev., January, 1850. *Lord Palmerston* retained the wealthiest farmers on his estates who were intending to emigrate, by causing the poor ones to emigrate at his own expense. The independent emigration of the Irish at their own expense which has been going on for some years, might become an incalculable gain to the English nation. By the poor law, 4 and 5 William IV., c. 76, the English parishes are authorized, with the approval of the central poor board, to assist emigration to the extent of £10 per capita. Between 1849 and 1853, they assisted 1,826 poor persons on an average per annum, who received for that purpose £10,352. (*Kries*, Engl. Armenpflege, 1863, 30.)

[2] It is an interesting thought of *R. von Mohl*, Polizeiwissenschaft, I, 130, that real overpopulation, when no one was willing to emigrate of his own accord, might be remedied by a species of emigration-conscription of young adults by the drawing of lots, the right of substitution etc. The ancient Italians sometimes realized this idea by the *ver sacrum*. Similarly in many cases of Greek emigration, by the worship of Appollo: Compare *W. H. Roscher*, Apollon und Mars (1873), 82 ff.

in one locality than in another which is easily accessible,[1] the workmen of the former place resolve much more readily on periodical migrations thither than on permanent settlements in the place. It is especially the difficult work of harvesting, where farmers are pressed for time,[2] and that of house-building,[3] which are undertaken by these birds of passage; and

---

[1] The locust-like emigration from Ireland to England takes three principal directions: from Dublin to Liverpool, from Cork to Bristol, from the North-East to Scotland. This even before 1835. (*Berkeley*, Querist, Nr., 526 ff.) Great increase since the fare has been reduced on the steamers to from 4 to 6 pence. (Edinburg Rev., XLV, 54 ff.; XLVII, 236 ff.)

[2] Thus mowers emigrate from Württemberg and the Odenwald into the valley of the Rhine; inhabitants of the Alps into the South German plains, and the inhabitants of the sandy and healthy localities into the Hanoverian marshes and Holland; inhabitants of the Brabant into France. Many go from Waesland, 5 and 6 miles distant from Holland, to sow a field manured and plowed by the owner with flax, and afterwards to weed and harvest it, etc., and at their own expense. (*Schwerz*, Belg. Landwirthschaft, II, 105.) Even in the sixteenth century, 20,000 Frenchmen went every year to Spain in harvest time. (*Boden*, Responsio ad Paradoxa, 49.) Migration of the East-goers (*Ostgeher*) from Wartebruch as far as Poland and Russia. (*Frühling*, N. Landwirthsch., Ztg., 1870, 451 ff.) Galicians go into the Polish plains, and Poles into the Prussian low country (*v. Haxthausen*, Ländl. Verfassung, I, 99); Russians from the populous district of Oreland Poltawa etc. into the Southern steppes (*Kohl*, Reise, II, 118), and also out of Northern woody districts to Jaroslay, where they give themselves to the cultivation of the fields (*v. Haxthausen*, Studien, V, 198); Gallegos into the Portuguese wine region; inhabitants of the Abruzzi into the Roman Campagna (*Galiani*, Della Moneta, V, 4); Calabrians to Naples. In Tuscany, almost the entire cultivation of the unhealthy plains is done by the inhabitants of the mountains. Even in Africa migrations by the *fulahs* into the plains before them (*Ritter*, Erdkunde, I, 349); of the inhabitants of the cataracts of the Nile into Lower Egypt, where they remain from six to eight years, and where they are in great favor because of their honesty as gate-keepers and pack-carriers. (*Burckhardt*, Travels, 147.)

[3] In Paris, a great many masons and carpenters from Lothringen and Limousin, who return after from 6 to 7 months. The number of these migratory building workmen is estimated at over 40,000. (*Wolowski*.) Thus thousands of brick makers migrate from Vicentini and Friaul into Austria and Hungary; from the vicinity of lakes Como and Lugan, masons have been spread over all Italy, and this, it is said, has been going on a thousand years. (*v. Rumohr*, Reise in die Lombardei, 135 ff.) Yearly migration of

mountainous regions, with their limited agriculture, their late crops and their longing look into the far-off which is found united with a deep-rooted attachment to home, are the places whence they come.[4] When their home is distinguished in certain branches of labor, they are wont to carry these with them abroad, and in such case their sojourn away from home is generally longer.[5] The shorter and the more vagabond-like their migration, the less apt is it to be an economic blessing to the wanderers themselves.[6] There must necessarily result, as a consequence, a species of equalization between the

about 3,000 brick finishers from Lippe-Detmold, which is very opportunely directed by the government. (*F. G. Schulze*, Nat. Œk., 606.)

[4] In the Appenines, almost every valley has its own migration-district. Thus the Modeneses go to Corsica, and the Parmesanes to England. The migration from the German Tyrol amounts yearly to between 16,000 and 17,000 men. (*v. Reden*, Zeitschrift für Statistik, 1848, 522.) In the Canton of Tessin, over 11,000 passes are given for this purpose yearly; that is, to more than 10 per cent. of the entire population. The majority go to Upper Italy, but some go to Russia. The cheese-makers, pack-carriers and dealers in chestnuts, migrate from fall to spring; masons, glaziers etc. in summer.

[5] Savoyards as "shoe-blacks" etc. in Paris (*L. Faucher*, La Colonie des S. à Paris); Portuguese, as peddlers and pack-carriers in large cities in Brazil (*Jahn*, Beitr., 33); Gallegos in the large cities of Spain and Portugal as water-carriers; Bergamasks, in Milan and Genoa as pack-servants, where they constitute a kind of guild; the inhabitants about Lake Orta (south of the Lago Maggiore) as waiters, and hence the inns there are very good; Bohemian musicians, who carry on quite a different business at home during the winter; Grisons, as confectioners all over Europe. Many villages obtain from this source 20,000 florins. (*Röder und Tscharner*, C. Graübundten, I, 337.) There are at this time about three million people from China, and almost exclusively from the conquered and oppressed province of Fokien, in Farther India, where they execute the finer kinds of labor. (*Ritter*, Erdkunde, IV, 787 ff.)

[6] In Tessin, the fields are tilled, and badly enough, by old men, women etc. The men spend in the taverns and in all kinds of vice what they saved during the working season. (*Franscini*, C. Tessen, 156 ff.) Those who migrate from the vicinity of Osnabrück into Holland are said to bring back with them yearly about 100,000 thalers; but their abstinence from warm food, their bivouacing etc., to which they have recourse for the sake of frugality, lays the germs of numberless diseases. (*J. Möser*, P. Ph., I, 14 ff.) There are serious complaints of the demoralization of women produced in England by the gang-system, in which roving workmen, mostly Irish, are employed

rates of wages in the country receiving and the country furnishing them.[7] This may be a great national misfortune for the latter, inasmuch as its working class may thus be forced to a lower standard of life, and all their providence and self-control in the founding of a family be made fruitless by the arrival of less capable foreigners.[8] The hatred existing among the members of a higher class for parvenus from a lower corresponds in this respect to the mutual hatred of two countries for the natives of the other. (*v. Mangoldt.*) Considered from the point of view of the country furnishing these migratory classes, temporary emigration has this advantage over definitive emigration, that the persons leaving the country always maintain their economic connection with their home.[9]

---

under a gang master to perform contract work. (*L. Faucher*, Etudes sur l' Angleterre, 2, ed. I, 383, ff.)

[7] Hence, for instance, Osnabrück complained bitterly of the migration to Holland, because it raised the wages of servants. However, the absolute freedom of removal from one place to another produces not only a leveling of wages, but also an absolute rise of the rate of wages, as may be seen by contrasting it with the *glebae adscriptio*. Compare *supra*, § 160.

[8] Great danger to the national life of the English people by immigration from Ireland. The Irish laborers, bare-footed and ragged, restricting themselves to potatoes and whisky, have carried their disgusting habit of living in cellars, and of congregating several families together into one room, even with pigs as companions, over to England. (*Th. Carlyle*, On Chartism, 28 ff.; *G. C. Lewis*, The Condition of the Irish in England.) It is said that, in 1819, in London alone, there were over 70,000 Irish; in 1826, over 119,000. (Edinb. Rev. XLVII.) Even *J. S. Mill* would have no hesitation to prohibit this emigration to prevent the economic contagion spreading to English workmen. (Principles, I, ch. 14, 6.) Fortunately now Irish emigration has taken the direction of America, where there is more room. Whether in future Chinese emigration may not greatly endanger the condition of the lower classes, first in America and Australia, and then indirectly in Europe, *quære*. It is estimated that between 1856 and 1859, 78,817 Chinese emigrated to the United States. In Australia, to deter them from immigration, a tax of £10 per capita has been imposed on their entry into the country. (*Fawcett*, Manual, 107.)

[9] Of the East Indian coolies who had gone to Demarara, 469 returned in September, 1869, after having saved in five years, £11.235. (*Appun*, Unter den Troppen, II, 34).

The most striking example of this is afforded by those merchants, ship-owners etc. who are, so to speak, pioneers in foreign markets for Switzerland and Bremen. Only there is always danger of a crisis when the usual flow is suddenly checked.[10]

SECTION CCLXIII.

CONCLUSION.

That the economy of no nation can continue to grow *ad infinitum* is, in general, as easy to believe[1] as it is difficult to point out with a specification of particulars what are the limits which cannot be exceeded. This would be possible first

---

[10] The Grisons had, during the 17th century, accustomed themselves to living some time in the Venetian territory as shoemakers, 1,000 at a time. The blow was all the more severe when Venice, in 1766, expelled all the families. Since that time most of the Grison confectionaries in the principal cities of Europe have had their origin. (*Röder und Tcharner*, C. Graudbundten, I, 56.) The practice of engaging mercenaries as troops was of great assistance, especially in the interior of Switzerland. During the war of 1690 ff., there were nearly 36,000 Swiss hirelings in the French army. Shortly before 1789, even during the period of peace in France, Italy, Spain and Holland, their number may be estimated to have been at least 30,000. (*Meyer v. Knonau*, Gesch. der Schweiz. Eidgenossenschaft, II, 104, 464.) No wonder, therefore, that the cessation of the Swiss guards caused a frightful crisis. Expulsion of the Tessinians from Lombardy, 1853.

[1] There are, indeed, different opinions on this matter, and they were preponderant during the second half of the eighteenth century. Compare *Condorcet*, Tableau histoirique, des Progrès de l' Esprit humain, especially Epoque X, in which he treats of future progress. Nevertheless, he obscurely alludes (Oeuvres, VIII, 350) to a time when no further increase of population should take place. *Malthus*, Principle of Population, III, ch. 1, thoroughly demonstrates that in regard to the great prolongation of human life which he foresaw, the idea of the indefinite and that of the infinite were confounded with each other.

In that young and vigorous country, the United States of America, we find a popular school which, to say the least, hints at the principle of infinite growth. Thus, for instance, *Peshine Smith* (Manual of Political Economy, New York, 1853) teaches that the means of subsistence consumed at the place of production are not destroyed, but may return just as much to

in the case of agriculture. Here there are points beyond which every man practically versed in the art can see, that an increase of the gross product must be attended by an absolute decrease in the net product.[2] But even supposing that a

the soil in the form of manure as they had previously drawn from it (ch. 1). Capital has a tendency to increase more rapidly than population (ch. 6). The rate of wages has a tendency to increase with the increase of population (ch. 5). Mechanical progress increases the value of human labor and causes that of capital to decline relatively (ch. 3). He reverses, with *Carey*, Ricardo's law of rent (ch. 2).

Carey, also, relying on the assumption that more fertile land is brought under cultivation as civilization advances, allows us to see no limits whatever to this growth. (Past, Present and Future, ch. 3.) Still more clearly is the principle of unlimited and continually accelerated growth laid down in his Principles of Social Science, I, 270. *Carey* illustrates this principle by means of the example of the continually accelerated motion of a falling body, without noticing the practical *ad absurdum deductio* involved in it, that at the end of the thousandth second a falling body reaches a velocity of 1,000,000 feet. (loc. cit., 204.) But even in England, at present, we find such thoughts at times. *Banfield*, for instance, can scarcely understand how the relative rates of wages, interest and rent can decrease, except by an increase of their absolute amounts. See his Organization of Industry, passim. And so *v. Prittwitz* entertains the most rosy-colored hopes. He has no doubt that all governments which are still bad will see the error of their ways and correct them. (Kunst reich zu werden, 79.)

The growth of capital and even of human wealth in general is capable of indefinite increase (81). The rate of interest would sink amost to zero if so much capital were accumulated that no "undertakers" could be found who care to use it (305). Large farming will entirely cease in the future (307), and when the system of railroads is entirely completed, the whole earth will present the appearance of one immense park (29). He would allay all fear concerning the exhaustion of combustible material by pointing out the possibility consequent upon improved means of communication, that a great many of the inhabitants of the colder regions of the earth might migrate in winter to a warmer climate (21). At the same time, artesian wells might be made to bring to the surface the internal heat of the earth, or metallic plates connected with the wings of a windmill, might be made to generate heat by their friction on one another (22). See the same author's Andeutungen über künftige Fortschritte und die Gränzen der Civilization, 21 Aufl., 1855.

[2] According to § 165, we might say: where the product of the workman last employed is not sufficient to meet his own wants. Thus *J. B. Say* says that only that can be considered a product, the utility of which is at least equal to its cost. He makes use of the example where a three days' journey is neces

people had reached this point in their entire agriculture, they might still carry on industries, commerce, perform personal services for other nations, and obtain remuneration therefor in the means of subsistence and manufactured articles. If our nation has once entered on this path, it is evident that every improvement of its industry, every advance made by foreign countries in the production of raw material, manufactures and the consumption of services must result in a growth of our economy. David Hume was of opinion that industrial preponderance was in a necessary and continual state of transition from one country to another. A very highly developed state of industry made a country rich in money but enhanced the price of the means of subsistence, and the rate of wages; until finally it became impossible for it to compete in the markets of the world with cheaper countries, and industry, in consequence, emigrated to these.[3] But it is easy to see how all such limits are extended by the modern improvements in transportation, and the consequent facilitation of importation; and how much the remedy mentioned in § 198 has gained in importance by the modern advances made in machinery and the preponderance in so many respects of machine over hand labor.[4]

---

sary to obtain the food requisite for one. As the limits of production he gives the following: too few human wants; too costly methods of production; too high taxes, natural obstacles created by infertility or too great distance. (Traite I, ch. 15. Cours pratique, I, 349.)

[3] *D. Hume*, Discourses, No. 3, On Money.

[4] England is especially well situated in this respect, in consequence of its excellent commercial position and its surplus of the principal auxiliary products, such as coal, iron etc. Should the coal-beds of such a manufacturing country be ever entirely exhausted, it is scarcely possible to see, from our present point of view, how the most rapid and most frightful decline of its national economy could be averted! Compare the opening address before the British Association, by Armstrong, at Newcastle (1863), who prophecies the exhaustion of the English coal-beds in 212 years at the rate at which coal had been consumed during the eight preceding years. According to the report of the royal committee on the coal question (1871, vol. III), Great Britain has still attainable deposits, that is 4,000 feet deep, 90,207,000,000 tons of coal in its coal beds already known; and in beds not yet worked,

But here it is necessary to distinguish between the "applied" and only practical political economy, and "pure political economy." (§ 217. A development thus continued would be attended with great difficulty even if the whole world constituted one great empire. We need only mention Austria, where some provinces have remained in a very backward, almost medieval condition, while others have for a long time manifested the symptoms of over-population. How much more in different states. An uncivilized nation will frequently not care to increase its consumption of our manufactures, if to do so it becomes necessary to carry on its agriculture more industriously. Another nation that has already tasted of the fruit of the tree of economic knowledge may not be satisfied with the mere production of raw material forever. In time it may want to carry on commerce and industry itself, and hence consider the breaking of its commercial course with us as a species of emancipation from us. And, further, how if other highly cultivated nations should compete with us in the markets of countries which produce merely raw material? if such rivals should wage war in which each party should harm his adversary for the mere love of doing harm, and not unfrequently in opposition to its own economic interests? I know of no period the development of which has not been attended by such disturbances, and hence they cannot be said to be entirely unnatural.[9]

56,273,000,000 tons. Compare, also, *Jevons*, The Coal Question (1866). It is estimated that the most productive French coal-field will be exhausted in 100 years. (*M. Chevalier*, Rapport du Jury international de 1867, 57

[1] Even *J. S. Mill's* views on the probability of perpetual peace on earth are altogether too rosy: Principles III, ch. 17, 5. This is still truer of *Buckle*, History of Civilization, I, ch. 4. In the modern state-system of Europe, there is wont to be in each generation, a peaceful half and a warlike one, which follow each other as ebb and flow. I need only mention the preponderance of peace between 1714 and 1740, between 1763 and 1793, and between 1815 and 1853. It happens frequently that at the close of the period of peace, intelligent and noble but unhistorical and therefore short-sighted minds begin to dream of perpetual peace. Even a man like *Dohm* (Ueber die bürgerliche Verbesserung der Juden, 227 seq.) expected, in 1785, that considering the size

And even at home and among highly civilized nations, there are wont to be many obstacles to advancement on this road of progress. Every great economic change is connected as cause and effect, with a variety of political, social and other reformations which are never accomplished without great hardship and hesitation.[6] Where the division of labor has been developed to any extent, the formerly existing circumstances which must be surrendered for the sake of progress are generally synonymous with the interests of some class. This class opposes the improvement, and a struggle becomes necessary to carry it out. But under certain circumstances, a long delay in effecting a necessary reform may paralyse or poison the minds of the people to such an extent that they may afterwards have neither the will nor the power to successfully advance. This is the most important exception to the rule laid down in § 24. The happier the ethnographic and social composition of a people, the better the national spirit, the more skillful the form of its constitution, the less frequently will it happen.[7] All this is true especially of over-population and the plethora[3] of capital which so easily injure the morality of a people. New inventions also, by means of which the limits of the possibility of production may be incalculably extended can

---

and quality of armies, and the mutual knowledge of all countries of one another, that instead of actually waging war, nations might send to each other well authenticated statements of the strength, for instance, of their navies and of the sums necessary to maintain them for a number of years.

[6] The Mongols saw the abandonment of their nomadic life in so gloomy a light that they seriously thought of turning all China with its countless human beings into pasture-land! *(Gibbon*, History of the Roman Empire, ch. 34.)

[7] It is a fact characteristic of the history of England, that Norman supremacy and afterwards bondage were wiped out so gradually that contemporary historians have nothing to say of the transformation. (*Macaulay*, History of England, ch. 1.) Repeal of the corn laws *vis-a-vis* of the most recent industrial advance of the country.

[3] Even *Ricardo* says that in a highly civilized country the continual making of savings is by no means desirable. Carried to an extreme, saving would lead to the equal poverty of all. (Principles, ch. 5.)

be expected only from nations where there is no intellectual decline.[9]

SECTION CCLXIV.

THE DECLINE OF NATIONS.

That, after a whole nation has reached the zenith of its prosperity, it is subject to old age and to decline, and cannot avoid them, is in general, a proposition susceptible neither of proof nor refutation.[1] This uncertainty is practically very useful, for were it otherwise, mediocre statesmen might become either discouraged or indifferent. However, we should not assume, as so many do,[2] without proof, the earthly immor-

---

[9] The *Beccaria*, Economia publica I, 3, 31, teaches that the limits of population are to be found at the point where agriculture cannot be made to yield an additional increase of products, and where foreign countries do not offer any more a counter value of their products in exchange for the manufactured articles and the services to be furnished them. Similarly, *Büsch*, Geldumlauf III, 7; otherwise, indeed, V, 15, in which, in opposition to *Adam Smith*, it is claimed that the work to be performed by one nation for others has no limits which cannot be exceeded. *Steuart's* theory of the limits to the production of every commercial nation: Principles, I, ch. 18. *Lauderdale*, Inquiry, ch. 5, 274 ff., says categorically, that all wealth which is produced by the transformation of raw material depends on the production of such raw material, and of the means of subsistence necessary for the support of the labor employed in such transformation. Excellent investigations by *Malthus* in the additions (1817) to the Essay on the Principles of Population, II, ch. 9-13. Compare *Roscher* Nationalöcon. des Ackerbaues, § 162. As early a writer as *Mirabeau*, Philosophie rurale, ch. X, was of opinion that a country whose industries were on as large a scale as those of Holland, dispersed its people indeed over the whole earth, made them independent at home, but almost destroyed their nationality.

[1] Even in the case of individuals, that death is necessary is not susceptible of absolute demonstration; but no one doubts it, because of the experience so frequently repeated; an experience, however, which cannot be had in the same degree in the case of whole nations.

[2] Remarkable controversy between *Hume* and *Tucker*. The former had charged the latter with holding the opinion that industry and wealth must necessarily continue to advance indefinitely; and yet all things had in them the germs of decay. *Tucker*, on the other hand, remarked that all he wished

SEC. CCLXIV.] THE DECLINE OF NATIONS. 385

tality of nations, provided only they observe a proper diet; nor call the science of the physiology or medicine of nations a chimera, simply because it confesses that it knows of no preventive against such old age. It has doubtless been the fate of many nations to die, that is, not precisely to be destroyed — just as in the physical world, not a particle of matter is lost — but to see their former national personality disappear, and themselves continue to exist only as component parts of some other nation.[3] This phenomenon, indeed, finds its analogon in every thing that is human, but seems to contradict a law of nature which very widely prevails, viz.: that it is easier to advance in a certain direction in proportion to the distance gone over in it already.[4]

The problem of decline, however, is solved by the enervating influence of possession and power, an influence which only a select few among men can escape. And yet to every external advance there must be a corresponding advance of the interior man, else there is a fall great in proportion to the height before attained. The greater number take their ease once they have attained the object of their ambition. I need only cite the example of the posterity of those men who have

---

to say was that no one could point out where progress must necessarily cease. All political bodies like all natural bodies might decay; but it is not necessary that they should. With good laws and morality they would become more vigorous with increasing age. A great deal depended here on the more general distribution of property, on the assurance that industry would meet with its reward, and on the removal of the principal defects in the English electoral system. (Four Tracts, 477 seq. Two Sermons, 30.) Most political economists are of the same opinion; thus *McCulloch*, Principles, II, 3. See, however, the last two sections in *Ferguson*, History of civil Society.

[3] We assume that a new nation has arisen, when, after the disappearance of an earlier and high civilization, combined with the taking up of new ethnographic elements, we perceive anew the easily recognizable symptoms of youthful immaturity.

[4] Expressed in the domain of religion in the words of the Savior: *Matth.*, 25, 29. But at the same time the equally well-known expression in *Luke*, 12, 48, must be fulfilled. Compare *H. Brocher*, L'Economie monétaire, 1871, 25 ff.

VOL. II. — 25

grown rich by unusual exertion. Success itself generates vanity and a feeling of false security, the latter especially, inasmuch as that is expected from the whole community, from the state for instance, from others generally, which should be the fruits of one's own vigilance and one's own endeavors. It should not be forgotten that the nation is made up of individuals.[5]

In addition to this there is the striving after the new for the sake of novelty; a striving promotive of progress in itself, and without which the full development of the forces of civilization would probably not be possible. But if the genius of no nation is possessed of infinite capacities, it must happen, at last, that, in case the best has been attained, and the demand for novelty continues, men will go over to that which is worse. Even very great competition has here a dangerous influence, since it raises the great mass of the incompetent to the dignity of judges, and endeavors to seduce them by illicit means; in the arts, for instance, sensuousness is made to take the place of the feeling of the beautiful.[6]

There is, further the process of undeceiving, inseparable from the prosecution of any ideal purpose. Such ideals have always very much of human weakness in them. The great crowd of ordinary men follow, as a rule, their material inter-

[5] Schools of art are generally ruined by mannerism. Of the two great means of education in art, the study of nature and the study of classic models, the latter is the easier, and the former is readily neglected for it. Then there is the endeavor to flatter the master, which is most effectually done by imitating his faults; and the fact that pretending connoisseurs are most cheaply satisfied by mannerism.

[6] There is a peculiar charm, very productive in itself, attaching to the cultivation of a field which has been but little cultivated, and which, therefore, has the advantage of promising something new. On the other hand, the decline of almost all literatures begins with this, that writers and readers no longer think out completely the forms of speech, modes of expression etc. to which they have become used, as their original creators did; a great temptation to have recourse to a more and more spicy literary style. *J. S. Mill* considers the stationary state (Principles, IV, ch. 6) a very pleasant one to contemplate, but he overlooks the very important fact, that as men are constituted it uniformly introduces national decline.

ests. Only occasionally do they rise to the height of ideal things; and here we discover the brightest points in history. Later there comes uniformly a period of disenchantment and of exhaustion after the debauch is over. When all the ideals accessible to the nation have been destroyed or outlived, nothing can be done to awaken the masses from their slumber, or induce them to shake off their inactivity.

As a rule, the influences which have accelerated a nation's progress and brought it to the apogee of its social existence end in precipitating its ruin by their further action. Every direction which humanity takes has almost always something of evil in it, is limited in its very nature, and cannot stand its extremest consequences.[7] All earthly existence bears in itself, from the first, the germs of its decay.

However, to calm the feeling of human liberty, we may boldly assert that there never was a nation remarkable for its religiousness and morality which declined so long as it preserved these highest of all goods; but then no nation outlived their possession.

SECTION CCLXV.

CONCLUSION.

All the separate nations which have lived side by side, or followed one another, are embraced under the general name, humanity. Who would deny the existence of a point, viewed from which humanity might be seen to constitute one great whole; all the variations and differences in its life only one great plan, one wonderful sovereign decree of the divine will, grandly and wonderfully executed by God? Or who is so bold as to say that he stands on this point himself? Theologians should be the last to do it, since even the apostle Paul calls

---

[1] Great rulers, of whom it is said that they conquered the world by following out their own ideas to their ultimate consequences, would most certainly have lost the world by reason of the same logic if they had continued it only fifty years longer. What would have become of Alexander the Great and Charlemagne if they had lived one generation more?

God's ways inscrutable. So long as we do not even know whether we live in one of the first or one of the last decades of humanity, every system of universal history in which each nation and period is made to take its place in due subordination to its superiors, can be only a castle in the air; and it is a matter of indifference whether the basis of the system is philosophical, socialistic, or natural-philosophical.[1]

The usual error into which the builders of such history fall, is that they consider the peculiarities of certain stages of civilization, which may be shown to exist among all nations in the corresponding period of their history as the national peculiarity of the single people with whose history they are, for the time being, concerned. They deduce wonderful consequences, from the premises they laid down, but which our increasing acquaintance with other nations immediately shows to be unfounded.

There is, however, a number of facts really peculiar to a people which make up the national character, and which may give to an observer endowed with an imaginative mind, an inkling to the special vocation in the economy of providence of a particular people. That a positive system can be constructed from the material of such facts, I do not, indeed, think. But they are at least a safeguard against false systems, against the improper application of analogies, against the idle, fatalistic exaggeration of the maxim: "nothing new under the sun!" It had almost become the fashion to compare our present with the period of decline of the Greek and Roman republics. Frightful parallel, in which the greatest and most undoubted differences were frequently overlooked for smaller and certainly questionable similarities. Is not the abolition of slavery, which has been accomplished among all

---

[1] I mean here, especially, the attempt so frequently made (by *Herder*, for instance) to draw a parallel between the periods of universal history and the age at different times of the individual, or with the seasons. If there were a great many humanities between which we might institute a comparison, we might accomplish something with the analogy, but——!

the most important nations of the present, something new and of great import from a moral and economic point of view?[2] Can the national wealth, which depends on labor and frugality, be in any way compared with that which was based on plunder? And so, no one can calculate the benefits which may be reaped by posterity from the mere continuation of the scientific and especially natural-philosophical results obtained by former generations. The discovery of the whole earth soon to be completed, and its probable consequence, the civilization of all nations of any importance, must remove the danger to which all the civilized nations of antiquity eventually succumbed, namely, destruction by entirely barbarous hordes. Nor should the significance of the state-system of Europe, which might be extended soon enough into a state-system embracing the world, be under-estimated. Macedonia would not so readily have subjugated the Hellenes and the Persians if the great powers of the west, Rome and Carthage, had intervened at the right time. And there, too, is Christianity, whose means of grace are at hand for every one at all times, for his complete moral regeneration.

In one word, the usual argument with which the "man of experience" meets the man of inventive genius, that there never was anything of the like seen before, may suffice in thousands and thousands of cases; but it affords no strict proof. It is the province of genius to compel rules to extend their limits. But science should never forget that self-denial is necessary to the discovery of truth.[3]

---

[2] However, even such a man as Minister *Stein*, thinks that a laboriously acquired wealth may affect a people's morality injuriously. "The striving after wealth is the striving for the possession of the means of satisfying chiefly sensuous wants. This striving may suppress all nobler feelings, whether it find expression in violence or industry." Contrariwise, it is possible that some of the noblest of human qualities may be found side by side with the forcible acquisition of wealth, viz.: courage, patriotism. (*Pertz*, Leben Steins, II, 466.

[3] Compare my discourse on the relation of Political Economy to classic antiquity in the transactions of the royal Saxon Academy of Sciences, May,

1849; also many excellent remarks in *Knies*, Polit. Œkonomie. *Chr. J. Kraus*, has zealously discussed the question whether the development of humanity turns about eternally in a circle, or whether it forever advances to a progressively better future. He strongly advocates the latter view, and on grounds which appeal both to the head and to the heart. (Vermischte Schriften, III, 146 ff.; IV, 277 ff.)

APPENDIX II.

INTERNATIONAL TRADE.

INTERNATIONAL TRADE.

SECTION I.

THE MERCANTILE SYSTEM.

The principal peculiarities of the so-called mercantile system depend on a five-fold over-estimation: of the density of population, of the quantity of money, of foreign commerce, of the industries concerned with the transformation of materials *(Verarbeitungsgewerbe)*, and of the guardianship of the state over private industry.[1] All these tendencies are very intelligible, and almost self-evident, in a sovereign city-economy *(Stadtwirthschaft)* as opposed to the governed and worked-out *(ausgebeuteteten)* country districts; as they are found even in the city-republics of later medieval times. But they are also natural in whole national economies, during that period of youthful and rapid growth in which the increasing density of population continues still, for a long time, to be really only a spur and an assistance, and in which, therefore, there can be no expression of anxiety concerning over-population; in which the new and rapidly growing division of labor draws attention particularly to the market-side of all businesses and to the circulation of goods; in which the progress from trade by barter to trade by money necessarily makes the volume of money needed even relatively greater; but especially are they natural in that world-period in which foreign trade suddenly increased enormously in consequence of the discovery of the

[1] Compare *Roscher*, Geschichte der Nationalökonomik in Deutschland, I, 228 ff.

whole earth; when the citizen classes of the people assumed immense importance as compared with the landed and clerical aristocracy, and when, in the internal affairs of state absolute monarchy, and in foreign politics, the system of equilibrium, through the instrumentality of the great compact-formation of states prevailed.

All these tendencies are most intimately connected with one another. If precious metal-money be really the essence of national wealth,[2] a people who possess no gold and silver mines themselves;[3] for instance, Italy, France and England, can be-

---

[1] Even the remarkable Florentine pamphlet of 1454 (*Jablonowski's* prize essay of 1878, app. Beilage, 4) complains of the decrease of industry principally on account of the diminution of money caused thereby. "Wealth is money," says *Ernestine*, essay of 1530, on the coin, and explains the smaller wealth of the silver-country, Saxony, as compared with England, France, Burgundy and Lombardy, by the greater exportation of commodities of these countries, by means of which they draw the silver of Saxony to themselves. (*Roscher*, Geschichte, I, 103.) *Bornitz*, Theorie wie sich der Staat diesen *nervus rerum* in grösster Menge verschafft: De Nummis (1608), II, 4, 6, 8. *A. Serra*, Sulle Cause, che possono far abbondare un Regno di Monete (1613), places excess of gold and silver and poverty as diametrical opposites, at the head of his work. *Hörnigk*, Oesterreich über Alles, wann es nur will (1684), says that it is " better to give two dollars which remain in the country for a commodity, than only one dollar which goes out of the country " (ch. 9). According to *Schröder*, Fürstliche Schatz-und Rentkammer (1686), the export of commodities is a blessing only " when we can turn them into silver through our neighbors." (LXX, 12.) Even *Locke* held similar views (Considerations of the Consequences of the Lowering of Interest, 1691. Further Considerations concerning Raising the Value of Money, 1698). On *Davenant's* inconsistency in this respect, compare *Roscher*, Geschichte der Englischen Volkswirthschaftslehre, 110 ff. The quantity of money remaining the same, a country grows neither richer nor poorer (Christ. Wolff, Vernünftige Gedanken vom gesellschaftlichen Leben, 1721, § 476). *J. Gee*, Trade and Navigation of Great Britain considered (1730), bewails the folly of those to whom " money is a commodity like other things, and also think themselves never the poorer for what the nation daily exports," p. 11). *Justi*, von Manufacturen und Fabriken (1759 seq.), considers it the principal object of industry simply to prevent the outflow of money. Similarly, *Pfeifer*, Polizeiwissenschaft (1779), II, 286. Even Frederick the Great considered it " true and obvious " that " a purse out of which money is taken every day, and into which nothing is put in turn, must soon become empty." (Oeuvres, VI, 77).

[3] The thirst for gold which, in the sixteenth and seventeenth centuries,

SEC. I.] THE MERCANTILE SYSTEM. 395

come richer only through foreign trade,[4] by means of a favorable balance produced by a preponderance of their exports over their imports; and only inasmuch as this excess is balanced by a payment in money from foreign parts. And so, too, in foreign trade, one nation can gain only what another nation has lost.[5] Gain is promoted not only by direct obstacles placed in the way of the exportation of the precious metals, but still more by the value-enhancement of the exported commodities, and by the value-diminution of the imported commodities.[6] And as commodities which have undergone the process of transform-

drove so many emigrants to the western Eldorado, reminds one, by reason of its enthusiasm, of the crusades to the Holy Land. The striving after the making of gold which the emperors Rudolph II., Ferdinand III., Leopold I., Frederick I. of Prussia, Christian IV. of Denmark, Christian II. and Augustus the Strong of Saxony, Heinrich Julius of Braunschweig, Frederick of Würtemberg, harbored, and also the Silesian and Brandenburg princes even during the Hussite war *(Riedel*, Cod. Dipl. Brandenb., II, 4, 151), was, to a great extent, misplaced philosophy; men went in search of the *materia universalissima*, the *spiritus universalis*, from which all that is receives its *esse et fieri*, the universal elixir, at once the life-power of man, the universal medicine and maturing principle of natural bodies. (*Roscher's* Gesch., I, 230.)

[4] *Schröder* justifies the little estimation in which he holds internal commerce by saying that "a country may indeed grow and become powerful by its means, but cannot gain in wealth;" just as a dress embroidered with pearls is not made more costly by taking the pearls from the cuffs and putting them upon the cape. (F. Schatz-und Rentkammer, XXIX, 3.) According to the Fredrickian theorizer, *Philippi*, "internal trade scarcely deserves the name of commerce." (Vergröss. Staat, 1759, ch. 6.) *Sir J. Steuart* still teaches that an isolated state may, indeed, be happy, but that it can grow rich only through foreign trade and mining. (Principles, II, ch, 13.) The same fundamental thought finds expression in the title of *Th. Mun's* celebrated book: England's Treasure by Forraign Trade, or the the Balance of our Forraign Trade is the Rule of our Treasure (1664).

[5] *Il est claire qu'un pays ne peut gagner, sans qu'un autre perde, et qu'il ne peut vaincre sans faire des malheureux (Voltaire*, Dict. phil., art. Patrie). Even *Verri* was, in his earlier period, of the opinion: *ogni vantaggio di una nazione nel commerzio porta un danno ad un altra nazione; lo studio del commercio è una vera guerra* (Opuscoli, 335).

[6] Even in 1761, the learned *Mably* could say: *la défense de transporter les espèces d'or et d'argent est générale dans tous les états de l'Europe . . . il n'y a point de voie moins sensée* (Droit public, II, 365).

ation are, on an average, more valuable than raw materials, the state can best carry out this policy by import duties, import prohibitions, and export premiums on manufactured articles, as well as by export duties, export prohibitions and import premiums on raw materials.[7] This is extremely necessary against those nations who are superior to others in culture, wealth, the cheapness of labor and capital; and hence the envy of the mercantilists was directed chiefly against Holland, and after Colbert's time also against France.[8] Such commodities as are not at all adapted to the nature of a country, because of its climate, for instance, the nation should produce at least in colonies of its own, that it might, in this

---

[7] The obstacles placed in the way of importation by governments originated, in great part, from views entertained on sumptuary legislation; in that of exportation, from a desire to prevent a scarcity of certain articles, as may be clearly seen in *Patricius* (De Inst. Reipublic, V, 10, I, 8), and even in *Sully* (Mémoires, XI, XII, XIII, but especially XII), *Bornitz, Besold, Klock* and *v. Seckendorf*. (Compare *Roscher*, Gesch., I, 191, 202, 215, 247.) But the mercantilistic germs show themselves even in *Hutten* and *Luther*. *(Roscher,* I, 44, 63.) The advance made between the police ordinance of the empire of 1530 and that of 1548, is very remarkable in this respect. The mercantile theory of duties appears very systematically elaborated even in *J. Bodinus*, De Republica, 1577, VI, 2; in Germany in *Hörnigk*, Oesterreich über Alles, ch. 9.

[8] The English jealousy of Holland is represented especially by *Sir W. Raleigh* (?), Observations touching Trade and Commerce with the Hollander and other nations, 1603, Works, III, 31 ff.; *Sir J. Child*, A new Discourse of Trade (1690), and *Sir W. Temple*, Observations upon the U. Provinces (1672). Compare *Roscher*, Z. Gesch. der englischen V. W. Lehre, p. 31 ff., 125 ff. The English jealousy of France: *Sam. Fortrey*, England's Interest and Improvement (1663). *R. Coke*, A Treatise, wherein is demonstrated that the Church and State of England are in equal Danger with its Trade (1671), and the anonymous, Britannia languens (1680). *Per contra*, especially the work: England's Greatest Happiness, wherein it is demonstrated that a great Part of our Complaints is causeless (1677). Here we find chapters with the title: To export Money our great Advantage; the French Trade a profitable Trade; Multitudes of Traders a great Advantage. *Petty* gave the best solution to the question in dispute, in his posthumous Political Arithmetic concerning the Value of Lands etc. *Hörnigk* would enlist his service in the cause of the jealousy against France, immediately after the disgraceful defeats which Germany in 1680 ff. suffered in the midst of peace, by Louis XIV.

way, emancipate itself from foreign countries.[9] As the clear distinction drawn to-day between money and capital has asserted itself only since Hume's time, the notion that prevailed for centuries, that much money, much trade and a large population mutually conditioned one another, was a very natural one.[10]

The younger and more refined conception of the mercantile system is distinguished from the coarse Midas-believing one, by two tendencies especially:

A. By the more thorough consideration of the balance of trade and the consequent limitation of the traditional supposition, that the excess of exports over imports would be always made up in cash money.[11]

B. By the extension of the field of view, so that not only the direct but also the indirect and more remote effects of international trade were taken into consideration.[12]

Concerning smaller works of the same period and in the same direction, see *Roscher's* Gesch., I, 299 seq.

[9] Even *Peter Martyr* considered the colonization of countries which yielded the same products as the mother country of no advantage (Ocean, Dec., VIII, 10). On Spanish maps the most flourishing portions of America at present are designated as *tierras de ningun provecho*. And the English for a long time, ascribed value to their New England possessions, so far as the mother country was concerned, only to the extent it was possible to provide the West Indies from that quarter with corn, meat and wood. *(Roscher* Kolonien, p. 262.)

[10] Compare *Botero*, Ragion di Stato (1591); *Law*, Money and Trade (1705), p. 19 ff.; and *Verri*, Opuscoli, pp. 325, 333. Meditazioni (1771), cap. 19.

[11] Thus *Child*, spite of all his esteem for the discoverers of the balance-problem, calls attention to cases in which exports suffer so much waste *(Abgang)*, or imports are sold so advantageously, that an apparently favorable balance made a people poorer, and an apparently unfavorable one, richer. From the value of the imported commodities the self-earned freight has to be deducted. Countries like Ireland, many colonies etc., have a preponderance of exportations, because they, by means of the same, pay a rent to absent capitalists or to landowners. (p. 312 ff.)

[12] *Mun* admits that, for instance, the East Indian trade makes England richer, although it causes the exportation of much English money. But the exporter of money who, in exchange for it, brings back reëxportable commodities, should be compared to the sower. (Ch. 4.) Similarly, C. Rob-

A certain over-estimation of the circulation of goods continued to characterize even the latest adherents of the mercantile system.[13] Yet the caricature drawn by the tradition of more recent text-books, of the mercantilists, is true only of the inferior ones among them.[14] The most distinguished of them, Botero,[15] for instance, approximate more closely to the science of the present day than is usually supposed.

erts, The Treasure of Trafficke (1641), and even *A. Serra*, III, 2. According to *Child*, the loss in the East Indian trade is compensated for chiefly by this, that England obtains there the saltpeter it needs to satisfy its demand, and that the ships engaged in that trade are peculiarly well fitted for war. (l. c.) *Saavedra Faxardo*, for similar reasons, declared the discovery of America to be a misfortune. (Idea Principis Christiani politici, 1649, Symb., 68 seq.)

[13] Thus *Law, Dutot, Darjes* and *Büsch*. Even the violent opponent of the mercantile system, *Boisguillebert*, could not entirely escape this view. Compare vol. I, § 96.

[14] This is true, especially of the protectionist weekly paper: British Merchant or Commerce preserved (1713 ff.), in the contest with the weekly Tory paper edited by *Defoe:* Mercator or Commerce retrieved, which Charles King systematized and published anew in 1721. Later *Ulloa:* Noticias Americanas (1772), cap. 12. *Adam Smith* also concedes that many of the best writers on commerce, at the beginning of their books, allow that the wealth of a country consists not only in gold and silver, but also in goods of every description; but that further on they tend more and more to forget this qualification of the meaning of wealth. (W. of N., IV, ch. 1.) Hence it is that, in recent text-books, so many are now called adherents and now opponents of the mercantile system.

[15] Even *Colbert* says: nothing is more precious in a state than the labor of men (Lettres, Instructions et Mémoires de C. publiés par P. Clement, 1861 ff., II, 105). The great trade with foreign countries and the small trade in the interior contribute equally to the welfare of nations. (II, 548.) I would not hesitate to do away with all privileges, the moment I found that greater or as great advantages attended their abolition. (II, 694.) His duty-system of 1664 was a simplification, but also an important diminution of his earlier chaotic tariff. (II, 787 ff.)

SECTION II.

REACTION AGAINST THE MERCANTILE SYSTEM.

The reaction against the mercantile theory of the balance of trade, which reached its height in Adam Smith, was based principally upon the following considerations:

A. Precious-metal-money is a commodity like all other commodities, and therefore useful only for certain purposes. It is as little to the wealth-interest of a people, by means of a continually favorable balance, to import infinite quantities of the precious metals, as it is to its power-interest, by means of its commercial policy, to accumulate infinite stores of powder. The person who possesses other exchangeable goods will be as well able, in case of need, to obtain gold and silver therewith as to obtain powder.[1] We part with no capital when

---

[1] Even *Petty* and *North*, with their deep insight into the nature and functions of money, could not possibly entertain the mercantile theory of the balance of trade. *Petty* considers the exportation of money useful, even when commodities are brought back in exchange for it, and which are of greater value in the interior than the exported money. (Quantulumcunque concerning Money, 1682.) According to *North*, no one is richer simply because he has his property in the form of gold and silver plate etc.; he is even poorer, because he allows his goods to lie in that shape unproductive. Hence the importation of money is, in itself, not more advantageous than the importation of logs of wood; at most, the difference that, in case of excess, it would be easier to get rid of the money than of the wood, is of importance. Therefore, a state need never care very anxiously for its supplies of money. A rich nation will never suffer from a want of money. (Discourses upon Trade, 1691, pp. 11, 17.) According to *Berkeley* (Querist, 1735, pp. 566 ff.), there is no greater error than to measure the wealth of a nation by its gold and silver. It is to the interest of a people to keep their money or to send it off, according as its industry is thereby promoted. *Quesnay* declares it to be impossible that the exports of a country should be permanently greater than its imports: *tout achat est vente et toute vente est achat*.

Adam Smith (W. of N., IV, 1) compares the Spanish discoverers who inquired on every island, first of all, for gold, to the Mongolians, whom *Rubruquis* (c. 32) was obliged to give information to concerning the cattle of France;

we export the precious metals and import other commodities instead; we simply exchange thereby one form of capital for another.[2] The notion that the gain in trade is coincident with the balance of account paid in cash, is just as palpably false in the trade among nations as in trade among private persons.[3] It would be a decided hardship to most men, if they were to receive payment at once in money for all that they possessed: and the nation is made up of individuals.[4] And even the reasons which make payments in cash more uniformly desirable, in the case of private persons not engaged in mercantile pursuits, cease in the case of whole nations.[5]

" of the two, perhaps the Tartar nation was the nearest to the truth." Precious-metal-money may be even more easily dispensed with than most other commodities, since, in case of necessity, it can, by reason of its greater transportability be readily obtained from without, and can also be supplied by exchange and by credit. "Money makes but a small part of the national capital and always the most unprofitable part of it.... Money necessarily runs after goods, but goods do not always or necessarily run after money." *J. B. Say* calls the exportation of money more advantageous than that of other commodities, because the former is of use, not through its physical qualities, but only through its value, and the value of the money which remains behind correspondingly rises by reason of the exportation. (Traité, I, ch. 17.) Compare especially *Bastiat*, Maudit Argent, 1849.

[2] Against *Ganilh*, Théorie de l' Economie politique, II, 200.

[3] Even *Mun* had, in every balance of trade, distinguished three persons who participated in it; the merchant might lose when the nation in general gained, and *vice versa;* the king, with his duties, always gained. (Ch. 7.) The British Merchant (p. 23) maintained even, that when the merchant himself gains nothing and takes his back-freight *(Rückfracht)* in money, his country gains the whole amount thereof.

[4] "Every individual is continually exerting himself to find out the most advantageous employment for whatever capital he can command. It is his own advantage, indeed, and not that of the society, which he has in view. But the study of his own advantage, naturally, or rather necessarily, leads him to prefer that employment which is most advantageous to the society." *(Ad. Smith*, W. of N., IV, ch. 2.)

[5] For the reason that money, in international trade, for the most part, loses its character as money, and appears more as a commodity. Exhaustively in *Adam Smith* and *J. B. Say*, l. c. The English state paid, during the French war of the Revolution, in subsidies to foreign countries, £44,800,000; and yet, up to the end of 1797, imperial loans and the payments of private indi-

B. But a continual over-balance *(Ueberbilanz)* is not at all possible. Every relative increase of the amount of money must enhance the price of commodities, lower the value of money, and thus produce an exportation of money until a restoration of the level with other countries.[6] The prohibitions of the exportation of money, so often resorted to, can avail nothing, because the precious metals are among the specifically most valuable goods; and because it is easier yet to smuggle them out of a country than to smuggle them into it.[7]

C. The signs by which the mercantile system supposed it could estimate the favorableness of the balance of trade are essentially deceptive.[8] We cannot, for instance, from the course of exchange, determine whether the payments made by us to foreign countries have been made for purchases, to absentees etc., or as loans; and yet, according to the mercantilists, the latter are as useful to us as the former are injurious.[9] And even the most accurate tariff-record *(Zollregister)* of

---

viduals included, not as much as one million in cash went out of the country. *(Rose*, Brief Examination into the Increase of the Revenue of Great Britain, 1799.) When France paid the five milliards to Germany, the plus value of English exportation to Germany above the English importation thence rose from 274,000,000 (1869) to 478,000,000 (1872), and the increase in the amount of French from 39,400,000 (1869) to 131,700,000 (1873). The entire German underbalance *(Unterbilanz)*, *Soetbeer* (loc. cit.) estimates at 878,000,000 of marks.

[6] Emphasized especially by *David Hume* who calls attention to the seeking of its level by water. (Discourses: On the Balance of Trade.) *J. B. Say* speaks of carriages, the increase of which over and above the need of them must infallibly produce a reëxportation of them. (Traité, I, ch. 17.)

[7] With all the severity of its export prohibitions, Spain, for centuries, served as a medium to conduct the streams of American silver to the other parts of Europe. As to how Spain, during the last third of the 18th century, was overflowed by copper money, see *Campomanes*, Educacion popular, IV, 272.

[8] *von. Schröder*, F. Schatz-und Rentkammer, XXVII, has a very ingenuous faith in the rate of exchange and a tariff-record *(Zollregister);* while *Child* had a much better insight into the defects of these two criteria. (Disc. of Trade, p. 312 ff.) Compare *Steuart*, Principles, III, 2, ch. 2.)

[9] Compare § 199. It was a discovery of *Locke's*, that borrowing from foreign countries was advantageous in all those instances in which the inland borrower earned more than the amount of his interest by means of the loan. (Considerations, p. 9.)

the exportation and importation of commodities affords no guaranty [10] that, in many instances, the rendering of the counter-value may not remain absent, by reason of bankruptcy, shipwreck, or the emigration of property.[11]

D. Every act of exchange is advantageous only because through it a greater value is received than the one parted with was. (?) Fortunately, in normal trade, where both parties satisfy a real want, and neither party is deceived, this is actually the case on both sides.[12] In accordance with all this,[13] Baudrillart is of opinion that the whole theory of the balance of trade no longer exists.

SECTION III.

FURTHER REACTION AGAINST THE MERCANTILE SYSTEM.

Simultaneously with this opposition, the theory of the international balance of trade underwent important refinements, a new and improved edition, so to speak, of old Colbertism.[1]

---

[10] *Ségur*, Mémoires, II, 298, tells how the Russian officers of custom were bribed by English merchants to represent the Russian imports from England *under*, and the exports to England *above* the true value. In addition to this, smuggling was carried on!

[11] *J. B. Say* calculates from the English tariff-record (*Zollregister*), from the beginning of the 18th century to 1798, an excess of exports over imports of £347,000,000; and yet the highest estimates of the amount of money actually in England, according to *Pitt* and *Price*, gave only £47,000,000. (Traité, I, IV, 17.) The Russian lists of exports and imports from 1742 to 1797, show a favorable balance of 250,000,000 rubles; to which must be added 88,000,000 rubles taken from the mines during the same time. But it is notorious that the stores of money diminished. *Storch*, Gemälde des russischen Reiches, XI, 12.

[12] Manuel, 310. *F. B. W. Herrmann* (Münch. gelehrte Anz. XXV, 540) also declares the whole theory of the balance of trade wrong. According to *Brauner*, Was sind Mauth und Zollanstalten (1816), 51, it is "a mere fancy."

[13] Recognized even by *Ch. Davenant*, On the probable methods of making a People Gainers in the Balance of Trade (Works, II, p. 11).

[1] Compare *Mengotti:* Il Colbertismo (prize essay of the Georgofili at Florence), 1791. If, with *H. Leo*, we were to designate the whole period from the issue of the struggles of the Reformation to the preparations of the French

Each school is wont to estimate the favorableness of the balance according to the preponderance of that which they consider the most important element in a nation's economy. Thus the population-enthusiasts, after the middle of the 18th century, distinguished the "balance of advantage" from the "merely numerical:" the former is favorable to the country which, by means of its exports, employs and feeds the greatest number of men; the latter to the country with a preponderating importation of money. And they call the former much more important than the latter.[2] The great advance which this view constitutes over the old system lies chiefly in two points: that the number and employment of men are evidently, so far as the whole national economy and national life are concerned, a much more important element than the quantity of money in a country; and further, that now, at least, the possibility of a simultaneous profit on both sides is admitted.[3] The best writer in this direction, Jos. Tucker, is among the great-grand-parents of the Manchester theory of to-day!

Revolution as the "age of the mercantile system," *Colbert* would be a very appropriate type of it.

[2] Compare § 254. Here belong *Forbonnais, Necker, Tucker* (Important Questions, IV, 11; V, 5; VII, 4; VIII, 5. Four Tracts, 1774, I, p. 36); *Justi* in his middle period *(Roscher,* Gesch. der N. O. in Deutschland, I, 451 ff.); but especially *Sonnenfels* (politische Abhandlungen, 1777, Nr. 1), who sees the best sign of a favorable balance in the increase of population. (Grundsätze, II, 333.) When Austria, for 2,500,000, purchases diamonds of Portugal, and sells Portugal linen to the amount of 2,000,000, it has the numerical balance against it, but obtains the "balance of advantage." (II, 329 seq.) With an admixture of physiocratism, this doctrine appears in *Cantillon,* Nature du Commerce, 1755, p. 298 ff.; with an admixture of free trade, in *Büsch,* Geldumlauf, V, 12.

[3] *Justi,* Chimäre des Gleichgewichts der Handlung und Schiffahrt (1759), supposes a gain on both sides in all commerce between nations. Hence, no nation can attain to a flourishing trade in any way except it be to the advantage of those with which it has to do. (p. 14 ff., 43.) Here, it may be presumed, *Hume's* Essay, On the Jealousy of Trade, exercised an influence. *Sonnenfels* distinguishes, in foreign trade, five grades of advantage: 1, most advantageous, when finished commodities are exported and cash money is imported; 2, when finished commodities are exchanged for raw materials;

A further advance was made by men who introduced the higher notions of nationality and of the stages of civilization into the theory of international trade. Thus, at about the same time, the socialistic J. G. Fichte, with his shut-in commercial state, and the romantic reactionary, Ad. Müller, with his organic whole of national economy.[4] Finally, Fr. List,[5] with his "National system of Political Economy," and his severe subordination of the mere "agricultural state" to the "agricultural, manufacturing and commercial state," acknowledges the favorableness of the balance in the nation which by means of the exportation of manufactured articles, the importation of the means of subsistence and of articles to be manufactured, demonstrates and promotes its higher stage of civilization.[6]

3, finished commodities against finished commodities; 4, raw material against raw material; 5, raw material against finished commodities. (Grundsätze, II, 202.)

[4] It is as necessary that every nation should constitute a separate commercial body as that it should be a separate political and juridical body. The person who asks: why should I not have commodities in all the perfection in which they are made in foreign countries? might as well ask: why am I not completely a foreigner? *(Fichte*, Geschloss. Handelstaat, 1800: Werke, III, 476, 411.) *Ad. Müller* compares universal freedom of trade to a universal empire, which will ever remain a chimera. (Elemente der Staatskunst, 1809, I, 283.)

[5] *List* (Werke, II, 31 ff.) had, after 1818, recognized that a *passive* balance for whole nations was possible, if they were not able to cover their wants, supplied from abroad and then consumed, by their income, but were obliged to make inroads on their national capital.

[6] *Ch. Ganilh*, who expects a real enrichment of a nation only from foreign trade (Dictionnaire de l'E. P., 1826, p. 131), ascribes the most favorable balance to the nation that exchanges dear labor against cheap; that is, principally to a nation of tradesmen as contradistinguished from a nation of agriculturists. (Theorie de l'E. P., 1822, II, 239 ff.)

SECTION IV.

PARTIAL TRUTH OF THE MERCANTILE SYSTEM.

But even among the successors of Hume and Smith, a deeper insight into, so to speak, the physics of money and of international trade must have led to the recognition of many a truth which the mercantile system had, indeed, badly formulated, insufficiently proved, but which it had, nevertheless, an inkling of. And, indeed, how frequently it happens that the progress of science proceeds from one one-sidedness, through another opposed but higher one-sidedness, to the all-sidedness which knows no prejudice!

A. Precious-metal-money is, indeed, a commodity, but of all commodities, the most current, the most many-sided in its utility, the most economically energetic, and at the same time of peculiarly great durability.[1] Money-capital, far from being the least useful portion of a nation's capital, is rather one of its most important parts; and especially in the higher stages of civilization, where the division of labor has been most largely developed, is it peculiarly productive and indispensable.[2] Here

---

[1] *Locke*, Civil Government (1691), § 49, seq., emphasizes this durability of the value-preserving metallic money, in opposition to the perishable articles of consumption, as a principal element in the development of private property and of economic civilization. But even *Petty* ascribes to the precious metals a higher quality as wealth than to any other commodity, for the reason that they are less perishable, and possess value always and everywhere. Hence, he esteems foreign trade more highly than inland trade, and would have those businesses which import the precious metals protected more than others against taxation. (Several Essays, 1682, p. 113, 126, 159.) *Adam Smith* also recognizes this, at least so far as intermediate trade is concerned. (W. of N., IV, ch. 6.)

[2] Even *Rau*, in his additions to *Storch* (1820), p. 397, concedes the peculiarly charming, vivifying power, which money possesses to an extent greater than any other commodity. Well distinguished whether the money-want of a country is already fully satisfied or not. (Ansichten der Volkswirthschaft, 1821, p. 157.) *Carey* exaggerates when he calls money the cause of the movement in society, out of which force is produced, what coal is to the lo

it is really more likely that the possessor of commodities may be wanting the wished for money, than that the possessor of money should be wanting in the wished for commodities. And, hence, the numerous half mystic expressions of the magical power of money, which have passed into literature from the common usage of the people, can be, by no means, considered mere errors.

B. Just as little, can the impossibility of the preponderant importation of money for a long time, be asserted. Hume's rigid theory of a level, by no means, exactly corresponds with the reality. The precious metal which is, indeed, imported, but which does not subsequently enter into the circulation, need exert no influence whatever on the prices of commodities in general; and may, therefore, remain permanently in the country. Think only of the articles made of the precious metals, which minister to luxury,[3] of buried private treasure, of the treasures of the state, which are idly stored up; as well as of a portion at least of most cash on hand.[4]

comotive, or food to the animal body (Principles of Social Science, ch. XXXII, 5), or the only want of life for which there is a universal demand. (Ch. XXXIII, 1.) But he rightly calls it the "instrument of association." Excellent demonstration, as to how, at the sudden outbreak of a war, of a revolution etc., all those who have money on hand, even when they had previously obtained it while peace still prevailed, in the form of a loan, are in an infinitely better position than the owners of the otherwise most useful commodities. (Ch. XXXVII, 12.) Earlier yet, *P. Kaufmann* placed the "principal character of money" in this, that it was "most perfect property *(Vermögen);*" and he calls its quality as a commodity, philosophically considered, in question; and judges the balance of trade according to this, that in commodities, interest-yielding as well as dead capital is exported, but in money capital, which is always gain-engendering. (Untersuchungen im Gebiete der politischen Œkonomie, 1829, I, 4, 74, 80.)

[3] In England, *Patterson* estimates the regular additional importation *(Mehreinfuhr)* of money at from four to five millions sterling, of which the greater part is devoted to purposes of luxury. (Statist. Jrl., 1870, 217.)

[4] *Fullarton's* view (Regulation of Currencies, 1844) suffers from exaggeration. *Knies*, Geld and Credit, II, 285, very well shows that the "hoards" are by no means mere idle stores, and that, therefore, their void produced by the exportation of money must be soon filled up again. *Adam Smith*, even, may be considered a predecessor of *Fullarton*. (W. of N., ch. 2, p. 250, Bas.)

From the other side, also, the over-balance or under-balance *(Ueber-oder Unterbilanz)* of a country may continue, a very long time, when its internal trade with its money-need is, in the first case, an increasing, and in the last, a decreasing one. So far, the preponderance of the importation of money may be called a favorable sign and the preponderance of the exportation of money an unfavorable one. And the person who thinks that a permanent preponderance of exports or imports is not at all possible in the way of commerce, overlooks the possibility of a very extensive national indebtedness.[5]

C. But a distinction should be made between the *balance of payments* and the *balance of trade* in the narrower sense of the expression.[6] In the case of the latter, to be complete, it is necessary to carry to the credit side of the account: 1. The exports of commodities; 2, the profit made by parties at home by realizing on *(Realisirung)* the exports in foreign countries; 3, the freight-profit made by parties at home on exports and imports, as well as in foreign carrying trade *(Zwischenverkehr);* 4, the sale of inland ships in foreign countries; 5, premiums and compensation for damage on account of maritime insurance from foreign countries. On the debit side, on the other hand, the corresponding items when foreigners have received from the home country, as in the case of imports etc. To obtain the general payment-balance, we have still, in addition, on the credit side: 1. The profit from home participation in enterprises in foreign countries and the transfers of capital originating therefrom; 2, the interest and repayments of money-

---

[5] Even *Büsch* (Werke, XIII, 26) says that the under-balance *(Unterbilanz)* of the Scotch vis-a-vis of England was for a long time made up in two ways, by the marriage of wealthy English heiresses and by Scotch bankrupts. Thus the troops, who, in the 17th century, were traded over to France, and in the 18th, to England by German princes, brought the money, in part, back again, which was exported by the unfavorable balance. According to *List*, the exported metals, after they have risen in price with us, flow back to us again; not, however, as exchangeable articles, but in the form of a loan, by which it is made possible for us to dispose of them again, and again to receive them in this shape. (Werke, II, 37.)

[6] Thus even *J. Steuart*, Principles, IV, 2, ch. 8.

capital loaned in foreign countries; 3, the sale of stocks *(Effecten)* to foreign countries as well as new loans to which the home country makes in foreign parts; 4, remittances from foreign countries to foreigners sojourning in the home country, and money brought with them by travelers and emigrants; 5, inheritances, pensions and extraordinary payments from foreign countries. Then, too, on the debit-side, belong the corresponding counter-items.[7] If we, in this way, take a survey of the whole world, we shall perceive a treble current of the precious metals. The first and most regular goes, in long lines, from mining countries, over to the commercial countries of the world, and distributes the newly acquired gold and silver as commodities according to the wants of the coinage, of manufactures etc. The second oscillates, as it were, in short waves from country to country, in order to adjust the *plus* or *minus* for the time being of payment-balances. Lastly, regular sudden currents, with slow subsequent counter-currents, when single economic districts require to make extraordinary drafts or shipments of the precious metals, by reason of bad harvests, war, a disturbed double standard etc.

D. Since international indebtedness has so much increased, precisely the richest nations may have the greatest regular excess of exports over imports; partly because of the great amount of capital etc., which they possess in foreign countries; partly because of the great development of their system of credit in the interior, by means of which they find substitutes for so great a part of the metallic currency.[8]

---

[7] Compare *Soetbeer* in *Hirth's* Annalen des deutschen Reiches, 1875, p. 731 ff.

[8] British Europe had from 1854 to 1863, a yearly surplus amount *(Mehrbetrag)* of imports of at least 266, and at most 1190 millions of marks, in the average, 764 millions; from 1864 to 1873, of at least 802 millions, and at most 1388 millions, an average of 1104 millions; whereas, on the other hand, Australia, besides its great exportation of gold, exhibits a great excess of exports of commodities over imports. France, too, from 1867 to 1869, had attained to an average surplus importation *(Mehreinfuhr)* of 211 million marks; which is related to the fact that, according to *L. Say*, it received about from

SECTION V.

THE ADVANTAGES OF INTERNATIONAL TRADE.

The truth that no exportation is permanently possible without importation, and that, in international trade, also, both sides better their condition, was clear to the Italians in the fifteenth century, and in the sixteenth and seventeenth centuries to the Netherlanders.[1]
Every nation can, through its instrumentality, for the first time, acquire not only those commodities which nature entirely refuses to it, but such also which it can itself produce only at a great cost.[2] And here it is not so much the absolute costs

---

600 to 700 million francs a year in interest from foreign countries; and that from 200 to 300 million francs were expended by foreigners etc., traveling in France. Similarly, in the case of governing countries vis-a-vis of their dependencies; whence even the old mercantilists entertained no doubt of the enrichment of the former. Thus France, in 1787 ff., had a yearly importation of 613 million livres, and an exportation of 448 millions, because the colonies sent to France 150 millions more than they drew therefrom. *(Chaptal*, De l'Industrie, Fr., I, 134.) Hungary, from 1831 to 1840, had a yearly exportation of 46 million florins to Austria, and an importation of only 30 millions. *(List*, Zollvereinsblatt, 1843, No. 49.) Algiers drew from France in 1844 to the amount of 83 million francs, and found a market there for only 8 millions (Moniteur), which no one will consider an enrichment of France. The great preponderance of French exports in 1831, 1848 and 1849, of Austrian, between 1874 and 1876, a sign of diminished purchasing capacity! When England, in March, 1877, imported to the amount of £35,230,000, and exported to the amount of £16,921,000 (against £27,451,000 and £17,739,000 in March, 1876), the Economist sees therein a sign that many outstanding debts were called in.

[1] *M. Sanudo*, in Muratori Scriptores, XXII, 950 ff., and the Netherland decree of February 3, 1501, in the Journal des Economistes, XIII, 304. Then, *Salmasius*, de Usuris (1638), p. 197. *Child*, *Becher* and *Temple* had all made their studies in Holland. Compare, besides, even *Plato*, De Rep., II, 371.

[2] *J. S. Mill* rightly calls it a remnant of the mercantile system that *Adam Smith* still saw the principal utility of foreign trade in the market for the home production which is thereby increased. But this utility is to be looked for not so much in what is exported as in what is imported. (Principles, II, ch. 17, 4.)

of production as the comparative which are decisive.[3] The country A may be superior to the country B in all kinds of productiveness; but when this superiority for the group of commodities x amounts to only 50 per cent., and for the group y, on the other hand, to 100 per cent., it is to the interest of A, which possesses only a limited quantity of the factors of production, to produce a surplus of the commodities y, and to exchange that surplus against what it wants of x.[4] B, also, would willingly agree to this, even if it were not to get the commodities y entirely as cheap as A might supply them, but still decidedly cheaper than their production would cost in B itself. But, if both parties derive advantage from international trade, there is no necessity whatever that this advantage should be equally great on both sides. As in every struggle over prices, the gain here also is greatest on the side of the nation whose desire to hold fast to their own commodities is farthest

---

[3] Compare v. *Mangoldt*, Grundriss der V. W. L., 185 ff. By the English, the discovery of this truth is attributed to *Ricardo*, Principles, ch. 7. Compare the further development in *J. Mill*, Elements (1821), III, 4, 13 seq.; *Torrens*, The Budget (1844) and *J. S. Mill*, Essays on some unsettled Principles of Political Economy (1844), No. 1, and Principles, III, ch. 18 ff. But even *Jacob*, Grundsätze der Polizeigesetzgebung (1809, p. 546 ff.), was acquainted with the truth that generally both sides gained, but the one party, possibly more than the other. According to *Lotz*, Revision (1811), I, 161, the gain and loss of each party rises and falls in proportion to the difference between the degrees of value which each party, so far as he is himself concerned, attaches to the goods given and the goods received. And even *Cantillon*, Nature du Commerce (1155), p. 226, 369 ff., had a presentiment of the reason why countries having a low value in exchange of money can continue notwithstanding to sell in foreign countries. And so, too, *Hume*, Essays (1752), On Interest, who, without looking through the spectacles of the mercantile system, perceived that countries with a flourishing trade must necessarily draw much gold and silver to themselves. Recently, *Cairnes* has shown by practical examples that Australia imports Irish butter and Norwegian wood, and the Barbadians meat and flour from New York, although both might themselves produce such articles cheaper. (Essays etc., 1873. Leading Principles, 1874, p. 379.)

[4] Thus a Kaulbach might more expertly ornament his own door and window frames than an ordinary room-painter, but does not do so, because he can employ his time to better advantage.

from being outweighed by the want of the foreign commodity, and which, at the same time, employs most productively the equivalent received in imports in exchange for its exports.[5] Yet, in estimating this productiveness, it is necessary to take the whole national life into consideration.[6]

The international distribution of the precious metals is subject to the same law. These, also, are procured most cheaply by the nation which, directly or indirectly (by the production of counter values wished for by the whole world), employs the most productive economic activity upon them, and at the same time (it may be by especially well developed credit), is in the least urgent need of them.[7] Therefore, on the whole, their value in exchange is wont to be lowest among the richest

[5] Even *Law*, Money and Trade, p. 31, was of opinion, that when a nation consumes its imports which are greater than its exports, it grows poorer, not in consequence of the importation, but of the consumption. *Quesnay* calls attention to the *plus on moins de profit qui résulte des marchandises mêmes que l'on a vendues et de celles que l'on a achetées. Souvent la perte est pour la nation qui reçoit un surplus en argent, et cette perte se trouve an préjudice de la distribution et de réproduction des revenus.* (Max. génér., 24.)

[6] *Rau* distinguishes principally whether importation brings articles of luxury or means of acquisition *(Erwerbstamm)* into the country. (Ansichten der V. W., 163.) Similarly, *de Cazeaux*, Elements d' Economie privée et publique (1825), p. 188 ff. *Schmitthenner*, Zwölf Bücher vom Staate (1839), I, 497. "A favorable balance of trade does not make a people richer because they receive the metals for other values, but because they produce and sell more than they purchase and consume; the result of which naturally is that the difference must consist in values capable of being capitalized." Kaufmann draws a distinction according as the imported goods come into the country in the form of dead or interest-bearing capital. He illustrates his view by the case of a peasant who sells his seed-corn in order to purchase a finer hat with the proceeds. (Untersuchungen, I, 96, 81 seq.)

[7] International trade makes imported commodities cheaper and exported commodities dearer, but the aggregate of consumers gain more in the former case than they lose in the latter, because they now enjoy the blessings of the international division of labor. But, even with this general enrichment, single classes of the people, and even the majority, may have to suffer; as, for instance, when in the exchange of corn against iron, the cheapening of the iron profits the people less than the consequent dearness of corn injures them. (*Fawcett*, Manual, 391.)

and most highly cultivated nations.[8] Such a relative cheapness of gold and silver is not only a symptom of economic power, but considering the preëminent energy of these very commodities, at the same time, a means to procure most foreign commodities with a smaller expenditure of one's own forces.[9] Hence, a great change in the distribution, hitherto usual, of the precious metals, produced, possibly, by great advances made in production here, or by an increase in consumption there, or by means of commercial prohibitions etc., may be just as advantageous to the country which receives more as hurtful for the country which pays more;[10] and both, all the more as the

---

[8] " Gold and silver are by the competition of commerce distributed in such proportions amongst the different countries of the world as to accommodate themselves to the natural traffic which would take place if no such metals existed and the trade between countries were purely a trade of barter." (*Ricardo*, Principles, ch. 7.) In most direct opposition to the mercantile system, he represents the distribution of the precious metals to be not the cause but the effect of national wealth. A nation rapidly growing in wealth will obtain and keep a larger quota of the general supply of gold and silver. (The high Price of Bullion, 1810.) On the other hand, it depends on the one-sided abstraction with which *Ricardo* loves to pursue certain assumptions, that every exportation of money is made to signify a peculiar cheapness of money, and *vice versa*. (Opposed by *Malthus*, Edinb. Rev., Febr., 1811.) *Carey's* frequently repeated assertion, that gold and silver always flow towards those markets where they are cheapest (Principles of S. Science, I, 150, and passim), confounds cause and effect.

[9] Compare § 126, and even *Kaufmann*, Untersuchungen, I, 75 seq.

[10] Let us suppose that, hitherto, the English had supplied their demand for wine from France, and paid therefor in commodities made of steel; and that now France prohibits the importation of the latter and requires gold instead. If the English take this gold out of their own circulation, the value in exchange of the gold which remains to them rises; the prices of all commodities fall, state debts and private debts become more oppressive etc. If, to avoid this, they send their steel wares, which France has rejected, to California, to obtain gold there in exchange, they find that California has as much of steel wares as it requires, and that it can be induced to extend its consumption of them only by a corresponding lowering of their price. But if, on the other hand, the gold which has flowed towards France has produced a rise in the price of commodities, and a decrease in the exportation of commodities; and has then flowed out of the country, to Germany for instance; England may in consequence be placed in a position to effect its payments for

revolution in prices enhances the most productive elements of the nation there, and here the most unproductive.[11] Hence, even when it cannot, in general, be said that one branch of commerce, carried on in a normal manner, should necessarily remain behind another in economic productiveness, those which have nothing to fear from a disturbance of their balance by the measures of foreign states are distinguished by the greatest security, and those are capable of the greatest growth which exchange articles to be manufactured *(Fabrikanden)*, and the means of subsistence against ordinary manufactured articles.[12][13]

French wine with the gold which its manufactured articles have been exchanged against in Germany. But all this always supposes that the prices of commodities have fallen in England and risen in other countries; that is, a changed and, so far as England is concerned, an unfavorable distribution of the precious metals — which is found in connection with a relatively decreased productiveness of English labor. The English cost of production may yet continue to be covered, notwithstanding; but, when it has been diminished by a lowering of wages, interest etc., the national wealth suffers in consequence. Compare *Torrens*, Budget, p. 50 ff., who precisely on this bases the greater security of trade between the mother country and its colonies; and which also found expression in the Peel reform plan of 1842 ff. *Adam Smith* approximated to this view when he ascribed a more favorable balance to the country which paid for its imports with its own instead of with foreign products. (W. of N., IV, ch. 3-2, p. 329, Bas.)

[11] Compare § 141. Strongly emphasized by *List*, Werke II, 31, 36 seq. 48, 137.

[12] *Torrens* imagines an English manufacturer who employs raw material $= 100$ quarters of corn and manufactured wares $= 100$ bales of cloth (the quarter of corn and the bale of cloth supposed to be of equal value) and whose product $= 240$ bales in value; and compares him with an American agriculturist who, by means of the same outlay of capital, harvests 240 quarters of corn. The trade between them restores to each not only his outlay, with twenty per cent. profit, but puts them in a position to repeat their production on a larger scale. Only the quantity of fertile land can put a limit to this growth; for corn and cloth help produce each other, and the cheapness of the one promotes the cheapness of the other, which can not, by any means, be said, for instance, of the exchange between vanilla and satin. (Budget, p. 268 ff.) Compare *Roscher*, Colonien, p. 277 ff.

[13] The important controversy concerning absenteeism may be answered in accordance with the principles laid down in this chapter. The mercantile system considered the rent sent to absentee landlords or capitalists as a trib-

SECTION VI.

INTERNATIONAL COMMERCIAL TREATIES.

All international commercial treaties have this object in common: to moderate the impediments to trade which arise

---

ute paid to foreign countries; but certainly improperly, as such rent is only the fruit of their property which the owners might have consumed in their own country, without giving any one a particle of it. Besides, these rents are not sent in cash to foreign countries, but in the form of those commodities to the exportation of which the country is peculiarly well adapted. Let us suppose, for instance, that the Irish absentees had all left the country at once. The tradesmen, personal servants etc., to whom they had hitherto furnished employment would be greatly embarrassed to find a market for their services etc., but the producers of linen and meat would have largely increased their exports, because an entirely new demand for their products would have arisen through the farmers of the absentees. The reverse would necessarily happen if all absentees were suddenly called home. Absenteeism which has lasted a long time injures no one economically. Many, recently, laud it even, because it permits every nation to devote their energies to the branches of production for which they are best qualified: Paris, for instance, to theatrical and luxury wares. The savings made by the English absentees on the continent, where things are cheaper, turn eventually to the advantage of England. (Thus, even *Petty:* Political Anatomy of Ireland, p. 81 ff. *Foster*, On the Principle of Commercial Exchanges between Great Britain and Ireland, 1804, p. 76 ff. Edinb. Rev., 1827. *F. B. Hermann*, Staatswirthschaftl. Untersuchungen, 355, 363 ff. *Per contra*, especially, Discourse of Trade and Coyn, 1697, p. 99. *M. Prior*, List of the Absenters of Ireland, 1730. *A. Young*, Tour in Ireland, 1780. *Sir J. Sinclair*, Hist. of the Public Revenue, 1804, III, 192 seq. *Lady Morgan*, On Absenteeism, 1825. An aversion for absenteeism plays a chief part in all Carey's writings. Thus, even in his Rate of Wages, 45 ff.

On medieval complaints concerning the absenteeism of monasteries: *Bodmann*, Rheingauische Alterthümer, 751. From a higher point of view, it cannot, indeed, be ignored that absenteeism, largely developed, cripples the organic whole of national life. The most highly cultured and influential classes become estranged from their country, the great mass remaining behind coarser, economic production more one-sided, and all social contrasts more sharply defined. Disturbances in Rome, when Diocletian removed his residence from there; the decline of the Netherlands, very much promoted by the discontent which Philip II.'s departure for Spain produced. It was estimated, however, in 1697, that the English absentees caused a gain to France

from the differences and even from the enmities of states. According to time and character, they fall into three groups:

A. *Medieval*, where a barbarous state for the first time promises foreign merchants in general legal security, without which regular trade is unthinkable. Such treaties, where their provisions are not a matter of course, must be certainly considered as a salutary advance; and they may, under certain circumstances, be necessary even to-day.[1]

B. *Mercantilistic* treaties, which close, perhaps, even a bloody commercial war carried on against a rival,[2] or which

of £200,000 per annum. (Discourse of Trade, p. 93.) It is said that about 1833, 80,000 Englishmen traveled on the continent, and consumed £12,000,000 there. *(Rau.)* According to *Brückner*, the Russians who travel in foreign countries take 20,000,000 rubles a year out of the country with them. *(Hildebrand's* Jahrb., 1863, 59.) That the countries which receive these travelers receive no very great benefit from them, see in *J. B. Say*, Cours pratique. In Paris, there were, even in 1797, so many strangers who so enhanced the rents paid for *maisons garnies* that their expulsion was proposed. *(A. Schmidt*, Pariser Zustände, III, 78.)

[1] The treaty of commerce between England and Morocco, of the 9th of December, 1856, specially covenants that the countrymen of a debtor shall not be held responsible for debts in the creation of which they had no part; that between England and Mexico, in 1826, guaranties, among other things, that prices shall be freely determined between buyers and sellers (art. 8), freedom from compulsory loans, and from forced conscription for military duty (10), the exercise of one's religion, and the inviolability of graves (13); things which were not yet matters of course in Mexico! Similar agreements between Spain and England in 1667; between Spain and Holland in 1648 and 1713; and even in 1786, between England and France. Commercial treaties of this kind are found very early and very frequently among the ancients. Compare the Arcadian-Ægean in *Pausan*, VIII, 5, 5, which strongly recalls the Russo-English trade over Archangel; further, Corp. Inscr. Gr., II, No. 1793, 2053 b and c, 2056, 2447 b, 2675-78, 3523. That in the suburbs of Jerusalem, from Solomon to Josias, places where Astarta etc. was worshipped, were maintained unhindered, depends, it is said, on commercial treaties with the Phœnicians, Moabites, Ammonites. *(Movers*, Phönikier, III, 1, 121 ff., 206 seq.)

[2] The two commercial treaties between Rome and Carthage, 348 and 306 before Christ *(Polyb.*, III, 22 ff.), are a clear proof that, in the interval, the mercantile superiority of Carthage had increased. While the Romans in 348 had still the right, under certain limitations, to carry on trade in Sardinia and Africa, it was in 306 entirely denied them.

by a closer connection with a state, whose rivalry is not so much feared, are intended to moderate the worst consequences of a general seclusion.³ Consistently carried out, and without any regard for consequences, the mercantile system really means a war of each state against all others, and it is no mere accident that after the cessation of the wars of religion (1648) and before the beginning of the war of the French revolution (1792), commercial wars occupy the foreground. Such economic alliances as are entered into in these treaties generally unite states which, by reason of the very different nature of their land and their different national culture, are adapted to production of very different kinds, and which, at the same time, have a common political interest.⁴ Each party here agrees with the other to give a preference to its subjects in trade, to not exceed certain maxima of duties etc.⁵

---

³ As guild-privileges make annual fairs *(Jahrmärkte)* and governmental fixed prices necessary.
⁴ Commercial treaty of the Venetians with the Latin empire in Constantinople, of the Genoese with the Greek after its restoration; in which, for instance, it was promised to the former, that no citizen of a state at war with Venice, should be permitted to sojourn in the Byzantine empire; to the latter, that they alone of all foreigners should enjoy freedom from taxation, and, with the Pisans, navigate the Black Sea. As long as the Dutch were the hereditary foes of Spain, they were much favored in France. Commercial treaty of 1596, putting them on an equal footing with the French; and which, considering their superiority at the time, was necessarily of greater advantage to them than to the French. *Colbert's* step to destroy this preponderance is coincident with the changed foreign policy. (Richesse de Hollande, I, 127.) In the peace of Nymweg, again (art. 6 seq.), France tried to separate the Dutch from their allies by the restoration of their former rights. In the Spanish war of succession, France entered into a treaty with the arch-duke, Charles, that a common commission should fix the duties on English commodities, transfer the trade with America to an English-Spanish company, but that the French should be excluded therefrom. *(Ranke,* Franz. Gesch., IV, 257.)
⁵ The king of Bosporos had the rights of citizenship in Athens, and enjoyed that of freedom from taxation of his property there. In consideration of this, the Athenians were released from his corn export duties of $\frac{1}{30}$. *(Isocr.,* Trapez., § 71. *Demosth.,* Lept., p. 476 ff.) Commercial treaty of Justinian with Ethiopia: the latter was to afford aid against the Persians, in

SEC. VI.] INTERNATIONAL COMMERCIAL TREATIES. 417

The art of the negotiator was employed to overreach the other contractant in relation to the balance of trade.[6] It was considered a special matter of congratulation to induce a less highly developed nation to abandon the traditional means employed to artificially elevate its industries. Hence it is, that such friendly treaties frequently contained the germs of the bitterest enmity.[7] A popular remnant of this second group

return for which Byzantium promised to supply its requirement of silk no longer from Persia, but from Ethiopia. Commercial treaty between Florence and England, 1490: England promised to permit all the wool destined for Italy, except a small quantity intended for Venice only, to go over Pisa, and as a rule, not through foreigners. Florence, on the other hand, was to receive English wool only through English ships. (*Rymer*, Foedera, XII, 390 seq. Decima dei Fiorentini, II, 288 ff.)

[6] The difficulties of such negotiations described by an experienced politician (probably *Eden*): Historical and Political Remarks on the Tariff of the French Treaty, 1787.

[7] The Methuen treaty (1703) was considered an English master-piece, because Portugal had actually exported a great deal of Brazilian gold to England. *Pombal* said, in 1759: "Through unexampled stupidity, we permit ourselves to be clothed etc. England robs us every year, by its industry, of the products of our mines....A severe prohibition of the exportation of gold from Portugal might overthrow England." (*Schäfer*, Portug. Gesch., V, 494 ff.) And yet the treaty only says that Portugal withdraws its prohibition of English woolen wares, and restores the former duties (15 per cent.), while England continues to permit Portuguese wine to pay a duty ⅓ less than French wines! Singular doctrine of *Adam Smith* (W. of N., IV, ch. 6), and still more of *McCulloch* (Comm. Dict., v. Commercial Treaties), that this commercial treaty was unfavorable to England and very favorable to Portugal, although, in fact, later a duty of only about 3 per cent. was imposed here on English commodities. (*Büsch*, Werke, II, 62.) The English-French commercial treaty of 1786 introduces in the place of the former prohibition, duties of 10, 12 and 15 per cent. for a number of industrial products. The French soon came to believe that they had been taken advantage of here. *A. Young* found the desire very general in the north of France, to get rid of the Eden treaty even through a war. (Travels in France, I, 73.) Many of the *cahiers* of the third estate demand that no treaty of commerce should be entered into without previous consultation with the industries interested. (Acad. des Sc. morales et polit., 1865, III, 214.) But in England, also, bitter complaints of the opposition, to which Pitt replied, that commercial treaties between agricultural and industrial countries result to the advantage of the latter, independent of the fact that England obtained a new

VOL. II. — 27

has been noticeable even in recent times, when in diplomatic negotiations concerning the reciprocal modification of duties, it was considered an overreaching and even as an outrage, in case one state made more "concessions" than it received:[8] evidently, a confusion of the producers of the industry in question with the whole nation.

C. *Free-trade* treaties, intended to pave the way to the general freedom of trade.[9] Two provisions especially are charac-

---

market of 24,000,000, and France of only 8,000,000 persons. Compare the extracts in *Lauderdale*, Inquiry, App., 14. Forcade: Revue des deux Mondes, 1843.

[8] Urged very largely in southern Germany against the Prussian-French commercial treaty of 1862. But is it really an "advantage" for France to have in the interior more toiling *(Plackereien)* for inlanders as well as for foreigners? Or that its consumers must pay high taxes to the producers of certain wares?

[9] Seldom in antiquity. Compare, however, Inscr. Gr., II, No. 256, and the reciprocal granting of the rights of citizenship of Athens and Rhodes. *(Livy,* XXXI, 15.) Among the moderns, Flanders followed free-trade principles similar to those followed later by Holland, at the beginning of the fourteenth century; for instance, it refused to gratify France by breaking off its trade with Scotland. *(Rymer,* Foedera, II, 388.) Florence, in 1490, promised the English, that in all treaties to be entered into with others, it would permit it to enter. In the French-Florentine commercial treaty of 1494, it is stipulated with the Florentines that their ships *Gallica esse intelli· gantur* and their merchants *tanquam veri et naturales Galli* etc. (Docima, II, 308.) Swedish treaty with Stralsund, 1574, that every privilege granted to a Baltic city should also be, of itself, to the advantage of Stralsund. Mutual equal treatment of subjects promised between Portugal and England, 1642; Portugal and Holland, 1661; mutual treatment on the basis of the most favored nation: between England and Portugal, 1642; Holland and Spain, in the peace of Utrecht; Spain and Portugal, 1713; Spain and Tuscany, 1731; England and Russia, 1734. But how far such principles were removed from the beginning of the eighteenth century is shown by the speech from the throne of the 28th of January, 1727, of George I., in which the Austro-Spanish treaty of 1725, that placed the subjects of Austria in the colonial empire of Spain on an equal footing with the English and Dutch, is described as a violation of the dearest interests of England, and in which it is said that England must defend its own unquestionable right against the covenant entered into to violate public faith and the most solemn treaties; that it might be that Spain thought of subjecting England once more to the popish pretender. Even in 1713, it was one of the principal points in controversy between the Tories and Whigs, whether, in a commercial treaty with

teristic here: putting the subjects of the other party on an equal footing with those of the home country in what relates to the ship-duties etc.;[10] and the promise that the products of the other party, as regards import duties, shall be treated like those of the most favored nation.[11][12] Whether this preparation for the universal freedom of trade is better made through the medium of an international treaty or of national legislation cannot be answered generally.[13] Besides, in our day, the preference of one foreign nation would be easily evaded through the perfection of the modern means of communication.

France, the latter should be accorded the rights of the most favored nations. Compare *Daniel Defoe*, A Plan of the English Commerce, and *per contra*, The British Merchant.

[10] English treaties with Prussia, 1824; the Hanse cities, 1825; with Sweden, 1826; France, 1826 (England removed the limitations still retained without compensation, in 1839); Naples, 1845; Sardinia, Holland and Belgium, 1851. Prussian treaties with Russia, 1825; Naples, 1847; Holland, 1851. French with Bolivia, 1834; Holland, 1846) in which reciprocity is extended even to the navigation of rivers); Denmark, 1842; Venezuela, Equador and Sardinia, 1843; Russia and Chili, 1846; Belgium, 1849; and Portugal, 1853.

[11] Marking an epoch in this respect are the treaties of the United States with Holland (Oct. 8, 1782), Sweden (April 3, 1783), Frederick the Great (Sept. 10, 1785), and England (Oct. 28, 1795); recently that entered into by Napoleon III. with England in 1860, and with the Zollverein in 1862.

[12] The expression "most favored" is not always strictly construed. Thus, for instance, France granted the right of coast-sailing proper *(cabotage)* only to Spain. States frequently promise only: *s'appliquer reciproquement toute faveur en matière de commerce et de navigation qu'ils accorderaient à un autre état gratuitement ou avec compensation.*

[13] Napoleon III. had a preference for commercial treaties, because these, as acts of foreign politics, lay in the plenitude of his imperial power (art. 6 of the constitution of 1852; senatus consultum of Dec. 23, 1852), while in legislation, his free trade tendencies were limited by popular representation. And so also Prussia, by its commercial treaty with him (1862), was actually freed from the hindrances which the free veto of the Zollverein-conferences would have opposed to its reform. Opposition to the treaty-form because too binding. *(Chaptal*, De l' Industrie Française, II, 242 ff.) The free-trade party lauds it precisely on this account. See the report of the Leipzig Chamber of Commerce for 1874-75, p. 41.

APPENDIX III.

THE

INDUSTRIAL PROTECTIVE SYSTEM

AND INTERNATIONAL FREE TRADE.

THE

INDUSTRIAL PROTECTIVE SYSTEM

AND INTERNATIONAL FREE TRADE.

SECTION I.

PROXIMATE ECONOMIC EFFECTS OF THE INDUSTRIAL PROTECTIVE SYSTEM.

That the principal measures which the mercantile system recommended, artificially to increase a nation's wealth, could not produce the immediate effects expected of them, has been shown, especially from the natural history of money. Their proximate economic consequences necessarily consisted in this, that they diverted the existing productive forces of the nation from their places of application *(Verwendungsplätzen)* hitherto, to others which the government thought more advantageous.

A. If home producers are in a condition to offer their commodities as good and as cheap as foreigners, all protection of the former by import duties, or even by prohibitions, is superfluous. The home producer has, as a rule, not only the advantage of the smaller cost of freight to the place of consumption,[1] but that of being earlier informed, because of his

---

[1] It is of course different in the working *(Verarbeitung)* of foreign raw material. Much also depends on the situation of the industrial provinces. For instance, manufactured articles can reach the interior of Spain and the Western states of the American Union only after they have passed the industrial coast-regions of both countries. In Russia, on the other hand, the center is the principal industrial region; and hence the coast may be actually nearer to foreign than to home manufacturers. Similarly, in France, at least for iron and coal. Compare *Adam Smith*, W. of N., II, p. 279 Bas.

proximity to consumers, of a change in their tastes.² If, indeed, foreigners could supply us better and cheaper, and if they are kept from supplying our market only by artificial means, the state compels our consumers to a sacrifice of enjoyment;³ and such a sacrifice as is not fully compensated for by the profit made by the favored producers in any manner. The latter are generally soon compelled by home competition to arrange their prices in accordance with the rate of profit usual in the country. If they had no "protection" they would simply employ their productive forces in other branches of production; and in those in which they were equal or even superior to foreign competitors. By means of the products thus obtained, the people might then get in exchange all those commodities from foreign countries, the production of which it is, according to the laws of the division of labor, better to leave to foreign countries.⁴ Since one nation can lastingly pay

---

¹ People would, however, have to calculate on the foolish luxury which despises the home product because "it came from no great distance." World-supremacy of Paris fashions! A manufacturer of excellent German *Schaumwein* (foaming wine) complained to me, in 1861, that, after suffering heavy losses, he was compelled by his customers to adopt French labels. Here, a wise prince may have a favorable influence by his example. Louis XIV. himself insisted, when his mother died, that the court should use only French articles of mourning Gee, Trade and Navigation, p. 46. Augustus I., of Saxony, always wore home cloth. (*Weisse*, Museum für Sächsische Geschichte, II, 2, 109.) Similar requirements by the prince of Orange (1749) of all officials: Richesse de Hollande, II, 317. Dutch executioners were dressed in calico. (Discourse of Trade, Coyn etc., 1697.) American popular stipulations not to wear foreign articles of luxury. (*Ebeling*, Geschichte und Erdbeschreibung, II, 481.) Rhode Island tailors placed the working wages for home stuffs much lower than for foreign. (II, 149.)

³ *Prince Smith* calls protective duties scarcity-duties (*Theuerungszölle*). Because of this increased dearness of the "protected" commodities, consumers can no longer pay for as many other home commodities. If the industry was previously in existence, the protective duty imposed is wont to enhance the price, not only of the foreign commodity, but also of the home commodity.

⁴ If, for instance, the English had never had a protective tariff on silk, nor the French a protective tariff on iron, the former would probably get all the silk commodities they want from France and pay for them in iron ware. In

another nation only with its own products, any limitation of imports must, under otherwise equal circumstances, be attended by a corresponding limitation of exports.[5] Directly, therefore, these hindrances to importation produce no increase, but only a change in the direction (*Umlenkung*) of the national forces of capital and labor; an increase, only in case that foreign producers are thereby caused to transfer their productive forces within our limits;[6] which may certainly be considered the greatest triumph of the protective system. Hence it is

---

this way, both nations would be well off in what concerns the relation between the cost of production and the satisfaction of wants. *Say* calls protective duties a fight against nature, in which we take pains to refuse a part of the gifts which nature offers us. He leaves himself open to the charge of exaggeration, however, when he compares a nation that wants to produce everything itself to a shoemaker who wanted to be tailor, carpenter, to build houses and cultivate a farm also. Although no nation is all-sided, yet every nation is a great deal more-sided than an individual.

[5] Whoever keeps a people from purchasing in the cheapest market, thereby prevents their selling in the dearest. (*McCulloch.*) It was no mere desire of revenge that induced Holland, in the 17th century, to threaten the Poles, in case the enhancement of their duties continued in Danzig and Pillau, they would supply their corn-want from Russia. (*Boxhorn*, Varii Tractat. polit., p. 240.) Thus the tariff-measures adopted by France against the German cattle trade and the Swedish iron trade promoted the growth of the Crefeld silk manufacture, and lessened the exportation of French wine to Sweden. When, in 1809, England heavily taxed Norwegian wood, in favor of Canada, the Norwegians began, instead of purchasing English manufactured articles, to supply themselves from Hamburg, Altona and France. (*Blom*, Norwegen, I, 257.)

[6] *Fr. List* assumed altogether too unconditionally such an effect from import duties to be the rule. The more developed the self-confidence of a nation is, the more vigorous the life of its industries, the more many-sided the commerce of its people; the less disposed are its industrial classes to give up their home and carry their market with them. But, for instance, Swiss labor and, still more, Swiss capital have been induced by the tariff systems of the great neighboring countries to settle in Mühlhausen, Baden and Voralberg, or at least to establish branch houses in these places. Similarly, Neumark cloth makers were induced to emigrate to Russia, and Nürnberg industrial workmen to Austria (*Roth*, Geschichte des Nürnberger Handels, II, 170) etc. Compare *Burkhardt*, c. Basel, I, 74; *Böhmert*, Arbeiterverhältnisse der Schweiz, I, 16 seq.; II, 17.

absurd when an equal extension of "protection" to all the branches of a nation's economy is demanded, as it is so frequently, in the name of justice. There is here no real protection whatever, analogous, for instance, to the protection afforded by the judge, but a favor which can be accorded to no one without injuring some one else.[7]

SECTION II.

EFFECT OF EXPORT DUTIES ETC., ON RAW MATERIAL.— EXPORT PREMIUMS.

B. Export duties on raw material, and prohibitions of the exportation of raw material, lower the price of such articles, by preventing the competition of foreign buyers.[1] To this loss of the producers of raw material, there is, in the long run, no corresponding gain to the manufacturers. Rather will there be, when freedom of competition prevails at home, an increased flow of the forces of production to the favored branch, because of its rate of profit, which is greater than that usual in the country, and a corresponding flow from the injured branch, until such time as the level of profit usual

---

[1] Compare *Alby* in the Revue des deux Mondes, Oct., 1869, and, *per contra*, Cairnes, Principles, p. 458. The misfortunes of war or internal disquiet have frequently driven away the best labor-forces of an old industrial state, and thus powerfully promoted a young protective system in the neighborhood. Reception of Byzantine silk-weavers in Venice, during the crusade to Constantinople, of Flemish wool-weavers in England, under Edward III. (*Rymer*, Foedera, III, 1, 23) and Elizabeth; of Huguenot industrial workmen under the great elector etc. The growth of the Zurich silk industry by the settlement there of expelled Protestants from Loearno.

England, indeed, had, up to 1849, protective duties both for industry and agriculture. But the protective duties were of no real importance, except in the case of the latter, because the greater part of England's industrial products were superior to foreign competition without the help of protective duties. Something similar is true of most duties on raw material in the United States.

[1] Rags in Silesia dearer than in Bohemia by the full amount of the Austrian export duties (Gutachten über die Erneuerung der Handelsverträge;

in the country is restored.² Hence here, also, the final result is only a change of the direction, not a direct increase of the productive forces.³

C. In the case of export-premiums, it is necessary to distinguish between the mere refunding back of the taxes which have been paid on the assumption of a home consumption which has not taken place (drawbacks), and the actual making of donations because of the exportation of goods (bounties). The former produces no result except to maintain the possibility of a production which would otherwise have been prevented by the tax. The latter, on the contrary, compels all

---

1876, p. 9). When the English export-prohibitions were extended to Scotland, the price of Scotch wool fell about 50 per cent. *(A. Smith*, W. of N., IV, ch. 8.) In the case of foreign raw material, the reëxportation of which is prevented, the object of such prohibitions may be largely frustrated. When England, to promote its dyeing industries, left the importation of colors entirely free, but allowed their exportation only under heavy duties (8 George I., c. 15), the importers provided the market always with somewhat less than the amount required, and thus raised the price.

² Export hindrances have been continued longest in favor of manufacturing industries *(Verarbeitungsindustrie)*, in the case of such commodities as are not intentionally produced, such as rags, ashes etc., but which are collected only as the remains of some other kind of production or consumption. "Negative production," according to *Stilling*, Grundsätze der Staatswirthschaft, 803, because it is desirable to produce as little as possible of such raw material. But the dearer rags, for instance, are, the more carefully are they collected.

³ When the French prohibition of the exportation of hemp was extended to Alsace, its production decreased from 60,000 to 40,000 cwt. *(Schwerz*, Landwirthschaft des Nieder-Elsasses, 378 ff.) Frederick the Great soon carried his prohibition of the exportation of raw wool to such an extent as to prohibit the exportation even of unshorn sheep, and to punish the dropping of a sheepfold by a fine of 1,000 ducats. (Preuss. Gesch. Friedrichs III., 42.) Here, also, belong prohibitions relating to the exportation of corn, which force considerable capital etc. into industry. The prohibition of the exportation of corn in England, and the permitting of the exportation of cattle, wool etc., was one of the principal causes why there were so many complaints at the time of the turning of land used for tillage into pasturage-land. When, in 1666, the exportation of Irish cattle to England was prohibited, it produced, at the outset, great need in Ireland, but afterwards a flourishing condition of Irish industry. *(Hume*, History of England, ch. 64.)

those who are subject to taxation to make a donation to one particular class of persons engaged in industry.[4] Moreover, all consumers are compelled to pay a higher price for the commodity to the extent that the market price, inclusive of the premium to be obtained abroad, is higher than the home market price hitherto usual. But, as the cost of production has not increased, this profit of the producers, which is greater than that usual in the country, must induce other productive forces to enter into the favored branch; so that here, also, the lasting result is not a higher rate of profit of the individuals engaged in the industry, but an extension of the industry itself. Foreign countries chiefly reap the greatest advantage from this course, since they obtain the commodities at gift-prices.[5] The premiums paid, not for exportation, but for the production of a commodity, have a meaning akin to this.[6] Either the industry could not maintain itself without premiums, in which case the state encourages a losing production,— and the more there is produced the greater is the loss to the national economy;— or the industry might exist without the payment of premiums, and then the newly increased profit

---

[4] The effect must be very much the same when the right of buying up all the raw material of a certain district is granted to one factory exclusively The elector, Augustus of Saxony, did this frequently. Compare *Falke*, Gesch. des Kurf., A. v. S., 190-212, 345.

[5] As to how, by means of German drawbacks *(Rückzölle)* it is possible for beet-sugar to be offered at a cheaper rate in Brazil than home cane-sugar, see *Wappäus*, Brazilien, 1830. The French export-premiums for sugar amounted, in 1856, to over 8,000,000 francs. Frenchmen subject to taxation were obliged to pay this amount, and thus add to the already increasing price which they had to pay for that article. (Journ. des Econom., Juill., 1857.) In England, in 1742, the export-premiums for linen were defrayed by enhanced entry-duties on cambrics. (15 and 16 George II., c. 29.)

[6] As to how English export-premiums sometimes made English commodities cheaper in Germany than in England, see *Büsch*, Werke, XIII, 82. There are, indeed, gifts which may ruin the receiver of them, as, for instance, when one gets his rival intoxicated at his expense before the decisive solicitation. *Timeo Danaos et dona ferentes* (cited by Fox and Burke against the Eden treaty: *Hansard*, Parl. History, 1787, Jan. p. 402, 488).

would lead to an extension of the industry. Exportation would follow, and all the effects of export-premiums appear.[7]

SECTION III.

THE FREE-TRADE SCHOOL.

From what has been said, we may understand why the so-called free-trade school, with its atomistic over-valuation of the individual and the moment, rejects all those measures of the industrial protective system.[1] As such measures really injure

---

[7] It is said that Maria Theresa paid 1,500,000 florins a year for this purpose. *(Sonnenfels,* Grundsätze, II, p. 179.) England, between 1806 and 1813, altogether, £6,512,170. *Colquhoun,* Wohlstand, Macht etc., Tieck's translation, I, 251.

[1] *P. de la Court,* in his freedom of trade, has in view not the interest of consumers — and least of all of the whole world — but the interest of the commercial class. Compare Tüb. Ztschr., 1862, p. 273. Similarly, *Child,* Discourse of Trade, 1690; whereas *D. North,* Discourses upon Trade (1690), may be called a free-trader in the sense in which the expression is used to-day. No nation has yet grown rich by state-measures; but peace, thrift and freedom, and nothing else, procure wealth. (Postscr.) *Davenant* also zealously opposes the craving of a people to produce everything themselves, to want only to sell etc. He considered very few laws on commerce a sign of a flourishing condition of trade. (Works, I, 99, 104 ff.; V, 379 ff., 387 seq.) *Fénélon's* antipathy for import and export duties in Télémaque, a part of his general opposition to the *siècle de Louis XIV.* The view of the Physiocrates *(La police du commerce interiéur et extérieur la plus sure, la plus exacte, la plus profitable à la nation et à l' état consiste dans la pleine liberté de la concurrence: Quesnay,* Maximes générales, No. 25) is directly connected with their deepest fundamental notions of *produit net* and *impôt unique. Turgot* vindicates the interests of workmen against protective duties, for whom no compensation is possible, where one industry gains by its being favored in the same way that it loses when another is favored. (Sur la Marque de Fer, I, p. 376 ff., Daire.) "Those who cry so loudly for protective duties are partly thoughtless persons who wish to avoid the consequences of bad speculations, and in part shrewd persons who would like to earn during the first years a rate of profit higher than that usual in the country." *(Rossi.) Bastiat* ridicules the advocates of a protective tariff by the petition of the lamplighters, lamp manufacturers etc., that to advance their industry, and indirectly almost all others, the mighty foreign competition of the sun might be re-

the oppressed portions of the people more than they help the favored classes, their introduction, it is said, uniformly depends on this, that single classes of producers understand their private interests better than others, and are better organized than other producers and especially better than consumers, to take care of their interests.[2] Adam Smith approves import hindrances for the purpose of artificially promoting an industry only in two cases:

A. When military safety demands it. Hence he calls the English navigation act, that great prohibitive and protective law intended to advance the merchant marine, the wisest perhaps of all English commercial regulations, although he clearly saw that it compelled England to sell her own commodities cheaper and buy foreign commodities dearer.[3]

---

moved from all houses. (Sophismes écon., ch. 7.) To him, the protective system is precisely the system of want; freedom of trade, the system of superabundance. Political economy would have fulfilled its practical calling, if, by means of universal freedom of trade, it had done away with all that is left of that system which excludes foreign commodities because they are cheap, that is, because they include *une grande proportion d'utilité gratuite*. (Harmonies, p. 174, 306.) *Cobden's* pet expression: " Free trade, the international law of the Almighty!" (Polit. Writings, II, 110.) *K. S. Zachariä* calls the protective system a step introductory to communism (Staatsw. Abh., 100), because it nearly always leads to over-population and *List's* system, a politico-economical absurdity (Vierzig Bücher vom Staate, VII, pp. 23, 92).

[2] Among the many frequently wonderful speeches by which persons engaged in industry are wont to support their motion for protective duties etc., the following are particularly characteristic. The long struggle of English manufactures against the East Indian Company, since the later portion of the seventeenth century. Compare *Pollexfen*, England and East India inconsistent in their Manufactures (1697), against which *Davenant*, at the solicitation of the company, wrote his Essay on the E. I. Trade (1697). Prohibition of East Indian commodities, 11 and 12 Will. III., ch. 10. The struggle did not stop until the middle of the eighteenth century, when India was outflanked by English machines. When Pitt, in 1785, labored for the abolition of the tariff-barriers against Ireland, English manufacturers, and among others Robert Peel, declared that they would be forced in consequence to transfer a part of their manufactories to Ireland! *(McCulloch*, Literature of Political Economy, p. 55.) *Say* tells of a proposition made by the hatmakers of Marseilles to prohibit foreign straw hats (l. c.).

[3] W. of N., IV, ch. 2. According to *Roger Coke*, England's Improve-

B. When the import duty is no more than sufficient to balance the tax imposed on the corresponding home product. Smith rightly remarks that a universally heavier taxation by the home country, but which affected all branches of its production equally, operated like diminished natural fertility, and hence does not make any equalizing tax for foreign trade necessary.

The person who has only a modest opinion of the power of his own reason, and therefore a just one of the reason of other men and other times, will not believe that a system like the industrial protective system which the greatest theorizers and practitioners favored for centuries, and which governed all highly developed countries in certain periods of their national life, proceeded entirely from error and deception. It really served, in its own time, a great and regularly occurring want; and the error consisted only in this, that, partly through improper generalization by doctrinarians and partly by the avarice of the privileged classes and the inertia of statesmen, the conditioned and transitory was looked upon as something absolute.[4]

---

ment (1675), ship-building in England became dearer in a few years by about one-third, on account of the navigation act; and the wages of sailors advanced to such an extent that England lost its Russian and Greenland trade almost entirely, and the Dutch obtained the control of it. This *J. Child*, Discourse of Trade, admits, but still calls the navigation act the *magna charta maritima*. Similarly, *Davenant*, Works, I, 397. Here the relation of the cost to the immediate product can as little decide as it can against the exercise of troops or the construction of forts. *Adam Smith* allows the same reasons to apply to export premiums for sail-cloth and gunpowder (IV, ch. 5). Recently, however, *Büllau* (Staatswirthschaftlehre, 339; Staat und Industrie, 220 seq.) has argued against all these exceptions of Adam Smith.

[4]*Schleiermacher* (Christ. Sitte, 476) calls the polemics which can see nothing but error in a refuted theory, immoral.

SECTION IV.

FURTHER EDUCATIONAL EFFECTS OF THE INDUSTRIAL PROTECTIVE SYSTEM.

The sacrifices which the protective system directly imposes on the national wealth consist in products, fewer of which with an equal straining *(Anstrengung)* of the productive forces of the conntry, are produced and enjoyed, than free trade would procure. But it is possible by its means to build up *(bilden)* new productive forces, to awaken slumbering ones from their sleep, which, in the long run, may be of much greater value than those sacrifices. Who would say that the cheapest education is always the most advantageous?[1] Only by the development of industry also, does the nation's economy become mature.[2] The merely agricultural state can attain neither to the same population nor the same energy of capital, to say nothing of the same skillfulness of labor, as the mixed agricultural and industrial state; nor can it employ its natural forces so completely to advantage.[3] How many beds of coal, waterfalls, hours of leisure,[4] and how much aptitude for the arts of

---

[1] *List*, Nationales System der polit. Oekonomie, kap. 12, contrasts two owners of estates, each of whom has five sons, and can save 1,000 thalers a year. The one brings his sons up as tillers of the ground *(Bauern*=peasants) and puts his savings out at interest. The other, on the contrary, has two of his sons educated as *rational (rationelle)* agriculturists, and the others as intelligent industrial workers, and at a cost which prevents the possibility of his accumulating any more capital. Which of the two has cared better for the standing, wealth etc. of his posterity; the adherent of the "theory of exchangeable values" or the adherent of the doctriue of "the productive forces?"

[2] The rent of the land of Gr. Botton, in Lancashire, was estimated in 1692 at £169 per annum; in 1841, at £93,916. *(H. Ashworth.)*

[3] The pottery district of Staffordshire was formerly considered very unfertile. It was industry that first showed how the rich and varied beds of clay at the surface, and the wealth of coal under them, could be fully utilized.

[4] Blind free-traders always like to assume that every man capable of work-

industry, can be turned to scarcely any account in a merely agricultural state? If, therefore, the protective system could materially promote a national industry, or if it made such industry possible, for the first time, the sacrifice connected therewith, in the beginning, should be considered like the sacrifice of seed made by the sower;[5] but this can be justified only on the three following conditions: that the seed is capable of germination; that the soil be fertile and properly cultivated, and the season favorable.[6][7]

---

ing always busies himself; whereas idleness frequently excuses the wasting of its time, by the plea that a remunerative market of the possible new products is improbable, or at least uncertain. Compare *J. Möser*, P. Ph., I, 4. *Kröncke*, Steuerwesen (1804), 324, 328 seq., and even the first German reviewers of Adam Smith in *Roscher*, Gesch. der N. Oek. in Deutschland, II, 599.

[5] *List* calls attention to the case of the stenographic apprentice who writes more slowly for a time than he was wont to formerly.

[6] Let us suppose that a country had hitherto produced $10,000,000 worth of corn, and that of this amount it had sent $1,000,000 worth into foreign countries as a counter-value for foreign manufactured articles. It now, by means of a protective tariff, establishes home manufactures, through the instrumentality of which a coal bed or water fall is turned to account. The workmen in the manufactories henceforth consume what was formerly exported. Of course such a change is not effected without loss; but this loss ceases as soon as the home industry becomes the equal of the foreign industry which was crowded out. And then the forces which have been made useful in the meantime appear as clear gain. *List* not unfrequently called special attention to the fact that a consumption of 70,000 persons engaged in home industries means as much to German agriculture as all that it exported to England from 1833 to 1836. (Zollvereinsblatt, 1843, No. 5.)

[7] *Adam Smith's* free-trade doctrine has always been contradicted in Germany. Even in 1777, his first great reviewer, *Feder*, says that many foreign commodities can be dispensed with without damage; and that industries which indemnify the undertakers of them only after a time but which are then very useful to the community in general, would not be begun always without special favor shown them. (*Roscher*, Geschichte der National Oekonomie, II, p. 599.) *Kröncke*, Steuerwesen, 324 ff., speaks of attempts towards the education of industries by taxation-favors: "If of ten, only one succeeds, even that is to be considered a great gain." But modern protectionists base themselves chiefly on their interest in the independence of the country, precisely as the free-traders do on that of individual freedom. *Id. Müller*, with his organic way of comprehending things, opposes the assump-

SECTION V.

PROTECTION AS A POLICY.

A. So long as a nation is, indeed, politically independent, but economically in a very low stage, it is best served by entire freedom of trade with the outside world; because such freedom causes the influences of the incentives, wants, and the means of satisfaction of a higher civilization to be soonest felt in the country.

tion of a merely mercantile world-market, in which all the merchants engaged in foreign trade constitute a species of republic. *(Quesnay.)* He also rejects on national grounds the universal freedom of trade as well as the universal empire akin to it; although as a means of opposing it, he suggests not so much a protective tariff as the intellectual cultivation of nationality in general. (Elemente der Staatskunst, 1809, II, 290, III, 215, II, 240, 258.) According to *Sörgel* (Memorial an den Kurfürst v. Sachsen, 1801,)commercial constraint *(Handelszwang),* by means of export and import duties, is useful in the childhood of manufactures, afterwards injurious, because the powerful incentive to perfection is wanting where no competition is to be feared (67). *P. Kaufmann,* the opponent of Smith's balance-theory, demands moderate protection against the otherwise irresistible advantages of already developed industrial nations. (Untersuchungen, 1829, I, 98 ff.) The principal advocate in this direction is *Fr. List,* with a great deal of sense for the historical, but with little historical erudition; and after the manner of an intelligent journalist, he reproaches the free-trade school with baseless cosmopolitanism, deadly materialism, and disorganizing individualism. He distinguishes in the development of nations five different stages: hunter-life, shepherd-life, agriculture, the agricultural-manufacturing period, the agricultural-manufacturing-commercial period; and he demands that the state should lend its assistance in the transition from the third to the fourth stage, in the nursing or planting of manufacturing forces in connection, throughout, with the enfeebling of feudalism and bureaucracy, the increase of the middle class, with the power of public opinion, especially of the press, the strengthening of the national consciousness from within and without. Compare *Roscher's* review in the Gött. gelehrten A. 1842, No. 118 ff. As to how List resembles, and differs from Ad. Müller, see *Roscher,* Gesch. der N. O., II, 975 ff.; *v. Thünen's* independent defense of a protective tariff: Isolirter Staat, II, 2, 81, 92 ff., 98; Leben, p. 255 seq. The socialist *Marlo* (Weltökonomie, I, ch. 9, 10) distinguishes common products *(Gemeinprodukte)* which

B. The further advance which consists in the development of home industries by the country itself, may, indeed, be rendered exceedingly difficult by the unrestricted competition of foreign industries, which are already developed. The carriers may be obtained equally well in every properly developed country, and peculiar products *(Sonderprodukte),* like coffee, wine etc. With respect to the former, he agrees with List; in regard to the latter, with Smith. A protective tariff exerts a constraint on consumers, compelling them to abridge their enjoyments somewhat, and to employ these now in the procuring of instruments of production, in the exercise of skill needed in production and the accumulation of capital. At the same time foreigners should be kept from utilizing home natural forces, and where possible, home manufactures should be helped to utilize foreign natural forces. *Marlo,* indeed, assumes, as one-sidedly as the followers of Smith do the contrary, that without the tariff the workmen in question would not be employed at all; but he is right in this, that the most fruitful employment of the forces of labor, and the keeping of them most completely busy, mutually replace each other. In France, even *Ferrier,* Du Gouvernement considéré dans ses Rapports avec le Commerce (1808), had defended the Napoleonic continental system. See *Ganilh,* the French List, Theorie de l' Economie politique (1822), who grades the branches of a nation's economy in a way the reverse of Adam Smith, and finds the protective system necessary for the less developed nations, to the end that they may not be confined to the most disadvantageous employments of capital (II, p. 192 ff.). Especially is a greater population made possible in this way (248 ff.). Similarly, *Suzanne,* Principes de l'E. polit., 1826. Further, *H. Richelot,* List's translator. *M. Chevalier,* who recommends free trade for France in our day so strongly, approves the system of Cromwell and Colbert for their own time, and for a long time afterwards (Examen du Système commercial, 1851, ch. 7): a view which *Périn* says is now shared by "all serious writers." (Richesse dans les Sociétés Chrétiennes, 1861, I, p. 510.) *Demesnil-Marigny,* Les libres Echangistes et les Protectionistes conciliés (1860), bases his protective system on this, chiefly, that it may greatly enhance the money-value of a nation's resources to the detriment of other nations, especially by the transformation of agricultural labor, estimated in money, into the much more productive labor of industry. The value in use of all the national resources is doubtless greatest where full freedom of trade obtains. In Russia, *Cancrin* demands that every nation should be to some extent independent in respect to all the chief wants to the production of which it has at least a middle *(mittlere)* opportunity; especially as all civilization, even the higher development of agriculture, must proceed from the cities. (Weltreichthum, 1821, 109 ff. Oekonomie der menschlichen Gesellschaften, 1845, 10, 235 ff.) America's most distinguished protectionist is *Hamilton,* Report on the Subject of Manufactures

on of industry in an old industrial country have a superiority over those in the new, in the amount of capital, the lowness of the rate of interest, the skill of undertakers *(Unternehmer)* and workmen, generally, also in the consideration in which the whole country hold industry, and the interest they take in it;[1] while in the country which has hitherto been merely agricultural, it happens only too frequently that industry is under-

---

presented to the House of Representatives, December 5, 1791. *Jefferson's* saying, that the industry should settle by the side of agriculture, leads us to *Carey*, who repeats the same idea with wearying unwearisomeness; at first for the reason that the "machine of exchange" should not be allowed to become too costly; but afterwards rather from the Liebig endeavor to prevent the exhaustion of the soil. He describes, indeed, how the East Indian producer and consumer of cotton are united with one another by a pontoon bridge which leads over England. (Principles of Social Science, I, 378.) A good soil and good harbors are the greatest misfortune for a country like Carolina if free trade prevails, because it is turned into an agricultural country (I, 373). The people who, after the manner of the Irish, gradually export their soil, will end by exporting themselves. *Carey* would force colonies to demean themselves like old countries from the first. If corn be worth 25 cents in Iowa, and in Liverpool $1, for which 20 ells of calico are brought back, the Iowa farmer receives of this quantity about 4 ells. Hence it would be no injury to him were he to supply his want of cotton from a neighbor who produced it at a cost four times as great as the Englishmen. Analogies drawn from natural history, as, for instance, that every organism, the lower it is in the scale of existence, the greater is the homogeneity of its several parts; also a deep aversion for centralization, and hatred of England, coöperate in *Carey's* recommendation of the protective system, often called in the United States the "American system," in opposition to the "British," advocated by Webster against Calhoun and Clay against Jackson. *John Stuart Mill*, Principles, V, ch. 10, 1, allows a protective tariff temporarily, "in hopes of naturalizing a foreign industry in itself perfectly suitable to the circumstances of the country." Peel's colleague, G. Smythe, said, in 1847, at Canterbury, that as an American (citizen of a young country) or as a Frenchman (citizen of an old country with its industry undeveloped), he would be a protectionist. *(Colton*, Public Economy, p. 81.) Even *Huskisson* admitted, in 1826, that England in the seventeenth century had been very much advanced by its protective system; and that he would continue to vote even now for its maintenance, if there were no reprisals to fear.

[1] What an advantage it has been to English industry and commerce that the state here so long considered it a matter of honor to have its subjects well represented in foreign countries, to extend their market etc.

valued, and that young industrial talent is, as a consequence, forced to emigrate. How frequently it has happened that England by keeping down her prices for a time has strangled her foreign rivals.² Even on the supposition of equal natural capacity, the struggle between the two industries would come to a close similar to that between a boy of buoyant spirits and an athletically developed man. What then is to be said of the cases in which the more highly developed nation is at the same time possessed of the more favorable natural advantages, such, for instance, as England possesses over Russia in her incomparable situation in relation to the trade of the world, and which gives her for all distant countries, without any active commerce, a monopoly-like advantage; farther, her magnificent harbors, streams, her well-situated wealth in iron and coal etc. The advantages of mere priority weigh most heavily, when the great development of all means of transportation almost does away with the natural protection afforded by remoteness; and when, at the same time, a certain universality of fashion, which, as a rule, is governed by the most highly developed nations, causes national and local differences of taste, which could be satisfied only by national or local production, to become obsolete.³ Under such circumstances, it would be possible, that a whole nation might be

---

² *Hume*, in the parliamentary session of 1828, uses the expression "strangulate," to convey this idea. As early as 1815, Brougham said: "It was well worth while to incur a loss on the exportation of English manufactures in order to stifle in the cradle the foreign manufactures." The report of the House of Commons on the condition of the mining district (1854) speaks of the great losses, frequently in from three to four years, of £300,000 to £400,000, which the employers of labor voluntarily underwent, in order to control foreign markets. "The large capitals of this country are the great instruments of warfare against the competing capital of foreign countries, and are the most essential instruments now remaining by which our manufacturing supremacy can be maintained."

³ Before the development of the machinery system, also, the preponderance of the greatest industrial power could not be nearly as oppressive as later; especially as in highly developed commercial countries, the wages of labor are always high. (*List*, Zollvereinsblatt, 1843, No. 44, 1845, No. 5, ff.)

made continually to act the part of an agricultural district (*plattes Land*), to one earlier developed, leaving to the latter, almost exclusively, the life of the city and of industry.[4] A wisely conducted protective system might act as a preventive against this evil, the temporary sacrifices which such a system necessitates being justifiable where some of the factors of industrial production unquestionably exist but remain unused, because others, on account of the mere posteriority of the nation, cannot be built up. The abusive term "hot-house plant" should not be used where there is question only of transitory protection, and where there is the full intention to surrender the grown tree to all the wind, rain and sunshine of free competition, and where it is foreseen that it shall be so surrendered.[5][6] The want of a certain economic many-sidedness which must

---

[4] "Shall the forester wait until the wind in the course of centuries carries the seed from one place to another, and the barren heath is converted into a dense wood?" (*List*, Gesammelte Schriften, III, 123 seq.) When the Romans had conquered an industrial country, its industries began generally to flourish better, because of the greater market opened to them; whereas, those which had no industries before, continued, for the most part, to remain producers of the raw material after the conquest, also. Related to this is the phenomenon, that the provinces not favored by nature, were much less backward in the middle ages than they are to-day. Compare the description of the misery of Mitchelstown, after the Earl of Kingston had ceased to consume £40,000 there: *Inglis*, Journey through Ireland, 1835, I, 142. The royal commission appointed to investigate the misery of Spessart in 1852, show that the home-made clothing had gone out of use there, and that the wooden shoes, so well adapted to wooded countries, had been changed for leather ones. This becoming acquainted with foreign wants in a region not adapted to industries, without a large market, greatly increased the distress. As soon as such a region becomes an independent state, a productive system would suggest itself.

[5] *List* very well remarks that otherwise most of our fruit trees, vines, domestic animals would be "hot-house plants." And even men are brought up in the hot-house of the nursery, the school etc. (Zollvereinsblatt, 1843, No. 36.)

[6] That a posterior people would never be in a condition to establish industries of their own, where full freedom of trade prevails, I do not by any means assert. Compare the list of industries which attained to so flourishing a condition without the aid of a protective tariff, that they were able to supply foreign markets, in *Rau*, Lehrbuch, II, § 206, a. But when Switzerland

be given to a nation manifests itself in a particularly urgent manner in times of protracted war. Here the error of so many free-traders, that different states should comport themselves towards one another as the different provinces of the same state do, is most clearly refuted.⁷

C. No less important is the political side of the question. Since the protective system forces capital and labor away from the production of raw material and into industry, it exerts a great influence on the relations of the classes or estates of a country to one another. The immense preponderance possessed in medieval times by the nobility, agriculture, the country in general as contradistinguished from the city, by the aristocratic and conservative elements, is curtailed in favor of the bourgeoisie, of industry, of the cities generally, and of the democratic and progressive elements. If when the history of a nation is at its highest point, there is supposed a certain equilibrium of the different elements, all of which are equally necessary to the prime of a nation's life, this height is now attained sooner than it would otherwise be. It is no mere accident that in almost every instance, those monarchs who humbled the medieval nobility and introduced the modern era, also established a protective system.⁸

---

is so frequently cited as an illustration in this connection (*J. Bowring*, On the Commerce and Manufactures of Switzerland, 1836), people forget the many favorable circumstances of another kind which coöperated here to elevate industry; a neutrality of three hundred years, during the French Huguenot War, the Thirty Years' War, the Wars of Louis XIV., and as a consequence of this, no military budgets, few taxes and state debts, etc. In addition to this, at an earlier period, the many mercenary troops, and afterwards the foreign travelers.

⁷ As free trade in Holland's best period was more an international law than a politico-economical system, so, afterwards, the Dutch protective system grew out of war prohibitions; and, in times of peace, the newly established industry was not abandoned. At last, in the time of its decline, all industries, with a strange logic, sought protection, even the most ancient one, the one whose growth was the most natural, the fisheries. (*Laspeyres*, Gesch. der volksw. Anseh., 134 ff., 146, 159.) The United States, during the war of 1812, with England, doubled their protective duties. (*A. Young*, Report on the Customs-tariff Legislation of the U. S., 1874.)

D. However, such an education of industry can be attempted with proper success only on a large scale, that is, on a national basis. The least hazardous *(unbedenklich)* measure of the system, import-duties, supposes a relatively short boundary line, such as only a great country, even where its formation is the most favorable imaginable, can possess.[9] The greater the tariff territory *(Zollgebiet)*, the less one-sided is its natural capacity wont to be, the sooner may an active competition in its interior be built up, while the foreign market always suffers from uncertainty. Hence all tariff-unions *(Zollverein)* between related states are to be recommended not only as financially but also as economically advantageous. Between states not related and of equal power, so far-reaching a reciprocity, embracing nearly the whole of economic policy, can scarcely be established; and it would be still harder for it to continue long. If the states not related are of very unequal power, the probable consequence would be the early absorption of the weaker by the stronger.[10][11]

---

[a] Hence, we should not judge the Russian and the American systems of industrial protection, for instance, by the same rule. In Russia, it may be necessary to strengthen artificially the still weak bourgeoisie, and to awaken numberless slumbering forces and opportunities by encouragement of their use by state measures. Here, also, the absolute ruler is called upon, and accustomed to educate his people. In the United States, on the other hand, there is no nobility; the whole nation belongs to the class of burghers, and even the cultivators of the land are raisers of corn, cattle traders, land speculators etc. Considering the universal activity and laborious energy of the people, it is to be expected that every really profitable opportunity will be turned to account in such a country, without any suggestion or assistance from the state. Here, therefore, *A. Walker's* saying is true: America should produce no iron, not because it does not know how, because it has not sufficient capital, because the nature of the country is not adapted to it, or because it has no natural protection, but "because we can do better." (Sc. of W., 94 seq.) Since a democracy cannot, properly speaking, educate the people, the protective duties of the United States are, for the most part, only attempts by one part of the people, who claim to be the whole, to prey upon the other parts.

[b] If we suppose three countries, each in the form of a square: A = 1 sq. m., B = 100 sq. m., C = 10,000 sq. m.; there is in A for every mile of boundary ¼ sq. m. of inland country; in B, 2½; in C, 25.

SECTION VI.

WHY THE PROTECTIVE SYSTEM WAS ADOPTED.

This explains why so many nations in the periods of transition between their medieval age and their higher stages of civilization, adopted the industrial protective system.[1][2][3][4][5][6]

---

[10] Towards the close of the middle ages, the vigorous commercial policy of Venice, for instance, towards Greece, or the Mohammedan power, was thwarted by other Italian cities, Genoa, Pisa, and later, by Florence especially.

[11] Why most of the reasons above advanced do not apply to a corresponding "protection" of agriculture by duties on corn, see *Roscher*, Nationalökonomik des Ackerbaues, § 159 ff.

[1] The fact that among the ancients there was so little thought bestowed on the protection of industry is related to the comparative insignificance of their industry. Compare *Roscher*, Ansichten der Volkswirthschaft, 3 ed., 1878, vol. 1, p. 23 ff. It occasionally happened in the east that workers in metal, especially the makers of metallic weapons, were dragged out of the country. I *Sam.*, 13, 19; II *Kings*, 24, 14 ff.; *Jerem.*, 24, 1, 29, 2. Among the Jews, certain costly products were subjected to export prohibitions for fear that the heathen might use them for purposes of sacrifice. *(Mischna*, De Cultu peregr., § 6. Persian law, that the king should consume only home products: *Athen.*, V, p. 372; XIV, p. c. 62. The Athenians went farthest in reducing such provisions to a system. Solon had strictly prohibited the exportation of all raw material save oil *(Plutarch*, Sol., 24), and a complaint was allowed against any one who scoffed at a citizen because of the industry he carried on in the market. *(Demosth.*, adv. Eubul., p. 1308.) The exportation of corn was always prohibited; also that of the principal materials used in ship-building. In war, prohibitions of the exportation of weapons; importation from enemy countries also prohibited. No Athenian was permitted to loan money on ships which did not bring a return cargo to Athens *(Demosth.* adv. Lacrit., p. 941), nor carry wheat to any place but Athens. *(Böckh.*, Staatsh. der Ath., I, 73 ff.) In Argos and Ægina, the importation of Athenian clay commodities and articles of adornment, prohibited. *(Herodot.*, V, 88; Athen., IV, 13; XI, 60.)

The Athenians imposed a duty of two per cent. both on imports and exports. Similarly, in Rome, where the higher duties imposed on many articles of luxury served an ethico-political purpose. We have, besides, accounts of prohibitions of the exportation of money: *Cicero*, pro Flacco, 28 (L., 2, Cod. Just., IV, 63). Plato's advice to prohibit the importation of luxuries and the

SECTION VII.

HOW LONG IS PROTECTION JUSTIFIABLE?

All rational education keeps in view as its object, the subsequent independence of the pupil. If it desired to continue

---

exportation of the means of subsistence *(De Legg.)* on ethico-political considerations; and the Byzantine prohibition of the exportation of certain articles of display from court vanity. (Porph. Decaerim, p. 271 ff. Reiske.)

¹ In Italy's best period, the protective system bears a specifically municipal complexion; in democracies, a guild-complexion; the former especially because of the many differential duties in favor of the capital.
A very highly-developed protective system in Florence. The exportation of the means of subsistence forbidden (Della Decima, II, 13), and so likewise the importation of finished cloths. (Stat. Flor., 1415, V, p. 3; Rubr., 32, 39, 41, 43, 45.) In the streets devoted to the woolen industries, it was not permitted to give the manufacturers notice to quit their dwellings, nor to increase their rent, unless the connoisseurs in the industry had admitted a higher rate of profit. (Decima, II, 88.) In order to promote the silk industry, the importation of silk-worms and of the mulberry leaf was freed from the payment of duties in 1423, the exportation of raw silk, cocoons and of the mulberry leaf forbidden in 1443; and in 1440, every countryman was commanded to plant mulberry trees. (Decima, II, 115.) When Pisa was subdued, the Florentines reserved to themselves all the wholesale trade, and prohibited there all silk and woolen industries *(Sismondi,* Gesch. der italienischen Republic, XII, 171). It was a principle followed by Milan in its best period, to exempt manufacturers from taxation. Yearly subsidies, accorded about 1442, to Florentine silk-manufacturers, who immigrated; in 1493, a species of *expropriation*, in case of houses which a neighbor needed for manufacturing purposes. *(Verri,* Mem. Storiche, p. 62.) Bolognese prohibition of the exportation of manuscripts, because they wanted to monopolize science *(Cibrario,* E. polit. del. medio. Evo., III, 166). Even in the seventeenth century, a city like Urbino forbade the exportation of cattle, wheat, wood, wool, skins, coal, as well as the importation of cloth, with the exception of the very costliest kinds. (Constitut. Duc. Urbin., I, p. 388 ff., 422 ff.)

² In England, since the fourteenth century, all genuinely national and popular kings always bore it in mind both to secure emancipation from the Hanseates, to invite foreigners skilled in industry to the country (the Flemings since 1331, although the English people disliked to see them come; *Rymer,* Foedd., IV, 496) and to adopt protective measures, especially when they had reason to rely on the bourgeoisie. *(Pauli,* Gesch. von England, V, 372.) The

SEC. VII.] HOW LONG IS PROTECTION JUSTIFIABLE. 443

its guardianship, the payment of fees etc., until an advanced age, it would thereby demonstrate either the pupil's want of

precursors of the navigation act, 1381, 1390, 1440. *(Anderson,* Origin of Commerce.) The prohibition of exporting raw wool (1337, 11 Edw. III., c. 1 ff.) lasted only one year. Wool remained a long time still so much of a chief staple commodity that in 1354, for instance, £277,000 worth were exported; of all other commodities taken together, only £16,400. *(Andersou.)* On the other hand, the prohibition to import foreign stuffs (1337), for instance, was repeated in 1399, and the prohibition to export woolen yarn and unfulled cloths in 1376, 1467, 1488. The statutes of employment operated very generally. The statutes provided that foreign merchants should employ the English money they received only to purchase English commodities, and their hosts, with whom they were obliged to live, had to become security therefor. Thus, in 1390, 4 Henry IV., c. 15, and 15 Henry IV., c. 9; 18 Henry VI., c. 4, 1477. Prohibitions of the exportation of money, 1335, 1344, 1381. Even in the case of payment by the bishops to the pope, the exportation of money was forbidden in 1391, 1406, 1414. Henry VIII. (3 Henry VIII., c. 1) threatened the exportation of money with the penalty of double payment. Even in 1455, the importation of all finished silk wares was prohibited for five years. See a long list of similar prohibitions in *Anderson.* The prohibitions relating to the exporting of raw materials, and especially wool, were exceedingly strict in Elizabeth's time, and stricter yet in the seventeenth century. The penalty of death was attached to their violation, and producers subjected to the most burthensome control. Moderated especially by 8 Geo. I., c. 15. In the eighteenth century we again find a series of import-premiums for raw material from the English colonies. Compare *Adam Smith,* IV, ch. 8.

⁴ *Sismondi,* Histoire des Français, XIX, 126, considers as the beginning of the French industrial protective system, the edict of 1572, by which, with a view of promoting the woolen, hemp and linen manufactures, the exportation of the raw material and the importation of the finished commodities are prohibited. *(Isambert,* Recueil, XIV, p. 241.) Yet even Philip IV., in 1302, had prohibited the exportation of the precious metals, of corn, wine and other means of subsistence. (Ordonn., I, 351, 372.) About 1332, the decision of the question whether the exportation of wool also should be forbidden was made to depend on who offered the most, the raw-producers or those engaged in industry. *(Sismondi,* X, 67 seq.) The third estate not unfrequently asked for protective measures from the parliaments: thus, in 1484, a prohibition against the importation of cloth and silk stuffs, and against the exportation of money *(Sismondi,* XIV, 673), claims which went much further in 1614, when freedom of trade, reform of the guilds etc., were desired. Opposition of Sully to the industrial-political measures of Henry IV., whose prohibition of foreign and gold stuffs lasted scarcely one year. *(Forbounais,* Finances de Fr., c. 44.) The edict of 1664, which, for the first time, created a boundary

capacity or the absurdity of its methods. The industrial protective system also can be justified as an educational measure

---

tariff-system for the greater part of France, with the removal of numerous export and import duties of the several provinces, and the abolition even of the duty-liberties of the King's court, marks an epoch. The introduction in which Colbert lets the King speak of his services to the taxation-system, the marine, colonies etc.; in which he describes the chaos of those earlier duties, and demonstrates their desirability of doing away with them, is very interesting. Colbert, inconsistently enough, allowed a number of export duties for industrial products to remain, that he might not alienate any domanial rights. (*Forbonnais*, I, 352.) The tariff, then very moderate, was, in 1677, doubled in part, and even trebled, which provoked retaliation, and led to the war of 1672. Hence, in 1678, the tariff of 1664 was, for the most part, restored. Colbert entirely prohibited these commodities, which were still imported, spite of the tariff: thus, Venetian mirrors and laces in 1669 and 1671. Among his characteristic measures are the export-premiums for salt-meats which went to the colonies in order to draw this business away from Holland to France. (*Forbonnais*, I, 465.) He caused the transit between Portugal and Flanders to be made through France by providing that it should be carried on by means of royal ships at any price. (*Forbonnais*, I, 438.) Compare *Clement*, Histoire de la vie et de l'Administration de C. (1846). *Joubleau*, Etudes sur C. ou Exposition du Système d'Economie Politique suivi de 1661 à 1683 (II, 1856). Lettres, Instructions et Mémoires de C. publiés par Clément (1861 ff.).

¹ In Germany, the tariff projects of the empire of 1522, contemplated no protection, inasmuch as imports and exports were equally taxed, but the importation of the most necessary means of subsistence was left free. Prohibition of the exportation of the precious metals in 1524; of the exportation of raw wool *mit grossen Haufen* (R. P. O., of 1548, art. 21; 1566, and in the R. P. O. of 1577, limited to the pleasure of the several districts. Hence, in Brandenburg, 1572 and 1578, the Saxons, Pommeranians and Mecklenburghers were prohibited to export wool and to import cloth, in retaliation. Individual states had much earlier adopted protective measures: Göttingen, in 1430, prohibited the exportation of yarn, and in 1438, the wearing of foreign woolen stuffs. (*Havemann*, Gesch. von Braunschweig und Luneburg, I, 780 seq.) Hanseatic politics recall in many respects the Venetian. After 1426, the sale of Prussian ships to non-Hanseates was made as difficult as possible; and in 1433, the importation of Spanish wool was prohibited in order to compel the payment of debts by Spain. (*Hirsch*, Gesch. des Danziger, H. 87, 268.) Prohibition of the exportation of the precious metals to Russia at the end of the thirteenth century. *Sartorius*, II, 444, 453, III, 191. The elector, Augustus of Saxony, forbade the exportation of corn, wool, hemp and flax (Cod. Aug. I., 1414). The Bavarian L. O., of 1553, prohibits

SEC. VII.] HOW LONG IS PROTECTION JUSTIFIABLE. 445

only on the assumption that it may be gradually dispensed with; that is, that, by its means, there may be a prospect of

generally the sale of corn, cattle, malt, tallow, leather or other *Plennwerthe* to foreigners; which prohibition was, in 1557, limited to cattle, malt, tallow, wool and yarn.

The protective system received its most important development in Prussia. Prohibition by the margrave, about the end of the thirteenth century, of the exportation of woolen yarn. *(Stengel,* Pr. Gesch., I, 84.) In the privilege accorded to the weavers of woolen wares, in 1414, the importation of the less important cloths is forbidden for two years. *(Droysen,* Preuss. Gesch. I, 323.) The prohibition of the exportation of wool of 1582 assigns as a reason of the prohibition, that the numerous leading weavers should not be ruined for the sake of a few unmarried journeymen and sellers. *(Mylius,* C. C. M., V, 2, 207.) In the prohibitions of 1611 and 1629, the domains, the estates of prelates and knights were exempted; similarly, in Saxony, 1613-1626; which is one of the many symptoms of the then growing *Junkerthum.* The great elector, who attached, both in war and peace, great value to the possession of coasts, men-of-war and colonies, forbade, for instance, the importation of copper and brass wares (1654), of glass (1658), of steel and iron (1666), of tin (1687); farther, the exportation of wool (1644), leather (1669), skins and furs (1678), silver (1683), rags (1685). Home commodities were, for the most part, stamped with the elector's arms, and all which were not so stamped were prohibited. The prohibition was generally preceded by a notice that the elector had himself established or improved a manufactory, or that the guilds *(Innungen)* had entered complaints against foreign competition. Not till 1682 did the idea occur to impose a moderate excise on the home product to be favored, and a much higher duty on the foreign one; thus in the case of sugar. *(Mylius,* IV, 3, 2, 16.) Frederick I. continued this system especially for the forty-three branches of industry hitherto unknown, and the introduction of which was contemporaneous with the reception of the Huguenots. *(Stengel,* 3, 48, 208.) Frederick William I., in 1719 and 1723, threatened the exportation of wool, under certain circumstances, with death. *(Mylius,* V, 2, 4, 64, 80.) The severity with which he insisted that his officials and officers should wear only home cloth is characteristic; and the fact that in 1719 he threatened tailors who worked foreign cloth, with heavy money fines and the loss of their guild-rights. At the same time all workers in wool were freed from military duty, and capitalists who had loaned money to wool manufacturers were given a preference (1729). Frederick the Great, who continued nearly all this, prohibited the exportation of Silesian yarn, with the exception of the very coarsest and finest, as well as of that which had been bleached. Its exportation was allowed to Bohemia only, because from here the linen went back again to Silesia to be bleached and sold there. *(Mirabeau,* De la Monarchie Pruss., II, 54.)

attaining to freedom of trade.[1] In the case of all highly civilized nations, the presumption is in favor of freedom of trade,

---

[*] Important beginnings of a protective system in Sweden, under Gustavus Wasa, and again under Charles IX., the violent opponent of the supremacy of the nobility *(Geijer*, Schwed. Gesch. II, 118 ff., 346); while Christian II., of Denmark, failed in all such endeavors. The founder of the Russian industrial protection was Peter the Great, who was in complete accordance with the native theorist, *I. Possoschkow:* Compare *Brückner*, in the Baltische Monatschrift, Bd. VI (1862), and VI (1863). Spain first adopted a real protective system under the Bourbons. The export prohibitions issued mostly at the request of the cortes between 1550 and 1560 *(Ranke,* Fürsten und Völker, I, 400 ff.) must be considered as a remnant of the medieval scarcity-policy, induced principally by a misunderstood depreciation of the precious metals.

[1] *Colbert* advised the companies in Lyons to consider the privileges granted them only as crutches, by means of which they might learn to walk the soonest possible, it being the intention afterwards to do away with them. (Journ. des Econom., Mai, 1854, p. 277.) Thiers said, in the chamber of deputies, in 1834: *Employé comme représailles, le tarif est funeste; Comme faveur, il est abusif; Comme encouragement à une industrie exotique, qui n' est pas importable il est impuissant et inutile. Employé pour protéger un produit, qui a chance de réussir, il est bon; mais il est bon temporairement, il doit finer quand l' education de l' industrie est finie, quand elle est adulte.* Schmitthenner, Zwölf Bücher vom Staate, I, 657 ff., admits that full freedom of trade between England and Germany would be advantageous to the world in general; but that England might here secure the entire gain even at the cost of Germany, in part. *Schmitthenner's* view is distinguished from that of *List's*, against which *Schmitthenner* zealously seeks to maintain the priority of his own (II, 365), disadvantageously enough, by this, that it contains no pledge of subsequent freedom of trade. *List,* on the contrary, considers universal freedom of trade, not only as the ideal, but also as the object which is to be striven for by temporary limitations on trade; an object, indeed, attainable only where there are a great many nations highly developed and in an equal degree, just as perpetual peace supposes a plurality of states equal in power. Ges. Schr., II, 35; III, 194. Compare, on this point, *Hildebrand*, N. O. der Gegenwart und Zukunft, I, 87. That *Carey* advocates a perpetual protective tariff is connected with his absolute inability to conceive the Malthusian law of population. *(Held,* Carey's Socialwissenschaft und das Mercantilsystem, 1866, p. 166.)

Thus, for instance, the prohibition of foreign cloths in Florence begins in 1393, that is, at a time when the protected industry had long been developed, so that its products were exported on a great scale, but when it began to fear the young, vigorous, competition of the Flemings.

both at home and abroad, and in such nations, the desire for a protective system must be looked upon as a symptom of disease.[2][3] It is true, that recently the inferiority of young countries, even when inhabited by a very active and highly educated people, is greatly enhanced by the improvement of the means of communication. But this is richly compensated for by the simultaneous instinct towards emigration, both of capital and workmen from over-full, highly industrial countries; whereas, the prohibitions by the state, that extreme of

---

[2] How frequently it happened in the conquests of the French revolution or of Napoleon, or when the Zollverein was extended, that two territories, now united to each other, feared an outflanking of their industries, each by the other, whose competition was formerly excluded; and that, afterwards, the abolition of the barriers to trade worked advantageously to both parties! *(Dunoyer*, Liberté du Travail, VII, ch. 3.) The Belgian manufacture of (coarse) porcelain flourished under Napoleon, spite of the competition of Sevres. It declined after the separation from France, notwithstanding protective duties of 20 per cent. *(Briavoinne*, Industrie Belge, II, 483.) The French cotton manufacturers feared, in 1791, that the incorporation of Mülhausen would necessarily produce their downfall.

[3] In Venice, the relations of a workman who had emigrated and refused to return home were imprisoned. If this was of no avail, the emigrant was to be put to death. *(Daru*, Hist. de V., III, 90.) It is said that this was still the practice in 1754. (Acad. des Sc. mor. et polit., 1866, I, 132.) Florence, in 1419, threatened its subjects who carried on the brocade or silk industry, in foreign countries, with death. Similarly, when the Nurnberg Rothgiessers were prohibited, under pain of the house of correction, showing their mills to a stranger. *(Roth*, Gesch. des N. Handles, III, 176.) In Belgium, enticing manufacturers of bone lace to emigrate was made punishable. Austrian prohibition for glass-makers, in 1752; for scythe-makers, in 1781. Colbert also approved of the imprisonment of manufacturers desirous to emigrate. (Lettres etc., II, 568 ff.) By 5 Geo. I., ch. 28, and 23 Geo. II., ch. 13, the soliciting of an artificer to emigrate to foreign countries is punished by one year's imprisonment and £500 fine; and even workmen who do not respond to a call home within six months lose all their reachable property in England, and their capacity to inherit there. Every emigrant had to certify that he was no artificer. The only effect of this law was that the emigration of artificers to the United States was made by the way of Canada; the poorer ones, at most, were kept back by the cost of this circuitous route. Hence the law was repealed in 1825. Compare Edinb. Rev., XXXIX, p. 341 ff.

exportation embargoes, formerly so frequently resorted to, it is no longer possible to carry out.[4][5] Now the young country has the advantage of being able immediately to use the newest processes of labor etc., without being hindered by the existence there of earlier imperfect apparatus. It is certain that international freedom of trade must be of advantage to a people's nationality the moment they have attained to the maturity of manhood, for the reason that they are thereby forced to make the most of that which is peculiar to them. Care must be taken not to confound many-sidedness with all-sidedness.[6] The best "protection of national labor" might consist in this, that all products should be really individually characteristic (artistic), all individuals really national, and national also in their tastes as consumers. This

---

[4] The first English prohibition of the exportation of machinery was made in reference to the Lee stocking frame, in 1696, the second in 1750; whereupon others followed very rapidly after 1774. As late as 1825, prohibitions of the exportation of a large number of machines and of parts of machines were still in force; but the Board of Trade might dispense with them. Here it was considered whether a greater disadvantage was caused to the industries by permitting the exportation, or to the manufacturers of the machines by prohibiting it. *Porter*, Progress, I, 318 ff., recommends full freedom of exportation especially for the reason that Englishmen can now procure all new machines, and sell the old ones to foreign countries. On the other hand, a French manufacturer purchased old machines *parceque sous le système prohibitif je gagnerai encore de l' argent avec ces metiers*. (*Rau*, Lehrbuch, II, § 209.) Similar cases in the United States. *Cairnes*, Principles, p. 485.

[5] *Baudrillart*, Manuel, p. 299. Every nation needs, in order to become fully mature, an industry of some magnitude. But it may just as well be the silk industry as the cotton which shall lead to this maturity; and when the nation has much greater natural capacity for the former than for the latter, it would do well to reach its object by the shortest course.

[6] *Riehl*, die deutsche Arbeit, p. 102 ff., 107. Shakespeare, the most English of Englishmen, and yet the most universal of poets! During the last centuries of the middle ages most nations had come to have national and even local costumes which were in strong contrast with the universality of fashions during the age of chivalry. This must have greatly contributed to the advancement of industry, even before the introduction of the state protective system.

ideal has been pretty closely approximated to by the French in respect to fashionable commodities, so that they will hardly purchase such from abroad, even without a protective tariff; and the cultured of most nations in respect to works of art. Here, too, it is worth considering, that even the most national of poets, when they are great enough to rise to the height of the universally human, possess the greatest universality.[7]

SECTION VIII.

INDUSTRIAL-PROTECTIVE POLICY IN PARTICULAR.

If it be once established generally that an industry is to be artificially promoted, and if there be question only of a choice between the different measures to be adopted to thus promote it, moderate[1] import duties are not only the most equable, least

---

[7] How much more convenient it is for the statesman, when he does not need to give any thought to the education of industry, is shown, especially by the great difficulty of striking precisely the proper height of a protective tariff. If too low, it fails of its object; and so, likewise, if too high; because then, in a very unpedagogical way, it lulls one into a lazy security. And how impossible it is to make the tariff vary with every variation in the cost of production, in price etc.; as List desired it should, not, however, without a good deal of variation in his own views. *(Roscher,* Gesch. der N. O., II, 989 seq.) How greatly would not List have been obliged to limit his assumptions, if he had lived to see the universal exposition of 1862, at which English connoisseurs expressed their pleasure that England had not remained behind France and Germany in locomotive building? (Ausland, 19 Oct., 1862.) Hence *Schäffle* opposes all protective duties as an educational measure, because the "protected" classes, by means of diets *(Landtage),* newspapers etc. so greatly influence legislation; that is, the educator is influenced by the pupil! (System, 409 ff.) The usual calculation of the cost for home undertakers *(Unternehmer)* can always only strike the average, and hence it is too high for some and too low for others. *(Rau,* Lehrbuch, II. § 214.) It frequently occurs that large manufacturers already existing desire a low protective tariff to facilitate their competition with foreign countries, possible even without such tariff, but not high enough to encourage others to compete with them at home.

[1] In general, *Müser* was in favor of *Colbert,* and opposed to *Mirabeau.* (P. Ph. II, 26.) He ridicules the prohibitions of the exportation of raw material

subject to abuse, but also attended by the greatest number of secondary advantages. Here the sacrifice is imposed on all the consumers of the "protected" commodity, that is, on the entire people, to the extent that they come in contact with the commodity in question. Export duties on raw materials, on the other hand, compel one single class of the people to make sacrifices in order to advance the favored industry.[2] Export premiums for commodities on which labor has been expended are distinguished from import duties as the offensive from the defensive: the former promote the artificial trade, the trade which has gone beyond its natural basis, the latter curtail it.

Premiums, advances without interest, gifts of machinery etc., to persons engaged in industry would operate very usefully under an omniscient government.[3] But they generally fall to the lot not of the most skillful manufacturers, but of the most acceptable supplicants, who now are doubly dangerous to the former as competitors.[4] The same is true to a still greater extent of monopolies granted to undertakings which

---

by saying that not only flax-seed, flax-yarn, but also the linen, must remain in the country. As Raphael Mengs once ennobled four ells of linen to a value of 10,000 ducats, a hundred Mengs should be sent for, to the end that all the linen should be exported painted. (v. 25.)

[2] *Rau*, Lehrbuch, II, § 214, would prefer to tolerate state premiums (politically so dangerous), rather than protective duties, because, in the case of the former, the magnitude of the assumed sacrifice may be exactly estimated in advance. Similarly, *Bastiat*, Sophismes, ch. 5.

[3] Many striking examples in *List's* Zollvereinsblatt, 1843, No. 47.

[4] Under *Colbert*, the granting of a monopoly had frequently no effect but to ruin an already existing rural industry in the interest of a city manufactory. Thus, in the case of lace, in Bourges and Alençon, and soap in the south, etc. The upshot of the matter in some places was simply that the carriers on of industry on a small scale were allowed to carry on their industries in consideration of a payment made to the owners of the privilege. (Journ. des Econ., 1857, II, 290). The King of Denmark bought back, in 1756, at a high price, industrial privileges which his predecessors had granted gratis. (*Justi*, Polizeiwissensch., § 444.) The Colbert monopoly of the Hollander v. Robais (1665), who was the first to manufacture fine cloths in France, was not abolished until 1767. (Encycl. Mech. Arts et Manuf., II, 345.)

it is intended to promote.⁵ They require, at least, to be vigilantly superintended in case of sale from one person to another; otherwise the individual to whom they were first granted is very apt to withdraw with the capitalized value of the privilege accorded, and his successors, loaded with a heavy debt in the nature of a mortgage, to derive no advantage from it.⁶

Further, import duties, besides the fiscal advantage which they afford, have the police advantage that they may, like quarantine provisions, prevent somewhat the inroads of many economic diseases: thus, for instance, gluts of the market, and still more, the severe chronic disease of ruinously low wages.⁷ But only very moderate hopes from protective duties should be entertained in all such respects as these.⁸

---

⁵ Thus, for instance, in 1863, the apothecary shops of the governmental district of Breslau had a value of 2,791,227 thalers, of which the land and inventories of stock were only 29 per cent. The concessions represented 71 per cent. The sick, in the entire state of Prussia, were obliged to contribute 1,780,000 thalers a year to compensate these monopolists. Compare *Brefeld*, Die Apotheken, Schutz oder Freiheit? (1863).

⁶ *Hermann*, in his review of Dönniges' System des freien Handels und der Schutzzölle (Münch. G. A. Sept. und Octbr., 1847) calls attention to the point that a decrease of the cost of production, by merely lowering wages, is no gain to the national resources, but only an altered distribution of them, for the most part a very unfavorable one. But when a nation is advancing on this road, it may strengthen its exportation by such means, as it might granting export premiums at the expense of the workmen. This would lead, on the supposition of entire freedom ot trade, to a corresponding depression of the lower classes in other countries; and against such contagion a protective tariff may operate in a manner similar to the quarantine. This is much exaggerated by *Colton*, Public Economy of the United States (1849), p. 65, 178. America needs a protective tariff more than any other nation, because of its dear workmen and capital. In Europe, the upper classes rob labor of its product, while in America, labor itself enjoys its products. Free trade would lower America to the level of Europe.

⁷ Severe crisis in the woolen industries of America in 1874 ff., spite of an enormously high protective tariff. The financial utility of a protective tariff can be scarcely great, because the intention of the tariff to permit as little as possible to be imported, and of the tax to levy as much as possible, are irreconcilable.

⁸ Frederick II., in 1766, forbade the importation of 490 different commodi-

Prohibition proper operates, as a rule, very disastrously.* It spoils those engaged in industry by a feeling of too great security (mortals' chiefest enemy: Shakespeare). It may even lead to complete monopoly, when the industry requires very large means and the country is small. The inducement to smuggling is peculiarly great here. But even duties, so high that they far exceed the insurance premium of smuggling, can be of very little advantage either to industry or to the exchequer. They can only promote the smuggling trade. However, the repeal of an import prohibition or the abolition of a tariff approaching to a prohibition should be announced long enough in advance to enable the capital invested in the protected industry to be withdrawn without too heavy a loss.

---

ties which, up to that time, had only paid high duties. *(Mirabeau*, Monarchie, Pr., II, 168.) In 1835, France still had 58 import and 25 export prohibitions.

They might, by way of exception, become necessary, in case a foreign state should desire to make our protective duties illusory by export premiums. But the exportation of Prussian cotton stuffs, for instance, has increased, with a moderate tariff, much more than the Austrian, with full prohibition. The English silk manufactures were, so long as the prohibition continued, inferior to the French, even in respect to the machinery system. (*McCulloch*, Statist., I, 681.)

* In the case of circulating capital this is generally done rapidly. The machines would have worn out, and care is taken not to renew them. Buildings also can, for the most part, serve other purposes. The most difficult thing of all is for the masses of men, gathered together at the principal seats of industry, artificially created, to distribute themselves. Between the two rules: "No leap, but gradual transition," and "cut the dog's tail off at once, not piecemeal," the right mean is struck in the abolition of a prohibitive protection, when, what it is intended to do, is announced long in advance without maintaining vain hopes, and a long space of time is left to enable people to make their arrangements accordingly. This plan was followed in a model manner in reference to the English silk prohibition, under Huskisson. It was announced as early as 1824 that protective duties of 30 per cent. would on the 5th of July, 1826, take the place of the prohibition. The duty on raw silk was immediately reduced from 4 sh. to 3d. per pound, and after a time, even to 1d., which so increased the demand that the number of spindles rapidly increased from 780,000 to 1,180,000. During the 10 years from 1824, the importation of raw and twisted silk amounted to about 1,941,000 pounds, and in the 10 years after, to 4,164,000 pounds. The English exports of silk wares

SECTION IX.

WHAT INDUSTRIES ONLY SHOULD BE FAVORED.

That as a rule only such industries should be favored which, by reason of the natural capacities of the country and of the people, have a good prospect of being able soon to dispense with the favors accorded, would be self-evident were it not for the fact that it has been ignored a thousand times in practice.[1] It is especially necessary to take the natural station *(Standort)*,[2] as well as the natural succession of the different branches of industry into consideration. Half manufactured articles of

---

had before 1824 a value of £350,000 to £380,000; in 1830, of over £521,000; in 1854, of almost £1,700,000; in 1863, of £3,147,000. Compare *Porter*, Progress, I, 255 ff. On the other hand, Austria was over-hasty when it went over from the prohibition of foreign silk stuffs to duties of 180 florins per cwt. Oest. Weltausstellungsbericht von 1867, IV, 140.)

[1] *Torrens* calls an industry which can, in the long run, bear no competition: "A parasitical formation, wanting the vital energies while permitted to remain, and yet requiring for its removal a painful operation." (Budget, p. 49.) Especially frequent in the case of luxury — industries in which the court was interested. The oysters which were sent for to Venice under Leopold I., in order to stock the artificial beds in the garden of the president of the Exchequer reached Vienna, dead. *(Mailath,* Gesch., IV, 384.) As to how Elizabeth, and Catharine II. in Russia, desired to compel the cultivation of silk, and caused the peasantry to be levied like recruits for that purpose; as to how the latter petitioned against it in a thousand ways, and endeavored to destroy the silk worms, mulberry trees etc., see *Pallas*, Reise durch das südliche Russland, I, 154 ff. Frederick II.'s silk-protection is characterized mainly by the order for church-inspectors to keep tables *(Tabellen)* concerning it, and to look after clergymen's and teachers' knowledge of the cultivation of silk. Tragico-comic endeavors of the Shah Nasreddin to establish manufactories in Persia: *Pollak*, Persien, II, 138 ff. One of the principal effects of the Mexican protective system, since 1827, was the establishing of manufactories on the coast only to cover up smuggling. *(Wappäus,* Mexiko, 83 ff.

[2] When Holland stunted its bleach-yards by high duties on linen, an industry in which it must always remain behind many other nations, was favored at the expense of another for which it possesses incomparable advantages.

foreign raw material should not be protected until the entire manufactured article has completely outgrown protection; which condition manifests itself most clearly by a strong, independent exportation of the article.[3] The celebrated tariff controversy between the cotton spinners and the weavers in the Zollverein was probably without any conscious plan, but certainly to the well-being of German industry, settled essentially in accordance with these principles. In such struggles of the different stages of a branch of production with one another, it is necessary not only mechanically to weigh the number of workmen, the amount of capital, etc., on both sides, but also organically the capacity for development and the influence of both sides on the entire national life.[4] Half-manu-

---

[3] Even before *Colbert's* time, French jewelry was prepared from Italian gold wire, and exported in great quantities. The mere rumor that it was contemplated to impose heavy duties on gold wire, provoked plans for the removal of the industry from Geneva to Avignon. (*Farbonnais*, F. de Fr., I, 275.) When France protects its raw silk, it makes the purchase of raw material in Italy cheaper to all its competitors.

[4] According to *L. Kühne* (Preuss. Staatszeitung, 17 Decbr., 1842), the cotton yarn consumption of Germany amounted to 561,000 cwt. per annum, of which the home spin-houses yielded 194,000 cwt. Weaving employed 311,-500 workmen with 32,250,000 thalers wages, spinning only 16,300 workmen with a little over 1,000,000 thalers wages. Even if the entire yarn-want (*Garnbedarf*) were spun in the interior, yet spinning would stand to weaving only as 1:5 in the number of workmen, and as 1:8 in the amount of wages. Hence the tariff of the Zollverein defended by Prussia, placed the tariff on tissues *(Gewebe)* 25 times as high as on yarn, while their prices stood to each other as 1:3-4. *List* (Zollvereinsblatt, 1844, No. 40 ff.) objected that only by spinning industries of its own could Germany's cotton-tissue industries become independent; since it was a very different thing to procure the material to be worked from the many mutually competing cotton countries, rather than from an intermediate hand; and indeed, from the most powerful industrial country of the world. (Compare, however, *Faucher's* Vierteljahrsschrift, 1863, Bd. I.) Besides, there is the great importance of the spinning industries, in order to come into immediate connection with America, the most rapidly growing market, to influence Holland, and also to advance navigation and the manufacture of machinery. In opposition to *Kühne's* calculation, *List* says: A man who lost eyes, ears, fingers and toes, would undergo only a small loss of weight.

factured articles of a very superior quality should not be kept away, since by promoting commodities of the first quality they have an educational influence on the whole industry. Thus, in the case of the duties on iron, it should not be forgotten, that they enhance the price of all instruments of industry.[5] Just as objectionable are protective duties for machines or for intellectual elements of training.[6]

---

[5] Special calculations on this matter in *Junghanns*, Fortschritt des Zollvereins (1849), I, 179.

[6] Frederick II. threatened the prosecution of one's studies at a foreign university with a lifelong exclusion from all civil and ecclesiastical offices; and, in the case of the nobility, even with the confiscation of their property. (*Mylius*, C. C. M. *Contin*, IV, 191, Noviem C. C., I, 97.)

INDEX TO NAMES OF AUTHORS
CITED IN THE PRINCIPLES.

[The references are to the sections.]

A.

Académie française, 42.
Agricola, 116, 120.
Ahrens, 16, 77.
Algarotti, 49.
Anacharsis, 116.
Anaxagoras, 38.
Anderson, A. (Origin of Commerce), 188.
Anderson, J. (Nature of Corn Laws), 152, 154.
Anonymous, authors of:
—— Britannia languens, 123, 196.
—— Discourse of Trade, Coyn and Paper-Credit, 48, 50, 90, 108, 123.
—— England's great Happiness, 196.
—— Interest of Money mistaken, 188.
—— Paying old Debts without new Taxes, 49.
—— Virginia's Verger, 9.
—— (W. S.) Compendious or brief Examination of certain ordinary Complaints, 137.
Antisthenes, 225.
Antoninus, 191.
Arbuthnot, 135.
Aretin, v., II, 118.
Aristippos, 225.
Aristophanes, 79, 202.
Aristotle, 1, 2, 5, 9, 14, 36, 38, 43, 49, 57, 63, 69, 70, 75, 79, 81, 100, 107, 116, 117, 190, 205, 250, 251, 253.
Arnd, 20.

Arnold, 184.
Asgill, 49.
Augustinis, de, 51.
Auxiron, 154.

B.

Babbage, 57, 58, 106.
Baboeuf, 79, 81.
Bacon, 13, 21, 24, 50, 55, 98, 108, 114, 191, 204, 254.
Bandini, 123, 188.
Banfield, 115, 157, 205, 263.
Bastiat, 2, 5, 9, 31, 35, 42, 54, 58, 81, 82, 84, 87, 97, 116, 117, 152, 167, 185, 210, 238, 242, 243.
Baudrillart, 21, 242.
Baumstark, 20, 154.
Bazard, 11, 53, 67, 84, 86, 90, 97, 205, 207.
Beaumont, de, 250.
Beccaria, 19, 49, 57, 79, 125, 126, 140, 256, 263.
Becher, J. J., 98, 114, 214, 254.
Beckmann, J., 225.
Bentham, J., 12, 71, 193, 232, 250, 256.
Berg, v., 76.
Berkeley, 9, 47, 57, 95, 116, 123, 212, 214, 231, 254, 255.
Bernhardi, v., 147, 154.
Bernhardinus, 191.
Bernoulli, 3, 246, 248.
Besold, 137, 191.
Bible, 11, 16, 36, 41, 63, 69, 81, 84, 190, 202, 204, 218, 225, 239, 245, 255, 264.

Biel, 22, 116, 120.
Blackstone, 42, 86 87, 199.
Blanc, L., 81, 82, 98, 167, 178.
Blanqui, 169.
Böckh, 135, 137.
Boden, 183.
Bodin, J., 37, 137, 254.
Bodz-Reymond, 97.
Boisguillebert, 1, 9, 12, 49, 96, 97, 100, 111, 117, 123, 154, 214, 215.
Booth, 243.
Bornitz, 3, 114.
Bossuet, 77, 191.
Botero, G., 9, 210, 241, 242, 245.
Boussingault, 32, 34.
Boxhorn, 39, 94.
Brentano, 166, 175, 176, 177.
Bridge, 238,
Brissot, 77.
Broggia, 9, 116.
Buat, 16.
Buchanan, 152, 153, 154, 164.
Buckle, 209, 263.
Bülau, 17, 97.
Buonarotti, 79.
Buquoy, Count, 22, 34, 129, 147.
Burke, 11, 220; II, 5, 106, 140, 155.
Büsch, 2, 9, 42, 95, 96, 117, 123, 126, 170, 183, 263.

C.

Cabanis, 37.
Cabet, 79, 82, 250.
Cæsar, Jul., 16.
Calvin, 49, 79, 114, 191.
Campanella, 79.
Canard, 22, 42, 47, 95, 101, 106, 123, 152, 188, 195, 215.
Cancrin, Count, 64, 98.
Cantillon, 47, 49, 90, 98, 106, 123, 126, 128, 137, 144, 154, 161, 167, 185, 193.
Carey, 5, 42, 148, 154, 155, 157, 166, 172, 199, 214, 243, 253, 263.

Carli, 137.
Casper, 246.
Cato, Cens., 43, 190, 222.
Cazaux, 22, 127, 145.
Celtes, 41.
Cervantes, 55.
Chadwick, 218, 248.
Chalmers, Th., 216, 217, 242.
Cherbuliez, 202.
Chevalier, M., 11, 40, 66, 70, 89, 97, 116, 120, 121, 124, 128, 129, 136, 137, 139, 142, 143, 173, 199, 216, 217, 220.
Child, Sir J., 42, 97, 98, 114, 123, 154, 157, 188, 192, 193, 197, 199, 241, 242, 254.
Chrysippos, 250.
Cibrario, 17, 137.
Cicero, 9, 46, 49, 75, 100.
Cieszkowsky, 89.
Clemens, Rom., 81.
Cleonard, 54.
Cliquot de Blervache, 108.
Cobden, R., 98.
Coke, R., 196.
Colbert, 232, 255.
Colton, 12, 25, 42, 116, 201.
Columella, 40, 59, 71.
Comte, Ch., 37, 71.
Condillac, 21, 49, 107, 129.
Condorcet, 263.
Considérant, 51, 88, 183.
Constant, B., 168.
Contzen, Ad., 49, 226.
Cooper, Th., 12.
Corpus Juris civilis, 69, 83, 117, 201.
Corpus Juris canonici, 41.
Corvaja, 82.
Cournot, 22.
Court, P. de la, 94, 97, 98, 108, 114, 185, 254.
Culpeper, Sir Th., 154, 188, 192, 199.

D.

Dankwardt, 16, 56.
Dante, 191, 250.
Darjes, 19, 76, 96, 106, 192, 254.
Darwin, 242.
Davanzati, 116, 123.
Davenant, 9, 10, 21, 97, 103, 116, 124, 157, 242, 254.
Decker, Sir M., 10, 41.
Defoe, D., 222.
Demosthenes, 21, 42, 43, 89, 231.
Diderot, 57.
Dietzel, C., 42, 90.
Diogenes, 225.
Dithmar, 19.
Dohm, 49, 263.
Doubleday, 242.
Drobisch, 13, 129.
Droz, 46, 92, 214.
Dufau, 18.
Dumont, 225.
Dunoyer, 16, 17, 21, 26, 38, 42, 50, 54, 111, 145, 178, 203, 216, 242.
Dupont de Nemours, 5, 97, 108, 147.
Duport, St. Clair, 139.
Dutot, 96, 100, 116, 212.

E.

Eden, Sir F. M., 57, 140, 213.
Edinburgh Review, 116, 154, 176, 242.
Eiselen, 51, 95, 195.
Enfantin, 250.
Engel, 161, 162, 214, 240, 243, 246, 248.
Epicharmos, 47.
Erasmus, 41, 79, 191.
Euler, 238.
Euripides, 37, 226.
Everett, 243.

F.

Fallati, 18, 21.
Faucher, J., 1.
Faucher, L., 178, 215.
Faust, M., 137.
Faxardo, Saavedra, 9, 254.
Fénélon, 225.
Ferguson, 11, 16, 21, 44, 50, 63, 115, 210, 217, 224, 225, 226, 255.
Fichte, J. G., 12, 82, 97, 123, 129, 204, 250.
Filangieri, 225, 254.
Fix, 4.
Fleetwood, 143.
Forbonnais, 68, 97, 116, 123, 173, 190, 200, 214, 254, 255.
Forster, 79.
Fortrey, Sam, 196.
Fourier, Ch., 51, 66, 81, 85, 97, 183, 207, 250.
Fox, 77.
Franklin, B., 12, 33, 41, 42, 49, 71, 89, 97, 98, 107, 116, 128, 173, 178, 203, 218, 219, 225, 232, 241, 242, 255.
Frégier, 223.
Friedländer, 4.
Friedrich II. (Emperor), 49, 83.
Friedrich, M., 16, 114, 244, 254.
Fullarton, 123, 125.
Fuoco, 11, 22, 121, 146, 154, 202.

G.

Galiani, 8, 9, 42, 47, 98, 100, 104, 116, 120, 126, 128, 129, 140, 142, 167, 187, 197.
Gallatin, 136.
Ganilh, 12, 42, 51, 52, 55, 116, 123, 147, 180, 188, 196, 214, 216.
Garcilasso, de la Vega, 9.
Garnier, 16, 50, 137.
Garve, 30, 50, 52, 99, 115, 173, 231.
Gasparin, 161.
Gavard, 17.
Gee, 116.
Geiler v. Kaisersberg, 39.

Genovesi, 4, 16, 64, 97, 102, 123.
Gerstner, 253.
Gessler, 261.
Gibbon, 234.
Gioja, 2, 30, 42, 47, 51, 64, 191.
Gobbi, 32.
Godwin, 243, 250, 254.
Goethe, 11, 25, 36.
Goldsmith, 254.
Gournay, 49, 108.
Graham, 243.
Graswinckel, 87.
Gratian, 47.
Graumann, 125.
Graunt, 245.
Gray, 243.
Gregorius Tolosan, 48, 55.
Grotius, H., 77, 87, 187, 191.
Guérard, 143.
Günther, 194.

H.

Hackluyt, 9.
Haller, K. L. v., 14, 256.
Hamann, 117.
Hamilton, 90, 152.
Hanssen, 40, 126, 139, 140, 144.
Harless, 81.
Harrington, J., 98, 205, 253.
Harris, 47, 57, 128, 180.
Hegel, 3.
Held, 146.
Helferich, 86, 137.
Helvétius, 11, 38, 231.
Herakleides, 225.
Herbart, 16, 22.
Herbert, 101, 142.
Herber, J. G. v., 265.
Hermann, F. B. W., 1, 2, 3, 11, 17, 42, 43, 44, 45, 50, 51, 101, 103, 106, 108, 110, 113, 115, 118, 129, 137, 142, 144, 145, 146, 147, 150, 152, 153, 154, 166, 172, 180, 181, 183, 186, 196, 196a, 199, 204, 208, 211, 212, 216, 219, 221, 246, 259.
Herodotus, 37.
Herrmann, E., 101, 207.
Heuschling, 154.
Hildebrand, B., 5, 13, 18, 79, 90, 146, 205.
Hippokrates, 37.
Hobbes, 42, 47, 50, 77, 107, 116, 118.
Hoffmann, J. G., 97, 117, 119, 159, 205; 246, 249.
Homer, 71, 250.
Hood, 168.
Hopkins, 159.
Horn, 245, 247, 248, 254.
Horneck, v. 19, 114, 116, 254.
Howlett, 39.
Hufeland, 2, 5, 12, 13, 46, 51, 59, 66, 87, 106, 107, 111, 118, 152, 195, 221.
Hugo, G., 24, 69, 81.
Humboldt, A. v., 32, 36, 61, 98, 106, 136, 139, 214.
Hume, D., 11, 36, 42, 47, 50, 71, 96, 98, 116, 117, 121, 123, 125, 126, 137, 154, 185, 200, 214, 225, 242, 263, 264.
Hutcheson, 5, 11.
Hutton, U. v., 225.

I.

Iambulos, 79.
Isokrates, 57, 231.
Ivernois, Sir F. d', 239, 246.

J.

Jacob, W., 120, 135, 137.
Jakob, H. L. v., 16, 49, 71, 106, 107, 127, 128, 147, 153, 195, 217, 219.
Jarke, 202.
Jevons, 22, 129.
Johnson, S., 93.

INDEX TO NAMES OF AUTHORS.

Jones, R. 148, 154.
Jselin, 67.
Jung, 76, 156; II, 53, 101, 173.
Justi, v., 9, 17, 116, 199, 237, 254.

K.

Kant, 11, 87.
Kauffmann, 3, 9, 126.
Kautz, 29.
Kees, v. 194.
King, Ch., 48.
King, G., 103.
King, Lord, 124.
Knapp, 246.
Knies, 4, 5, 6, 7, 11, 18, 28, 42, 89, 95, 107, 116, 117, 139, 169, 189, 213, 265.
Kosegarten, 117, 202.
Kraus, 17, 128, 137, 197, 265.
Krause, 170.
Kröncke, 22, 147.
Krug, L., 192, 254.
Kudler, 49, 128.

L.

Lafitte, 202.
Lang, 22.
Laspeyres, 129.
Lassalle, 45, 84, 163, 196a.
Lau, 245.
Lauderdale, Lord, 8, 9, 50, 51, 99, 103, 104, 106, 117, 128, 132, 147, 200, 214, 217, 221, 231, 263.
Lavergne, L. de, 139.
Law, 42, 96, 101, 107, 115, 116, 117, 121, 123, 127, 254.
Legoyt, 245.
Leib, 48, 237b.
Leibnitz, 13, 114, 140, 254.
Leopoldt, II, 87, 145.
Leplay, 65.
Letronne, 137, 214.
Libanios, 174.
Liebig, J. v., 162.

Linguet, 69, 174.
List, Fr., 45, 46, 50, 64, 98, 154, 260.
Liverpool, Lord, 118, 120, 142.
Livy, 231.
Locke, J., 5, 42, 47, 77, 100, 107, 116, 123, 129, 152, 154, 158, 188, 191, 193, 194, 199, 254.
Lotz, 5, 17, 20, 49, 50, 98, 99, 100, 115, 123, 128, 144, 166, 169, 195, 202.
Louis XIV, 221.
Lowe, 129, 219.
Lueder, 37, 50, 117.
Luther, M., 41, 49, 57, 114, 128, 191, 254.

M.

Mably, 79, 81.
Macculloch, 21, 40, 42, 43, 47, 50, 93, 107, 112, 113, 151, 164, 166, 173, 188, 197, 212, 253, 264.
Machiavelli, 21, 191, 238, 242, 244.
Macleod, 89, 90, 107, 115, 123, 154.
Macpherson, 143.
Malthus, 3, 9, 33, 42, 43, 50, 55, 79, 80, 98, 100, 107, 111, 112, 128, 129, 147, 152, 153, 157, 159, 163, 164, 166, 183, 185, 188, 205, 214, 216, 217, 239, 241, 242, 243, 244, 247, 258, 263.
Malthusians, 217, 254.
Mandeville, 11, 57, 225.
Mangoldt, v., 6, 16, 22, 30, 43, 51, 53, 59, 63, 71, 106, 129, 146, 149, 153, 157, 167, 177, 181, 195, 205, 220.
Mariana, 100, 114, 231.
Marlo, K., 71, 79, 178, 207, 242, 250, 251, 258.
Martineau, H., 176.
Marx, K., 22, 42, 47, 107, 189.
Masius, 237.
Massie, 42.
Melanchthon, 79, 100, 191.
Mélon, 42, 90, 91, 97, 123, 225, 254.

Menander, 174.
Mendelsohn, 77.
Menger, 2, 5, 101, 112.
Mengotti, 50.
Mercier de la Rivière, 22.
Mercantilists, 9, 47, 48, 96, 97, 116, 121, 126, 225, 236, 254; new, 116.
Merivale, 172.
Meyer, G., 246.
Michaelis, 135.
Mill, J., 47, 126, 216.
Mill, J. S., 5, 20, 22, 34, 38, 40, 42, 46, 51, 74, 79, 88, 90, 97, 106, 107, 111, 113, 121, 126, 150, 152, 153, 157, 163, 164, 166, 170, 172, 176, 177, 178, 180, 183, 186, 188, 192, 195, 197, 213, 216, 221, 243, 250, 259, 262, 264.
Minard, 223.
Mirabeau, Marq. de, 95, 97, 98, 117, 144, 147, 191, 210, 214, 254, 263.
Mirabeau, Son, 256.
Mischler, 1.
Mittermaier, 94.
Mohl, R., 242, 253, 258, 259, 262.
Moleschott, 162.
Moncada, 137.
Montaigne, M., 98, 236.
Montanari, 100, 116, 123, 125, 127, 188, 220.
Montchrétien de Vatteville, 9, 16, 48, 57.
Montecuccoli, 16.
Montesquieu, 37, 77, 89, 95, 116, 118, 123, 185, 192, 199, 205, 220, 221, 237, 238, 240, 248.
Moreau de Jonnès, 18.
Morelly, 79.
Morhof, 19.
Moritz (Marschall von Sachsen), 255.
Morrison, 176, 178.
Mortimer, Th., 173, 175; II, 53.
Morus, Th., 79, 98, 117, 147, 166.
Möser, J., 42, 63, 69, 91, 117, 161, 169, 173, 191, 200, 226, 242, 248, 254, 256.

Müller, Ad., 3, 5, 11, 12, 22, 28, 42, 50, 55, 64, 116, 117, 120, 202.
Mun, Th., 48, 116.
Muret, 239.
Murhard, K., 52.

N.

Nau, 19.
Nebenius, 89, 120, 137, 150, 182, 184, 186, 187, 195, 199, 219.
Necker, 103, 163, 204, 254.
Neri, P., 100, 118, 120.
Neumann, F. J., 6, 16, 100, 246.
Newmarch, 137.
Niebuhr, B. G., 92.
North, Sir D., 9, 12, 47, 48, 97, 98, 114, 116, 121, 123, 152, 154, 179, 191.

O.

Obrecht, 238 a; II, 164.
Oppenheim, 116.
Oresmius, 116, 120.
Ortes, 16, 34, 38, 117, 194, 217, 242.
Owen, R., 66, 128.

P.

Pagnini, 100, 137.
Paley, 50, 254.
Palmieri, 9.
Paoletti, 173.
Paris, Comte de, 176.
Patricius, 48, 246, 254.
Paucton, 143.
Paullus, Jul., 116.
Perikles, 231.
Périn, 11, 254.
Petty, Sir W., 16, 47, 48, 57, 107, 116, 123, 127, 129, 154, 164, 193, 214, 254.
Philemon, 69.
Physiocrates, 5, 8, 47, 49, 97, 101, 106, 128, 147, 154, 159, 214, 221, 225, 254.

INDEX TO NAMES OF AUTHORS.

(Pinto), 90, 98, 123, 221, 225.
Pitt, 254.
Plato, 9, 12, 21, 23, 42, 57, 61, 62, 79, 116, 190, 211, 250, 251.
—— Eryxias, 116.
Plinius (Major), 71, 79, 117, 120, 225, 231.
Plotinos, 79.
Plutarch, 73.
Pölitz, 17; II, 194.
Pollexfen, 9.
Porter, 129, 205.
Postlethwayt, 173.
Price, 238.
Prittwitz, v., 17, 51, 214, 263.
Proudhon, 5, 66, 70, 77, 81, 82, 85, 97, 185.
Puchta, G. F., II, 14.
Purves, 253.

Q.

Quesnay, 42, 44, 47, 49, 98, 101, 116, 121, 123, 125, 137, 147, 154, 214, 221, 254.
Quételet, 18, 248.

R.

Rae, 45, 59.
Raleigh, Sir W., 140, 241, 252, 254.
Rau, K. H., 3, 5, 6, 9, 20, 22, 33, 38, 42, 43, 49, 50, 58, 64, 101, 106, 109, 110, 111, 112, 116, 118, 120, 129, 131, 137, 143, 144, 145, 146, 147, 153, 156, 161, 166, 168, 179, 181, 194, 195, 208, 212, 216, 225, 253.
Raumer, F. v., 49.
Raynal, 49, 62, 214.
Read, 195.
Reformers, 47.
Reitemeyer, 135.
Reybaud, 78, 79.

Ricardo, 1, 5, 22, 43, 44, 66, 90, 106, 107, 109, 111, 126, 129, 147, 148, 150, 151, 152, 153, 154, 157, 164, 173, 175, 183, 184, 185, 186, 188, 195, 197, 201, 202, 212, 216, 263.
Ricardo's School, 47, 128, 157, 183, 197, 200.
Richelieu, 16.
Riedel, 16, 31, 65, 106, 118, 179, 195; II, 139, 187.
Riehl, 41, 56, 169, 230.
Ritter, K., 37.
Rivet, 258.
Rodbertus, 97, 135, 154, 201.
Roesler, 90, 157, 173, 193, 195, 207.
Rossi, 9, 42, 46, 243, 248.
Rössig, 19.
Rousseau, J. J., 16, 57, 62, 79, 169, 202, 205, 229, 254.
Rümelin, 18.

S.

Sadler, Th., 239, 242, 243, 245.
St. Chamans, 8, 90, 116, 123, 144, 214.
St. Just, 79.
St. Simon, 54, 70, 80, 84, 86, 90.
St. Simonists, 54, 70, 80, 84, 86, 90.
Sallustius, 14, 21.
Salmasius, 89, 97, 114, 116, 191, 193.
Sartorius, 29, 128.
Say, J. B., 1, 12, 16, 20, 22, 42, 43, 47, 50, 51, 53, 55, 58, 71, 87, 90, 98, 104, 106, 108, 115, 129, 137, 144, 145, 147, 151, 154, 169, 183, 195, 199, 200, 212, 216, 218, 223, 231, 243, 256, 263.
Say, L., 4, 9.
Scaruffii, 134.
Schäffle, 1, 2, 3, 4, 12, 30, 42, 43, 44, 47, 79, 89, 102, 110, 114, 117, 129, 152, 159, 176, 196a, 207, 208, 218, 246, 250, 251, 258.
Schiller, Fr., 30, 169, 204.

Schleiermacher, 16, 55, 63.
Schlettwein, 128, 145.
Schlözer, U. L. v., 18, 144.
Schlözer, Chr. v., 42, 116, 117, 128, 168, 185, 254.
Schmalz, 17, 19, 152, 195.
Schmitthenner, 42, 44, 50, 54, 95, 99, 108, 116, 117, 121, 224, 253.
Schmoller, 42, 147.
Schön, J., 11, 50, 97, 195.
Schröder, v., 9, 19, 42, 53, 54, 90, 116, 199, 210, 221.
Schulze, F. G., 20, 69, 96.
Schüz, 11.
Scialoja, 13, 17, 38, 41, 51.
Seckendorff, B. L. v., 19, 114, 116, 237, 254.
Seneca, L., 51, 69, 79, 100, 190, 214.
Seneca, M., 251.
Senior, 2, 22, 33, 34, 40, 46, 58, 102, 110, 112, 115, 121, 126, 129, 130, 142, 143, 148, 152, 155, 161, 165, 166, 167, 169, 173, 180, 181, 183, 185, 187, 189, 195, 200, 212, 242.
Serra, 33, 48, 181.
Shakespeare, 191.
Shuckburgh, 132, 137.
Sismondi, 12, 22, 44, 50, 54, 55, 93, 97, 98, 106, 109, 117, 123, 128, 144, 145, 147, 153, 154, 168, 174, 195, 201, 210, 214, 215, 216, 221, 231, 242.
Smith, Ad., 1, 2, 5, 11, 12, 20, 39, 40, 42, 44, 47, 48, 49, 52, 55, 57, 58, 59, 66, 71, 81, 91, 97, 98, 104, 106, 107, 111, 112, 113, 116, 117, 119, 120, 121, 123, 125, 128, 129, 130, 131, 134, 135, 137, 144, 147, 148, 153, 154, 157, 161, 163, 164, 166, 167, 168, 171, 172, 174, 176, 179, 183, 185, 186, 192, 193, 195, 197, 202, 213, 214, 218, 221, 226, 236, 238, 242.
Smith, Th., 116, 137.
Socialists, 6, 9, 12, 22, 53, 62, 66, 81, 82, 85, 88, 97, 117, 147, 148, 202, 205, 214, 242, 254, 265.

Soden, Graf, 16, 51, 92, 129, 194, 212.
Soetbeer, 138.
Socrates, 9, 71, 100, 250, 251.
Solera, 120.
Solly, 214.
Sonnenfels, v., 160, 194, 254.
Spinoza, 88, 254.
Spittler, 81.
Stahl, F. J., 24, 78.
Stein, K. v., 254, 265.
Stein, L. v., 14, 16, 46, 79, 98, 207.
Steinlein, 30, 47, 61.
Steuart, Sir J., 16, 20, 25, 34, 42, 71, 100, 104, 117, 123, 127, 134, 137, 147, 157, 199, 201, 213, 224, 239, 242, 253, 254, 263.
Stoics, 72.
Storch, H., 2, 3, 5, 7, 8, 10, 17, 27, 46, 50, 53, 55, 62, 71, 91, 96, 106, 115, 116, 117, 120, 145, 147, 165.
Strabo, 37, 61.
Struensee, v., 90, 96, 119, 210.
Süssmilch, 239, 245, 247, 254, 256.

T.

Tacitus, 41, 238, 250, 251.
Temple, Sir W., 41, 57, 98, 104, 115, 157, 185, 188, 214, 222, 231, 254.
Tengoborsky, 40, 139.
Thaer, 69, 112, 129, 131.
Thiers, 77.
Thomas, Aquin, 21, 49, 57, 191.
Thomasius, Chr., 19, 114.
Thornton, H., 101, 123, 125, 193.
Thornton, W., 164, 166, 176, 253.
Thucydides, Pref., 16, 36, 63, 229.
Thünen, v., 22, 106, 117, 149, 151, 154, 158, 161, 165, 173, 178, 183, 195.
Tocqueville, 71.
Tooke, Th., 100, 103, 104, 107, 108, 109, 112, 113, 123, 128, 137, 139, 157, 179, 188, 193.

Torrens, 9, 58, 107, 126, 130, 157, 164, 260, 262.
Townsend, 242.
Tucker (Progress of the U. S.), 71.
Tucker, J., 1, 16, 54, 57, 97, 98, 102, 130, 200, 216, 219, 254, 256, 262.
Turgot, 5, 9, 37, 42, 47, 49, 57, 70, 71, 90, 92, 95, 115, 116, 117, 152, 159, 163, 178, 188, 191, 193, 194, 221, 232.
Twiss, 121.

U.

Ulloa, 116.
Umpfenbach, 39, 82, 152, 173.
Ure, 173, 176.
Ustariz, 241.

V.

Varro, 71.
Vasco, 192, 194.
Vauban, 9, 78, 147, 254.
Vaughan, R., 107.
Verri, 8, 9, 16, 42, 49, 55, 97, 98, 100, 101, 116, 123, 159, 205, 214, 232, 254.
Viaaxnes, 191.
Villegardelle, 81.
Virgilius, 117.
Voltaire, 11, 98, 210, 225, 254, 255.

W.

Wagner, Ad., 13, 90.
Wakefield, D., 51, 64, 89.

Vol. II. — 30

Wakefield, E. G., 130, 185, 259.
Walker, A., 151, 152, 176, 195, 202, 206, 242.
Wallace, 242.
Wappäus, 246, 248.
Watts, 176.
Weinhold, 258.
Weishaupt, 214.
Wells, 10.
West, 154.
Weyland, 242, 243.
Whately, 17, 21, 110, 149.
Wirth, M., 185.
Wit, J. de, 92, 108.
Wolf, Chr. v., 175, 256.
Wolkoff, 35, 42, 43, 161, 186.
Woodward, 88.

X.

Xenophon, 9, 21, 57, 98, 100, 116.

Y.

Young, A., 32, 40, 42, 110, 137, 143, 242, 254.

Z.

Zachariä, K. S., 29, 37, 83, 87, 97, 128, 214, 229.
Zeno, 98.
Zincke, 49.
Zwinglius, 191.

www.ingramcontent.com/pod-product-compliance
Lightning Source LLC
Chambersburg PA
CBHW022103300426
44117CB00007B/569